WORLD POLITICS

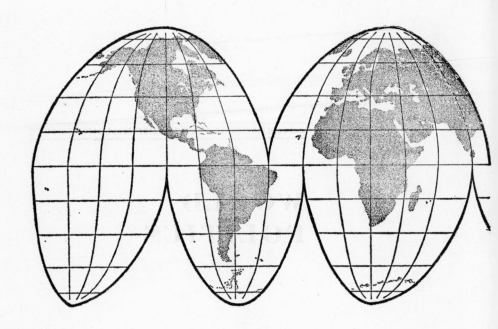

by *A.F. K. Organski*

The University of Michigan

NEW YORK

World

POLITICS

SECOND EDITION

ALFRED · A · KNOPF

THIS IS A BORZOI BOOK,
Published By Alfred A. Knopf, Inc.

Library of Congress Catalog Card Number: 68-13160

Manufactured in the United States of America.

Published 1958, reprinted seven times
Second Edition, revised and reset, 1968
Second Printing, December 1968

In Memoriam
V. O. Key, Jr.

PREFACE
to the Second Edition

❖❐❖

Ten years have passed since this book first appeared and within that time world politics have moved in directions predicted in the first edition. Yet time has also brought unforeseen developments. Some of the views expressed in the early edition were plainly wrong. New emphases were clearly needed. Ten years is a long interval—as such things are measured —between the first and second editions. However, the longer span of time has permitted a greater amount of thought, research, and care to be invested in this edition. I can only hope this has improved the work from what it otherwise might have been.

The major theme and purpose of this book have been kept intact. It is still my view that those who approach world politics need most a framework within which to organize their data. And it is still my view that the overall patterns of world politics in the modern era are caused by sharp differences in social, economic, and political modernization among and within nations. Differential modernization in turn causes shifts in the distribution of world power among states. It is these changes that underlie the wars and other conflicts of our era. The immensely complex patterns that create these shifts in power, the shifts themselves, and their consequences are not easily deflected by diplomacy or by military power.

In this edition I have made these views far more explicit, discarding, revising, and adding to the ideas first presented in 1958. Nearly every chapter of this book has been amended to include new thoughts and new data. In addition I have added new chapters on national growth and on the influence of nuclear weapons upon international politics.

Second editions are ungrateful work. They are slow, uncertain, and agonizing labor, and any sentimental attachment to the first edition of a book—such as I had for this one—only compounds the problem. Thus my gratitude goes to a number of people who have generously helped in carrying this work to a conclusion.

My wife, Katherine, as in all my previous work, has helped me at every stage of the undertaking. She discussed with me the new material introduced in this edition and helped me pare the final version. Her analytical bent of mind and her editorial skills have again saved me from errors and improved my prose. I am very grateful to her for all she has done.

A number of colleagues helped me in clarifying my views on the influence of nuclear weapons on international behavior. They read some of the early drafts, argued with me, and gave advice. I wish to record my indebtedness to Professors Abraham Bargman of The City University of New York at Brooklyn College, Inis L. Claude, Jr., of the University of Michigan, Walter Goldstein of the Bendix Corporation and of The City University of New York, and J. David Singer of the University of Michigan. I should also like to thank the members of the security seminar of the University of California at Berkeley and particularly Professor Aaron B. Wildavsky, then its chairman. The seminar proved a stimulating and helpful setting for a first public presentation (in April 1966) of my views on the influence of nuclear weapons on world politics.

I need hardly add that those who have helped me most have not always agreed with me. The responsibility for what I have written is mine alone.

Ann Arbor, Michigan   A.F.K.O.

PREFACE

to the First Edition

It has been my conviction for many years that to understand international relations one requires most of all a framework within which to organize the mass of detailed information to which we are all exposed. This book is an attempt to offer such a framework to the reader. And if, after having read it, the scattered parts of the international jigsaw puzzle fall into place, this work will have achieved its purpose.

Two people contributed directly to the writing of this book.

My wife, Katherine, edited for style and content every line of the following pages. She discussed with me every idea before and after it was written down. She generously contributed many ideas of her own and much of the interesting and original results of her own research. My debt to her cannot be fully expressed in any acknowledgment here.

V. O. Key, Jr., of Harvard read the entire manuscript and made suggestions. No writer could ask for a more perceptive, kinder, or fairer critic. His trenchant comments were of great help, and I am very grateful to him both for his criticism and for his encouragement.

But my intellectual debts extend much further, and it seems only fair in a first book to try to acknowledge some of the major ones.

The attempt to set down a coherent framework for the understanding of international affairs required pulling together information and ideas that had been formed over a period of many years. It is ironic now that I look back that four men, at least three of whom would undoubtedly disagree with large portions of this book, influenced my thinking most when my ideas were taking shape. James Burnham gave an exciting and inspiring presentation of those great Italian and French writers, Pareto, Michels, Sorel, Mosca, and Machiavelli. The ideas of these great authors underlie the substance and the approach I use. Clyde Eagleton's lectures on international law and organization were my first introduction to the field of international relations. His love of the field was contagious and led me to a choice of life work that I have never regretted for an instant. I also owe a great deal to Clyde V. Kiser of the Milbank Memorial Fund, whose lectures on world population problems opened up to me new vistas of what could be understood in international relations through an interdisciplinary approach. Finally I want to thank Dr. Herbert L. Hayward, a fellow student, but much my intellectual superior, who with his brilliant, original, and argumentative turn of mind led me on many exciting explorations of uncharted terrain in international relations.

However, I alone take full responsibility for what I have written.

A.F.K.O.

CONTENTS

PART TWO: *International Relations*

PART THREE: *International Organizations*

CONCLUSION

WORLD POLITICS

1

Introduction to a Field of Study

International relations is a study that is plagued with platitudes. It is a field where every man plays expert, where every teacher, every speaker, every preacher, every cabby, every table-thumping dinner guest has special insight and the inside story. Popular writers give us laboriously contrived and elaborately presented glimpses of the obvious. The morning papers serve up a daily dose of cautious optimism and variations on the theme that justice will triumph. It is enough to weary Job.

And what a grave injustice, for if ever there was a field where clear, hard thinking would bring immediate rewards, international relations is one. The importance of its study today is obvious. None of us cares to come to his final rest as a bit of fall-out. The fear of war has terrified us all and nearly paralyzed our thinking processes as well. Like primitives engaged in magic, we ritualistically repeat the procedures that have failed us before. We resemble the man who, faced with a foreigner who could not understand his language, shouted a little louder in order to make himself understood. We are well aware of the problems that need to be solved, but we would get further if we stopped shouting and examined the problems in a less excited frame of mind.

This is not to say that the study of international relations lacks excitement. Quite the contrary. There is plenty of drama in international relations, perhaps too much. The world's most colorful characters stride its stage. The world's most significant events make up its history. Relations between nations have been exceptionally turbulent in the years since 1914. Two great world wars have shaken us to our roots, and we dread that somehow we will set off a third. These same years have seen the United States rise so rapidly in wealth and power that almost nonchalantly we have taken over the leadership of the world from Britain, only to find that what was grasped without effort may require great effort to hold, for new and jealous giants are growing up beside us.

Beneath the fast-paced melodrama of war and of contests for world leadership, there is a deeper drama going on. Modernization is changing the face of the globe, creating new nations, and altering the nature of international politics. This is a creeping change, economic and social in its roots, but its progress is marked by political upheavals. The colonial world has shaken itself free, and colonialism as we have known it is coming to an end. The distribution of power among the major nations of the world is shifting. The period when white men ruled the world is drawing to a close.

One of the most exciting things about the age in which we live is that we find ourselves between two eras. We were born in one world, and we will die in another. Our lives span the passage between them, and from where we shall stand in a few years, we shall be able to see them both. Most of those who lived one hundred years ago, even sixty years ago, had limited horizons. They did not question the rules by which they lived or the accepted explanations of events. They took it for granted that the world as they knew it, with minor corrections in the line of progress, would continue to exist forever. Those who live a hundred years hence will also have a restricted view. For them the past will assume the nature of a myth carefully tailored not to disturb existing prejudices and conceptions, while the present will be accepted as eternal. But we are living in one of those brief periods when both the past and the future can be seen in clear perspective and the differences between them identified and traced to their causes. It is an age in which the social sciences, international relations among them, have blossomed forth.

As a science, international relations today is in its infancy; it is still less a science than a mixture of philosophy and history and art. Its theories are few and shockingly untestable. Writings on the subject are largely descriptive. However, the descriptive-historical approach has resulted in the collection of an immense amount of data, and the daily papers provide us with more. Now theorists are beginning to provide the kind of theoretical framework that is necessary for ordering and interpreting the facts. We are on the verge of great discoveries. Those who work in the field today are still groping, but within the next few decades, the basic foundations of a new discipline will be laid. Perhaps the readers of this book will help to build them.

The Scientific Approach

This book approaches international relations in the tradition of the sciences rather than that of the humanities or the arts. We must be careful not to claim too much, for the social sciences in general and international relations in particular are still a long way from being sciences in the manner of physics or chemistry. It is a matter of controversy whether they can be called sciences at all. However, there are unquestionably ways in which a scientific approach to international relations has proved and will continue to prove highly useful.

To be scientific, a study must have certain characteristics.[1] First of all, it must be rational and conform to the rules of logical thought. Most serious writing in the field of international relations meets this requirement.

Second, a scientific study must be concerned with empirical facts, that is, it must be testable by evidence that is available to the senses. In this respect, science differs from philosophy, which may be concerned exclusively with ideas and theories that cannot be proved or disproved by any empirical test. Much of the writing in international relations is partly or mainly philosophy. In particular, many works are concerned primarily with what kind of international relations *ought* to exist in the light of some defined (or often undefined) set of values. This book, however, is primarily a study of the kind of international relations that *do* exist.

Every scholar has a set of values. These help to determine which phenomena he chooses to study. Certainly the values of others determine what use is made of his findings, but during the course of the investigation, the scientist lays aside his values and treats his data objectively, as if it did not matter to him what he found. The plant biologist may know perfectly well how he thinks corn ought to grow, but he will not succeed in developing better breeds unless he first finds out how corn does grow.

The same principle holds true for the social scientist, although it is not always honored. It is easy to be blinded by our own values and to see only what we want to see, but such behavior does not contribute to man's control over his social environment. It may well be that the ultimate social purpose of science is to enable man to manipulate his

[1] See Bernard Barber, *Science and the Social Order* (New York: Free Press, 1952), chap. 1.

environment to conform more to his values, but he cannot manipulate it unless he first understands how it works, and this is best learned through a scientific approach. We are a long way from understanding the determinants of man's social behavior, but we will increase our understanding rapidly if we can learn to look at human behavior in an objective manner. A sincere effort has been made in this book to view the facts objectively and to follow them where they lead, even when the findings are discomforting.

But science must not only describe the facts, it must explain them. This is done through the construction of theories, which are extremely general abstract statements or "laws" according to which empirical phenomena behave. If the theory is good, it should be stated in such a manner that it can be tested with empirical evidence. If the theory is correct, it should be borne out by every test, with no exceptions. Practically speaking, almost none of the theories of international relations will meet this test, but this is the kind of theory at which we should aim.

The present book is focused largely on current and recent events of which it is assumed the reader has some knowledge. It is *not* a history of recent happenings. Concrete incidents and cases are used throughout for illustration and to test generalizations put forward, and the reader is invited to fill in other cases wherever they are relevant. The emphasis, however, is on a search for general principles, for regularities, for patterns that recur in case after case, and at a deeper level, for the causal explanations that underlie these regularities.

The book contains a little philosophy, for values have a way of intruding no matter how carefully one tries to segregate them, and it contains a good deal of description. It contains few "laws" but a great many of the generalizations and hypotheses that are the first step in the formation of theory. Some of the generalizations are crude and need refinement. Some of the hypotheses are probably downright wrong. The reader is invited to refine and correct wherever he can, for only by such steps does knowledge grow. Beginnings must be big and breezy; refinements follow later.

The Interdisciplinary Approach

This book also utilizes an interdisciplinary approach. The central focus, of course, is political. International relations is traditionally considered to lie within the confines of political science. The nation, after all, is primarily a political unit, and the study of international relations is concentrated upon political relations among nations, upon diplomacy and wars and struggles for power.

Political science in and of itself, however, does not provide all the concepts necessary for a full understanding of relations among modern nations. All of the social sciences deal with the same raw data, the actual behavior of specific men in their relations with each other and their relations to their environment, but each of the sciences abstracts out a different aspect of these relations. Political science deals with the power aspect of human relations, with the ways in which individuals and groups control the behavior of others and with the institutions through which such control is exercised. Economics deals with the ways in which men produce, distribute, and consume wealth and with the institutions that regulate these processes. Sociology, a more imperialistic science, includes both political and economic behavior within its purview as well as other areas such as family life, religion, and recreation, but concentrates primarily upon the structure and the operation of groups rather than upon individuals. Psychology deals with individual behavior and attitudes and their determinants. Social psychology sits astride the boundary that divides sociology from psychology. Geography, primarily a physical science, becomes a social science when it considers the effect of geography upon human life and the ways in which man, in turn, has changed the physical features of the earth.

Each of these sciences is valuable in its own right, and each requires specialists who concentrate on relatively narrow areas, but more and more we are coming to realize that the study of many topics is best conducted by men who are capable of crossing the conventional boundaries between disciplines or by cooperation among specialists of several fields. This is particularly true when concrete, practical problems are considered, when the prediction of actual future events is attempted, or when the determinants of a particular human act are sought.

Indeed, the search for the determinants of action in one sphere almost invariably leads the seeker into several disciplines. Voting behavior, for example, is certainly a political phenomenon, but recent studies have shown that the way a man votes is determined not only by his political philosophy and by the political actions of the parties and the candidates, but also by his social class, his income, and his religious, ethnic, or racial group. Psychology also plays a role.

Similarly, market research has revealed that consumer demand for goods is not to be explained only by economic theories, for the real consumer, unlike the theoretical "economic man," is strongly influenced in his purchases by desires to improve his social status and by psychological considerations. Still again, the birth rate, a biological phenomenon studied by sociologists who specialize in population, is affected not only by social and psychological factors, but also by economic events such as depressions and political events such as wars.

The need for an interdisciplinary approach in the study of international relations is quite obvious. The major units to be studied—nations—are not only political entities but geographic, social, and economic units as well. Moreover, they are groups of individuals held together by strong psychological ties. Nor are their actions in the international arena explainable in terms of power alone. Even power itself, however it may seem to be an exclusively political characteristic of nations, cannot be understood without reference to other disciplines, for the power of a nation is determined by such factors as the size of its population and the level of its economic development.

This is not to say that the student of international relations must be an expert political scientist, economist, sociologist, social psychologist, and geographer rolled into one, but he should have at least a nodding acquaintance with these disciplines. It will serve him well if he can develop an interdisciplinary outlook from the start. This book attempts to develop such an outlook, starting on a level that can be understood by the student who is not yet a specialist in any of these disciplines.

Things to Come

In the chapters that follow, we shall deal with a wide range of topics. The book is divided into three broad sections: one, on the nation and its characteristics; two, on international relations; three, on international organizations. A conclusion sums up the findings and makes predictions.

We begin with an examination of the basic unit of all international relations, the nation, setting out to determine what it is that makes this particular group of people a unit. We shall explore the characteristics and sentiments shared by fellow nationals and analyze the nature of the ties that bind them together. We shall see whether the nation is gaining or diminishing in importance and what the chances are of its being replaced by more extensive units such as regional federations or a world state.

Next we shall examine how nations grow and change, and then consider two of the characteristics of nations that are particularly important in shaping their international behavior: national goals and national power. All nations do not have the same goals, and we shall devote a chapter to considering some of the different kinds of goals that nations may have. The following chapter deals with the determinants of national goals. Why are some nations warlike while others pursue peace at any price? Why do some nations seek to impose their ideologies on others while other nations ask only to be left alone? Why do some nations have narrowly nationalistic goals and others humanitarian goals? We shall try to find answers to these questions.

We shall devote major attention to analyzing national power, defining the concept of power in some detail and discussing the determinants of power at length. We shall consider the influence of such factors as geography, resources, population, economic development, political development, and national morale, and then decide which factors are most important and devise an index by which the power of a nation can be measured. Finally, we shall prescribe the ways in which an underdeveloped country can best increase its power and the ways in which a nation such as the United States can best maintain the power advantage it has.

Part Two treats relations among nations, starting out with the kind of relationships that characterize dealings between very strong nations and very weak nations and moving on to relations among the great powers.

Colonialism first claims our attention, as the kind of relationship that results when the discrepancy in power between two political units is greatest. Modern nations are often reluctant to call their colonies colonies, but we shall try to define the term in such a way as to include them all. We shall explore the nature of colonialism and outline the steps by which colonies achieve their independence, noting why some freed themselves long ago while others are achieving their freedom only now. We will go beyond formal political colonialism to examine the new forms that are replacing it—the economic dependencies of the United States and the satellites of the Soviet Union. We shall give particular attention to the appeal and the dangers of communism to former colonies that have recently won their independence from the West.

A particularly important section of the book is the discussion of the balance of power and the balance of terror and the suggestion of a new theory to take their place. The balance of power and the balance of terror are two of the few real theories in the field of international relations. My treatment of them here is highly critical, but the reader is entitled to disagree. Following the rejection of the balance of power and balance of terror theories, the book sets forth an alternative view of the way power is distributed among nations and traces out a recurring pattern in international relations which we have called the power transition. The fundamental causes of war and the conditions under which war is most likely to occur are discussed in this chapter. The section closes with a discussion of diplomacy and an assessment of its importance in altering the course of international politics.

Part Three deals with international organizations. A preliminary chapter examines the idea of collective security, a mechanism that has been proposed as a way of keeping international peace and that the League of Nations and also the United Nations, to a lesser extent, were designed to put into effect. The next chapter focuses on the contradictory forces of national sovereignty and international interdependence and shows how the attempt to reconcile these forces has affected the structure, the powers, and the procedures of international organizations. A concluding chapter treats the working of the League of Nations and of the United Nations in more detail, showing what can reasonably be expected of the United Nations and what cannot.

In the conclusion, significant patterns of international relations identified throughout the book are reviewed, and on the basis of them, predictions are made about the future. Will nations continue to be the significant units in world affairs? How will the distribution of power among nations be altered in the years ahead? Will the United States retain its present leadership of the world? Will there be a third world war? We are rash enough to venture answers to all these questions.

Part One

THE UNIT
OF ACTION:
THE NATION

2

Nations and Nationalism

❖❮❮

The story we are about to tell is a tale of nations. Nations are the major characters, and it is with their actions, their goals and plans, their power, their possessions, and their relations with each other that we shall be concerned. Acting in the name of national honor, national aspiration, and national defense, men have behaved so badly in recent years that the temptation is great to regard nationalism as an evil force and the nation as an unfortunate form of political organization. It is nations that fought each other with a fury that killed and maimed millions of men and blasted the cities and countryside of Europe and Asia in two world wars, and it is nations that stand toe to toe today, suspicious and hostile, skirmishing in smaller wars, retaining the power to blow up the world whenever national interest commands it. Small wonder that we sometimes wish for some form of political organization with less explosive potentialities.

It has been charged that national governments are not only dangerous but obsolete, that modern weapons, modern trade, and modern communications have made the people of the world dependent upon each other to such an extent that it is ridiculous to have them divided into 143 independent political units. It is argued that only a handful of nations are truly in command of their own destinies and that for the others, national independence and national sovereignty are myths. The convulsions of the present age, the growing discontent with national organizations, and the growth of new international institutions are taken as evidence that the era of the nation-state is drawing to a close and that the beginning of a new era is at hand.

Perhaps. But a burial requires a corpse, and for better or for worse, the nation still shows considerable signs of life. The flags still fly, the anthems sound, the armies march. The same wars that have aroused our intellectual suspicions about the merits of national political organization have also filled us with patriotism. Germans, driven by nationalistic excesses into a war that left their country split in half and under foreign occupation, today wait impatiently to be reunited; Americans, jolted out of their isolation and made to feel their interdependence with the rest of the world, have lost none of their feeling of being different and somehow superior because they are American, and their distrust of "un-Americans" is as great as ever.

Nor is nationalism restricted to the old and established nations of Europe and America. In the course of the twentieth century, whole belts of new nations have broken out like a rash across the map of the world. Even a partial list of new nations formed since 1900 is imposing:

In Europe: Albania, Austria, the Baltic states (Estonia, Latvia, and Lithuania—later reabsorbed by the Soviet Union), Bulgaria, Czechoslovakia, Finland, Hungary, Iceland, Ireland, Malta, Norway, Poland (an old nation reborn), Yugoslavia. Overseas: Australia, Nauru, New Zealand, Western Samoa. In the New World: Barbados, Guyana, Jamaica, Trinidad and Tobago. In the Middle East: Bahrein, Cyprus, Iraq, Israel, Jordan, Kuwait, Lebanon, Saudi Arabia, Syria, United Arab Republic, Yemen. In South and East Asia: Burma, Cambodia, Ceylon, India, Indonesia, North and South Korea, Laos, Malaysia, the Mongolian Republic, Pakistan, the Philippines, Singapore, North and South Vietnam.

In Africa: Algeria, Botswana, Burundi, Cameroon, Central African Republic, Chad, Congo (Leopoldville), Congo (Brazzaville), Dahomey, Gabon, Gambia, Ghana, Guinea, Ivory Coast, Kenya, Lesotho, Libya, Malagasy, Malawi, Mali, Mauritania, Mauritius, Morocco, Niger, Nigeria, Rhodesia, Rwanda, Senegal, Sierra Leone, Somalia, Sudan, Tanzania, Togo, Tunisia, Uganda, the Union of South Africa, Upper Volta, and Zambia.

And nationalism remains an active force throughout the parts of the world that are still colonial. Citizens of the Portuguese colony of Angola in Africa do not consider themselves Portuguese no matter what Portuguese lawyers may say on the subject, and Hungarians, nominally independent, have died resisting the de facto rule of Russians. Increasingly, client nations in the Communist world have insisted on their right to defy their patrons or to change patrons. Albania switched her allegiance from the Soviet Union to China. North Korea and North Vietnam have broken away from total dependence on China, and Rumania has done the same with Russia. Within the Western Alliance, France and Germany are showing increased independence in their relations with the United States. It takes strange vision, indeed, to look at the world today and proclaim that nationalism and the nation-state are dying.

There is, of course, no reason to assume that nations will exist forever. They have been created by men as one form of social organization and what men have created they can destroy and replace with other forms if they wish. It is even probable that such a change will eventually take place.

For the moment, however, the nation is far and away the dominant form of political organization. Local units are subordinate to it, and international organizations are as yet powerless. Anyone who wants to understand the modern world and in particular its power structure must, of necessity, deal with nations.

Individuals, Groups, and Nations

It could be argued, of course, that nations should not be our main concern, that it is really individual human beings with whom we are dealing. The nation, after all, is nothing more than a convenient abstraction to cover a large group of individuals who have some things in common but who also differ in many ways, a group whose members have some common interests but also some separate interests, a group that sometimes feels a strong unity and sometimes does not, a group whose members sometimes act in concert and sometimes work at cross purposes. It is all very well to say that America is beginning to exercise her world leadership or that India is playing the role of peacemaker or that China is threatening world peace, but when one looks at individual citizens of these nations the picture may be quite different. There are many Americans who are not leaders at all. They may read a little—not much—about international events in the newspaper. They vote—usually —and they make up part of that vague entity called public opinion, but they don't have a foreign policy or even a very well-defined attitude toward the rest of the world.

Or look at the people of India. Indian leaders and diplomats may be trying to be peacemakers, but how many of India's millions know much about communism or democracy or the struggle between East and

West? How many individual Chinese are threatening anyone? Isn't it likely that they, too, are more concerned with the problems of their own daily lives than with China's role in world politics? Surely it is a mistake to think and write as if a nation were a collection of people who always thought and acted as one and who shared all the views expressed by their leaders.

It would be an even greater mistake, however, to treat national leaders as individuals representing no one but themselves. National leaders can and do commit the citizens of their nations to many activities, among others to the activity of making war. It is true that only individuals can act, feel, speak, form policies, threaten or attack, and it is true that small groups of leaders often form the policies and speak in the name of a nation, but to the extent that the citizens of the nation will back up these words with actions, it is the nation with which one contends and not merely a handful of leaders or a collection of individuals. Ivan and John may have no personal quarrel, but they will kill each other if their nations are at war. We will never understand why they do so, or how to prevent them from doing so, if we limit our inquiry to the characteristics of Ivan and John.

It remains to be explained why, of all the groups to which men belong, the nation should be so important. Everyone shares some characteristics with different groups of individuals. He feels himself to be a member of many groups, and he feels many and sometimes conflicting loyalties. Most of these groups do not have the same membership as the nation; some are smaller, some larger, some cut across national lines. For example, an individual belongs to a family, to a circle of friends, to a neighborhood, to a work group of some kind—all small groups— and the demands which they make upon his loyalty, his time, and his efforts are often greater than those demanded by his nation. Indeed, in peacetime, the nation may make so few demands as to be virtually unfelt.

An individual also belongs to groups that are larger than his nation. He may be a European or a Latin-American; he may be a member of the free world; certainly he is a member of humanity. Still other groups cut across national lines, uniting the individual with some of the people of other nations and dividing him from some of his countrymen. Religious, class, and racial groups may be of this nature, and a man may feel a strong bond with his fellow Catholics, his fellow proletarians (or princes), or his fellow whites even though they do not all share his nationality.

All these groups are important. All of them make demands upon the individual and help determine his attitudes and his actions. It should be noted, however, that most groups do not conflict with the nation. Small ones are generally contained within the nation, and it is a relatively rare individual whose family, circle of friends, or work group contains people of a different nationality than his own. His family pride may be strengthened, not weakened, by the feeling that it is an *American* (or a Japanese or an Icelandic) family. He may find his ties to his friends strengthened by the knowledge that they are all Germans or Irishmen or Finns. There may be some conflicts of interest between these small groups and the larger nation of which they form a part. For example, should a young man enlist in the navy or stay home and take care of his mother? Should a businessman make goods as cheaply as possible for the army or should he concentrate on making money for his company in his war contracts? Such conflicts exist, but the areas where interests coincide are probably much greater.

The large groups are somewhat similar, particularly those that consist of groups of nations. The American government does not mind at all if Americans consider themselves to be members of the free world; in fact it is pleased if they do so. The government of the United Arab Republic does not object if Egyptians consider themselves part of the Arab world; in fact it uses that feeling to stir up a sort of double-barreled nationalism. Difficulty arises only if individuals allow their larger loyalties to supersede their national loyalties in a dispute between their own nation and another. Patriotism demands that an Englishman be loyal to the Western Alliance to which his nation belongs, but not to such an extent that he sides with the United States in a dispute with England because he thinks England is damaging the alliance. In this case, he is liable to find himself accused of being pro-American, not pro-alliance. Loyalties to humanity are somewhat more dangerous to nationalism, for one's nation is almost always at odds with some part of humanity, and an honest concern for those particular members will always be unpopular.

The most divisive groups and loyalties are those that cut across national lines. A selfish businessman may do less than his full bit for his country at war, but a businessman who belongs to a cartel including enemy nationals may be tempted to treason. An underprivileged worker with a grievance may make himself a nuisance to his employer, but a disgruntled worker who belongs to a foreign subsidized revolutionary party may commit deliberate sabotage. Religious feelings may act as a strong bolster to nationalism, as in Japan or Israel or other one-religion countries, and they may help tie blocs of nations together, as in Catholic Latin America or the Arab world. But they can also divide a nation against itself, as they do in Holland and even to some extent in the United States. Racial animosities can be even more damaging to national unity.

National interests and loyalties seem to win out in the most crucial tests, however. In time of war, loving sons go off to fight; war contracts are renegotiated and profits cut; enemy property is confiscated, cartel or no; and saboteurs are shot. Socialist Germans shoot at socialist Frenchmen, Catholic Americans bomb Catholic Italians, and South African natives volunteer to form labor battalions in the armies of their white oppressors.

National organizations and nationalistic sentiments must be explained if we are to understand why the people of the world feel and behave toward each other as they do. And if we are looking for a unit of action, that is, *for the largest group of people who can be treated as if they acted together in world politics,* it seems obvious that the nation is a far better choice than the corporation, the labor union, the social class, the church, the race, the continent, or humanity as a whole.

What Makes a Nation?

We have written a good deal about nations and their importance, but up to this point we have not said much about what a nation is. What is it that makes this particular group of people a unit? What are the characteristics and the sentiments they share?

POLITICAL TIES

The nation is first and foremost a political unit. It is, more specifically, the largest political unit that recognizes no political superior. Members of the same nation can and usually do share much more than the same government and the same territory. They may also have a common economy, language, culture, religion, political ideology, and history. It is important to note, however, that these other traits, though usual, are not universal. One can, in fact, think of exceptions in almost every case. The one characteristic that all members of a nation share, and to this there can be no exception, is that they are all under the political jurisdiction of the same government.

Thus it is political behavior which defines the extent of each nation and the population it includes. In addition, political institutions play a large part in keeping the nation separate and distinct from other nations, in promoting unity within the nation, and in defending it against interference or attack from the outside.

To keep the nation separate from the rest of the world, political agencies watch over the national frontiers, arbitrary lines that separate the national territory and population from the outside world. They control the movement of people and goods across these lines, and they pass upon the applications of outsiders who wish to move into the national territory or to become members of the national group. To become an American or a Chinese or a German or a Brazilian, one must go through a political process and meet political standards. All national governments reserve to themselves the right to refuse admission or citizenship to any outsider they do not want.

National political agencies also act to prevent people and territory they control from breaking away from the nation. Only two countries today nominally grant their constituent units the legal right of secession: the USSR and Burma, but in the case of the Soviet Union, at least, this right is an illusion. The right of the American states to secede was denied by war, and most national governments would treat in a similar manner any attempt by some of its citizens to take the territory they lived on and withdraw it and themselves from the control of the national government.

Even individuals who wish to depart without territory are limited in their right to do so. No matter how free the country, the granting of passports is a right that national governments jealously guard, and although some governments allow some of their citizens to emigrate to other countries and become citizens there, other governments do not give passports to anyone whom they suspect of wanting to shift his political allegiance. To leave such a nation, an individual must trick his government into giving him a passport or flee illegally across an armed border; once he is beyond reach of his government, he must find another that will accept him despite the objections of his own nation. He must eventually fall under the control of one nation or another: he cannot simply secede from the nation-state system.

To promote unity within the nation, national governments engage in many different activities. They act to remove obstacles to the movement of men and goods within the national territory, to improve internal communications, and to spread and promote common characteristics of the people such as language, culture, and political ideology. They try to stamp out forms of localism that interfere with national unity, and they punish individual treason as the worst political crime a man can commit.

National governments provide and enforce many of the rules that allow the individuals in the nation to work together without getting in each other's way and doing one another harm. It seems obvious that, particularly in the great and complex industrial nations of modern times, life as we know it could not be carried on unless the government made and enforced rules governing the use of highways and railways and plane routes, of radio and television stations, of the mails; rules setting standards of safety and honesty in the production and distribution of goods and services; rules about money and banking and selling stocks; rules about labor relations; rules providing for the handicapped and the underprivileged. All these governmental activities are necessary for the smooth functioning of a nationwide economy and a nationwide culture. Government rules help to minimize conflicts between individuals who are dependent on each other.

When conflict does occur, the government again stands by to set limits on the kind of struggle that can be permitted and to help settle or even to impose settlement of cases that cannot be left for private solution. In this area of governmental activity, it is usual to think first of institutions such as courts, which are designed specifically for this task. In actuality, however, the process of settling differences that might tear the fabric of national society goes on constantly in many political institutions. Political leaders at political conventions, lawmakers in legislatures, bureaucrats in executive offices—all are frequently engaged in accommodation or negotiation, for the peaceful reconciliation of differences is an integral part of the political process.

If all goes well, differences within the nation are settled without the use of force. Enlightened self-interest keeps the citizens of a nation working together a large percentage of the time, and respect for law and order keeps them in line on most occasions when self-interest runs against the interests of others. But when self-interest and a respect for law are not enough, the overwhelming force at the disposal of the national government comes into play.

An excellent example of the many ways in which a national government helps settle and control disputes among its citizens is provided by the Negro revolution now taking place in the United States. National political institutions are busily engaged in mending the fabric of society and weaving a new pattern. The courts upset old rules and legitimize new ones; legislatures write new laws; executives mediate between warring groups, cajoling those entrenched in the existing power structure to give way, urging that new demands be made and met in a conciliatory fashion. And if all else fails, governmental forces move in to control outbursts of violence.

Another way in which political institutions help hold the nation together is by providing the symbols that evoke the idea of the nation in the minds of its citizens. The process through which people identify with the nation will be treated more fully later, but it should be noted at this point that the main national symbols—for example, the flag, the words of the national anthem, the king, the nation's founder—are all political symbols representing the national government, its personnel, and its actions. Without them, the expression of the emotional attach-ment people feel for their nation would be difficult indeed.

In addition to separating the nation from the outside world and helping to unify its people, the national government performs the crucial function of protecting the nation from outside interference or attack. The government has the exclusive right to deal with officials of other nations; it regulates all dealings of its own citizens with the people of other nations; and it mobilizes the population and resources of the nation in any armed combat with outsiders.

In short, the nation is primarily a political unit, for membership in it is defined in political terms, and political agencies have the main responsibility for defining the territorial boundaries, controlling move-ment across them, deciding who can belong to a nation's population and who cannot, preventing secession, promoting unity within the nation by encouraging internal trade and communications, making rules to keep the peace, settling disputes through control of a monopoly of force, providing the symbols that stand for the nation, and protecting it against outsiders. It is hard to overestimate the importance of political ties in binding a group of individuals into a nation.

TERRITORIAL TIES

National governments have jurisdiction not only over a group of people but also over the territory in which they live, and with very few excep-tions the territory consists of an uninterrupted piece of land or a group of islands located near each other. Pakistan is one exception, for it is divided into two widely separated parts. And with Alaska and Hawaii admitted to statehood, the United States consists of three separate bodies of land. Colonies, of course, are often far from the mother country, but nations as a rule are groups of people who live clustered together on adjacent pieces of land.

It is sometimes said that individuals feel an attachment to the soil of their homeland and that this sentiment about a common piece of territory is one of the ties that bind the people of a nation together. The claim seems somewhat exaggerated. The natural attachment of an individual is to the place of his birth, or, more exactly, to the place of his childhood, to the street on which he lived, to his hometown, to the area surrounding it, perhaps to the countryside where he spent his vaca-tions. This emotional attachment to places where one has had important personal experiences can be transferred to the national territory, but it requires a good bit of propagandizing. Left to his own devices, the in-habitant of the American Great Plains will feel a good deal more at home in the countryside of western Canada or even the Ukraine than he will in New England, and the mountaineer of Italy will find the mountains of Greece more congenial than the Italian seaside 30 miles away. The automobile is acquainting Americans and other motorized peoples with many parts of their national territory, but until quite recently, a love for the soil of one's whole native land was based more on stories and legends, books and pictures than upon personal experience. If love of the home-land tied men together, it was largely a creation of national literature and propaganda.

The validity of the argument that size is a determinant of national unity is also doubtful. Granted that extensive personal acquaintance with the same locality will give people something in common, the area about which people can have such feelings depends less upon its size than upon the means of communication and upon the presence or absence of social and economic barriers. The United States is an immense country, but it is probably safe to say that its residents have a wider knowledge of various sections of the country than do the residents of a much smaller country such as Yugoslavia, where communications are poor, travel rare, and provincial feelings strong.

It seems clear that the national territory in itself is not an important factor in keeping the nation together. Quite the contrary. Strong ties to local territory tend to divide a nation. It is because the nation is a political unit within whose boundaries travel is relatively easy and across whose boundaries travel is difficult that people come to experience and to love the land, and it is because of national literature and propaganda that people come to have strong sentiments about the national territory they have never seen.

ECONOMIC TIES

The modern nation is also to some extent an economic unit. The day of local self-sufficiency is past in all the industrialized nations and is passing rapidly even in the underdeveloped ones. Farmers who could conceivably live on what they produce prefer to specialize in cash crops and sell their produce in the cities for money to buy the many manufactured goods and nonlocal foods they require. A nation is tied together through a vast web of commercial transactions among its citizens, who are dependent upon each other and also sometimes upon the people of other nations.

The growth of international economic interdependence is often stressed in books on international relations. It is an important phenom-enon with great significance for the future, but it should not be allowed to obscure the much greater economic interdependence that exists *within* each nation. If the United States were suddenly cut off from all external trade, it would find crucial industries crippled for lack of raw materials until some inferior substitute could be devised. Profits would be sharply cut in many industries, workers laid off their jobs, and consumers compelled to do without many foreign products that they take for granted. We might even be thrown into a depression. Certainly serious economic reorganization would be required. But if New York City were suddenly cut off from trade with the surrounding countryside, it would be deserted in a week, and if a slice of American countryside were cut off from trade with the rest of the country, it would soon revert to a peasant economy. It is almost impossible to imagine what our lives would be like if the American economy were not nationwide.

One of the driving forces behind this national economic unity is modern technology. Because of it, the wants of the nation are increasingly standardized. Economical production of goods with modern machines requires mass production, and mass production requires a large market, preferably the entire nation. The assurance of a market large enough to consume the vast quantities of goods produced requires a constant stimulation of demand. All the great American producers engage in national advertising, and the public is subjected to a constant din of buy, buy, buy. Under the double influence of national advertising and national brands, local differences in tastes and wants tend to disappear. The nation becomes more of a unit. The same development occurs in planned economies such as that of the Soviet Union, where advertising to increase consumer demand has recently made its appearance and where the standardization of products is even more marked than in America. Fifty years ago, a man set down on a street in an unknown town in the United States would soon have been able to guess fairly accurately what part of the country he was in. People dressed differently, houses were different, each place had a distinct local flavor. Today, an American set down on the edge of a new highway or in the middle of a new suburb would have a hard time guessing whether he was in Oregon, Kansas, or Maine. And a woman placed suddenly in a strange kitchen would have a hard time telling whether she was on a farm or in the middle of a major city. The tremendous standardizing influences of mass production and mass advertising have spread a new commercial culture from one end of the country to the other.

Left free from political interference, the dynamics of modern technology and mass production would soon create a worldwide economy, and to a limited extent, this has already occurred. However, national governments cannot afford to ignore the economic lives of their subjects, and even the most laissez-faire of governments takes steps that prevent the free flow of international trade. Often the government tries to preserve the national market for her own producers by setting up barriers against the entrance of foreign goods. The United States has accomplished this through protective tariffs that have made American consumers pay higher prices for foreign goods but have protected American producers from foreign competition. The Soviet Union accomplishes its ends by having the government itself handle all foreign trade, buying and selling only those goods that fit in with the national plan. Political techniques for controlling international trade in the national interest are many and varied and sometimes unbelievably complex. Suffice it to say that no modern national government allows goods to enter and depart freely across its borders in the fashion that they circulate within the nation's territory.

Government planning also operates to increase economic unity within a nation. In a planned economy, the unit for planning is the nation. In a mixed economy, such as that of the United States, private economic organizations plan alongside the government, but even local businesses are affected by the government's tax policies, credit and banking regulations, and other fiscal policies, which are designed with the entire nation in mind.

In conclusion, we can say that modern technology and mass production have greatly expanded the size of economic operations and have acted to produce ever-larger economic units. National governments have encouraged this process within their national boundaries but have discouraged the free formation of economic ties that extend beyond the nation. There is no question that growing international economic interdependence is the most corrosive force at work on the nation-state system, but as long as that system is strong, nations will continue to be economic as well as political units.

THE NATIONAL LANGUAGE

Members of a national group usually share a common language that sets them apart from the people of other nations. The most common and the simplest way of identifying the nationality of a man is by the language he speaks.

The existence of a national language has a double effect. On the one hand, it makes communication quick and simple between fellow nationals, a necessity if they are to have extensive relations with each other and thereby develop a strong feeling of common identity. At the same time, a national language accentuates the differences between people of the same nationality and outsiders, because it makes it extremely difficult for such people to communicate easily and satisfactorily. The flood of American tourists who have traveled in non-English speaking countries know full well the truth of this statement. After a day of sight-seeing, when ordering a simple meal or planning a trip to the bathroom is a bitter struggle with an enigmatic environment, it is a great relief to return to a hotel with an English-speaking staff. It is easy to become irritated with people who do not understand you, and it is difficult to form a friendship with someone with whom you cannot speak at any length. Some of the difficulties posed by separate national languages can be overcome by learning a second or third language—a common practice among educated Europeans—but one is never as thoroughly at home in a second language as in his native tongue.

Sometimes language differences do not coincide with national boundaries. Occasionally a language is spoken by the people of more than one nation, as in the case of English, the common language of Englishmen, Americans, Australians, New Zealanders, most Canadians, and some South Africans; or French, which is spoken by Belgians as well as Frenchmen; or German, which is shared by Germans and Austrians; or Spanish, the language of most of Latin America. In such cases, language may be an integrative force within the nation, but it does not serve as an obstacle between people of the various nations that speak it. However, language is more than just words and grammar; it is also a question of accent and intonation. American English is quite different from British English, and Canadian French cannot be mistaken easily for the French spoken in France. Even where a common language is shared by two or more nations, differences in accent may set the nations apart.

Sometimes two or more languages are spoken by the same national group. The Swiss with their four official languages are the classic case, but Canadians have two different languages and so do South African whites. Dozens of different languages are spoken in the USSR and in India, and the Chinese, although they share one written language, speak dialects many of which are mutually incomprehensible.

It is difficult to say with precision to what extent the multilingual national group loses cohesion because its members do not all speak the same language. The split between English- and Afrikaans-speaking South Africans is serious, and the French-English rift in Canada is significant, but language differences here are probably more symptoms than causes of the difficulties. The Swiss, on the other hand, are as cohesive a group as one could wish for. Certainly the lack of a common language is a serious handicap for some of the new nations such as India—witness the language riots of 1966—or the African states, and one can predict that efforts will be made to spread some national language to all their citizens so that national unity can be increased.

Nations have even gone so far as to resurrect dead languages in order to have a common language of their own distinct from that of outsiders. At considerable effort, Jews in Israel have learned Hebrew, and Irishmen who have spoken English from birth must learn Gaelic if they are to speak their "native tongue." National languages are sometimes ordained by political officials, and often spread and standardized by governmental action, but once established, they do help to create a feeling of unity among those who speak them.

THE NATIONAL CULTURE

Language, however, is only one element of the culture that members of a nation often share. Culture includes all the things that people are taught by other people: what language a man speaks, how he dresses, which food he considers delicious and which disgusting beyond words, and how he behaves in the thousands of different circumstances that make up his daily life.

There is no question that people who share the same culture feel much closer to each other than those who do not. Of course, there are subtle differences in culture between social classes and between different regions of the country within a nation, but as members of a nation travel around and meet each other and as they are exposed to the same national influences, schools, literature, advertising, television, and movies, they tend to become more and more alike. Even where they do not become exactly alike, they gain enough acquaintance with their fellow citizens to know what to expect from them. It is very comfortable to deal with people who behave as one expects them to behave, who have the same manners and the same outlook on life, who have the same opinions, and who laugh at the same jokes. One feels close to them: they are "his own people."

The possession of a common culture also sets a group apart from those who do not share it. An individual who has always been surrounded by people who do things the same way he does is likely to be shocked or amused when he first meets someone from a different culture. European travelers who first encountered African natives were shocked at their nakedness, while the Africans for their part thought the Europeans were ridiculous to put their arms and legs in little bags in such hot weather. Americans find the sanitary arrangements in India appalling, but well-bred Indians are disgusted to see Americans blow their noses on pieces of cloth and then put the cloth in their pockets.

Sometimes differences in national culture involve fundamental attitudes. Americans, for example, are trained from early childhood to compete, and tests show that they do their best work in competitive situations. At the same time, they are trained to be good losers. Japanese, on the other hand, are taught to avoid competition. They do their best work when working alone and measuring their performance against their own past record and are liable to go to pieces when confronted with a competitor. Losing out to a competitor may make a Japanese depressed or angry for a long time.[1] An American is trained that it is a sign of maturity to be able to admit occasionally that he has been wrong, if this is the case. A Japanese, however, is taught by his culture that it brings dishonor to his name to admit he is wrong. These are fundamental attitudes, and a person holding one of them will find it difficult to deal with someone holding the other.

Sometimes the differences in national cultures are more trivial, and it is often these differences that are recognized as most "national": whether a man eats spaghetti or tortillas or frog's legs or bird's nest soup; whether he wears *lederhosen* or a kilt or a kimono. If you pass a cricket field and hear a restrained "good shot" and a quiet ripple of applause, make no mistake, you are among Englishmen. Or if you see a howling crowd eating small sausages in buns and drinking bottled drinks while a man swings horizontally with a bat at an almost invisible ball, you can be sure you are looking at Americans. Anyone acquainted with sartorial styles can tell at a glance whether men in a room are Russian, Italian, English, or American. But a good observer does not rely on dress alone: the way men talk, the way they stand, their range of facial expressions, the way they use their hands give anyone familiar with several national cultures enough clues to make an informed, and probably correct, guess at their nationality.

These differences of dress and diet and sport may seem trivial, but it is highly probable that a foreign conqueror who made all Americans wear long robes, deprived them of their familiar diet (say, made them teetotalers and vegetarians), and forbade them to watch television or play any games, would find himself as thoroughly hated as a conqueror who made major changes in the political and economic system but left the daily habits of Americans untouched.

Possession of a common culture is one of the strongest bonds holding the members of a national group together, and anyone who has been brought up in one national culture and later tried to switch to another knows how difficult it is to feel the new identification completely. No matter how fully conversant with the new culture he becomes, some of

[1] Ruth Benedict, *The Chrysanthemum and the Sword* (Boston: Houghton Mifflin, 1946), pp. 153–54.

its nuances will escape him, and he will not have all the built-in emotional responses of natives. For the latecomer, certain responses will always be, at least to some extent, an intellectual exercise.

RELIGIOUS TIES

It should be made clear that the national culture includes not only ways of behaving but also ways of thinking and systems of belief. Common religious beliefs have often helped reinforce feelings of national unity, particularly when a nation is faced with enemies whose religion is different. Religion has been relegated to a secondary place by most modern governments, but its power as a unifying—or as a divisive—force should not be discounted.

One of the most impressive examples of the unifying force of religion is the contribution of religion to the establishment of the state of Israel, in which Jews split apart politically for almost two thousand years drew back together to form a nation. Through all the period of separation, a feeling of national identity had been kept alive almost entirely through religious institutions and beliefs. This is admittedly an extreme case, but religion has played a nationalistic role in other countries, giving the Spaniards a feeling of common unity against the Moors, the Irish an additional point of difference from the English, the Arabs of North Africa a separate national identity from the French settlers with whom they legally shared a common nationality.

Religions, however, do not respect national boundaries. Often the religious group is greater than the nation, and sometimes it cuts across national groupings. In the first case, religion may be a factor in causing common *international* action by nations that share the same system of religious beliefs, as when the South American republics gave unanimous support to Catholic Italy and Spain in their attempts to be admitted to the United Nations or when a number of Muslim countries joined to form the Arab League.

Religions that cut across national lines may be a cause of serious disunity, as in Belgium and the Netherlands or, more tragically, as in India and Pakistan, where millions of Hindus and Muslims found themselves in the "wrong" country when British India was divided and felt compelled to leave their homes and possessions in order to join their coreligionists. Israel and its Arab refugees provide another case in point.

Most modern nations, however, are capable of containing more than one religious group. The Soviet Union, whose people are mostly Eastern Orthodox Christians or atheists, contains large minorities of Muslims and Jews. The United States finds three of the world's major religions well represented among its people, and both India and China contain a considerable variety of religious groups.

In general, it can be said that common religious beliefs are an important source of group unity, and that religious sentiments can be used to bolster nationalistic feelings in one-religion countries, but that they are not emphasized where religious differences might divide a nation against itself.

POLITICAL IDEOLOGY

Better suited than religion to the nationalistic purposes of governments is that secular system of beliefs sometimes referred to as political ideology. In its strongest form, such ideology has some of the elements of a religion about it. Communism, for example, or Nazism and fascism in the past, are more than forms of government; they include systems of belief, mythologies, frequent and stirring ceremonies and rites, and codes of behavior. Even Americanism includes some ritualistic elements: parades, flags, oaths, the recital of past history and the listing of past heroes on the Fourth of July and in election speeches. Being an American is not a mere fact about which one feels the same as he does about being a public accountant. It involves emotional feelings of love and pride and dedication.

Schoolchildren of every nation are taught an immense amount of factual detail about their form of government and the political philosophy that lies behind it, partly in order to understand their rights and obligations as citizens, to be sure, but also partly to arouse their feelings of patriotism. A look at the content of courses in political science, particularly those taught in American primary and secondary schools, makes the purpose fairly clear. Observe the emphasis on glorious events and political heroes in contrast to the treatment given less colorful events and personalities of the present day. Look at the amount of time spent reading statements of principle, constitutions, and the like compared with the time spent studying political behavior. A good citizen should know how tax rates are assessed, how to go about getting decent schools from his local government, how the political machine in a big city actually operates, how party leaders are chosen, how primaries work, and how pressure groups and lobbies operate. But these are not the things our schools emphasize, for what they are transmitting to the young is not so much a working knowledge of practical politics as the ringing phrases and the tribal lore that will produce a strong feeling of national identity.

COMMON HISTORY

The past history of a nation is most useful in stirring up strong feelings of national unity. For one thing, the citizens of a nation have experienced together that part of the national history that has occurred during their lifetime, and shared experiences always create a bond among people. But historical events create a feeling of national unity not only among those who participate in them, but also among those for whom they are re-created later. The Boston Tea Party, the Gettysburg Address, and Pearl Harbor all help to unify Americans, and we grieve for the assassination of Lincoln as we do for that of Kennedy.

As far as the effect of common experiences on national identity is concerned, one is almost tempted to say that it is not important what kind of experiences the nation has had. What is important is that the experiences be widely shared and that the members of the nation not think less of themselves because of them. Germany, for example, has recently lost two world wars, suffering humiliating and total defeat, but these misfortunes have had no visible effect on the solidarity of the nation, although they seem to have dimmed her military ardor, at least for the moment. Common suffering creates a bond as strong or stronger than common victory; again, witness the history of the Jews.

Of all the experiences that nations have, the one that seems to add most to a feeling of national unity is war. The dates and details of battles and the names of generals and wartime leaders of the nation figure prominently in the history of almost every nation. This should not be surprising, for war is one of the very few national experiences in which the nation works and thinks as one and where the good of the whole is generally considered to be more important than the good of the component parts. One of the reasons Texans are so proud of their state and have retained such strong local feelings is that more than one hundred years ago they fought against Mexico and were independent for a time. They have a separate history from the rest of the United States in this respect, and they are proud of it. Or take the American South, which fought and lost the Civil War. Oddly enough, it is Southerners, not Northerners, who are most likely to hark back to the War Between the States as a period of glory. Proud of their showing and hurt by their defeat, Southerners of today regard the leaders who took them down the road to defeat as heroes of their stillborn nation.

Founders of the nation are also important symbols of national unity. Legends grow up around them, and their real lives and characters, though of interest to scholars, grow dim beside the heroic figures that national pride creates. The combination of a new nation born in battle is irresistible; and when it comes to re-creating patriotic feelings in later generations, nations created in strife have an immense advantage over those formed more peaceably. The Revolutionary War is known to every

American as a glorious war of major proportions, whereas to the British, it is merely a minor skirmish in their long military history.

The idea that wars have such a unifying force suggests the dangerous idea that in order to remain truly united, a nation ought to fight a war every now and then. Fortunately, this is not necessary, for old wars will serve as well as new ones, perhaps better, for they are all glory and no sacrifice. Any past experience can be shared by nonparticipants if they know about it and can identify with the actors. This is one of the major reasons for the study of national history in the nation's schools. It is not simply an academic interest in truth or in the past roots of the present that leads nations to teach their histories to their young. Such teaching is based on the correct assumption that the students will develop a feeling of identity with their own nation in exploring an expurgated and glamorized version of its origin and development.

This is why national heroes and events that have brought luster to the nation are constantly paraded for the reflected glory that nationals can feel in being associated, however vaguely, with such great men and events. Political and military leaders head the parade, but great or merely colorful men of any sort will do. Artists, writers, thinkers, inventors, adventurers, all have their place as national heroes. Nations that have a long history have an advantage, but recently formed nations can make up some of their loss by claiming as theirs the great men among their ancestors in the days long before the present political unit was formed. Thus the Greeks go back to Homer, Plato, and Praxiteles, the Italians claim Caesar and Virgil, Dante and Michelangelo and all the thinkers and artists of the Italian city-states. The Americans have incorporated the Pilgrims (Englishmen all) into their national history. Even Columbus is ours for discovering our continent, although by that event he brought glory also to Italy as the country of his birth and to Spain as the country that employed him.

Thus a common history is one more tie that binds the members of a nation together, first, because they actually share a small part of that history, and secondly, because through history books and stories they vicariously experience great events that occurred before they were born.

SUMMARY

We have seen that individual members of a national group have many characteristics in common. Although these vary somewhat from one nation to another, it is possible to generalize. Nations usually have a common language, some have a predominant religion. Most have a common culture, a common predominant political ideology, a common history and a certain amount of economic unity, and the tendency toward national differentiation along these lines is strengthened by governmental action. However, the major tie that holds the members of a nation together is political, for the nation is essentially and without exception a political unit.

Second, it is a psychological unit, that is to say, a group of people who feel that they constitute a unit, who feel they have many important characteristics in common, whether they actually do or not. It is a group of people who choose to emphasize the ways in which they are alike rather than the ways in which they differ. This feeling of unity is every bit as important as the actual homogeneity upon which it is supposedly based.

It will be useful here to make a distinction between three ideas that are sometimes confused. The individual members of a nation share certain characteristics, and to the extent that they actually *are* alike, one may speak of national homogeneity.

In addition, or even apart from this, members of a nation may *feel* that they are alike and may think of themselves as constituting a unit. We may call this their feeling of nationalism.

Finally, as a result of these nationalistic feelings, the individuals who make up a nation may *act* together as a unit, submerging their own individual interests in the common good and presenting a united front to the outside world. We may call this nationalistic behavior.

Such terms as national unity, national cohesion, nationalism, and patriotism refer to these last two phenomena: to the way the people of a nation feel and to the way they act. These feelings and actions by themselves create additional strong ties that hold the people of a nation together. It is to a consideration of them that we turn next.

Nationalism

There is no doubt that nationalism is a powerful force in the modern world. We have seen impressive demonstrations of the capacity of members of the same nation to feel and act as if they were a unit. Nationalism is not limited to small, homogeneous nations whose citizens are in fact very much alike and who do share an almost identical set of interests. It seems to be equally characteristic of giant nations such as the United States and the Soviet Union, whose citizens vary tremendously from each other in many ways. Millions of Indians, differing from each other in language and culture and religion and economy, sharing very little except dislike of their British rulers and reverence for a great leader, managed to act together in a program of passive resistance which compelled the British to grant them political independence. And the new Arab nations of the Middle East, strange conglomerations of feudal princes, illiterate peasants, urban mobs, and a handful of Westernized politicians and businessmen have shown themselves capable of sudden and inflammatory nationalistic action. What is this strange feeling that leads men to behave in such unpredictable ways? When did it arise and why?

We do not know exactly when nationalism first began to appear, but we do know that it is a recent phenomenon. Nationalism, in the modern sense, did not exist at the time of the Romans or the ancient Greeks. It was not present in medieval times. Some trace of nationalistic feeling can possibly be found at the very beginning of modern times when the nation-state was first becoming an important form of political organization. Indeed, it is doubtful that without some such feeling to back them up, the leaders who unified the first nations politically would have been so successful. However, the modern mass identification of common folk the world over with the nation to which they belong is much more recent.

When it comes to describing what nationalism is, we are on somewhat firmer ground. Nationalism is essentially a strong feeling of personal identification with the collection of people, places, and patterns of behavior that make up a nation and its way of life. The strong emotional attachment of the individual to the nation comes about through the transfer to the large, impersonal, and somewhat abstract group called the nation of a portion of those attitudes and feelings that the individual has developed for small face-to-face groups of which he is a member. Through daily association, he develops real feelings of love and identity and loyalty toward his family, his friends, and to a lesser extent toward his co-workers and his neighbors. It is these feelings that form the basis for his attachment to the nation.

The exact nature of the devotion felt for the country and its political leaders varies greatly from one nation to another, but it is interesting to note how closely it parallels the feelings toward the family and the home. The national territory is the "homeland" or the "fatherland" or the "motherland." Soldiers from farms in Nebraska felt they were home when ships bringing them back from war sailed into New York harbor or Seattle, although in many ways New York and Seattle might actually have been as foreign to them as Liverpool. Political leaders are often regarded as fathers: The founder of a nation is the "father of his country," Russian tsars were "little fathers," and some American Presidents have owed their election to the fact that they were father-images. The British royal family is, in sentiment, the family of every loyal subject, and Britishers follow the fortunes of the royal family with all the interest customarily bestowed on relatives. The elaborate obligations of the Japanese toward his senior relatives find a reflection in his obligations to his emperor. The authoritarian tradition of the German family has often found expression in an authoritarian political structure. The child-centered American family produces citizens who are highly democratic but often disrespectful of authority. Given a thorough knowledge of the relations between parents and children in a given culture, one could predict with a fair degree of accuracy many of the political attitudes these people would have.

The likelihood that such a transference of sentiments from family to nation will be made is much greater in a modern, industrial nation than it was in preindustrial society. In a peasant society, face-to-face ties are very important. What is more, an individual is likely to spend his entire life as a member of the *same* face-to-face group. His family, his friends, his co-workers, and his neighbors all belong to the same local group. It is easy for him to identify himself completely with it without feeling the need for any larger loyalty. Religion is extremely important in such societies, and the needs people have for group ceremonies and rituals and for orienting themselves in relation to mankind, to the past, and to the future, are amply met by religious institutions.

In modern society, however, the old face-to-face ties are fractured. Families are small and mobile, parents and children become separated from each other by distance and by differences in interests. Neighbors come and go, and improved transportation and communication break down the old self-contained neighborhoods and with them the feelings of neighborliness. The people one meets at work are known only partially and are viewed instrumentally. A man may know virtually nothing about his employer. A clerk may have no interest in her customers. Even friends may change from year to year, as one moves to a new town, rises socially, joins a new club, or develops a new interest. The number of friends retained from childhood to old age is very few, indeed.

As an individual moves from group to group, working with one, playing with another, living next to a third, he finds that he does not belong completely to any group, that he is very much alone. He may turn to religion in an effort to find some meaningful relationship to his environment, but the religion of today encompasses less of his life than did that of his forefathers, and many of its claims to his faith are challenged. Small wonder that he sometimes feels lonely, helpless, and anxious and that he yearns for some group that can mean to him what his family meant to him in his childhood.

It has been suggested that a feeling of national identity helps to compensate for the helplessness and insecurity created by modern society, for here is one group to which the individual belongs from birth to death, a group that remains the same despite its changing personnel, a group that must accept him simply because he exists. In the highly competitive environment of modern society, few can hope to reach their goals, but frustration may be partially avoided if the individual can find in the successes of his country some emotional compensation for his own failure to succeed. Aggressive feelings may be poured out upon the national enemies, and with the full approval of other patriotic citizens, the individual may participate in attitudes and actions usually forbidden. As Werner Levi writes:

> The moral code applying to him individually is greatly relaxed for him as a member of the national community. He would be thoroughly rebuked for following the principle "Right or wrong, Myself" whereas he might be praised for doing so as a member of the collectivity of individuals called the state. This double standard permits the citizen to enjoy vicariously through the group a behavior that would never be permitted him as an individual within it. By setting the state apart from himself in a quasi-personalized form the citizen can approve with a clear conscience national actions against other states, i.e., groups of people, which he would severely condemn if performed by an individual.[2]

It is easy to see what an attractive force nationalism can be to the lonely and anxious individual of modern times.

NATIONAL SYMBOLS

Before the individual can transfer to the nation those sentiments he customarily feels toward his family and other small groups, certain simplifications must be made. A nation, after all, includes a great many people, most of whom a single individual will never meet and many of whom he would not like if he did meet them. How can an individual feel a warm, personal tie to a large group of people with whom, individually, his dealings are impersonal or nonexistent?

Through the use of symbols it becomes possible. A symbol is a relatively simple, concrete thing—a bit of colored cloth (the flag), a picture of an imaginary person (Uncle Sam or John Bull), a stirring poem set to music (the national anthem), or better yet, a real person who is the leader of his nation. Men have always found it difficult to deal directly with abstractions. (Note the tremendous amount of symbolism in most religions, for example.) But through the use of symbols, men find it possible to feel warm, personal emotions about distant, abstract ideas.

The nation is such an abstraction. The patriot is not deeply moved by his daily, face-to-face encounters with his countrymen, but he feels a great identity with them when he thinks about them in the abstract, and

2 Werner Levi, *The Fundamentals of World Organization* (Minneapolis: University of Minnesota Press, 1950), p. 25.

he may be moved to a state of high excitement when he watches or participates in rituals where living people and objects constitute symbols of the nation. Take a group of fine-looking, healthy, young men, put them in colorful uniforms and march them in perfect unison to a martial tune, and what heart will not be thrilled? And yet the same group of young men in civilian clothes on their day off would attract no notice at all, for then they would be merely themselves, not symbols of the nation.

Flags make excellent national symbols, for they can be carried into battle and thus share in the glory of victory or the nobility of defeat, and they are all alike so that any single flag can be made to stand for all the other flags of the same pattern that have been associated with glorious events in the nation's past. The flag is raised over conquered territory, placed on the coffins of heroes, carried into new lands by explorers, posted on the tops of mountains, even shot into space. A new flag is raised when a colony becomes independent, and an enemy's flag is burned as a sign of disrespect. The elaborate ritual with which the flag is handled, the fact that it must never touch the ground, that no other national flag may fly above it on American soil, that it must never be destroyed except by burning or burial, all of this makes no sense at all if one thinks of a flag as simply a piece of cloth, but it makes a great deal of sense if one thinks of it as symbolizing the national honor.

Leaders of the nation also make excellent symbols, especially if they are not actually engaged in the daily strife and controversy of practical politics. When it comes to symbolizing the entire nation, a ceremonial leader such as the Queen of England or the Emperor of Japan has marked advantages over the premier or president, who must, after all, make enemies if he is to rule. And the leader who holds his office for life or at least for a long period has an advantage over the democratically elected official whose term is brief and who must engage in partisan political campaigning in order to serve any term at all. We say that we revere the office of the Presidency, not the man who is President, but it is difficult to separate the two, and a man in an office makes a much better symbol of the nation than the office itself, which is simply another abstraction.

Democratic leaders who are active in politics do sometimes serve as national symbols, however, particularly in troubled times when the nation is united. During the blackest days of World War II, Winston Churchill came close to personifying England. An earlier generation of Europeans gave Woodrow Wilson a hysterical ovation after World War I, which expressed their feelings toward America not their feelings toward the man who was visiting their country. Most diplomatic protocol is based on the fiction that diplomats are nations. The Belgian ambassador may be personally obnoxious, but another diplomat cannot refuse to attend his receptions without insulting Belgium. He is, in short, a symbol and must be treated as if he were what he represents.

In addition to persons and things, there are verbal symbols—names and events and phrases that are recited, not because they add to the factual content of a statement, but because they evoke feelings of patriotism. To list such phrases would appear to mock them, and that is not my intention. It is enough to say that they abound in political speeches and in all celebrations of a patriotic nature. If the reader takes careful notes on the next Fourth of July address or the next speech on foreign policy that he hears, he will find that the main factual argument could have been expressed in a very few words, but that it has been embroidered with ringing phrases that could be transposed freely from one part of the speech to another or even put into an altogether separate speech on a different subject without changing the meaning. Indeed, such phrases gain a patriotic flavor mainly from the fact that they have been used so often. They are symbols, not descriptions of fact.

Enough has been said to make it quite clear that nationalism is less a natural force than a learned response to certain symbols. Nor is it a rational force, although it is put to rational uses. It is essentially an emotional feeling expressed in action.

NATIONALISTIC BEHAVIOR

The ways in which nationalistic feelings can be expressed are many. They may be expressed in parades and speechmaking, cheering and singing, in pulling in one's belt and cheerfully accepting a rationing system, in the organized discipline and deprivation of war, or in riots, arson, and rape. Nationalistic feelings are noted for getting out of hand and leading to excesses, but they can also provide a powerful harnessed force under the direction of a national government.

Such a force can be used to throw out an oppressor or to oppress others, to repel an invasion or to start one, to wrest new land from the sea or to wrest new territory from a neighbor, to build a peaceful and prosperous nation or to reduce a continent to rubble. Nationalism, in itself, is neither good nor evil. It is a powerful emotion that leads large groups of men to act in unison. It is frequently deplored because, as a feeling of unity that ends at the national boundaries, it is often expressed in actions by one nation against another, that is, because it is a force dividing nations. But nationalism is also a unifying force within the nation, tying together groups that would otherwise be divided against each other. It can be harnessed for any constructive purpose that requires the united action of all the citizens of a nation.

We have treated national unity of action as if it were solely a *result* of the degree to which a group of people are alike and of the degree to which they feel they are alike. In fact, however, unity in action is also a *cause* of nationalistic feelings and national homogeneity. One can say that because people are similar to each other in many important characteristics they have a feeling of common identity which leads them to act together as a unit. This is true. But it is equally true that when a group of people acts together to achieve a common goal, this increases their feeling of unity, and when people feel that they share a common identity, they become more like each other in fact.

National unity, however, is always a matter of degree. Just as there is never complete homogeneity, there is never a complete feeling of national identity. The degree of national unity (or cohesion) varies greatly from one nation to another and from one time to another. It is difficult to locate all the determinants of these differences. We shall discuss some of them when we come to a consideration of national morale,[3] but it should be noted here that national unity increases greatly whenever the nation is attacked from outside, a characteristic of many social groups.

Whatever the causes, a certain degree of unity of action is an essential characteristic of the nation. As long as its members stick together and act together, the nation will survive. Its power in dealing with others will be greatly influenced by the strength of the cohesive forces within the nation. A group of people may share a common government and a common territory, constitute an economic unit, have a common language, culture, religion, political ideology, and history, but without a feeling of unity and the capacity to act together they will not long remain a nation. More than any other characteristic, it is this capacity to unite its members in common action for a common purpose that makes the nation the most important unit in world politics today.

Summary

Our consideration of the ties that bind the people of a nation together has shown how many different ties there are: political, territorial, economic, cultural, linguistic, religious, ideological, historical, and psychological. In particular we have seen the strength of nationalism, the needs that it fills for the individual—and for the state.

At the beginning of this chapter, the question of whether the nation was diminishing in importance, whether is was about to be replaced by some more extensive unit, perhaps even a world state, was raised. It was granted then that such a change may eventually come to pass, but we

[3] See Chapter 8.

are now in a better position to see why it is unlikely to occur in the near future. The forces that created the nation have been a long time in the making, and the adjustments that individuals have made in accepting this new unit have been severe. It will take new forces at least as powerful and new adjustments at least as painful to destroy the nation-state. Nor is nationalism an ancient force, weary and spent. On the contrary, it is a relatively new development that is only now coming into its own in much of the world. To believe that nationalism will vanish because it is dangerous or that nations will wither away because there are better ways of organizing mankind is naive. The nation is the major unit in world politics today, and it is likely to remain so for some time to come.

3

The Process of
National Growth

The nation was not always so important. Five hundred years ago, there were no nations as we know them, and even three hundred years ago, national loyalties were not the major group loyalties of most people. The nation is a relatively recent development, and it has changed a great deal during its brief history.

In its broadest outlines, the historical development of the nation can be seen as a process involving an ever-increasing number of people in the fortunes of the state. The earliest nations were little more than groups of kings and nobles with the rest of the population constituting properties to be fought over. Gradually, the nation came to include the bourgeoisie as responsible participants who felt a national identity. Recent years have seen an increasing involvement in the nation of the great mass of common people until today the more advanced nations are units that include the entire population living under a common government.

Other broad changes can be traced. In nation after nation we find a long-term increase in the efficiency with which the government is able to use the human and material resources of the nation for the realization of national goals. Still other changes include increased differentiation of governmental structure and, according to some writers, increased rationali-

40

zation of authority and increased acceptance of the state as the final arbiter of fundamental disputes within its jurisdiction.[1] Even more important are changes in the primary function of government that occur as nations progress from one stage of political development to another.

For purposes of discussion, the political development of the nation-state can be divided into four recognizable stages: (1) the politics of primitive unification, (2) the politics of industrialization, (3) the politics of national welfare, and (4) the politics of abundance. This division, of course, is merely a convenience. In actuality, the changes that have occurred have been continuous, and there are no sharp dividing lines between one stage and another.

Nations have moved from one stage to another at different dates. Today the great majority of nations—most of the underdeveloped countries—are still in stage 1. Others (China, most of Eastern Europe, and much of Latin America, for example) are in stage 2, whereas the United States, the Soviet Union, and Western Europe are all at various points in stage 3. Stage 4 lies in the future.[2]

Before we examine each stage in detail, two cautions are in order. All the nations in the world have not followed exactly the same path and certainly all of them will not become exactly like the United States or the other highly developed nations of today. But all do seem to be headed in the same direction: through a series of changing functions of the political system toward increased political efficiency and broader participation.

We must also be careful in comparing the experiences of different nations as they go through each stage. There are, of course, vast differences between stage 1 in England under Henry VIII, in Algeria under French rule, and in India today. There are dramatic contrasts between stage 2 in the United States under McKinley, in Russia under Stalin, and in Italy under Mussolini. But there are also similarities. Generalization covering such diverse cases is legitimate, *provided* we remember that generalization is an intellectual exercise that selects what is common and ignores what is not. We are not trying to describe the total reality; rather, we are looking for similarities in order to construct a framework in which to organize our knowledge of the growth of nations.

[1] Samuel P. Huntington identifies the three major elements of political development as the rationalization of authority, the differentiation of structure, and the broadening of participation. ["Political Modernization: America vs. Europe," *World Politics,* XVIII, 3 (April 1966), 378–414.] Kalman Silvert has suggested that modernization is to be traced through the increase in acceptance of the state as the final arbiter of fundamental disputes within its jurisdiction.

[2] More detailed treatment of the political growth of nations can be found in A. F. K. Organski, *The Stages of Political Development* (New York: Knopf, 1965).

Stage 1: The Politics of Primitive Unification

The first task of government in any emerging nation is to provide at least a minimum of national unity among the diverse peoples and groups within the national boundaries. Without such unity political leaders may *speak* for the entire nation, but they cannot organize or command its resources for any national purpose, nor can they proceed with the task of economic modernization that so often preoccupies them today.

The problems of creating this early unification beset most of the countries in the world today, and the rest have solved similar problems at some time in the past. The stage of primitive unification therefore includes a wide variety of experience. At least four types of politics of unification can be identified:

1. Dynastic politics, where nations are built by absolute monarchs, as in Western Europe in the sixteenth, seventeenth, and eighteenth centuries. Dynastic systems still exist in such states as Ethiopia, Iran, Saudi Arabia, and Thailand.
2. Colonial politics, where national unity is first created under the rule of a foreign colonial ruler. This was the origin of most of the African and American nations and of many of the nations of Asia.
3. The politics of newly independent preindustrial countries. Here former colonies continue the process of primitive unification under their own governments. India, Indonesia, and Nigeria are examples, to name only a few.
4. The politics of old and established countries that are still economically underdeveloped and less than fully unified politically. Iran, Egypt, and some of the nations of South America are examples.

There are important differences among these four types of political systems, the most obvious being who rules: king, colonizer, revolutionaries, or landed aristocracy. There are also striking similarities in the way the nation was created; in the way central control was achieved, perpetuated, and exercised; and in the political tools available to carry out the job of unification.

THE BIRTH OF NATIONS

There is a depressing similarity in the way nations are born: they are born by force. Regardless of other differences, there are few nations that have not been given both life and shape by force of arms. The major distinction seems to be whether the force of arms came from within or without.

In dynastic Western Europe, major nations owed their origins to feudal lords (sometimes the king) who fought their fellow lords into submission and drew boundary lines around their conquered lands, imposing their rule upon communities of peasants who were poor, economically inefficient, politically divided, local in their loyalties, and unified in nothing but their rulers.

In the European colonies, the force came from outside. Again local lords and chieftains were conquered, new boundaries were drawn to stake a claim to the conquests, and central rule was imposed upon poor and divided peasants. Again the resulting unity was of the thinnest and most fragile sort.

The politics of primitive unification do not end with national independence but continue—sometimes for centuries—under the new rulers. The difference, however, is fundamental, for it is only after political colonialism is over that the slow struggle to develop a central authority capable of unifying the nation from within begins in earnest. It is only then that *local* control is wrested from the sheiks and feudal lords and maharajahs, the priests, or bonzes, or mullahs. It is only then that the fiefs and principalities and tribes are finally destroyed. The struggle is seldom completely won by the end of stage 1, for the political tools available to the central authority are primitive and not sufficient to accomplish this task.

THE TOOLS OF UNIFICATION

Political authorities seeking to unify fledgling nations have relied heavily upon two major institutions: the standing army and the bureaucracy. The importance of the army should be obvious. In European experience the military forces of feudal times consisted of a large variety of separate armies, each responsible to the lord who raised it. To destroy the power of the lords, Europe's emerging national monarchs found it necessary to create armies of their own—armies of professionals, paid from the king's treasury and responsible only to the king.

In the colonies, too, the new rulers substituted a single professional army of their own for the variety of local forces that had previously existed. An important difference, however, was that the army came from the outside, and when the colonies became independent they were often (though not always) left without efficient, unified military forces loyal to the new central authority. This lack has complicated the task of primitive unification for the newly independent nations.

Throughout the underdeveloped world—in the new nations and in the old—military forces are generally too small, too poorly trained, and too poorly armed to be of much use in prolonged warfare with other states. But they are of great value in maintaining internal order, and their leaders often play important roles in internal politics.

The second major tool of primitive unification has been the national bureaucracy.[3] In dynastic Europe, the gradual creation of a professional national bureaucracy responsible to the monarch from the top level down to the local level of government was a significant departure from feudal practice. Without it, it is doubtful that the new monarchs could have kept their hold over their conquests and created the nations we know today.

Similarly in the colonies, a relatively small number of bureaucrats provided the spinal cord of colonial rule. The top levels of the bureaucracy were always staffed by Europeans while natives were used at the lower levels, but regardless of the differences from colony to colony and from time to time, regardless of differences between direct and indirect rule, decision and control remained in European hands.

The fact that the bureaucracy, like the army, was largely imported has also had serious consequences for the newly independent nations, which have been hard put to find trained and competent personnel to fill the gaps left by their departing rulers. In a few of the more fortunate colonies a small operating native civil service was left in control when the Europeans departed, but in many cases the rule of the colonial bureaucracy was resisted from beginning to end, and even now the whole notion of impersonal rule by trained specialists is far from accepted by the present authorities and their citizens.

In nearly all the nations presently in stage 1 of political development the bureaucracy, though crucial, is very primitive by modern standards. Nearly always short-handed, it is often inefficient and corrupt as well. Its domain is generally limited to the cities and its hold upon and understanding of the countryside is often extremely limited.

The political party also plays a role as a unifying institution. In Western Europe the expansion of the franchise and the growth of political parties did not occur until well along in stage 2, but in the newly independent nations of today the political party has already appeared and it fills a different function. Because of their preoccupation with national

[3] By bureaucracy we mean a corps of full-time, professional specialists who work for wages in a large, centralized, hierarchical organization (in this case the government). See Max Weber, "The Essentials of Bureaucratic Organization: An Ideal-Type Construction," and Carl J. Friedrich, "Some Observations on Weber's Analysis of Bureaucracy," in Robert K. Merton *et al.* (eds.), *Reader in Bureaucracy* (New York: Free Press, 1952).

unity, the new nations have tended to be one-party states, and the whole apparatus of elections, rallies, slogans, and speeches operates not so much as a means of expressing popular will as a way of spreading nationalistic sentiments and creating national unity.

REMAINING TASKS

The nation in stage 1 with its national army and its national bureaucracy is a significant departure from the past, but it is not yet a nation in the full sense of the term. What unity there is remains almost entirely political and is only the thinnest net of control stretched over a varied and divided society. Cities are divided from countryside, province from province. Geographic, ethnic, racial, and religious differences are often marked. Separatist tendencies are strong, and it is often a major task of the national government simply to maintain the nation's existence. Even the elite is divided within itself with particularly sharp conflict between the traditionalists and the more modern elements.

A vast chasm separates the rulers from the ruled, and the great majority of the people living within the national boundaries cannot truly be considered members of the nation. In the dynastic states, in the colonies, and in many of the new states they are in reality subjects whose major function is to be taxed. Even in the new nations where there is talk of social welfare or even socialism, the national government provides the mass of people with virtually nothing in the way of services; and the people in turn feel little loyalty to the national government and not even much national identity. The vast majority of the population consists of peasants whose loyalies and interests are local and they are often hostile to the national government and all it represents.

Economic unity is also primitive. Subsistence agriculture occupies most of the population and the movement of goods and people from one part of the country to another is not great except among a handful of major cities. Labor is not very mobile, and the great urban migrations lie in the future.

Nevertheless, the beginnings of economic unity exist. Mercantilists, colonial rulers, and the leaders of new nations today are all alike in building new road networks and other means of communications and in stimulating manufacturing and commerce. This helps to break down local particularism and begins, if only in a rudimentary way, to increase the dependence of the peasant population upon a national economy.

In summary, it can be said that the governments of nations in the first stage of political development are preoccupied almost entirely with creating national unity, that is, with consolidating political rule, with preventing separatist movements, with compromising, wiping out, or covering over internal dissensions, and with arousing nationalistic sentiments.

The major tools of unification are the armed forces, which are used more to maintain internal order than to fight external threats, the national bureaucracy, and to a lesser extent the political party. All these tools are primitive in nature—the army small and badly armed, the bureaucracy understaffed and inefficient, and the party neither a channel for representing the popular will nor an efficient means of reaching the masses.

During this first stage the beginnings of political unity are laid. Equally important, a setting is provided for economic unification to commence. Full participation of the population in the national life, however, must await the tremendous economic and social changes that occur in the second stage.

Stage 2: The Politics of Industrialization

With the coming of industrialization the nation-state undergoes important changes not only in its economic life but also in its political system. The two are related—so closely, in fact, that we can say that without the political changes industrialization could not have occurred. Indeed, the major function of national government during the second stage is to permit and to aid economic modernization.

The government of an industrializing nation has several important contributions to make if industrialization is to proceed. First, it must see that predominant political power is shifted out of the hands of the traditional landed aristocracy, which opposes economic change, to the new industrialists who wish to modernize the economy, be they private capitalists or governmental managers. If the shift from one elite to another is quick and thorough the change will be revolutionary, as it was in France in 1789, in Russia in 1917, and in China in 1949; or it may be as slow as in England in the eighteenth century.

Second, the political system must permit and assist the accumulation of savings in the hands of those who will reinvest a large part of them in the capital goods—machinery, factories, and so on—that make industrialization possible. This means keeping much of the nation's wealth out of the hands of the mass of the population who would from necessity spend it on better food, better housing, and other immediate improvements in their living standards. Governments of industrializing nations, both democratic and totalitarian, have helped hold down mass living standards during this period by outlawing effective labor organizations, by spending extremely little on welfare measures, by repressing popular protest, and perhaps most important, by denying the masses any effective participation in the decisions of the national government.

Third, the governments of nations in stage 2 must aid or at least permit the massive migration from countryside to city that breaks up the old peasant system and provides the modern industrial workers to man the new factories, fill the new cities, and create the new way of life. Ideally, the speed of this migration should be regulated so that it flows neither too slowly to provide needed labor nor so quickly that it swamps the cities with unemployed. In practice, however, such regulation has often been lacking or ineffective.

To date, industrialization has been achieved under three different political systems: bourgeois democracy; Stalinism; and fascism, or syncratic politics as I prefer to call it. Other varieties may develop in the future. These three forms of government have differed in their response to common problems, as a brief examination of them will show, but all three have brought the industrializers to political power, assisted the formation of capital, and permitted mass rural-urban migration. All have held down mass living standards, and none have been democratic in the sense of giving the common people a major voice in political decisions.

BOURGEOIS POLITICS

This type of politics takes its name from the bourgeoisie who dominated the economy and the government during the stage of industrialization in nineteenth-century northwestern Europe, the United States, and—with significant variations—in Japan at a later date.

During stage 1 of political development, political and economic power lay in the hands of the nobility, who owned the land that was the major source of wealth. Because these aristocrats considered trade beneath them, and because they needed managerial and entrepreneurial talents they themselves could not provide, a new class emerged beneath theirs and grew in wealth. This was the "middle" class—the bourgeoisie. National monarchs unifying their nations and quarreling with each other came to rely more and more heavily upon the wealth of this new group, and the bourgeoisie in turn demanded and won an increasing voice in national politics.

The bourgeoisie never ruled alone. In the early years it shared its rule with the old aristocracy and toward the end of stage 2 it was crowded by representatives of the masses. Bourgeois politics forms a bridge between the dynastic state and the mass state and it touches on both. Under bourgeois rule the nation was extended to include the new middle classes as well as the nobility, but the population at large was still excluded from political participation, although it was drawn more closely into a nationwide economy and culture. The political institutions of the later mass democracies were shaped during this period, and the legislatures (strongholds of the new industrialists) gained power at the expense of the executive (stronghold of the old aristocracy). Voting, however, was nearly everywhere limited to those who owned property, that is, primarily the bourgeoisie and the nobility.[4]

The political power of the bourgeoisie was used to promote and to protect the economic interests of those who industrialized the nation. Popular myth has it that the governments of that day kept their hands off the economy and let it develop as it would, but this is far from true. Everywhere the bourgeois governments passed new laws that undermined the legal basis of the old aristocratic privileges, feudal obligations, guild regulations, and peasant rights. The governments played an important part in ripping the web of economic arrangements that had held the old society together and thus clearing the way for a new economic order. The new national governments also helped industrialization directly by building and subsidizing nationwide networks of roads, canals, and railroads; by expanding currency and credit through the creation of national banks; and by protecting national industries through tariffs on foreign goods, to mention only three of the many forms of assistance given to industry. Some national governments of the period even built their own factories and mines and ran them for a time as government enterprises.

Government activity was equally valuable in preventing interference with the accumulation of capital for reinvestment in industry. To accumulate capital, that is, wealth that is not consumed but rather used to produce more wealth, in a basically agricultural subsistence economy entails holding down the living standards of the mass of the population. It means paying most workers so little that they cannot afford decent clothing and housing or adequate food. In the long run, industrialization enriches the masses, but for several generations at least it means great sacrifices. Such sacrifices were not made voluntarily for future generations by the masses of Western Europe and the United States but were imposed on them by a political, social, and economic system that gave them no choice.

During the early industrialization of the West, wages were unbelievably low, hours long (72- to 84-hour work weeks were common), working conditions deplorable, and housing squalid. Whole families commonly shared a single room (and often a single bed), damp, unlighted, and without any sanitary facilities whatsoever.

Welfare measures were virtually nonexistent, for the welfare of the

[4] In the United States, however, the franchise was widely expanded under Jackson, even in advance of industrialization.

population was not a major concern of the government or of the industrialists. Health and housing were considered private matters. Even a worker injured on the job had no claim on his employer. The needy were regarded as improvident and responsible for their own misfortunes. Charity was given to those who would otherwise have starved to death, but even this limited charity dated from a previous era. When workers attempted to organize to improve their lot, they were savagely repressed. Labor unions and strikes were outlawed, political demonstrations forbidden, and of course the workers could not vote. It is no accident that in country after country industrialization progressed most rapidly in the period between the death of the guilds and the legalization of labor unions.

Finally, the bourgeois governments encouraged that most important shift, migration from country to city. Government help was most dramatic in England, where the enclosure acts literally expelled large numbers of peasants from the countryside. On the Continent, liberation of the serfs eventually, though not immediately, achieved the same result. In the United States, much of the early rural-urban shift took the form of migration from European farms to American cities, a movement which was, of course, greatly encouraged by the free immigration policies of the American government.

It is hard to see what more the bourgeois governments could have done to grant political control to the new industrialists, to provide them with the labor force they needed, and to assist them to accumulate capital at the expense of mass living standards—or perhaps we should say it *would* be hard to see, if we did not have the example of Communist industrialization before us today.

STALINIST POLITICS

The Soviet Union, China, and the other Communist nations have also embarked upon the course of industrialization. However, with the example of Western production and wealth before them, they have pursued their goals more consciously, more thoroughly, and more ruthlessly, and they have achieved results more rapidly and at a higher cost in human suffering.

Let us call the political system of this period of Communist industrialization "Stalinist politics" to distinguish it from the period that follows. The Soviet Union, indeed, has already forsaken the Stalinism of stage 2 in her political development and entered the third stage. This in itself explains much of her bitter quarrel with China, which is still fiercely committed to Stalinist politics.

There are a number of parallels between bourgeois and Stalinist politics, though of course the differences are also great. Both systems, for example, brought an industrializing elite to political power, but the Stalinists, unlike their bourgeois predecessors, never shared their power, neither with the old aristocracy whom they exterminated through revolution, nor with the proletariat in whose name they ruled. The bourgeois elite gained its first toehold of power in the legislature and eventually asserted the supremacy of the legislative branch, but the Stalinist industrializers lodged themselves in the executive, and to this day the legislature remains a withered arm of the Communist governmental system.

Both systems denied ordinary workers any effective voice in defense of their own interests. The bourgeoisie denied them the vote; the Stalinists insisted they vote in one-party elections. The bourgeoisie outlawed all trade unions; the Stalinists encouraged union membership but perverted unions into an instrument for disciplining labor and encouraging higher production.

Once in control, the Stalinist industrializers threw the full power of government into a massive drive to industrialize the nation. Bourgeois governments had permitted and encouraged; Stalinist governments took the lead. With control over the allocation of the human and material resources of the country, the government single-mindedly pursued the goal of increased production. All savings that could be scraped together were poured into capital investment to build tools to make it possible to build more tools to expand consumer goods sometime in the future.

Like the bourgeoisie before them, the Stalinists invested heavily in capital goods, but they gave much greater priority to heavy industry, with the result that both industrial production and overall production increased even more rapidly than they had in the West.

Governmental power was also used to hold down consumption. In spite of rising production, consumption was held at the old preindustrial subsistence level while the increase went into capital goods. Consumer goods were scarce, rationed, and of poor quality. The Soviet government has recently begun to relax its iron grip on the standard of living, one indication that Russia has now passed out of stage 2 of political growth and entered stage 3, but during the early years of industrialization, life for the Russian consumer was grim indeed. In China, the story is very much the same. Rationing and improvement of distribution have raised the lowest level a bit, eliminating the mass starvation that characterized China in the past, but the standard of living remains extremely low.

In Stalinist countries the role of government in holding down mass living standards has been much more direct than it was in the bourgeois nations, for wages and hours are government controlled, with a large part of the working population employed by the government. It also determines which goods will be produced in what quantity, sets prices, and regulates distribution.

The price of industrialization in the Stalinist countries has been high in terms of human suffering, for they started from a lower economic base and industrialized more rapidly than the West. They have driven the workers close to the limits of endurance, and they have employed constant indoctrination and stern repression to still all protest or even questioning of the course they have chosen. Where other means have failed, they have used forced labor and military labor extensively to accomplish tasks that workers would not perform voluntarily.

On the other hand, Stalinist governments have instituted some welfare measures at a far earlier stage than in the West. Massive efforts and improvements have been made in health and education, and though wages are low, free medical care, low rents, and low-cost holidays are available. Welfare provisions have eased the lot of those who cannot work because of illness, pregnancy, incapacity, or age.

Finally, Stalinist governments have played an important part in regulating rural-urban migration. In Russia, ruthless collectivization of the land despite fierce resistance broke up the old peasant society forever, severing the tie between peasants and the land, and driving large numbers of peasants to the cities. The growth of Russian cities during the early years of industrialization and the shift from agricultural to nonagricultural work were extremely rapid. This vast social dislocation placed great strains upon the system, which had to provide housing, schools, transportation, and jobs for the moving millions.

In China, too, communization of the land and rapid industrial growth have been accompanied by large-scale movement of peasants to the cities, but here the role of government has been somewhat different. Though expanding rapidly, Chinese industry has not been able to create new industrial jobs as fast as China's population is increasing. Thus the problem has been to control the flow of rural-urban migration lest it swamp the small modern section of the economy.

We see, then, that the Stalinist governments, despite their protestations to the contrary, have followed the lead of the bourgeois governments in many ways. In the pursuit of economic power and wealth through industrialization, they too have given control of the government to "capitalists" (in this case government bureaucrats and managers). They have pushed their workers as hard as possible to create capital, and they have presided over a mass rural-urban movement that has destroyed the old life and provided needed industrial labor but, ironically enough, given rise to many of the social problems we face in the West.

At least one other variety of political system has accompanied indus-trialization in several nations—in Italy, Spain, Argentina, and Batista's Cuba, for example. Such regimes are generally called fascist because of their resemblance to Fascist Italy. However, the term "fascist" is used very loosely by most people to refer to almost any authoritarian, national-istic, aggressive political system that is not clearly Communist. Using the word in this general fashion, one may call fascist such diverse political systems as those of Dominican dictator Trujillo (a stage-1 family autoc-racy), Mussolini (a stage-2 totalitarian government), and Hitler (a nondemocratic variant of the stage-3 politics of national welfare).

But a more exact term is needed to describe the type of stage-2 political system with which we are dealing here, and for this purpose I have coined the word "syncratic." It has the advantage of separating out a group of regimes that have approached the problems of industrialization in a similar way, and it has the further advantage of being applicable not only to the fascist systems of Italy, Spain, and Argentina, but also to past and future regimes that may share this approach but are almost certain not to call themselves fascist. It would exclude Nazi Germany.

One distinguishing characteristic of a syncratic political system is the period of economic development at which it occurs. Syncratic systems typically arise when industrialization is already well under way but when the industrial sector does not yet dominate the economy. If we use a rough measure and consider a nation's economy industrial when 50 percent of its economically active males are engaged in nonagricultural work, we can say that syncratic politics is most likely to originate when the per-centage in nonagricultural work lies somewhere between 40 and 55 per-cent. This is later in the development process than either communism or bourgeois politics takes hold. These two systems both see a nation through its industrialization from start to finish, whereas syncratic politics have typically developed in the latter half of stage 2 after a period of bourgeois rule. In this sense syncratic rule represents a sort of derailment of bourgeois politics.

A second characteristic of syncratic politics that distinguishes it from both bourgeois and Stalinist politics is a peculiar political com-promise between the new industrial elite and the old aristocracy, who unite to hold down any threat from below. A deep conflict of values, outlook, and economic interests between these two elites exists in any industrializing society. As the industrial sector of the economy grows at the expense of the agricultural sector, the new industrializers seek to rewrite the laws and replace the old aristocrats as the dominant group in the government.

In country after country the two groups have battled it out. In a Stalinist system the industrializers win through violence at the beginning; in a bourgeois system the two continue to struggle throughout most of stage 2. In a syncratic system, however, special circumstances lead the two groups to make a temporary peace. For one thing, a period of strife and increased worker agitation leads both groups to feel threatened by possible revolt from below. Second, the compromise occurs at a time when the new and old elites are nearly equal in power, and each group sees a potential advantage in neutralizing the power of the other. Hence the appearance of syncratism at such a late stage of economic development.

The heart of the political compromise lies in an agreement, usually tacit, that each elite be left free to run its own sector of the economy. The agricultural elite for its part does not resist industrial progress and permits the government to aid industrialization through loans and grants, through heavy military purchases (a form of aid which accords well with traditional values), through the building of roads and schools, and through assistance to employers in their struggle to hold down labor costs. As in other stage-2 political systems, wages are held down, strikes outlawed, and political protest prohibited.

The industrial elite, for its part, keeps hands off the agricultural sector of the economy. Landlords are exempted from major tax contributions and land reform is taboo. Within the agricultural world, old privileges are protected, and in the case of Italy even the migration of peasants to the cities was restricted. This protection of the agricultural sector from change and from making a full contribution in human and material resources to the modernization of the country is probably the fundamental difference between syncratic industrialization and the bourgeois and Stalinist systems. The result is almost certainly to slow the process of industrialization, since under a syncratic system the capital for economic expansion must be derived almost exclusively from the industrial sector rather than from the economy as a whole.[5]

Industrialization is not prevented, however, merely slowed, and with time the industrial elite becomes strong enough to end its compromise with the agricultural elite. At this point syncratic rule collapses and is replaced by bourgeois rule, and the nation moves on to stage 3. This has been the pattern in all historic cases but one.[6]

[5] In this regard as in several others, Peron's Argentina presents a variant form of syncratism. See Organski, *op. cit.*, pp. 150 ff.
[6] Cuba, which became a Communist state rather than a mass democracy after its syncratic period ended. Reasons for this are discussed in *ibid.*, pp. 147 ff.

One heritage of the syncratic past remains: though mass democracy may follow, it is less than complete. National unity is hampered by the severe split that remains between the industrial sector which has modernized and the agricultural sector which has not, particularly where industry has tended to concentrate in one section of the country, as in the north of Italy and the north of Spain. Economic progress is hampered by the hold of old-fashioned landlords on the country's agriculture, and mass participation in democratic politics is limited by the backwardness of the peasant population.

It must be stressed that these three paths through industrialization—bourgeois, Stalinist, and syncratic—are by no means the only possible ones. It is, of course, highly likely that many nations industrializing in the future will follow roughly in the footsteps of those who have preceded them; it is also probable that some at least will clear new paths. The choice of a political system for stage 2 is particularly important, for that choice in large part determines the kind of political system a nation will have in stage 3.

Stage-2 politics are important for another reason. Industrialization brings with it a tremendous increase in the power of a nation, not only because of the increase in material goods, but also because the concentration of more people in cities, improved communications, and increasing participation of the masses in politics all give the government greater ability to mobilize its human and material resources for national goals. The speed of industrialization is important in determining how fast a nation grows in power relative to its neighbors and rivals. And the choice of a bourgeois, Stalinist, or syncratic governing elite helps shape a nation's goals. We shall return to these topics in later chapters on national goals and national power.

Stage 3: The Politics of National Welfare

Political development is a relative concept, not an absolute state at which a nation eventually arrives. When all the nations in the world were still in stage 1, the most politically developed nations were those with the highest degree of national unity. In stage 2, a politically developed nation is one that has unified its people and is successfully encouraging the industrialization of the economy. Today, a number of nations have entered the third stage of political development and a new task has been thrust upon their governments: the promotion of the economic and social welfare of the masses.

Curiously enough, this new function of government is the direct opposite of its main function in the previous stage. In the early years of industrialization it is the function of government to protect the accumulation of capital against the demands of the masses for higher living standards, but once industrialization is achieved, higher standards of living become possible—indeed, necessary, for the smooth functioning of the economy requires a mass market. Thus the main function of government shifts from protecting capital from the people to protecting the people from capital.

To date almost all countries that have reached stage 3 in their political development have done so via the road of bourgeois industrialization, and the bourgeois democracies of stage 2 have gradually evolved into the mass democracies of stage 3. This has happened in the United States and in most of Western Europe. However, there have also been totalitarian forms of the politics of national welfare in Nazi Germany and in the Soviet Union.

MASS DEMOCRACY

The rise of the masses to political power can only be briefly sketched here. The process began at the very start of stage 2 when the bourgeoisie enlisted the masses to help overcome the power of the landed aristocracy. In the name of the people the bourgeoisie took over. The basic principles of mass democracy date from this period although they were originally intended to apply primarily to the bourgeoisie. With time, however, the masses gained enough power to apply some of these principles to themselves. In this they were greatly aided by the very process of industrialization, which collected workers in large numbers in great urban concentrations where, unlike their peasant fathers, they were susceptible to effective organization. The factory system provided a model for union organization, and the increased training and literacy required for skilled workers to perform their jobs strengthened their bargaining power and ability to defend their economic and political interests. The conscription of citizen armies also helped unite and arouse the masses.

The means by which the masses obtained some control over the national government was through the extension of the franchise. Once able to vote, the common people increasingly used their voting power to enlist government protection against the hardships wrought by industrialization. Low wages, long hours, poor working conditions, child labor, unemployment, lack of economic security, restrictions on the right of labor to organize, all were attacked through legislation and government regulation. A review of the major domestic activities of the welfare states of stage 3 will show a heavy emphasis upon such welfare measures as labor legislation, social security, health services, and education. The national government is also heavily involved in overseeing the operations of the complex national economy in order that it may provide the citizenry with full employment and a high standard of living.

It is this extensive activity that distinguishes the politics of national welfare from any other. There are in the world today few countries that do not have some welfare legislation on their books, but for the governments of stages 1 and 2, such laws represent hopes rather than realities. No matter how humane the intentions of governmental leaders, welfare politics cannot exist unless the means to create welfare for the masses exist as well, namely, a modern productive economy under effective political control.

Nor are welfare politics possible without a massive expansion of executive power. With the arrival of the politics of national welfare, the center of governmental power shifts back to the executive. This is true for two reasons: first, because the legislatures in stage 2 became the stronghold of bourgeois power and it was therefore natural for the masses to seek power elsewhere; second, because the new welfare and regulatory tasks of government require a vast bureaucracy for their performance. Gigantic political parties also assume new importance as channels for the orderly transmission of popular demands to the central authorities.

Throughout stages 2 and 3 of political development, the mutual dependence of people and government grows. The mass of the population—industrial workers, clerical workers, even farmers—find themselves dependent for their survival upon the successful operation of a national economy so vast and so complex that only the government can control it. And with the increased mechanization of warfare, the masses also come to depend upon the government to protect them from destruction in modern war.

The government, for its part, finds itself increasingly dependent upon mass participation to achieve its goals. National wealth in the modern nation depends not upon treasure or upon the contributions of a few rich burghers, but upon the labor—and the taxes—of the entire population. And national power requires mass armies and mass citizen support.

Finally, mass democracy is a rational political system. The demands made of government are rational, they are specific, they deal with material benefits, they are negotiable, and they can be compromised. It has been aptly remarked that the democratic system reduces the political arena to a marketplace. In other words, mass democracy represents the rational aspect of man, and though the individual has many irrational drives that influence his desires and his behavior, a successfully operating mass democracy does not represent the more irrational forces loose in any polity. Limits are set to arousing the hates and fears of the electorate, even in a heated campaign, and the divisions of race, religion, and class are minimized rather than sharpened by most responsible politicians.

These, then, are the essential characteristics of mass democracy. The national government adopts as its primary concern a responsibility for the economic and social welfare of the entire population. It seeks to keep the economy running smoothly enough to provide relatively full employment and it intervenes in the economic process to raise the living standards of ordinary people and particularly of the underprivileged. It gives the common people a considerable voice in the political process, and it appeals primarily to the rational desires of the electorate.

WELFARE POLITICS AND NATIONAL SOCIALISM

Welfare politics are also possible under a totalitarian system, as the example of Nazi Germany makes clear. Though often described as "fascist," National Socialism was in reality something quite distinct from the syncratic systems of fascist Italy, Spain, and Argentina. Nazism was not a system for coping with the problems of industrialization—Germany was already fully industrial—nor was it ruled by a coalition of industrialists and big landowners, though both were important.

Nazi Germany is a case (so far, the only one) of a totalitarian welfare state that arose out of the failure of a mass democracy. The Weimar Republic which came to power after Germany's defeat in World War I was a mass democracy, but it was severely shaken by the terrible inflation of the early 1920s and overwhelmed by the worldwide depression of the 1930s. The Weimar Republic failed in its fundamental responsibility as a welfare state, for it could not keep the economy running and it could not guarantee the population a high standard of living or even employment. The depression eroded the power of the major forces that had supported democracy in Germany: the unions and the Social Democratic party. Frightened by the depression, the masses and the industrial leaders lost faith in mass democracy. The army officers, the landed gentry, and the bureaucrats had always disliked the democratic order. Under attack from both the left and the right, democracy fell, and Germany turned to totalitarianism under Adolf Hitler.

The new regime was supported by an elite composed of four mutually suspicious and antagonistic bureaucracies: the army, the higher civil service, the industrialists, and the Nazi party. The four were held together first by hope and then by fear of what would happen if they stopped collaborating. They found they could agree on little except repression of the masses below and military conquest of foreign enemies. The other three soon found themselves dominated by the Nazi Party with consequences that were distressing to all.

Under Hitler, the welfare state was immediately restored. Germany's economic recovery was extremely rapid: Unemployment dropped, farm prices rose, and the country's industries began to hum. Welfare services were, if anything, expanded. Welfare politics were restored, but with a difference; they were no longer democratic. Parliament ceased to exist as an independent force, and voters had no control at all over national policy. Workers could no longer organize or strike, and peasants were bound to their farms. Dissent was stifled and opposition crushed with terror.

These two policies—restoration of the welfare state and suppression of the masses—were important in maintaining support for Nazism, for the first appealed to the masses and the second appealed to the elites, but these policies were also fundamentally contradictory. That the Nazis were successful in pursuing both policies for as long as they did was due in large part to the headlong preparations for war upon which Germany embarked. Rearmament stimulated the economy and, at least in the beginning, improved the economic welfare of the masses. War, first threatened and then actual, provided a rationalization for the political suppression that characterized Nazism.

Warfare, however, provided another set of contradictions. The increasing demands of producing guns before butter eventually reduced German living standards, and the war itself destroyed not only the welfare but also the lives of a substantial number of Germans. The older elites also found the war detrimental to their interests, for it eroded their entrenched positions of privilege and exposed them to rapid infiltration by their new competitors, the Nazi party bureaucracy. A few examples will suffice. Preparation for war rendered the industrial elite dependent upon the party for war contracts. The expansion of the army and the course of the war necessitated changes in the officer corps, and the higher civil service, thinned out by the expansion of its responsibilities, found its ranks replenished by new members of the party. In the end the war proved disastrous not only for the masses and the old elites but for the Nazi party as well.

Nazism as a system was profoundly irrational. Hitler fomented an ideology so emotional and incoherent it must be read to be believed possible. He appealed to the deepest fears and hates of the German people and unified them first for a mad attack upon the Jews and then for an equally mad assault upon the democracies and Communist Russia. It was a war that could only end in the destruction of Germany, for the countries Hitler attacked were overwhelmingly more powerful than Germany and her allies, as World War I should clearly have indicated.

After World War II, West Germany returned to mass democracy while East Germany had foisted upon her a third variety of welfare politics: the Communist kind.

COMMUNIST WELFARE POLITICS

Whereas Nazism seems to represent a temporary derailment of the democratic system (in this sense it is like syncratism), Communist welfare politics represents an orderly development from stage-2 Stalinism. Here again there are few examples, for with the exception of East Germany and Czechoslovakia, both of whom had communism imposed upon them from outside after they were already welfare states, the Soviet Union, Hungary, and Poland are the only Communist nations to reach stage 3 of political development. China will probably offer considerable variation when she finally gets to stage 3.

In Russia as in the West the differences between stage-2 and stage-3 politics are quite clear though an exact dividing line between them is difficult to locate. Under Khrushchev and his successors, the Soviet government has become increasingly occupied with raising the living standards of the Russian masses, both by expanding welfare services and by reapportioning production to provide more and better consumer goods. As in the West, the Soviet economy now generates sufficient capital to provide for future expansion without depriving consumers of the goods they need and want. Indeed, rational use of its giant productive plant requires a higher level of mass consumption.

It would appear that the government of any economically developed nation, be it democratic, Nazi, or Communist, must undertake the welfare function if it wishes to obtain the full contribution that the population can make to the nation's wealth and power. Welfare politics will therefore arise even where the masses lack the political power to demand a better life for themselves.

The Soviet Union is also liberalizing its political life in stage 3 of its development. The more obvious signs of repression are gone; the labor camps closed, most forced labor abolished, the secret police subjected to tighter control. There is more freedom of inquiry, more freedom of discussion, and a "thaw" in the arts.

Thus far, however, liberalization has stopped well short of democracy. The masses have no political control over the government and voters have no choice between competing candidates. This is the essence of democracy, and there is no indication that the Soviet Union is proceeding in that direction. Political democracy requires decentralization of economic power and its separation from political power, conditions that are lacking in the Communist world.

Stage 4: The Politics of Abundance

It would be a mistake to think that stage 3 represents the end of political development. Recent achievements in the realm of technology promise to be as important for the politics of nations in the future as industrialization has been in the past. Atomic power, rocketry, and automation are already posing problems with which political institutions must deal, and their future use will both shape and be shaped by the various political systems of the world.

It is usual to emphasize the effect of nuclear weapons upon relations among nations, and we shall devote Chapter 13 to this consideration, but it should also be noted that such weapons have an internal effect on the nation as well. They have strengthened the executive at the expense of the legislative branch of government and decreased popular participation in decisions of war and peace. Nuclear weapons have increased government expenditures, altered the allocation of national production and scientific research, and affected educational systems. Quite apart from military use, atomic power will inevitably alter national economies and patterns of urbanization just as rockets will inevitably revolutionize transportation and communication within and among nations.

Automation promises a second industrial revolution that will almost certainly increase human economic productivity to the point where man can look forward to material abundance for all—a most significant change indeed, for all the political systems of the past have been forced to spend much of their energy dealing with problems of economic scarcity. Automation will surely alter the occupation structure and the labor force. It will probably reduce the power of labor unions, intensify the concentration of economic power in fewer, larger companies, and increase the power of national governments over the economy. It remains to be seen how these changes will affect the continuation of mass democracy or even the survival of the nation-state.

4

National Goals

Before we can understand the ways in which nations treat each other, there are two things that we must know about each nation: what does it want to do, and what is it capable of doing? In other words, we must know its goals, and we must assess its power. This chapter and the one that follows are devoted to a consideration of national goals.

The subject is not an easy one, for national goals are intangible, and discussions of them abound in contradictions and misinformation. Of necessity, we can deal only with words and wishes, and how are we to know which words are true and which wishes real? There are great discrepancies between what men aim at and what they attain, and there is often a discrepancy as well between what men *say* they aim at and the things they do.

The Romans said they wanted peace. They are known today for having brought peace and law to much of the world they knew—they even gave their name to a particular type of peace. And yet the Romans in their search for peace were always at war. The famous Roman saying, in which many still believe, "If you want peace, prepare for war," takes on added meaning when we realize that the Roman social and economic system could not have existed without war.[1]

Similar confusion exists about the goals of nations in the world of

[1] Joseph Schumpeter, *The Sociology of Imperialism* (New York: Meridian, 1955), pp. 51–54.

the last fifty years. The continent of Europe is forested with the tomb-stones of millions who died in wars for peace. It is by no means simple to say what the goals of nations are.

What Are National Goals?

Before discussing the different kinds of goals that nations have, it will be useful to make clear what a national goal is. A goal is a future state of affairs that someone considers desirable and worth spending some effort to achieve. Goals do not exist in the abstract; they exist in someone's mind.

Our interest here is in the goals of nations, but it should be clear that to speak of nations in this fashion—as acting and having goals—is to use a kind of shorthand. Only individual human beings can act, and only individuals can have goals. However, because individuals may share common goals, and because they have national governments that act for them, we can speak of national goals.

We are not interested here in all the goals that nations may have, but only in those that affect people and areas beyond the boundaries of the nation. Unless they do this, the goals are domestic and do not concern us in this study. For example, a national goal to improve housing or to provide better child care may be considered domestic. On the other hand, a goal to raise national productivity that results in an increase in arms or in trade with other nations may be considered international.

The line dividing domestic from international goals becomes ex-tremely thin, and it is often difficult to make a clear distinction. A goal that is essentially domestic (full employment for shoemakers, for example) may have international implications if it results in a tariff on foreign shoes. However, one cannot take at face value all the arguments that seek to justify specific domestic policies in terms of more general (and more popular) international goals. Because it is assumed today that all Amer-icans are opposed to communism, it has become common to drum up support for the most diverse causes by claiming that they will help in the fight against communism.

Do you oppose discrimination against Negroes? Do you want higher wages? Are you against inflation? Do you like labor unions? Do you fear labor bosses? Do you favor government spending? Do you oppose it? Whatever your views, there will be someone to tell you that you are helping to defeat communism. We cannot throw out all arguments of this nature, for domestic policies do indeed have international repercussions, but we shall try to confine ourselves to cases where the international im-plications are obvious.

Our interest, then, is in goals that are: (1) shared by a sizable, or at least an important, segment of the national population; (2) promoted by the national government; and (3) directed toward or having considerable effect upon the people of other nations.

Nations may have a variety of goals. Some members of the "realist" school of international relations assume that for purposes of study all national goals can be reduced to one: the goal of national power.[2] According to them, power is the immediate goal of every nation that engages in politics, no matter what its ultimate goals may be. This seems, however, to be an oversimplification. Power is surely one of the most important goals that nations pursue, but it is not the only goal, and it is not always the principal one. If we are to understand the actions of nations in their dealings with each other, we must understand not only the goals they share, but also the differences in their hopes and aspirations.

As a start, we can divide all national goals into four broad categories: power, wealth, cultural welfare, and peace. Having goals of one kind does not exclude the others, for it is possible for a nation to pursue goals in all these categories at one and the same time. Indeed, one goal may be necessary to achieve another, and the same action may be a means to several different ends. Wealth may bring power, and power may bring peace, and peace may be necessary to preserve the cultural heritage of the nation.

Competitive and Absolute Goals

An important distinction can be made between goals that are competitive and goals that are absolute. Some objectives may be desirable in themselves, quite apart from what other nations do; for example, a higher standard of living or the preservation of the national culture. Such goals we shall call absolute. Others have meaning *only* in relation to other nations, for example, a desire to be as rich as another nation or to be the most powerful nation in the world. Such goals are competitive.

The nation with competitive goals can never rest, even though it may be winning for the moment. Regardless of whether it is competing with one other nation or with the whole world, regardless of whether it wants to be better than the nation just ahead of it or whether it wants to be the best, success will always be precarious. The chances of success always rest in some part in another nation's hands.

If the national goal is absolute, the nation may make a great effort

2 See Hans J. Morgenthau, *Politics Among Nations,* 4th edition (New York: Knopf, 1967), pp. 25–26.

to achieve its aim, but once it is reached, the nation can relax. It does not matter that others are outdistancing it or that those who were behind are catching up. Instances of absolute goals are hard to find, partly because they have been reported less thoroughly than the more dramatic situations in which nations compete with each other, but absolute goals are not so rare as a reading of current headlines would lead one to believe. Japan, until she was forced to establish contact with the West, pursued absolute goals. Many of the smaller countries still do. The level of living in Switzerland is high, but it was not raised in order to compete with other nations. Consider Denmark or Ceylon or Mexico. None of these nations could be said to have primarily competitive goals.

It is not always easy to tell whether a nation is competing with others or not. In the case of India and her efforts to industrialize, for instance, the standard of living is so very low it would be natural for any Indian government to seek to raise it. However, it is very difficult to say at this time whether India's attempts to increase productivity are aimed simply at improving living standards regardless of what other nations do or whether they are part of an effort on India's part to become a major world power. The same action would serve both ends.

If a nation's leaders constantly say that it is competing with others and if its behavior supports these assertions, no such problem exists. It is not hard to find cases of this sort. Hitler made it quite clear that Germany's cultural goals were an assertion of German superiority over others, and German behavior toward the Jews and the Poles in particular made it all too clear that Hitler was telling the truth.

Or take the case of the Russians. They are modernizing their economy at a rapid pace. This fact in itself might raise the question of whether they are competing with the West in economic production or merely raising their own standard of living, but all doubts may be laid aside in the light of statements made time and again by Russian leaders that they intend to catch up with the West—in living standards, in armaments, and in power.[3] There is no question that Russian goals are competitive.

The same is true of the United States. We are the richest and most powerful nation on earth, but we are not content. We are very much concerned with keeping our lead over the rest of the world, and we are

[3] Nikita Khrushchev, noted for his bluntness, once told an American television audience: "We have overtaken such great industrial powers as Britain, France and Germany, and now occupy the second place, second only to the United States. And now we are faced with the fundamental task of catching up with the advanced capitalist countries as far as production per capita is concerned." *The New York Times,* June 3, 1957, p. 6, col. 1.

anxious not to allow the Communist world to close the gap between us. Our goals, too, are largely competitive.

In spite of the fact that such knowledge is not always easy to come by, it is often crucial for a nation to know whether other nations are competing with it or not, for if the goals of a nation are determinedly competitive, those with whom it competes must not make the mistake of granting it concessions unless they are ready to concede supremacy in the area of competition. Concessions will not satisfy a competitor; they will merely bring it nearer to victory. Take the classic case of Germany before World War II. Power was a major goal of Germany, and the goal was competitive. What Germany wanted was to be undisputed master of Europe. England and France allowed Germany to take over several of her neighbors in the vain hope that she would be satisfied, a serious mistake for which the English and the French paid dearly. The English in particular did not seem to understand that Germany was competing with them and would not stop until she became more powerful than England—or until she was stopped by force. Whether the Chinese are fundamentally competitive or not, as far as power is concerned, is the subject of bitter debate today.

National goals do not remain competitive or absolute forever. For the time being, Germany seems to have forsaken many of her competitive goals. Certainly, other nations have changed the nature of their goals in the past. For much of her history, the United States had absolute goals in the field of power, seeking only enough power to assure her own independence, but toward the end of the nineteenth century, her goals began to fluctuate. Between the two world wars, the United States turned back to absolute goals, but since the end of the 1930s her goals have been clearly competitive. The assumption of world leadership allows no other choice. The reverse is true of Sweden. Once a proud and dangerous aggressor, Sweden no longer competes in the field of power. In this area her goals are as absolute as goals related to power can ever be.

The distinction we have been making between competitive and noncompetitive goals cut across the power-wealth-culture-peace classification. Although it is true that power is always to some extent competitive, a distinction can be made between the kind of goal that consists of only enough power to guarantee national independence and the goal of great-power status or world domination. Peace, on the other hand, is always an absolute goal. Wealth and cultural welfare, however, can be pursued either competitively or for themselves. The competitive-noncompetitive distinction should be kept in mind as we proceed to a more detailed discussion of the different kinds of national goals.

POWER AS A NATIONAL GOAL

It is sometimes claimed that the drive for power is inherent in human nature and that this drive makes nations intrigue and fight against each other. However, such reasoning seems dubious. If such a drive were a part of human nature, it would be present in all men at all times, without exception, as are sex and hunger. But most men in history have not exhibited this so-called universal human drive, and many do not exhibit it today. On the national scale, power is a conspicuous goal of some nations but by no means of all, and the emphasis that different nations place upon it varies greatly.

Every nation, however, seeks to be master in its own house and to be free of external control. To this extent, it can be said that all nations seek to maintain at least a minimum of power, if only to survive as political entities, for if a nation does not control even its own domestic affairs, then nationhood is an illusion.

In addition, power over other nations can be extremely useful in achieving other desired aims, such as wealth or colonies or peace and security. Power, in other words, is an important means to other goals. Indeed, it is valued primarily for this reason, and only rarely is it sought as an end in itself.

Finally, it must be noted that nations occupy positions in an international power system—that is to say, they have a certain amount of power relative to that of other nations. As we shall see in later chapters, this characteristic of nations is extremely important in explaining much of their international behavior.

Our concern here is with power as a conscious goal or subgoal. Important though it may be, particularly for the great nations that occupy the major part of our attention, it is by no means the only goal that nations pursue.

WEALTH AS A NATIONAL GOAL

Wealth is another goal that is sought to some extent by all nations. Every nation seeks adequate territory, resources, and production to maintain at least subsistence for its population with enough surplus to provide the ruling group with whatever standard of luxury it is accustomed to. Indeed, national existence demands a certain minimum of national wealth. Above and beyond this minimum, however, many nations, the United States among them, pursue wealth as a major national goal.

It might be thought that the poorest "have-not" nations would be those most interested in increasing their wealth, while the wealthy nations would be less anxious to accumulate further riches, but in reality this is not the case. The poorest nations are poor in part because wealth has *not* been a major national goal. We must make a distinction here, of course, between the personal greed of a backward ruler seeking to build up his own personal fortune and a nationwide desire for a higher standard of living. The quest for national wealth in the form of higher living standards is a modern phenomenon, a product of the industrial revolution, which has made better living for all a genuine possibility instead of a utopian dream. The poorest nations are stage-1 nonindustrial nations like Ethiopia and Burma, whose people accept their poverty as natural and whose rulers have only recently become aware of the possibility of raising the national standard of living. It is the richest nations on earth that are so extraordinarily concerned with wealth, and it is the nations just behind them that are consumed with an envious desire to "catch up."

The pursuit of wealth may be either competitive or absolute. It seems abundantly clear that most Americans are not concerned solely with achieving the increased comfort and satisfaction that goods and services can provide. They are also concerned with being the "best." Abroad as well as at home, publicly as well as privately, there is a tendency to regard wealth as a sign of status. Americans constantly remind themselves and the rest of the world that theirs is the highest standard of living in the world. This fact is a great source of national pride. The Russians, too, congratulate themselves constantly on the speed with which their standard of living is increasing, claiming that this proves the superiority of communism.

It would appear that most rich nations view their high living standards as an indication of their general superiority over their less wealthy neighbors, but again it is possible to distinguish between nations such as Russia and the United States, which seek wealth in order to prove their primacy, and those like the Scandinavian countries, which seem to value better living for its own sake.

In some cases, however, it is difficult to tell why a nation is seeking wealth. This difficulty is increased by the fact that wealth and power are so closely connected. Wealth in the form of increased national production can be converted into either military or civilian goods. In the first case, wealth is clearly being used to increase national power and not to improve living standards, but even if the emphasis is on civilian goods, it may be that power is a major consideration. For example, great efforts may be made to secure capital investment to develop heavy industry, which can be used to turn out tractors one day and tanks the next, airliners today and bombers tomorrow. As we shall see, even the most harmless types of civilian goods may be a source of national power if they are used adroitly in international trade.

Wealth is not only a major source of power, power may also be a major source of wealth. As concepts, however, wealth and power are quite separate. Confusion is caused by the fact that these two goals are so often pursued jointly, but it should be clear that they may also conflict with each other. Often a nation must choose between guns and butter, and the choice it makes will shed great light upon its national goals. Even a nation as wealthy as the United States may find that its military expenditures jeopardize domestic programs—for example, the cost of the war in Vietnam probably caused a cutback in the expenditures planned for the fulfillment of the Great Society. This is difficult to measure, for funds are generally more readily forthcoming for military purposes than for domestic reform that upsets important interests, and while lack of action for reform may be blamed on military needs, it is by no means certain that the funds voted for war efforts would be equally available for other purposes. In World War II, the United States proved itself capable of conducting full-scale war without any reduction in American living standards. For less wealthy nations, however, the choice is more pressing. England made her choice not so long ago, when she gave up many of her international responsibilities because of the tremendous cost to the British taxpayer. Nazi Germany and Communist Russia, on the other hand, have both chosen in the past to increase their power, even at the expense of living standards.

CULTURAL GOALS

Apart from power and wealth, a nation may have cultural goals. In fact, the preservation of the national culture is a goal of every nation. As we have seen, profound sentiments grow up around the national way of life, and most of the people of the world have a deep preference for their own language, their own ways of dressing and eating and building houses, their own political and economic and religious institutions. These preferences are shared by the men who fill the top governmental positions (particularly in modern times when rulers are of the same nationality as the population) and are thus translated into governmental policy. Indeed, national governments often encourage such nationalistic sentiments as a means of unifying the nation and increasing the power and effectiveness of the government in its dealings with other nations. Most nations today are not simply political units, they are also cultural units.

Nations seek to preserve their cultures in many different ways. A major reason for desiring national independence or for opposing foreign conquest is that independence allows the assertion of the national culture, whereas foreign conquest may threaten to submerge it or change it drastically. It is surely a libel to say that American soldiers in World War II were fighting to preserve ice cream sodas and apple pie, but it is also erroneous to suppose that they were fighting solely for the power and wealth of their country. The triumph of Nazism would have meant a serious threat to the American way of life, and most Americans knew it.

Immigration restrictions are another means by which nations seek to preserve their national cultures. Canada and Australia, for example, could greatly increase their wealth and power by throwing open their gates to all who desire to come. Australia in particular is badly in need of a larger population, which overpopulated India and Japan would be happy to provide. But Australia chooses to limit immigration to Europeans, preferably northwestern Europeans at that, for she fears that a flood of Asian immigration would destroy her European culture or alter it beyond recognition. American immigration laws until 1965 were written in such a way that the more different in culture a nation from the United States, the smaller its quota. The new immigration law abolishes the quota system, but limits total immigration to a small number (170,000 per year), many of whom will probably continue to come from similar cultures. (Probably most nations underestimate their capacity to absorb people from different cultures and overlook almost completely the cultural contribution that could be made by immigrants simply because they *are* different.)

Much of the resistance underdeveloped nations offer to technological change stems from a fear that modernization will destroy the old culture, as in fact it will. Such resistance may be extremely damaging in terms of wealth and power, but if cultural goals are primary, who can say that the resistance is mistaken? Actually, many of the leaders of underdeveloped countries seem to be ambivalent about modernization in general and foreign aid in particular. On the one hand they want very much to possess the higher standard of living and increased power that modernization would bring, but on the other, they do not want the changes in the local culture that modernization would require. Caught in a conflict between cultural and other goals, they want somehow to wish away the conflict and achieve both sets of goals at once.

Another example of the pursuit of a cultural goal even at the expense of economic goals may be found in the determination of India to substitute Hindi for English as the official governmental language, an immense undertaking that will cost a great deal and will probably mean at least a temporary setback in the efficiency of communication among Indian officials, since all educated Indians now speak English and existing records and communications are all in English. Such a switch represents an economic waste, but it may pay off eventually in terms of power, if it helps to make educated Indians more conscious of their national unity and hence more nationalistic. In any case, the goal that motivates this policy is cultural, not economic or political.

As in the case of the other goals examined, cultural goals can be pursued competitively or absolutely. The distinction is between nations that try merely to preserve their own culture within their own borders and nations that try to impose their culture on others. Here again, the United States must be placed on the competitive side, for not only are we convinced that our culture is superior to others (many nations have a conviction of this sort), but we also have a great desire to spread American political institutions, economic practices, technological efficiency, and material culture throughout the world. In this respect, we resemble the great colonial powers of Western Europe, most of whom believed they had a mission to "civilize" the natives as well as the right to exploit them. Today, the Soviet Union and China also have distinctly competitive cultural goals. Their leaders are imbued with missionary spirit and are as determined to spread communism as Americans are to spread their way of life. It would be a mistake to overlook the importance that cultural goals may play in determining the behavior of modern nations.

PEACE AS A NATIONAL GOAL

Last on our list of major national goals is peace, but "peace" is a word so general and so worn with use that it means all things to all men. As used here, peace means the absence of war, with emphasis upon the absence of lengthy, terribly destructive wars. Certainly not the only meaning that can be given to peace, it is the best definition for our present purposes, for when nations dream of peace, they do not think of a higher standard of living, nor do they necessarily aspire to better international understanding or the brotherhood of man. What they want, and they want it desperately, is to avoid another world war.

In the twentieth century, peace has become a more important national goal than ever before. The destructiveness of World War I, the first major conflict between fully industrialized nations, came as a shock to the world. It was felt at the time that another war of this sort would destroy humanity. We now know that the first war was but a beginning. Although humanity has survived a second world war and will perhaps survive a third, the invention of weapons such as the hydrogen bomb, guided missiles, and bacteriological weapons has greatly intensified the search for peace. The nature of warfare has changed drastically since the eighteenth and nineteenth centuries, and so has the importance of peace as a national goal.

Under modern circumstances, it can be argued that peace, or at least the absence of *world* wars, has become an end in itself, to be sought no matter what effect it may have upon other national goals. It can be argued that nothing could be worse than the utter devastation that would result if the United States and the USSR or other nations possessing the latest weapons should be locked in a fight to the finish. Although this view is widely held, it is not unanimous, and the governments of major nations continue to contemplate war as a real possibility and to prepare for it with programs that are given top priority. Even now, peace is only one of many goals, and although it is important, it is not necessarily supreme.

Sometimes peace is complementary to other goals; sometimes it is even a prerequisite for the achievement of other goals. Generally, when a nation is declining in power, peace is necessary if it is to preserve whatever power and wealth it possesses. For example, England and France were extremely concerned to preserve world peace in the years before World War II, so much so that they refused to understand the clear meaning of many of Germany's actions. Those who led England and France understood that another world war would mark the beginning of the end for them as major powers, and in large part they were right. Finally, Germany left them no choice but to fight, and by the end of the war, both nations had suffered irreparably in power and in wealth.

On the other hand, it is possible to find instances where peace is an obstacle to the achievement of other goals. This is particularly the case for powerful nations that desire changes in the status quo which other nations are not willing to make peacefully. Wars, after all, are waged because at least one side believes it has something to gain from victory. That is to say, war is a common means by which nations attempt to achieve goals of wealth or power or cultural preservation. In cases where war is not terribly destructive or where victory is certain and the destruction is likely to be almost exclusively at the enemy's expense, a nation may well weigh the advantages of peace against other goals. India, for example, found it to her advantage to seize Kashmir by force, China to seize Tibet. North Vietnam and the United States both believed it to their advantage to fight for control of South Vietnam despite great cost to both sides. In recent years, most wars have been of a minor nature, and the destruction involved has not been enough to discourage those who are thinking of starting others.

In a sense, the goal of peace, which nearly all nations consider desirable, other things being equal, limits the pursuit of other goals. Many goals that will be sought if they can be achieved peacefully may be foregone if war is required to achieve them; few are worth the price of a major world war. For example, England would have liked very much to retain her colonial empire, but not at the cost of constant warfare to put down rebellions, and so she gave up India and liquidated her African holdings as well. Similarly, the United States would like very much to see Eastern Europe liberated from Soviet domination, but she has not been willing to risk world war to bring this about.

The terror of modern warfare may have increased the price nations are willing to pay for peace, but no nation seeks peace at any price. A powerful nation like the United States will fight if just the outer limits of its power and wealth are challenged, and even a tiny nation will fight to preserve its national independence. Surely the Dutch did not think they could defeat the troops of Nazi Germany, nor did the Hungarians who revolted in 1956 seriously believe that they could defeat the Russians, but they fought nevertheless. Even a conquered people who possess no national independence may rise in revolt if minimum goals of subsistence and culture are threatened.

Types of National Goals

It is not enough to determine whether a nation's goals are competitive or absolute and whether it is seeking power, wealth, cultural goals, peace, or some combination of them all. Other questions must be answered if one is to understand the goals that motivate international action.

Specifically, we will want to know: Who is it that holds the goal? Is this so-called national goal truly a goal of all the nation or is it only the goal of some special group within the nation? Or to put it another way, are the international goals of various groups within the nation the same or do they differ? Are the national goals unified or divergent?

Next we will want to know who is expected to benefit from the achievement of the goal—the nation itself, a whole group of nations, or humanity at large? That is, is the goal strictly national or is it humanitarian?

Another important question concerns the time at which the goal is expected to be reached. Is it an immediate or a long-range goal?

Then there is the question of how well defined the goal is. Is it specific or is it general and perhaps ambiguous?

In addition, we will want to explore the possibility of a discrepancy between the goals a nation says it has and the goals it actually holds. Is the "goal" we are examining a real goal or is it simply said to be one for purposes of public relations?

Finally, we will want to know whether the future state desired is a continuation of the present state of affairs or whether it must be brought into existence—that is, does achievement of the goal involve maintaining the status quo or does it require change?

UNIFIED VERSUS DIVERGENT GOALS

The claim is often made that disarmament or freer trade or the return of a lost colony or some other future state of affairs is a national goal with the firm backing of the entire national population. However, such claims are made more often than they are justified. In truth, the majority of the ordinary citizens of a nation are often not deeply interested in international affairs, at least not unless some crisis exists where they can see that their immediate interests are likely to be affected. Even in a democracy where the expression of opinion is invited, the public is likely to remain apathetic and to rely on experts to form opinions on international affairs which the public later adopts. This kind of behavior is perhaps more characteristic of the United States than of some European democracies, but it is difficult to find a nation where international goals are *formed* by the entire population. In any nation, democratic or totalitarian, there is a power structure, headed by a relatively small group of men who make the major decisions, although in a democracy (and even, to a limited extent, in a totalitarian country), the public must ultimately approve these decisions or at least accept them.

Under the circumstances, it is not to be expected that a nation's international goals need always be in accord with the best interests of the entire population. Indeed, the entire population may not even have the same interests, so that a single goal to suit them all would be impossible. It seems safe to say that national goals are always the goals of those who hold the most power in the national government. Whether the goals of this group are shared by the entire population or even the majority varies from situation to situation.

There are, however, significant differences in the degree to which the public at large participates in approving the nation's goals and in adopting them as its own. For nations in the stage of primitive unification, when the nation consists of the king and his nobles, or of a small group of colonizers or ex-revolutionaries, national goals are the goals of the rulers. Ordinary subjects do not share their rulers' aspirations, nor are they important in achieving them. Particularly in the realm of international affairs, the public does not count. One can almost say it has no international goals.

In the period of the politics of industrialization, national goals are primarily the aims of the powerful bourgeoisie, of Stalinist managers, or of fascist leaders, and although the achievement of some goals is of importance to a large group, relatively few participate in the formulation of the great majority of national goals or in the execution of policies to achieve them.

Only in the third stage of political development can one speak of truly national goals, and even here the majority of the population does not form them, but merely adopts and supports them in varying degrees. Once adopted, however, such goals may be felt with deep conviction and supported with great fervor. To the extent that this is true, we may speak of them as genuinely national goals.

Sometimes a nation is split within itself over the international goals that it desires. The degree of unity, in fact, is a major determinant of the success a nation will have in achieving its goals, and as we shall see in a later chapter, the amount of national unity affects the nation's power.[4] Agreement on national goals may range from the apparently solid support characteristic of an efficiently functioning, totalitarian dictatorship such as the Soviet Union to the wide and open differences that divided the United States over the war in Vietnam. Of course, it is not always easy to judge the amount of agreement on national goals in a nation where a one-party government and a firm system of censorship prevent the free expression of disagreement with official policies. In Russia, for example, there has been no open deviation by the public from official policies for many years, but the friendly interest in America that individual Americans traveling in Russia so often encountered during the years of the Cold War seemed to indicate widespread attitudes that did not jibe with the official Soviet attitude toward the United States. However, a one-party government and firm censorship do not merely smother opposition; they also help to create support. It would be a mistake to suppose that after so many years of indoctrination the vast majority of the Russian people did not go along with the major foreign policy goals of the Soviet government. Popular support sets limits on the possible international goals, but the limits are much broader in a dictatorship than they are in a Western democracy.

In any nation, but particularly one like the Soviet Union, disagreement on goals among the leaders themselves is more significant than a

4 See Chapter 8.

disagreement between the leaders and the public at large. In 1957, a controversy between those who wished to raise living standards at the expense of capital investment and those who wanted to continue a high level of capital investment with an eye to increasing power helped cause important changes in the top leadership of the Soviet government. Disagreement between Nikita Khrushchev and the Presidium about his handling of the dispute with China was in part responsible for his fall from power in 1964. However, most such disagreements among leaders are resolved within the top organs of government, and once national goals and policies have been adopted, full support is given to them even by officials who originally had other ideas. The possibilities of disagreement on goals, even among the top leaders, are severely limited in a totalitarian dictatorship.

At the opposite extreme lies a nation such as pre-Gaullist France, where the public expressed whatever views it had vociferously and where it seemed to be almost a rule that no two prominent public figures should have the same goals for their nation. In the decade before De Gaulle came to power, the French found it virtually impossible to reconcile the conflicting goals of various powerful interest groups within the nation. French action in Algeria was crippled for years by the fact that the government could not devise any single course of action that would satisfy the goals of the various parties involved. There were the French settlers who wished to perpetuate French rule and privilege no matter what the cost; there were important business interests in France who would have liked to keep Algeria but had no intention of paying higher taxes to pay for costly military action; there were young Frenchmen who mutinied rather than be sent to North Africa for military service; there were a few prominent idealists who felt Algeria should be given her liberty immediately.

France under the Fourth Republic and the Soviet Union represent extremes; most nations fall somewhere between the two in the degree of unity on their national goals. And, of course, the amount of unity varies from issue to issue. The United States, for example, has found herself considerably less united over goals in the Vietnamese and Korean wars than she was in World War II. It is important to know how much unity on goals exists in order to understand why a nation behaves as it does. Action will be most effective where goals are most unified. Similarly, goals will be most specific where there is the most unity behind them, for one of the ways of hiding disagreement and providing for some kind of government position even in the face of divergent interests is to make the national goals vague and general. However, action in pursuit of such vague goals is almost impossible, since it is no longer clear exactly what future state is desired by the nation, and any clear-cut action will reopen the controversy that the vague goal was designed to obscure.

In analyzing national goals, the second question to be asked is: Who will profit from the future state of affairs that a nation desires? Is the achievement of the national goal to be of advantage solely to that nation, or will other nations also benefit? Important consequences depend upon whether the goal is strictly national or humanitarian, for if the nation that holds the goal is to be the sole beneficiary, it cannot really expect other nations to support its aims, whereas if other nations are to benefit as well, their cooperation can be expected. We are not asking here whether other nations will be *affected* by the achievement of the goal, but whether they will *benefit*. If other nations were not affected, the goal would not be international and would not concern us here.

Great advantages accrue to the nation that has goals believed by its people and by others to be steps toward universal good. The nation that wants to persuade other nations to do as it wishes must have these nations believe that it is working for their interests as well as its own.

Humanitarian goals, then, are essential to dominant nations wishing to hold together their allies and followers. A major source of power of such nations is their ability to generate humanitarian goals, and when such goals cease to be put forward or cease to be believed, disastrous consequences follow. One of the reasons great leaders—Woodrow Wilson, Lenin, Franklin D. Roosevelt, Winston Churchill, John F. Kennedy—are assets to their nations is their ability to convince others of the righteousness of their cause. This is not as simple as it sounds, however. If a nation is to convince others that its goals are in the general interest, there are several "musts" to be observed. First, the nation itself must believe it. The national group and particularly its leaders must believe firmly that what they do is done for the common good.

The United States and the Soviet Union are good cases in point. Both have been successful in getting others to believe that many of their national goals are in the general interest, and Americans and Russians, by and large, have not the slightest doubt that, given a choice, the world would choose their way of life. We Americans are certain that all the world desires wealth and freedom such as ours, and we feel sure all honest men must recognize that our policies toward other nations are designed with their best interests at heart. An American Secretary of State once set forth this naive view quite openly. James Byrnes quotes himself as telling Soviet Foreign Minister Molotov: "No one in the world fears the United States or its intentions."[5] A later Secretary of State, John Foster Dulles, said in a press conference in 1957: ". . . we do fear and think we have reason to fear that under certain circumstances that [sic] the Soviet Union might attack. I don't think that the Soviet Union has any legitimate ground to fear any attack from anywhere in the United States or any of our bases."[6]

The Russians, for their part, are equally certain that they are on the side of right and that in the long run they will triumph. As we seek to save the world from communism, they seek to save the world from "capitalist imperialism." Each side charges the other with insincerity and claims that if the people of the world could be reached with the truth and released from bondage, they would happily embrace its way of life.

A good example of a people fundamentally sure of their mission to benefit mankind is the British. Indeed, their own assuredness on this point was the chief reason why so much of the rest of world came to agree with them. Cecil Rhodes, the great English empire builder, wrote: "I contend that we are the first race in the world and that the more of the world we inhabit the better it is for the human race."[7] Or consider the words of a noted nineteenth-century English journalist, W. T. Stead: "The English-speaking race is one of the chief of God's chosen agents for executing coming improvements in the lot of mankind."[8] Examples of this kind are legion.

It is not enough for a nation to believe it acts for the good of the world: the world must believe it, too. For this purpose, the nation must have an ideology that will appeal to others, beliefs such as "all men are created equal" or "liberty, equality, fraternity" or "from each according to his ability, to each according to his need." The fact that the nation voicing these beliefs may not live up to them in daily life is not a fatal fault. The fact that when many American Southerners say all men are created equal they do not include Negroes, the fact that it never occurred to most Frenchmen to grant liberty, equality, and fraternity to their colonials until they were forced to do so, the fact that the Russians have not achieved anything approaching pure communism, these facts do not destroy the usefulness of such lofty principles. They are pointed to as ideals with progress always being made in their direction, or it is claimed that these principles represent what citizens really believe while the practice is simply a temporary aberration or expedient. Each side contrasts its own ideals

---

[5] James Byrnes, *Speaking Frankly* (New York: Harper & Row, 1947), p. 129.
[6] *The New York Times,* June 12, 1957, p. 12, col. 2.
[7] E. H. Carr, *The Twenty Years' Crisis* (London: Macmillan, 1954), p. 76.
[8] *Ibid.*

with the actual practice of its rival, and the world is, in fact, moved by these principles, even though it learns from each side that the other does not live up to its fine declarations.

Unless humanitarian ideals and traditions are present, a nation will not be believed in its protestations of altruism. Nazi Germany and Imperial Japan both believed in their missions, but they were never successful in getting others to believe in them, for neither nation possessed a humanitarian ideology suitable for export. The fact that humanitarian principles are useful, however, does not lead to their creation. Such beliefs and attitudes evolve over centuries and cannot be created from one day to the next, nor can they be feigned because it would be convenient to be believed humanitarian. Russian rulers will not allow freedom of speech simply because this would make them more popular with us, and Americans will continue to discriminate against Negroes even though their acts may damn the United States in the eyes of the world.

Even when a nation says its goals benefit mankind and others believe this to be so, it does not necessarily follow that this is true. Usually the assertion that a nation's goal is the welfare of humanity is not an outright lie but a half-truth. A major task in the realistic analysis of national goals is to differentiate between the interests of one's own nation and the interests of other nations (or the general good). The fact of the matter is that national goals truly in the general interest are extremely rare, if they exist at all.

What are generally confused for goals that aim at the general good are in reality goals that benefit more than one nation. These are not in the general interest, because they do not benefit all nations but only some, and even those they benefit do not gain equally. Let us consider first the case of a nation whose national goals have long been believed to benefit mankind, and then let us consider a goal traditionally thought of as benefiting all and harming none. The nation is England. The goal is peace.

As head of an international system that dominated the world for almost the entire nineteenth century, England could and did claim that she was providing the world with peace and order. Her allies accepted this claim, and even some of her enemies occasionally wavered. Carr quotes a German professor as writing in the 1920s: "England is the solitary Power with a national programme which, while egotistic through and through, at the same time promises to the world something which the world passionately desires: order, progress and eternal peace."[9]

Why did so many nations believe this claim of England's? Mainly because the international system that England headed provided distinct

[9] *Ibid.*, p. 82.

benefits for many of the major European nations and for the United States as well. When these nations thought of humanity, they thought of themselves, not of those who occupied the bottom rungs of England's international order and benefited hardly at all from her rule. The German professor might speak for Europe, but he could not speak for India or China or Africa. It was possible for Englishmen and other Europeans to argue that England's goals were for the benefit of humanity because they assumed that what was good for them was good for the world.

Or take the goal of peace. It is generally believed that this is truly a humanitarian goal, since all nations gain by peace and no one loses. In fact, wars do not hurt all nations equally, and they may even benefit some. In World War II, Germany and Japan suffered terribly. England and France also suffered, but the total balance for the USSR is not so evident. Russia lost millions of people and much of her industry, but when one compares the position of Russia before the war with her position today, it is not so clear whether she lost or gained. The United States became the undisputed leading nation in the world, and India won her independence.

To take even a more extreme example, consider World War III. For more than two decades, there has been a Niagara of statements that a third world conflict would mean the end of the world. It is quite possible that the United States and Russia might annihilate one another in such a war and destroy much of Europe in the process, but Russia, the United States, and Europe are not the world. Even the much-feared disappearance of Western civilization would not mean the end of the world. It would mean the end of *our* world. But would China lose? Would Southeast Asia lose? Would Africa lose?

The point here, however, is not that wars are good, for surely on balance they cause more misery than benefit, but that peace—particularly if peace means the preservation of the status quo—does not benefit all nations equally, and that those who pursue peace as a national goal while claiming that they are interested in the welfare of all men are often more seriously interested in avoiding the destruction of their own wealth, which war would cause, and in perpetuating their own positions of privilege, which peace helps to guarantee. Peace is as close to a truly humanitarian goal as we are likely to find, but even peace is often pursued for selfish reasons.

The brief section above shows that humanitarian goals have some distinct advantages for the nations that hold them. The main advantage is that other nations will help to put them into effect. No one, unless fooled into doing so, will help a nation realize goals of which it is the sole beneficiary, but many will help in what appears to be a common cause. Humanitarian goals are not invented simply because it is advantageous to have them, but if they are available, they can be extremely useful. It should be remembered, however, that many of the goals considered to be in the general interest are of benefit primarily to a relatively small group of nations and are of greatest benefit to the nation that holds them.

Let us now glance at the more narrowly national goals. Here our task is far simpler. By narrowly national, we mean goals where only the nation holding the goal will receive whatever benefits follow from achievement of the desired end. Since one nation is the sole beneficiary, it will usually carry the entire burden in making the goal a reality. If a nation cannot fulfill its desires through its own efforts, it cannot afford to have narrowly national goals; its goals must be broad enough to interest more powerful neighbors. The only alternative for a nation that cannot carry out its projects alone but still insists upon having the kind of goals from which it alone will benefit is to content itself with daydreams and to resign itself to doing nothing much on the international level. In this case, however, the goals become, in effect, hopes—desired future states of affairs that the nation intends to spend no effort attempting to achieve. In international affairs, as in individual life, selfishness is a luxury that only the rich and powerful can afford.

Thus nations of little power are almost compelled to have international goals that appear, at least, to be humanitarian, whereas powerful nations have more of a choice in the kind of goals they hold. However, great nations may sometimes find it more effective to emphasize narrow national goals, particularly where the major weight of sacrifice in achieving the goal must fall on the nation itself. When Russia was fighting against German aggression in World War II, she dropped her emphasis on the humanitarian goals of communism and hammered home to the Russian people that they were fighting for Mother Russia and for their own survival. When Churchill offered the British blood, toil, tears, and sweat, the goal was England's safety, and when Americans are asked to pay high taxes, the goal presented to them is America's security. The greater the sacrifice demanded of the nation, the more likely it is that the goals will be narrowly national.

There is one other instance in which a tradition of narrow national goals will prove more useful than a humanitarian tradition. If the government wishes the nation to take action that is clearly against the interests of other nations, it will find it difficult to sell such a program to a nation accustomed to thinking of itself as the benefactor of mankind. One of the reasons England lost so much of her colonial empire in recent years is that the English came to believe their own myth that they were ruling for the benefit of the colonial populations. Consequently, the English could not in good conscience take the steps that would have been necessary to hold onto the colonies.

LONG-RANGE VERSUS IMMEDIATE GOALS

Another important consideration concerns the amount of time that is expected to elapse before a national goal is realized. Long-range goals are in a sense "safer" for a national government, since it is harder to tell whether they are achieved. On the other hand, it is difficult to whip up great enthusiasm for extremely distant goals, since people seem most easily motivated to work for benefits that they themselves or at least their children will receive. It is hard to work for posterity without some intermediate rewards along the way.

Ideally, immediate goals and long-range goals should be in accord with each other, the long-range goals determining what the immediate goals will be and the immediate goals being steps toward the long-range goal. In fact, however, there is often conflict between the two. In such cases, the short-term goals more often win out, first because they are often more concrete, and second because there is more pressure from the population to receive immediate rewards.

On the whole, countries with popularly controlled governments are under much more pressure to pursue immediate goals. The result, as a look at either American or British foreign policy indicates clearly, is all too often a course of action that does not seem headed clearly toward *any* long-range goal but is rather a hauling and tacking from one crisis to another. Autocratic governments, on the other hand, are much freer to make long-range plans since their government structure facilitates resistance to immediate popular demands.

GENERAL VERSUS SPECIFIC GOALS

Still another distinction can be made between goals that are specific and goals that are general or vague. We have already noted that irreconcilable specific goals held by various important groups within a nation are likely to result in vaguely stated national goals. Perhaps the best example of such general goals is to be found in the election platform of either American political party. By keeping the platform extremely general, the party hopes to appeal to people holding opposite points of view. Thus "fair relations between labor and management" is a phrase supposed to appeal to militant labor leaders and to violently anti-labor employers alike. Such generalities are also found in international politics.

Thus the government that pledges itself to seek world peace presumes that it can count upon the support of all, although it has not made it clear whether it means to pursue peace through disarmament and lower taxes or through arming to the hilt and taxing its citizens heavily. Peace is perhaps the prime example of a vague international goal. Peace of what kind? At what price? At whose expense? Unless these questions are answered, it is impossible to know what actions a nation proposes to take for the sake of peace, for we are treated daily to the spectacle of nations taking diametrically opposed actions all in the name of peace.

Vague, general goals, useful to cover disagreement within the nation, are also useful to keep one's rivals guessing. Perhaps the ideal international situation for a nation is to have complete internal unity behind both general and specific goals but to confine public statements to the realm of general goals. This provides the government with freedom of action and with maximum bargaining power on any specific occasion.

Finally, it should be noted that general goals can also serve the purposes of hypocrisy. Specific goals may be narrowly nationalistic and highly offensive to other nations, and to state them outright would arouse opposition from other nations. In such a case, vague, general goals, which are often humanitarian in nature, can be extremely useful. Disguised in this way, putting down a colonial revolt becomes "restoring order," subverting a rival government is "opposing tyranny," and preparing for conquest is "assuring peace."

The danger in relying heavily upon the use of general goals is that the nation may forget that for effective action it must know, at least privately, what its specific goals are. It is possible to talk in generalities, but action is always specific. To act without definite goals is to run the risk of producing consequences quite other than those intended.

STATED VERSUS ACTUAL GOALS

The point that national goals are not always what they are claimed to be or what they appear to be leads us to the next distinction to be made about a nation's goals. Do the statements made by a nation's leaders really represent its goals or are they statements made in error or with the intent to deceive? This is crucial information for those who must deal with that nation. Indeed, a major function of the intelligence services of any country is to find out the true international goals of other nations. Mistakes in this area can be extremely costly, even fatal. Germany lost two world wars because she did not understand that American goals ruled out the possibility of allowing Germany to defeat England and France. England, for her part, *almost* lost World War II because she did not understand that Germany's goal was war and world supremacy but thought that

Hitler's goals were more limited and could be satisfied through concessions.

The diary of the Italian foreign minister, Count Ciano, reports a very interesting conversation on this topic about a month before World War II began. Ciano says he asked the German foreign minister: "Well Ribbentrop, . . . what do you want? The Corridor or Danzig?"

The answer was brief and to the point: "Not that anymore, we want war."[10]

If a nation professes to have one set of goals while in reality it holds another, it is usually possible to find some evidence of this. If there is a discrepancy between what a nation says and what it does, it is safer to stick to behavior as a guide.

It is also useful to check what a government says for internal consumption against what it says to the outside world, for here again, it is not possible to mislead one's own citizens too drastically if they are to be relied on later for support and even sacrifice in pursuit of the nation's goals. For example, during the early years of World War II, Russia and Germany had a treaty of nonaggression and were officially friends. Soviet officials in direct touch with the Russian people, however, kept preaching that the Germans were not to be trusted and that Russia must be ready for any eventuality.

It is advisable, then, to check a nation's stated goals against its behavior and against what it tells its own people, even though neither guide is infallible. As we have noted, the same behavior may be appropriate for several different goals. Mobilization may indeed be a preparation for aggression, but it may also be a sign of fear or a preparation for self-defense. Russian industrialization can be interpreted as a move to build up her armed might for future wars, but she may also be interested primarily in raising her standard of living.

Nor are statements for internal consumption always a good index of national intentions. It is quite possible for a government to lie to its people or to be working for goals that the majority of the population might not accept if they were stated clearly. This appears to have been the case in the early years of both world wars, when the American government clearly considered Allied victory a more important goal than keeping America out of war but when public statements to the contrary were frequently made. In the Vietnam conflict, the discrepancy between American policy statements and governmental actions involving the United States ever more deeply in the war was great enough to cause a "credibility gap," or, to put it less politely, a considerable number of Americans

---

[10] Galeazzo Ciano, *The Ciano Diaries, 1939–1943* (Garden City, N.Y.: Garden City Publishing Co., 1947), p. 580.

decided their government was lying to them about its goals and plans in Vietnam. Discrepancies between the actual goals and the stated goals of nations are common, but they are not always easy to identify.

Often a discrepancy between actual goals and stated goals confers an advantage upon a nation by misleading others and diverting attention from unpopular goals, but at times such a discrepancy can be a marked disadvantage. This is particularly true when the stated goal is humanitarian, whereas the actual goal may be narrowly nationalistic and much less laudable. Enemies of the nation may seize upon the discrepancy to embarrass the nation abroad and to undermine the support of the government at home.

America's goals for the colonial world were of such a nature. Our stated goal for years had been the end of imperialism and the freedom and independence of all nations. However, confronted with armed struggles between ou. European allies and their colonies, we almost invariably sided with our European allies. The Russians were quick to point out this discrepancy and to use it to discredit us abroad. The nation that can state its actual goals quite openly has a much easier time in some respects, for it is not open to this kind of attack. Nazi Germany's policies toward what she believed to be "inferior races" were reprehensible, but they were perfectly consistent with her goals. It was not possible to undermine the determination of the Nazis by pointing to discrepancies between words and deeds.

One way to handle the discrepancy is to refuse to see any difference between the two. It is difficult to undermine a nation like nineteenth-century England, which could truly believe that her conquest of an empire was designed primarily to bring civilization to the heathen. The United States, Russia, and China all protect themselves today with some of this brand of self-righteousness. Such nations admit grudgingly, if at all, that in the process of saving the world they always happen also to strengthen their own position, fill their own pockets, and increase their own prestige.

STATUS QUO VERSUS CHANGE

One final observation remains to be made. We have spoken of goals as desirable future states to be achieved, but there are many nations that are quite content with many aspects of the present world. For them, the achievement of many national goals merely means perpetuating the status quo. It is important to know whether this is the case or whether realization of the national goal requires change.

Those whose goal is to upset the status quo are often viewed as troublemakers, as disturbers of the peace who pursue narrowly nationalistic goals at the expense of the common good, while those who seek to perpetuate the status quo are the defenders of peace, law, and order. The so-called troublemakers countercharge that those who seek to perpetuate the status quo are against justice and freedom and are really interested only in preserving their own positions of privilege.

There is some truth in both these charges. Those who defend the status quo are certainly those who are most contented with it, that is, those whose power and privilege are greatest. On the other hand, those who are discontented and seek to change the status quo often find that they cannot do so within the existing set of rules or without disturbing the peace. Neither side can claim a monopoly of morality or of humanitarian goals.

Summary

We have defined a national goal as a future state of affairs considered desirable by the nation, promoted by the national government, and calling forth the efforts of the population in order to achieve it. Goals concerned with international affairs have been classified into four broad categories: power, wealth, cultural welfare, and peace. It has been demonstrated that it is not always easy to tell whether a specific action is directed toward one or another of these goals, since the same action may be a step toward several of them at once.

National goals may be pursued either competitively or as absolute goals desirable in themselves. Power is always to some extent competitive, whereas peace is always an absolute goal. Wealth and cultural welfare, however, may be pursued either competitively or in an absolute manner.

We have seen that it is also useful to distinguish between national goals that are unified and those that are divergent, between goals that are humanitarian and those that are strictly national, between goals that are long-range and those that are immediate, between goals that are general and those that are specific, and between goals that a nation truly holds and those that it merely claims to hold. Finally, we have seen that it is important to know whether the achievement of a nation's goals requires a change or whether it involves perpetuation of the status quo.

In the chapter that follows, we shall deal with some of the factors that determine the goals of nations and the differences among them.

5

Determinants of National Goals

Once we understand a nation's international goals, we are well on the road to understanding why it behaves as it does in international relations, but the question remains: What makes a nation choose the goals it has? Why does one nation concentrate on achieving a higher standard of living while another taxes its citizens severely to build a mighty war machine? Why does one nation seek to convert the world to its way of life while another asks merely to be left alone? Why does one nation take foolish risks and provoke its enemies and neighbors while another seems to seek peace at almost any price? In short, what are the determinants of national goals?

At best, we can provide only partial and tentative answers to the questions asked. As a beginning, let us divide the possible determinants into two broad categories. That is to say, there are two places where we can search for determinants: (1) within the nation itself, among the characteristics of the nation and its population; and (2) in the external situation in which the nation finds itself in relation to other nations. We begin with the internal determinants.

It is sometimes claimed that national character is a major determinant of a nation's goals. Thus Americans are said to be materialistic and American foreign policy therefore largely a policy in pursuit of national wealth; Indians, more spiritual, and India's foreign policy consequently more concerned with morality and ideals. A few decades ago, German militarism was blamed for German conquest, and Japan's attempt to establish a new order in Asia was traced back to the necessity for the Japanese to be surrounded by an orderly world in which everyone occupied his rightful place in a well-defined hierarchy.

At first glance, it may not seem unreasonable to believe that the character of the millions of individuals who make up a nation will have an influence in shaping the nation's goals. However, it is not enough for a view to seem reasonable: we must see if it is valid and if it increases our understanding of world politics.

The theory that national character is an important variable in shaping national goals rests upon three assumptions: (1) that the individual citizens of a nation share a common psychological make-up or personality or value system that distinguishes them from the citizens of other nations, (2) that this national character persists without major changes over a relatively long period of time, and (3) that there is a traceable relationship between individual character and national goals. It is necessary to examine each of these assumptions more closely, for if any of them turns out to be false, the whole theory is disproved.

The first question, then, is whether it is possible to identify national character traits. Sociologists, anthropologists, and psychologists are showing revived interest in modal personality structure, value orientations, and the relationship between personality and culture, but it is not quite clear that any of these add up to national character. The idea that certain personality types are more common in some nations than in others is an interesting one, but existing studies are of small homogeneous groups, not entire nations.

We have seen in Chapter 2 that members of a nation do share a common culture to some extent. Particularly when we deal with parts of the culture that are related to bringing up children, it seems logical to assume that the culture would have an effect upon the kind of personalities developed. However, we are only beginning to learn what kind of child-rearing produces what kind of personality, and we do not have anything like complete information on the child-rearing practices of entire nations or on the personalities of entire populations. We know that there are vast differences from class to class and from group to group within a nation, and there are also great differences in the way different individuals respond to the same cultural background.

The study of national character, when pursued with any scientific rigor, is beset with difficulties. There are problems of defining what national character is in the first place, and there are problems of method. Existing studies generally offer insufficient evidence and most are plagued with a sampling problem. A small group of people or a small body of literature is examined very carefully, but the sample is not representative of the nation as a whole. In short, the studies now being conducted are highly interesting, and the field as a whole is a fascinating one. We may hope for progress in the years ahead but we are a long way from any generalizations about personality that can be applied with confidence to entire nations.

At this point the reader should be warned to differentiate sharply between the serious work being done in the area of national character, fragmentary though it is, and the statements that have little connection with scientific inquiry sometimes made in writings in international relations. We are referring to the common-sense observations and the biased stereotypes of the psychologically unsophisticated public, in which Germans are described as innately militant, brutal, industrious, and orderly; Americans as inventive, frank, generous, materialistic, and naïve; Frenchmen as logical, witty, cynical, and fickle; Englishmen as unemotional, pragmatic, and hypocritical; Russians as slow, stolid, and patriotic, and so on.

In practice, however, it is possible to find numerous examples of naïve Frenchmen, cynical Americans, kind-hearted Germans, witty Russians, etc. No nation has a monopoly on these widespread human characteristics, and common impression to the contrary notwithstanding, it has never been scientifically determined that even in a general way one national population has a higher incidence of any one of these traits than any other national population. The truth is that these descriptions are stereotypes, and like other stereotypes, they owe as much to the one who looks as to the one who is seen. Every nation has a relatively favorable stereotype of its own national character, a faintly hostile stereotype of the character of its allies, and a distinctly unflattering stereotype of the character of its enemies. We are far from the realm of science.

These stereotypes of national character are often supported by so-called evidence, but it is highly questionable. The usual process of reasoning seems to be as follows: first, characteristics displayed at particular times and in particular circumstances by individuals belonging to a nation are extended to the entire national group. Second, when the resulting generalization is questioned, the original actions are brought forth as evidence. In other words, the event that aroused the suspicion in the first place is used as proof that the suspicion is correct. For example, we notice the immense cruelty of some Germans in World War II. Cruelty, then, is said to be a trait of the German national character, and if anyone doubts it, the cruelty of some Germans in World War II is brought up as irrefutable evidence that the belief is correct. It may well be that such a thing as national character exists, but if so, we have yet to locate precisely which character belongs to which nation.

The second assumption, that national character is somehow innate and changes slowly if at all, is open to even more serious question than the first. The premise is that if we understand the national character, we will know what to expect from a nation and will not be misled by apparent changes in ideology or government. This would be convenient if it were true, but there is no reason to believe that it is true. Indeed, most of what we know points to the opposite conclusion.

We know that human culture has changed greatly in the past few hundred years. It is even possible for us to witness dramatic changes in the culture of nations as they take place. Nations that have industrialized have changed their whole way of life, and the colonial world has been subjected to entirely new influences that have resulted in dramatic changes in the culture of those nations. Economic life has changed markedly and new political institutions have been invented. The influence of religion has diminished with increasing secularization, and new secular religions have arisen. Family patterns have changed very much, and children today are brought up and taught and disciplined in ways that differ even from one generation to the next. Under the circumstances, it would seem a miracle if national character did not change, too, and yet the myth persists that Americans still have the character of backwoods frontiersmen, that Russians under the commissars have the same character as Russians under the tsar, that Italians have not changed since Machiavelli.

The stereotypes themselves deny the permanence of national character. "Swashbuckling, adventurous" Vikings have become "phlegmatic, contented" Scandinavians. The "sweet and doll-like" Japanese of Perry's day became "leering, bespectacled sadists" when they invaded China. Or take the English and the French. In the first half of the twentieth century, the English had a reputation as politically staid and faithful while the French were considered to be fickle and politically unstable, but in the sixteenth and seventeenth centuries it was the British who were known for political volatility while the French were reputed to be faithful to their monarchs and their institutions.[1]

The international behavior of nations also puts a strain on the notion that national character is permanent, for if national behavior is determined by national character and national character is fundamentally unchanging, how can we explain the fact that the Swedes, so peace-loving today, were once raising military havoc from one end of Europe to the other or that Frenchmen, so militant and confident under Napoleon, became so defeatist after World War II, and then rebounded again, or that Americans, so firmly isolationist for years, are now engaged in settling the problems of the entire world?

It would be very nice, indeed, if the world would remain the same, so that once having figured it out, we would not need to think again, but reality is not so kind. The world is ever-changing, and there is no reason to believe that national character is any exception to the rule.

The third assumption, that there is a direct relationship between national character and national goals, is also open to question. Granted that individual citizens have goals and that these are influenced by their character and personalities, there is still a big gap between the goals of individual citizens and those of the nation as a whole. Before the wishes of individual citizens are translated into collective action by the nation, they must be filtered through many institutions and channeled through many intermediaries. In the process, many alternative possibilities appear, so that the same character traits of individual citizens may be expressed on the national level in a great variety of ways.

The same kind of process can be seen on the individual level. An aggressive individual may express this personality trait in a number of ways, some antisocial, some socially acceptable. His character may determine his actions, but the way in which he chooses to express himself is not predictable. And the same is true of nations. It could be argued, for example, that the Japanese people had a great desire to be recognized and accepted by other nations and that it was this desire that led them to military aggression and ultimately to defeat in World War II. Having tried this method and failed, however, the Japanese then turned to other policies, so it could be argued equally convincingly today that this same desire to be recognized and accepted led Japan to emphasize peaceful cooperation to the point where she was reluctant to arm at all. The connection between national character and national goals is nowhere near as clear as one might wish.

In view of the shakiness of these three assumptions, the case for na-

[1] Frederick Hertz, *Nationality in History and Politics* (New York: Oxford University Press, 1944), p. 42.

tional character as a major determinant of national goals does not stand up very well. Perhaps some kind of national character does exist, but we have not yet been successful in identifying anything better than rather crude stereotypes. The characteristics most often attributed to members of a nation turn out to be widespread human attributes that cut across national lines. Certainly, there is no such thing as a semi-permanent national character that remains constant over long periods of time. Finally, even if such a thing as a national character can be established, it is not possible to trace a direct line from the character of individual citizens to the behavior of the nation as a whole.

If we are to find a satisfactory explanation of national goals, our best hope does *not* lie in examining the character or the psychological characteristics of the individuals who make up the national population.

The Ruling Classes

If the character of ordinary citizens does not provide a key to the nature of national goals, what can be said about the character and interests of the ruling group? One does not have to subscribe to any great-man theory of history to admit that it makes a difference whether a nation is governed by a theocracy, a group of businessmen, or a military clique, nor does one have to be a Marxist to admit that some people are more influential than others in forming a nation's goals. If it is offensive to call these people "a ruling class," we can call them something else, but if we are going to be realistic we must admit that even in a democracy such as ours, there are powerful men who have considerably more influence over the actions of our government than do common citizens.

As we have noted before, it is individuals, not nations, that have goals. It is individual people who consider certain future states desirable enough to be willing to work to bring them about. However, most individuals do not have international goals for their nation, at least not goals that are of much importance to them. Their major goals are for themselves and their families. On the whole, they tend to become interested in international affairs only when there is some dramatic issue that catches their imagination or when their own interests are vitally affected, as when they are likely to be drafted or have their taxes raised. Not surprisingly, American interest in international politics rose sharply during the Korean and Vietnamese wars. Interest also rises when an individual is affected by some particular issue. For example, a man who manufactures bicycles will be interested in tariffs on foreign bicycles, and a farmer will be aware of government policy in regard to selling farm surpluses abroad. In truth, ordinary citizens are affected by many of the international actions taken by their nations, but unless the relationship is fairly obvious and immediate, they do not feel involved. Even when they are concerned, they often do not focus their sentiments sharply enough to have anything that might properly be called international goals.

There are, however, some organized groups that have a more definite and focused interest in international affairs, and these groups have international goals. Many American oil companies, for example, have a very real stake in the Middle East and consequently are very much concerned about American policy in that area. There are organized Jewish groups with an equally important stake in the Middle East (an emotional and not a financial commitment, but a stake nevertheless), and they, too, have definite goals that they would like the American government to adopt in its dealings with the nations of the Middle East. Businessmen form lobbies to enlist government support for many divergent goals: to protect their sources of raw materials (as in South Africa), to facilitate American investment abroad, and to broaden the market for American goods through freer trade. Military leaders and companies with defense contracts have an immediate and direct interest in defense policies.

In wartime, the interests of all these groups tend to converge in the single goal of military victory, but in ordinary times there may be considerable range and even outright contradiction between the international goals of various groups within the nation. The national government considers these various conflicting interests and forms goals for the nation as a whole.

The role of the government in the formation of national goals is crucial. Private citizens may or may not have international goals, but the government *must* have goals if it is to act at all. Private citizens may have conflicting goals, but the government must reconcile these differences and arrive at some conclusion before it can act, for it cannot act in pursuit of two contradictory goals at the same time. The government must hammer the divergent desires of many organized groups within the nation into a single set of national goals, for it is the government that must act for the nation in its dealings with other nations. No other group has this responsibility.

Theoretically, a democratic government does no more than act as the agent of the national population it represents, but actually, the government itself is a group of people with its own international goals. As such, the government competes with other groups to have its own goals accepted as the goals of the nation. In this competition, the government has certain marked advantages over other groups: it has superior information as to what is going on, both at home and abroad; it receives superior publicity and has access to superior means of convincing the populace that it is right; and it has the job of implementing whatever decisions are reached.

In advanced industrial societies, government officials constitute only one of many organized groups with interests and goals in the international field, but in some of the more backward preindustrial nations, the national government has the field to itself. In Saudi Arabia or Outer Mongolia or Nepal or Yemen, nobody but the government cares two whoops about international affairs. The rulers *are* the nation, and their goals are the national goals. In a modern state, the situation is more complex, but even here national goals tend to be shaped primarily by government officials and by the influential groups upon whom they depend most closely.

The groups competing for supremacy within a nation are not all equal in power and prestige. In every nation, some groups are more influential than others, and the government necessarily depends more heavily upon the powerful groups and represents their interests more carefully than it does the interests of the general public. Although modern governments, both democratic and totalitarian, must depend upon at least the tacit support of the whole population to avoid the possibility of revolution, public opinion sets only broad limits upon what the government can do, particularly in the field of international relations. The reliance of the national government upon the most powerful groups within the nation is much more direct. It relies on them for the internal support necessary to remain in office. It relies on them for funds and for personnel.

The identity of these most powerful groups varies from one nation to another. In much of Latin America, for example, the military appears to hold the key to power, and without the support of important military leaders, a government is doomed. In the United States, on the other hand, the military has comparatively little power, although its leaders are a great deal more powerful today than they were before World War II. The most important groups in the United States are first, leaders of the business community, and second, leaders of major labor unions and farm organizations as well as leaders of the military establishment and the professions. Government bureaucrats have also become a group of increased importance in the years since the New Deal. In Spain, the big landowners, the Catholic Church, the military, and the governmental bureaucracy appear to be the major power groups within the nation. In the Soviet Union, power is shared among the top bureaucrats of the Communist Party, the top industrial managers, the top military leaders, and, until recently, the leaders of the secret police. China, formerly controlled primarily by Westernized businessmen and regional war lords, is now in the hands of a Communist bureaucracy, although military leaders continue to be important.

The groups mentioned above are usually not completely distinct from one another. There is likely to be considerable overlapping of membership among them. In the Soviet Union, for example, leading industrial managers, top military men, and leaders of the secret police are all members of the Communist Party. In Spain, the Church holds great wealth, and men of wealth often send their sons into the Church or the bureaucracy. In the United States, business executives go into government, the generals become corporation executives or even Presidents upon their retirement.

It is a vast oversimplification, however, to consider a nation to be run by a single, unified ruling class. The most powerful groups within a nation may be highly unified, as they are in the USSR, or they may be hopelessly split, as they have recently been in France and in China. In most nations, the picture is extremely complex. Not only do economic institutions compete with military, religious, and political institutions, but smaller groups within each of these institutions also compete. Thus the armed services fight among themselves as well as with nonmilitary groups. Steel companies fight with coal companies, and religious institutions compete for control of the toll road to heaven. When it comes to foreign policy, the most powerful groups within a nation are often far from agreed on the goals they have or on the course they would like the nation to pursue.

Nevertheless, these groups determine in large part what the national goals will be. The advantages of having the nation espouse one's goals are too obvious to require extended discussion. When these powerful groups agree upon a goal, it is accepted as a national goal almost without question, certainly without serious opposition. When they disagree among themselves, either their disagreement blocks the national government from acting effectively, or the difference is settled through the intervention of government officials or, in some cases, through an appeal to the public, as when the disagreement becomes a major campaign issue in a national election.

Thus, to a great extent it is the goals of these powerful groups that become the national goals. Whenever this happens, it is important that the public as a whole should feel that the goals are beneficial to the entire nation. Often, this is indeed the case, but even when it is not, efforts are made to make the public believe so. Such efforts are not necessarily motivated by dishonesty. It is always easy to identify one's own selfish interests with the common good. Years ago Charles Wilson, then

Secretary of Defense and a former president of the General Motors Corporation, stated publicly: "What is good for General Motors is good for the country." The statement caused an uproar, but Wilson was not alone. Many an honest man sincerely believes that what will benefit him will benefit humanity, and if the honest man is important enough and if he states his case with care, a good part of the general public will agree with him.

If one is seeking to establish why the international goals of a nation are what they are, much of the explanation is to be found in the nature of the dominant group upon whom the government depends most heavily. Once this group (or groups) has been identified and its interests and goals specified, it is not hard to predict what the goals of the nation in international politics will be.

The Character of Individual Leaders

We have still to consider what influence an individual leader may exert upon the formation of national goals. Common sense and modern history indicate quite clearly that it does make a difference who happens to lead a nation at a particular time. Nazi Germany is inconceivable without Hitler, and the First French Empire cannot be separated from the person of Napoleon Bonaparte. The United States might have floundered hopelessly or turned to an extremist solution in the Depression without Roosevelt, and the bloodless achievement of Indian independence would probably have been impossible without Gandhi.

However, it must be remembered that leaders, no matter how dynamic, must work within the framework set by the interests of the major power groups within the nation. Without the support of at least one such group, the leader will not rise to a position of power in the first place, and once in office, he still cannot afford to offend those upon whom he depends for support. Nkrumah in Ghana, Sukarno in Indonesia, Ben Bella in Algeria, and Khrushchev in the Soviet Union were all powerful leaders who offended and antagonized those on whom they depended for support, and thus fell from power.

Perhaps the most dramatic instances of the importance of leadership are to be found in revolutionary situations where a leader opposed by the previous power groups is thrown to the top, and begins to create new institutions and present a new ideology, but even here, one must look behind the leader to the group he represents. Usually he is the representative of a new power group that has been growing in strength for some time, and he brings into office with him a whole new ruling elite. In no case does he rise alone, completely detached from other changes going on in the power structure of the nation.

It may sometimes appear that there is no explanation for some action by a nation other than a peculiar twist in the personality of its leader. Surely the goals Hitler set for Germany were in part the personal dreams of a madman. But, as we indicated earlier, one must still ask, what is there in the social structure, the character of the mass, and the interests of the powerful within a nation that allows this kind of leader to rise to the top?

If one wishes to understand in full depth the meaning of a nation's actions at a particular moment of history, then, it will be useful to understand the personality and aims and aspirations of its major leaders. They must be seen, however, in reference to the groups whose interests they further and in reference to the institutions that allow them their place of power. It is not helpful to exaggerate the role they play.

External Factors

Some of the factors that determine what a nation's international goals will be lie outside the nation itself, for goals, in any realistic sense, are determined not only by the desires of important groups within the nation, but also by what is possible. Theoretically, there is no limit to what such groups may want, and utopian dreams may even be incorporated into long-range goals.

National governments, however, must also have short-range goals that are possible of achievement in the relatively near future, and here reality intrudes. International goals, by definition, involve more than one nation. Consequently, some part of the responsibility for success or failure in achieving them also rests on other nations. The power, the goals, and the behavior of other nations set limits on what any single nation can accomplish, and although it may be possible to influence the behavior of these other nations to some extent, they cannot be ignored.

The behavior of other nations not only influences whether goals can be achieved or not; it also helps determine what those goals will be in the first place. Indeed, the very idea that a particular goal was desirable may have come from outside. In most of the colonial world, for example, the idea of political nationhood and the idea of political freedom in the modern sense were kindled by the conqueror. Similarly, the achievement of a previously unknown standard of living by the United States has set new standards for many other nations. Particularly where a goal is pursued competitively, the accomplishments of one nation become the goals to be surpassed by another.

But while the power and wealth of other nations may stimulate a powerful rival to expand its own goals, these same factors may limit the goals of lesser nations. Holland, for example, was once a great world power, and as such she entered into the race for colonies, power, and prestige with full competitive spirit. Such a role for the Netherlands today would be out of the question. No matter how competitive the Dutch might be, there would be no sense at all in their trying to vie with giants like the United States, the Soviet Union, and China. The Netherlands, therefore, has abandoned the struggle for world power and has turned her attention to the goal of raising Dutch living standards, quite apart from what the rest of the world may do.

The power of a nation is a particularly important determinant of the kind of international goals that nation can afford. Any nation may attempt to raise its own standard of living, but only a very strong nation can pursue power competitively with other great nations. Indeed, a great nation is almost compelled to compete for power because of the activities of other great nations. It is not primarily a change in the American character or in the American ruling class that has led to the nation's abandoning isolation for a competitive struggle to remain the most powerful nation in the world. It is the simple fact that having once become so powerful, we find that our standard of living, our way of life, and even our ideology have come to depend upon remaining powerful.

Furthermore, it is not only the amount of power a nation has at a given moment that influences the nature of its goals. It also makes a difference whether the nation is expanding in power or contracting. It is primarily the great powers that are still expanding that seek to impose their rule and their way of life on other nations. England in the nineteenth century was intent upon "civilizing" the rest of the world, and in the process, she conquered one quarter of the earth's surface. Today it is the United States, the Soviet Union, and China who seem determined to spread their way of life. It really should not surprise us that the missionary spirit has hit the Chinese as hard as it has, and if past experience is a reliable guide, it should hit the Indians equally hard as soon as they begin to industrialize in earnest.

Nations that are just beginning their ascent to great power necessarily have more moderate goals. They tend to be less imperialistic and often ask only to be left alone to pursue their own ways. Isolation of the sort that the United States enjoyed during her early years is probably not possible for a major nation today, but we find a reflection of the same attitude in the policies of India and other nations seeking to maintain a neutral position removed from the conflict between East and West.

Declining nations also tend to be more tolerant and more modest in their goals. England is an excellent example of a nation on her way down, asking to remain on top a little longer and seeking no more than to hold on to what she has. Gone is the White Man's Burden of earlier English imperialists. Gone is the desire for power and glory. What remains is mainly a desire to be left alone to live in peace without the necessity of new and costly battles.

These same factors, the power position of the nation relative to others, and its movement up or down in the international power hierarchy, are important in determining whether a nation's goals will involve changing the status quo or preserving it. Generally speaking, nations that have been powerful for many years have already made use of their power to establish for themselves a place in the international order that is to their liking. Nations still in the process of rising to power, however, or nations that have become powerful only recently frequently receive fewer benefits from the existing order than they feel they are entitled to. Consequently, it is often true that nations rising rapidly in power have goals that involve serious changes in the status quo (for example, Russia and China); that nations at the peak of their power are more satisfied but may be willing to accept some changes provided they can control them (for example, the United States). Nations on the way down do not follow so predictable a path. Some cling desperately to the existing order lest any change dislodge them. Others seem to accept change realistically. Still others (for example, Gaullist France) seek to return to the status quo ante.

Still another external factor that influences the goals of nations is something that might be called the climate of the times. This is undoubtedly an overly vague term for a factor or a set of factors that ought to be identified more exactly. What is meant is a giant force such as industrialization, which sweeps up every nation and focuses human attention upon new goals. Today, there is scarcely a nation on earth that does not seriously desire to raise its standard of living, but this was not so a century ago. The current emphasis on economic goals is thus a temporary phenomenon, rooted in the historical events of the recent past and perhaps destined to pass in the not too distant future, once the entire world is industrialized and satisfactory living standards have been attained for all. Much the same can be said of the intense and widespread desire of the elites of underdeveloped countries to forge viable national political institutions. In a previous age of great religious ferment, one goal that nations almost invariably had was to extend their religious faith to other nations.

A final factor remains to be considered, one that is neither specifically internal nor external: the factor of chance. Even when we know the national character, the most influential groups within the nation, the personality of the leaders, the power position of the nation, and the climate of the times, we are still a long way from being able to predict with any accuracy exactly what the international goals of a nation will be. Obviously, there are other factors at work. We can call them chance or historical accident, but whatever we call them, the simple truth is that we do not know what they are. It must be emphasized that the whole area of national goals is one where the discussion is far from final. Much work remains to be done, particularly in identifying the determinants of national goals.

Summary

On the basis of material from this chapter and the previous one, it is possible to make a limited number of generalizations about the determinants of national goals. Among the major determinants that we have identified are the interests of the most influential groups within the nation, the personalities of the most important leaders, the power position of the nation, and the general climate of the times. Other factors that seem to have an influence on goals are whether the national government is democratic or autocratic, and whether the ruling elite is united or divided. National character as it is currently defined does not appear to be a major factor. At least, its influence has not yet been clearly identified.

Although it is not possible to specify all the determinants of each of the kinds of national goals distinguished earlier, these generalizations may be suggested:

Wealth is most often sought by wealthy nations, just as power is a more important national goal for strong nations than for weak ones. Peace is a more important goal for declining nations or for nations at the peak of their power than for nations that are rising in power. However, the industrial revolution has greatly increased the importance of wealth, and particularly of higher living standards, as a goal for every nation. Similarly, the increased destructiveness of weapons of war has increased the importance of peace as a national goal.

Powerful, expanding nations are most often competitive in their national goals, whereas weak nations and nations that are declining in power are more apt to pursue absolute goals. Expanding nations, particularly those that have recently risen in power, are most likely to have goals that involve changing the status quo, whereas declining nations and nations near the peak of their power are most concerned to preserve the existing order.

Powerful nations may have goals that are either humanitarian or nationalistic; weak nations, however, cannot afford to have goals that are too narrowly national. Nationalistic goals are also more likely when a high degree of sacrifice is required of the national population.

Nations with totalitarian governments are more apt to have unified goals than democratic nations are. Autocratic governments also find it easier to work toward long-range goals since they are under less pressure than democracies to produce immediate rewards for the public. Finally, national goals are most likely to be specific when the nation is unified, for vague goals may be needed to cover up fundamental disagreement among important groups within the nation.

6

The Nature of National Power

❖⟨C❖⟨C❖⟨C❖⟨C❖⟨C❖⟨C❖⟨C❖⟨C❖⟨C❖⟨C❖⟨C❖⟨C❖⟨C❖⟨C❖⟨C❖⟨C❖⟨C

One of the most important characteristics of a nation is its power, for power is a major determinant of the part that the nation will play in international relations. World politics consists primarily of the doings of America and Russia, of Britain and China, and of the other great nations. It is not much concerned with relations between Iceland and Liberia or with the latest twist of foreign policy in Paraguay. And what is the reason for this? Surely not that Icelanders are less moral than Americans or Liberians less deserving. They are simply less powerful. What they or their governments do does not have much effect on the rest of the world. They seldom intrude on the lives of the rest of us, the major international meetings do not include them, the newspapers do not write about them, and students of international relations do not spend much time studying them. The importance of power is obvious.

It has long been fashionable, particularly in America, to denounce power as evil and to consider "power politics" a noxious practice. We prefer to speak of morality and principles, of legality and justice, not of power. Somehow we assume that those who have power have no principles and that those with principles have no power, but why should this be so? We reject the cynic's statement that God is on the side of the largest battalions, but it is no more reasonable to assume that the smallest battalions always fight for the right. "Power corrupts," the saying goes, but is it merely that corruption is more conspicuous when it is practiced on a large scale? Certainly it would be difficult to prove that powerful governments are more corrupt than weak ones, or that rich men are any more dishonest than poor.

There is no intention here of glorifying power. That would be to fall into the opposite error, one that has also been popular in its time and place. Above all, the exercise of power should not be confused with the use of force and violence, for these are but one way of using power.

In short, power itself is neither good nor evil; what the reader should remember is that it is universal. There is a power aspect to every relationship, and the study of that aspect is the study of politics. On the international level, a nation must have power if it is to carry out its goals, whether they be good or evil. The goals and the men who hold them may be judged moral or immoral, but not the power with which they are pursued. The study of power is essential to an understanding of international affairs. We must not allow a misplaced moral judgment to cloud our analysis in this area.

Power Defined

What, then, is power, this quality that is so important in international politics? In a way, it is easier to list those nations that are powerful than to specify of what their power consists. Everyone knows that the United States is powerful and that Luxembourg is not. Everyone knows which nations' reactions must be considered when foreign policy is formed and which can be ignored except for purposes of courtesy. In a rule-of-thumb way, everyone can make a list of nations in the order of their power and find that this list would be generally agreed upon except for a minor difference here and there.

But what is it that makes a nation powerful? The answer to this question is not so simple. One thinks of size, of nations that possess great expanses of territory peopled by a large and growing population. One thinks of wealth, of nations that are rich in resources, that possess mighty industries, that are blessed with fertile land and good crops. One thinks of military strength, of nations with modern armies and missiles and bombs. But no one of these things alone gives power. Brazil is huge (nearly as large as the United States), Pakistan has a large population (larger than Germany's), Belgium is throughly industrial, and Switzerland has a first-class army, yet none of these are powers of the first rank.

Let us take an even more startling case, China. In the late 1940s, China possessed a large territory, the largest population in the world, not much industry, to be sure, but a large army armed with modern weapons supplied by the United States. Yet she was a great power by courtesy only. She did not even have firm control of her own affairs at home, and her international influence was slight. In the early 1950s China rose to the status of a great power in fact as well as name. Her area had not changed much, her population had not increased substantially, industrialization was still a dream of the future, and her armies were now supplied by the Soviet Union, a less generous ally than the United States. Yet China had become a major power. Her resources—land, people, and industry—had not changed, but her use of them had. Mere possession of resources does not guarantee power. To confer power, these resources must be used, and they must be used in such a way as to influence other nations, for power is the ability to determine the behavior of others.[1]

Let us take another example, Germany. Before World War II, Nazi Germany was one of the strongest nations in the world. After the war, defeated in battle, shorn of her conquests, split in two, deprived of her government, and disarmed, Germany counted for nothing. Now, she is again beginning to emerge as a great power. Although Germany was deprived of people, territory, and wealth, her major loss was her capacity to influence other nations. West Germany, in particular, still possessed enough of the first three to rank as a good-sized nation. Without armed forces, however, she could neither fight nor threaten to fight. Ruled by occupation authorities, she could make no decisions that would affect other nations. She had no power. By the same token, the restoration to Germany of control over her own government and her own economy has restored to her the ability to make decisions in which other nations are interested. She can again grant or withhold her industrial goods, her experts, her friendship, and her troops. She again has power, not simply because she possesses things that other nations want, but because she can dispose of them as she wishes and can thus bargain with them in such a way as to determine the behavior of others. This is the essence of power.

[1] Power is sometimes defined as control over men's minds, but there is little advantage in such a definition. Influence over men's minds is only one way of exercising power. Where such control leads to the desired behavior (as it does in most cases), it is the least costly and most lasting way available to the party who wishes to exercise power. In many cases, however, control of behavior can be obtained without control of men's minds. This is particularly true in cases where force is used. Moreover, whether men's minds are controlled or not is often most evident in their behavior.

Power, then, is the ability to influence the behavior of others in accordance with one's own ends.[2] Unless a nation can do this, it may be large, it may be wealthy, it may even be great, but it is not powerful.

Power, moreover, is not a thing; it is part of a relationship between individuals or groups of individuals. The very existence of power presupposes at least two individuals or groups having some kind of relations with each other, and it further presupposes that in some matter where they disagree, one has the ability to make the other do what it wishes.

After World War II, the United States wished to rearm the West Germans as a bulwark against Russia, but France, fearing the Germans more than the Russians, did not wish to do so. The French executed a series of intricate diplomatic steps and managed to stall off a decision for several years, but in the end, they agreed. One may say that the United States had exercised its power over France.

Or look at India. The British, happily installed in India for many years, had no intention of departing, but after World War II an increasingly nationalist India demanded they get out. In 1947, Britain withdrew and granted India her independence. One may say that India had gained power relative to Britain. It would *not,* however, be accurate to say that India had become more powerful than Britain. Had she wished to remain at all costs, Britain could undoubtedly have stood her ground, but by utilizing her new-found ability to nag and if necessary to fight, India managed to raise the price to the point where Britain no longer considered it worthwhile. India by her actions had influenced the behavior of Britain in such a way as to make her behave as India wished on a point where the two nations disagreed. In short, India had exercised her power.

There is a power aspect to every relationship. One could almost accept this as a definition of their being related. Whether two nations are friends or enemies or merely potential allies, whether they fight together, trade together or have only certain cultural interests in common, each nation cares what the other is doing, and the minute one nation cares, the other has the power to influence it.

Suppose, for example, that two nations have cultural and historic ties, although at present they are politically separate, as in the case with France and Canada. One would not think of this as primarily a power

2 See Herbert Goldhamer and Edward A. Shils, "Types of Power and Status," *American Journal of Sociology,* XLV, 2 (September 1939), 171–82; Peter Bachrach and Morton S. Baratz, "Two Faces of Power," *American Political Science Review,* LVI, 4 (December 1962), 947–52; Robert Dahl, "The Concept of Power," *Behavioral Science,* II, 3 (July 1957), 201–15; Harold D. Lasswell, *Power and Personality* (New York: Norton, 1948); Harold D. Lasswell and Abraham Kaplan, *Power and Society* (New Haven: Yale University Press, 1950).

relationship, and yet it could be used for purposes of power. France, for example, could direct propaganda at the French-speaking population of Canada in such a way as to influence Canada to grant greater military or political support to France than she would otherwise grant. Because the French Canadians care what happens to France, France is able to influence the behavior of Canada. The power aspect may be more or less important, but it is always present.

The power part of a relationship, however, is not a separate unit that can be manipulated apart from the rest of the relationship. The kind of relationship determines the kind of power that can be exercised. The United States and Britain, for example, are close friends of long standing. They share a common language and a common culture, they have many economic ties, and they are military allies. Thus many avenues for influencing each other are open to them which are not open to, let us say, the United States and China. The United States can offer to share atomic developments with Britain in return for closer military cooperation, but she would be ill-advised to make a similar offer to the Chinese, who might well use such information against the United States.

Similarly, the United States would be unwise to attempt to use on Britain the power techniques that have proved effective against China. The United States may forbid Americans to trade with China in retaliation for Chinese policies that she opposes, but she cannot very well apply the same methods to Britain when Britain takes a line that is not favored. The entire alliance would be upset. Hotheads may howl, but a good diplomat knows that a nation cannot treat its friends like enemies every time they misbehave a little, just as he knows a nation cannot treat its enemies as friends simply because they make sweet noises now and then. The ways of power must be appropriate to the relationship of which they form a part.

The reverse is also true. If a nation seriously alters its power relations with another nation, the rest of their relationship will also change. When Indochina won her liberty from France, a fundamental change occurred in the power relationship between the two countries, but this was not all that changed. With freedom, the flow of benefits that had gone to France from her richest colony stopped. The sale of French goods in Indochina dropped off sharply. The flow of raw materials to France dwindled to a trickle. The army that Indochina and the United States had paid for was sent elsewhere to be supported by French tax-payers. These benefits had been the result of a colonial relationship. They could not possibly remain the same once France's hold on her colony was broken.

The same holds true for India. The difference between India the colony and India the member of the Commonwealth is not to be found solely in a different power relationship between India and Britain. The rest of the relationship has changed as well.

We see, then, that power is a part of a relationship. Indeed, it is a part of every relationship. As such it cannot be disentangled from the rest of the relationship but is influenced by it and changes with it. For power is that aspect of a relationship in which each party is able to influence the behavior of the other, and almost any tie between two nations may be utilized in this fashion.

The Instruments of Power

It becomes clear that the qualities we think of as conferring power— wealth, resources, manpower, arms—may indeed bring power, but not unless they are used to influence the behavior of others. They are only the instruments of power; their effectiveness depends upon their use.

For example, wealth is so frequently used as an instrument of power that we tend to think of it as bringing power automatically, but this is not the case. Just as a wealthy recluse may choose to count his millions in private and may exercise no power at all, so a nation may decline to use its wealth for power purposes. Although surely wealthy enough, the United States for many years possessed far less power in international affairs than she might have.

Riches by themselves may even be a source of weakness. Ancient Burma spent enormous resources, both human and material, in the search and capture of sacred white elephants and in the adornment of its pagodas with jewels. No one wanted the elephants, but the undefended treasure was a tempting prize that gave the British an added inducement to conquer the country. Colonies provide an excellent example of the perils of undefended wealth, for in nearly every case, these areas became the colonies of others because they were both rich and defenseless, and because their undefended riches excited the greed of more powerful nations.

In general, however, wealth is an instrument of power. In addition to serving as a reward, it can also be used to purchase still other instruments of power, in particular the instruments of coercion. Now, as in the past, arms, mercenaries, resources, and allies are all available if the price is right.

It would be a mistake to consider only the tangible instruments of power, for intangibles can also be used to influence the behavior of others. The esteem of a friend or the jealousy of a rival may be as important a reward as any material possession, and this is as true on the international level as it is on the personal level. There is power in ideals, in propaganda, and in the granting of good will. A wide variety of objects and attitudes may be used to influence the behavior of others, but no object or attitude confers power upon a nation unless it is used in this way.

Skillful use of even meager resources can give a nation power considerably greater than one might expect from looking at its material resources alone. The nation that knows its own strength possesses by that very fact an additional source of power, for it can utilize its power to the maximum in every case. Switzerland, for example, stood up to Nazi Germany and to the Allies during World War II, refusing the demands of nations that could have obliterated her. She did so, not because of any illusions that she could defeat these giants in a military contest, but because she understood that neither the Nazis nor the Allies considered it worth their while to fight for the advantages that Switzerland had to offer. This understanding gave Switzerland as much power as a military machine the size of Germany's would have given her, for it enabled her to ignore the military might of her potential conquerors. The game was a dangerous one, but it was a success.

Even a bluff may work, provided it is not called, but on the whole, it is extremely dangerous to threaten action that cannot be delivered, particularly if one overestimates his own power. Just as exact evaluation of one's power is itself a source of power, so overestimation of it is a source of weakness. The nation whose bluff is called will find its future power seriously diminished, with even its legitimate threats falling on deaf ears.

There is equal danger in overestimating the power of an enemy, for this may lead a nation into excessive timidity and make it fail to exercise even that power which it does possess. Oddly enough, overestimating the strength of one's enemies is fairly common, perhaps because the practice is so useful for propaganda purposes both within and outside the nation. It is usual for aggressors to justify their actions by exaggerating the dangerousness of their victims. Thus Poland "threatened" Hitler's Germany, Ethiopia "attacked" a neighboring Italian colony, Finland "endangered" the USSR, and a leftist Dominican Republic "menaced" the United States.

This technique may be useful when the other party is a small, helpless nation against whom military action is imminent, but when the other party is a large and powerful state likely to grace the international scene for some time to come, self-deception as to the power of the enemy may be more serious. There is no question that both the United States and the Soviet Union, at least in their public statements, have seriously over-estimated each other's strength in recent years. It has been the practice in the United States to blame a whole crop of international ills upon the USSR, China, and international communism and to see in every discontented sheik, in every anti-Yankee Latin-American, in every anti-Western Asian, and in every land-hungry peasant the world over the evil hand of the Kremlin or of Peking. This may be useful for stirring up the kind of popular sentiment required to keep Americans paying heavy taxes for defense and to guarantee united action should the United States actually be attacked, but it is not conducive to a sober analysis of Russia's or China's real strength or to the selection of appropriate measures for counteracting that strength.

Similarly, the Soviet Union and China suffer serious misconceptions about American strength. If anything, their hallucinations seem even worse. American "imperialists" and their lackeys are believed to be lurking everywhere, ready to pounce upon the Russians and the Chinese if they falter for a moment, and American "spies" are found even in the uppermost reaches of the Chinese and Russian hierarchies. To the extent that Communist rulers believe these myths, they have seriously handicapped themselves by imposing upon reality a world that does not exist. Such exaggerations and simplifications massively distort the complex reality they are supposed to portray.

The practice of overestimating the power of one's enemies owes its commonness to its usefulness for propaganda purposes, to its value in creating national unity, and to the fact that it is psychologically satisfying to conjure up horrors as explanations for situations for which no rational explanation is available or, as in a good number of such cases, for situations where rational explanation would challenge beliefs cherished by the people in question. Strange though it may seem, people prefer to be scared to death rather than remain without a plausible explanation of events.

The Subjectivity of Power

A good part of a nation's power therefore seems to depend not only upon its genuine ability to influence the behavior of other nations, but also upon its own estimation of its ability and upon the estimation made by other nations. It is possible to imagine that an objective scientist, armed with all the crucial facts regarding every nation's power resources and looking at the world from an appropriate distance, could accurately assess the relative power of all the nations in the world. Knowing how the leaders of each nation would react in each particular case, he could predict just what would happen in any test of power. The mere mortals who run governments, however, are not possessed of such an array of facts, of such insight into the probable reactions of their rivals, nor, most important of all, do they possess such objectivity. As a result, they must guess how strong other nations are and how strong they are themselves, and they must make these guesses in advance of any actual test of strength. The interesting thing is this: If a nation guesses wrong about its power relative to other nations, this miscalculation may actually alter its relative power. That which is guessed at alters with the guessing. Let us look at an example.

During the 1930s, Mussolini's Italy was considered to be a major power and her wishes were given serious consideration in the international diplomacy of that day. In particular, she was felt to possess a military force with which it would be unwise to tangle. World War II proved that Italy's power had been vastly overrated, but until the proof was given on the battlefields, Italy benefited greatly from the overrating. Because of it, she was able to influence the behavior of other nations just as if she actually possessed the military might they feared she had. Or take the case of France and Germany during the 1920s. The fear that France had of Germany at the end of World War I, even though Germany lay prostrate at France's feet, considerably lessened the power of France and was at least in part responsible for her eventual defeat by Germany in World War II.[3] A reputation for power confers power, whether or not it is justified.

For this reason, nations that have been great powers in the past may continue to trade upon their reputations for some time. The France of the Fourth and Fifth Republics is a clear example of this. Although France has slipped considerably from her position in the days of Louis XIV or Napoleon, she has not slipped as far as her objective ability to influence others would warrant. France was unquestionably a great power in the past, and so she continues to be treated like one today.

The expectation of future power may also be traded upon, and a nation expected to be great tomorrow may find its present power position improved for that reason. India is a good example. Part of India's ability to influence other nations rests upon the peculiar moral position that her leaders, Gandhi and Nehru, came to occupy, but another part of her present power is due to more material considerations. India, with her

[3] Arnold Wolfers, *Britain and France Between Two Wars* (New York: Harcourt, Brace, 1940).

gigantic population, possesses one of the important prerequisites for being a great power. If she ever modernizes and mobilizes that population, she will, indeed, be a nation to contend with. It is with one eye on the future that East and West are vying for the friendship of India.

It is difficult to say how long the reputation for power outlasts the actual possession of power or by how much it precedes the time when power is a reality. If peace prevails and there are no major military contests or diplomatic crises, the great power of yesterday may remain untouched, clutching its reputation while the corrosion within escapes the notice of friends and foes alike. At the same time, the emergence of new powers may be more difficult to detect. In times of international strife, however, there are more frequent and more dramatic tests of power, and a reputation that is not in accord with reality is more difficult to maintain. The rise of Japan, for example, escaped unnoticed for many peaceful years, but the Russo-Japanese War of 1904–1905 rocketed Japan into the ranks of the great powers while it seriously damaged the power reputation of Tsarist Russia. Similarly, the humiliating defeat France suffered in the Franco-Prussian War of 1870–1871 signaled to all the rise of Germany and the decline of France.

The French example brings out another point. France has remained a great power, in name at least, partly because although damaged grievously in the two world wars, she was on the side of the victors. Had France fought Germany alone and lost, the story would have been quite different. Similarly, Britain has slipped from her position as number-one power in the world, but she has done so gracefully, retaining her lead as long as possible and falling the minimum distance required by reality. She has managed this in part because the new American giant that took her place was a friend and not a foe. We may expect a shift in power from the Soviet Union to China at some future date, but Russia will keep her reputation for power longer if she manages to avoid an open conflict when China becomes stronger. In short, it matters whether a great nation of the past must test its present power against its nearest rivals or whether it can ride on the coattails of a new great power.

Power, then, is not a static characteristic. It is part of a nation's relations with other nations, and it grows and diminishes with use. The power of a nation depends in part upon what other nations think it is, and in part on what a nation *thinks* other nations think. There is constant anticipation by one party of the other party's response. Into the formation of every policy goes an automatic calculation: "If I do this, then he'll do that." In terms of national power, this means that a nation may choose not to exercise all the power it has at any given moment, because if it does, it may stir up resistance so strong that in the long run its ability to influence others will be less rather than more.[4] The United States today possesses the power to do a great many more things than she does. She could seize colonies here, overthrow governments there, attack in this place, and apply economic sanctions in that, but she will not, and one of the reasons is that if she did, she would soon be friendless and, in the long run, less powerful.

The nation that throws off the customary restraint and launches an unexpected action in spite of the generally anticipated response by others gains the advantage of surprise. This may be a tremendous advantage in the short run, but in the long run a nation cannot ignore the reactions of others. Hitler's blitzkrieg, which made him for a time the master of Europe, eventually resulted in the shattered cities of Germany. The unprovoked attack on Pearl Harbor by the Japanese eventually led to the atomic destruction of Hiroshima and Nagasaki. In both instances, the Axis nations miscalculated the response—and the concerted power—of the Allies. They overlooked the fact that a maximum use of Axis power would bring into being power among the Allies that had not existed before.

Power is a subtle thing. It consists of the ability to influence the behavior of others, and this ability may be enhanced both by the possession of certain instruments of power and by the skillful use of whatever instruments exist. Material resources there must be: land, men, raw materials, industries, and military forces. No amount of bluff can take their place completely. But above and beyond these necessities, a nation can increase its power by shrewdly estimating its exact power relative to other nations, by knowing just what it can and cannot do, and by making the most of a past reputation or a future promise of power. We have yet to see just how power is exercised, just how one nation can influence the behavior of another.

Methods of Exercising Power

In any real situation, there are a great many different actors, each with his own particular aims and each trying to influence the others. However, it will be easier to understand the way in which power is exercised if we begin with the simplest case: two nations and one issue. Let us assume that Nation B wishes to do one thing while Nation A wishes it to do

[4] See Carl J. Friedrich, *Constitutional Government and Democracy* (Boston: Ginn, 1950), pp. 589–91. Also Seymour M. Lipset and Reinhard Bendix, "Social Status and Social Structure, a reexamination of the data and interpretations: II," *British Journal of Sociology*, 2 (1951), 253–54.

something else. Furthermore, let us pretend that all the power is operating in one direction. In any real case, Nation B would be trying to influence Nation A at the same time that A was trying to influence B. In our case, however, we are concerned only with the ways in which Nation A can get Nation B to do what it wants. How can Nation A influence the behavior of Nation B? How can it exercise power?

There are four things Nation A can do: It can by argument persuade B that it really wants to do what A wants it to do; it can offer B a reward for doing what A wants; it can threaten B with punishment if it doesn't do what A wants; or it can take direct action and force B to do what A wants whether B wishes to or not. These are the four ways of exercising power: persuasion, reward, punishment, and force. We shall look at each in more detail.

PERSUASION

Persuasion is by far the easiest method of exercising power as far as Nation A is concerned. Voluntary action by Nation B is a good guarantee of lasting results, and once B is persuaded, no further effort need be made by A. What the representatives of Nation A do in such a case is to redefine the situation so that the representatives of Nation B change their minds about what their nation ought to do. This redefinition may take the form of appealing to sentiments and principles, of bringing out facts that B had overlooked, or of suggesting consequences that B had not taken into account. Nation A may point out rewards and punishments that will fall to Nation B if it pursues one course or the other, but as long as A sticks to persuasion, it will not offer any new rewards or punishments. It will merely point out those that already exist. Much of diplomacy consists of this kind of persuasion. International conferences are largely contests in persuasion, and most of the work of international organizations consists of efforts by the delegates to persuade each other. Persuasion is particularly popular with small nations who lack the power to coerce the great nations and whose ability to reward and punish is also somewhat limited, but great nations, too, may benefit from the judicious use of the arts of persuasion. They are always widely used because they are so effective—and so cheap.

REWARDS

The second way of exercising power is by offering rewards. Nation B, faced with a choice between two courses of action (the one it prefers and the alternative preferred by A), makes up its mind on the basis of which behavior will bring the most benefits. If the decision is a sound one, and if all the facts are taken into consideration, B will select the course which is best for it, that is, the course which is most rewarding. But if A can intervene in the situation and offer B rewards for choosing the course desired by A, the balance may be tipped. Depending upon the amount and kind of rewards A can offer, B may now find that it is genuinely to her advantage to do as A wishes.

The rewards that one nation can offer to another are many and varied. They may be merely psychological. A diplomat may change his nation's policies to win the approval of his fellow diplomats from other countries. This, presumably, is the fate that Americans fear will befall our diplomats if they are allowed to negotiate with rival nations. The myth is widespread that Americans are apt to be outsmarted in international conferences, that they will somehow be talked into giving away valuable concessions. Whether the fact corresponds to the myth is another matter, but certainly the technique of offering psychological rewards to rival diplomats does exist. In this case, the line between persuasion and reward is a thin one, for the only reward consists of the approval of the other negotiators.

More usually, the rewards are material and accrue to the country represented, not merely to its representatives in a personal sense. They may consist of territory; of military aid in the form of weapons, troops, bases or training facilities and personnel; of a promise to allow passage to troops or a promise not to interfere in some dispute with others. The rewards may be economic and take the form of loans or gifts (the chief method of the United States in recent years), of trading contracts or concessions, of lower tariffs, or of access to strategic materials. Nor should we overlook the possibilities of technical assistance as a form of international reward. Political rewards might include a grant of political freedom or increased self-government to a dependent area, support for another nation's position at an international conference, votes in an international organization, or even a promise not to embarrass another nation by calling to public attention some controversy that would better remain hidden.

PUNISHMENTS

A third way of exercising power is by threatening punishments. Here an unpleasant consequence is promised if Nation B persists in behavior that Nation A considers undesirable. Rewards and punishments are closely related, for one of the most effective punishments is to withhold a reward, and vice versa. In both cases, A intervenes in a situation, altering the balance of relative rewards and punishments so that it becomes to B's advantage to do what A wants. There is a difference, however. The granting of a reward sometimes occasions gratitude, and if the strings attached are not too obvious, it may increase the good feeling between Nations A and B. The threat of punishment, however, is certain to arouse ill feeling, the more so if it is effective.

Acts of punishment are common on the international scene, but for maximum effectiveness, punishment should be threatened in advance, not slapped on unexpectedly in retaliation. When Secretary of State James Byrnes cut off American aid to Czechoslovakia because the Czechs at an international meeting applauded Russian criticisms of the United States,[5] the action was not very effective in influencing the behavior of Czechoslovakia. The hapless Czechs presumably learned that they should be careful whom they applauded in the future, but the particular offense in question had already been committed and could not be undone. Nor was there any suggestion that American aid would be restored in the future if the Czechs learned when to clap their hands. The most effective punishment is never meted out, for the very threat of it succeeds in preventing the action. If punishment must be administered, it should be given in such a form that it can be withdrawn once the offending party mends his ways to the satisfaction of the punishing power.

We have spoken of punishment taking the form of withholding a reward, but actually punishment may consist of any action that is unpleasant to Nation B. Common international punishments include unfavorable propaganda, political support for enemies of B, annoyances and inconveniences for B in matters of immigration, trade, and transport (the Berlin blockade by the Russians would come under this heading), economic sanctions, and even military action.

FORCE

With military action, we cross the border from punishment into force as a means of exercising power. The same concrete action may serve as both punishment and compulsion, but the essential difference is this: punishment is designed to influence Nation B of its own free will to undertake the course of action A desires. Punishment is threatened as a preventive, that is, it is designed to prevent the action disapproved. When punishment is actually administered, it is intended to show that Nation A was not bluffing and thus to prevent future occurrences of the same sort. Compulsion, on the other hand, is designed to produce results in the present. Compulsion operates not by changing the balance of rewards and punishments so that B will make the proper choice, but by taking the choice out of B's hands altogether.

Wars represent the primary use of force or compulsion on the international scene. Through warfare, nations act to seize territory or

[5] James F. Byrnes, *Speaking Frankly* (New York: Harper & Row, 1947), p. 143.

riches which they cannot gain in any other way or to topple governments with which they cannot deal. As a means of influencing others, warfare is a last resort. It is used only when a nation cannot persuade, buy, bribe, or threaten its way to a desired goal, and even then the price of warfare is so high, even to the victor, that its use is much discouraged. Compulsion is also possible short of war, but only in cases where the preponderance of force on one side is so great that the other yields in advance rather than face annihilation. Thus Czechoslovakia gave in and accepted a Communist coup d'état in 1948, not because she agreed or even because she wished to avoid punishment, but because resistance was hopeless.

The Choice of Methods

Whether a nation chooses to use persuasion, rewards, punishment, or force in influencing the behavior of another nation will depend somewhat upon the amount of agreement between the two nations:

1. In the extreme case of complete agreement between two nations, power need not be exercised at all. If two nations see completely eye to eye on some matter, there is no need for either to try to change the behavior of the other. One nation may be stronger and may possess the ability to influence the other should they disagree, but this power will lie dormant and not be apparent to either party. So long as the Soviet Union and Czechoslovakia agree, the overwhelming power of the USSR does not matter, but when Czechoslovakia wanted to join the American-sponsored Marshall Plan and Russia did not want her to, the difference in power meant that Czechoslovakia had to abide by Soviet wishes. It is perhaps for this reason that the relative power of friends is so seldom mentioned. The American press bristles with references to the strength of Russia, but it rarely mentions America's power over Britain, or the power Britain could exercise over the United States. A preoccupation with the power of the other party is one of the first signs that all is not well between friends. It is a sign that the relationship is not altogether satisfactory, that there is disagreement with the course of action determined by the stronger partner, or that there may be such disagreement in the near future.

2. If disagreement is slight or superficial and a large body of agreement exists between two nations, persuasion is apt to be prominent in the exercise of power between them. Rewards may also be used, but persuasion is particularly appropriate to such a relationship because persuasion is most effective where common values are shared. It is in such

cases that statesmen are most successful in influencing one another's behavior by force of argument and by appeals to common principles, sentiments, and interests. This is the method so often used in internal politics, where a wide body of agreement exists among the citizens of a nation. This is the method best used among close allies such as the United States and Britain. It is *not* particularly effective when used among nations that differ widely in their outlook and interests. Appeals to principle are then apt to be viewed as hypocritical or for propaganda purposes only, and Nation B finds it hard to believe that Nation A would suggest a course of action that really coincided with B's best interests.

3. If somewhat more disagreement is present, but the relationship between two nations is still fundamentally friendly, the granting and withholding of rewards becomes a major way of exercising power. In practice, persuasion and rewards are often mingled on the international level, but rewards become progressively more important as persuasion becomes more difficult because of increasing disagreement. Most economic relations are of this nature, one nation rewarding another in return for goods or services that it desires. Governmental aid to other nations is a striking example of this method of influencing others. Significantly, such aid is nearly always limited to friends. Military alliances also include a heavy element of mutual rewards, and again, such alliances are limited to friends. No clear line can be drawn between the granting and the withholding of rewards, for the power to withhold is inherent in the very act of rewarding. If it were not, the giver of rewards would possess no power over the recipient. If Nation B were going to get what it wanted in any case, the motive for modifying its behavior would vanish. The power to withhold must always be present, but even so, it makes a difference whether the emphasis is placed upon the reward, with the possibility of its being withheld only implied, or whether B is constantly reminded that benefits it now enjoys are contingent upon its continued good behavior. An emphasis upon the rewards themselves is more appropriate if the relationship is friendly.

4. If disagreement between two nations is widespread, there is likely to be less emphasis upon rewards and more on punishments as a means of exercising power. If relations between the two nations are already bad, the threat of punishment cannot make them much worse and so is not attended by the disadvantages that would accompany the use of threats against a friend or ally. Also, in efforts to influence unfriendly nations, punishments may be stressed simply because persuasion and rewards are ruled out. Suspicion between two nations may be so great as to make persuasion difficult if not impossible, and ill-feeling

may be so great that a political representative of Nation A dares not offer rewards to Nation B for fear of being accused of aiding a potential enemy. Until very recently, this was somewhat the situation in relations between the United States and the Soviet Union. American leaders would have liked to alter the policies of the Soviet Union, but they did not feel that persuasion was likely to be very successful, and they were afraid to offer substantial rewards to the Russians. Hence the heavy emphasis on threats in American attempts to influence the Soviet Union. Russia, too, relied heavily upon punishing the United States in various petty and annoying ways and then bargaining to gain concessions in return for the reward of removing the punishments. True rewards are rarely offered by one unfriendly state to another; more often, the only rewards consist in the removal of punishments. The threat of punishment may occasionally be used to influence a friend, particularly if other means have failed. Thus in the 1950s the French were finally compelled to agree to German rearmament not by persuasion or by promised rewards (though there had been plenty of both), but by the threat that the United States would go ahead and arm Germany without French approval or participation if the French persisted in their opposition. Significantly, however, this approach was adopted as a last resort only after years of persuasion and rewards had failed to produce results.

5. If punishments are inappropriate as a means of influencing friendly nations, the use of force is even more out of place. Indeed, the mere threat of force would probably be enough to terminate any international friendship. For this reason, force as a means of exercising power is used where disagreement between two nations is most profound, and it is appropriate only in such relationships. Within a well-regulated nation, there is such a wide area of agreement among the citizens that force is not usually used to settle disputes except with isolated, individual criminals. Industrial or racial strife may sometimes flare into violence. A fundamental split between two powerful groups may in an extreme case produce a civil war, but in the everyday conduct of affairs, force is not the means by which groups and individuals within a nation influence each other. On the international level, however, agreement is not so well grounded nor are instruments of force monopolized. Consequently, the resort to force as a means of exercising power over others is much more frequent. Nations will hardly forego the use of force in areas where disagreement is so fundamental that persuasion, reward, and punishment are without result.

In summary, the choice between alternative ways of exercising power will be influenced by the amount of agreement and the degree of friendliness between the nations concerned, and the emphasis will tend to shift from persuasion to rewards to punishments to force as the amount of disagreement and unfriendliness increases.

Other factors also affect the choice of methods in any particular case. Different methods of exercising power require different instruments, and a nation may possess the means for excelling in one method but may lack some of the requirements for practicing others. Thus a nation with a small military force can hardly make much use of force to influence the behavior of a larger neighbor. Acts of political terrorism may be possible and even effective, but large-scale military operations will be out of the question. Similarly, a poor nation cannot make much use of economic rewards, much as it might like to. Nor can a nation with a nonexportable ideology make as effective use of persuasion through propaganda as one whose ideology has universal appeal.

The choice of method for exercising power will also depend partially upon the goal which the nation has in mind. If Nation A wishes Nation B to make some minor change in policy, persuasion may be highly effective, but if A wishes B to give up territory to which it has a strong historical and emotional attachment or to abandon policies which it believes essential to its security, persuasion will hardly suffice, and even rewards and punishments may not be enough to induce B to behave in the fashion desired by A. It is not necessary that A resort to force in such a case. It can simply abandon the attempt to exercise power over B in this matter. But if A insists upon altering the behavior of B, it will have to choose force as the only method capable of producing results. Here the choice of method is determined not by any characteristic of Nation A, but by Nation B's determination to yield to nothing but force. The use of force by one nation usually leads to a retaliation in kind, not necessarily because the nation attacked wants to fight, but because under the circumstances force is the only effective means of stopping the attack.

Positive and Negative Power

We have been talking about power as the ability of one nation to make another nation do what it wants. In actuality, however, a more common form of power on the international level is the ability of one nation to *prevent* another nation from taking action it considers undesirable. This might be called negative power. Almost every independent nation possesses that minimum of negative power necessary to prevent other nations from interfering seriously in its internal affairs. Within the nation, the national government customarily possesses positive power as well, for it can direct, regulate, and determine the actions of its own citizens, not merely prevent them from doing certain undesired things. As far as *other* nations are concerned, however, a national government finds its positive power limited by the negative power of others. Thus power on the international level is largely negative. It is perhaps for this reason that so little can be done by international organizations.[6]

To be perfectly clear, we should not speak of a nation's power in general, but should distinguish between its positive and its negative power. Remembering that we are dealing with a relationship, we must consider not only A's ability to influence B but also B's ability to influence A. To put it in other terms, when we talk of Nation A's power relative to Nation B, we are really including both A's positive power to exercise influence over B and its negative power to resist the influence of B over it. Power in this sense has two dimensions. In practice, both are usually lumped when national power is spoken of, but they can be considered separately.

The Measurement of Power

The question remains: can the power of a nation be measured, or is it so subtle it escapes measurement? It is clear that even in the simplest case of two nations and one issue, it is not easy to predict in advance which nation will succeed in influencing the other, since this ability rests not only upon the possession and use of appropriate means for persuading, rewarding, punishing, or if necessary using force, but also upon the mutual appraisal these nations make of each other and of their possible reactions. There are many intangibles to be considered. Excluding hindsight, how could one measure the hypnotic power that Hitler had over Mussolini, or the degree to which one nation believes the promises of reward or threats of punishment by another? Worse still, in a good number of cases no promises of reward or punishment are actually made; they are anticipated by those who are to receive them. And if all these complications exist when only two nations are involved, how much more complicated must it be to measure power when we consider all the nations in the world and all the matters on which they differ. Nevertheless, such a measurement must be made, and *is* in fact made every day in the conduct of international affairs.

One could begin by setting up an imaginary tournament in which each nation fought it out with every other nation, one pair at a time. This would involve asking: "If Nation A and Nation B were brought to

[6] See Chapters 17 and 18.

the ultimate test of battle, which would win?" This would afford some approximation of the relative power of nations, but it would at best be very rough, for the ability to win a war, although important, is by no means the only kind of power. Power in war and power in peace are obviously related, but they are not the same. A militarily weak nation might have substantial influence in times of peace. Professional neutrals such as Sweden and Switzerland are cases in point. Neither has exercised any military influence in over a hundred years, but it would be inexact to call either nation powerless.

Even if power in battle were the only kind of power that mattered, few wars really measure the relative power of the combatants, for nations seldom battle one by one. More usually, they line up in groups, each side gathering all the allies that it can muster, and the weakness of one ally is counterbalanced by the strength of another. An occasional pair of small neighbors may fight it out alone. A major power and one of its colonies have sometimes become involved in a dispute in which no one else took part. Usually, however, the influence of other parties is to be found, if only behind the scenes. When the great powers fight each other, they almost never fight alone. With half the world in flames, it is impossible to determine the individual contribution of each nation and preposterous to consider being on the victorious side as a sign of individual power. A combination of efforts by the United States, Britain, the Soviet Union, and numerous lesser powers defeated Germany, Italy, and Japan in World War II. If Germany sided with the United States and Britain, could the three defeat the USSR? Or if Germany sided with the USSR, could these two defeat Britain and the United States? If we were to succeed in winning the USSR to the Western side, could we together defeat China? We cannot look to wars as they are actually fought to provide more than an occasional clue to the relative power of individual nations.

It would be better to consider individually each instance where two or more nations desire a different outcome and to see whose view prevails. By observing such instances over a period of years, one could construct a sort of score card and see which nations usually have their way. Here, too, however, there are difficulties if one attempts to reduce this method to anything approaching scientific accuracy. To begin with, it is not always easy to know when an international difference exists. Nations do not publicly declare their desires on every issue, particularly when their desires would not be likely to have any effect upon the outcome. A small nation may be seriously opposed to action taken by a larger neighbor, but believing opposition hopeless, it may never make its objections publicly known. Even in formal negotiations, a nation may give in on certain points in advance, just as it may adopt positions that it does not really care about and hold to them with vehemence in order to gain advantage by surrendering them later in the bargaining. The issues that are publicly contested do not always provide the most important tests of power.

Assuming, however, that it were possible to know the position taken by every nation on every matter of consequence, and that one could then locate all the areas of disagreement and determine who won out in each case, it still would not be easy to assess the overall power of each nation, for how is one to weight the various victories won? Is a victory over the date on which a conference is to be held equivalent to a victory over who gets control of a dependency? Clearly not. But is it worth half as much or a third as much? What about the nation that wins a string of minor victories and then loses out in one major dispute? Is it more or less powerful than the adversary who gives in on all the minor controversies but stands fast on the one big issue?

Still another difficulty lies in the fact that power cannot really be separated from the relationship of which it is a part. We cannot with complete accuracy say that a nation has a given amount of power in the abstract, but only that it has so much power relative to that of another particular nation. To return to the analogue of the tournament, the separate matches may come out in such a way that the final score for the entire tournament does not tell us all we want to know. A separate match between the United States and China, for example, would show the United States to be more powerful. So would a total score for all the matches won. However, if only matches involving Southeast Asian nations were considered, China might well turn out to have as much power as the United States. It would be nice to tally victories in controversies and arrive at a "score" in national power, but the result would be a burlesque of reality.

Nevertheless, with all its shortcomings, this is the method actually used, in a rule-of-thumb way, by most observers and participants in international relations. We look at the major controversies of which we are aware, and we see whose view prevails. We separate in a rough way the minor issues from the important issues, and we consider a nation powerful if it customarily wins out in major differences with other nations. It is on this basis that we assign to the United States the position of number-one world power, for we have seen her view prevail, time and time again, against the objections of friends and foes alike. On the same basis, the second most powerful nation in the world is the Soviet Union, for she is the nation whose behavior the United States has the greatest difficulty in influencing.

The difficulty with this method of measuring national power is that it is based exclusively on past performance. After a controversy is over, we can tell who won it, but we do not know who will win the controversy that begins tomorrow. Looking at a period of years in the past, we can tell which nations were the most powerful, and we can see the shifts in power from one nation to another that have occurred, but we do not know who will be most powerful tomorrow. It is not safe to assume that a nation's power will remain the same indefinitely.

For predicting more than the very immediate future, we need more than an understanding of past results, more than a simple tally of who has won past struggles for power. We need an understanding of the determinants of these results. What were the characteristics of these nations that enabled them to influence the behavior of others so successfully? Which are the nations that possess these characteristics today, and which are the nations likely to possess them in the future? In the chapters that follow, we shall examine the determinants of power.

Summary

Power is the ability to influence the behavior of others in accordance with one's own ends, and as such it is not a thing but a part of a relationship. Indeed, there is a power aspect to every relationship, and that part of the relationship cannot be clearly separated from the rest.

There are certain qualities and possessions which are useful for purposes of power—wealth, resources, manpower, arms, diplomatic skill—but they are only instruments. They confer power only if they are used in such a way as to influence the behavior of other nations.

There are four ways in which one nation can influence the behavior of another: it can use persuasion; it can offer rewards; it can threaten punishments; it can use force. The choice among these methods will depend somewhat upon the amount of agreement and the degree of friendliness between the nations concerned, with a tendency to use persuasion and rewards where relations are most cordial and a shift to punishments and force where they are not. Other factors will also influence this choice: the means available, the goal, and the anticipated response.

Much of the power on the international level consists of negative power, that is, of the ability to prevent undesired action by other nations. Positive power, the ability to bring about desired action by others, is somewhat rarer.

The measurement of international power is not an easy matter, since so many intangibles are involved. The outcome of a war does not provide an adequate test of power because nations do not fight their battles alone, nor is power in war the only power that matters. The method of measuring power most often used, rough as it is, is to locate the matters of most obvious international disagreement and to see which nations customarily win out. For predicting future power, however, it would be useful to know not only the results of past contests but also some of the determinants of those results.

7

Natural Determinants of Power

✦❬❁❭✦❬❁❭✦❬❁❭✦❬❁❭✦❬❁❭✦❬❁❭✦❬❁❭✦❬❁❭✦❬❁❭✦❬❁❭✦❬❁❭✦❬❁❭✦❬❁❭✦❬❁❭✦❬❁❭✦❬

We have described what national power is. Now let us look at its determinants. What are the factors that make one nation more powerful than another? Granted that many intangibles are involved, what can we isolate? We will not be able to discover all the determinants of power, nor will we be able to weight them in such fashion as to arrive at an exact estimation of a nation's strength; but by looking at the nations that we know to be powerful by their performance, we should be able to discover certain characteristics that they have in common, and by thinking it through we should be able to see just how these characteristics might be expected to increase a nation's power.

Let us start with a simple list:

1. Geography
2. Resources
3. Population
4. Economic development
5. Political development
6. National morale

The list covers the people of a nation (population), the physical environment in which they live (geography and resources), their forms of social organization (economic and political), and something of their state of mind (national morale). It should be possible to fit most of the determinants of national power under one or another of these headings.

Simply as a convenient way of organizing the material for study, we have made a distinction between natural and social determinants of power. The natural determinants (geography, resources, and population) are concerned with the number of people in a nation and with their physical environment. The social determinants (economic development, political development, and national morale) concern the ways in which the people of a nation organize themselves and the ways in which they alter their environment. In practice, a clear distinction between natural and social elements is impossible—for example, resources are certainly a natural factor, but the degree to which they are utilized is socially determined. Population factors, in particular, straddle the dividing line.

It must be understood at the start that no single factor is responsible for power. Determinism of any kind, whether geographic, demographic, economic or ideological, is clearly out of place. Each factor plays its part, and each one affects the others. For example, political institutions certainly have an influence on national morale, but at the same time national morale affects the kind of political institutions that can exist and function. Again, the population structure (for example, the number of people of working age) affects the degree of industrialization of a nation, but, as we shall see, the process of industrialization, in turn, greatly alters the composition of the population. One can start at any point and trace the influence of one factor on all the others, but this is mere mental gymnastics. It may well be that some determinants of power are more important than others. But it does not make sense to try to reduce all the determinants to one, to say: "This and this alone is what makes a nation powerful."

The interaction of all the factors listed gives each nation the amount of power it has, so that if we seek a measurement of power other than past performance, we must put all the determinants together. In this and the following chapter, however, we shall try to isolate each of the determinants and to analyze its influence on national power. Then we shall combine them to construct an index of power.

To be considered a determinant of power, a social or a natural phenomenon must increase the ability of a nation to influence the behavior of other nations. Specifically, it must increase the ability of a nation to persuade, to reward, to punish, or to apply force to other nations. If it does not do this, the phenomenon may be an interesting one and well worth studying, but it is *not* a determinant of national power. There are far too many sloppy statements and giant generalizations that this or that is important for national power, and far too few careful studies of the specific ways in which a particular factor increases the ability of a nation to influence others. We shall try to be as specific as possible.

Geography

To the geopoliticians, geography is the handmaiden of power. To them, and to some political scientists as well, national power is firmly rooted in the geography of the nation. The extreme claims sometimes made for geography are exemplified by Mackinder's famous statement:

> Who rules East Europe commands the Heartland:
> Who rules the Heartland commands the World-Island:
> Who rules the World-Island commands the World.[1]

Unfortunately for the accuracy of such claims, those who have ruled East Europe to date have *not* commanded the Heartland of Eurasia, and those who have ruled the Heartland have *not* commanded the World Island (Europe, Asia and Africa). Moreover, while one may safely wager that if, someday, one nation should rule all of Europe, Asia, and Africa, it would be well along the way to world rule, the question could still be raised: Is that power due to geography? Extremists like Mackinder have clearly gone too far.

Our own approach to the importance of geography for power is more modest. First of all, the notion of geography can be broken down into more specific factors that appear to have some effect on national power. At least four such factors can be listed:

1. The size of the land area a nation controls
2. Its climate
3. Its topography
4. Its location[2]

Armed with this list, we can begin to specify the ways in which each factor affects a nation's ability to influence the behavior of other nations.

[1] Sir Halford J. Mackinder, *Democratic Ideals and Reality* (New York: Holt, Rinehart & Winston, 1942), p. 150.
[2] Natural resources are sometimes included under the heading of geography, but because of their importance, we have chosen to deal with them separately.

The size of the land area that a nation controls is not a matter of geography alone, for the number of square miles that lie within a nation's borders depends upon where its boundaries are, and boundaries are made by man, not Nature. Geography may have an influence on where the boundaries lie, but it does not determine them. A land mass may contain a single state, like Australia, or it may be shared by several states, like India and Pakistan or the nations of North America, or it may contain a multiplicity of nations, as Europe does. Even islands are not always political units. A single island may house two nations, like Haiti and the Dominican Republic, or a group of islands may fall under a single sovereignty as in the cases of the British Isles, Japan, and Indonesia. Man draws his own political lines upon the surface of the earth.

Nor are these lines as stable over time as they would be if they were determined by geography alone. The size of a nation often varies from one period to another. No more common phenomenon exists in international politics than the expansion, shrinkage or even disappearance of political units. Through the ages, the size of China has fluctuated with the fortunes of the dynasty in power. The boundary between France and Germany has swung back and forth, now favoring one and now the other, depending upon the course of European politics. If at any one time the size of a nation is considered fixed, it is not because of some geographic feature on the boundary, but because the people inhabiting the area differ from their neighbors, possibly in language, customs, and loyalties, but certainly in being under a common political authority that is ready to defend the area that it controls.

The size of nations varies from one nation to another and varies in a single nation over time because of such factors as the nation's social organization, its capacity for political unity, and its ability to defend itself. In short, a nation's size is largely determined by nongeographic factors. However, once size of area is taken as given, as it is when one considers the actual situation at any particular time, then the size of a nation can be seen to have an influence on its power.

That size is related to power can be seen even in the most superficial examination. Surely it is not altogether an accident that the two current world powers, the United States and the Soviet Union, are both extremely large in area. Nor is it accidental that no very small nations are great powers, although some of middle size have made the grade. Interestingly enough, the powerful nations of middle size have ruled large colonial empires, extending their size in this fashion. England in the day of her greatest power controlled a larger land area than any other nation in the world. Size is obviously of some importance.

Yet size alone is not enough to make a nation powerful. This fact is amply proved by listing the ten largest nations in the world (see Table 1).

TABLE 1

Nations of Largest Area

Nation	Square Miles of Territory	Nation	Square Miles of Territory
USSR	8,649,000	Australia	2,968,000
Canada	3,852,000	India	1,176,000
China	3,691,000	Argentina	1,072,000
United States	3,615,000	Sudan	967,000
Brazil	3,286,000	Algeria	920,000

SOURCE: United Nations, *Demographic Yearbook, 1965* (New York: United Nations, 1966), Table 2.

The list does not coincide very well with our common-sense notion of national power. It includes the United States, the Soviet Union, China, and India, as one would expect, but it does not include Britain, France, Germany, Japan, or other nations which we know by their behavior to be powerful. And it does include newly independent Algeria and the Sudan, obviously not major powers.

The question of whether size gives power or whether power brings size may also be raised. France and Britain began their rise to power when they were relatively small in area, and as they grew in strength they used that strength to build tremendous empires. Germany and Japan tried to use their power to seize more land and failed. When power and size are found together, it is not always easy to say which is cause and which effect. More likely each has influenced the other, with the influence of power on size the greater of the two. A powerful state can add to its territory by conquering its neighbors or by winning colonies, but new territory, once won, may further increase the power of the nation that controls it.

A large area contributes to a nation's power in two ways. First, a large habitable land area can contain a large population and a large and varied supply of natural resources. A list considering mere square miles of territory, however, is too crude. On this basis, Canada with its frozen wastes, Brazil with its jungles, and Australia with its deserts rank near the top in size, but not in power. It is not even enough for land to be capable of supporting a large population; it should have some population on it if it is to serve as a source of power. Otherwise, a rich but empty area may be a source of weakness, serving as a cause of envy and a temptation to people of other nations who would like to settle there. Not without reason is Russia anxious about the rapidly multiplying Chinese who live across the border from empty Siberia. Not without reason does Australia fear the teeming Asian nations. Japan in the past has cast covetous glances on the empty spaces of Australia and has publicly declared that, deserts notwithstanding. Australia could support several times its present population. Uninhabited lands may, of course, contribute to a nation's power if they are rich in resources, but here again, the nation must have the strength to defend them if the lands, the resources, and the advantage gained by owning them are not to be lost.

A large area may also add to a nation's power by providing certain military advantages. Size gives a nation room to retreat without surrendering. Space helped defeat the armies of Napoleon and Hitler in Russia and the armies of Japan in China. It would be an advantage if ever the United States were invaded. Hitler was quite right when he observed that the state with a small territory can be most easily overrun and have its life snuffed out in battle.[3] If he had followed his own advice, he might still be with us.

Before the era of thermonuclear bombs and ballistic missiles, size was also an advantage because it made possible the location of vital centers of industry and government far from the nation's frontiers. This situation provided a military advantage, for troops stationed at the frontier could begin defending their country's major centers at a great enough distance to cut down the danger of their being quickly captured. Political control of neighboring nations acts as an extension of size in this regard, for it moves the region of first battle still closer to the enemy and farther from the center of the homeland. Where nuclear weapons cannot be used, size still confers this important advantage. In view of the new possibilities of air war, however, such an advantage is rapidly being reduced.

Finally, size confers a military advantage because once conquered, a large area is difficult to occupy and control, particularly *if it is heavily populated*. The task of occupying a hostile Europe proved demanding on German manpower. The occupation of China would be formidable: it would require more soldiers and administrators than the United States possesses. Similarly, the difficulties of successfully occupying the United

[3] Adolf Hitler, *Mein Kampf* (Boston: Houghton Mifflin, 1940), p. 177.

States would give an invader pause. The occupation of a large foreign area is not impossible. England occupied India for many years, and as Kingsley Davis points out, that giant nation was ruled by such a small group of Englishmen that they could all have been put into a single American football stadium.[4] On the other hand, one of the reasons that India, of all English colonies, became free first is that England realized well the difficulties of holding on to such a large country once the Indians had organized to oppose their colonial status. Even here, it was far more Indian organization than Indian geography that was responsible for independence.

Size of area, then, is a factor associated with national power. In itself it does not have much influence upon a nation's ability to persuade, reward, or punish other nations. It may, however, make possible the support of a large population and the possession of large amounts of vital resources, and these, as we shall see, are important aids to power. Size of area does have a direct effect upon the ability of a nation to use force in self-defense, and it helps give a nation those powers of persuasion that follow from the ability to defend itself.

CLIMATE

Another geographic feature often assumed to have an influence on national power is climate. It is true that extremes of climate may make an area virtually uninhabitable and that even where the land is habitable, climate may rule out the kind of agriculture required to support a large population. In this sense, climate does affect a nation's power through its effect upon agricultural production and upon the size of the population.

Most writers go further, however. It is often assumed that a nation must have a temperate climate to be a major power, for it is claimed that the Arctic is too forbidding and the tropics too enervating to allow the kind of activity required of a modern, industrial people. The evidence offered in support of this conclusion is first, the fact that all the great powers of modern times have been located in the temperate zone, and second, the fact that languor seems to overcome Europeans who go to the tropics, making them incapable of doing the kind of work they did in cooler climes.

The first of these statements is certainly true. No great power lies outside the temperate zone, but is this because of climate or is it perhaps an accident of history? It must be remembered that if we look at human history on a broad enough scale, we have only one example. Only one

[4] Kingsley Davis, *The Population of India and Pakistan* (Princeton: Princeton University Press, 1951), p. 96.

industrial revolution has occurred. It began in Europe, in the temperate zone, but this does not constitute proof that it could not have happened elsewhere. Many of the great preindustrial civilizations of the past—the Indian, the Aztec, and the Mayan—flourished in tropical climates quite different from those of Northern Europe. Egypt, Greece, Rome, and Carthage arose in climates that a Northern European today finds uncomfortably hot. So far, there are no major *industrial* nations outside the temperate zone, but there is no reason to believe that this situation will not change. Soviet development of Russia's northern regions is already putting a dent in some of our preconceptions about what can be done in the Arctic.[5] Modern industry as now developed is best suited to the temperate regions, but new developments such as air-conditioning and automation may adapt it better to other regions as well.

The second argument, that industrialization outside the temperate zone is proved impossible because Europeans do not work well in the tropics, is open to more serious question. The fact that Europeans seem to slow down in the tropics does not prove that climate is the cause. It may well be "social climate," not the weather, that slows down the new and over-eager European. After a period of hurrying and trying in vain to get the people of another culture to hurry for him, the new arrival generally gives up and accepts the prevailing pace. The acceptance will be hastened if the European joins one of those tropical communities which believe that whatever else the white man's burden may include, it does not include manual labor. Where all the heavy work is left to "natives," the European learns to live a life of leisure very rapidly. In the end, it is not easy to say whether manual work is done by non-Europeans because Europeans cannot work in a tropical climate or whether Europeans do not work because there is someone else to do it for them. That the latter may be the case is strongly suggested by what has happened in Queensland in Australia. In Queensland the climate is tropical, but because of Australia's white labor policy, there are no nonwhites to do the work. Here, European labor has worked out very well.[6]

In any case, it is the native inhabitants, not Europeans, who must build industrial societies in most of the nontemperate world. Even if one assumes that Europeans cannot work well in the tropics, it does not mean that others cannot work there. To some extent, comfort is a question of what one is used to. The average African would probably find the climate of England as incapacitating as an Englishman would find the

[5] See Hans W. Weigert *et al.* (eds.), *New Compass of the World* (New York: Macmillan, 1949), chaps. 1 and 9.
[6] See A. Grenfell Price, *White Settlers in the Tropics* (New York: American Geographical Society, 1939).

Arctic, while the average Finn would probably find summer in New York City as impossible as a New Yorker would find the Congo.

A more relevant question that can be raised is: Why do the natives of the tropics, who are thoroughly accustomed to the climate, resist the patterns of work that are a prerequisite for the wealth and power European nations possess? Here, again, the answer may be climate, but other answers can be given as well. It is fairly well established that many of the tropical peoples are diseased and that much of their slovenliness and absence of energy is due to the fact that they are sick throughout much of their lives. In addition, their diet is frequently insufficient. Still another factor to be mentioned is that in many cultures hard work is not held in high esteem. Indeed, the work habits of Northwestern Europeans and their cousins overseas are historically unique, part cause and part effect of that historical occurrence we call the industrial revolution.

Although it is widely believed that a tropical climate makes an industrial way of life impossible or at best extremely difficult, this view must be questioned. Remembering the exaggerated claims that once were made for racial differences and their effect upon a people's way of life, one may gain courage to question the current claims that are made for climate. This is not to say that considerations of climate must be rejected altogether. Climate may have an influence on the way the people work. A temperate climate may even turn out to be a prerequisite for a modern, industrial system, but we do not *know* that this is so. It is reasonable to assume that it is not.

One final claim made for the importance of climate concerns the use of force and will probably be familiar to the reader. The argument runs that an intemperate climate (extreme heat or cold or periods of torrential rain, for example) hinders offensive military operations, thus favoring the defender against the attacker. The major example is usually Napoleon's defeat in Russia, though other examples are also given.

The weakness of this thesis is revealed in a statement attributed to Hitler in reply to generals who wished to delay an offensive because of the rains: "It rains on the enemy, too." Harsh climatic conditions do indeed make military operations more difficult, particularly for soldiers who are not accustomed to them, but the difficulties affect both sides and those unaccustomed to the climate are not always the attackers. Consider, for example, the American ground defense of South Vietnam. Even the Napoleonic example has been undermined by recent research revealing that the weather during the initial period of the Napoleonic rout from Moscow was unusually mild that year.

Climate, therefore, does not seem to be a very important determinant of national power. The most that can be said with certainty is that extremes of climate can make impossible the support of a dense population and that excessive heat or cold *may* rule out the development of a modern, industrial society. In neither case does climate have any direct effect upon the ability of a nation to persuade, reward, punish, or use force on other nations. Its effect seems to be wholly indirect. Certainly climate cannot be used to differentiate among the scores of nations that lie in the temperate zone, including all the major powers of the present day. All possess the climate believed necessary for modern national power. If one wishes to understand the reasons for the gradations of power among these nations, one must look to other factors.

TOPOGRAPHY

Topography may have some influence on the relative power of nations. Like climate, it may help determine the density of population which a region can support. Indeed, much of climate is determined by topography. Wind, rainfall, temperature, and consequently soil conditions, all are influenced by the lay of the land and by the relative positions of land and sea and mountains.

The influence of topography does not end here, however. The location of mountains, valleys, rivers, and plains may affect the ease of communication within a nation. If communication is quick and frequent, there is a greater likelihood of cultural unity among the citizens of different regions. Political control by a strong central government is also easier. Ease of transport is important in the economic development of a nation, and it also affects the ease and speed with which military forces can be gathered and deployed. Of course, the communication and transportation network within a nation has never depended exclusively upon topography. In recent years especially, the development of air transport and radio and television communication has greatly reduced the importance of topography.

Although topographical features may sometimes determine natural boundaries between nations and thus set limits to their natural expansion, their importance should not be overestimated. The Himalayas, the Alps, and the Pyrenees mark national borders, but the Rockies and the Urals do not. The Rhine, the Rio Grande, and Yalu rivers are boundaries, but the Mississippi, the Amazon, the Nile, and the Yangtze, the Po, and the Volga are not. Even oceans and deserts that once formed impassable political barriers have been overcome in recent times. The French, for example, managed to control land on both sides of the Sahara, and the British Empire straddled the seas.

Where natural barriers lie along a nation's frontiers, they may have some effect on its military power. Thus the Pyrenees are said to make a fortress out of Spain, the English Channel to guard the coasts of England, and the Atlantic and Pacific oceans to provide a natural protection for the United States. However, this is only partly true. A geographic obstacle may indeed slow up the military force (though not the missile) that has to cross it, but whether this is an advantage or a disadvantage depends upon whether the nation in question wishes to attack or defend itself. The English Channel helped keep Hitler's armies out of England, but it was distinctly *not* an advantage when the tide of battle turned and the Allied armies wished to reconquer Europe. The same is true of America's prized oceans. We tend to think of them always in terms of defense, where they are surely valuable, but overlook the tremendously complicated logistic problems that arise when America wishes to use her armed forces overseas, the major place they have been used in the twentieth century.

Even for defensive purposes, a geographic barrier is not much help unless it is garrisoned. More than two thousand years ago, Hannibal crossed the Alps and proved the folly of expecting a natural barrier to defend itself. In more recent times, the Chinese Communists took over Tibet with ease in spite of some of the most difficult terrain in the world. Caesar and his legions had little difficulty crossing an undefended English Channel, and in parallel fashion, modern American troops in the Korean and in the Vietnamese wars have easily crossed the seas.

America has been protected by her oceans not only because they are wide and deep, but because throughout the nineteenth century, a friendly Britain ruled their waves and because the American navy controls them now. If the fleets of our enemies controlled the seas around us, our textbooks would not be so filled with glowing references to our oceans. This protection has all but vanished in the age of intercontinental ballistic missiles. The movement of masses of troops is still important in modern warfare, but the first attack and the major destruction of any major modern war is far more likely to be delivered by missiles and bombers for which topography is meaningless. Of course, distance itself may still serve as a barrier to some extent by increasing the difficulty of moving troops and by lengthening the missile warning by at least a few minutes. In this sense, an ocean is a barrier if only because it separates two nations by a certain distance.

Topography, then, is no longer the determinant of power it may once have been. The extent of the advantages or disadvantages imposed by distance and topography depend upon the resources, technology, and ingenuity of the nations concerned.

The discussion of distance brings us to consideration of the fourth geographic factor that has an influence on national power—location. It is often said that the location of a nation has a great effect upon its role in international affairs and upon its power.

Specifically, it is claimed that location is a major determinant of whether a nation is a sea power or a land power. The explanation given for England and Japan's achievements on the seas has been that they are islands. The explanation offered for the massive land strength of the USSR and Germany has been their location, one in the heart of Europe, the other in the center of the "world island." The United States, presumably, possesses a location relative to land mass and seas that enables her to be both a land and sea power.

Certainly it is reasonable to grant that the possession of some sea coast is necessary for the maintenance of a navy and that therefore Switzerland and Austria are not to be numbered among the sea powers of the world. It also seems reasonable that Russia's lack of warm-water ports for many years hindered her attempts to have a powerful navy, and that Britain's island position made it natural for her to turn to the seas. However, the claims for location are pushed too far. The Japanese and British isles are seats of naval power, but Indonesia and the Caribbean islands are not. The United States and France, with lengthy coastlines, possess great navies, but where are the navies of India, South Africa, and Peru? To be a great naval power, one must first of all be a great power with all that implies. The possession of a lengthy coast is no guarantee of naval strength. It does not even seem to be a prerequisite. Holland, a great naval power of the past, never possessed more than a little strip of coast. Germany in the past and the Soviet Union today have both overcome their geographic handicaps to build formidable navies.

The same kind of doubts can be cast upon the simple notion that nations have large armies because they occupy the center of a land mass. The nation with a large army requires first a large population and a military bent; only after that does geography enter the picture. It may usually be assumed that a nation with lengthy land frontiers must possess a large army if it wishes to defend them, but even here oversimplification is a danger. The United States, for instance, has a large land force today, but she did not build it up in order to protect herself from Canada. Location relative to land and sea may motivate or aid or hinder a nation in building military strength, but it is not a very important factor. A look at the location of the nations of the world will not tell us which are land and which are sea powers today or which will have this status in the future.

It is also claimed that certain regions of the world are inherently strategic and that location relative to them therefore influences a nation's power. Areas traditionally recognized as strategic include narrow passages between two seas such as the Dardanelles, the Strait of Gibraltar, and the Strait of Malacca (commanded by Singapore), or artificial passages such as the Suez and Panama canals, or level plains that form the easiest invasion routes, such as the approach to France through the Low Countries.

Other regions are strategic because men make them so. Greenland and Okinawa were once of strategic importance primarily because the United States wished to have bases within easy bombing range of her potential enemies. Small countries that lie between two giants are strategically located only because each of the giants wants to be sure the country on its borders does not lie in unfriendly hands.

In a real sense, it is the powerful nations and not geography that confer strategic importance upon their own locations and upon the routes to their possessions, to their allies, and to their enemies. It is no accident that strategic routes almost always lie between powerful nations and the places in which they are interested. Suez and Gibraltar were not of much importance during the Middle Ages. They became important when they lay along the sea lane from Britain to her richest colony, and they are becoming less important again today. Venice was once a strategic point along the trade route between the Near East and the heart of Europe, but that was the route at least partly because powerful Venice put it there.

Political control of areas that become strategic at any given time may be a source of power, *provided* the control is firm. But the power benefits of owning a strategic territory rarely fall to the original inhabitants who live there. If they possess the power to ward off others and to dispose of their strategic territory as they wish, granting its use to other nations or withholding it as they see fit, the fact that they control an area that other nations wish to use may be a source of power. More often, however, some great power will seize the area and subjugate its inhabitants. Thus Gibraltar is not controlled by Spaniards, and Singapore and Suez have only recently been returned to their inhabitants. Belgium has twice in the twentieth century felt the brunt of invasion and conquest, and the strategically located buffer states between the Soviet Union and Germany are now firmly in the control of the USSR so that their location is certainly no source of power to them. The weak nation located in a strategic spot may find this fact a curse, leading not only to a loss of power but to a total loss of independence.

There remains one way in which the location of a nation affects its power. Consider the location of a nation in relation to the location of other powerful states. As we have just observed, small nations bordering on a great nation may find their power suffering in consequence. Conversely, a moderately powerful nation surrounded by nations of no consequence may find its power enhanced by this fact. Canada, for example, is almost completely overshadowed by the United States, a fate not likely to befall a nation of her size and strength if it were not located next door to the most powerful nation on earth. Japan, on the other hand, has gained in power from the fact that she was for many years the only great power in Asia, although the rise of China may put her in a position not unlike that of Canada.

Power, it will be remembered, is revealed in relationships with other nations, and nations generally have the most extensive relations with countries that are near to them. As a result, the relative power of neighbors is often more important than that of nations separated by great distance, particularly if the nations concerned are small. Geography does not determine the relative power of neighbors, but geographical location does determine who the neighbors are, that is, it determines the countries with which a nation must compete in power most actively.

SUMMARY

In summing up the influence of geography on power, we find that influence usually much exaggerated. What influence there is seems greatest on the use of force, and that much greater in the past than in the present. The ability of a nation to wage war successfully is determined in part by the size of its territory (a large area has certain defensive advantages); by its topography (natural barriers on the frontiers may aid defense, while an absence of natural barriers within the nation will aid troop movements); by its location relative to other nations (distance may aid defense); and by its control of strategic places.

Geography, however, has little *direct* effect upon the ability of a nation to persuade, reward, or punish other nations. The control of strategic areas and the ability to grant or withhold rights of passage, use of bases, and so on, may place important rewards in a nation's hands, but aside from this, the influence of geography outside the realm of force is due primarily to its effect on other determinants of power. Thus size of area, topography, and climate may help in small part to determine whether a nation can support a large population and whether it is rich in natural resources. Topography may also have some effect upon the ease of internal communication and transport, and this in turn may affect the cultural unity, political unity, and economic development of a nation.

Finally, geographical location plays a role in determining the power of a nation because it may place a nation near smaller states it may dominate or near giants by whom it will be eclipsed.

Our examination has shown, however, that many of the claims made for the importance of geography do not stand up. The size of a nation is determined not by geography but by politics, and natural barriers may be overcome. Geography does not determine who controls the areas that are strategic, nor does it have the importance claimed for it in directing military development toward land or sea. The whole relationship of climate to economic development is open to serious question.

Although geography does have an effect on national power, its influence has at times been much exaggerated. Its reputation as one of the most important determinants of national power does not seem merited.

Natural Resources

The second of the "natural" determinants of power to be considered is resources, by which is meant primarily minerals (fuels and metals) and the soil and its products. The importance of these for the exercise of national power is obvious.

Resources are essential for the use of force. From the great flint industries of prehistoric times up to the present, man has relied on minerals for fashioning weapons. The medieval knight required iron for his armor and his blade. The modern military force requires not only iron but high-grade steels and alloys for missiles; aluminum for planes; oil and rubber for tanks and trucks; and now uranium for bombs. Practically all the natural resources known to man are used to keep a modern army in fighting trim, and it would be hard to dispense with a single one of them. A lack of oil was one of Hitler's greatest handicaps, a handicap never completely overcome even by the skillful use of substitutes or by the conquest of Rumania with its rich oil fields. Italy, lacking both the real thing and the substitutes, was never capable of supplying a first-class army. Indeed, her entrance into World War II should be of equal interest to the psychoanalyst and to the political scientists, since she entered the war with only enough military supplies to last three months.[7] Even a nation as wealthy in resources as the United States finds it advisable

[7] Galeazzo Ciano, *The Ciano Diaries, 1939–1943* (Garden City, N.Y.: Garden City Publishing Co., 1947), p. 257.

to stockpile huge quantities of raw materials because they are so necessary for the waging of modern war.

To produce the arms and the supplies necessary for a modern army requires not only the use of raw materials but also an extensive, modern economic system, and this in turn requires still more resources, the materials of which modern machines are made.

In short, a nation cannot wage modern warfare, or threaten to do so, without making use of a tremendous amount and variety of natural resources; and without the ability to wage war—offensive or at least defensive—a nation is severely handicapped in any test of international power.

Aiding the exercise of force, however, is only one of the ways in which resources contribute to national power. Quite apart from warfare, nations use resources to reward and punish other nations. Among the most important rewards that a nation can offer to others are agricultural products, mineral resources, and the manufactured goods that can be made from these resources.

The possession of raw materials desired by other nations can give a nation power it would not otherwise possess. Thus Arab nations of little present consequence in other terms have been very carefully treated by Washington because of the oil they possess. Agricultural products may serve in the same fashion. Argentina has used her beef (raised on her rich grasslands) to political advantage in negotiations with Britain, her major customer. Ceylon, rich in rubber, has been courted by both East and West.

The nation that can turn its raw materials into manufactured goods possesses even greater powers of reward. The great manufacturing nations have always been great powers: England, France, the United States, Germany, Japan. One of the greatest sources of American power today is the fact that so many people want the products that America produces. Industrial organization is, of course, the key to this kind of power, but without the use of large quantities of raw materials, it could not exist.

POSSESSION AND CONTROL

Natural resources are seen to be a very important determinant of power, necessary for waging modern war, for running an industrial machine, and for possessing the raw materials, agricultural products, and manufactured goods with which to reward other nations through trade and aid. However, one must distinguish between the *use* of natural resources and the physical possession of them within a nation's boundaries. These two things are not the same.

Let us take three natural resources considered particularly crucial as determinants of national power: iron, coal, and oil; and let us see which nations possess the greatest supplies of each within their borders. The list is somewhat startling (see Table 2).

TABLE 2

Nations with Largest Reserves*

Iron†	Coal‡	Petroleum**
USSR	United States	Kuwait
Brazil	China	Saudi Arabia
India	USSR	Iran
United States	West Germany	United States
China	United Kingdom	USSR
Canada	Poland	Iraq
France	South Africa	Venezuela
Sweden	Canada	Indonesia
West Germany	India	Kuwait, Neutral Zone
Guinea	Australia	Algeria

* Most figures for 1960 and 1961.
† Measured, indicated, inferred, and potential reserves.
‡ Probable reserves.
** Proved reserves.

SOURCE: *Encyclopedia Britannica World Atlas* (Chicago: Encyclopedia Britannica, 1966), pp. 204–05.

The United States and the Soviet Union, as one might expect, are among the top ten possessors of each of these three important resources. The rest of the list, however, shakes any simple idea that physical possession of resources is either a guarantee of national power or a prerequisite for it. Guinea and Kuwait are among the richest political units in the world, as far as iron and petroleum are concerned, but no one would claim that they are major powers. On the other hand, Britain, Germany, and France, lacking oil; Japan, lacking iron and oil; and Italy, lacking all three resources, have managed to achieve the status of great powers without these crucial raw materials.

Thus the physical possession of resources may give a nation more power than it would otherwise have, but it is clearly not a major determinant of a nation's power position. Nor is the reason for this any mystery. Power is influenced by the natural resources that a nation has at its command, not by the amount that lies within its boundaries.

Mineral resources are not a source of power unless they are developed; in their raw state, they are of no use to anyone. The great Mesabi iron deposits were of no use to the American Indians who lived near Lake Superior, and Arabian oil was of no interest to the nomads who camped above it a hundred years ago. To be used, these minerals must be extracted from the earth, processed, and marketed. If the nation that possesses them cannot do these things, it must make a deal with those who can. The result (assuming that the possessor manages to remain politically independent) is usually some form of concession-granting in which the possessor of the resource gains something in terms of goods and cash and international influence, but in which the full power potential of using the resource or of deciding who will use it goes to the concessionaire. Iran, for example, finds her power increased by the fact that large deposits of oil in her territory are developed and marketed by foreign oil firms (British for many years, now American and Dutch as well). However, her power is for the most part reduced to haggling over the price of the oil. The most Iran can do is withhold her oil from the world market altogether, for she cannot pick and choose among the various possible customers. That power lies with Britain and the United States. Iran's one attempt in 1951 to seize the power advantages connected with disposition of her own resources ended in failure when Britain's friends refused to touch her oil unless she came to terms with Britain.

To have even the limited amount of power that Iran derives from her resources, a nation must maintain political control of the area in which the resources lie. This is not always easy, for if resources are badly wanted by some great power, the power may be tempted to seize outright control of the area in question. The quest for raw materials has been one of the major reasons for colonialism. To cite an example, the copper of the Congo lies under Belgian control. Under colonialism it was the Belgians who gained in power from this resource, not the Africans who inhabited the country where it lay. To a lesser extent, this is still the case today in the state of economic dependency that has replaced old-style colonialism.

As in the case of the possession of strategic places, the physical possession of natural resources is not a source of power unless: (1) they are developed; and (2) the possessor maintains political control over their disposition. Resources confer the greatest power upon the nation that not only controls the territory that contains them, but that also extracts, processes, and markets its own resources. Obviously, then, a nation can contain great wealth in natural resources and still not be a major power.

Conversely, a nation may be one of the most powerful in the world without containing rich resources within its boundaries. It can make up for its deficiencies in several ways. One time-honored method is to conquer the resources that belong to others, hold the areas as colonies, send in (or follow) companies from the homeland to develop the resources, and provide the kind of laws that allow the operation to run smoothly. This has been the method of all the great powers that did not possess ample resources at home—for example, Spain, Portugal, France, England, Belgium, and the Netherlands. Germany, Italy, and Japan tried to do the same, but started at a time when many of the colonies they wished to possess were already in the hands of other major powers who were ready and able to defend them. Among the great powers of the present day, only the United States, the Soviet Union, and China have not resorted to political colonialism as a means of providing themselves with desired resources—and all have adequate resources at home. Also, the United States and the Soviet Union have developed other techniques for achieving some of the results of colonialism. What China will do when her power becomes greater remains to be seen.

A second method is to develop (without conquest) resources located in other countries. Short of outright political colonialism, control over the resources of other nations can be gained through concessions, political manipulation, and a judicious use of force. These are the methods that the United States and Britain have used to great advantage in Latin America, in Saudi Arabia, and in Iran. Sometimes private companies undertake the actual operations, but it is common for individuals engaged in such enterprises to have governmental backing.

In an age of nationalism run riot, this kind of economic penetration, sometimes called neocolonialism, has many advantages over political colonialism and has practically replaced it. In the first place, when penetration is economic, the domination by outsiders can be disguised, avoiding to some extent the irritation felt by the natives of a territory when they are compelled to accept an inferior political status. Second, this method lightens the burden of responsibility the colonizer has for the welfare of the colony. A colonial government might be expected to provide health services, education, and political training; an oil company is expected only to produce oil, and if it goes so far as to provide adequate housing for its workers, it is considered very public-spirited indeed. Finally, this method relieves the "colonizing" nation—at least to some extent—from responsibility for what its citizens do abroad, and if things somehow go wrong, the government, after all, is not responsible. Control is not so tight under this method as under political colonialism, and the country that develops the resources will have to pay a higher price to whoever nominally owns them; but in the long run control will probably be as efficient as it would be when dealing with a nationalistic and rebellious population, and the price paid for the resources will probably be no greater than the cost of the military and administrative forces that would have been required to hold a colony. Economic control has obvious advantages.

A variant of this method that leans more on force and less on payment and that provides more complete political control was practiced by the Soviet Union in the ten or fifteen years after World War II. Here the pattern was for the dominating government to enter into joint "corporations" for the development of resources in the dominated area. Again, the nations possessing the resources were nominally sovereign, but the actual disposition of their resources was decided by the Soviet Union.[8]

A third method of obtaining natural resources from other nations is to buy them. Even without resources of its own or colonies, a nation can obtain the raw materials it needs through international trade. This method is perfectly adequate in peacetime, all the arguments of aggressors to the contrary notwithstanding. Japan and Italy, after all, did succeed in becoming major world powers even without the colonies they claimed they needed for survival. The advantage in getting them from colonies, economic dependencies, or satellites is that they are cheaper if a dominant power position can be used in setting the price.

In time of war, however, a lack of natural resources within a nation's boundaries or within its colonies may be a serious handicap. Even in a period of "cold war," potential enemies may refuse to sell resources to each other. In recent years, the United States exerted every effort to prevent the flow of strategic materials from the West to the Communist world. In a hot war, efforts to prevent the enemy from getting strategic materials are intensified. Each combatant tries to cut its enemies off from any source of raw materials outside the boundaries of the state. Sales are stopped, diplomatic pressure is applied to neutrals, blockades are set up, and submarines deployed. During World War II, for example, German U-boats came within a few miles of the American coast to sink American oil tankers right outside our harbors.

Looked at in these terms, attempts at national economic self-

[8] More detailed discussion of the advantages of economic dependencies and satellites is contained in Chapter 11.

sufficiency are not so ridiculous as they are sometimes depicted. Although such attempts are expensive and wasteful, they do make sense as war policy.

In conclusion, a nation does not need to possess within its own boundaries all the natural resources it requires, though having them is an advantage in case of war. If a nation does not possess sufficient resources at home, it is a power advantage to have them in its colonies, for then the nation can control the sale of the resources to others. Also, the price paid to the people of a colony will probably be lower than it would be if the area were not politically controlled. Even without adequate resources at home or in its colonies, however, a nation can obtain the resources necessary to be a great power through neocolonial economic domination or through purchase.

SUMMARY

There is no question that the utilization of large quantities of natural resources is essential for the exercise of power by a modern nation. They are necessary for waging war, for operating a modern industrial system, and for rewarding others through trade and aid in the products of modern industry and in the raw materials themselves. However, a nation can utilize resources without possessing them within its own geographic boundaries. A strong nation can conquer the resources that lie in other countries. A skilled nation can develop and market the resources that belong to others. A rich nation can buy what it needs from other countries.

It is true that the possession of rich resources at home is a power advantage, particularly in time of war, but the mere possession of resources does not make a nation strong. A strong nation without resources will obtain them by one method or another; a weak nation with resources is liable to lose not only its resources, but its freedom as well.

Population

With population, we come to a resource whose claim as a determinant of national power rests on firmer ground. At a first, superficial glance, the importance of a large population for the power of a nation seems obvious. All the great powers of today have giant populations: there is not a single major power with a population under 50 million.[9] On the other hand, all the dependent (and therefore powerless) areas have very

[9] France, with a population of 49.4 million in midyear 1966, is over 50 million today.

small populations: only five have more than one million inhabitants.[10]

The relationship of population size to power is clearly indicated by a list of the most populous nations in the world (see Table 3). All the

TABLE 3

Nations with Largest Population

Nation	Population* (in millions)	Nation	Population* (in millions)
China	710	Brazil	85
India	499	West Germany†	61
USSR	233	Nigeria	59
United States	197		
Indonesia	107	United Kingdom	55
		Italy	52
Pakistan	105	France	49
Japan	99		

* Midyear 1966.
† Including West Berlin.
SOURCE: United Nations, *Demographic Yearbook, 1966* (New York: United Nations, 1967), Table 4.

major powers are present, although we do not find them listed in the order of their power and a few outsiders are in their midst. In any case, the list is closer to a power ranking than those based on size of area or resources. The major discrepancy between this listing and the power rank of nations is that the Asian nations are rated too high if one considers population alone.

A role for population size in the determination of national power is also indicated if we review modern European history. In 1800, France was the most powerful nation in Europe, and with the exception of Russia she was also the most populous. Her population was larger than Germany's or Britain's and almost as large as Russia's. In 1869, Germany passed France in population size, and two years later won over France a military victory that established her as the major power of continental Europe. Today, that place is filled by the Soviet Union, whose population has grown until it far surpasses that of France and Germany together.

Or consider the United States and Britain. The United States passed Britain in population size in about 1850, many years before she could claim to rival British power. If we credit all the British dependencies

[10] Mozambique, Angola, Hong Kong, Puerto Rico, and New Guinea.

to Britain, however, we find the big shift in relative size did not come until after World War I and culminated in the loss of India after World War II. This is also the period during which the United States took Britain's place as the most powerful nation in the world. The parallel between population size and power should not be overstressed, for it is not exact. Many other factors have an influence on power, but some parallel exists (see Table 4).

TABLE 4

Population Growth of Selected Countries (in millions)

Year	U.S.	Britain	France	Germany	Russia
					European Russia
1700	0.3	7	20		17
1750	1	8	25		
1800	5	11	28		38
				Prussia	
1850	23	21	36	16	61
1860	32	23†	37	18	63
				Germany	
1870	40		36	41	77
1880	50	30†	37	45	89
1890	63		38	49	95
1900	76	37†	39	56	103
1910	92		39	65	111
1920	107	44	39	62	
1930	123	46	41	65	
					USSR
1940	132	48	40	70	192
				West Germany*	
1950	152	51	42	50	180
1960	181	52	46	55	214
1965	195	55	49	59	231
1975	217	56			275

* Including West Berlin.
† 1861, 1881, 1901.

SOURCES: Pre-1920: United States, National Resources Planning Board, *The Problems of a Changing Population* (Washington, D.C., 1938), p. 21; Herbert Moller, *Population Movements in Modern European History* (New York: Macmillan, 1964), p. 5; United Kingdom Royal Commission on Population, *Report,* cmd. 7695 (London: H.M.S.O., 1949), p. 8; A. J. P. Taylor, *The Struggle for the Mastery of Europe 1848–1918* (Oxford: The Clarendon Press, 1954), p. xxv. Figures for 1920 through 1965: United Nations, *Demographic Yearbook, 1956* (New York: United Nations, 1956), Table 3; United Nations *Demographic Yearbook, 1965* (New York: United Nations, 1966), Table 4. Projections for 1975: United Nations, Department of Economic and Social Affairs, *The Future Growth of World Population* (New York: United Nations, 1958), Appendix C.

The importance of population as a source of national power has long been recognized in international politics. The French were well aware that Germany was outstripping them, just as German leaders worried about the growing size of the USSR. Mussolini called upon Italians to produce a larger population, saying: "Let us be frank with ourselves: what are 40 million Italians compared with 90 million Germans and 200 million Slavs?"[11] Nazi Germany, Fascist Italy, and Imperial Japan all tried to foster high birth rates for purposes of power. More recently, the British observed the widening gap between the number of Europeans and the number of Asians and began to worry publicly about the prestige and the influence of the West.[12]

However, the fact that population size and power are associated does not prove that it is size that determines power and not the other way around. In fact, we know that to the extent that population growth is the result of conquest of neighboring peoples or of colonial subjects, it is the result of national power, not the cause. Before reaching any final conclusions as to the importance of population as a determinant of power, it is necessary to examine in more detail the ways in which a large population contributes to the ability of a nation to influence other nations.

HOW POPULATION CONTRIBUTES TO POWER

The first and most obvious use that can be made of a large population is as manpower in military action and in economic production. Push-button war remains a dream; in spite of the complicated machinery with which modern war is waged, a modern army requires as many men as ever. Planes and guided missiles and atomic artillery require men to operate, to service, to transport, and to repair them. A modern infantryman, equipped with all the paraphernalia modern science has provided, requires many men behind the front lines to keep his equipment and supplies flowing to him. Above all, there is still a need for common infantry. The Korean and Vietnamese wars have proved without a doubt that there is still no substitute for foot soldiers.

To some extent, a nation can rely upon troops drawn from populations other than its own. In the recent past, colonial troops and foreign mercenaries (such as the French Foreign Legion) have expanded many national armies. Allies, too, may sometimes fight each other's battles. But if a nation wishes to be sure its interests will be defended, a strong

[11] Speech quoted by David V. Glass, *The Struggle for Population* (Oxford: Clarendon, 1936), p. 34.
[12] United Kingdom, Royal Commission on Population, *Report* (London: H.M.S.O., 1949), p. 134.

fighting force composed of its own nationals is essential. Supplementary troops may be gathered from other sources, but the core must be native to the country concerned.

Manpower and armed forces are not the same thing, of course, and a nation with a large population may not have a military force to match. India, for example, has a tremendous population, but her military forces are small. Nor is a large military force a source of much power if the nation that controls it is reluctant to commit it in battle. A large part of Fascist Italy's power during the 1930s was due not to great military strength but to the fact that Mussolini was willing, even eager, to fight, while the governments of England and France were not. The government of a reasonable nation committed to preserving the lives and the property of its citizens will always be at a slight disadvantage (other things being equal) vis-à-vis a fanatical government willing to go to war to achieve its goals.

A large population also provides another military advantage quite apart from its direct use in battle. A large and densely settled population is more difficult to conquer and to hold once conquered. The military occupation of such a territory ties down many men and may lead to the creation of manpower shortages at home for the conqueror. Nazi Germany found the occupation of Europe almost more than it could manage, and during the height of its expansion, Germany suffered from acute labor shortages at home.

A second major area where a large population contributes to a nation's power is in economic production. A nation's economic output depends on many factors, but one of these is the size of the labor force involved. Modern technological improvements may someday lead to an economy requiring fewer human workers, but so far this has not been the case. The machine age finds as many men at work as in the past. They tend machines and sit at desks instead of working with their hands and backs, but still they work. The coming age of automation may mechanize clerical work and change our occupations in other ways, but it is not likely to leave us unemployed, for as the amount of goods we can produce grows, it will be matched for a long time by our increasing needs. We will not reach in the near future (nor perhaps ever) the point where we can all sit back and leave economic production to a few specialists guiding a nation filled with machines. Now and in the foreseeable future, a nation wishing to produce a large amount of goods and services will require a large labor force, all working hard.

As in the case of military manpower, it is possible for a nation to rely on foreign workers to some extent. Slavery (and slaves are usually foreign) has been a major institution of the past, banished from the

United States barely a hundred years ago. More recently, the institution was revived in Nazi Germany, where there were more than eight million foreign workers (most of them there involuntarily) in 1944, and by Soviet Russia, which employed large numbers of war captives for many years after the end of World War II. The colonial powers relied heavily on forced labor, more or less thinly disguised, to do much of the work in their colonies. The immigration of free labor from other countries may also increase a nation's labor force, but unless the laborers are absorbed as permanent immigrants, this creates other problems, both for the migrants and for the receiving country. A large source of voluntary, nonforeign laborers, however, would seem to be essential for the nation that aspires to economic strength.

People not only produce, they also consume, and a large consumer population can be a source of strength. Although major industries can and do find markets for their products abroad, such industries are more likely to arise where there is a large home market. Detroit is the automobile capital of the world not only because of the superior productivity of American workers, but also because the existence of a tremendous American market for cars assures manufacturers of the full advantages of mass production. The power advantage conferred by these great industries need hardly be elaborated.

A large population can also provide a good potential market for producers in other nations, a fact that can be used to increase a nation's power over others. The use by one nation of its purchasing power to bring other nations to heel is common enough in international practice. Nazi Germany was a master at this practice, and the USSR, through a government monopoly of purchasing, uses its buying power today as a political tool, often placing orders to achieve political goals. Even where the government does not monopolize buying, purchases can be made or refused in an attempt to influence not only the seller's price but also his general behavior. America's refusal to buy Cuban sugar after Castro came to power must be viewed in such a light.

A large labor force with many skills and a large body of consumers with diverse needs make possible the development of a rich and varied economy such as is necessary for any attempt at economic self-sufficiency. We have already observed that such attempts do not make much sense in peacetime, but that a lack of dependence upon other nations may be a marked advantage in war. Self-sufficiency is out of the question for a modern nation with a small population, but for the populous nation it can at least be approximated.

It must be stressed that a large population does not guarantee powerful armed forces or great productive wealth. These depend upon many other factors as well, particularly upon the degree to which a nation has industrialized and modernized its military forces and its productive machine. A large army without modern weapons cannot give a very good account of itself in battle. A large labor force is not a source of power if it is engaged in subsistence agriculture and peasant handicrafts or if it is unemployed because of a depression, nor does a large population constitute a large market if it cannot afford to buy consumer goods beyond the bare necessities. A large population may even be a source of weakness to a nation if the existing population is already living close to the subsistence line and if a growth in numbers cannot be absorbed into productive work. India, for example, would seem to suffer from overpopulation at the present time, her growing numbers constituting a liability and not an asset. No claim is made here for demographic determinism as far as power is concerned. Population size is only one of many factors contributing to national power, and it must be properly related to the others to be effective.

So far, we have discussed only the total number of people in a nation as a determinant of power. However, all the people of a nation are not equally important in the contribution they can make to a nation's strength. Old people and children may help make up an economic market, but they cannot contribute much to the labor force or the military forces. By and large, the working ages can be said to lie between 15 and 65 or 70, although backward economies may make some use of the labor of younger children. The fighting ages are even more restricted, prime fighting men being from the age of 17 or 18 up to about the age of 35. Sex, too, is involved here, since most armies do not make extensive use of women.

When considering such limited groups as those of working and fighting age, we are concerned not only with the total size of a nation's population but also with the *proportion* of the population that is in these groups. The United States, for example, has 63 percent of its population in the ages 15 through 69, while England and Wales have 69 percent in the same age bracket. India, on the other hand, has only 57 percent of its population in the working ages because of the much larger proportion of small children.[13] The nation with a relatively large percentage of its population of working age is doubly blessed. Not only does it have more potential workers than it might otherwise, it also has a smaller nonworking population for these workers to support. The proportion of potential fighting men also varies from one country to another.

[13] Figures for the United States and England and Wales are for 1966; India, for 1961. United Nations, *Demographic Yearbook, 1966* (New York: United Nations, 1967), Table 5.

Fourteen percent of the population of the United States consists of men aged 15 through 34. The corresponding figure for Brazil is 19 percent.[14]

Our interest in a nation's population does not end with a consideration of total size and the proportion in the working and fighting ages. If these remained the same for each nation over long periods of time, that would be all we would have to know. But nations grow and shrink in size, through political conquests and border changes, and also through immigration and the natural workings of the birth rate and the death rate. If birth and death rates change, the size of the population will change too, and so will its age structure (the proportion of people of various ages). Differences in population size between one nation and another at any one time are but one side of the demographic picture. Also important are differences in rates of growth. To understand the full significance of demographic factors for international power, we must know not only how large each nation's population is, but also how fast it is growing.

POPULATION GROWTH

We live in an age of tremendous population growth. Nearly every nation on earth is expanding its population. Some countries are increasing as rapidly as 4 or 5 percent each year, others hardly at all, but together they have since 1940 added more than one billion people to the world's total population (now around 3½ billion).

The reason for this large and unprecedented growth, stated simply, is that men today do not die at as fast a rate as they are born. In theory, population increase in any particular country can be caused by higher birth rates, lower death rates, greater immigration, or smaller emigration. In fact, the population explosion we are witnessing is due almost entirely to a drop in death rates. Economic and political modernization have brought better food supplies, better living conditions, and better sanitation. Modern science has brought dramatic improvements in medical care. The result is a startling drop in human mortality, even when the effects of modern war are taken into consideration.

Birth rates have also dropped in much of the world, for reasons that are somewhat more complex. In a general way, falling birth rates can be attributed largely to family planning by people in the more industrial and urban sections of the world who have decided they want fewer children than their peasant ancestors had.

Falling birth rates might be expected at first glance to cancel out falling death rates, but this is not the case. In country after country, the drop in the birth rate has come many years after the drop in the death

[14] The U.S. figure is for 1966; Brazil, for 1960. *Ibid.*

rate, leaving a gap between the two rates that brings continued population growth.

As the nations of Western Europe and the European-peopled nations overseas experienced these population changes, they followed a pattern that was labeled "the demographic transition" by demographers. These countries grew fairly slowly and unevenly during their preindustrial periods. Then, as they began to industrialize, death rates fell while birth rates remained high, causing rapid population growth. Once they became fully industrialized their birth rates fell, too, and it was once believed that they would level off and eventually decline in population. However, with the end of the Great Depression and World War II, birth rates rose again to moderate levels, and today these nations are all increasing in population, although more slowly than they did during the period when they were first industrializing.

Much of the rest of the world, however, has followed a different pattern of population growth. Many of the underdeveloped nations today are growing rapidly in population long before they have modernized their economies to any substantial degree. This is a development of the last ten or twenty years. What has happened is that nations whose economies are still backward have been able to borrow the science and technology of more advanced nations to reduce their own death rates. In doing so they have shown a degree of social organization and a sense of social responsibility far beyond anything the West possessed at the equivalent stage of economic development.

The result has been a great improvement for the people of these nations insofar as increased length of life and improved health are blessings, but these blessings have also brought problems. Death rates have fallen early and fast, but these nations probably face a long period before the peasant attitudes producing high birth rates also change. In the meantime, their populations will continue to grow rapidly, perhaps more rapidly than their faltering economies can provide for. India, for example, must find the food and lodging to provide for more than 10 million additional people each year. At a rough guess, 19 million new babies are born each year in India and perhaps three-quarters of them will survive to enter the labor market, where they will require jobs that do not now exist. In future years the figures will be bigger. Such rapid growth may *reduce* rather than add to the wealth, power, and political stability of nations like India.

In considering the effect of population upon national power, we must distinguish between population size and the rate of population growth. We have seen that large size confers many power advantages in providing military manpower, labor power, and the potential for a large market. But rapid growth is another matter. Rapid growth is an asset only for the nation that is politically and economically efficient enough to employ its growing numbers productively. Starving peasants and rioting unemployed do not increase a nation's power. Indeed, they may act as a tremendous drag upon economic advance and reduce the political system to chaos.

For industrial nations and for those that are successfully industrializing, continued population growth is a source of power, but for those that are only beginning to modernize their economies, rapid population growth has a mixed effect. On the one hand it is undoubtedly increasing the power base that these nations will have to build on in future years, but on the other hand it probably helps to slow their economic modernization.[15]

SUMMARY

The population of a nation is a relatively important determinant of that nation's power. Particularly important is the number of people a nation has in the most productive ages. As military personnel, these people can be armed and used directly as an instrument of force. Military forces may also be offered or withheld from participation in the battles of other nations, constituting a very significant reward or punishment for the other nations involved.

As civilians, the population (especially if it is large and densely settled) may make the task of military occupation much more difficult for any potential conqueror.

As workers, the population of a nation helps determine the amount of national production. The goods and services that they produce can be given, loaned or sold to other nations as a reward for desired behavior, or they may be withheld as punishment.

As consumers, the population helps determine the size of the home market for various goods. A large market may encourage the development of great industries based on mass production. A market can also be offered to or withheld from producers of other nations as a political reward or punishment.

Finally, a large population that is growing rapidly may engender in its own members a kind of confidence and instill in other nations a kind of fear that greatly aid the national government in its efforts to use persuasion on other nations.

Population size and composition are by no means the only factors

[15] Further material on the relationship of population to power may be found in Katherine and A. F. K. Organski, *Population and World Power* (New York: Knopf, 1961).

that affect a nation's power. A large population does not guarantee a large armed force, a mighty productive machine, or a large market, but it is a prerequisite for these important means to national power.

Population *growth,* on the other hand, is not always an advantage. If the population is increasing so rapidly that the increment cannot be absorbed into useful work, the result is to slow economic growth and to increase the danger of political instability.

8

Social Determinants of Power

✧《

We turn next to those determinants of power we have labeled "social": economic development, political development, and national morale.

Economic Development

One of the most important determinants of a nation's power is its economic organization, or more specifically, the degree to which it has industrialized. We have already seen that natural resources do not contribute to a nation's power unless they are developed, and their development is a question of technology and economic organization. We have seen that a large labor force is not a source of power unless it is organized to produce the wealth of goods and services characteristic of a modern, industrial economy. And we have seen that even a large army is not of much importance unless it possesses the weapons and supplies produced by modern industry. We have also seen that a large part of the importance of both population and resources as determinants of power lies in the contribution they make to a strong and efficient economy. Again and again, we have hinted at the importance of economic development. Now it is time to look at this factor directly.

To begin, what is meant by a modern, industrial economy or an efficient economic organization? What is the essential difference between a modern and a backward nation, between a highly industrialized nation and an underdeveloped one? An impressionistic answer is easy to give, for the mental images summoned up by these two kinds of nations are quite different. One thinks of modern industry and one thinks of molten steel and flowing oil, of miles of tall chimneys belching smoke, of sooty, squalid factory towns, of skyscrapers and suburbs, of miles and miles of highways and railroad tracks, of telephones and packaged foods and gadgets. An industrial society is characterized by great factories, great cities, and machines and their products. It is a society that produces tremendous quantities of goods and services, and herein lies the key. An industrial economy is one characterized by great efficiency of production.

In a backward economy, each worker produces barely what he needs for his own subsistence. There will be some surplus, enough to support a royal court, a few rich men, an army of sorts, but most of the production goes into providing the minimum of food, clothing, shelter, and amusement. Sometimes even this minimum is not met. Acute poverty is always present and starvation a constant threat.

In a modern, industrial economy, each worker produces far more, for he is part of an elaborate and efficient economic organization where tools, techniques, motivation, and opportunity combine to make him productive. He finds placed at his disposal a vastly superior technology. Most important, he has the use of the machine. Compare the peasant with his horse-drawn plow, his scythe and flail with the modern farmer with his tractor and his combine. Compare the man who transported goods by team and wagon with the modern trucker. Or a scribe and a typist, a seamstress with a needle and one with a sewing machine, a mathematician with an abacus and one with an electronic brain. Unquestionably, the greatest boost to productivity has come with the machine. Aided by what is in fact an extension of himself, the modern worker in an industrial economy produces infinitely more than the worker of a nonindustrial society could possibly produce, no matter how diligently he applied himself to his work. The modern worker produces far more than he requires for his own subsistence. He produces a surplus, and it is this surplus which contributes to a nation's power.

INDEXES OF ECONOMIC DEVELOPMENT

How are we to know, however, which economies are most developed, which nation's workers produce the largest surplus? Size of area could be measured in square miles, resources weighed, and population counted, but how is economic development to be measured? We need some simple index.

One way would be to measure the productivity of workers. It is possible, by means of statistical techniques known and used in modern nations, to set a total monetary value on all the final goods and services exchanged in a nation during a given year (the GNP or Gross National Product).[1] This figure could then be divided by the number of man-hours worked to give a measurement of productivity (output per man-hour), or it could be divided by the number of workers in the nation to give a measurement of output per worker, a somewhat cruder measurement of productivity. Unfortunately, figures on man-hours or even on the number of workers are hard to find. For many of the most backward nations, they simply do not exist, and so we must turn to some less satisfactory measure.

One possibility is to divide the gross national product by the number of people in the nation (per capita product). This gives a measurement of production per head of population, which is not exactly the same thing as productivity per worker. The two are related closely enough, however, to serve our purpose. High per capita product accompanies high productivity per worker and can be used to give a rough idea of it. Per capita product, therefore, is the index we shall use for productivity. The more developed a nation's economy, the higher its per capita product.

Another way of looking at the process of economic development (or industrialization) is to view it as a shift from agricultural to industrial work. When a nation industrializes, each worker not only produces more; he also produces different kinds of goods and services than he did before. In a preindustrial society, the great bulk of the working population is engaged in agriculture, and indeed, it must be, for methods of production are so inefficient that the labor of nearly every worker in the nation is required simply to produce the food required for life. In a developed or industrial society, however, agricultural methods have so improved that a few farmers can produce enough food for many, thus freeing the others to provide the multitude of goods and services that characterize industrial life. This shift away from agricultural work is one of the most dramatic changes that occur with industrialization.

Another way to measure economic development, then, is by the

[1] More exactly, the gross national product of a nation consists of the sum of all personal consumption expenditure on goods and services, plus governmental expenditure on goods and services, plus gross investment expenditure on all new machines and construction. Paul Samuelson, *Economics* (New York: McGraw-Hill, 1964), p. 191.

percentage of a nation's workers engaged in nonagricultural work. As a rough measure, a nation can be considered industrial when more than half its workers have left the land.

Following a procedure that is now familiar, let us take these two indexes of economic development and see which nations rank the highest. Which are the most economically developed nations in the world, and how does their rank compare with their relative power? Consider the nations with the highest per capita product (see Table 1).

TABLE 1

Nations with Highest Per Capita Gross National Product

Nation	Per Capita GNP*	Nation	Per Capita GNP*
United States	$3,312	Australia	$1,789
Canada	2,273	Denmark	1,766
Sweden	2,215	Luxembourg	1,735
Switzerland	2,043	West Germany†	1,724
New Zealand	1,847	Norway	1,694

* Estimates for 1965 in constant 1962 prices.
† Including West Berlin.
SOURCE: United States, Agency for International Development, *Gross National Product, Growth Rates and Trend Data by Region and Country* (Washington, D.C.: U.S. Agency for International Development, June 1966), Tables 3a–3g.

This is a list of the ten richest and most productive nations in the world, but it is clearly not a list of the most powerful, for some of these are tiny nations, eliminated from great power status by their small populations. Of all the nations that are usually classified as great powers, only the United States and West Germany are on this list. The other great powers are scattered from top to bottom of the international range.[2]

The other index gives a list that includes many of the same nations (see Table 2). Again, it is far from being a list of the most powerful nations in the world. It is true that most of the great powers are industrial nations with well over 50 percent of their working men in nonagricultural work,[3] but even here, generalization is tricky, for China and India, surely

[2] France in 1965 had a per capita GNP of $1,664; the United Kingdom, $1,663; the USSR, $1,271; Italy, $863; Japan, $684; and India, $81. United States, Agency for International Development, *Gross National Product, Growth Rates and Trend Data by Region and Country* (Washington, D.C.: U.S. Agency for International Development, June 1966), Tables 3a–3g.
[3] France, 79 percent in 1962; Italy, 72 percent in 1961; Japan, 66 percent in 1955; USSR, 54 percent (both sexes) in 1959. United Nations, *Demographic Yearbook, 1964* (New York: United Nations, 1965), Tables 9 and 10.

TABLE 2

Nations Most Industrialized

Nation	Percent of Economically Active Males in Nonagricultural Pursuits*
United Kingdom	95%
Belgium	92
United States	90
West Germany†	90
Netherlands	87
Israel	87
Australia	87
Luxembourg	86
Switzerland	85
Canada	85

* 1960–1961.
† Including West Berlin.

SOURCES: United Nations, *Demographic Yearbook*, 1964 (New York: United Nations, 1965), Table 9. For Great Britain, 1961 censuses of England and Wales, Scotland, and Northern Ireland. For Belgium, Institut National de Statistique, *Recensement de la Population, 1961*, vol. 8, Table 9.

major powers, are among the most heavily agricultural nations in the world.

This does not mean that economic development is not a major determinant of national power, but it does show vividly that no one determinant alone explains a nation's power. The influence of economic development on power is obscured when small nations are compared with giants. Switzerland, Luxembourg, and Israel, for example, are economically developed enough to be great powers, but they are too small in population. It becomes apparent, however, if nations of the same size are compared (see Table 3). Britain is much more powerful than Nigeria, but here the difference cannot be attributed to population size. The big difference between them is in economic development. Or take Australia compared to Peru, or Israel compared to El Salvador. Again a big difference in power is found paralleled by a difference in economic development.

THE CONTRIBUTION OF ECONOMIC DEVELOPMENT TO POWER

¶ *Persuasion.* It is not hard to see why economic development contributes to a nation's power, for the amount that is produced beyond the needs

TABLE 3

Population, Per Capita GNP, and Power Rank of
Selected Pairs of Nations

Nation	Population* (in millions)	Per Capita GNP†	Power Rank
United Kingdom	54.6	$1,663	1
Nigeria	57.5	104	2
Australia	11.4	1,789	1
Peru	11.6	267	2
Israel	2.7	1,160	1
El Salvador	2.9	280	2

* Midyear 1965.
† 1965 per capita GNP in constant 1962 prices.
SOURCES: United Nations, *Demographic Yearbook, 1965, 1966* (New York: United Nations, 1966, 1967), Table 4. United States, Agency for International Development, *Gross National Product, Growth Rates and Trend Data by Region and Country* (Washington, D.C.: U.S. Agency for International Development, June 1966), Tables 3a–3g.

of bare subsistence can be used in many ways. This surplus can be used to increase the living standards of everyone within the nation, thus helping to create a contented and loyal population. Possessed of plenty, these people will be admired and envied by the people of other nations, particularly since we live in a world where only a few nations are industrialized and most are not. To be the object of admiration by others gives a nation an additional source of power far beyond any abilities at persuasion that its diplomats may possess. In a sense, every citizen becomes a diplomat, and wherever industrial and nonindustrial people come into contact with each other, the poorer, nonindustrial folk can easily be induced to change their ways to conform to those of the industrial people. This has happened again and again all over the world, and the change is always in one direction: there is no case of an industrial nation changing to a nonindustrial way of life.

A good part of America's power today rests on the fact that the people of poorer nations would like to be like us, at least as far as their material lives are concerned. Russia, too, has capitalized on this source of power, using the example of her own improved living standards as an inducement to less developed nations to follow the Russian way and to raise their own standards. If China succeeds in industrializing, her example alone will give her tremendous power in Asia.

The advantages in persuasion conferred by a high standard of living may boomerang, however, if those who possess them are not careful. Admiration accompanied by envy can all too easily turn to resentment and then to hatred, particularly if those who possess tremendous wealth also appear to feel superior to others. In such a case, the power of the rich to influence the poor through persuasion will decrease.

Industrialization increases the powers of persuasion of a nation in still another way. It not only provides a persuasive message; it also provides the means by which this message may be delivered. In convincing others, personal contact is most effective, but since mass contact between the citizens of one nation and those of another nation is not usually possible, the media of mass communication must be used in any attempt to reach the common people of other nations. To set up a giant system of mass communication and to keep it running requires wealth and engineering skill that are not possessed by backward nations. There may be something in the Iraqi way of life that would appeal to Americans, but if there is, we are not likely to find out about it, because the citizens of Iraq have no way of reaching us and telling us about it.

As the high standard of living of an industrial people enables them to influence others through persuasion, so it also enables them to resist persuasion by others. The Americans and the British, for example, have a high stake in their nations as they are. These people do not often make envious comparisons between their lot and that of other people. Indeed, where comparisons are made, the result will be to solidify the wealthier people, making them even more resistant to the arguments of others who would change their way of life. No fully industrial nation has ever voluntarily turned to communism.

¶ *Rewards.* The major power use that can be made of economic wealth lies in the realm of reward and punishment, for economic rewards are among the most important that one nation can offer to another. One way in which rewards are granted is through international trade, and here industrialization is a great advantage. Underdeveloped nations may produce raw materials for other nations, but they do not turn out the manufactured goods that figure so importantly in international trade. Airplanes, automobiles, tractors, farm machinery, electrical equipment, mining machinery, machine tools, guns—these must all be purchased from industrial nations, and the fact that only industrial nations make them gives these nations great power. The United States today produces goods that all the world would like to have, and this is perhaps her greatest source of power. Before World War II Germany and Japan threatened the power of England and France not only by military action but also by their sudden and successful appearance as salesmen in markets all over the world. Their ability to produce goods wanted by other nations gave them spheres of influence that did not make the Allies happy.

An industrial nation possesses a second significant economic reward for other nations in its ability to buy their products. Underdeveloped nations may *want* the goods that other nations produce, but they often do not possess the means to buy them. A few rich men may order Cadillacs and refrigerators, but the average citizen cannot afford more foreign goods than an occasional piece of cloth, a few simple tools, perhaps a gadget or two. An industrial population, on the other hand, requires vast amounts and varieties of goods from other nations, and its ability to choose among several sources in buying these goods gives it great power over those who depend for their living upon selling their products.

The ability to buy and the ability to sell may both be used to enhance a nation's power, but whether they are actually used in this fashion will depend somewhat upon the type of economy and upon the type of government involved. During the nineteenth century, the age of laissez faire, most international trade was in private hands. The individual buyer or seller was indeed interested in rewards, but for himself, not for his country. He bought where goods were cheapest and sold where they were dearest without much thought about the power advantages this might or might not confer upon his nation. The twentieth century, however, has seen a growth in governmental control over international trade. In an extreme example, such as the Soviet Union, the government takes over a monopoly of international purchases and sales. In such a case it is to be expected that many transactions will have political as well as economic significance, and in recent years the Soviet Union has offered prized machinery to its international friends, and she has half-promised orders to nations troubled with surplus goods, hoping for political concessions in return. Britain has long designed her trade and customs policies with an eye to favoring her friends. Even the United States has allowed power considerations to influence her trade, though economic considerations generally still come first.

It is primarily through foreign aid, however, not trade, that the United States has used her economic power to influence the behavior of other nations. Her whole policy of opposing communism has been based upon the assumption that by giving needed goods to friendly nations, she can win their friendship and prevent them from turning to communism. There is no question that quite aside from force and principles, one of the strongest ties binding the free world to the United States is the tie of economic benefits that flow from an association with this industrial colossus. The Soviet Union too seeks to help her friends with aid, though she has had to be much less generous than the United States, and China has sought in vain to compete with the Soviet Union and the United States in this field. Britain and the other major Western European powers give some aid to poorer countries, but for the immediate future, only the United States is able to maintain large-scale foreign aid on a continuous basis. The giving of extensive international aid requires a highly developed economy, for only if a nation's workers produce a large surplus above their own needs will a government be allowed to give away goods to citizens of other nations. Only a rich nation can afford to invest so heavily in international friendship.

Another form of international economic reward is capital. The greatest resource of the industrial nations and the greatest need of underdeveloped lands is capital, the wealth that is not used by consumers and can therefore be used to produce still further wealth. Without extensive capital, modern industry could not exist, for it is only by plowing large amounts of production back into the building of still further production facilities that great industries can be created. In the long run, it is as important to build steel plants as it is to produce the steel itself, and if a nation wishes to produce airplanes or bridges or elecrtic lights, it must first produce the tools to make the tools to make the goods desired. What the economy of a nation will produce tomorrow depends in large part upon the capital investments made today.

Rich, industrial nations have capital to spare, but poor nations must deprive their citizens of badly needed goods if they are to raise the capital so needed for development. (Indeed, the USSR allowed her people to starve that she might build up her industries.) It is perhaps an irony that the nations that need capital most are those that have the least of it, while those that have the most of it need it least. One solution is for the most developed nations to give or loan their capital to others. This, of course, has gone on for many years, and industries all over the world owe their existence to American and European capital. Capital is never free, however. If private individuals provide the capital, they expect to share in the control and the profits of an enterprise. If governments give capital to foreign countries, they expect a political return.

Still one more economic reward which an industrial nation has at its disposal is technical assistance. We have said that capital is the greatest resource of an industrial nation, but perhaps that statement should be qualified. At least as important as capital is industrial know-how, another product of an industrial way of life. All the money, all the machinery, and all the workers in the world will not make one modern factory unless they are combined in the proper fashion and unless the workers are trained to use the equipment. Backward nations know this, and they go to great expense to hire foreign experts and to train their own nationals in the ways of modern industry. Soviet Foreign Minister Molotov once told an American newsman: "We are for American technique. That is one thing we want to take from the United States."[4] By providing technical experts, an industrial nation can provide a greatly valued reward to less developed nations.

Military aid, though generally given for strategic reasons, can also be used as a simple reward. Renewed Soviet military assistance to the United Arab Republic after her defeat by Israel in 1967 was clearly designed to gain friendship rather than effective military support for Soviet goals.

It should be understood that trade, aid, capital, experts and arms are not sent to other countries solely as rewards in the narrow sense of payments made for desired political behavior. Even by totalitarian countries, most economic actions are taken because they are advantageous to the nation that makes them, quite apart from any effect they have upon the recipient. Even out-and-out aid is not given solely as a bribe to win or keep the friendship of other nations. Gifts may be given in part to keep an international friendship, but they are also given because the giver is genuinely anxious to build up the strength of its friends and allies. The Marshall Plan was sold to the American Congress as a means of keeping Europe from going Communist, and in the case of France and Italy the argument may have had some merit. England, however, was in no danger of falling to the Communists, but she was our international friend, and we wanted to see her solvent again. Military aid, in particular, is not usually distributed primarily in order to win friends and influence nations, but rather to assure that nations already friendly will be able to bear their share in any fighting for a common cause. Thus aid is given for many reasons quite aside from its serving as a reward.

It is difficult, however, to give such aid without attaching any strings, particularly when every politician interested in other nations tries to tie in his favorite project as a quid pro quo for foreign aid. It is a generous nation, indeed, that can refrain from sometimes indicating that a certain gratitude would be appreciated for gifts received or from occasionally suggesting more or less obliquely that aid might be withdrawn if the recipient offends too greatly.

¶ *Punishments.* The withdrawal of any of these economic rewards constitutes a punishment. Again, it should be stressed that there are many possible reasons for breaking off an economic relationship between two

4 *The New York Times,* Apr. 24, 1955, p. 37, col. 2.

nations. The buyer may have found a lower price elsewhere. The seller may have found a better market. Particularly where economic dealings are in private hands, trade ties may be made and broken for purely private ends. However, national purposes may also be served. Contracts can be withheld or tariffs raised or exports forbidden for punitive purposes. The boycott, after all, has a long political history. Or a nation may refuse, as the United States has done, to sell strategic goods to its potential enemies in a deliberate effort to prevent them from developing their own power by means of these goods. Here, governmental regulation serves as well as a monopoly on foreign trade. A government cannot tell its private traders where to buy and sell their wares, but it *can* tell them where *not* to buy and sell. Thus the American government, while leaving trade in private hands, nevertheless managed to cut off virtually all trade in a long list of goods with Communist nations. Government aid to other nations, of course, is much more easily withheld as punishment, for here the role of private interests is much smaller.

¶ *Force.* We have seen that goods and services can be used as an aid to persuasion and as rewards and punishments, and that industrial nations have a great advantage in the use of economic power because only they possess the higher living standards, the abundance of goods, the capital, and the know-how that are so valued by others. The role of economic development in the use of force is even clearer. As we have said, modern armies require modern weapons and vast quantities of supplies that only an industrial nation can produce. Indeed, strategists in a modern war know that they must concentrate their attack as much upon the enemy's industrial centers as on its military forces. The nation that attempts to fight with antiquated or inadequate weapons fights under a tremendous handicap, no matter how brave or numerous its soldiers.

Arms need not be produced at home. They can, of course, be purchased from other nations or even received as gifts, provided one's allies are rich enough. During World War II, America served as an arsenal for the Allies, and today the United States and the Soviet Union provide a large part of the weapons possessed in their respective camps. With luck, arms can even be captured from one's enemies. Thus the Chinese Communists built up their initial store of weapons from supplies surrendered to them by the Japanese at the end of World War II and from aid provided by the Americans to the Chinese Nationalists, large numbers of whom surrendered, deserted, or sold their equipment.

It is a foolish nation, however, that depends exclusively or even mainly upon outside sources for its military supplies. A great nation must make its own arms, for to depend on other nations for the power to defend oneself is to put oneself completely in the hands of others. There are many reasons for the strong power position of the United States in Central America, not the least of which is that none of the Central American nations manufacture enough military equipment to amount to anything. The shipment of a few planes or tanks from the United States can tip the balance in any struggle among or within them.

Unfortunately for nonindustrial nations, the field of military production is one of the most difficult to enter. The most complicated and advanced techniques known to man, the most expensive plants and operations have been put at the disposal of military science. Electronic devices, nuclear bombs, and intercontinental missiles are not to be built by amateurs or beginners. The industrial nation finds itself with great advantages when it comes to influencing other nations through persuasion, through rewards or punishment, but its superiority is greatest of all when it comes to the exercise of power through the use of force.

THE INDUSTRIAL WAY OF LIFE

If industrial development is such an important factor in national power, then the determinants of industrial strength must also be important in any consideration of what makes nations powerful. We have defined industrialization in terms of economic productivity, but high productivity is only part of a whole way of life. The shift from peasant agriculture to modern, industrial production is accompanied by many changes in other areas of life, without which industrialization would not be possible. It is hard to dissect a social system and see just which changes are essential for the development of modern industry. It is particularly difficult because changes in the rest of the system accompany industrialization, and are part cause and part effect of changes in production. We can, however, separate out several that seem to be particularly important. Our treatment of them will be brief.

¶ *Urbanization.* One of the changes that has accompanied the growth of modern industry everywhere is the growth of cities. The correlation between the two is very close. Those nations that are most industrial are also most urban, and those nations whose industries are growing fastest also have the cities that are growing fastest.[5]

The growth of cities is in part a result of the industrial revolution, for in a world without machine production, the great majority of people

[5] The correlation between the percentage of males engaged in nonagricultural work and the percentage of the population living in large cities for all the countries in the world that have good census data is above 0.9. Hilda Hertz Golden, formerly of the Bureau of Applied Social Research, Columbia University, personal communication.

must work in agriculture and must live near the land they till. Under such conditions, a large number of great cities is impossible.

Once cities begin to grow, however, they help speed the process of industrialization. If modern industries are to cluster together and take full advantage of the economies of being near each other, they require great concentrations of workers. City life provides this, just as it provides a concentration of talent, skill, and industrial training, which in turn makes it easier for new industries to arise. City living also contributes to the growth of industry by breaking down the old-fashioned habits and attitudes, some of which are incompatible with efficient industrial work, that immigrants from the countryside bring with them. Urbanization, then, contributes to industrialization both by providing concentrations of brawn and brain for factory and office and by helping to create an urban outlook more compatible with industrial life than the peasant mentality.

Great cities and industrial concentrations are in some respects a disadvantage to a nation as far as power is concerned. They are not easily defended, and in an age of thermonuclear weapons, they are subject to instant destruction. It has sometimes been suggested that perhaps our cities and industries ought to be decentralized in the interests of defense. However, this is not likely to be done, since the economic advantages of concentration far outweigh the military disadvantages.[6]

¶ *Education.* Widespread, formal education is another essential part of an industrial way of life. All the major industrial nations have so educated their populations that illiteracy has been reduced to insignificant proportions, and one of the first steps taken by a modern government attempting to industrialize its economy is to institute a high-speed literacy drive. There is little place in an industrial system for the worker who cannot read or write. City living, even for the nonworker, requires a rudimentary ability to read.

Beyond mere literacy, many special skills are needed by a modern industrial system, skills that can be best learned through formal education. Some skills can be learned through apprenticeship or through experience on the job, but others require many years of training. A nation's physical resources may be destroyed, but if its people retain their skills and the ability to teach them to others, they will build again. Destroy a nation's educational system, and within a generation its power will be gone.

---

[6] See Ansley Coale, *The Problem of Reducing Vulnerability to Atomic Bombs* (Princeton: Princeton University Press, 1947); David M. Heer, *After Nuclear Attack; A Demographic Inquiry* (New York: Praeger, 1965).

¶ *Mobility.* Geographic and social mobility are essential to an industrial system. Unless individual workers can be shifted from place to place and from job to job, the ever-changing needs of industry cannot be met. Social mobility—the possibility of rising from one social class to another through accomplishment in work—is also necessary. The possibility of rising is a powerful spur to effort and encourages hard work. It enables industry to select workers on their merits, hiring and promoting those who produce the most regardless of their social origins.

¶ *Family Organization.* A contribution here is also made by family organization. Both social and geographic mobility tend to be stifled in a peasant community where strong family ties lead to the social identification of people according to their families, not according to their accomplishments, and where sharing of property and income among a large number of relatives ties each worker down. The smaller family characteristic of industrial society enables the breadwinner to take his wife and children with him and move to the place where opportunities are greatest, allowing him to rise in social status if he is able, and granting him the full benefits of the rewards that flow to him from occupational success. A man can carry his wife and children up the social ladder with him, but he will not travel far if he must also take with him his parents, his brothers and sisters, his aunts and uncles and cousins and in-laws. Strong ties to relatives may also hamper industrial efficiency by leading to excessive nepotism. If a man who has a job to fill hires his brother-in-law instead of looking for the man best qualified to fill the job, his brother-in-law may benefit, but the enterprise will probably suffer. No system has ever completely abolished nepotism and favoritism, but modern industry has come as close to this result as any system has. This is one additional reason for its great efficiency.

¶ *Acceptance of Innovation.* Another prerequisite for industrial development is the acceptance of change. Science and technology have reached the peaks they have through constant innovation. The habit of asking, "How can this be done better?" rather than, "How has this been done before?" is deeply rooted in industrial society, so much so that we tend to take it for granted, overlooking the fact that traditionalism has ruled in the past and that it still reigns supreme in all but the most advanced nations. Until this attitude is vanquished, backward nations will not advance. The nation whose citizens try to do their jobs exactly as their fathers before them have done theirs will be by-passed by the stream of economic progress.

¶ *Secularism.* Religious beliefs and attitudes may help or hinder economic development. Particularly in this matter of accepting innovation, a religion that relies heavily upon traditionalism and ritual may hold back economic changes. A religion that stresses other-worldly values or mysticism may divert people from the economic tasks at hand or prevent the growth of scientific inquiry. It is usual to decry the materialism of the present age and the growing secularism that removes so many areas of life from the control of spiritual values, and yet materialism and secularism of a sort would seem to be essential to industrial development. This is not to say that ideals and faith do not continue to be important. Protestantism has been intimately connected with the rise of capitalism,[7] and the Communist world has its own ideological substitute for religion in the creed of communism. But both these systems of belief lay heavy stress upon the world we live in. There is nothing in them that is incompatible with the pursuit of higher productivity.

SUMMARY

Economic development, then, is an important determinant of national power. The only way a nation can achieve great power status without industrializing is by possessing a tremendous population. For a middle-sized nation, industrialization is essential.

An industrial economy contributes to a nation's power in many ways. It produces the weapons and supplies that are required for modern warfare. It provides important international rewards (withheld, they become punishments) in the form of consumer goods and capital equipment for use in trade and aid, in the form of markets for the goods of other nations, and in the form of technical assistance. It helps a nation use persuasion in influencing other nations by providing the technical means for mass communication and by assuring a high standard of living at home, thus helping to create a loyal population and winning the admiration of the citizens of other nations.

Industrial development cannot be considered by itself, however, for it is merely the economic side of a whole way of life. Other changes must also occur if an underdeveloped nation wishes to industrialize. Specifically, industrial development is aided by political modernization, by the growth of cities, by widespread formal education, by geographic and social mobility, by the rise of the small family, by the acceptance of in-

[7] Max Weber, *The Protestant Ethic and the Spirit of Capitalism* (London: George Allen and Unwin, 1930); R. H. Tawney, *Religion and the Rise of Capitalism* (New York: Mentor Books, 1950).

novation, and by the growth of secularism. Without all these developments, industrialization, and the power it brings, could not occur.

Political Development

Another extremely important determinant of national power is the level of political modernization. We have examined at length the contribution made to a nation's power by its human resources (population) and by its material resources, both natural and man-made, but we have omitted one important consideration: the capability and more particularly the efficiency of the national government in utilizing these resources in pursuit of national goals. Such efficiency—and this is what is meant by political development—is crucial for the realization of a nation's full power potential.

Unfortunately, there is at present no generally accepted method of measuring political efficiency. People and goods can be counted, and economic efficiency can be approximately measured, but political efficiency is more elusive. The development of a good scale for measuring political efficiency is one of the most important tasks facing political scientists today.

Broad judgments of "more" or "less" efficient can be made. The government of present-day Belgium is certainly more efficient than that of the Congo; the government of the United States is more efficient than that of South Vietnam. One cannot say how much more efficient—twice as efficient, ten times as efficient—but one can say "more" or "less." Even this judgment becomes difficult, or at least subject to disagreement, when nations of not too dissimilar strength are compared. Is the government of Britain more or less efficient than that of France? Is the government of the United States more or less efficient than that of the Soviet Union? Differences over time are equally difficult to judge. We can say that the government of the Soviet Union is more efficient in mobilizing the nation's resources than that of the tsars, but was the government of John F. Kennedy more efficient than that of Franklin D. Roosevelt?

Though an exact quantitative measurement of political development cannot be made, it *is* possible to characterize most national governments roughly as being in one of three stages of political development: the politics of primitive unification, of industrialization, or of national welfare.[8] Even here the question is one of emphasis, with no clear line separating one stage from the next.

It is also possible to examine the state of development in two of

[8] See Chapter 3.

the most important governmental institutions: the bureaucracy and political parties. Both are crucial, for it is through them that the central government reaches and mobilizes its citizens for national purposes. No government can be considered to be developed (or modern) unless these institutions are effective. In countries with underdeveloped political systems (those still in stage 1), bureaucracy and party do not extend their influence out into the mass of the population. As a result, the central government can reach directly only a small fraction of the total population nominally under its control. Some of the public can be reached for limited purposes through intermediaries such as regional warlords or local authorities, but for most purposes the separation between the masses and the central government is quite complete. Government leaders may make speeches and announce programs, but 20 miles from the capital one will find another world populated by peasants only dimly aware of those who rule them.

BUREAUCRATIC DEVELOPMENT

The single most important tool available to any national government for mobilizing its human and natural resources is the governmental bureaucracy. Military bureaucrats provide the backbone of the armed forces that defend the existing social and economic system both from outside attack and from internal rebellion. Civil bureaucrats collect the governmental revenues, regulate or perhaps even run the economy, and provide governmental services that establish justice and promote the general welfare. In the stage of industrialization, the governmental bureaucracy has a crucial role to play in pushing through modernization of the economy, as we have seen in Chapter 3. With full economic development, the governmental bureaucracy experiences a further growth in power and in numbers in order to carry out the welfare programs necessary to ensure a productive and loyal population.

The relationship between the governmental bureaucracy and the economy can take a variety of forms. In socialist countries the government runs the economy through its own bureaucracy, but in nonsocialist countries most industries remain in private hands and are run by private bureaucracies. Other bureaucracies can be private as well. Taxes can be collected by private individuals who take their pay out of the tax proceeds. Even armies can be private. Many of Nationalist China's military forces were private armies,[9] and as late as 1966, semi-private armies were fighting with government troops in the Congo and in South Vietnam. Govern-

[9] Joseph W. Stilwell, *The Stilwell Papers* (New York: William Sloane Associates, 1948); F. F. Liu, *A Military History of Modern China* (Princeton: Princeton University Press, 1956).

ments, in fact, may function with almost no bureaucracy at all, but when the major bureaucracies in the nation are private it can be taken as a sure sign that the nation's political system is underdeveloped.

Control of the military bureaucracy is particularly important. A monopoly of the use of force must rest in the hands of any effective government. Without control of the armed forces, a government's authority at home rests on precarious grounds, and its ability to influence other nations through the use of force is strictly limited.

For effective action, control of the armed forces and control of the rest of the nation's governmental machinery must be in the same hands, but it makes a difference whether the army controls the government or the government controls the army. Roughly, one can distinguish three kinds of nations:

1. Nations in which the army runs the government, and in which the defection of a division is enough to make a government fall —for example, Greece, Iran, most of the Arab and African nations, many of the Southeast Asian countries, and some of the Latin-American republics.
2. Nations in which the army is an important power, but in which there are also other sources of power upon which the national government can rely. Here the national government seeks the support of the armed forces, but they are not supreme. Examples would be Nazi Germany, prewar Japan, and China during the Cultural Revolution of 1966–1967.
3. Nations in which the armed forces do not play a leading role in government, although individual military leaders may rise to important positions in the civil government. This is usually the case in most of the developed nations.

It is not easy to say which of these systems contributes most to a nation's power. One might expect that military forces would be the largest and best prepared in countries run by the army, but in actuality other factors seem to be more important: for example, the level of economic development, the perception of military threat, and the amount of foreign military aid.

POLITICAL PARTIES

Political parties also serve as a valuable link between the government of a nation and the masses of its citizens, particularly in the more developed political systems. In the advanced mass democracies of the West, political parties fill two important functions for the government:

1. They serve as a channel for the expression of the popular will.

Through elections officials who have pursued unpopular policies are removed from office. Between elections, political parties generally encourage consensus politics by discouraging the nomination of candidates thought likely to lose the next election. Political parties and contested elections provide the government with valuable information on the views of the voters, encouraging the formation of policies that will find considerable short-run support.

2. Political parties in the mass democracies also provide a channel from the government back to the masses, helping the government to manipulate the voters by propagandizing them, by arousing their partisan enthusiasm, and by limiting the policy choices of the electorate to a small number of practical alternatives.

Both in the bourgeois democracies in stage 2 of their political development and in the mass democracies of stage 3, the function of representation tends to be emphasized. In the totalitarian governments of stages 2 and 3, however, manipulation is more heavily emphasized, although representation is not totally absent.

In the new nations now undergoing primitive unification, the political party is filling a new function: aiding in national unification. In these countries an interesting reversal of the Western experience is taking place. In the West, the expansion of the franchise and the growth of political parties followed economic and political modernization, but in the new nations, political parties and universal suffrage are preceding and helping to expand the political consciousness and national identity of the masses. Elections help focus attention upon the policies and actions of the national government, and through voting, even in elections where there is often no real choice, the citizens perform one of their few truly national acts.

Newly independent nations are often one-party states, either legally or in actuality, but it would be a mistake to write off their elections as therefore meaningless. Divided into separate ethnic and regional groups as these nations often are, they find in a one-party government perhaps their only significant nationwide institution. The party provides the government with an important means of increasing national consciousness, spreading nationalistic sentiments, and furthering national unity.

EFFECT UPON NATIONAL POWER

It is clear, then, that an orderly process of political development can be identified that is roughly parallel to the process of economic development. In country after country we have seen increasing governmental efficiency in mobilizing national resources as the nation moves through recognizable stages of political development. There remains the task of showing that political development contributes to national power.

Unfortunately, it is not possible to repeat with political modernization the procedure we have used in calculating the effect of other variables upon the power of nations. Lacking a common scale of measurement, we cannot list the most politically developed nations and see how the list accords with our ideas of their relative power.

A grouping of nations according to *stage* of political development can be made, however. It would show some association of political development with power. With the possible exception of India, no major world powers would be found among the nations in stage 1, and with the exception of China, none in stage 2. In other words, all the major world powers are characterized by highly developed political systems unless they possess extremely large populations that may compensate to some extent for political underdevelopment. However, political modernization alone is clearly not enough to guarantee great power status, for such nations as Switzerland, New Zealand, and Israel are highly developed politically but of only moderate power.

Knowing as we do that many factors affect the relative power of nations, the best procedure for showing the influence of political efficiency would be to hold constant some of the other important factors, such as population size and level of economic development. Let us look for nations that are roughly equal in population size and economic development but that differ significantly in political development. Will there be a parallel difference in their power? It is not easy to find such pairs, for if two nations are similar in economic development they generally do not differ much in the level of their political modernization. It is possible, however, to find few examples.

North and South Vietnam provide one such pair. They do not differ greatly in population size (North Vietnam is a little larger), and their level of economic development is roughly similar (North Vietnam is slightly more advanced), but there is a marked difference in their political efficiency in mobilizing resources. The government of North Vietnam has been stable for many years, has thorough control over its population, and operates a planned economy. The government of South Vietnam, on the other hand, has been subject to constant upheaval, with military coups, regional and religious divisions, and a full-scale civil war against the Vietcong. It does not control large parts of the territory and population within its national boundaries, and it has difficulty obtaining sacrifice and service from the citizens it does control. The difference in power between these two nations is what we would expect it to be. Because of effective mobilization of its resources, North Vietnam is considerably more powerful and would undoubtedly defeat the South Vietnamese in battle if American military assistance were withdrawn.

An even clearer illustration of the generation of power through political modernization is provided by the Vietcong in the South. There were in 1968 perhaps 250,000 Vietcong rebels helped by some 60,000 North Vietnamese resisting an American army of some 525,000 helped by some 700,000 men of the South Vietnamese army and backed by the immense industrial might of the United States. In terms of foreign aid, American expenditure in the Vietnamese War from 1965 to early 1968 was estimated at roughly $35 billion; Russian and Chinese aid to the rebels, at $1 billion. The estimates are rough but they reveal the magnitude of difference in men and resources. Only the highly modern political organization of the rebels made it possible for them to resist.

A less dramatic example of the importance of political development is provided by a comparison of the Philippines and Thailand, two nations that are again roughly equal in population size (33 as against 32 million) and in level of economic development (per capita GNP $136 as against $126). Here again the level of political development differs. The Philippines is a bourgeois democracy with some of the governmental forms of a mass democracy. There is an active if not highly efficient nationwide bureaucracy and competing nationwide political parties. Thailand, on the other hand, is an old-fashioned monarchy run by a traditional elite, clearly a stage-1 government. Again the difference in power is as expected; the Philippines carries far more weight in international councils than Thailand.

Still one more instance of the importance of political development can be provided, this time in a single country that has undergone sudden changes in its political efficiency: mainland China. In 1949 China was at a low ebb of power. The country was exhausted by civil war, Chiang Kai-shek's armies had disintegrated or fled to Formosa, and the new Communist government was just beginning to assume control. Yet only one year later, China successfully took on the United States in a limited war in Korea and held her own against the greatest military power on earth.

This case amounts almost to a natural experiment. Geography, resources, population size, and economic development remained constant or nearly so. Only one major determinant of power had changed: there had been a massive modernization of the political system, and for the first time in centuries the central government of China had the capacity to reach and to mobilize the Chinese masses.

More recently, Communist China has provided an example of a

different sort. Throughout the 1950s and the early 1960s China's growing power was increasingly recognized until she was considered by many to be not only the major challenger of the Soviet Union but also the major challenger of the United States. Then deep fissures appeared within the Chinese Communist political system, culminating in the Cultural Revolution of 1966–1967. China's leaders quarreled among themselves, military revolts broke out in some of the provinces, and the activities of the Red Guards disrupted life from one end of the country to the other. The effect upon China's power was immediate. Her prestige and influence in Southeast Asia plummeted. Her satellites reasserted their independence, and her influence over Communist nations in Eastern Europe and over Communist movements in the underdeveloped areas waned.

Political development, then, has a major influence upon the power of nations. Let us examine more closely the ways in which this influence is exercised.

¶ *Persuasion.* Political efficiency increases the ability of a nation to persuade others (and to resist their persuasion in turn) by increasing unity within the nation. A government whose people are united behind its policies can speak firmly in international councils. A nation whose own political system works smoothly can offer its political ideology as an example for others to follow. To realize the tremendous importance of effective political control at home one need only consider the immense damage done to the image of the United States and to the effectiveness of American propaganda abroad by the race riots that annually break out in American cities. Though sporadic and temporary, these breakdowns in law and order indicate that the American political system has not yet found effective ways of dealing with critical economic and social problems in the field of race relations.

The major task of influencing the policies of other nations through persuasion falls to a country's diplomats and to its propagandists. When it comes to diplomacy, the level of political development does not seem to make quite so much difference. The individual diplomats of a nation may be highly skilled, even though the nation as a whole is backward. It is the job of the diplomat to make the most of whatever power resources his nation possesses. In one respect his job is difficult, for while skilled diplomacy cannot add much to the power of a small, weak nation, poor diplomacy can detract considerably from the power of a great nation.

Attempts at persuading other nations are aimed not only at official representatives; they are also aimed directly at the people of other nations. Through propaganda broadcasts, publications, and speeches that will be reported in other nations, a government reaches over the heads of the other governments with which it deals and appeals directly to their citizens. Skills in propaganda vary greatly from one nation to another, but again level of political development does not seem to be the main determinant of the differences in skill.

¶ *Rewards and Punishments.* The role of political efficiency is perhaps clearer in the meting out of rewards and punishments to other nations. Foreign aid is granted to other nations primarily by governmental action, and only a relatively developed government controls enough resources and has firm enough control of its population to give away or to loan any significant amount of the nation's production to other nations for political purposes. One form of foreign aid positively demands a highly developed government: the granting of technical assistance to other nations in modernizing their own political institutions.

The national government must also decide what amount of trade and what kind of trade to allow with other nations, what export and import regulations to impose, and what financial decisions to make that affect the international community. All these decisions are better made (and certainly better enforced) by a highly developed political system.

Not only does the government select the proper time and manner of granting rewards; it also helps create the rewards that can be given. This is particularly true in the realm of economic rewards, for what the government does or does not do has a tremendous effect upon a nation's economic life.

Without the proper political setting, an industrial system cannot develop and cannot persist. Modern industry requires that there be peace within the nation, that banditry, warlordism, and civil disturbances be prevented. It requires machinery for the peaceful settlement of economic disputes. Negotiation may be left in the hands of labor and management and strikes may be allowed, but the government must stand ready to prevent a resort to violence to settle industrial disputes. Industry requires a stable national currency and a credit system closely enough controlled to be trusted. Taxes may be high but they cannot be arbitrary, for businesses must have in advance some idea of what their expenses will be. Above all, the financial program of the government must be one that allows the accumulation of capital, by private individuals or by the government itself, for use in further modernization. Since the American government provides all these conditions, and has for many years, we tend to be unaware that without them our industrial structure would collapse.

Beyond providing these minimum requirements, a government can take positive steps to aid industrialization. We noted in Chapter 3 the wide range of governmental activity undertaken in the past by bourgeois, Stalinist, and syncratic governments to encourage economic modernization. We see today many examples of the ways in which political modernization is preceding and hastening economic modernization, helping to create the many economic rewards and punishments which a modern government has at its disposal to help influence the behavior of other nations.

Government policies influence not only how much a nation produces, but also what kind of goods and services are produced and how they are allocated. This is obviously true where the government runs the economy directly, but to a lesser extent the same result can be achieved where the economy is privately controlled, through the use of taxes, credit regulations, import and export policies, and government purchases. Even in the United States, the federal government is responsible for spending roughly one-fifth of the national income[10] (much more in time of major war). A customer as large as this has a good deal to say about what the economy produces.

Economic decisions important to a nation's power must be made by any national government. The government participates in the decision as to how much production is to go into consumer goods and how much into heavy industry, a very important decision for a nation's power in the long run. The government determines how much production will be devoted to military output and how much to goods and services for civilians. It is not an easy matter to determine how large a military budget a nation can afford. Too small a military output will handicap a nation in the use of force; too large a share for military goods may damage the economy, cut down the economic rewards that can be offered to other nations, and create consumer discontent at home. This is a political decision of the first importance.

¶ *Force.* It is probably in the use of force that political modernization helps a nation the most, for the ability to collect young men from all over a nation and organize them into units that will fight effectively at the risk of their own lives is a crucial test of that nation's ability to mobilize its resources. The efficiency of a nation's armed forces is directly related to its political modernization, as the wars between politically modern Israel and her well-equipped but badly organized Arab neighbors showed conclusively.

[10] The national budget in fiscal 1967 amounted to 19 percent of the 1967 national income.

One question remains: Is there any one form of government that provides a power advantage over other forms of government? It would seem fairly obvious that political systems which have reached the stage of national welfare have marked power advantages over political systems still struggling with primitive unification or industrialization. They have behind them more unified citizens and a richer economy. Their government bureaucracies and political parties are better instruments of popular representation and control. In short, they are more efficient in mobilizing the human and material resources of the nation in pursuit of national goals.

However, the question still remains: Among the more politically developed nations, what are the relative merits in terms of power of democratic and totalitarian government, other things being equal?

This is not an easy question to answer. Convinced as we are that democratic government is the best government, that it provides its citizens with the highest standard of living, with the greatest spiritual, artistic, and scientific freedom, and that democracy is the system under which men live the happiest lives, we also tend to assume that this is the system that provides the greatest national power and that it will therefore win out in any competition or combat with totalitarianism. We want so badly to believe in the victory of all that we value most, we have such a large emotional investment in believing that right is might, that we tend to overlook any facts that might indicate the contrary. Most writers in democratic countries come to the conclusion that democratic government is not only best but also most powerful. This is not to say that their conclusion is incorrect, but merely that it is somewhat suspect. It is not easy to examine a question scientifically when you know what you want the outcome to be.

Our purpose here, however, is to attempt such an objective examination of the relative power of democratic and totalitarian government. Even if we can set aside all emotional bias, the problem is not an easy one. So many incomparable things must be compared. The best that can be done is to indicate some of the obvious power advantages of each kind of system, leaving the final balancing of these different advantages to the reader.

In the formation of foreign policy, a totalitarian government no doubt finds it easier to form a single, unified, specific policy, since disagreements within the government are suppressed. Because fewer people have a voice in the formation of foreign policy, it can be formed more rapidly and reversed more easily if the situation demands a rapid shift.

However, these totalitarian advantages of speed and unity must be weighed against the democratic advantage of representativeness. In a democracy, the foreign policy adopted is open to criticism from within the government and from the public. Before such policy is set, many divergent opinions will be considered, thus guaranteeing a broader view of the situation to which the policy relates. Under these circumstances, one might expect democratic foreign policy to be more carefully considered, less bound by dogma in its assessment of other nations, and therefore more appropriate.

The major requirement for the formation of effective foreign policy, however, would seem to be that the men who make the policies be intelligent, realistic, and well informed. This is a factor that does not appear to have much connection with the form of government. Both democracies and totalitarian governments have had their share of brilliant statesmen and of miserable failures.

When it comes to the use of persuasion, totalitarian governments have certain definite advantages. Internally, a totalitarian government can use propaganda to gain support for foreign policy in a way that is impossible in any democratic country. A totalitarian government, controlling the media of mass communication, can tell its people anything it pleases, and particularly in the field of international relations, where the factual evidence may lie in other countries, the government can lie with relative impunity. Thus President Nasser of the United Arab Republic was able in 1967 to withhold from most of his people the fact that Israel unaided had defeated Arab forces and that the war was over.

Deception on this scale is impossible in a democratic country, where official statements must be exposed to possible contradiction. The political opposition, after all, rises on the misfortunes of those in office, and one of the main tasks of the opposition in a democracy is to find fault with official decisions and policies. In addition, the news media conduct their own relentless search for the truth, particularly for scandalous or derogatory truths that officials might wish to hide. Consider the war in Vietnam, for example, in which the American public was treated to opposition speeches, peace protests, and even to daily television coverage of the battlefields. Indeed, one important reason for widespread American disenchantment with the war in Vietnam was undoubtedly the television coverage in which real war, with all its confusion and brutality, was for the first time in history experienced directly by civilians at home.

Monopolization of the media of mass communication and the ability to lie unchallenged are powerful tools in the hands of totalitarian governments. So, too, is the use of professional agitators, whose job is to whip up support for government decisions.[11] These are tools a democratic government does not want and would not use, but there is no question they provide a great advantage when it comes to selling government foreign policy to the public. The counterbalancing advantage that democratic governments can claim is that their policies do not need so much selling in the first place because they are more closely based on what the public wants.

Government propaganda directed at other nations also seems to be a totalitarian specialty. For some reason, democratic nations have been slow to make as much use of this method of international persuasion as totalitarian nations. The government of Nazi Germany specialized in propaganda and in retrospect seems to have been almost unbelievably successful in convincing large sections of the American and British publics in the 1930s that Hitler's intentions were peaceful. The Soviet Union has also mounted gigantic propaganda campaigns, but with the possible exception of the war years, neither the United States nor Britain has made similar efforts. For all the current talk about psychological warfare, Voice of America, Radio Free Europe, and so on, American expenditures on foreign propaganda have been comparatively small.

One problem faced by democratic governments propagandizing foreign citizens is that official efforts are always supplemented by private communications that are beyond the control of the government. American movies, TV series, and magazines have spread a picture of American life that has influenced the way many foreigners react to American policy. Sometimes the influence is beneficial; sometimes it is not. In depicting a life of plenty, these private media have been helpful in "selling" the American way of life, but they have also painted other pictures that may not be so favorable to American prestige. It is said, for example, that American magazines have quite a following in India, not because of their stories or their editorial comment, but because they are so filled with ads of women in their underwear. Obviously, government films and publications can be more closely controlled so that they carry the message the government wants carried, but for this very reason, they are sometimes less effective. Totalitarian propaganda is better controlled but it probably suffers from lower credibility.

When it comes to economic power, so important in dispensing international rewards and punishments, it is not altogether clear where the advantage lies. The totalitarian government, of course, has much closer

[11] The city of Moscow was said in 1950 to have one agitator for every thirty members of the population. See Alex Inkeles, *Public Opinion in the Soviet Union* (Cambridge, Mass.: Harvard University Press, 1950).

control over the national economy and can use it for power purposes even in the face of popular opposition. Especially in its control over foreign trade, the totalitarian government possesses a political weapon that democratic governments lack. Most important of all, a totalitarian government can force the pace of economic development, exacting greater economic sacrifices from a population that cannot vote it out of office.

Totalitarian governments, then, have certain advantages in developing their national economies rapidly and in using national wealth for power purposes once it is developed. However, to date, these advantages have been completely offset by the superior wealth of the democratic nations. Democratic governments may control a far smaller proportion of their nations' wealth, but these nations are so much richer that even so, the government has at its disposal a far greater supply of goods and services than any totalitarian regime. With all its waste and freedom, the American government controls resources beyond the wildest dreams of any Russian dictator. This shows up clearly in the field of foreign aid. No totalitarian government can begin to afford the kind of foreign aid programs that America has had for two decades. Again, totalitarian regimes may be able to industrialize their people more rapidly, but the long, slow development under democratic rule in nations like the United States and Britain has produced a kind of economic wealth that totalitarian newcomers are still a long way from approaching. The crucial question is this: Can totalitarian nations develop economies as rich as those developed under democratic governments? If they cannot, the democratic nations may maintain superior economic power because of their greatly superior wealth. If they can, however, we are in for serious trouble, for a fully developed industrial economy together with centralized direction of that economy for power purposes is a combination that must give us pause. The one fully industrialized nation to become totalitarian was Nazi Germany, and before she was stopped by defeat in war, she gave the world quite an illustration of the effectiveness of controlled economic power.

The military area is the place where one might expect a totalitarian government to have the greatest advantage, for certainly it is in times of war that centralized control, immediate decisions, unity within the government, secrecy, unquestioning obedience, and other qualities characteristic of totalitarian government are most required. Oddly enough, this expectation is not justified. In wartime, democratic governments suddenly transform themselves. The national government takes firm control of many areas that are usually beyond its scope, and the public voluntarily agrees to many temporary restrictions upon its customary liberties. Whatever power advantages totalitarian governments may possess largely vanish in war, for then the people of democratic nations voluntarily adopt a sort of "dictatorship-for-the-moment," a dictatorship which is the stronger for being voluntary and temporary. To make a just comparison of the military power of democratic and totalitarian nations, we must compare them not only in periods of peace when the totalitarians seem to have an edge in belligerency and in military strength, but also in the long swing of war and peace. We see then that the democracies possess a flexibility of structure that enables them to reap the military advantages of centralized control and discipline without losing the advantage of voluntary popular support.

In conclusion, the power position of the democratically governed nations in the world today is far superior to that of the totalitarian nations. Many factors contribute to this state of affairs, and form of government appears to be one of them. Democratic foreign policies take more account of public opinion at home. Democratic efforts to persuade other nations are more firmly based on truth. Democratic economies are far richer than those of the totalitarian nations, and democratic armies are equally effective. What totalitarian government does provide is a way of making up for some of the deficiencies of totalitarian nations. Totalitarian governments can "sell" unpopular foreign policies through their monopoly of the means of mass persuasion. They can use propaganda heavily larded with lies to cover up truths that might mar their arguments. They can develop their economies more rapidly, and they can utilize to the full the power potentialities of whatever wealth their nations have.

The most powerful nation in the world today is a democracy. This is not a coincidence. But the second greatest power in the world is a totalitarian dictatorship. This should give us food for thought.

SUMMARY

Political development is another important determinant of national power, for it is largely through govenmental direction that the human and material resources of a nation are mobilized to influence the behavior of other nations. Political development increases internal unity, stimulates economic development with all its important consequences for power, and organizes men and material into effective fighting forces.

The relative advantage of democratic over totalitarian government in terms of power is not easy to calculate, but it is clear that highly developed stage-3 political systems—whether democratic or totalitarian —enjoy a marked power advantage over those in stages 1 or 2.

There remains one important determinant of national power: an elusive quality which, for lack of a better term, we shall call "national morale." It consists of a state of mind. Sometimes it is called patriotism or love of country. It is an important ingredient of nationalism. What it amounts to is a willingness by a large percentage of the individuals in a nation's population to put the nation's welfare above their own, or to see the two as one.

This willingness to sacrifice has an important effect upon the ability of a nation to influence the behavior of other nations. One of the places where this effect is most obvious is in the nation's military forces. "Morale," indeed, is a term most often used to refer to the mental condition of troops. The army whose men are more concerned with preserving their lives or with enriching themselves than with winning battles does not fight effectively. No matter how large and how well-equipped, it is not a great source of strength to the nation that possesses it.

To see that armies differ widely in their morale, one need only look at recent international history. Remember the fanatic dedication of the Japanese soldiers in World War II, willing to fight to the last man if ordered to, preferring suicide to surrender, or the fierce determination of Israeli soldiers in their wars against the Arabs. Compare the behavior of the French army defeated by the Nazis, or of the Chinese Nationalist armies, retreating before the battles were fought, deserting to the enemy by divisions, giving up one of the largest countries in the world with hardly a single major military encounter.[12] Again compare the dedication of soldiers in North Vietnam with the general behavior of Vietnamese soldiers of the South.

One can distinguish between the morale of officers and men. It is possible to imagine an army of valiant and loyal soldiers that surrenders because its top officers sell out to the enemy. It is possible to imagine an army with dedicated officers whose men won't fight, but generally the morale of officers and men rises and falls together. Particularly does the attitude of the officers affect the men. Widespread differences between a privileged officers corps and the body of common soldiers may help to lower morale among the soldiers, but this is not universally true. Although privileges for officers produce gripes among American G.I.s, they seem to have helped, not hurt, morale in the Japanese and German

[12] See F. F. Liu, *A Military History of Modern China* (Princeton: Princeton University Press, 1956), chap. 19.

armies, whose soldiers apparently wanted officers they could look up to. We are involved here with cultural differences, and it is better not to generalize too broadly.

A willingness to sacrifice and to stand up under attack is also important among the civilian population. Modern warfare is not confined to battlefields. Civilian populations are subjected to merciless bombing and strafing. Even when they do not participate directly in military action, they must make extra efforts and submit to real hardships. They are called upon to work harder, to produce more, to consume less, to do without luxuries and even without necessities, and to bear up cheerfully while friends and members of their families are taken away for governmental service, many of them never to return. In the extreme case, civilians may have to undergo the rigors of enemy occupation.

Differences in national morale can be seen from one nation to another and from one age to another. The will of the Italians in World never strong, crumbled under a series of Allied victories in World War II. The English, on the other hand, withstood a punishing air assault with courage and good spirits which astounded everyone. Since the Civil War, the American population has never had its morale severely tested. Since then, Americans have fought all their wars far away from home, and they have been on the winning side in every case. They have been called upon to send their boys to war, but other than that, few serious sacrifices have been asked of them. During World War II, civilian living standards actually increased in spite of greater military production. How the Americans would act under heavy bombing or in defeat is anybody's guess. Our record for minor sacrifices is not good. We grumbled at rationing and took to the black markets all too readily in World War II (compared to the English, for example, who pulled in their belts without a complaint). During the Korean and Vietnamese wars, few civilians seemed ready to give up any of their comforts. However, it may be that if we were fighting for our lives, as the English were, we would respond more heroically.

Sacrifices for one's country may also be required in peacetime, though on a lesser scale. Poor countries, in particular, may be called upon to reduce consumption for military spending or for capital investment needed to industrialize, and even moderately rich nations may be called upon to accept austerity programs. Businessmen may be required to accept smaller profits than they feel they are entitled to, workers to accept smaller take-home pay, consumers to do without many of the things they would like to have, because a nation is arming or because it is building industries for the future. Civilian sacrifice in peacetime takes its most common form in the payment of taxes to the government, and it is interesting to note the different attitudes toward taxes that people have. No one likes to pay his taxes, but the tax rates that will be tolerated vary greatly from one country to another, and the amount of evasion of taxes also varies. Since the war, the British have paid taxes that appear staggering to Americans. Americans, though complaining and cheating a little here and there, themselves pay tax bills that are considerable. Before De Gaulle, however, the French considered it an outrage to pay taxes.[13] It is said that many Parisian businessmen kept three sets of account books—one to show the tax collector; the second to be produced when the tax collector demanded to see the true books; the third to be used when the businessman wanted to know how much he really made.

Military service may also come under the heading of peacetime sacrifice. Mothers are never happy to see their sons sent off to training camps, nor are most young men pleased about interrupting their education or their work careers to serve in the army. The British, the French, and the Italians, however, accept universal conscription of young men as a matter of course, while in the United States the idea that every young man should serve for a year or two in the army has never been accepted outside of wartime. Various proposals to set up such a system have been abandoned because of popular opposition.

DETERMINANTS OF MORALE

What causes this willingness of individuals in some nations and the refusal or reluctance of individuals in other nations to put the national welfare above their own? One important factor is surely the degree of identification that individuals feel with the nation. Is the nation a significant unit in their lives? Do they often think of themselves as Americans, Frenchmen, Chinese, etc., or do they usually think of themselves as members of some other group such as Republicans or farmers or Catholics or Parisians or members of the Chen family?

Identifications and loyalties that extend beyond the nation can sometimes be used as motives for national sacrifice if the nation as a whole can in turn be identified with some larger unit. Thus Egyptians, nearly all of whom are Muslims, may fight against Israel out of loyalty to Egypt or out of loyalty to Islam. Practically speaking, the result is the same. Similarly the USSR may exhort her people to fight for communism or for Russia, and Americans may fight "to make the world

---

[13] Note the Poujade movement of 1955, in which small French shopkeepers literally terrorized the government into changing its tax laws by refusing to pay their taxes, by assaulting tax collectors, and by threatening political action. See *The New York Times*, Jan. 18, 1955, p. 1, col. 1.

safe for democracy" or to protect "the American way of life." Other supernational loyalties, however, may be held by only part of a nation's population and may therefore have a divisive effect, preventing these people from aiding their nation against other members of the same group. American Jews will find it hard to support any American policy that favors the Arab nations over Israel, just as many German-Americans found themselves with a severe problem of conflicting loyalties in World War I and to a lesser extent in World War II. Socialists before World War I were supposed to be so devoted to each other and to peace that they would refuse to fight in national armies, although the war proved that when the chips were down, nationalism was a stronger force than their professed principles.

Loyalties to smaller groups within the nation also sometimes compete with national loyalties and make the members of these groups less willing to make sacrifices for national goals. A national war effort may require a cessation of labor disputes, but devoted members of a militant union may find it hard to accept the idea that they should sacrifice their union's interests even temporarily for the sake of war production. The national interest may call for freer trade and lower tariffs throughout the world so that America's allies can sell their goods and so that American consumers can buy foreign goods at reasonable prices if they want to, but the particular American industry that will make less money if the protection given it by tariffs is taken away may be unwilling to suffer the loss.

The strongest loyalty and identification for many people is to and with themselves and their immediate families, but nationalism and patriotism demand that this, too, give way to national interests. The sacrifice demanded may be simply an inconvenience, a few hours taken from pleasure for work in civil defense, or it may involve actual discomfort, as when taxes are paid with money that could have been spent on badly need clothing or better housing or medical service. The sacrifice may require the absence of a father or husband or sweetheart for many years. The greatest sacrifice—and this, too, is demanded by nations—is that an individual be willing to die for his country.

The balance of these conflicting loyalties to nation, region, religion, class, family, and self varies from one nation to another. One need only compare the Germans and the Israelis with their strong (but differing) ethnic loyalties, the Japanese with their devotion to the emperor as a symbol of the nation, the English with their calm insistence on remaining English, the Italians with their loyalties to city and to region, the Chinese with their emphasis on family (a loyalty their Communist rulers are seeking to supersede), the French filled with love of France but torn by class conflict and a sort of super-individualism.

Faith in the national government is certainly an important determinant of individual willingness to make sacrifices for the nation. A man may love his country, but if he feels that the national government does not represent the nation, he will not leap to sacrifice himself for causes the government calls "national."

Willingness on the part of individuals to make sacrifices for the nation depends not only upon identification with the nation and upon confidence that the national government does indeed represent the nation, but also upon the prevailing political ideology. Every political system has its ideology, a system of ideas as to how the world is and how it ought to be. Each ideology includes a definition of the relations between citizens and state, and to the extent that this ideology is genuinely believed and followed by the population and is not simply a statement of hopes by the political administration, it can have an important influence upon willingness to sacrifice.

Obviously, ideologies that emphasize the role of the group and particularly the role of the state while minimizing the importance of the individual will be more apt to produce that blind devotion and fanaticism that characterized Nazi Germany and Imperial Japan than will democratic ideologies. The essence of democracy lies in its assertion of the importance of the individual and his welfare. A democratic government cannot command and does not seek blind devotion and fanaticism. It relies upon enlightened self-interest combined with feelings of duty and affection to bring its citizens to its support when help against the outside is required.

Ideologies are important in another respect. As ideas held in common by many individuals, an ideology helps to unify the nation, and as a systematic statement of the nation's aims, it helps to justify the goals and actions of the government. It is therefore an aid to the government in finding support from its citizens. However, there are also dangers here. No ideology conforms exactly to the facts as they exist, but an ideology that paints a picture of the ideal world too different from reality may leave those who hold it open to exploitation by enemy propaganda. Communist propaganda in the United States hammers so heavily upon the theme of race relations partly because this is one area where American ideology and practice are not in accord. (The solution, of course, is to alter the practice, not the ideology, but the point is that the gap between them leaves Americans vulnerable.) Americans have used a similar propaganda opportunity in emphasizing the difference between Communist ideology against imperialism and Communist practice in the Russian satellite nations. One of the most effective propaganda techniques is to use a people's own ideology to turn them against their government.

Finally, a political ideology can be exportable. Communism is such an ideology, for in theory it is tied to no single political unit but is phrased in terms that appeal to people of many different nationalities. Nazism, on the other hand, was too thoroughly bound up with ideas of a German master race to have widespread appeal among non-Germans. Democracy, by all rights, should have a worldwide following, for its ideology is rich in ideas that have a universal appeal. A crucial task for the Western world in the immediate future is to rephrase and reshape the democratic ideology in such a way that it can stand up against the challenge of communism not only in Western countries that have already known political freedom, but also in poverty-stricken, underdeveloped nations that have lived under tyranny for centuries.

National morale, then, is our last determinant of national power. It is in part a consequence of political organization and in part an extension of nationalism, of political ideology, and of cultural identifications. High morale makes it possible for the government to devote a greater proportion of the nation's resources to the pursuit of national goals. Morale is always important, but it is crucial in time of war.

Summary

The determinants of national power are many. Size of territory, geographical location, the possession of natural resources, population size, age structure of the population, rate of population growth, industrial development, urbanization, education, geographic and social mobility among the population, family structure, intellectual attitudes toward innovation, religious beliefs, political development, skill in diplomacy and propaganda, military strength, military and civilian morale, and political ideology, all contribute to the ability of a nation to influence the behavior of other nations.

The nation that wishes to achieve its goals must have the power to do so. Many of the materials and the qualities that give power to a nation will be sought as good things in themselves. Other qualities, however, particularly in the realm of social and political organization, will not be sought by all, even though they do increase a nation's power, for power is not the only goal of nations. Power is necessary for the pursuit of other goals, but to give up those goals in the very search for power would be a fool's solution.

9

The Road to Power

The task of this concluding chapter on national power is fourfold: first, to show some of the interrelationships among the major determinants of power and to locate the overall patterns of change in the determinants; second, to evaluate the relative importance of the various determinants of national power; third, to form a simple index by which the power of a nation can be measured; and fourth, to determine what a nation should do to keep or to increase its power in international politics.

Relationships Among Determinants

Up to this point, we have considered the determinants of national power one by one, isolating each factor in order to see more clearly its contribution to the power of the nation. Here and there, we have dropped broad hints that these various factors have some relationship to each other, but for the most part we have treated each one independently. The reader may have been left with the impression that major changes in one determinant, say, economic development, can occur quite independently of what is happening to the political system or to the population size of the nation.

Nothing could be further from the truth. All the determinants, and most particularly the social determinants, are related to each other,

190

and major changes in any one will be accompanied by changes in all the rest. In broad outline, we can see a definite pattern of change where several determinants appear to change together, going through a recognizable and predictable process. Specifically, we can see definite connections between changes in political development and economic development and definite connections between both of these and changes in the population.

THE PATTERN OF ECONOMIC CHANGE

Economic changes are among the most dramatic that have occurred in modern nations, and the pattern of economic change is one that is both obvious and thoroughly familiar to the reader; it is the pattern of industrialization. Nation after nation has gone through this process, and in each case a number of similar changes have occurred. The division of labor has become much more complex, and economic specialization has increased. Machines have been introduced, and production has been rationalized and standardized.

Perhaps the most basic change has been a steady increase in productivity per man-hour, so that the amount of goods and services that the workers in a nation produce goes up and up. Living standards rise along with this increased production.

There is also a pattern of change in the way that people earn their living. In a preindustrial economy, the majority of people are subsistence farmers. Early in the industrialization process, however, a revolution in agriculture occurs. New methods and new equipment greatly increase agricultural efficiency and free workers for other jobs. In the early stages of industrialization, many of these people go into mining and manufacturing. At a still later stage, a great expansion occurs in the jobs connected with distributing goods and with providing various services. Thus, a look at the occupational statistics of a nation going through the industrialization process reveals first, a vast majority of the population in agriculture, then a shrinkage of the proportion of workers in agriculture accompanied by a great swelling of the proportion in mining and manufacture, and finally, a shift out of mining and manufacturing into distribution and services with a continued decrease in the proportion in agriculture. Future efficiencies in distribution may well bring about still another shift, out of distribution and into the various professions such as teaching, medicine, and entertainment.

New forms of economic relationships also appear. Self-sufficiency and barter vanish to be replaced by a complex, monetary economy laced with whole networks of credit. Impersonal economic dealings replace the old personal, semisocial transactions.

It is fascinating to note that these same changes have occurred in every single nation that has industrialized, no matter how different their original cultures were. If one looks at details, great differences can be found between the industrialization of, say, England, the United States, Russia, and Japan, but in broad outline, such as we have sketched above, the process was the same, and we can predict that it will be the same for other nations in the future. What's more, the changes are always in the same direction. Nation after nation has moved from peasant agriculture to modern industrialism, but there is not a single case to date of an industrial nation reverting to a peasant state. Industrialization provides a pattern of major importance. Indeed, it is the pattern that, more than any other, characterizes the age in which we live, an age that might well be called "the worldwide industrial revolution."

THE PATTERN OF POLITICAL CHANGE

Political development also appears to be a one-way process, as nation after nation moves toward increased political efficiency. Several trends become evident as we review the history of modern nations. One basic trend is the constant expansion of the political system through the absorption of new groups. Beginning with a small elite group, the modern nation has enlarged its political institutions to include the participation first of the middle classes and eventually of the masses, both in totalitarian and in democratic systems. This process of political mobilization has continued in the most developed nations to the point where only a small number of citizens are bypassed and excluded from political awareness and participation.

It should be stressed that this process of political mobilization or recruitment of new members into the political system is not to be confused with what Karl Deutsch has called "social mobilization,"[1] or the prying loose of individuals from a traditional setting, making them available for participation in more modern forms of behavior. *Political* mobilization occurs when an individual (in or out of a traditional setting) is reached by one of the capillaries of the political network and becomes a person who must be taken into account in politics. Social mobilization and political mobilization often accompany each other; one may even cause the other; but they are not the same.

A second pattern of political change that we have identified is the alteration in the primary function of government as the political system moves from one stage of development to another: the shifting emphasis from creating national unity, to encouraging the creation of capital for

[1] Karl Deutsch, "Social Mobilization and Political Development," *American Political Science Review,* 55 (September 1961), 493–514.

economic development, to protecting the economic and social welfare of the masses. This pattern stands out clearly in the experience of nations already developed and can be expected to be repeated in the countries that have yet to modernize their governments.

As national governments broaden their base and change their function, they also change their structure. An almost universal trend toward big government, with increasing numbers of civil servants, increasing governmental budgets, and increasing differentiation of the political structure is discernible. We have noted the enhanced importance and effectiveness of governmental bureaucracies and political parties.

It is not possible to identify a clear trend toward increasing democratization, that is, toward giving the common people an important voice in the making of political decisions. Though this has been the history of the West, it has not been true of other areas of the world. Democratic and nondemocratic governments have both appeared at all three stages of political development.

Political modernization, as we have seen in Chapter 3, is intimately related to economic modernization, though their relative priority has varied from one nation to another. In nations such as England and the United States, where the motive force for industrialization was found outside of government, the modernization of the economy proceeded a considerable distance under archaic forms of government better suited to a preindustrial economy. Modernization of the government, particularly political mobilization, came *after* modernization of the economy.

In nations that have industrialized more recently, however, specifically in the Soviet Union and in Japan, modernization of the government has *preceded* modernization of the economy. Indeed, the industrialization of the nation has been planned and controlled by governmental officials. Nations that are just starting to industrialize today are also beginning with the modernization of the government, whether they are following the Communist or the Western road to industrialization. China, for example, has established a highly organized government, much like that of the Soviet Union, although her economy is still in a very primitive stage. India, borrowing from the West, has similarly set up a modern government as a first step to industrialization—she has established universal suffrage and a responsible government although most of her peasant population cannot even read and write. Both nations are thoroughly aware of the important role that government can play in hastening industrialization.

The degree of governmental control of the economy does not appear to be directly related to the degree of industrialization. Highly centralized governments controlling virtually the entire economy can be found in China, a nation that has barely started to industrialize, in Hungary, a nation that is about midway in the process, and formerly in Nazi Germany, one of the most highly industrialized nations in the world. On the other hand, governments that regulate industry that remains almost entirely in private hands can be found in India, in Ireland (about midway in the process), and in the highly industrialized United States and present-day Germany.

The *degree* of industrialization, then, does not appear to be directly related to democratic-totalitarian differences. The *speed* with which industrialization is achieved, however, has a very marked relation to the form of government. The first group of nations to industrialize (the nations of Northwestern Europe, the United States, Canada, Australia, and New Zealand) did so under democratic forms of government and did so relatively slowly, whereas the major nations to industrialize most recently (Italy, the Soviet Union, and Japan) have done so very rapidly under totalitarian governments. It is a matter of deep concern to the democratic countries that nations wanting to industrialize today may turn to dictatorial forms of government as the quickest way to achieve their goal. China has already chosen this path, and India may do likewise.

Is it merely a coincidence that totalitarian nations have been able to industrialize more rapidly than their democratic predecessors? Are their advantages when it comes to speed due perhaps to the fact that they have industrialized more recently and thus can borrow from other nations and learn from the experience of others rather than due to the form of their government? Unfortunately not. Rapid industrialization requires far-reaching changes that a national population may not be willing to make voluntarily. In particular, it requires the formation of capital at great sacrifice. The difficulties encountered in trying to get a nation to make these changes and accept these sacrifices voluntarily have the unfortunate result of easing the country toward a dictatorial form of government.

This argument is controversial and deserves to be spelled out in more detail. Let us begin with a consideration of the need for capital (tools, machinery, factories). It is obvious that a functioning industrial economy requires vast amounts of capital. The tremendous quantities of consumer goods (houses, clothing, food, etc.) that modern industry and modern agriculture produce are possible only because of the great quantity of capital goods that are used to produce them. It is equally obvious that in the short run a nation must choose between capital goods and consumer goods. At any given moment, a nation has only so many workers, so much material, and so many tools and machines. If it elects to use them all to produce things that can be used immediately by consumers, it cannot increase its capital. If, on the other hand, it elects to use a large proportion of its productive capacity to turn out more capital goods, this may make it possible to make even more houses, automobiles, and the like in the future, but the immediate effect will be to reduce the amount of consumer goods that could otherwise be produced, for the workers, the raw materials, and the tools and machines that could have been used to make them will be occupied elsewhere.

Once an economy is fully industrialized, the rate of capital investment need not be particularly high. Capital laid aside in the past can continue to be used, and the total national production is so high that even a small proportion of it provides a lot of capital. But in the early years of industrialization, the picture is quite different. At that time, capital must be created from scratch. Factories are still to be built, machinery still to be manufactured. Also, the country is poor, total national production is low, and even a moderate amount of capital will constitute quite a slice of the national production. A high rate of capital investment is required in the early years if a nation wishes to industrialize at all. If the nation wishes to industrialize rapidly, the rate required is even higher.

Thus the provision of capital is one of the most serious questions facing a nation that sets out to industrialize rapidly. Fundamentally, there are only three ways in which capital can be provided:

1. Obtaining it from other nations
2. Raising production
3. Lowering consumption

Each of these methods presents certain difficulties.

¶ *Obtaining Capital from Other Nations.* At first glance, the most attractive method of obtaining capital might appear to be to get it from other nations, and in fact, this method has been much used. There are three possibilities here. The nation desiring capital can force other nations to give it, it can accept loans from them, or it can receive gifts. In other words, the nation in need of capital has the age-old choice of whether to beg, borrow, or steal.

More capital than we realize has changed hands under duress. A major reason why empires have been conquered has been to enable the conqueror to take the riches they possessed. A well-established practice at the end of past wars was to take tribute from the vanquished. This practice has largely vanished, but capital may also change hands in the form of reparations. For example, Russia stripped East Germany of much of its machinery at the end of World War II. Many of the economic relations between strong nations and weak nations or colonies take the form of squeezing the weaker nations to provide wealth that can be turned into capital in the stronger nations.

This method of obtaining capital, however, is usually not open to nations just beginning to industrialize. Particularly today, when such nations must compete with others that are already fully industrial, pre-industrial nations are usually too weak to obtain capital by exercising compulsion. We should note one exception. Many underdeveloped countries have been successful in turning the tables on the industrial nations and extracting capital from them by nationalizing foreign holdings. This practice has many dangers, not the least of which is that such practices tend to sour private investors on risking their capital in countries where they consider such a thing likely to occur.

Borrowing capital from abroad is more promising, but here, too, there are difficulties. Wealthy nations are indeed willing to lend skills and material capital to less developed nations—but at a price. The return in interest or in profits that private investors demand (and reasonably so, for they can obtain a high return on their money at home) is often higher than a preindustrial nation can afford. That is to say, foreign capital may be invested in an underdeveloped country, but much of the increased wealth that such capital produces is likely to flow right out of the country again into the hands of those who provided the capital.

Capital may also be borrowed from foreign governments, but here the price demanded is liable to be political. Particularly if the nation wishing to borrow capital is a former colony or has been exploited by rich nations in the past, its rulers may be very chary about accepting aid if there are any strings attached, and there is little aid that does not have some kind of string. Wealth is too valuable a source of power for it not to be used in this fashion by those who possess it.

Not least of all, it must be noted that the total amount of capital available in loans from other countries is not large. Even small nations may have trouble trying to borrow the amount of capital they require for rapid industrialization. The amount required by giants such as China and India is simply not available.

Gifts from other nations are even rarer than loans. The United States is the only nation that has ever provided gifts to others on a large scale. Such gifts are given only to her international friends to be used for purposes of which she approves, and the supply is by no means steady but is subject to revision every year. In addition, the gifts have been largely in the form of military aid and have gone primarily to other industrial nations, not to underdeveloped areas seeking to industrialize.

Finally, it must be stressed that capital is not simply a matter of machines and tools, but also involves the attitudes and skills of the population. The physical equipment of a modern factory can be obtained from abroad—even the top management can be imported—but the bulk of the labor force must be provided by the nation itself. Deep social and psychological changes are required to turn illiterate peasants into satisfactory industrial workers, but there is no short-cut here. Human capital, in the form of attitudes and skills, cannot be borrowed or stolen; it must be developed from within.

In summary, then, the chances of getting capital from abroad are small. Nations setting out to industrialize usually do not possess the power to steal much capital from others, while loans and gifts are likely to be unduly expensive both economically and politically. In addition, the amount of capital available for loans and gifts by other nations is not large enough to meet the needs of a nation of any considerable size, and the attitudes and skills required for a modern labor force cannot be borrowed in any case. The nation wishing to industrialize in a hurry must itself provide most of the capital.

¶ *Obtaining Capital by Raising Production.* If a nation produces more than it consumes, that surplus is available for capital investment. For example, if a nation raises more wheat or more rice than its population needs, the surplus can be traded abroad for machinery. If the efficiency of agriculture can be increased so that a smaller number of people can grow the same amount of food, the surplus labor can be used to build factories and manufacture machines. One way of raising capital, then, is to increase production while holding consumption constant, or to increase production *faster* than consumption is increasing.

It is not too hard to increase production once industrialization is in full swing. The application of machinery to tasks that were once done by hand brings tremendous increases in productivity, and improvements due to the efficient organization of labor in a modern factory bring additional gains in the amount each worker can produce. Once industrialization is well under way, production practically multiplies itself.

The problem is at the beginning. Capital begets capital, but where is the *first* capital to be obtained? How is one to wring capital from an economy that is not yet mechanized? How is capital to be squeezed out of peasant farmers tilling the soil in the age-old, traditional, inefficient manner? How can a handful of industries be made to produce more without the introduction of new machinery?

Gains can be made through organization alone. Peasant agriculture conceals a large amount of underemployment, people who work a few hours a day at this or that but whose labor would never be missed if they could be pried loose from the countryside and put to work at other tasks. But peasants are not eager to forsake their traditional way of life, particularly if the alternative is steady, hard, unpleasant work in a mine or foundry or construction gang.

Gains in production are also possible through the use of improved methods that do not require much capital. Agricultural yields can be increased greatly through the use of better seed and more rational procedures, but this, too, is easier said than done. To introduce scientific agriculture means to consolidate small family plots into larger units, to reorganize the agricultural labor force, and to take the decision-making power out of the hands of the traditional village elders and family heads and put it into the hands of younger men with more modern ideas. It is not surprising that those who are most powerful in the traditional society resist such changes.

It is also possible to make up for a lack of machinery in some cases by substituting human muscle-power. The methods are fairly simple and have long been known to those who employed slave labor or who had access to a labor force so desperately in need that it had no choice but to work, whatever the conditions. Back-breaking tasks, longer hours of work, neglect of safety and health in working conditions, these are the ways of forcing more production out of an industrial labor force that lacks machines, but these again are methods that free men will not accept voluntarily.

In short, it is possible to increase production rapidly, even before capital is available in large quantities, but the price in human terms is staggering. Forced migration, compulsory reorganization of agriculture, forced labor, these methods bring results, but they are not compatible with democratic political institutions. This is the world of the secret police and the concentration camp. It is not a world where democracy can flourish.

¶ *Obtaining Capital by Lowering Consumption.* A final method of obtaining capital is to produce the necessary gap between production and consumption by reducing consumption or by preventing it from rising to keep pace with an increase in production. The consequences of such a policy should be obvious. America is the richest nation in the world, but the government that set out deliberately to lower the American standard of living, even a little bit and even for the worthiest of purposes, would be greeted by a howl of protest that would remove it from office at the first opportunity. Imagine how much more violent must be the opposition to any attempt to lower living standards in a poor, peasant nation where the majority of the people are already living at a level little above bare subsistence. Reducing consumption in such a nation means stripping not only the rich but even the moderately well-to-do of all that distinguishes them from the rest of the population. For the masses, it means acute hardship, perhaps even starvation in cases. Attempts may be made to justify such sacrifices as providing the base for future prosperity. A high spirit of nationalism and revolutionary ardor may even produce a minority who are willing to make such sacrifices voluntarily, at least for a short time, but the majority will never accept such a policy, if they have anything to say about it. To push through such a program in the face of popular resentment and resistance is a task that no democratic government can undertake. Only a government with powerful instruments of repression can compel a recalcitrant population to reduce its standard of living.

¶ *Summary.* Rapid industrialization poses tremendous problems for the government of an underdeveloped nation. It is extremely difficult to impose upon a peasant population the techniques, attitudes, and social organization of an industrial people. Difficult at best, the task becomes truly formidable if rapid industrialization is demanded.

If better living conditions could be provided at the start, the population might be given sufficient incentive to make the required changes voluntarily, but this is seldom possible. Capital is required for industrialization, and since it is impossible to borrow from other nations a sufficient quantity for rapid industrialization, capital must be provided by raising production through inhuman work conditions and by cutting consumption to the bare minimum. Thus the lure of a higher standard of living cannot be used immediately. On the contrary, living standards are cut.

The result, after the first flush of enthusiasm for modernization has worn off, is deep and widespread popular discontent. Government officials may wish to continue to press ahead, but they must face growing popular discontent. Under such conditions, there are only two choices: slow the pace of industrialization, or repress popular resistance through authoritarian governmental institutions and push through a program of rapid industrialization by force.

The choice for anyone who believes in democracy and human freedom is obvious; slow the pace of industrialization. No promise of a higher standard of living or greater national power in the future is worth the price in human happiness and human life that must be paid for rapid industrialization. But the leaders of underdeveloped nations are not always democrats. Governments desiring industrialization at any price are likely to find themselves turning totalitarian, whatever the philosophy under which they came to power. We see that the speed of industrialization and the form of government are intimately related. Only a totalitarian government can industrialize a nation at breakneck speed, and for this reason those desiring rapid industrialization are likely to turn to totalitarianism even though the human and moral price of doing so may be made quite clear.

The pattern of population change is familiar to the reader: a change from relatively high fertility and mortality to relatively low fertility and mortality. That is, in the earlier demographic stages the birth rate is generally high (though it varies considerably from one country to another), families are large, and there is a high proportion of children in the population. The death rate is also high; many of these children—perhaps the majority—die before they reach adulthood. The average person does not live to a ripe old age and those who do often suffer from disease. In the latest demographic stage the birth rate is much lower, families are smaller, and a much higher percentage of the children born survive. The death rate is also much lower. The expectation of life at birth is somewhere in the seventies. Health in general is much better, and there is a much larger proportion of old people in the population.

Here again change has always proceeded in the same direction, although wars, depressions, and cultural variations have produced considerable fluctuation. It can also be said that in every country going through these changes in population, the death rate has dropped before the birth rate and has dropped to lower levels so that some population growth occurs through nearly all of the transition. The amount of growth and its timing, however, have varied.

There is a close connection between demographic changes on the one hand and economic and political modernization on the other. Falling death rates, falling birth rates, and the resulting population growth have been a direct result of economic and political modernization.

The connection with economic modernization is easy to see. The drop in the death rate has been brought about by better food supplies, improved sanitation, and medical advances, each of which can be traced directly to technological and economic improvements. Quite early in the process of economic modernization, better methods and the use of newly invented tools (and eventually agricultural machines) increase agricultural yields. Thanks to the improved methods of transportation that are also part of the industrialization process, food supplies can be distributed widely and rapidly, thus putting an end to local famines. With industrialization, man achieves firm control of his food supply; famine, one of the greatest killers of peasant society, is vanquished. Modern sanitation and scientific medicine are also accomplishments of industrial society, and thanks to them, smallpox, typhoid, malaria, pneumonia, tuberculosis, and other great killers of the past have been brought under control.

Industrialization has also been responsible for the drop in the birth rate, for it is urban living and a monetary economy that have made large families an economic expense and a social handicap. In a rural society, children are an economic and social asset, for they go to work early and soon contribute to the family as much as they consume. When they are grown, they usually remain at home, continuing to add to the wealth of the family. Under these conditions, parents with many children are socially rewarded with the esteem of others. An industrial economy, in which the family income is provided by the wages of the father and in which the mother who stays home to care for her children cannot perform any service that is paid for, provides quite a different set of conditions. In this setting, children, economically speaking, are merely extra mouths to be fed, not extra hands to work. A large number of children cuts down the family's standard of living, impedes its social mobility, and subjects it to a vague but nevertheless real form of social disapproval.

The effect of political modernization upon population trends is perhaps less obvious. There is little if any direct effect of political modernization upon reducing fertility except insofar as political modernization is a prerequisite for industrialization. But political modernization plays a real part in reducing mortality. Political efficiency is required to improve the nationwide distribution of food supplies in time of famine. Government has an all-important role to play in improving sanitation and in launching the nationwide health programs required to wipe out epidemic diseases. So important is political modernization that it can be used, even in advance of industrialization, to reduce mortality to very modern lows. This, in effect, is what is happening throughout the underdeveloped areas today, where political modernization is preceding economic modernization and where it is being used to distribute foreign aid and to apply foreign technology far in advance of industrialization.

In a rough way we can say that death rates drop sharply as soon as political modernization is achieved, whereas a substantial drop in birth rates has depended thus far upon industrialization and urbanization. In Western Europe, where economic and political modernization went more or less hand in hand, the result was rapid population growth during the early years of industrialization that tapered off to moderate growth as industrialization became well established. In much of the non-European world, however, political modernization is occurring at a relatively earlier economic stage. Death rates are being reduced far in advance of the expected fall in birth rates, bringing massive population growth to much more primitive economies and increasing both the length of the growth period and the amount of growth.

Evaluation of the Determinants of Power

We have seen that there are many determinants of national power and that these determinants are related to each other. However, if we are to devise an index by which the power of a nation can be measured, we must first know the relative importance of the various determinants that we have listed. Let us begin by disclaiming once more any one-factor determinism. Economic determinism is *not* the answer, nor can it be said that population size is the key to national power, or that it is "really" political organization that determines whether a nation is powerful or not. Each of the factors that we have discussed in the two previous chapters has an influence on national power, and the interrelationship among the different factors is complex.

It is a gross oversimplification to claim that any one factor determines by itself the power of a nation. We must not, however, fall into the opposite error of assuming that because each of these factors plays a role, all are of equal importance. Some factors are clearly more important than others.

Our task is somewhat complicated by the fact that there is no objective measurement of some of the factors. We can count heads and determine population size exactly, we can even measure the productivity of workers (or at least the per capita gross national product), we can estimate the amount of natural resources that a nation possesses, but how are we to measure the degree of national morale? We can say in a rough way that the government of a nation is efficient or inefficient, but how are we to measure the relative merits of a government with extremely shrewd leaders who can form effective foreign policy rapidly and a government whose leaders are less able but whose policies are assured of more widespread popular support? We can measure the size of a nation's territory, but how can we assess the relative advantages of ease of internal communication and easily defended frontiers?

Even assuming that we could measure each separate determinant of power fairly accurately, there is no common currency into which we can translate our separate measurements. When is a nation more populous than its government is efficient? How much economic productivity is required to make up for a lack of resources?

Finally, as we have observed at length, the various determinants of power are interrelated, and the value of one determinant often depends upon the presence of others. Resources alone do not bring power, but resources coupled with the economic organization to exploit them and the power to defend them *do* increase a nation's power. An immense population with a backward economy may have some power, but add an efficient political structure, and the gain in power is tremendous, even in the absence of an industrial economy.

The difficulties are real, and because of them, any evaluation of the relative importance of the various determinants of power is bound to be impressionistic and based on personal opinion. The reader has been warned. Now, let us proceed.

POPULATION

Any comparison of the nations of great power and the middle-range powers leads one to the conclusion that a large population is the most important single determinant of national power. As we have noted before, there is not a single major power with a population of less than 50 million. An excellent example of the primary importance of population size is Canada. Rich in resources and large in area, Canada is highly industrial, has a thoroughly modern government, and from all reports has high national morale. All of this makes Canada a leader of the middle powers, but she is a middle power and not a great power. It seems reasonable to infer that what dooms her to secondary rank is her small population. All the other attributes of power that Canada possesses are not enough to compensate her for the lack of some 30 million Canadians.

China, on the other hand, possessed little *but* population before the Communists came to power. She had a large area, to be sure, and resources (though they were largely undeveloped), but she was extremely backward economically, had a government of very low efficiency, and abominable morale, as the easy victory of the Communists proved. And yet, because of her gigantic population, China was accorded a place as one of the world's great powers, named as one of the "Big Five," and given a permanent seat on the United Nations Security Council. India, too, has been accorded an important place as a leader of the middle powers almost completely because of her large population.

Again, take the cases of Indonesia, Pakistan, Brazil, and Nigeria. These four are the only nations among the lesser powers that have populations larger than 50 million. It seems clear that these four nations are not as important as India because their populations, although large, are not large enough to compensate for their inadequacies in political development and their lack of industrialization. However, their populations are large enough to make them middle powers. Should their numbers be halved, all four would automatically drop out of sight among the small powers.

We can say, then, that population size is the most important determinant of national power. With it, a lack of other determinants of power can be overcome. Without it, great power status is impossible.

POLITICAL DEVELOPMENT

It is not so easy to assign second place, for the next two factors, political development and economic development, are almost equally important as determinants of national power. We give the edge, however, to political development.

The key role played by efficient political organization can be seen in the tremendous boost in power gained by a nation when this determinant is added to any other combination. The main difference between the China of Chiang Kai-shek and the early China of Mao Tse-tung was a substantial improvement in the efficiency of political organization. Similarly in North Vietnam, efficient political organization would seem to explain how Ho Chi Minh, ruler of a relatively small and backward nation, has managed to defy the powerful industrial nations of the West for twenty years. In Russia, modernization in the political area ushered in modernization of the economy. Even in Western Europe, where full modernization of the government waited until after industrialization was well under way, governments with organized bureaucracies and with firm control over their national territories led in the economic expansion that gave Europe dominance over the rest of the world.

It is probable that, before the Industrial Revolution, the degree of political modernization had even more influence on national power than it has today. Differences in industrial strength are so great among nations today that they sometimes seem to overshadow all else, but in the pre-industrial world, while differences in economic development certainly existed, they were not so great. Thus differences in political efficiency were relatively more important.

Efficient government is not only a core factor in the determination of national power; a minimum degree of efficiency is necessary for national existence. Above this minimum, the degree of efficiency in government is a major determinant of power: First, government is the tool by which all the resources of the nation, both human and material, are mobilized to influence the behavior of other nations. Second, power that is wielded internationally is exercised through the agency of government. These two facts give to political development the high rank it has as a determinant of national power.

ECONOMIC DEVELOPMENT

Right behind political development comes economic development, the third most important determinant of a nation's power. The importance of industrialization in adding to a nation's power has been stressed repeatedly. Most of the great and middle powers are strong because they are industrial. The two exceptions are China and India, but even their present power rests in part upon the promise of the power they will have when they become industrial in the future.

There is little question that the main reason for the supremacy of the United States today in international politics is its amazing economic productivity, nor can there be much doubt that England ruled the nineteenth-century world because she was the first nation to industrialize. Indeed, the industrial countries have held the rest of the world in vassalage because (1) they were better organized politically, and (2) they possessed the goods and the guns that industrialization had given them.

It is difficult to untangle the respective contributions of modern political organization and an industrial economy, since at least a moderately effective political structure is a prerequisite for industrialization. We cannot say that a high degree of economic efficiency makes up for a backward government; we can say, however, that an industrial economy may enable a nation to compensate for poor resources and small territory. To some extent, a high degree of industrialization can even offset the disadvantages of a small population. None of the nations of medium rank that possess small populations would count for anything in international politics if they were not among the most economically developed countries in the world. It is this factor that enables them to exploit to the full whatever power potential they possess.

NATIONAL MORALE

The other three determinants of power—national morale, resources, and geography—are of considerably less importance. Added to the others, they make a difference, but even the most favorable position imaginable in all three is not enough to make up for a lack in one of the crucial determinants that we have already discussed.

Of the three, national morale appears to be the most important, for a nation can achieve first rank without adequate resources or favorable geography, but at least moderately high morale is required if a nation is to maintain its power position. Citizens who will not pay their taxes, obey the law, or willingly place the national welfare above their own in time of war may seriously handicap even a rich and populous nation. They can make effective government impossible.

There is no difficulty in determining that, logically, national morale must be a relatively important determinant of national power. In fact, we feel certain it is more important than the two determinants that remain to be discussed. The difficulty is in proving it by empirical facts. National morale is one of the most intangible and elusive factors with which we have dealt—even a simple statement that one nation's morale is high while another's is low is necessarily highly subjective. Proof that morale is low is sometimes found in the fact that a nation's soldiers have been easily defeated or have surrendered rapidly, but such a judgment is open to question. So many factors enter into the determination of a military victory. Is Denmark to be accused of low morale because she surrendered immediately to the blitzkrieg of Nazi Germany? Would resistance that might have made the conquest of Denmark take a day or two longer really have made any contribution to Denmark's power? Again, we credit high morale to soldiers who fight on to the death against hopeless odds. This is perhaps a sounder judgment. Surely the fanatical will of Japanese soldiers in World War II greatly increased the power of Japan's armies, undermanned and undersupplied as they were. Surely the behavior of British civilians under German bombardment added to the power of Britain in her hour of need.

RESOURCES

We have already noted the ways in which the power of a nation is influenced by the natural resources that it has at its command, but we have also observed that a nation need not possess the resources it needs within its own boundaries, for it can conquer them or buy them from other nations. Thus, the physical possession of rich resources within the national territory cannot be considered a major determinant of power. The facts bear out this argument nicely, for such major nations as Britain, Germany, and France lack oil, while Japan and Italy are seriously lacking in many resources. On the other hand, some of the nations that are richest in resources have achieved their independence only recently.

All other factors being equal, possession of resources should increase a nation's power, but even here the contribution does not appear to be great.

GEOGRAPHY

Last in importance as a determinant of national power is geography. We have seen that a large land area may enable a nation to support a large population and may confer certain advantages of military defense, but size of territory is determined by politics, not by geography alone. Climate and topography have a small indirect influence upon power through their effect upon agricultural production, ease of communication, and defensibility of boundaries. Strategic location may be an asset, provided a nation has the ability to defend itself, and location relative to other nations may increase or diminish the power a nation can exercise.

On the whole, however, geography does not appear to be a major determinant of national power. If we were given a list of nations containing information about the size of their territories, their climate, their topography, their location, and *nothing else*, it would be impossible to evaluate their power. Other things equal, favorable geographic factors probably increase a nation's power, but in any real situation, the influence of geography is almost completely obscured by the operation of other, more important factors.

An Index of National Power

At this point, we are ready to construct an index of national power, a formula by which we can take into consideration how a nation rates in the various factors which determine power and give the nation a "score" that will tell us at a glance whether it is more or less powerful than other nations with different scores. Ideally, the index should take into consideration all six determinants of power that we have located, but practically, this is impossible. We must limit ourselves to those that can be measured with some exactness, but even with this limitation we can construct an index that will be of use.

The fact that the various determinants are interrelated simplifies our task. We have seen that the two least important determinants, geography and resources, make a relatively small contribution to national power by themselves, that they contribute to power almost entirely through their effect upon the other determinants, that is, size of area, topography, and climate may help to determine whether a nation can support a large population and whether the territory is rich or poor in resources. Similarly, resources contribute to power largely as they are developed and used in industrial production, not by their mere existence within the national territory.

The influence on power of favorable geographic factors and adequate resources will be taken into account to some extent when we measure population size and degree of economic development. If a country has a large population, it is axiomatic that it must have territory large enough to hold it. Of course, this measure does not register the presence of vast stretches of uninhabited or sparsely settled territory, but such territory makes little contribution to power. Similarly, if a nation has an efficiently functioning, industrial economy, we can assume that it has access to adequate resources. The presence of undeveloped resources or of resources that are exploited and used by other nations is not registered in our index, but again, resources of this nature do not contribute to the nation's power. Location relative to other nations, another minor factor, will also not be reflected in our index.

The measurement of national morale, too, will be left out of our index, because it is extremely difficult to measure objectively. This is a loss, but not a major one, for the contribution of national morale to power is only fourth in importance. Also, it is related to political structure, and its influence will show up to some extent in the workings of government. If we could measure the efficiency of political organization, we would be taking into account to some extent the influence of national morale.

Our index of power, then, ought to be based upon the three most important determinants of national power: population size, political development, and economic development. The index we are about to suggest falls short of this ideal, for it is based solely upon population and economic development. This is a serious shortcoming, but there is no way to avoid it. A quantitative index by which to measure the effectiveness of political institutions does not exist at the present time; its creation is one of the major tasks that remains for political scientists to accomplish in the years ahead.

Our limited index will, however, tell us something about political efficiency. As we have mentioned, modernization of political institutions is an integral part of the process of industrialization. Thus we can assume that if a nation is highly industrialized, its political institutions are at least moderately efficient, that they include, for example, an organized governmental bureaucracy and at least one truly national political party. In other words, if we know that the degree of economic development in a nation is high, we can at least estimate within a range the degree of efficiency of political institutions; we can set it for sure above a certain minimum level. However, if the degree of economic development is low, no inference about the efficiency of government can legitimately be made. The low state of economic development does not tell us anything. Most underdeveloped nations, to be sure, have highly inefficient political institutions, but China and India provide good examples of nations in which the level of economic development is still extremely low but political institutions are effective enough to reap substantial benefits in terms of power.

The index of national power that we propose is a simple one. Population size can be measured directly and presents no problems. We require only census figures. The index of economic development that we have chosen is per capita gross national product.[2] Multiplied together, these two figures give us the gross national product (GNP), a figure

[2] See Chapter 8.

which reflects the influence of both population size and level of economic development. At the risk of being obvious, let us explain more clearly: The more efficiently the national economy is organized (that is, the more "developed" or industrial the nation is), the greater the amount of goods and services produced, that is, the higher the GNP. The size of the GNP will also be determined in part by the size of the nation's population, quite apart from the level of efficiency. Even an economically backward nation can produce a sizable GNP if it has an immense population. On the other hand, a relatively small nation can produce a high GNP if its economy is highly developed. The two factors operate independently, and both are reflected in the final figure of GNP.[3]

Let us make another thing clear. It is not the GNP itself that confers power upon a nation. The GNP is simply a figure representing the value of all the goods and services exchanged during a given year. We have seen that goods and services, insofar as they are used to persuade, reward, punish or coerce other nations, do make a *contribution* to national power, but we are more interested here in the fact that a high GNP indicates that the economy is highly efficient or that the population is large or both. An efficient economy and a large population by their very existence imply a certain amount of efficiency in government, access to adequate resources, and a sufficiently large national territory to contain the population. We are interested in the GNP, not because the goods and services it represents contribute to power directly, but because the GNP is determined by so many of the same factors that determine national power. Those nations with the highest GNPs should be the most powerful nations in the world; those with the lowest, the least powerful.

Let us see if this is in fact the case. Following the procedure established in earlier chapters, we shall list the major nations of the world in order according to their GNP. The best recent listing was compiled by the U. S. Agency for International Development for the year 1965. For purposes of comparison, we shall list the GNPs for 1965 and 1950. In spite of the fact that the GNPs of various nations are not exactly comparable and that the figures for the poorest nations are probably unreliable, the lists are invaluable (see Table 1).

The lists in Table 1 do not deviate much from our common-sense conception of the relative power of nations. There is general agreement

---

[3] Either gross national product or national income may be used as an index of national power. GNP is used here because a wider range of comparable figures is available. The writer is indebted to Kingsley Davis for his idea of using national income as an index of national power. See Kingsley Davis, "The Demographic Foundations of National Power," in Morroe Berger *et al., Freedom and Control in Modern Society* (Princeton, N.J.: Van Nostrand, 1954), chap. 10.

in the world today that the United States is the most powerful nation and that the Soviet Union is second, though it is perhaps surprising to note that West Germany and not Britain occupies third place in 1965. France and China are fifth and sixth, with some uncertainty as to which is higher.

The position of West Germany, substantially above that of Britain, gives a slightly inflated indication of her power. There seems little doubt that Britain still ranks third in power, but our index suggests that this would not be the case if the military restrictions on Germany were lifted. West Germany's position may be unexpected considering Germany's decisive defeat in both world wars and her present division. Her rapid economic recovery would seem to indicate, however, that the pattern of German growth in wealth and power, which has continued for more than a century now, was interrupted only briefly by her massive defeats of 1917 and 1945.

The closeness of China and France on our list raises serious doubts as to which country is really ahead of the other, particularly because the figure of $81 billion for China is highly unreliable and is an estimate for 1962, at which time the French GNP was estimated at $72 billion. In recent years French rates of growth have been high while the Chinese economy has suffered from the Cultural Revolution, and it may well be that France has pulled ahead.

Canada may be ranked a trifle higher than her actual power warrants. It seems likely that Canada's proximity to the United States reduces her power somewhat—perhaps below that of Italy. The relatively low ranking of India is to a large extent the obvious result of that country's inability to date to begin industrialization in earnest. Her position on our list—below such middle powers as Canada and Italy—is compatible with her defeat by China in the armed conflict over their borders.

All in all, the list appears to give a highly accurate picture of the power of the top ten nations. As we move down the list, its value becomes

TABLE 1

Power Rank as Indicated by GNP and Its Components

Nation	1965 GNP (in billions)[a]	1965 Rank in Per Capita GNP	1965 Rank in Population	1950 GNP (in billions)[a]
United States	$644.5	1	4	$375.6
USSR	285[b]	15	3	121
West Germany[c]	101.7	9	8	37.8

TABLE 1 (*continued*)

United Kingdom	90.8	13	10	58.9
France	81.7	12	12	41.5
China	81^d	—	1	38
Japan	67.0	22	6	23.3^e
Canada	44.6	2	23	23.2
Italy	44.4	19	11	19.5
India	39.6	63	2	22.8
Australia	20.4	6	31	11.3
Mexico	17.4	33	13	7.2
Spain	17.2	26	16	6.5
Sweden	17.1	3	42	9.6
Poland^f	—	—	17	—
Netherlands	15.7	16	29	7.8
Belgium	14.6	14	34	8.8
Brazil	14.4	51	7	7.0
Switzerland	12.2	4	46	6.1
Argentina	11.7	27	22	7.6
Pakistan	10.0	61	5^g	5.9
South Africa	9.8^b	29	24	—
Denmark	8.5	7	48	4.8
Austria	8.2	18	44	3.7
Turkey	7.2	44	15	3.4
Venezuela	7.0	21	38	2.5
Norway	6.3	10	52	3.4
Colombia	5.1	39	25	2.6
Greece	5.1	25	40	1.8
New Zealand	4.9	5	58	—
Nigeria	4.5	59	9	—
Philippines	4.4	56	14	2.0
Chile	4.0	31	39	2.4
Thailand	4.0	57	18	—
Portugal	3.6	34	37	1.6
South Korea	3.3	58	19	—
Peru	3.1	41	30	1.4
Israel	3.0	17	59	0.6
Malaysia	2.7	38	35	—
Ireland	2.4	20	56	1.7
Morocco	2.3	52	27	1.7^h
China (Taiwan)	2.3	50	28	0.8^h
Iraq	1.9	42	45	—
Burma	1.8	65	20	0.8
Ghana	1.7	46	41	—

TABLE 1 (continued)

Nation	1965 GNP (in billions)[a]	1965 Rank in Per Capita GNP	1965 Rank in Population	1950 GNP (in billions)[a]
Ceylon	1.6	55	32	—
Guatemala	1.4	37	50	0.7
Uruguay	1.4	28	57	—
Sudan	1.4	60	26	—
Ecuador	1.0	48	47	0.5
Ethiopia	1.0	67	21	—
Rhodesia	0.9[b]	45	51	—
Tunisia	0.8	51	49	—
Jamaica	0.8	32	63	—
El Salvador	0.8	40	55	0.4
Kenya	0.8	62	36	—
Tanganyika	0.7	66	33	—
Bolivia	0.7	53	54	0.5
Luxembourg	0.6	8	69	0.4
Panama	0.6	30	66	—
Trinidad & Tobago	0.6	24	67	—
Zambia	0.6[b]	54	53	—
Uganda	0.6	64	43	—
Nicaragua	0.5	36	64	0.2
Costa Rica	0.5	35	65	0.2
Honduras	0.5	47	60	0.2
Jordan	0.5	43	62	—
Paraguay	0.4	49	61	0.2
Cyprus	0.4	23	68	—
Iceland	0.3	11	70	0.2

a U.S. dollars, in constant 1962 prices.
b 1964.
c Including West Berlin.
d 1962; probably higher than France by 1965.
e 1953.

f No comparable GNP figure is available for Poland, which probably ranks among the top 15 nations. No GNP figures are available for East Germany, Indonesia, the United Arab Republic, Finland, Czechoslovakia, Yugoslavia, Rumania, or Hungary, most of which would rank in the middle ranges, or for a number of smaller nations.

g Indonesia would rank fifth in population if it were included in this listing.
h 1951.

SOURCES: United States, Agency for International Development, Gross National Product, Growth Rates and Trend Data by Region and Country (Washington, D. C.; U.S. Agency for International Development, June 1966), Tables 3a–3g. United Nations, Demographic Yearbook, 1965 (New York: United Nations, 1966), Table 4. Independent estimates for the USSR and China.

harder to assess, although the nations of recognized middle rank are roughly where we would expect to find them, and the small powers are at the bottom of the list. The relative power of the small nations is to be taken with a grain of salt, however, since many of them are underdeveloped areas for which the figures on GNP are only rough estimates.

The magnitude of differences in power between nations is also brought out clearly. The GNP of the United States is startlingly higher than any of the others, more than twice as great as that of the Soviet Union, for example. Our index is not exact enough to allow us to say that the United States is therefore twice as *powerful* as the Soviet Union, but it is perfectly clear that its lead in power is very great, whatever the exact mathematical dimensions. The GNPs of the United States, West Germany, France and Britain added together are greater than those of all the rest of the world. Again, it would not be accurate to conclude that these four nations together are therefore more *powerful* than the rest of the world combined, but it is clear that the power of the four major Western allies is very great, perhaps greater than we realize.

Comparison of the figures for 1955 and 1965 brings out some interesting facts. All the major nations have increased their gross national products in the ten-year period covered, but not at the same rate (see Table 2).

Different rates of increase have changed the ranks of some of the nations. The sharpest increases have been scored by Japan, West Germany, Italy, and the USSR. The lowest increases have been those of Britain and the United States. As a result, Germany has moved up, passing Britain, and Japan's phenomenal advance has placed her ahead of India and Canada. India's power potential remains very great, of course, but by the end of the period she had dropped to tenth place. The Soviet Union has remained decisively in second place with the United States still enjoying a commanding lead. Indeed, the distance in wealth between the two top nations is even greater than it was in 1955, for despite Russia's more rapid rate of growth, America's *amount* of increase has been greater, since she started with a bigger base. For considerations of power, however, it is the ratio between the various GNPs, not their absolute amount, that matters. In terms of ratios, the Soviet Union has gained on the United States but remains in second place.

Before concluding our discussion of gross national product as an index of national power, we should make clear what the limitations of such an index are. The most important difficulties arise when this index is used to measure the national power of underdeveloped countries. Because the gathering of statistics is in itself a function of development, it should not surprise us that the data from underdeveloped areas are

TABLE 2

Increase of GNP for Major Nations, 1955–1965

Nations	GNP 1955*	GNP 1965*	Amount of Increase*	Percent Increase
United States	$463.1	$644.5	$181.4	39.1%
USSR	173	285 †	112	64.7
West Germany‡	59.5	101.7	42.2	70.9
United Kingdom	67.2	90.8	23.6	35.1
France	50.7	81.7	30.0	59.2
China	56	81 **	25	44
Japan	26.8	67.0	40.2	150.0
Canada	29.1	44.6	15.5	53.3
Italy	26.0	44.4	18.4	70.8
India	27.7	39.6	11.9	43.0

* In billions of U.S. dollars, in constant 1962 prices.
† 1964.
‡ Including West Berlin.
** 1962.

SOURCES: United States, Agency for International Development, *Gross National Product, Growth Rates and Trend Data by Region and Country* (Washington, D.C.: U.S. Agency for International Development, June 1966), Tables 3a–3g. Independent estimates for the USSR and China.

very unreliable. Moreover, a good portion of the economic transactions in the underdeveloped countries is not paid for in money and therefore not reflected in such measures as GNP. Even more significant for use on underdeveloped countries is the fact that our index does not directly measure political modernization. In the twentieth century substantial political modernization often precedes economic modernization, and the increments of power due to such political modernization are entirely missed by our index. Take, for example, the case of China. Between 1948 and 1950 China abruptly ceased to be a great power by courtesy and became a great power in fact, a change entirely due to political developments within her borders. It could not, however, have been noted by observing shifts in Chinese GNP for the years in question. Economic modernization took longer.

Our index is somewhat defective in the case of the most highly developed countries as well. It seems probable that beyond a certain point increases in economic efficiency as measured by per capita GNP do not indicate a proportionate increase in power. In other words, the initial burst of industrialization (say the increase in per capita GNP from $300 to $800) probably contributes more to a nation's power than a similar increase later (say from $2,300 to $2,800). Thus GNP is most effective as an index of national power when a country is industrializing. It probably underestimates the power of some of the economically underdeveloped nations that are about to "take off" and it probably overrates the power of the most developed nations. It does, however, give a good indication of relative *rank* in power.

Gross national product figures are very much worth watching. In the years ahead, we can expect that whenever a nation experiences an increase in GNP, it will also grow in power. If we could measure the efficiency of political institutions and include this measurement in our index, we would have a highly accurate index of national power.

Ways of Increasing National Power

Assuming that we now know the determinants of national power and that we know which determinants are most important, we should be able to state what a nation must do in order to increase its power in international relations. However, the most advantageous course differs according to whether the nation is industrial or not. Let us consider the two categories of nations separately.

NONINDUSTRIAL NATIONS

Of all the determinants of national power, the one that can be manipulated with the greatest and most permanent results is economic development. Particularly for the nation with an underdeveloped economy, the gains in power to be achieved through industrialization are tremendous. Russia and Japan are cases in point, as were Britain and the United States at an earlier date. Similar gains could be realized by India or China or any of the nations with an extremely low level of economic development. India, for example, is near the bottom of the list in per capita GNP. Consider the power she would gain if she could raise her per capita GNP up only to the level of, say, Japan or Mexico. Consider the power China would possess if she could modernize her economy to the degree that Portugal has, or Chile.

If, however, industrialization is to be carried out most effectively, modernization of the political structure should precede it. This is true whether the nation has a democratic or a dictatorial government. We have already noted that if the pace of industrialization is extremely rapid, the government is likely to become totalitarian, but even if democracy is highly valued and the pace of industrialization is deliberately slowed to one that can be achieved without compulsion and repression, the national government has an important role to play. A traditional economy has strong vested interests that wish to perpetuate the status quo. Without the power of government on their side, those who favor modernization will have a hard time of it. In addition, government action may be needed to borrow funds from abroad, to further the creation of capital at home, and to channel it into productive enterprises. Certainly, the government has a tremendous educational job to perform to train a peasant population to fill the economic roles of a modern economy. Modernization of the political structure is crucial and, if it precedes industrialization, will make economic modernization much easier. Real gains in power can be made by modernizing political institutions, even before industrialization gets seriously under way.

The third major determinant of national power (indeed, we rated it first among the big three), population size, is more difficult to change deliberately. Internal policies aimed at raising the birth rate have never been very successful, but public health measures and improved medical facilities to cut down the death rate can be effective. As we have seen, changes of this nature are the fundamental cause of the population growth that much of the world has experienced. There is nothing to prevent a nation from instituting such measures deliberately for purposes of power as well as national welfare.

In any case, whether the nation is concerned about its population size or not, the population will increase if the nation modernizes its economy, for as we have seen, population growth has always accompanied industrialization. The increment in power to be gained through this method, however, depends largely upon the size of the nation before it begins to industrialize. Guatemala, with a population of about four and a half million, can expect only a relatively small number of additional citizens if she industrializes, certainly nowhere near enough to make her a power of any importance. China, on the other hand, with some 700 million people already, can probably expect a minimum increase of 350 million during the process of industrialization. Britain's population increased more than three times between 1800 and 1900. Russia's population doubled between 1900 and 1950. A 50 per cent increase for China seems highly conservative. If such an increase can be absorbed peacefully into the economy and into the political system of China, the increase in power will be greater than anything the world has seen heretofore. It pays to be big at the beginning.

Population can also be increased through conquest, but such a course is always dangerous and is especially risky for nonindustrial nations at the start when they are likely to be weak because of their backward economies. For underdeveloped nations that are small in size, conquest of any substantial number of people is impossible. On the other hand, if the country is large in size, it can add to its size still further by absorbing some of its smaller neighbors. India added to its power by taking over Kashmir, and China increased its size by conquering Tibet. Again the advantage lies with nations that are already large.

Small nations have one course open to them as a means of increasing population size. They can combine with other small nations to form a new and larger political unit. The United States, Germany, and Italy all provide good examples of the power than can be gained through political unification. The lesson they have taught the world is clear. The new, rising nations of Africa could learn by our example. If they wish to have a major voice in the international politics of the future, they would do well to form a single state rather than remain divided on the European pattern. But such unions are extremely difficult to form and consequently are rarely formed.

In summary, preindustrial nations can best increase their power by industrializing, but to do this most effectively they should modernize their governments first. They can also expect certain gains in population as they modernize their governments and their economies. For large nations, conquest of other states may be effective but is dangerous. For small states, political union with other states is the only way to major power status.

INDUSTRIAL NATIONS

For nations that are already industrial, the road to increased power is necessarily different. The dramatic differences in power caused when a nation first industrializes are, for them, events of the past that cannot be repeated. The United States, Britain, Germany, France, indeed, all of Western Europe, and Russia and Japan as well, cannot hope to change their position in the power hierarchy as radically as can such nations as China, India, or the nations of Africa and Latin America.

It is still possible, however, for industrialized nations to make further improvements in technology and economic organization. Russia, for example, having built an industrial economy, is now trying to catch up with the United States in per capita production. She has a long way to go, since she was only 16th in per capita GNP in 1955, and 15th in per capita GNP in 1965. Japan has even farther to go, having ranked 31st and 22nd in 1955 and 1965, respectively. Real gains are still possible for these nations if they can reach the level of productivity that the United States has already achieved. Even in the most advanced nations, there is still room for much improvement. Automation and the application of atomic power will increase productivity still further, and even in the

American economy, there are many inefficient backward areas. Gains in economic efficiency are particularly easy for those that are already efficient, for wealth begets wealth, and productivity begets still higher productivity. The best example of this is, of course, the United States. While the Soviet Union is trying to catch up, the United States will be advancing on its own. It has a tremendous head start.

Political efficiency can also be improved among the most industrial nations. Granted that the first gains of national unification and the creation of an organized bureaucracy and national political parties lie behind, many improvements can still be made. To consider only the United States as an example, national unification can be increased by absorbing into the political process those culturally and racially deprived groups that have been largely excluded. Vast gains can be made in encouraging more able men to enter government, in enabling them to form more effective and more stable foreign policy, in enlisting unified and enthusiastic popular support for national policies, and in implementing policies with greater diplomatic skill. Governmental intervention in the economy is not always as effective as it might be. Even in military spheres, governmental action leaves much to be desired. The kind of interservice squabbling that plagues America's military establishment, for example, costs much in efficiency of operation. It is impossible to think of a single nation that could not increase its power by improving the operation of its governmental institutions.

As far as population is concerned, the striking changes caused by rapid population growth also lie in the past for the industrial nations, but the demographers who predicted in the 1930s that population decline was just around the corner proved to be wrong. Contrary to expectation, the birth rate in most of the advanced nations rose sharply after the Depression ended and then stayed relatively high for many years, while the death rate continued to fall even lower than had been thought possible. As a result, even the most highly industrial nations continued to experience some population growth. Rates of natural increase (the difference between birth rates and death rates) for the ten most powerful nations in the world are given in Table 3.

Industrial nations can also increase their populations through conquest. Some of the nations that have pursued this policy in the past owe their present position at least partly to their success. England and France conquered great empires, and Russia acquired satellites that contribute to her power. Today, however, there are drawbacks to this method of increasing national power. With the world divided as it is, it is virtually impossible for a major nation to conquer an area without running the risk of a major war with other great powers who feel their

TABLE 3

Rates of Natural Population Increase for the Ten Most Powerful Nations

Nation	1966 Natural Increase per 1,000 Population
United States	9.0
USSR	10.9
West Germany*	6.5
United Kingdom	6.1
France	6.8
China	—
Japan	6.9
Canada	13.8†
Italy	9.4
India	25.5‡

* Not including West Berlin.

† 1965.

‡ 1963–1964.

SOURCE: United Nations, *Demographic Yearbook,* 1966 (New York: United Nations, 1967), Tables 7, 17.

interests threatened. Conquest through military force is always danger-ous, for failure in such a venture may spell disaster for decades to come. Germany's fate in World War I and the fate of Germany, Italy, and Japan in World War II are cases in point.

As in the case of nonindustrial nations, industrial nations can gain power by uniting politically with others. If the nations of Western Europe could ever combine to form a single political state, they would constitute a nation more powerful than the Soviet Union, second only to the United States. European union has long been the dream of an influential minority of Europeans and of some Americans as well, but the death of the European Defense Community and the difficulties of the Common Market should prove clearly, even to the most optimistically inclined, that voluntary mergers are most difficult to bring about between developed countries and that little reliance should be placed upon their successful accomplishment.

Summary

We have closed our discussion of national power with an evaluation of the determinants of power and their interrelationships and with an indication of some of the uses to which a knowledge of the determinants may be put.

We have seen that the separate determinants affect each other and that they tend to change together. In particular, industrialization has been accompanied by political modernization, and both have brought population growth in the past, and there is reason to believe that this will continue to hold true in the future. We have also noted that rapid industrialization has tended to go hand in hand with totalitarian government.

We have evaluated the importance of the separate determinants of national power, ranking population size first, political development second, and economic development a close third. Of lesser importance are national morale, resources, and geography, in that order.

A simple index of national power based on two of the three most important determinants is the gross national product, which reflects the contribution of both population size and economic development as well as that of the other factors to a lesser degree. The index would be much improved if a reliable quantitative measure of political efficiency could be found.

Finally, we have considered the ways in which a nation can best manipulate the determinants in order to increase its power in international relations. For nonindustrial nations we have recommended modernization of the government followed by industrialization which will be accompanied by a certain amount of population growth. For large nations, conquest provides another possibility, but one that is not recommended. For small nations, political union with other states is highly effective but difficult to achieve. For nations that are already industrial, the best hope for increased power lies in continued economic advance, in improving the efficiency of government, particularly in the realm of foreign policy, and in political union with other nations. Some internal population growth can be expected to continue, but conquest of other nations involves too serious a risk of world war to be practical. The roads to power are many: the choice in the hands of the modern nation is wide.

Part Two

INTERNATIONAL RELATIONS

10

Colonialism

❖❘❖❘❖❘❖❘❖❘❖❘❖❘❖❘❖❘❖❘❖❘❖❘❖❘❖❘❖❘❖❘❖❘❖❘❖❘❖

In moving from a consideration of the characteristics of nations to a discussion of the relationships among them, we will find that our lengthy discussion of national power will stand us in good stead, for the kind of relations nations have is deeply influenced by their relative power. As we have said before, our main concern is with the major nations, that is, the most powerful. However, there is a significant difference between the kind of relations that great powers have with each other and the kind of relations they have with weaker nations. At one extreme, we have the high politique that occupies the headlines and sets the tone of international relations. At the other, we have colonialism, where the lesser party to the relationship is not even an independent state. Colonial relationships do *not* occupy the headlines as a general rule, unless two major powers are squabbling over a colony or unless the colony is attempting to free itself and causing trouble. Both kinds of relations are important, however, and each merits full discussion.

International politics is now changing rapidly, and the shifts are especially conspicuous in the relations among the great powers. The main protagonists in international politics have changed. We no longer take particular interest in the policies and actions of Spain and Portugal and Holland or of Prussia and Austria-Hungary (some of these no longer exist as political entities). Even France and Germany, once such major powers, are receding in importance. Today, the United States and

Russia occupy the center of the stage; waiting in the wings are China and India.

Changes are also apparent in colonial relationships. Indeed, the whole institution of colonialism in its traditional form is dying out, and new forms are taking its place. Nation after nation has emerged from colonial status in the last few years. Those that are powerful enough will eventually take their place among the great and middle powers. Those that remain weak find themselves subjected to new forms of domination by the strong, but these forms are not the same as the old colonialism.

Changes in these two areas, in the politics of the great powers and in the relationships between the weak and the strong, constitute the major trends of international politics in the present period. We begin with a consideration of the relations between the weak and the strong, starting with colonialism in its classic form, for their colonial past will shape the actions and the plans of the new nations.

A Historical Sketch

Most of the world has enjoyed (or suffered) colonial status at one time or another, for colonialism as a system goes back to the ancient world. Great colonial empires were created by the Phoenicians, the Greeks, the Romans, and the Carthaginians. The Indians, the Chinese, the Arabs, and the Turks all had colonies. For the most part, however, the ancient empires colonized territory near the homeland where both the climate and the population were not too dissimilar from those at home.

Modern colonialism, on the other hand, is basically a European phenomenon, and with a few exceptions, the colonies have all been far from the homeland and inhabited by populations different from their conquerors in both culture and race.

Over the past 400 years or so, European nations have subjugated two-thirds of the non-European world and then watched it free itself again, bit by bit. Spain and Portugal were the first of the modern colonizers, but after 1600, their supremacy was challenged by Holland, England, and France, who staked out new colonial claims and took colonies from each other as well. The first peak in modern colonialism was reached about 1775, when the entire American continent as well as large parts of Asia and Africa were ruled from Europe. Then, in the next fifty years, while the Americas freed themselves, the European powers extended their hold in Asia. Africa remained, for the most part, unexplored until the last quarter of the nineteenth century, when it, too, was gobbled up in a mad colonial scramble. A second peak in European colonial expansion was reached about 1900, when half the earth's surface and a third of its population were colonial possessions. England alone held more than half of this; France was second; and Germany, third.

Since 1900, the colonial world has crumbled away. It is crumbling still. More than seventy new, independent nations have been created since 1900 out of what was once colonial territory,[1] and it is not improbable that within the lifetime of the reader, traditional colonialism will have disappeared.

The old colonial powers today stand shorn of almost all their richest possessions. In recent years the retreat of colonial rulers has become a rout. For example, as late as 1957 the colonial world still comprised 160 million people and 10 million square miles of territory. Eleven years later the total colonial population had shrunk to 31 million. Portugal, with 13.9 million people under her rule in 1968, had become the number one colonial power. Britain held second place with 7.2 million people, having freed or lost some 75 million colonial subjects in the preceding ten years. Third place was occupied by the United States, with a colonial population of 3.9 million, and Australia held fourth place with 2.2 million people under her colonial rule. The French empire, second only to that of Great Britain in 1957, was fifth in 1967, having shrunk from 40 million people to 1½ million. The Belgian empire had disappeared altogether. The remaining colonial holdings were lilliputian. The Netherlands, Spain, and the Union of South Africa had some half a million people each in their colonial possession. Denmark and New Zealand had 78,000 and 28,000 colonials, respectively.[2] Colonialism is dying rapidly, but it is not yet dead.

Definition of a Colony

Listing the United States as a major colonial power raises the interesting question of just what is a colony and what is not. Americans do not customarily think of their dependencies as colonies. Puerto Rico is a "commonwealth," the Carolines, the Marianas, and the Marshall Islands are "trust territories," while our rule of the Ryukyus (including Okinawa) and the Bonin Islands is "custodial and temporary." Nor are

[1] See list of new nations since 1900 on p. 14. Most of these were formerly colonies.
[2] All figures are 1966 population estimates for territory that was colonial in 1968. United Nations, *Demographic Yearbook, 1966* (New York: United Nations, 1967), Table 2.

we the only people to call our political dependencies by terms other than "colony." Not long ago France insisted that Algeria was a part of metropolitan France and that Morocco and Tunisia were "protectorates," and Portugal still considers Angola part of Portugal. Other terms in wide current usage are "dependencies" and "non-self-governing territories."

This shyness of the last two decades about calling a colony a colony can be traced to several causes. One is simply a matter of public relations, a desire to continue to receive the benefits of a colonial relationship without suffering the consequences of the unpleasant publicity that is likely to follow in a world where colonialism is unpopular. In such cases, the new names do not change the relationship, and the colonials understand very well what their status is, but their rulers hope the outside world will be given a better impression.

A second cause of this new terminology is not so much to avoid unpleasant publicity abroad as to meet objections from the home population. For example, the American public, because of America's own colonial past, considers "colony" a term with many evil connotations. It is largely because of strong views at home that the United States has found it necessary to gloss over her change in role from colony to colonizer.

To a lesser extent, the same problem must be met by other nations as well. There are many people today who do not like the master-subject relationship that has characterized colonialism in the past. The colonial relationship also runs counter to Christian morality and to the democratic ideals of the Western European nations. The argument that colonies, their people, and their riches were a sacred trust of the Europeans provided a way for the colonizers to keep their principles without any loss of national interest. As we shall see later, the bad conscience of the Europeans was an Achilles heel that the colonials found extremely useful when it came to freeing themselves from colonial control.

One notion that must be exploded here is the idea that so-called trust territories are fundamentally different from other colonies. In fact, they are not. The idea that colonies are a trust and that the Europeans are trustees for the welfare of the natives is an old one; it was incorporated in the Covenant of the League of Nations with reference to the mandates, colonies taken away from Turkey and Germany after their defeat in World War I and given to nations that had been on the winning side. One group of mandates (class A: Palestine, Jordan, Syria, Lebanon, and Iraq) was slated for eventual independence and did, in fact, become independent after a relatively brief period of colonial rule, but the others (class B: the Cameroons, Togoland, Tanganyika, and Ruanda-Urundi, all in Africa; and class C: Southwest Africa and some South Pacific islands) were to be ruled like any other colonies. The mandatory powers were supposed to adhere to certain principles and to submit annual reports on their mandates to the League, but there was no way of disciplining them if they abused their privileges or violated their trust. The necessity for reports subjected the government of the mandates to a certain amount of publicity, but otherwise they were treated no differently from other colonies.

The concept that colonies are really trusts was enlarged in the United Nations Charter to apply to all colonies, but this was merely a pious wish. In practice, the United Nations continued in somewhat modified form the mandate system (now called trusteeship) and added to the original group of trusts some new territories detached from the defeated powers of World War II (the Pacific Trust Territories and Italian Somaliland). Other colonies continue to be colonies, pure and simple, beyond the jurisdiction of the United Nations. The administration of the trust areas must be reported on annually to the United Nations Trusteeship Council, which can make recommendations to the nations governing them, but again there is no way of compelling nations to follow these recommendations, and in practice the trusts, like the mandates before them, are governed as if they were ordinary colonies.

The word "colony" is unpopular today, and if the reader prefers, he may substitute the more emotionally neutral term, dependency, wherever this book refers to colonies. However, we shall use the term colony when we speak of a territory that is governed by a foreign country and whose inhabitants are not granted full political rights.

The Benefits of Colonialism

Colonies in their day have been great sources of profit and power to their owners. They have provided plentiful raw materials at low prices and protected markets for manufactured goods. They have supplied cheap labor for economic enterprises within the colony and military manpower for use outside the colony; both England and France, for example, made extensive use of colonial troops in both world wars. Finally, colonies have been used for military purposes. One thinks of Gibraltar, Suez, and Singapore as classic examples, but it should also be noted that America's present colonies in the Pacific are held primarily for strategic reasons.

The contribution of colonial possessions to a nation's power should be obvious. England was the strongest nation in the world in 1900 not only because her home population was economically developed and politically well-organized, but also because she ruled a quarter of the earth's surface and a fifth of its population. France suffered a serious blow in the loss of Indochina, and the loss of the last French colonies in North Africa spelled the end of France as a great power. Small wonder the great powers of yesterday scrambled for colonies and even fought wars over them. Small wonder the great powers of today seek other arrangements to perpetuate some of the advantages of colonialism under new political forms.

Colonial rulers have been almost unanimous in claiming that their subjects also benefited from colonialism, and in some ways they did. These countries were enriched by having their primitive political unification partly completed for them, by having their resources developed, and by the addition of new productive facilities and improved transportation networks. The population benefited by better public health measures and the acquisition of new skills. These facilities and skills could be put to good use once the colonial rulers departed, but as long as they were present, the amount of benefit received by the native population was extremely small.

This shows up clearly when the standard of living in the colonies is considered. Three hundred years of Dutch rule left the Dutch East Indies (now Indonesia) in 1949 with the lowest per capita income of any of the seventy countries for which figures were available. The figure was $25 per person per year.[3] The average per capita income in the remaining African and Asian colonies in 1948 was less than $50 per year.[4] French rule in Indochina was well known for its exploitative character, but it is not generally known that in India, the amount of food per capita went *down*, not up, during the period of British rule, although commercial crops for export were greatly increased. The average colonial subject has not seen himself as benefiting from European rule, and he should know.

What benefits the native inhabitants of the colonies received from colonial rule were largely incidental by-products of measures instituted for the benefit of the colonial rulers. Resources were developed in order that they might be exported. Roads were built so that troops could be moved rapidly to keep the country under control. Railways were located not to serve the needs of the domestic economy, but to enable goods from

[3] United Nations, Department of Economic Affairs, *National and Per Capita Incomes of Seventy Countries in 1949 Expressed in United States Dollars* (New York: United Nations, 1950), p. 15.

[4] W. S. Woytinsky and E. S. Woytinsky, *World Commerce and Governments* (New York: Twentieth Century Fund, 1955), p. 666.

the interior to reach seaports for export. Health measures were instituted partly for the benefit of the natives, but the major concentration was on the cities and other areas where Europeans were gathered in the largest numbers. Native workers were sometimes the recipients of improved housing and diet, but the motive for the improvement was most often to increase their efficiency as workers. Altruism on the part of colonial rulers has been highly publicized wherever it existed, but the instances are few.

We must conclude that colonies have been highly profitable to those who owned them and that colonialism has been a benefit to the ruled largely because it laid the groundwork for a better life once the colonial rulers were thrown out. The judgment will seem a harsh one to those who identify themselves with the rulers, but it will not seem unfair to anyone who has ever been a native of a colony. The key to the colonial relationship lies in the fact that it is a relationship between superiors and inferiors. It is, in essence, an exploitative relationship. The inferiority of the colony is most obvious in the realm of political rights, but it extends to economic and social spheres as well. Not only the political institutions, but also the major economic enterprises within a colony are controlled by foreigners.

Europeans, particularly northwestern Europeans, also have had a practice of considering the non-European inhabitants of their colonies as socially, culturally, and racially inferior. Coming into contact with people whose race and culture were different from his own, the European took it for granted that his own ways were superior. If the natives did not share his religion, they were "heathens," if they did not have his sex complexes and taboos, they were "immoral," if they did not have his compulsion to work, they were "lazy," if they did not share his opinions or possessed a different kind of knowledge, they were "stupid," if they behaved in ways that he could not predict because of his own ignorance of their culture, they were "childlike." In short, the European judged the natives as if they were Europeans who were misbehaving. Accepting his own standards as absolute, he judged every departure from the European way of life in negative terms, with never a thought that the natives might have different standards of their own.

Cultural relativism and tolerance for the ways of others are more widespread today than they were in the heyday of colonialism, but even now the average European or American considers himself superior to non-Europeans in general. This attitude is an essential part of the colonial frame of mind. Without it, colonialism would probably never have existed, for one does not hold in permanent subjugation and exploit people whom one considers equals. But if this feeling of superiority helped to make colonialism possible in the first place, its continuation in later years helped to hasten the end of colonialism. As we shall see later, one of the strongest forces that has helped to unify colonial people in their fight for freedom has been their common resentment at the refusal of their conquerors to accept them as equals. There is one area where the Europeans were clearly superior; they were superior in power. Their firm belief that they were superior in every other area as well had the effect in the beginning of increasing their power over their colonial subjects, but in the long run, it undermined their ability to influence the behavior of the rest of the world.

Types of Colonies

We have been discussing colonies as if they were all the same, but actually there have been wide differences among them. These differences help to explain why colonies have developed as they have.

POINT COLONIES VERSUS TERRITORIAL COLONIES

One fairly obvious distinction that is often made is between what are called "point colonies" and "territorial colonies." Point colonies are those that are very small in area, a mere dot on the map. They originated mainly as trading stations for dealing with an unconquered hinterland, as coaling stations along important sea routes, or as fortresses controlling strategic passages. Some of the African colonies originated as point colonies and then spread inland. Point colonies still in existence include Gibraltar, Hong Kong, and the Panama Canal Zone.

Territorial colonies, as their name indicates, include a larger area. Most of the colonies in the world have fallen into this category, so it is primarily with them that we are concerned.

SETTLEMENT COLONIES VERSUS EXPLOITATION COLONIES

Territorial colonies, in turn, can be subdivided into two groups: settlement colonies and exploitation colonies. Settlement colonies are those where a substantial number of European colonists have settled permanently. On the other hand, if the European population is extremely small and consists largely of administrators, traders, missionaries, soldiers, and others who do not consider the colony their permanent home, the colony is an exploitation colony, that is, the Europeans only exploit the colony, they do not settle it. The term should not create confusion. In a broad sense, all colonies are exploited, but in a settlement colony, exploitation is largely for the benefit of the European settlers, who constitute a majority, or at least a large minority, of the total population, whereas in the other kind of colony, exploitation is exclusively for the benefit of the mother country and the handful of Europeans who represent her interests. In both cases, of course, the original natives of the colony are exploited (if they are allowed to remain in the territory at all).

Whether Europeans have settled in a particular colony or exploited it from a distance has been determined largely by climate, for Europeans on the whole have not adapted themselves to living permanently in the tropics. It is the temperate regions that have attracted great numbers of European settlers.

The nature of European control has also been determined partly by the number of native inhabitants who occupied the territory when the Europeans first arrived. Considering these two factors together—climate and density of native population—we can divide the world into four kinds of areas: temperate and densely settled, temperate and sparsely settled, tropical and densely settled, and tropical and sparsely settled. (The Arctic regions, with the exception of Alaska, have not been colonized and are only beginning to be used by the nations that nominally own them. It is not even clear who owns most of the Antarctic continent.) The colonial history of each of these four kinds of areas has been quite different. Let us look at them, one by one.[5]

TEMPERATE AND DENSELY SETTLED AREAS

The temperate regions with relatively dense native populations have not been colonies in modern times. On the contrary, it is they who have provided the colonizers. Such regions include the nations of Europe, and China and Japan.

Our previous discussion of national power should make it clear why Europe provided by far the great majority of modern colonizers. Europe went through the industrial revolution first, and the gigantic social and economic changes resulted in a huge population increase. Thus the Europeans possessed both the power to impose their rule upon the non-European world and the excess population with which to colonize any areas that were suitable for settlement.

Japan has never been a colony in modern times, either. Once her own industrialization was under way, she too set out upon a course of colonial conquest that was halted only by her defeat in World War II.

The status of China is less clear. China has been dominated by European powers in the past and was once divided into spheres of in-

[5] This classification and the discussion that follows are based upon Katherine Organski and A. F. K. Organski, *Population and World Power* (New York: Knopf, 1961), chap. 3.

fluence. Certainly she was penetrated and to some extent exploited economically, but she was never politically ruled from Europe. She, herself, has sent out large numbers of immigrants who have settled throughout Southeast Asia and who dominate much of its economic life while retaining their own national identity as Chinese. However, they are not exactly colonists, for they have not brought the areas in which they settled under the political domination of China.

The only real exceptions to our generalization that temperate, densely settled areas are not colonies are Formosa, Korea, and Manchuria, all of which were Japanese colonies for a brief period before World War II.

TEMPERATE AND SPARSELY SETTLED AREAS

The temperate regions with sparse native populations have made up what we have called the settlement colonies. Examples are the United States, Canada, Australia, New Zealand, and the southern part of South America.

The similar climate and sparse population of these regions attracted European immigrants, who felt it would be possible to create a "new Europe" in such surroundings. Labor in these lands was performed by whites, the original inhabitants having been run off or exterminated. This meant that labor was scarce and wages high, and a migrant of moderate means could count on improving his lot in such a colony.

Because the colony was his new home, the European migrant soon developed an attachment to it. Before long, divided loyalties began to cause problems, for the settlers put the interests of the colony above those of the mother country. Eventually, through warfare or through wisdom on the part of the country that controlled these colonies, they were granted their independence. All are independent nations today.

TROPICAL AND DENSELY SETTLED AREAS

The tropical colonies, on the whole, have been exploitation colonies. However, those that were densely settled won their independence before those that were sparsely settled. Examples of densely settled, tropical colonies are India, Indochina, Indonesia, and Egypt.

Europeans never migrated to these colonies in large numbers because they did not like the climate and because the ambitious poor, who would be most strongly motivated to emigrate, could not hope to make a decent living in a place where manual labor was performed by non-Europeans who worked for a pittance. Europeans who did go out to administer the government or to direct the labor of the natives often found life trying in a land that was fundamentally foreign. A gay and sometimes decadent social life grew up in the European quarters, but it was largely make-believe. These people were in semivoluntary exile. For them, "home" was not Indochina or Egypt, but France or England, and at the end of their tour of duty, that is where they went. Their aim was to get as much as possible out of the colony in the shortest possible time at the cheapest possible price. The pattern of exploitation was clear.

Today, these areas are nearly all independent, having won their freedom in the recent past. Their large and dense populations have stood them in good stead, for in the end, foreign control of such a population, once it is determined to free itself, has proved impossible. For a while, the Europeans hung on, increasingly isolated, increasingly afraid, surrounded by a sea of people they had taught to hate them. When independence was granted, the soldiers, the officials, and most of the businessmen packed their bags and left for home.

TROPICAL AND SPARSELY SETTLED AREAS

Tropical areas without dense populations made up the bulk of the last remaining colonial areas. Examples are tropical Africa, New Guinea, the West Indies, and the lands bordering the Caribbean Sea. Today, most of these areas are also independent.

These, too, were mainly exploitation colonies, though they were less profitable than the more populated colonies because of the shortage of labor. In some areas the problem was met by importing slaves (the West Indies and the Caribbean coast) or indentured laborers (the Pacific islands), but in others (Africa) the labor shortage remained a problem to the end. The sparse and often primitive populations of these colonies proved easier to control than the more densely settled colonies, with the result that they were the last to win their independence.

MIXED CASES

There is one type of colony that does not fit the classification above. It includes colonies that are temperate or semi-tropical, where a sizable number of permanent European settlers have been attracted, but where the native population is numerous enough to remain the majority. If the two groups mix, as they have in Mexico, for example, the basis for a unified nation can be laid, and once the colony wins its freedom, its future is fairly clear. But where the two groups retain separate identities while at the same time becoming dependent upon each other, especially where an effort is made to hold the original natives in a subordinate position politically, economically, and socially, there is likely to be trouble. Examples are the Union of South Africa, now European-ruled and independent; Rhodesia, now European-ruled and revolting against colonial domination; and Algeria, now ruled by its native inhabitants.

Where the European settlers had made themselves an overwhelming majority, new European-peopled nations have been established with the original population exterminated, absorbed, or relegated to reservations. Where Europeans have never constituted more than a tiny minority, the end result appears to be a non-European nation from which most of the Europeans depart once independence is won. For the mixed cases, however, there is no such simple solution. To continue European rule (as in South Africa) is a gross injustice to the native population. Furthermore, it is a highly unstable solution, for the native protest against it increases as time goes on. To evict the European settlers from homes where many of them have lived for generations (as in Algeria) is a tragedy of a different sort. The sane solution, a working arrangement whereby the two groups could live together in peace as equals, appears to be unlikely if one considers the actual cases in all their complexity.

In summary, the history of the four kinds of areas identified has been quite different. The temperate, densely settled areas (mainly European) have been colonizers, not colonies in modern times. The temperate, sparsely settled areas were settled by Europeans and won their independence early. The tropical, densely settled areas (largely Asiatic) have won their independence more recently, while some of the tropical, sparsely settled areas still remain colonial today. In addition, we have indentified a fifth kind of colony where Europeans have settled in the midst of a native majority. On occasion, the pattern has been for the two groups to combine and form unified nations, but in the Union of South Africa and Rhodesia, for example, friction between the two groups has caused brutality and bloodshed, and obscures the future.

The Steps to Freedom

The overwhelming majority of the colonies in the world have already won their independence, and it can safely be predicted that most of the few remaining colonial possessions will do so in the not too distant future. This is not surprising, for colonialism sows the seeds of its own destruction. No sooner is a colony conquered than its population begins to move, slowly and imperceptibly at first, then quickly and noticeably, toward political independence. When and how freedom comes depends, of course, on both the colonizer and the colonials. In particular it depends upon their relative power and upon the moral code and the wisdom of the colonizer.

Imperial rulers may bow out gracefully, like the British in India and West Africa, or they may fight, like the French in Algeria (or the British in America long ago), but they all ultimately leave.

FIRST STEP: UNIFICATION OF THE NATION AND CREATION OF LEADERS

In the discussion that follows, we shall be primarily concerned with the exploitation colonies, for the last of this group are now in the midst of achieving their independence. The settlement colonies have long been free. Indeed, some of them are themselves colonizers today. Certain differences in the development of the two groups of colonies will be noted, but the major emphasis will be upon the path to freedom of the exploitation colonies.

In the case of the latter, European conquest in itself was the first step to freedom, paradoxical as this may sound, for it provided the natives with a grievance and a desire to be independent once more. However, between this first desire and its fulfillment lay many other steps. The power discrepancy between the European colonizing nations and their colonies was initially so great that early revolt, though often attempted, proved fruitless. The colonials had much to learn from their masters before they could hope to tip the balance against them.

It is therefore not surprising that the settlement colonies were the first to break with colonial rule, for these colonials were Europeans who did not need to learn new values and new forms of social organization before they could combat a modern, European ruler. To gain power, they needed only numbers, provided by immigration, and an opportune moment when their rulers were unreasonable, foolish, or distracted elsewhere.

In the exploitation colonies, the picture is almost reversed. Here the native colonials were many and the colonizers few, but differences in culture assured the natives an inferior power position. It took time before the natives could absorb enough of European culture to be in a position to eject their rulers, but the rulers unwittingly helped them in the task.

In such colonies, the first steps to eventual independence were taken by the colonizers. First, they caused resentment by their conquest. Then they unified the conquered into a nation and provided them with nationalistic leaders. Such a course was not as foolish as it sounds. It may be ironic that the colonizer starts the colonials on their march toward independence, but in a sense, he has no choice. To make the colony pay, he is forced to set in motion the forces that eventually spell his ruin.

The creation of a colony means the establishment of new political boundaries where none existed before. Rarely have the limits of European conquest coincided with the old lines of political jurisdiction. More often, European territorial divisions have been superimposed upon a patchwork of smaller native units. Sometimes the new lines divided native peoples from others to whom they were closely connected by ties of blood and politics, but within the new European-imposed boundaries, unification has taken place. People ruled by the same overlord developed a feeling of identity. This was the first step toward their becoming a modern nation.

If only for the sake of pacifying the colony and keeping it under control, the colonizer was forced to build roads and establish better communications between one part of the colony and another, and if economic activities were to be pursued efficiently, local wars within the colony had to cease. The unavoidable result of this increased internal peace and ease of movement was greater movement on the part of the native population and increased mingling among various native groups. This again contributed to the creation of national unity.

One kind of native movement was actively encouraged by the colonial authorities. That was the movement of able-bodied young men from the back country to the centers where their labor was required in mines, on plantations, and in other European enterprises. These were the activities that made the colony profitable to its owners, but here again they were also a contribution to the unification of the native population against its rulers.

Almost everything the Europeans did increased the potential power of the natives. Laborers whose work was required for production could strike or demand higher wages. Customers whose purchases were required for profit could boycott European goods. Taxpayers whose funds were required to run the colonial government could refuse to pay their taxes. As long as the native population continued to carry on its own subsistence economy, there was little it could do to hurt the Europeans or to resist them, but once the natives had been drawn into the European economy, as they had to if the colony was to be profitable, once the Europeans began to depend upon them, their power was increased, for they could withhold their services and their trade—if only they could organize.

Two things were needed before the native population could organize to resist its colonial rulers: a feeling of unity and modern leaders. The colonizers helped provide both. Nothing unifies a people more than common misfortunes caused by a common enemy. Initially, the native population may have been deeply divided against itself, tribe against tribe, or kingdom against kingdom, nobles against commoners, or caste against caste; the colonizers, however, persisted in treating them all alike. High or low, rich or poor, clever or stupid, they were all "natives," to be treated as inferiors. And sooner or later, the high and the low, the rich and the poor, the clever and the stupid came to realize they had a common cause. A single cry rallied them all: "Throw the foreigners out." Once the Europeans were evicted, old rivalries reasserted themselves, but for the duration of the struggle for national independence, the people were united as they had never been before, and as they may never be again.

Racial discrimination has been the most dangerous of all the forces brought by the Europeans to their colonies, for it is a two-edged sword. In the hands of the colonials, it could become a truly terrifying thing. Riots, mob violence, indiscriminate terrorism, these have been the other edge of the sword with which the Europeans held the colonials in subjugation, and in the end, this weapon, more than any other, forced their departure.

The Europeans also trained the natives in modern leadership. Particularly if the number of Europeans was small, the colonizers had to rely upon colonials for many of the economic and political tasks required by the European regime. The army, the police force, the lower levels of the government and business hierarchies were staffed by natives. Slowly but surely, these people began to learn the European techniques and skills that were such an important ingredient of the conqueror's power.

The upper classes among the native population often became quite Europeanized. Through close contact with the Europeans, they learned that the Europeans were superior in power and in possessions, and because the Europeans looked down on them, they often accepted the idea that the Europeans were superior in culture as well. They adopted European clothing, learned to speak the language of their conquerors flawlessly, sent their children to Europe to be educated—and still they were not accepted. This was the rub. The native could not and would not accept the idea that he was innately inferior. He might agree that his culture, religion, system of politics, and living standards were inferior, and so he might change them all. But his European education and his acceptance of the colonizer's ways were not enough to win him the recognition he sought. He had reached the limit of his ability to adapt to European standards; he could not change his race. He was left with two alternatives: he must deny himself or he must destroy the colonial rule that institutionalized his inferiority. Denied admittance to European society, he turned against it and led his people in revolt.

Nearly all the leaders of modern colonial independence movements have been educated in Europe or America: Gandhi and Nehru of India, Mohammed Ali Jinnah of Pakistan, Ho Chi Minh of Vietnam, Nkrumah of Ghana, Azikiwe of Nigeria, and often it has been in the name of European principles that they fought for liberty. The brotherhood of man, the freedom of the individual, these were the principles they cited, principles with which colonialism is sadly at odds.

The colonizing nation was caught in a painful dilemma. If it pacified the colony and controlled it thoroughly, if it developed the colony economically and taught its workers skills and its leaders Western ideals, it was hastening the day of its own departure. If, on the other hand, it chose to be content with partial control over a backward area, that is, if it left the colony little changed, a long and quiet rule was probably assured, but the colony would not provide its rulers with much in the way of wealth and power. In actual practice, no colonial power has deliberately chosen to leave its possessions undeveloped in order to keep them. Nations like England and France have developed their colonies with no clear realization of the consequences. Nations like Portugal have left their colonies political and economic backwaters, but not because they were seeking any advantages this would confer. Nevertheless, it is worth nothing that the Portuguese have been troubled relatively little as yet by colonial agitation for independence. Their empire will eventually go the way of the other colonies, but it will be the last to go.

Colonial rulers *have* held back native developments in areas where they could see that it would contribute clearly to a drive for independence. One of the chief complaints of colonies seeking independence has been that the colonizer willfully postponed the day of freedom by not training natives to fill the top administrative and technical posts, and the charge has often been justified. When colonies first win their independence, their greatest lack is trained personnel. When the Indonesians were fighting the Dutch, their hurriedly assembled department of foreign affairs included a large number of medical men because that was one of the few areas of advanced education for Indonesians encouraged by the Dutch.

For similar reasons, colonial rulers have almost always opposed allowing natives much authority over military forces. When the French were fighting Communist rebels in Indochina, a struggle developed between American officials in charge of aid to the French and the French military officials. The French were using loyal Indochinese troops to fight the Communists, but officers and even most noncommissioned officers were French. The Americans argued that the Indochinese would fight harder if they were led by their own men, but the French feared that an army controlled by Indochinese might be turned against them. From the French point of view, there was little point in saving the colony from communism to lose it to the nationalists. In a sense, the French were right, for the nationalists (with American support in this case) soon won at least a nominal independence, but French policy was undoubtedly largely responsible for the Communist victory in the North.

We have outlined the ways in which colonizers unintentionally have helped their subjects to take the first step toward independence by unifying the colony and by providing it with Western-trained leaders who were hostile to European rule. Once the colony was united and led by able men, it took the rest of the steps to independence alone, though here again, the European rulers helped.

The first step, then, was unification of the people and the emergence of native leaders. The second step occurred when the colonials began to appeal for the redress of minor grievances within the colonial framework. In the third step, the colonials demanded and obtained political rights that eventually led to political independence. In the fourth step, which still lies ahead for most former colonies, the new nation must achieve its economic independence. Let us examine briefly each of these steps.

STEP TWO: APPEALS FOR HUMAN RIGHTS

In the second stage of the movement to independence, the colonials began to ask for certain basic human rights. This put the colonial rulers in an embarrassing position, for the natives, in seeking the end of forced labor, in appealing for better schools and health services, for higher pay, and for better living conditions, were doing no more than voicing the values of the Europeans. Such appeals were certain to arouse support in some liberal and humanitarian sections of the public in the mother country, and particularly if the colonizing nation viewed itself as a benefactor of mankind, the appeals brought limited results.

None of the grievances voiced at this stage challenge colonial rule directly. South African natives are still in this stage. It has been said of them, they do not demand "Africa for the Africans"; they merely ask "Africa for the Africans, too."

Native success in having some of these early demands fulfilled has been due partly to the bad conscience and to the genuine humanitarian instincts of some of the colonizers and partly to the fact that many of the reforms requested contributed to the economic development of the colony. Once colonial rule was well established and the effect of European contact began to be felt, voluntary workers proved more efficient than forced labor, healthy workers were more productive than sick ones, and a certain amount of education was necessary if natives were to fill many of the new jobs in the economy.

Grievances in these areas remained until full independence was achieved (and even afterwards), but a certain amount of progress was to the advantage of colonizer and colonized alike. One particular advantage has accrued to the colonial subjects alone, however. In expressing unity of purpose and in presenting their demands to the Europeans through their leaders, the native population learned political skills and gained good experience for the stiffer political struggle that lay ahead.

STEP THREE: DEMANDS FOR POLITICAL INDEPENDENCE

In the third step, the natives began to ask for political rights. These demands pointed clearly and unmistakably toward political independence. At this stage, native political aspirations received powerful help from the desire of the mother country to govern its colonial subjects with the least expenditure of funds. In the case of a settlement colony, local government was put largely in the hands of the European settlers, and the native population was given over to their charge. In the case of an exploitation colony, however, native institutions were relied upon to carry on many of the functions of government. The penuriousness of English taxpayers lay at the bottom of the traditional British policy of governing colonial people through their own authorities, for if the native structure remained almost intact and the Europeans could control the native leaders, this form of rule was the least expensive possible.

Traditional forms, however, were rarely adequate to meet the new demands of government in a European-controlled society with a semi-modern economy. New institutions were invented—the natives providing the necessary funds and the Europeans deciding how they would be spent. Wherever the natives were allowed to participate in their own government, however, these institutions became important rallying points in the fight for independence. The British, in particular, complicated their lives by creating a whole raft of political bodies, boards, legislatures, and councils in an effort to placate the natives by giving them the forms of self-government without the substance. In practice, the boards had limited powers or European heads, the "legislatures" and councils were largely advisory, and colonial administrators showed their mettle by turning down importune demands made by native bodies.

The difficulty was that in seeking to postpone unpleasantness and to pacify native demands, the colonizer could be trapped into admitting that eventual greater self-rule was a legitimate aim. Inevitably, the pretense did not satisfy the natives for long; soon enough they began to demand real power. For example, they might ask for a different system of representation to replace one that allowed a few thousand whites a greater voice in elections than millions of natives, or for the abolition of the colonial governor's veto in specific native affairs, or that the advice given by their advisory bodies be heeded.

The process of chipping away at the colonizer's rule did not go unchallenged, however. As native leaders became more aggressive in their demands, a counterbalancing force grew up on the side of the colonizer —a group of imperialist die-hards who felt that one concession only led to another, that all compromise with agitation for independence had to be stopped and a "firm hand taken with the natives."

An important factor in determining how rapidly and how easily the colony achieved its independence was the number of permanent European residents. We have already noted that if the European settlers constituted an overwhelming majority, if they had virtually exterminated the native population or were numerous enough to control the natives without outside assistance, they were usually successful in winning their freedom early and turning the settlement colony into an independent nation. The situation, however, was different for exploitation colonies or for those settlement colonies where the Europeans constituted such a small minority that they relied upon the support of the home government to maintain their supremacy within the colony.

A relatively large number of Europeans in a colony of this sort may have hastened the first steps toward independence, creating native unity and political sophistication fairly rapidly, but their presence delayed the final achievement of political independence. Generally, the home government was much more willing to make concessions to native nationalists than were the resident European settlers. Holding onto a colonial population that is determined to be free is an expensive business, and in the last analysis, the home country often decided to cut its losses and let the colony go, with the hope of preserving at least some of the economic ties. The resident European settlers, however, could not take so cavalier an attitude. For them, independence of the colony would mean immediate and far-reaching changes in their personal lives, new laws, new restrictions, higher taxes, the loss of privileged positions in government and in the economy. Perhaps worst of all, from their point of view, it would mean being ruled by people they had always regarded as inferiors, and so they resisted native demands for independence.

If the settlers were numerous, their views postponed independence, sometimes for years, but even their firm resistance was not enough to stem the tide if the natives made up the majority, were united in their views, were led by able leaders, and were determined. When the colonizers were adamant in the face of peaceful native pressure, it was not uncommon for the natives to turn to terrorism and make the life of the settlers unbearable.

Examples of the role played by European settlers can be found in the recent history of both the French and British empires. When nationalist pressure mounted to a high pitch in North Africa, the French granted independence to Morocco and Tunisia, where the number of French settlers was not so great, but tried to hold on to Algeria, where the French population was relatively large. Britain first granted independence to her possessions in Asia and West Africa, where permanent European settlement was almost nonexistent, while Kenya and other East African possessions, where a more temperate climate had made European settlement possible, waited years more for their liberty.

STEP FOUR: ACHIEVING ECONOMIC INDEPENDENCE

The last stage of the struggle for colonial independence occurs after political independence has been won. Even though political freedom has been achieved, foreign rule is not necessarily entirely eliminated. Indeed, it is almost inevitable that immediately after independence, the former mother country should continue to have a great deal of influence over her ex-colony. The new channels of control are economic and social rather than political, but they are important nonetheless. They result from the fact that the new nation is not yet in a position to manage the complex machinery of a modernizing economy.

First of all, the new nation will be in need of technicians. Because of the policies of its former rulers, its own educated people will be few, and of those who have received good training abroad, a disproportionate number are likely to have been trained in such subjects as law and philosophy, subjects that were important during the fight for independence but not sufficient in themselves once independence has been won. Second, the new nation will be in need of capital, and for this, too, it will have to look beyond its borders.

The former colonizer is in a good position to continue to supply these needs—at a price. In this respect, the former ruler has a number of advantages over possible competitors. It still shares a language with the ex-colony, and it probably has some supporters among the population. It has a first-hand knowledge of the problems the colony faces, and its people have a tradition of working in the colony. It has until recently been the principal market for whatever the colony produces and the major supplier of the colony's needs. Finally, it already has a substantial investment in the new nation, and will want to salvage what it can in the way of economic control. Other advanced nations may be reluctant to invest in a new nation whose policies they do not yet know and of whose stability they cannot yet be sure.

Yet even with all these advantages, the colonizing nation has a difficult time maintaining economic control over its former colonies once they are politically free. Three factors operate to split them further and further apart. First, there is the residue of bitterness between the two nations engendered during the final phases of the struggle for independence, especially if it has been a violent one.

Second, once the colony is free, there will inevitably be problems with which the new nation cannot cope effectively. Although not all these problems stem directly from colonial rule, the temptation is great to blame the former rulers for all the problems and failures of the new nation. It is a great convenience for a new and shaky government to be able to channel popular resentment against an outside target. However, such action makes it extremely difficult for the former colonizer to take an active role in the new nation's economy, for anything it does is bound to be criticized as a continuation of imperialism.

Finally, if the new nation is large and if it develops its economy rapidly, foreign domination of any kind is difficult to maintain. England would have found it impossible to hold onto the United States after the latter had begun to grow even if there had been no war of independence. British influence in India today is precarious for the same reason.

However, the fact that political ties with the old colonizer have been broken does not mean that foreign domination is at an end. The break with the colonizer simply means that the colony has freed itself from the rule of that particular nation. Even though politically free, the new nation is still a weak nation, dependent on other countries for the fulfillment of its most important economic needs, and this dependence means that veiled foreign control will be continued.

Summary

One of the characteristic forms of relationship between the weak and the strong in modern world politics has been colonialism. We have defined a political colony as any territory that is governed by a foreign country and whose inhabitants are not granted full political rights. In most cases, the native inhabitants of the colony are also treated as inferior to those of the mother country in economic and social spheres. We have distinguished between settlement colonies (largely sparsely settled, temperate regions where European colonists became the majority of the population and soon won their independence) and exploitation colonies (largely tropical areas that have become independent only recently).

Political colonialism reached its most recent peak around 1900. Throughout the twentieth century, this form of colonialism has been crumbling away, for it has proved to be a self-liquidating system. European rule has furthered primitive unification within the colonies and stimulated the rise of native nationalist leaders. These leaders have demanded—and generally won—first minor reforms and eventually political independence. Full economic independence, however, still lies in the future for most of the former colonies. Before the new nations can become fully free, they must learn to use their people and resources efficiently. In economic and social fields, independence cannot be won by enthusiasm and self-sacrifice alone or by mob action, armed ambush, and terrorism. Victory in these areas is infinitely more difficult to achieve. Unless it is achieved, however, the revolt of a colony may mean only a change of masters, for foreign control, which is the essence of colonialism, will be continued.

11

The New Colonialism: Economic Dependencies and Satellites

❖❧❧❧❧❧❧❧❧❧❧❧❧❧❧❧❧❧❧❧❧❧❧❧❧❧

Classic colonialism is all but dead, but new forms of colonialism are taking its place. Nations that have won their nominal political independence are not necessarily free. No one observing the present international scene can ignore Russian domination of the nations of Eastern Europe, nor is it possible to overlook the control exercised by the United States over large portions of Central and South America as well as various outposts in Asia such as Taiwan, South Korea, and South Vietnam. Colonies that have just managed to win their political independence, and also some nations that have never been colonies before, are falling prey to new forms of colonialism. In fact, the modern international order is grounded on these new colonial relationships, and the nations that lead the world today, the United States and the Soviet Union, are also the greatest modern colonial powers.

The study of this new colonialism is far more difficult than the study of classic political colonialism, in part because the new colonialism is so recent. Economic dependencies, it is true, have existed for quite some time, but until recently, say until the end of World War II, their importance was overshadowed by that of the traditional, political colonies. Satellites existed in their extreme form no more than a dozen years or so; now they too are changing.

Another cause of difficulty is the fact that it is not generally recognized that these new relationships are really colonial in character and deserve to be studied as such. No admission that these are colonial ties can be expected from the nations involved in these new relationships. The United States, for example, would deeply resent being called a colonial power ("imperialist nation" is the Communist phrase), and the representatives of the Soviet Union have stated again and again without so much as a blush that the Communist bloc is a voluntary assemblage of entirely free states. Moreover, the new colonies of the Western and Communist powers would probably not consider themselves to be colonial possessions.

Again, because the new colonialism is so recent, we cannot be certain whether or not these colonies will eventually free themselves, and if so, what road to freedom they will follow. Nevertheless, it is important to understand these new forms of dependency, for they are an important part of the modern international scene.

Modern Colonialism Defined

There are in the world today four distinct types of colonies. Alongside the remnants of classic colonialism, or "political colonialism" as we prefer to call it, three other types are growing in importance: economic dependencies, military dependencies, and satellites.

ECONOMIC DEPENDENCIES

An economic dependency is a nominally independent nation whose major economic enterprises are controlled by a foreign country. Obviously no hard and fast line exists between economically dependent and independent nations, for foreign control can be exercised in varying degrees. Nevertheless, we can identify many nations that clearly are not their own economic masters.

In practice, all economic dependencies today are economically underdeveloped nations. They are all controlled by nations that make a clear separation between their own economic and political institutions, that is, the home economy of these nations is not owned and operated by the government. Thus businessmen of such a nation can control the economy of another nation without involving their government in direct political control of the economic dependency.

As in the case of the political colonies, the people of the dependency generally differ in race and culture from those of the controlling nation, and the latter often believe themselves to be superior in race and culture as well as in power and standard of living. There are also exploitative elements to the relationship, although the benefits accruing to the dependency are greater. Finally, as with the political colonies, the relationship is highly profitable to the controlling nation.

One may argue that the dependence of an underdeveloped nation upon a more powerful and more economically modern country is not colonialism at all because the relationship is voluntary and because both benefit from it. One may argue that the benefits enjoyed by the stronger nation are merely its due. This may be true, but none of these statements denies the fact that the underdeveloped nation *is* dependent upon another nation and will find it difficult to break away. It seems odd to contend that international voluntary servitude is not servitude at all. Because an economic dependency may benefit from its lack of freedom does not mean that it is free, nor does the fact that it *thinks* of itself as free. Indeed, the fact that neither colonizer nor colony thinks of the relationship as colonial helps to perpetuate it.

MILITARY DEPENDENCIES

A military dependency is a nominally independent nation whose national existence is dependent upon the presence of foreign troops. Examples would be South Vietnam and South Korea, both dependent upon the United States. Such nations not only are host to large numbers of foreign troops, but also have their own military forces armed, supplied, and controlled by a foreign power. The controlling nation places limits upon the action permitted to the dependency's military forces. For example, they may not cross into neighboring territory, even that of enemies, unless it is the policy of the controlling nation that they do so.

The internal government of a military dependency rests nominally in the hands of its own nationals, but again the controlling nation places limits upon the actions of the national government, not only in foreign policy but also in internal affairs.

Military dependency is not a new form of colonialism. Many great imperial powers have had allies that were really military dependencies— certainly the protectorates of England and France in the nineteenth century were military dependencies in the beginning, although they sometimes became full-scale political colonies later.

As in the case of economic dependency, military dependency can vary greatly in degree, and it is difficult if not impossible to say exactly when national independence disappears. In extreme cases the nation is virtually occupied by foreign troops and its government heavily controlled from abroad. In other cases (for example, Taiwan), national existence is guaranteed by the controlling nation, foreign military bases exist, and the national forces are armed and supplied by the controlling nation, but large numbers of foreign troops are not present. Presumably they would be in case of conflict, but for the moment they are not. In still other cases nations may rely heavily upon foreign military aid and upon the territorial guarantees of foreign allies, but they retain control of their own government and military forces. The United Arab Republic, for example, although armed by the Soviet Union, did not seek Russian advice before provoking hostilities with Israel in 1967.

Military dependency is further complicated by the fact that most such dependencies are also the recipients of large amounts of economic aid and are often economic dependencies or satellites as well. At least in theory, however, it is possible to separate the two kinds of dependency.

SATELLITES

A satellite is a nominally independent nation that is dependent both politically and economically upon a more powerful foreign country. This form of dependency is peculiar to Communist nations. At present the Soviet Union is the only nation to have satellites, although for a few years in the late 1950s and early 1960s China seemed well on her way toward developing satellites of her own, beginning with North Korea, North Vietnam, and, to a lesser extent, Albania. However, internal Chinese upheavals, particularly the Chinese Cultural Revolution that began in 1966, destroyed much of China's influence in the Communist bloc and permitted the North Vietnamese and the North Koreans to reassert their independence.

Four features distinguish the satellites from the economic dependencies:

First, there is the degree of control. Because the government runs the major economic enterprises in a Communist nation it is impossible for one Communist nation to dominate the political institutions of another without also dominating its economy. Thus the control exercised over satellites is more complete than that exercised over the economic dependencies.

Second, a satellite is controlled largely through its leaders, who belong to the same political party as those of the dominant nation. Ideological unity is great between the leaders of the two nations.

Third, nations with satellites rely much more heavily upon political ties as a way of exercising power, whereas the controllers of economic dependencies rely more heavily upon economic rewards and punishments. In both cases, however, the existence of superior force in the background is felt.

Fourth, the satellites have nearly all been European nations, adjacent to the Soviet Union. Outer Mongolia, North Korea, and North Vietnam are exceptions. Interestingly enough, China sought to bring all these nations into her orbit, where again they would have been adjacent in territory and similar in race and culture to the nation that controlled them.

With these essential points in mind, let us now look more closely at the most important of these new forms of colonialism.

Economic Dependencies

Historically, economic dependencies have originated in three ways. (1) There are former political colonies that have won their political freedom but are still tied economically and socially to the nation that formerly ruled them. (2) There are former political colonies that have freed themselves both politically and economically from the mother country only to fall under the economic control of another great power. (3) There are nations that have never been political colonies.

There are few examples of this last sort, since most of the non-European world has been under the political yoke of the Europeans at one time or another, but Liberia belongs in the third category. Although this African nation has been politically independent since its creation more than a hundred years ago, it is economically controlled by the United States and always has been. Thailand, Afghanistan, and Iran are other nations that have escaped direct European rule.

Former colonies still under the economic control of their old masters are more numerous, although for reasons discussed in the previous chapter, this relationship does not generally last long. Recently independent underdeveloped nations almost always find it difficult to stand on their own economic feet at first, and consequently they must lean upon some nation more developed than they. As we have noted, the former colonial ruler usually tries to perpetuate a relationship in which the ex-colony remains economically dependent upon the mother country for capital and expert personnel in production, for markets for raw materials and handicrafts, and for handling the distribution of its products to other nations.

Once political ties have been severed, however, the continuation of such a relationship is a difficult feat for the former colonizer to carry off. Generally, therefore, within a short time after all political ties have been cut, the new nation is likely to forsake its old masters and become the economic dependency of some other nation instead. Indonesia, for example, continued to be controlled economically by the Dutch for a few years after her independence, but within a decade she broke all economic ties with the Netherlands. The Middle East continued to be dominated by Britain and France even after they had relinquished formal political control over the area, but these nations are now gravitating into the spheres of Russia and the United States. Most of the former British and French colonies in Africa will probably remain economic dependencies of their former rulers for a time at least. A relatively rare example of a former colony that remained an economic dependency of the same nation for many years is Cuba, which has been politically independent since 1902, but which continued to the day of Castro's revolution to have its economy dominated by American interests.

Far and away the most common circumstance is for the recently freed colonies of one nation to drift into the economic sphere of another. Thus England took over economic control of many of Spain's colonies in Latin America when they first revolted, and the United States took them over from England at a later date. The United States today has picked up as economic dependencies many of the colonies relinquished by other nations. Not only has she taken over colonies from her former enemies, such as South Korea and Formosa from Japan, but she is also falling heir to many of the colonies of her best friends, who may not have died, but who are retiring (with a nudge from us) from world domination. Thus America is replacing Britain and France as the major power in that part of the Middle East that is still free from Soviet influence. The United States has replaced France as the dominant power in Vietnam, and Americans are playing an increasingly important role in Africa.

Russia, too, is seeking economic dependencies, although in her case this is presumably an introductory step to full political control. Her bids for power in the Middle East, Latin America, and elsewhere, have aroused anxieties about areas long considered safely under the control of the West. China may be expected to make similar attempts at economic domination of small Asian nations in the future.

ECONOMIC CONTROLS

As we have indicated, the key to economic dependency lies not in any legally defined political status but in de facto control of the economy. The way to spot an economic dependency is relatively simple: if the major economic enterprises in the nation are run by foreigners (especially production and export marketing), the nation is an economic dependency. Sometimes foreigners of several nationalities combine or compete with each other for control of the economy, but in such cases, there is usually one nation whose interests are predominant.

It should be clear that even in an economic dependency, much of the economy remains in native hands. In an underdeveloped area, the majority of the population consists of peasant farmers engaged primarily in raising crops for their own subsistence. This sector of the economy continues to be owned and controlled by the natives—by tribal groups, by individual peasant owners, or by landlords, resident or absentee. Handicraft work remains in native hands, to the extent that it can continue to exist at all in the face of competition from mass-produced imports. Retail trade may also remain in native hands, though often this is carried on by a separate group of foreigners (Chinese through much of Southeast Asia, Indians in East Africa, and Levantines in much of West Africa), and the professions, such as the law and medicine, may be staffed largely by the native elite. Industry, finance, commercial agriculture, and the export-import trade, however, are heavily controlled by foreigners in such countries. Often they own outright the plantations, mines, industries, commercial houses, and banks; and they fill the top managerial and technical positions.

It is difficult to devise a foolproof measurement for determining when the economy of one nation is controlled by the nationals of another. In some instances, foreign control may be disguised. Firms may have local names and important local people may share in their profits and even in their management, but still they may be controlled by foreign interests or by foreign firms whose affiliates they really are. Even fully developed, powerful, and completely independent nations may allow foreign firms to operate within the nation, so the mere existence of foreign businessmen is no proof of economic dependence. When the country is weak and underdeveloped, however, and when the major part of its modern business is controlled by foreigners, the difference is one of quality as well as quantity.

Theoretically, it should be possible to determine that when a given percentage of the national income, say 51 per cent, not including subsistence agriculture and retail trade, is earned by foreigners, the nation is an economic dependency, but practically such a measurement would be almost impossible to make. National income statistics are notoriously poor for underdeveloped countries, and in addition, many of the payments in which we are interested would show up as part of the national income of the outside country. In the absence of a reliable yardstick, we must use common sense in determining which nations are economic dependencies and which are not, and such conclusions are always open to question, particularly by those who for reasons of financial advantage or national pride are interested in disguising the true nature of their economic dealings.

We should at this point take brief notice of another form of economic control which differs from that we have been discussing. Since World War II the United States and to a lesser degree the Soviet Union, Britain, France, and even some smaller nations like Israel have offered extensive economic aid to friendly governments. As a reward, such aid always represents some exercise of power by the donor. In many cases it is simply an effort to bolster friendly governments and to assure their continued friendship. However, where the donor is strong, the receiving nation weak, and the aid extensive, economic aid becomes a form of control of one government by another. In extreme cases where a government finds a substantial part of its budget provided by foreign economic and military aid, there exists a state of economic dependency quite apart from other intervention in the economy by foreign private citizens.

THE EXERCISE OF INDIRECT POWER

Officially, an economic dependency is a free and sovereign state with a government that makes its own decisions in the national interest. Practically, however, any national government is responsible to a large extent to the most powerful interests within the nation, and this is particularly true of preindustrial nations that are not mass democracies. It stands to reason that if foreign nationals control the major concentrations of economic power within a nation, they will have a large voice in its government, and this is in fact the case. Sometimes the path of influence is obvious, as in Saudi Arabia, where the bulk of the government's revenues is provided by royalties from resources developed by foreigners. In other situations, however, more subtle techniques may be used and the influence may be more difficult to trace. Outright bribery of important officials in the form of money or jobs for relatives and protégés is not uncommon, but such arrangements are not likely to be announced publicly. Sometimes influence can be exercised informally through semisocial relationships between government officials and important foreign businessmen whose good will is valued both because they are personal friends and because their enterprises are important in providing jobs for the local population and taxes for the government. If it is known that important foreign interests "favor" certain candidates or certain policies, their wishes will carry weight.

It is difficult to write of such relationships without implying that they are somehow immoral or illegal. They are sometimes both, but this is not necessarily so. The point is simply that wealth is a tremendous source of power. Possessing it, foreign business interests in an under-developed area would be foolish if they did not use it to secure for themselves the most advantageous arrangements possible and to protect themselves from competitors and from unwelcome interference by officials whose laws and customs differ from their own.

¶ *Disadvantages.* Control through such mechanisms as these is much more precarious, however, than outright colonial control. For one thing, "the controllers" are not colonial administrators who can be hired or fired at will and whose actions can be determined by the policies of the home government. They are private firms and individuals who may have aims of their own quite different from those of their governments.

Second, the control that these individuals exercise over the foreign government is much less thorough. Their interest in controlling the government is limited to certain specific areas that affect their business dealings, to tax policies, labor legislation, import restrictions, etc. Whether the dependency is willing to grant America an air base or vote on America's side in a dispute in the United Nations may be of no direct concern to American businessmen abroad. In certain basic matters, however, the interests of home government and businessmen abroad will coincide. Both, for example, will be highly interested in seeing that the government of the dependency does not go Communist or become markedly anti-American (or anti-British or anti-French, as the case may be).

This lack of direct control over the government of an economic dependency may be a serious handicap. Granted that powerful foreign interests generally have an important influence on the government, there is little they can do if the national government chooses to oppose them openly. The foreigners can throw their weight behind rival politicians hoping to swing an election or engineer a coup d'état, but this may be dangerous, for the government can always enlist nationalistic sentiment against them. In the last analysis, the national government controls preponderant force in the form of military forces and police. The foreigners cannot count on the support of the official security forces as they could if the country were a political colony. They can call for support from the troops of their home nation, as Americans did in the Dominican Republic in 1965, but it may or may not be forthcoming. If it is, the whole nature of the relationship between the two countries is changed, and direct political control is substituted for the indirect economic control that has functioned successfully up to that point.

There are instances, of course, in which troops from the dominant nation are stationed in the dependency, but it is necessary to look closely at the role these forces play before jumping to conclusions. American troops stationed in England or even in Iceland did not exercise any power over the government of their hosts. American Marines in the Dominican Republic, on the other hand, were direct agents of full political control. England and Iceland are allies, not dependencies, of the United States. The Dominican Republic was, at the time the Marines were there, a political colony in all but name. It reverted to being an economic dependency when the Marines departed.

¶ *Advantages.* Although there are many disadvantages of indirect economic control as opposed to direct political control, it also has advantages. Indirect economic control through private individuals is much more difficult to detect and hence much less open to opposition. This is an important asset today when so many of the economic dependencies are former colonies whose citizens are highly nationalistic and whose leaders are particularly sensitive about foreign domination. If control is exercised behind the scenes, the symbols and the trappings of power can be held exclusively by natives of the country. Formal diplomatic relations between the two can be scrupulously correct; the representatives of the stronger nations can exercise great care to preserve the appearance of independence.

The public may not even be aware of the extent to which the nation is dominated by foreign interests, for unless there are protracted labor troubles or particularly ugly social behavior on the part of resident foreigners, the activities of the economic colonizers are seldom such as to create the feelings of unity and hatred necessary to sever the relationship. If antiforeign feelings *should* flare up, there are few concrete symbols of foreign domination to attack. There are no foreign troops to battle, no foreign officials to assassinate, no large foreign population to terrorize. A mob may loot the embassy or destroy an information center, but such incidents can be glossed over without stirring up too much permanent hard feeling.

For the colonizer, then, economic dependencies have an advantage over political colonies in that they permit the appearance of independence to be maintained and obscure the real dimensions of control that one nation has over the other. Such an advantage may be difficult to maintain indefinitely, however, in an age of increasing communication and rabid nationalism, particularly in countries where other major powers competing for domination of an area keep up a barrage of propaganda exposing the control exercised by the dominant nation.

Another advantage of indirect economic control is that it absolves the dominant nation of many responsibilities. A colonial ruler is held responsible for the living standards of the populace, for its health facilities and schools, but the nation that dominates an economic dependency has no such responsibilities. A private firm is considered generous if it provides decent housing for its workers and sets up a plant dispensary; it has no responsibility for the rest of the population. If Arabians are poor, something is wrong with Arabia. Aramco would hardly be blamed.

The dominant government is also in the position of not having to take responsibility for what its citizens do abroad, although here the escape is not so complete. It is true that the government is not legally responsible, nor is it politically responsible as far as its own home population is concerned. A government can stand by calmly and accept the benefits while its citizens abroad bribe and threaten and topple governments and generally behave in ways that it would be reluctant to allow its own officials to behave. Liberals and humanitarians at home may deplore such actions, but again, they are less likely to blame the government for them. Citizens of the abused dependency, however, may not make this fine distinction. Once antiforeign feeling gets to running high, it is almost certain to be directed against the innocent and the guilty alike. A handful of misbehaving individuals can bring down upon all their fellow countrymen the wrath of the dependent population, and the dominant government's interests will suffer along with those of the businessmen abroad.

FEELINGS OF SUPERIORITY

Feelings of superiority on the part of the dominant Europeans or Americans are particularly likely to cause trouble of this kind. Such feelings are usually carried over from the colonial period and are likely to be even more marked among businessmen who come and go than among colonial administrators who stayed long enough to gain some first-hand knowledge of the culture of those they ruled. Businessmen are not generally trained in cross-cultural tolerance, and when they find production schedules upset by unskilled, untrained native labor and by officials and suppliers whose pace of work, business ethics, and value systems differ greatly from their own, they are liable to develop highly derogatory stereotypes of "the natives." The fact that foreign businessmen are dependent upon the good will of a government of "natives" and consequently cannot express their prejudices openly merely increases their frustration and hostility.

The native population, particularly if it has recently emerged from colonial status, is highly sensitive to any suggestions that it is inferior. The faintest nuance of such a feeling is picked up, as if by psychological radar. Such sentiments are hard to hide, for they crop up in a hundred different ways, in the turn of a phrase, in a lift of the eyebrows, in an impatient gesture. Those who deal with the Europeans are all too well aware of what the Europeans think of them, and they resent it deeply. On the surface, everything may seem calm, but a small, even trivial incident may suddenly bring to the surface emotions that are shocking in their depth and in their violence.

EXPLOITATION AND THE SHARING OF BENEFITS

Despite these undercurrents of animosity, relations between a nation and its economic dependencies are generally less troubled than those between a nation and its political colonies toward the end of the period of colonial rule. As we have indicated, foreign control of an economic dependency is much less obvious and therefore less open to attack, and feelings of superiority, although still present, are expressed less openly and less brutally. In addition, the whole relationship is less exploitative. The discrepancy in power between the two nations, although great, is not as great as in the case of a political colony, and as a result, some of the more naked forms of exploitation vanish. Forced labor, for example, is replaced by free labor—underpaid perhaps, but free.

Also, natives of the country receive a substantially larger share of the benefits. Royalties, rents, taxes, shared profits, and wages help to enrich the local economy to an extent that was not true when the colonizers controlled the government as well as the economy of the dependency. A disproportionate share of these benefits, however, usually flows into the hands of a relatively small native elite while the majority of the population continues to have an extremely low standard of living. But the fact that a group of powerful natives benefits directly and substantially from the ties that bind their nation to a foreign power proves useful to the foreigners. It means that they can count on important friends at court. In case of trouble, the first line of defense will be made up of natives who will exercise all their influence in favor of the foreign interests that benefit them so heavily.

Economic dependency is profitable, both to the dominant foreigners and their nation and to at least a small group of the citizens of the dependency. To realize how profitable our own economic dependencies are, one need only imagine what would happen to the American economy if we were suddenly stripped of them all. The temporary closing of the Suez Canal in 1957 brought home quite sharply to England and France how dependent they were on Middle Eastern oil and what a large stake the West had in continued economic control of that part of the world. Economic dependencies may not be quite as profitable as peaceful colonies, but they are profitable enough that the nations that control them go to considerable lengths to retain them.

Political and economic colonialism are by no means incompatible. It is quite possible for a nation to have political colonies in one part of the world and economic dependencies elsewhere. In practice, however, nations seem to lean toward one form of domination or the other. England and France have been the great modern political colonizers, whereas economic penetration has been the form favored by the United States.

There are, of course, underlying reasons why political colonialism flourished in the past, whereas economic dependency is more widespread today. For one thing, the level of economic development, both of the colony and of the colonizer, must be considered. Economic dependency is a subtler and in some ways more rewarding form of control than political colonialism but it is not possible as long as the colony has a primitive economy and lacks a national political organization. As the old colonies completed more and more of their primitive political unification and began to undergo more economic development, they threw off their old rulers, but at the same time, they became ripe for economic dependency. The level of economic development of the dominant nation is probably also a factor.

The United States has been peculiarly fitted for the role of economic colonizer. Its own colonial past has made political colonialism unpopular with the American people. In addition, the United States was still concerned with its own internal development during the years when England and France were occupying all the available colonial areas. However, as the American economy developed, it was only natural for American economic interests to look abroad for raw materials and for markets. Moreover, the United States became the politically and economically dominant nation in the world at just the time when the old colonial empires were beginning to break apart. It was practically inevitable that many of the newly freed nations, unable to stand alone, should gravitate toward such an industrial giant, a source of aid and arms, a gigantic market for their raw materials, and a practically inexhaustible warehouse of the machines and manufactured goods they are so anxious to acquire.

THE FUTURE OF THE ECONOMIC DEPENDENCIES

But what is the future of the economic dependencies? Will they, in their turn, become free and win their economic independence as they have already won their political freedom? The probable answer is that some will, and some will not. Political freedom is achieved when the colonizer unites the colonial population against itself and gives it a sense of nationhood, but economic independence can be achieved only when the dependency becomes fully modern economically, politically, and socially.

A small dependency can never become a major world power, nor can it hope to equal the power of the nation that dominates it. However, through industrialization or through complete modernization of its agriculture, it can hope to achieve a position such as that of Switzerland or Denmark or New Zealand. In short, it can learn to manage its own economy and to enter into economic dealings with other nations on more equal terms. Large dependencies, such as Indonesia, may even become major world powers if they are able to modernize their economies.

In a world split between East and West, however, the industrialization of the economic dependencies raises some major political problems. Broadly stated, the issue is this: Which path to industrial strength will they choose, the way of the West or that of the Communist bloc? If they choose our way, then, although the particular nation that controlled them may lose out, the Western alliance as a whole will gain through the acquisition of a newly effective member; but if they elect to travel the Communist road of industrialization, the Western world will suffer a double loss. Most of the economic dependencies have barely begun to industrialize and have yet to make their final and definitive choice between Western-style democracy and communism. This fact creates considerable anxiety for the West, which presently controls them.

The question has often been raised: Why don't the United States, England, and France help their economic dependencies to modernize in the democratic way and thus end once and for all the fear that these nations will desert to the Communist camp in their desire for rapid progress? The full answer to this question is lengthy and complex. Parts of it have already been suggested, but some of the main points can be summarized here.

1. The Western nations controlling economic dependencies are not wholeheartedly in favor of their modernization, because this would alter the relative power of the nations involved and compel a major readjustment in their relationship, a readjustment that would probably end most of the privileges and advantages currently enjoyed by the dominating nation and its businessmen. The Western alliance as a whole might gain. Even the dominating nation as a whole might gain, for a far greater volume of profitable trade can be carried on with a modern nation than with a backward one, but the particular individuals and firms now thoroughly established in the economic dependency would

probably lose out. Consequently, they will not exert much effort to upset a situation that is currently satisfactory for them.

2. Nations controlling dependencies indirectly through private businessmen do not control them closely enough to force through the changes that may be necessary for modernization but that are unpopular with important segments of the local population. Far from being in a position to foster social progress, foreign business interests are closely related to the most powerful elements of the existing social order, generally men who favor the status quo because they benefit greatly from it.

3. Industrialization requires large sums of capital which no one is in a position to supply. The government of the controlling nation is not responsible for the economic development of its dependency and cannot, within the existing political relationship, take over the responsibility of expediting capital formation. Private businessmen of the controlling nation do provide limited amounts of capital for the particular enterprises in which they have interests, but in a free economy, it is not their responsibility to make long-range plans for the national economy or to organize the dependent population to produce more capital. The government of the dependency is powerless to raise the required capital because it does not control the economy of the nation. Moreover, the type of modernization fostered by economic dependence on the United States and the Western European powers, with its emphasis on consumption, is not conducive to the kind of structural changes in the local economy that will lead to self-sustaining economic growth in the future.

4. The major effort in industrialization must be made by the people of the dependency themselves, but the obstacles to be surmounted are great. Left to their own devices, many people in the dependencies find it easier to indulge in fantasies that they are already modern. Governments may encourage such fantasies by buying a few guns and uniforms and the latest jet planes for the armed forces, by building a few modern houses and hotels, by laying down some modern highways and importing some shiny, foreign cars. This gives a superficial impression of rapid modernization, but it is an illusion. Two basic problems are not fully faced: first, that industrialization cannot be achieved painlessly; second, that a nation cannot successfully pursue at the same time the contradictory goals of a Western standard of living and preservation of the traditional way of life.

5. One final fear that plagues the West is this: as matters now

stand, the economic dependencies, backward though they may be, are in the Western camp. Their current rulers have no real choice between us and the Communists, for the coming of communism to their lands would mean the end of all their own wealth and privileges. However, once these countries begin to industrialize in earnest, who knows what changes may occur, what groups may rise to power, or what their aims may be? A little aid, a modest improvement in living standards and health and education, we certainly approve, but a thoroughgoing social revolution such as rapid industrialization produces may be dangerous. Granted that there are risks of Communist revolt if the present mixture of poverty and privilege is left undisturbed, there are also grave risks in upsetting the apple cart through rapid modernization.

Many of the facets of this problem are beyond the scope of this chapter, but two questions should be touched upon. What is the Communist appeal to these nations, and who in these nations is most susceptible to Communist promises?

THE APPEAL OF COMMUNISM

Communism (more properly "Stalinism") is, among other things, a means of industrializing rapidly, and this is its great attraction for the nonindustrial world today.[1] The slow process by which the Western world industrialized, which may well be necessary if a democratic society is to emerge at the end of the process, has severe drawbacks for people anxious to enjoy the economic fruits of industrialization within their own lifetimes. Western admonitions about the necessity of slowing the tempo of change appear to the economic dependencies as ill-disguised attempts to keep them at their present stage of economic development. Stalinism is appealing because it includes no such cautions. "Go ahead as rapidly as you can," say the Communists, not bothering to mention the price that must be paid for such rapid change—a price of compulsion, terror, social disorganization, and even *lower* living standards for the time being.

Stalinism is also appealing because it is offered by nations that have had few relations with the economic dependencies in the past. Western democracy, on the other hand, is offered by the same nations that have exploited the dependencies during their colonial past and that exploit them still in their present state of economic dependency. Because of their own past history, the dependencies are highly suspicious of any system

[1] See Chapter 3.

advocated by the West. Colonial administrators have done the West a vast disservice by claiming that they were acting in accordance with the principles of Christianity, democracy, and capitalism, when in fact they were engaging in age-old forms of repression and exploitation, for they have soured the only words we have to express our highest ideals. Communist propaganda is likely to be taken at face value in the economic dependencies, but Western propaganda has long ago been thoroughly discredited. We will be a long time living down our colonial reputation.

Another appeal of Stalinism lies in its promise of equal treatment for all races and nationalities. Again, the West has created its own liability in this regard. Quite probably Russians three hundred years ago or even a hundred years ago would have treated colonies filled with Africans or Asians as badly as the Western Europeans did, but the fact is that it was the Western Europeans who had the colonies and therefore had the opportunity to behave so badly. Once born, a tradition of racial superiority does not die easily, and even today, large numbers of Americans and Western Europeans consider themselves superior to Africans and Asians. The treatment of Negroes in America does not make matters any better. All of this gives the Communists a very decided advantage in dealing with former colonial nations who have experienced Western intolerance.

Interestingly enough, the Chinese, though never colonial rulers in the Western sense, have migrated throughout Southeast Asia and have exposed other nations to enough of their own feeling of cultural superiority to arouse considerable resentment. Indonesia's savage rejection of communism in 1965 was as much anti-Chinese as anti-Communist in inspiration.

Finally, it should be noted that the economic dependencies are faced with a great temptation to use the threat of going Communist as a bargaining tool against their Western dominators. One of the classic techniques by which a subordinate may increase his power is by playing off two masters against each other. This is a dangerous game, but skillfully played, it can win great prizes.

The second question is: Who in the economic dependencies is most susceptible to Communist promises? It is generally believed that communism makes its strongest appeal to the underprivileged masses, but this is not the case. Mass discontent provides a powerful revolutionary force once it has been channeled by Communist leaders, but the leaders themselves are rarely drawn from the underprivileged. Almost without exception, the leading Communists in underdeveloped areas are either members of the new, rising, Westernized bourgeoisie or they are Western-educated sons of wealthy landowners.[2] Strange as it may seem, this same group provides the leadership both for Western-inspired democratic movements and for Communist revolutions. It is they, not the masses, who are most vulnerable to Communist propaganda and indoctrination. It is the loss of them which is most dangerous for the future of the West.

The appeal of Stalinism to these people is fairly obvious. As Westernized individuals who have absorbed many of the values of an industrial society, these people no longer belong to the old, traditional society, but they are not Europeans either, and the Europeans reject them and look down upon them. They are, in a sense, men without a country. Their own society has no fitting place for them; it does not offer them positions where they can make full use of their skills. Although these nations badly need competent administrators and technicians, they cannot even provide enough jobs for the handful of trained young people that they have. Unused and embittered, many of these young people are highly attracted by an ideology that promises to overthrow the existing social order and place them in positions where they will be needed and respected and where they can use their skills to create the world of their dreams.

These are the people with the biggest stake in rapid industrialization, for it will destroy the social order that presently bypasses them. It will destroy also the poverty and ignorance and superstition that make them ashamed of their country. To such people, Western warnings to go slowly are infuriating, for they wish to reach the promised land within their own lifetimes so that *they,* not merely their children's children, can enjoy the thrill of leading a nation that is powerful and rich.

One may wonder, are not such educated people aware of the tremendous price in human suffering that must be paid for rapid industrialization? Some of them are and for this reason prefer the slower and more democratic way, even though it may be more frustrating to them personally, but others apparently are not, or if they are, easily gloss over it. After all, it is not they who will pay the price for rapid industrialization, for they will be the leaders of the changing society. It is not they whose living standard will be cut to provide capital. It is not they who will be forced—at gun point if necessary—to change their way of life.

The racial argument of communism also has great appeal for these people. The average citizen of an economic dependency has few direct dealings with Europeans, but the educated native who deals with them daily, who has been to their schools and read their books and visited their countries, has felt the full brunt of European prejudice. What a pleasure

[2] See Morris Watnick, "The Appeal of Communism to the Peoples of Underdeveloped Areas," in Reinhard Bendix and S. M. Lipset, *Class, Status and Power* (New York: Free Press, 1953).

it must be for him to dream of the day when he will lead a country that is rich and strong, when he can tell the hated Westerner: "Go home. We do not need you. We do things in our own way here."

It is by no means certain whether the economic dependencies will choose the Stalinist or the Western way to industrial strength. The appeal of communism to these areas is potentially great, but the West has great advantages in its superior power, in the wealth of aid (capital goods, consumer goods, and technical assistance) it can offer, in the very real appeal of personal freedom, and in the fact that the West currently controls these nations. Given a will to modernize its dependencies and to treat their people as equals, the West should win this particular struggle hands down, but in the absence of such a will, the outcome is less certain. Most of the dependencies are beginning to modernize today. Which way they choose is one of the most important international decisions of our time.

Satellites

Let us now turn to a brief examination of the satellites. On the whole, control over satellites is much tighter than control over economic dependencies, and the process through which it is exercised is also different from the manner and method used by Western powers to control economic dependencies.

For the first decade of the lives of the satellites the degree of control exercised by the Soviet Union was truly amazing. The sight of the representatives of Poland, Czechoslovakia, East Germany, Rumania, Bulgaria, Hungary, and Albania aping the words and actions of the Soviet representatives at international meetings, the never-ending eulogies of the leaders of the Soviet Union, the introduction of Soviet methods of organization in the economy and in the military forces, the creation of vital political institutions similar to those of the USSR, and the constant submission to the will of Moscow gave a fair idea of the degree of Soviet control over the satellites.

After 1957, however, a marked change occurred in Russo-Eastern European relations: The satellites began to act with a considerable amount of independence compared with the earlier period. The change was so great and so startling that many observers maintained that the term "satellite" no longer expressed the relationship between the USSR and the Eastern European countries under her rule. This view, perhaps, carries things too far, for the degree of control that the Soviet Union exercises remains high. It does seem fair to say, however, that the changes in

Eastern Europe are important enough that the decade before 1957 and the years since then should be treated as two separate periods.

It helps, perhaps, if we think of the satellites of the Stalin era as resembling political colonies more than economic dependencies, whereas after 1957 they increasingly resemble economic dependencies. It must be stressed, however, that throughout both periods the satellites have kept unique features of their own that differentiate them from economic dependencies or political colonies.

RESEMBLANCES TO POLITICAL COLONIALISM

In some ways, Soviet control over the satellites during the first period resembled classic political colonialism. Russia had virtually complete control over the governments of the satellites. These governments were staffed by nationals of the satellite nations rather than by Russian colonial administrators, but Soviet control over their actions was complete. Changes in Soviet government policy were reflected almost immediately in the satellites. This was not a coincidence, nor did the changes originate in the satellites.

If anything, Soviet control over the political life of the satellites was even more complete than that exercised by the colonial rulers of the past, for totalitarian government reached into every nook and cranny of the land and affected even the private lives of those under its control. Colonial rulers in the past were interested primarily in the maintenance of order, the collection of taxes, and a certain amount of economic exploitation of the colony. Beyond this, they did not care much how the natives lived. The Russians, however, had and still have broader aims. In addition to maintaining order (and their own control) and to exploiting their possessions economically, they also wished to communize them, to turn each satellite into a miniature edition of the Soviet Union. This meant changing not only the behavior but also the values of the entire population, a task that required very firm political control, indeed.

A second similarity between the satellites and the political colonies lay in the use of compulsion to maintain control over them. The presence of Russian military forces within these nations or on their borders was a decisive factor in the maintenance of Soviet control. The importance of these troops and of the fact that the satellites knew they would be used should they try to sever their ties with the Soviet Union cannot be overestimated. The use of large contingents of Soviet troops to put down the Hungarian revolt against Communist rule in 1956 left no doubt whatever in the minds of satellite peoples of the consequences of attempting to desert the Communist bloc. The brutal repression of the revolt also gave the rest of the world a clear picture of the exact relations between the Soviet Union and her neighbors to the west.

During this first period the national governments of the satellites were creatures of a foreign power. Their control over their nations rested on the military might of Soviet forces. Each of these governments was placed in power by the victorious armies of the Soviet Union at the end of World War II, when the territory was occupied by the Red Army. These governments did not enjoy a monopoly of force within their own boundaries, but depended completely upon the support of Soviet forces.

The exceptional case of Yugoslavia proves the point, for Tito did not owe his power to the Russian Army. He established his power as a leader of partisan fighters against the Germans, and his country was never occupied by Soviet troops. Thus the local military and paramilitary forces within the nation were under the control of the Yugoslav government. When Tito chose to break with the Russians, he took these forces with him, and there was no organized force in Yugoslavia to oppose him. It is perfectly true that the USSR controlled enough military might to have obliterated Tito's forces, but to have done so would have constituted an open act of war, which the Soviets apparently deemed too dangerous, given the international situation at the time.

Again in this first period the satellites resembled political colonies in the high degree to which they were economically exploited by the Soviet Union. It is hard to measure the extent to which one nation exploits another, but the impression is that the amount of exploitation lay somewhere between the great amount common in political colonies and the lesser amount characteristic of economic dependencies. The forced growth of economic ties with Russia at the expense of potentially profitable economic relations with the Western nations was similar to the kind of control that the great imperial nations of the past exercised over their colonies. Major economic enterprises, especially those concerned with the production of important resources, were often jointly owned by the Soviet and satellite governments with much of the direction openly in Russian hands.

It is interesting to note that early relations between the USSR and Communist China, a nation too large and too independent to be controlled tightly as the satellites were, followed more the pattern of the economic dependencies than that of outright political colonialism. Chinese political and military institutions were under firm Chinese control. Economically, however, China was in dire need of outside help and the only possible source of such aid was the USSR. In giving this assistance, Russia apparently tried to exploit China through such methods as joint economic enterprises. However, a change of Soviet regimes (plus China's growing strength) brought an end to these arrangements after the death of Stalin.

In the second period China destroyed whatever illusion there had been that she was a client state of the Soviet Union in any form, for she not only emerged as a great power in her own right, but openly challenged Soviet control of Eastern Europe and Soviet leadership of the world Communist movement.

RESEMBLANCES TO ECONOMIC DEPENDENCY

We have said that in the first decade of their existence the satellites resembled traditional colonies in the firm political control that was exercised over them, in the use of force to maintain that control, and in the high degree to which their economies were controlled and exploited by foreign interests. But even during this period, they resembled economic dependencies in some ways, most particularly in the fact that they were legally independent and that control over them was exercised indirectly rather than through direct political relations between the two governments concerned.

In the economic dependencies, control is exercised through foreign businessmen who, because they control the country's major economic enterprises, have a considerable influence upon its government. In the satellites, control is exercised through the Communist parties, to which the leaders of both nations belong. In both cases, the appearance of political independence is maintained in formal relations between the governments and in official statements. Beneath the pretense of independence, however, the satellites possess considerably less freedom than the economic dependencies.

Even the pretense of satellite independence has not been very skillfully utilized by the Soviet Union. In the first decade of Soviet rule this potential asset was totally dissipated by the absolute conformity and obsequiousness demanded of the Soviet satellites, behavior that rendered absurd any claim that these nations were really free to make their own decisions. Not only in the outside world, but also in the satellites themselves, people understood very well that they were not free. This policy had serious consequences for the USSR, for it completely spoiled the elaborate masquerade, enabled the peoples of the satellites to understand who their real rulers were, and led them to make the Soviet Union a target for their dissatisfaction. After 1957, however, when controls were loosened, the Soviet Union began to enjoy—more nearly—the benefits (and suffer the headaches) that the United States enjoys in her relations with her economic dependencies.

The reasons for the growing independence of the satellites since 1957 are immensely intricate, but it is possible to summarize them under three headings.

First among all the factors contributing to the change is the liberalization process within the Soviet Union after Stalin's death. Russia's entrance into the national welfare stage of politics and her moves to turn away from Stalinism at home had immediate and inevitable repercussions in Eastern Europe. Khrushchev's denunciation of the fake Moscow purge trials in the 1930s stimulated denunciations and opposition to the equally fake anti-Titoist trials and purges of the 1950s in Eastern Europe. On the other hand, official denunciation of past repression in the USSR immobilized Stalinist leaders in Eastern Europe, accustomed to aping their masters in the Kremlin, and kept them from repressing unrest in their own countries.

The second group of reasons for change in Soviet-satellite relations is related to the first. The Soviet Union, through her control of Eastern European governments, had exacted great sacrifices from the peoples of those countries, in part because of Soviet economic exploitation and in part because of the Soviet drive to force the satellites through rapid industrialization. Economic want and political repression made life in Eastern Europe hard and hopeless. The sacrifices were great and they were being imposed by an outside power, which made them doubly difficult to bear. By permitting—and indeed encouraging—disapproval of past Stalinist repression at home, the Soviet leaders allowed discontent to come to the surface in Eastern Europe. When it surfaced, it was directed not only against political leaders at home, but also at the foreign power that had pulled the strings and made them act.

One must distinguish between de-Stalinization and desatellization, however. Pressures for de-Stalinization have been greatest in the economically more advanced satellites. Three of the four most advanced (Poland, Hungary, and Czechoslovakia) have moved far in the direction of de-Stalinization at home but have at the same time remained faithful to the Soviet Union. Liberalization within these nations has been favored by the same forces at work in the USSR, and the almost parallel development has not interfered with a continued close relationship with the Soviets. East Germany alone has remained Stalinist but may change after Ulbricht is gone.

Among the economically less developed satellites, the reverse has been the case. Two out of three (Rumania and Albania but not Bulgaria) have shaken loose from Soviet control while remaining Stalinist internally.

Their assertion of independence has been at least partially in response to liberalization within the Soviet Union, which local Stalinist leaders considered to be out of step with their needs. This has also been a source of disagreement between the USSR and China.

A third major factor leading to the liberalization of Soviet control of Eastern Europe and indeed greater freedom for satellites everywhere was the emergence of China after 1958 as an open challenger of Soviet leadership. China was too large and too powerful to be browbeaten or bullied into submission by Russian power. While Stalin lived, the Chinese leadership was ready to defer to a man who had always been recognized as leader of the Communist camp, but the new leaders of Russia could not expect the same regard and did not receive it. The deepening conflict between the two Communist giants created anguish, confusion, and uncertainty among the smaller nations over which leader to follow, but it also created a setting in which the giants had to court favor with their clients, who were therefore given a measure of independent choice.

Understandably the loosening of Soviet controls appeared to many in the West as even greater than it was because of the unbelievable conformity demanded earlier. The cumulative impact of the defiance of Tito in Yugoslavia, of Gomulka in Poland, and of Ceauşescu in Rumania, to mention only three, was interpreted as a trend indicating early disintegration of the Soviet international system. It would appear more realistic to suggest that ties between the USSR and her dependencies will continue to loosen and that loose ties will permit modified Russo-satellite relations to have a better chance of surviving in a modern world.

UNIQUE FEATURES OF THE SATELLITES

Communist colonialism, though it resembles other forms of colonialism, is unique in several respects. First, nearly all the satellites border on the nation that dominates them. This was a characteristic of ancient colonialism, but it is rare in modern times. The nearness of the colonies has several effects. It makes them easier to control militarily, and it also means that military control can be maintained even without actually stationing troops within the satellite, for with modern means of transportation, Soviet troops can be across the border in short order.

Again, the satellites differ from other modern colonies and resemble the colonies of ancient times in the fact that their population is not racially or culturally very different from that of the dominant nation. This is important, for it eliminates the problem of racial discrimination, one of the most objectionable characteristics of Western colonial rule. Eastern Europeans are not on an equal footing with Russians because they are politically and economically dominated by the latter, but they are not considered socially inferior. Indeed, many Eastern Europeans consider themselves culturally superior to the Russians. Their resentment of Soviet domination may be strongly nationalistic, but it can never take the racial twist that is so important an ingredient of the attitude of those who inhabit the economic dependencies and the political colonies controlled by the West.

Another unique feature of Communist colonialism is the use of a political party as an instrument of domination. This is a feature of great strength, for it creates a strong bond between the ruling elite of the satellite and that of the dominant nation, a tie that cuts across the national loyalty that would incline these leaders to seek political independence. Certainly at the time of Stalin, but also today, the existence of a common ideology has enabled the ruling elite of the satellite to see its subservience to foreign interests as loyalty to an ideal rather than as betrayal of the nation. Thus the dominant nation can depend upon nationals of the satellite to help maintain control over the government without having to send in its own administrators. It is true that nationalistic tendencies arise, even among trained Communists, but they are less of a threat to Soviet domination than are the corresponding sentiments of the leaders of the economic dependencies of the West.

Soviet colonialism differs from that of the West in still another respect: The Soviets seem bent on industrializing their dependencies. In Western colonization, industrialization takes place *after* the colony has broken away from the mother country politically, and once industrialization is achieved, it spells the end of economic dependency. The Russians, on the other hand, have used their control over the satellites to hasten their industrialization, and by the 1960s much of Eastern Europe could no longer be considered preindustrial.

It may seem strange that the same process that frees the Western colonies should be actively fostered by the Soviets in their own colonies, but the policy is not so foolish as it seems. Several things should be kept in mind. First, industrialization of the satellites has meant a tremendous growth in the social and economic relations between the USSR and her satellites and among the satellites themselves. The Russians, through their control of major institutions in the satellites, had hoped to be in a position to supervise and direct all phases of the change and to see that it increased the economic dependence of the satellites upon the USSR. In actuality this has not occurred. With economic modernization the more crudely exploitative relationships have tended to diminish and the satellites have been exercising increasing economic autonomy. With industrialization the degree of Soviet control has lessened. Nevertheless, within this looser framework it is the industrial satellites that have maintained the closest ties with the Soviet Union.

Second, industrialization of the satellites has cost the Soviet Union little. The bulk of the capital necessary for industrialization has not come from the colonizer but has been squeezed out of the colonies by reducing living standards. Dictatorial governments have been able to force through changes even though they may have been extremely unpopular with the bulk of the people.

Although the Soviet Union has certain advantages over the West in industrializing its dependencies, we must not fall into the error of thinking that Stalinist industrialization is easy. The violent Hungarian revolt and the earlier abortive revolt in East Germany were both caused at least in part by popular resentment over reduced living standards. Such outbursts attest to the fact that a government cannot cut the standard of living of its people below a certain point with impunity, no matter how powerful the instruments of repression at its disposal. In the satellites, nationalistic sentiments are strong. Discontent with the hardship of life under Soviet rule found a natural channel in nationalistic uprisings.

THE FUTURE OF THE SATELLITES

Once again, we must ask: What of the future? Can the satellites ever become free? And once again the answer must be largely speculative. A return to the crude and bitterly repressive controls of the Stalin era is not likely. It is more likely that relations between the Soviet Union and the Eastern European countries will change and loosen even more. As the satellites develop their economies further, hardship and repression should diminish and internal liberalization increase. In other words, de-Stalinization seems a permanent trend. So does a certain amount of desatellization. Strong centrifugal forces exist, in part because of the attractions of trade with the West and in part because of the reluctance of the wealthier satellites to continue supporting the poorer ones. But centripetal forces are also present in the ideological and organizational ties between the ruling elites of the various nations and in the sheer economic and military power of the Soviet Union. Dependence of the satellites upon the USSR may become even looser, but the new arrangements now developing are more likely to survive the inevitable stresses and tensions of a modernizing international system than the bonds they have replaced.

Summary

Stripped of the verbiage that often surrounds it, colonialism turns out to be a relationship between a strong nation and a weak one, a relationship in which the power exercised by the strong nation is so great that the weaker nation cannot be considered independent. Classic, political colonialism is going out of existence, and we shall soon see its end, but domination and exploitation of the weak by the strong continue under new forms. It is instructive to compare the new forms with the old.

In political colonialism, external domination of the colony is openly and legally recognized, and the government of the colony is administered directly by officials of the stronger nation. In the more modern forms of colonialism, however, the nature of the relationship is not openly admitted. Economic dependencies are controlled indirectly through the fact that businessmen who are nationals of the stronger nation control the major economic enterprises in the weaker nation. Military dependencies are controlled through their dependence upon foreign military forces. Satellites are dominated through membership of the officials of both nations in the Communist parties of their respective countries.

Political colonialism has proved to be a self-liquidating relationship, but economic, military, and satellite dependency show indications of surviving for many more years. All are flexible arrangements in which the degree of foreign control can vary from absolute domination to barely noticeable influence. For the economic dependencies, independence will come with economic modernization. For the satellites, however, industrial status seems compatible with continued—though lessened—political domination from abroad. Military dependency will probably never cease completely and indeed may even increase with the growing complexity and cost of modern weapons.

It is the strong nations that set the course of international politics, but in our concern with them we should not overlook the dependencies that make up such a large part of the world. The modernization and the shifting allegiances of these areas will have a major influence upon the future of world politics.

12

The Balance of Power

❖❖❖❖❖❖❖❖❖❖❖❖❖❖❖❖❖❖❖❖❖❖❖❖❖

In the previous two chapters we have studied the changing relationships between the great powers and the small, between the handful of most powerful nations in the world and the collection of colonies, satellites, and economic and military dependencies whose affairs they control. We turn now to an examination of the relations among the great powers them-selves, and as we do so, we approach the heart of our story, for it is largely upon these relations that the peace and progress of the world depend.

The political relations of independent nations, and especially of the great powers, traditionally have been explained by the theory of the balance of power. Contemporary writers have called the balance of power "a basic principle of inter-national relations,"[1] "a manifestation of a general social principle,"[2] and "as nearly a fundamental law of politics as it is possible to find."[3] It is a tool that scholars may use to interpret

[1] Norman D. Palmer and Howard C. Perkins, *International Relations* (Boston: Houghton Mifflin, 1953), p. 309.
[2] Hans J. Morgenthau, *Politics among Nations*, 4th ed. (New York: Knopf, 1967), p. 163.
[3] Martin Wight, *Power Politics* (London: Royal Institute of International Affairs, 1946), pp. 45–46.

events and that statesmen may use as a guide to practical politics. It is a statement of the political facts of life—or so they say. Many of the political scientists interested in international politics see the great powers as constantly engaged in building, maintaining, and defending the international balance, and the balance, of course, is a balance of *power*. This balance is said to be difficult to achieve and even more difficult to maintain, but no matter how weary, the statesman must never turn from his task, for the maintenance of the balance is necessary for international peace and stability.

The balance of power has both its critics and its defenders. Idealists have long condemned power politics in general and the balance of power in particular, feeling that the pursuit of power is devoid of moral meaning and that nations engaged in this pursuit often run roughshod over moral principles. Realists have defended the balance of power on contradictory grounds: first, that the moral rules that govern individual behavior simply cannot be transferred to nations in the international field; and second, that the pursuit of the balance results in the greatest good for the greatest number. In short, realists and idealists may disagree as to whether the balance of power *should* be sought, but they are in substantial agreement that the theory of the balance of power adequately explains the conduct of nations as it actually occurs in this presently imperfect world.

The writer disagrees. It seems fairly obvious that if the theory of the balance of power explains adequately the political relations among nations, it would be wise for statesmen to use it as a guide for their foreign policies. But the crux of the problem is just this: Is the balance of power theory of any value? Does it explain correctly the facts of international politics? I shall argue that it does not, that it distorts grossly the meaning of events, that it is an alien plant plucked from another discipline and forcibly transplanted in the field of international power relations. What is more, the theory is not even consistent with itself.

Good or bad, the theory is widely held, however, and before moving on to the principles that seem to me to explain political relations among modern nations, we had best examine the balance of power. We shall first consider the theory itself and then what is wrong with such a view of international politics.

The Theory of the Balance of Power

The theory of the balance of power is rarely stated with crystal clarity. As we shall see, the theory is plagued with ambiguities, and writers who discuss the balance of power often do not define their terms with any exactness. Assumptions are often unstated, and contradictory conclusions are implied. To cut through the mass of words that have been written about the balance of power over several hundred years and to extract the nub of a coherent theory is a big order, indeed. The exposition that follows is surely oversimplified, but an effort has been made to present the main points fairly. The reader who feels that an injustice has been done is invited to read any of the treatments of the topic by other modern writers and to draw his own conclusions.[4]

The main points of the theory of the balance of power can be set forth as follows: Given a large number of nations with varying amounts of power, each one striving to maximize its own power, there is a tendency for the entire system to be in balance. That is to say, the various nations group themselves together in such a way that no single nation or group of nations is strong enough to overwhelm the others, for its power is balanced by that of some opposing group. As long as this balance can be maintained, there is peace, and the independence of small nations is assured.

Let us look into this in more detail. The idea of a balance of power is often explained by reference to an old-fashioned set of scales such as Justice is pictured holding in her hand. On the two dishes of the balance are nations, varying in weight according to the amount of power they possess. Power is balanced when the nations in each camp (on each scale) are of equal power.

Two different types of balances are sometimes distinguished. One is the simple balance we have just described. It may involve only two nations, or it may involve a large group of nations, but in either case, they are divided into two opposing groups of roughly equal strength. The other type is the multiple balance, which can be likened to a chandelier or to a Calder mobile, with many nations and many groups of nations balancing one another and with further balances within balances where the members of one of the major world blocs balance off each other as far as minor disputes within the bloc are concerned. There is no limit to the variations and combinations that are possible in a multiple balance of power.

It is an underlying assumption that nations are in conflict with each other, not only because many of their interests differ but, far more important, because each nation is bent on maximizing its own power. If one nation were to be successful in achieving a tremendous preponderance of power, it is assumed that this would endanger the liberty of all

[4] Two recent texts that treat the balance of power at length are Morgenthau, *op. cit.*, part 4, and Palmer and Perkins, *op. cit.*, chap. 9.

the rest. Consequently, the other nations must rise to this danger and meet power with power. As Nation A increases its power, B will strain to equal the achievement of A. If B cannot do so alone, she will join with other nations, and together they will offset the power of A. Thus any single nation's attempt to maximize its power will be blunted by the power drive of another nation or group of nations, and a balance is supposed to result.

In peaceful times, there may be many separate balances in different parts of the world, but in times of crisis, the simple balance will prevail. This is to be expected, because a major struggle for power spreads. As the main contenders seek to maximize their power, other nations that have not yet taken sides will be drawn into one of the two competing factions, and the complex, multiple balance (which once included balances within balances and independent or semi-independent balances) will slowly change into a simple balance between two groups of nations, one on each scale.

Sir Winston Churchill has given a good description of the simple balance that is said to have operated before World War I.

> The great Powers marshalled on either side, preceded and protected by an elaborate cushion of diplomatic courtesies and formalities, would display to each other their respective arrays. In the forefront would be the two principal disputants, Germany and France, and echeloned back on either side at varying distances and under veils of reserves and qualifications of different density, would be drawn the other parties to the Triple Alliance and to what was already now beginning to be called the Triple Entente. At the proper moment these seconds or supporters would utter certain cryptic words indicative of their state of mind, as a consequence of which France or Germany would step backward or forward a very small distance or perhaps move slightly to the right or to the left. When these delicate rectifications in the great balance of Europe, and indeed of the world, had been made, the formidable assembly would withdraw to their own apartments with ceremony and salutations and congratulate or condole with each other in whispers on the result.[5]

Other examples of the simple balance would be the approximately equal distribution of power between the Anglo-French combination and the Axis nations of Germany and Italy just before World War II. It is sometimes claimed that a similar balance exists today between the Western democracies and the Communist bloc.

[5] Winston Churchill, *The World Crisis* (1931 ed.), p. 43, quoted in Wight, *op. cit.,* p. 44.

The picture we have presented so far is far too static to do justice to the theory of the balance of power. Balancing is a dynamic affair, and there are constant shifts in the total power in each scale of the balance. Continuous adjustments are necessary in order to preserve an equilibrium.

Writers have identified at least six distinct ways in which nations may act in order to maintain the balance. Whenever the weight of power on one side of the scale is growing too heavy, the nations on the opposite side have two alternatives open to them: they can act to increase their own power, or they can attempt to diminish that of their adversaries. More exactly, they can arm, seize territory, set up buffer zones, form alliances, intervene in the internal affairs of other nations, or divide and conquer. Let us examine each of these suggested possibilities in turn.

¶ *Armaments.* Perhaps the quickest and most visible way of gaining a power advantage over a rival or of catching up with a successful competitor is to arm. As long as war is the ultimate arbiter, known ability and suggested willingness to fight at the drop of a hat will be a source of power. Whenever one nation suddenly increases its military strength, its rivals have little choice but to try to catch up. If the first nation can preserve the advantage it has gained, the balance of power is upset, but if its rivals can erase the advantage through arming themselves, the balance of power is preserved, though at a somewhat more explosive level. One need not search far for illustrations of this practice. Today's armament race between East and West, or more specifically between the United States and the Soviet Union, is probably the greatest and most spectacular ever seen.

In a similar fashion, disarmament, too, could be used to destroy or to restore a balance of power, but in practice this is rarely done. The nation that arms first stands to gain in power terms, but the nation that disarms first runs a serious risk. In consequence, disarmament is often discussed but rarely practiced unless there are assurances that all will disarm together in such a way as not to disturb the current distribution of power, whatever it is.

¶ *Seizing Territory (Compensation).* A second important method of increasing the power of a nation is for it to seize more territory and more people. When such an act occurs, the nations on one of the scales gain in power and tip the balance, unless the nations on the other side take immediate steps to increase their own power in compensation. In such cases, a powerful nation about to absorb a smaller one may be ordered by its powerful rivals to share its prey with them or at least to allow them to compensate themselves elsewhere at someone else's expense. The first partition of Poland in 1772 is sometimes cited as a case in point. Austria presumably was unhappy about the whole affair but could not afford to stand aside while Russia and Prussia carved up Poland, and so she joined in and received a share in order to preserve the power status quo. The division of the world into colonies and spheres of influence is sometimes justified on these grounds. The colonies lose all their power, of course, but the nations that seize them can justify their actions on the grounds that if they did not act, their rivals might, and then the balance of power would be upset.

¶ *Buffer Zones.* A different manner of preserving a given distribution of power between two powerful rivals is to set up a neutral buffer state between them. A buffer is a weak nation located between two large and not too friendly nations or their spheres of influence. Its function is to keep the two giants apart and thus reduce the chances of friction between them. Poland, for example, has been the traditional buffer between Russia and Germany; Belgium and Holland have been buffers between France and Germany; and there has been talk of neutralizing substantial portions of Southeast Asia as a buffer between areas of Communist and Western interest.

Since an addition of territory and people to one side would tend to upset the balance between two major competitors, neither of them can allow the other to absorb the small, independent nations sandwiched between them, and the buffer, in a way, owes its existence to the competition of the giants. The difficulty, however, as the reader may have anticipated, is that the balance can be maintained just as well if the two giants decide to divide the buffer zone between them in equal shares. Buffers often vanish in this fashion. Witness today divided Germany, Korea, and Vietnam, neatly cut in half in the interests of power.

¶ *Alliances.* In addition to increasing its individual power, a nation may improve its power position by the right selection of allies. The making and unmaking of alliances, the constant switching from one side of the scales to the other, this is the stuff of international politics, according to the accepted view. If Nation A is becoming powerful enough to threaten the balance, then its opponent, Nation B, will ally itself with C to right the balance again. It is maintained that the greater the number of nations involved, the greater the chance that the balance of power will work in a satisfactory manner; the smaller the number of nations involved, the more rigid and unworkable the balance is likely to become. Obviously, if there are many nations, the number of possible combinations by which a balance can be achieved will be greater, and consequently it will be easier to make the adjustments necessary to keep the scales equal. The large number of major powers in the eighteenth century is one of the things that made that period the golden age of the balance of power. On the other hand, if the number of major nations is small, the defection of one state from one side to the other will cause too large a shift to be made up easily by new alliances and counteralliances, and the equal distribution of power may be irreparably destroyed. Indeed, one of the chief reasons given for the failure of the balance of power to work satisfactorily today in the fifteen years after World War II, was the bipolarization of power between the United States and the Soviet Union.

¶ *Intervention.* It is not always possible to be sure of the loyalty of allies. Self-interest may lead them to switch sides or to try the dangerous game of playing one side against the other. In such cases, it is not unusual for a major nation to regain a lost ally or perhaps pick up a new one by intervening in the internal affairs of a smaller country and establishing a friendly government in power. This method is used more often than nations like to admit. Britain intervened in Greece at the end of World War II to see to it that the nation did not fall into the hands of local Communists. The Soviet Union intervened in the affairs of all its European satellites at the end of the war to establish Communist governments. The Middle East has been the scene of almost constant intervention by one or another of the great powers, and the United States has manipulated internal affairs in many a Latin American republic. Guatemala and the Dominican Republic are the most recent cases in point. In a sense, the United States has intervened in the affairs of all the nations to which she has given military and economic aid, and the Soviet Union and China have followed suit.

¶ *Divide and Conquer.* A final method of altering the distribution of power is to detach allies from the opposing side, leading them into neutrality or at least into isolated opposition where they cannot benefit by pooling their strength with others. England has pursued this policy with great success in many of her colonies. Germany made many efforts to separate England and France in the years preceding each of the two World Wars, and Russia today is continually trying to detach England and France from the American camp, just as we encourage Eastern Europe to assert itself and talk somewhat wishfully about the possibilities of getting Russia to join our side against China.

These, then, are the methods employed by nations that are said to be engaged in maintaining the balance of power. Those who seek to redress a balance that is turning against them may increase their own power by arming, by insisting on a proportionate share of the enemy's territorial loot, or by allying themselves with other nations. On the other hand, they may decrease the power of their competitors by injecting discord and division among their ranks or by intervening and placing friendly governments in power. Finally, they may stake out neutral buffer zones with an agreement that they are to belong to neither side.

We shall save our major criticisms of the balance of power theory until later, but it should be noted here that these six methods, described as ways of maintaining or regaining a balance of power, are in fact simply ways by which a nation can increase its power. There is nothing about the methods themselves to prevent their use by giants to achieve a tremendous preponderance of power over the rest of the world, or by hopelessly overpowered small nations that merely wish to improve their position slightly. All these methods of gaining power have been used and will be used again, but whether or not the actual distribution of power that results is a *balance* remains to be seen.

THE SELF-REGULATING BALANCE AND THE BALANCER

The result of all of these manipulations is said to be a balance of power. Each individual nation, of course, is seeking a preponderance of power for itself, but because there are many nations and because they are in competition with each other, no single nation is allowed to achieve a preponderance; a balance results, instead. Thus, in a fashion reminiscent of classical economics, the quest for private gain is assumed to result in public good. The system is self-regulating, at least in theory.

In practice, however, the balance sometimes breaks down. At this point a new concept is introduced: the concept of the balancer. The balancer is a nation or a group of nations that remains aloof from the rivalries of others. Its interests are best served if the international balance of power is maintained, and consequently, as long as the other nations are in balance, the balancer does not intervene. If, however, one side gains enough strength to tip the scales, the balancer acts, joining the weaker side and bringing the scales back into balance. The balancer, presumably, is motivated primarily by a desire to keep the balance. Whichever side becomes stronger, he will join the other.

The concept of the balancer is the keystone of the entire theory. It takes consummate skill to be a balancer, and the nation or group that fills this role must possess great power, for it must be strong enough to tilt the scales decisively in favor of the side it joins. It is claimed that the balance has not worked very well recently because there was no balancer strong enough to affect the distribution of power between the United States and the Soviet Union and because all the major nations had chosen sides in the ideological struggle, with none reserving their freedom to switch from one side to the other.

There have been balancers in the past, however, according to the theory. The nation that is believed to have filled this difficult role for the longest period and in the most successful manner is England. A classic statement of England's role was written in 1906 by Sir Eyre Crowe, England's Permanent Under Secretary for Foreign Affairs:

> History shows that the danger threatening the independence of this or that nation has generally arisen, at least in part, out of the momentary predominance of a neighboring state at once militarily powerful, economically efficient, and ambitious to extend its frontiers or spread its influence, the danger being directly proportionate to the degree of its power and efficiency, and to the spontaneity or "inevitableness" of its ambitions. The only check on the abuse of political predominance derived from such a position has always consisted in the opposition of an equally formidable rival, or of a combination of several countries forming leagues of defence. The equilibrium established by such a grouping of forces is technically known as the balance of power, and it has become almost an historical truism to identify England's secular policy with the maintenance of this balance by throwing her weight now in this scale and now in that, but ever on the side opposed to the political dictatorship of the strongest single state or group at a given time.
>
> If this view of British policy is correct, the opposition into which England must inevitably be driven to any country aspiring to such a dictatorship assumes almost the form of a law of nature.[6]

De Gaulle has dreamed of a Europe led by France filling the role of balancer today.

CONSEQUENCES OF THE BALANCE

Successful maintenance of the balance of power is said to have two important, beneficial results. First, it preserves the independence of small nations that would probably be swallowed up if one ambitious

---

[6] Sir Eyre Crowe, "Memorandum on the Present State of British Relations with France and Germany," in G. P. Gooch and Harold Temperley (eds.), *British Documents on the Origins of the War 1898–1914* (London: H.M.S.O., 1928), vol. 3, p. 402, cited in Robert Strausz-Hupé and Stefan T. Possony, *International Relations* (New York: McGraw-Hill, 1950), pp. 242–43.

state were allowed to achieve a tremendous preponderance of power. Granted that the great powers occasionally get together and agree to carve up their smaller neighbors, the situation is felt to be better than it would be if a single nation dominated the world without opposition. As long as the great powers must vie for the favor of smaller allies and as long as the great powers fear each other, the small nations are assured a certain amount of independence.

The second benefit often claimed for a successful balance of power is that it produces peace, for when power is equally distributed among various nations and coalitions of states, no one side can achieve a great enough superiority to be sure that aggressive action would be crowned with success. This uncertainty is said to help prevent aggression.

Thus the balance of power can be and has been defended on moral as well as practical grounds. Such achievements as peace and the independence of states are held to justify the occasional lack of ethics displayed by nations attempting to keep the balance by dissecting buffer nations, overthrowing unfriendly governments, or abandoning allies for their opponents.

THE HISTORY OF THE BALANCE

If the balance of power is in truth a fundamental law of politics, it should be possible to trace its workings in the history of international relations. Scholars have done just this, seeing balance after balance in the shifting history of modern times.

Some writers have traced the operation of the balance of power back as far as the Greek city-states, but although this may be somewhat doubtful, there is general agreement that the balance of power was operating by the sixteenth century. Indeed, the sixteenth, seventeenth, and eighteenth centuries are believed to have been the golden age of the balance of power, the period when this complicated international mechanism worked best. The nineteenth century saw a continuation of the operation of the balance of power. It is only in the twentieth century that the mechanism is believed to have broken down, and already, new balances are seen to be emerging.

It would be both impossible and undesirable to trace here the full details of international history for the past 450 years, but a few examples of the major balances can be given. In the sixteenth century, the major rivalry was between the Hapsburg Empire (Austria and Spain) and France, with England playing the role of balancer. At least that is the way in which Henry VIII saw his role, for he had as his motto, *cui adhaero praest* (whomever I shall join will triumph), and he is said to have had his picture painted holding a pair of scales with France on one side and Austria on the other.[7] His daughter, Queen Elizabeth, continued the policy, breaking off England's alliance with Spain and throwing England's weight on the side of France as Spain rose in power. Venice is also credited with playing balancer in the sixteenth-century rivalry between the Hapsburgs and France.

Another classic example of the balance of power in operation is drawn from the eighteenth century, when a multiple balance of great complexity is said to have existed. As fortunes rose and fell, the great nations switched partners, maintaining the balance. Thus in 1740, Britain and Austria stood together against France and Prussia, while a short sixteen years later, Britain and Prussia were allied against France and Austria.

The rise of Napoleon upset the apple cart, but after the Napoleonic Wars were over, Prussia and Austria together balanced the Russian Empire, and all three together with the help of England formed a counterbalance against the recovery of France. By the end of the nineteenth century, the multiple balance had once more been reduced to a simple balance, thanks to the rapid rise of Germany. The Triple Alliance of Germany, Austria-Hungary, and Italy was balanced by the Franco-Russian alliance, while England once more acted as the balancer.

England is seen as continuing to try to play the role of balancer in the twentieth century, uniting with France against Germany when Germany was strongest and helping to strengthen Germany again after both her major defeats.

In the decade and a half immediately after World War II, a simple balance is said to have existed between the American-dominated Western bloc and the Russian-dominated Communist bloc. The simple balance was worldwide. Because of the breaks and conflicts within the two blocs, it is now argued that a new multiple balance is emerging. Smaller balances are seen in the Western Hemisphere, in the Middle East, and in the Far East. There is even talk of an emerging balance in Africa. However, it is generally agreed that the balance of power has not functioned very effectively in the twentieth century.

Criticisms of the Theory

The idea of a balance of power is certainly plausible and surely interesting. Indeed, it has been proclaimed so many times and by such august authorities that it has entered into that realm of ideas that people almost take for granted. In view of this, it is shocking how badly

[7] Morgenthau, *op. cit.*, p. 280.

the theory stands up under even the most cursory critical examination. The sad truth is that the balance of power is neither a logical abstraction nor an accurate description of empirical fact. Let us begin with some general criticisms before getting down to cases.

THE SEARCH FOR A LAW OF INTERNATIONAL POLITICS

The balance of power theory appears to owe at least part of its acceptance to a deep-felt desire on the part of some students of international politics to have a law of their own as other sciences have. Many other disciplines have adopted a concept of equilibrium. There is a balance between flora and fauna, and there is a state of equilibrium in the human body. The concept of equilibrium plays a part in modern economic theory and in the functional approach that is popular in contemporary sociology and anthropology. However, because a concept is useful in one discipline is no proof that it will be useful in another. Certainly, it does not justify elevating the public relations statements of sixteenth-century monarchs and nineteenth-century diplomats to the status of scientific theory.

The popularity of the balance of power theory derives not only from the general desire for a law of politics but also from the fact that this theory purports to describe processes that are *automatic* (or at least semi-automatic). Reference has often been made to the fact that the balance is natural and therefore inevitable, and this natural law has been seen to operate for the ultimate good of the whole of international society. As one political historian has commented:

> It [the balance of power] seemed the political equivalent of the laws of economics, both self-operating. If every man followed his own interest, all would be prosperous; and if every state followed its own interest, all would be peaceful and secure. Only those who rejected *laissez faire* rejected the Balance of Power—religious idealists at one extreme, international socialists at the other.[8]

It was extremely useful to regard the balance of power as a natural law that worked semi-automatically, for this shifted the burden of moral responsibility from the shoulders of individual nations to the impersonal forces of Nature. A reply was possible to those who charged that nations committed immoral acts in their attempts to preserve the balance. After all, one could not very well charge Nature with immorality. In recent years, there has been less attempt to justify the balance of power on

[8] A. J. P. Taylor, *The Struggle for Mastery in Europe 1848–1918* (Oxford: Clarendon, 1954), p. xx.

moral grounds, but the idea remains that its operation is somehow inevitable.

Perhaps the major reason for the general acceptance of the theory of the balance of power today is the fact that it is such an old and respectable idea, but this again is no proof of its merit. On the contrary, one cannot help noticing that the international scene has changed greatly since the sixteenth century and so have the units of action (the nation-states). Under the circumstances, it would be strange, indeed, if the explanations offered by practicing politicians in that preindustrial age turned out to coincide exactly with the best explanations that can be devised to explain the world today.

The desire to have a law coupled with the existence of a time-worn explanation is not sufficient grounds for saying that a law of modern politics exists. A good theory must be clearly formulated and logically sound, and it must be consistent with the data it seeks to explain. Furthermore, it must explain something about the data that one would not otherwise know, and it must provide a more satisfactory explanation than any rival theory can offer. As we shall see, the theory of the balance of power does none of these things.

QUALIFICATIONS AND AMBIGUITIES

In the past few decades, those who have written about the balance of power at any length have had to hedge and qualify in order to explain the discrepancies between what ought to have been happening according to the theory and the actual events. They have practically qualified the theory out of existence, and under the circumstances, it might appear that to attack the balance of power is to beat a dead horse. But the theory survives. It would appear that many of the qualifications have been made not to improve the theory, but to protect it from attack.

In general, two lines have been adopted. The first is to claim that the principles of the theory are correct but that altered conditions have prevented the balance from operating correctly. The other is to use terms in such a vague manner that the same explanation covers diametrically opposed events.

Hans Morgenthau presents the first of these arguments:

> It will be shown . . . that the international balance of power is only a particular manifestation of a general social principle to which all societies composed of a number of autonomous units owe the autonomy of their component parts; that the balance of power and policies aiming at its preservation are not only inevitable but are an essential stabilizing factor in a society of sovereign

nations; and that the instability of the international balance of power is due not to the faultiness of the principle but to the particular conditions under which the principle must operate in a society of sovereign nations.[9]

Specifically, one popular contention is that the marked decrease in the number of political units and the bipolarization of power between the United States and the Soviet Union which existed for almost two decades after World War II made it difficult for the balance to operate, for all the major nations of the world were firmly committed to one camp or the other, and no single nation was strong enough to tip the balance between the two giants anyway.

The argument does not stand up, however. Granted that the number of political units had shrunk since the days of sixteenth-century European principalities, there still remained roughly one hundred independent nations in the world, surely enough to balance off in any number of ways. Nor is the picture of a world bipolarized around two giants of equal strength correct. It would be more accurate to picture the United States as possessing a tremendous preponderance of power over *all* her potential enemies, a situation not unlike that of England in the nineteenth century. It also seems an exaggeration to picture the other nations as so inconsequential in power that the United States and Russia need not worry about their tipping the scales. Surely the defection of China to the Communist bloc in 1949 was a major, perhaps crucial, loss to the West, and surely the successful maintenance of the Western Alliance was a necessity to the United States. One cannot blame the paucity of nations and the bipolarization of power for the defects in the operation of the balance of power. In the last few years new nations have appeared in large numbers and the once tight East and West blocs have lost control over many of their members. And still the balance does not work.

The disappearance of the balancer is not so much an explanation as to why the balance no longer works as it is a challenge to the idea that it *ever* worked. If it was to England's advantage to act as balancer in the nineteenth century, why is it not to America's advantage to act as balancer today? Why does Russia not balance the United States and China? If the balance of power is a permanent law, how *can* the balancer disappear? If it has disappeared today, the suspicion arises that perhaps it was never more than an illusion in the first place. This, indeed, is the fact. It is the principles, not the conditions, that require revising.

A second reason why the idea of the balance of power has sur-

[9] Morgenthau, *op. cit.*, p. 161.

vived so long is that it is phrased in highly ambiguous terminology, so ambiguous that it is virtually impossible to check the accuracy of the theory against known empirical facts. A theory couched in such terms is almost impossible to refute, for if one interpretation of its concepts is shown not to fit the facts, a different interpretation can always be offered.

The major ambiguity of the theory lies in the key definition of what constitutes a "balance." How is power distributed among the nations of the world when a "balance of power" exists? Given the analogy of the scales, one would think that this was perfectly clear. The power of two nations or two groups of nations ought to be "balanced" when it is roughly equal, when neither side is noticeably stronger than the other. But this is not the case. Through most of the nineteenth century, England and her allies enjoyed a tremendous preponderance of power over their rivals, and yet England is said to have been maintaining the balance of power. How can this be? Is a balance an equal distribution of power or an unequal distribution of power?

Martin Wight has pointed out that one must distinguish between an objective and a subjective view of the balance of power:

> The historian will say that there is a balance when the opposing groups seem to him to be equal in power. The statesman will say that there is a balance when he thinks that his side is stronger than the other. And he will say that his country *holds* the balance, when it has freedom to join one side or the other according to its own interests.[10]

This is a useful distinction. The difficulty is that at least two of these three definitions of a balance are mutually exclusive. We cannot accept them all as equally valid and then erect a theory around a word which means sometimes one thing and sometimes another. Yet this is exactly what has been done. In reading any discussion of the balance of power, the reader must keep his wits about him, for he will find that sometimes the term balance of power is used to refer to an equal distribution of power, sometimes to a preponderance of power, sometimes to the *existing* distribution of power *regardless* of whether it is balanced or not, sometimes to *any* stable distribution of power. Worst of all, the term is sometimes used as a synonym for power politics in general. The balance is all things to all men.[11]

[10] Wight, *op. cit.*, p. 45.
[11] See Inis Claude, *Power and International Relations* (New York: Random House, 1962), chap. 2; Ernst Haas, "The Balance of Power: Prescription, Concept, or Propaganda," in James Rosenau (ed.), *International Politics and Foreign Policy* (New York: Free Press, 1961), pp. 318–29.

When it comes to the concept of the balancer, we encounter still other ambiguities. Indeed, the very need for a balancer contradicts many of the assumptions of the theory. If the system is self-regulated, no balancer should be required. Even if we assume that a balancer is necessary, there are difficulties. If we are going to look at history and see whether the balance of power does in fact operate, we must know just what it is that the balancer does. What is the distribution of power before it intervenes, and what is it after it intervenes? Again the theory is far from clear.

When the system is working correctly, a balance of power is supposed to exist in the normal run of events. If the balance is upset, the balancer intervenes and restores it. We gather, then, that the distribution of power is initially balanced (equally distributed) among the major nations or groups of nations. The balancer itself apparently does not count in this calculation, because it remains aloof.

Then events change, and the balance is upset. One side becomes stronger than the other, but the difference in power cannot be very great, for the balancer is supposed to intervene immediately to rectify the balance. The balancer, then, intervenes when the scales are just beginning to tip, throwing its weight on the lighter side. This is supposed to redress the balance (restore an equal distribution of power). But does it? The balancer is always a major nation (England, for example, is said to be too weak to act as a balancer today), and if a major nation moves to either side of the scales, the result should be a great preponderance of power on its side, not a balance. Thus, intervention by the balancer brings about the very thing it is said to be designed to prevent. This is the point where it becomes useful to call a preponderance a balance, for otherwise the balancer is not a balancer at all. Thus, the ambiguity as to what constitutes a balance obscures a basic contradiction in the theory.

It also seems that the balancer is somehow different from all the other nations. All other states are said to be bent on maximizing their power and thus would make use of a preponderance of power to upset peace and conquer their neighbors, certainly a state of affairs to be avoided. This quest for maximum power is a universal law, but it apparently does not apply to the balancer (another contradiction, alas), for the balancer is different. The balancer is aloof, derives its power from outside the balance, and uses it only to maintain the balance. Unlike its fellow nations, the balancer does not strive to maximize its power and so will not press the advantage it gains by having a preponderance of power. The balancer derives full satisfaction from rebuilding and maintaining the balance. The balancer is reserved, self-restrained, humane, moderate, and wise.

The English modestly and the rest of the world credulously assigned this role to England. England was the balancer because Englishmen believed that she was, said that she was, and the rest of the world believed them. The specifications for the role of balancer have been written with England in mind: the balancer must be a big power slightly removed from the center of controversy, preferably an island and mistress of the seas.[12] Later, the fact that England met these specifications was used as added proof that England was the balancer.

Just why England's motives should differ so from those of other nations has never been explained. Why a preponderance of power in England's hands should be a balancing factor while preponderance for anyone else upsets the balance is not explained either, nor can it be, for it is not true. The theory of the balance of power is shot through with contradictions that would immediately be apparent if it were not for the obscurities and ambiguities.

In the discussion that follows, let us try extremely hard not to fall into the same kind of ambiguity. When the term balance is used, it will mean an equal or approximately equal distribution of power. Preponderance will be called just that. And when a distribution of power is referred to without regard to whether it is balanced or unbalanced, it will be called a distribution of power.

ERRONEOUS ASSUMPTIONS

Once the ambiguities are penetrated, the basic errors of the balance of power theory become apparent. To begin with, it is based upon two erroneous assumptions: (1) that nations are fundamentally static units whose power is not changed from within and (2) that nations have no permanent ties to each other but move about freely, motivated primarily by considerations of power.

¶ *Unchanging Units.* The concept of the balance of power is said to be dynamic, and yet the units involved in the balancing are strangely static. The system described assumes a number of nations of roughly equal strength. Furthermore, it assumes that the strength of each nation remains about the same unless it increases its armaments, conquers new territory, or wins new allies. Apparently, a nation can suddenly become ambitious and aggressive and can prepare to fight, but it cannot actually gain in power without infringing upon the rights of other nations, and the other nations, of course, will act to prevent this. Two nations can ally themselves against a third creating a bloc of greater power, but this does not change the power of each individual nation involved. It merely adds their power together for certain common purposes.

[12] Wight, *op. cit.*, p. 45.

In such a world, international politics becomes a giant chess game or quadrille, to use two of the figures of speech that are often applied. The pieces are of a given power, but they are skillfully manipulated in various ways as the game is played. The dancers remain the same but the figures of the dance change. In such a world, skill in political intrigue and in manipulation is of crucial importance. In the last analysis, the outcome may depend upon victory in warfare, but war is viewed as a breakdown of the system. When the balance is working, success in international politics depends primarily upon the skillful formation of alliances and counteralliances. The dynamism of the system is provided by occasional wars and peace settlements that redistribute territory and by the constant shifting of allies.

It is possible that these were in fact the major dynamic factors in international politics until about the middle of the eighteenth century, but as we have observed repeatedly, the nature of international politics has changed considerably since then. Back in the dynastic period in Europe, "nations" were kings and their courts, and politics was indeed a sport. A king could increase his power by raising an army, by conquering a province, by marrying a queen, or by allying himself with a powerful neighbor, but all of this was considerably removed from the daily life of ordinary citizens, who cared little about kings and their wars.

Two modern forces, nationalism and industrialism, have transformed the nature of international politics. Under the influence of nationalism, the hundreds of principalities and city-states that lay scattered across Central Europe were collected into nations, and more recently the same thing has happened in other parts of the world. These unifications have not merely created new and larger units; they have created a new kind of unit—nations whose citizens can be mobilized into an awesome instrument of power by the ruler who is skilled in new techniques. Napoleon was perhaps the first of these new national leaders, but we have seen many since. The time-honored defenses of the balance of power do not stop these men, for their initial power stems from within the nations they rule, from a place beyond the reach of jealous and fearful neighbors.

And if this is true of the power springing from nationalism, how much truer is it of the power that comes with industrialization. The theory of the balance of power takes no account whatever of the tremendous spurt of power that occurs when a nation first industrializes. It was England's factories, not her diplomats, that let her dominate the nineteenth-century world. Until the nations of the world are all industrialized, the distribution of power among nations will continue to shift, and any momentary equilibrium will be upset. A theory which assumes that the major road to national power lies in the waging of wars and in the formation of alliances has missed the most important development of modern times.

¶ *No Permanent Ties.* A second major assumption underlying the whole concept of the balance of power is that nations have freedom of movement, that they are free to switch sides from one coalition to another whenever they desire and that in so doing they are motivated primarily by considerations of power. This applies particularly to the nation acting as the balancer, since this nation *must* be free to join the weaker side in order to redress the balance.

Such an assumption appears to divorce power considerations from the rest of life, in particular from the hard facts of economic life. Again, this assumption may have been more true of preindustrial, dynastic Europe. In those days, subsistence agriculture occupied the great majority of people, trade was mostly local, and although international trade existed and was growing in importance, economic relations between nations were not of great importance. However, the assumption surely does not hold for the present-day world, or even for nineteenth-century Europe. England was the center of an international economy, much as the United States is today, and she could no more switch to the side of those who sought to upset the order she headed than she could move to Mars. Sixteenth-century monarchs might make or break alliances through a royal marriage or in a fit of royal temper, but modern rulers cannot. Years of propaganda are required before a population will believe that a former enemy is a friend or vice versa. A democratic government may be unable to switch sides in some cases, and even a totalitarian government may find its efforts embarrassed by popular resistance to too sudden a switch. Nor is a government likely to want to shift sides suddenly when its economy as well as its sentiments are intricately meshed with those of other nations.

It is claimed that after the Napoleonic Wars, England acted as the balancer, siding with France most of the time but reserving her freedom to turn against France if the need should arise. In reality, England and France were firmly tied together. Failure to understand this was one of the most serious blunders Germany ever made. World War I also revealed that there was a silent partner in the Anglo-French coalition— the United States. The strong tie between the United States and the two European powers was only beginning to be vaguely understood in the days before World War I, and even after the war, the United States went through a period of isolation during which she pretended that she had no permanent international ties. World War II put an end to that myth, and today the United States is determined not to let Russia miscalculate the strength of Western unity as Germany did twice. Even though the United States is finally beginning to understand the depth of its commitment to Western Europe, some still persist in thinking that other nations are free to switch sides at will. It is most improbable that either Russia or China, split by their rivalry as they are, can be won over to the West.

But is this to say that nations never change sides, that they are unalterably committed to their present friends? Of course not. Nations can and do switch occasionally, but often these shifts turn out to be temporary aberrations or deceits. The sudden alliance between the Soviet Union and Germany just before World War II was marked by hypocrisy on both sides and was ended as abruptly as it started when Germany invaded Russia a few years later. Yugoslavia appeared for a time to have deserted the USSR, and it looked as if it might be possible to include a Communist nation in the anti-Russian bloc, but this too turned out to be an illusion. Italy fought World War I on the side of the Allies and World War II on the side of Germany, but in between she had undergone great internal changes through fascism and through industrialization. What's more, her new loyalties were by no means secure. Throughout World War II, the king of Italy kept his money in an English bank,[13] and long before the war was over, Italians were fighting side by side with Allied soldiers against the Germans.

There have been a few permanent shifts. China appears to be one. The movement of West Germany, Italy, and Japan into the Western Alliance may be another. Some of the newly independent colonies may switch sides in the years ahead if they decide to turn to communism. However, shifts by nations from one side to the other have been extremely rare if one considers only the period since industrialization became widespread, and where they have occurred, they have usually been preceded by far-reaching internal changes or by defeats in war. Certainly the idea that nations have shifted sides in order to balance a power score is far-fetched, indeed. International politics is not a game of chess, and modern nations are not isolated individuals who can arrange themselves in combinations as they wish. Modern nations are tied to each other by subtle, deep, and intricate ties that are political, economic, and psychological in nature. Their quest for power is but one aspect of a far more fundamental set of relationships.

[13] Galeazzo Ciano, *The Ciano Diaries 1939–1943* (Garden City, N.Y.: Garden City Publishing Co., 1947), p. 279. Also *The New York Times,* Sept. 21, 1956, p. 5, col. 1.

If nations were in fact unchanging units with no permanent ties to each other, and if all were motivated primarily by a drive to maximize their power, except for a single balancer whose aim was to prevent any nation from achieving preponderant power, a balance of power might in fact result. But we have seen that these assumptions are not correct, and since the assumptions of the theory are wrong, the conclusions are also in error. We must take exception to two of the major conclusions: (1) that a balance of power is the usual state of affairs and (2) that a balance is desirable because it assures world peace.

¶ *Maintenance of the Balance.* If the mechanisms that maintain the balance of power operate as they are said to operate, we should be able to look at modern history and find some sort of balance in existence most of the time, that is, the cases in which one nation and its allies enjoy a great preponderance of power ought to be the exception, not the rule. However, this is not the case, at least not since the industrial revolution got seriously under way. Those nations that industrialized first gained a tremendous power advantage, and although it might be possible to arrange these giants and their smaller friends in such combinations that groups of nations would balance each other, this is not the kind of arrangement that nations actually formed.

Let us be specific. During the Napoleonic era, the two most powerful nations in the world, England and France, were on opposite sides, and it appears that the power of the French camp and that of the English camp were roughly equal for a number of years. It is claimed that after the defeat of Napoleon, England, Prussia, Russia, and Austria together balanced France. Even if this had been the actual alignment, the result would not have been a balance, for it is generally accepted that England emerged from the Napoleonic Wars the greatest single power on earth. If she was more powerful than France by herself, surely together with three other major nations she possessed an overwhelming preponderance of power. In fact, the actual alignment was even more unbalanced than that, for England and France soon drew close together, forming an unsurpassable bloc of power in many of their dealings with the rest of the world.[14]

In the second half of the nineteenth century, the unification of Germany and the rapidly continuing industrialization of that nation altered the distribution of power in Europe. Germany pulled up to a position where she and France were roughly equivalent in power. Toward the end of the century, the coalition of France and Russia was balanced

[14] See Taylor, *op. cit.*, pp. 284–85.

approximately by that of Germany, Italy, and Austria. This is called a balance of power, but it was not a balance if we add England to the side of France, where she was committed, and surely it was not a balance when we consider that the United States also turned out to be a member of this alliance.

A more accurate view of the distribution of power in the years from 1815 to 1914 would see England as the senior partner in a combination of overwhelming power, supported at the beginning of the period by the second most powerful nation of Europe and underwritten at the end of the period by the growing giant who was soon to take her place.

Nor did World War I reestablish any balance of power. The end of that war found the United States in possession of a great preponderance of power, and her withdrawal into isolation did not alter this fact. It is possible to see a balance of power just before World War II with England and France on one side and Germany and Italy on the other, but the balance vanishes if we throw in Russia and the United States, both of whom were bound by ideology and by economic facts as well as by power considerations to oppose any drastic expansion of German power.

After World War II it was said that the balance of power was between the United States and the USSR, who were roughly equal in power, as were the entire Western and Eastern blocs, but this belief, too, seems to be wide of the mark. In reality the power advantage of the West over the East was, and is, very great. The United States alone had more than twice the power resources of the Soviet Union in 1965, and in 1950 American preponderance was even greater. Together with her powerful allies in Western Europe, the United States is much more powerful than the Soviet Union and China combined. As they continue to modernize their economies, the distribution of power will undoubtedly change somewhat, but the present distribution is greatly in favor of the West, a fact of which the Communist leaders seem to be well aware, even if it is sometimes forgotten in the West.

If we look at the whole sweep of international history for the past 150 years, we find that balances of power are the exception, not the rule.

¶ *Conditions Producing World Peace.* Finally, it is often claimed that a balance of power brings peace. We have seen that there were periods when an equal distribution of power between contenders actually existed or was thought to exist by the parties involved, but examination revealed that these periods were the exception rather than the rule. Still closer examination reveals that they were periods of war, not peace.

In the eighteenth century, the last century of the period called the golden age of the balance of power, there were constant wars. In the nineteenth century, after the Napoleonic Wars, there was almost continuous peace. The balance of power is usually given a good share of the credit for this peaceful century, but as we have seen, there was no balance at all, but rather a vast preponderance of power in the hands of England and France. A local balance of power between France and Germany erupted into the Franco-Prussian War, and German miscalculations that her power balanced that of her probable enemies resulted in World War I, bringing an end to the century of peace.

In the years between the two World Wars, there again was peace and a preponderance of power on the side of the Allies. Once Germany rose again to the point where the power of the Axis nations in fact approximated that of the European allies, war broke out again, the attack predicated on the erroneous assumption that the power of the United States was not involved. Now there is again a period of relative peace, in which the United States holds the preponderance of power.

The relationship between peace and the balance of power appears to be exactly the opposite of what has often been claimed. The periods of balance, real or imagined, are periods of warfare, while the periods of known preponderance are periods of peace. If this is true, the time to worry about the dangers of a third world war is not now, when the predominance of the West is so obvious, but in the future, when industrialization may bring the Communist world abreast of the West in power.

The claim that a balance of power is conducive to peace does not stand up. Indeed, it is not even logical. Nations are reluctant to fight unless they believe they have a good chance of winning, but this is true for both sides only when the two are fairly evenly matched, or at least when they believe they are. Thus a balance of power increases the chances of war. A preponderance of power on one side, on the other hand, increases the chances for peace, for the greatly stronger side need not fight at all to get what it wants, while the weaker side would be plainly foolish to attempt to battle for what it wants. The conditions that make for international peace will be dealt with more fully in a later chapter. Suffice it to say here that one of them is *not* an equal distribution of power.

There is one last point that must be raised about the balance of power. According to the theory, the danger of aggression is to be expected from the stronger nation. A powerful nation intent on maximizing its power is expected to press its advantage and make war upon its neighbors if it ever succeeds in achieving a clear preponderance of power. Here again, the facts do not back up the theory. Nations with preponderant power have indeed dominated their neighbors, but they have not been the ones to start the major wars that have marked recent history. This role has fallen almost without exception to the weaker side. The theory of the balance of power provides no possible explanation for Germany's action in the two World Wars or for Japan's attack upon the United States. It does not explain the two great wars of recent history.

Uses of the Theory

One may well wonder why a theory with so many flaws has endured so long. The answer is twofold. As we shall see in Chapter 14, the theory of the balance of power became truly obsolete after the Industrial Revolution. Popular interpretations of socioeconomic and political events, however, are slow in dying: a century and a half is not unusually long for a theory to outlast its relevance.

Second, mistaken concepts are often useful. Theories that do not accord with the facts may nonetheless be useful in practical politics. For statesmen, the theory of the balance of power often provided a good slogan and a ready justification for what they did. Today, there is a new slogan: world peace. Whatever nations do, they justify it in terms of its contribution to peace. If they disarm, the action helps world peace. If they arm, that too will guarantee world peace. If they negotiate with others, it is in the interest of world peace; and if they refuse to negotiate their firmness will also help bring peace. In its heyday, the balance of power was useful in much the same way. An example will show this clearly.

One of the most quoted instances of England's acting to maintain the balance of power stems from a speech made in the House of Commons in 1826 by the foreign minister of the day, George Canning. Here is the case:

During the Napoleonic Wars, the Spanish colonies in Latin America had seized the opportunity presented by Spain's difficulties and had revolted. Unable to see the handwriting on the wall, Spain, as colonizers are wont to do, temporized, made impossible demands, and refused to look reality in the face. She wanted her colonies back on the old basis, and the revolt dragged on. Spain turned to England for help, but England advised moderation and negotiation. To a Spanish attempt to bribe England into helping her by giving England special commercial privileges in Latin America, the British returned a peremptory refusal.

The foreign minister wrote: ". . . you will perceive that the Prince Regent has never sought for any exclusive advantages. He has always recommended the commerce of South America to be opened to all nations upon moderate duties, with a reasonable preference to Spain herself."[15] This liberal and moderate request of England's was not, of course, as disinterested as it seemed. As the historian C. K. Webster has observed: "Owing to the superiority of Britain at this time over all her rivals in Europe, this open and liberal policy gave her all that she wanted."[16] English attempts at mediation between Spain and the insurgents drew an even more caustic judgment from John Quincy Adams, then the American ambassador to Britain: "In all her [England's] mediations or offers of mediations, her justice and policy will be merely to serve herself."[17] In view of the unreasonableness of Spain, this was a hard judgment to make, but it was largely grounded in fact. The colonies were important trading possessions, and England traded with the insurgents and extended commercial (or de facto) recognition to them. The fact that she did not extend de jure[18] recognition and that, due to her influence, the United States and the other European powers also refrained from doing so did not change any important part of the reality. This was the situation when France invaded Spain in 1823.

At that point, the American President James Monroe issued the Monroe Doctrine, and Canning, the new British foreign minister, extended de jure recognition to the former Spanish colonies. According to the theory of the balance of power, the invasion of Spain by France upset the balance constructed after the Napoleonic Wars, and England should have intervened on the side of Spain to restore the balance. Canning was severely criticized for his failure to do so.

In his famous speech to the House of Commons, Canning answered the criticism and turned the tables on his critics. He argued:

> But were there no other means than war for restoring the balance of power?—Is the balance of power a fixed and unalterable standard? Or is it not a standard perpetually varying, as civilization advances, and as new nations spring up, and take their place among established political communities? . . . Was there

[15] C. K. Webster, *The Foreign Policy of Castlereagh* (London: G. Bell and Sons, 1947), p. 409.
[16] *Ibid.*, p. 409.
[17] *Ibid.*, p. 416.
[18] There are two types of recognition that can be given to a new government: de facto and de jure. De facto recognition means recognition that a new government is in fact in control of the country. De jure recognition is an admission that the new government is the legally constituted government of the country.

no other mode of resistance, than by direct attack upon France —or by a war to be undertaken on the soil of Spain? What if the possession of Spain might be rendered harmless in rival hands—harmless as regards us—and valueless to the possessors? . . . If France occupied Spain, was it necessary, in order to avoid the consequences of that occupation—that we should blockade Cadiz? No. I looked another way—I saw materials for compensation in another hemisphere. Contemplating Spain, such as our ancestors had known her, I resolved that if France had Spain, it should not be Spain *"with the Indies."* I called the New World into existence, to redress the balance of the Old.[19]

But Spain had lost "the Indies" years before Canning's recognition. In fact, the insurgents had been free for years, and their de facto independence had been recognized by England. The subsequent de jure recognition at most formalized a situation that already existed. It certainly did not and could not change the situation one iota. Mr. Canning was taking credit for something that had already happened. His act of recognition did not affect the balance of power.

Things were obviously quite other than Canning portrayed them to be. How then can one make sense of Canning's famous remarks? Hans Morgenthau writes of Canning: "In order to disarm his critics, he formulated a new theory of the balance of power."[20] C. K. Webster sums up the whole event in a trenchant passage:

> The magnificent gesture which Adams made [the Monroe Doctrine] on behalf of a cause already determined and the wonderful reply which the oratorical genius of Canning was alone capable of producing were both false and both wonderfully successful.[21]

Cannings's critics had attacked his inaction and accused him of allowing the balance of power to be upset. Canning cleverly made inaction a virtue and defended his policy in the name of the balance of power, but all this had little to do with any theory of international politics. Canning's famous speech was very poor political theory but excellent politics. It is in such cases as these that the balance of power "theory" has proved of greatest use.

[19] *Speeches of the Right Honourable George Canning* (London: J. Ridgway, 1828), vol. VI, pp. 109–11.
[20] Morgenthau, *op. cit.*, p. 184.
[21] Webster, *op. cit.*, p. 436.

The basic outline of the balance of power theory has been summarized above, but the main points can be restated briefly. In a world of nation-states where each nation is seeking to maximize its own power and where nations are free to switch sides at will according to the dictates of power considerations, competition between nations in this quest for power will lead them to ally themselves in such combinations that no single nation or group of allies will be allowed to achieve a preponderance of power, that is, there will be a balance of power. The system is seen as essentially self-regulating. If, however, the self-regulating features do not work properly, a powerful nation with no selfish interests of its own (the balancer) may intervene against any nation that threatens to become preponderant. As a result of the self-regulation plus the actions of the balancer, a balance of power is the usual distribution of power in the world. As long as the balance can be maintained, the independence of small nations is safe and there will be world peace.

The theory of the balance of power is shot through with flaws, but the vagueness of its key concepts has made these flaws difficult to locate. The concept of the balance is never clearly defined. As we have noted, the term balance of power is used sometimes to describe an equal distribution of power between two rival nations or groups and sometimes to describe a preponderance of power in the hands of the balancer. However, if we insist that "balance" means an equal distribution of power, the flaws in the theory become clear:

1. Not all nations are bent primarily upon maximizing their own power. They do pursue their own national interests, but as we have seen in an earlier chapter, nations have many different goals, and power is merely one of them. In particular, economic and cultural interests may not coincide with considerations of power.

2. Nations are not static units that increase their power only through such means as military aggression, territorial aggrandizement, and alliances. They can change from within by mobilizing nationalistic sentiments, by improving the efficiency of political and social organizations, and, most particularly, by industrializing. Such shifts in power cannot be counteracted completely through the traditional mechanisms of the balance of power.

3. Nations are not free to make and break alliances at will for power considerations alone. They are tied to their friends by political, economic, and psychological interests. Even the so-called

balancer is not free to switch from one side to another whenever the distribution of power changes. In fact, a nation selects its friends on the basis of its own national interests. It supports those nations that uphold the international order from which it benefits, and it opposes those who seek to upset it or who insist upon a rival order.

4. The result of these actions by many independent nations each pursuing its own national interests is *not* a balance of power. Indeed, such balances are rare in recent history. At least since the Industrial Revolution, the usual distribution of power in the world has been uneven, with first England and then the United States heading a coalition of nations that enjoyed a vast preponderance of power over its rivals.

5. There is no such thing as a "balancer" and there never has been. No single nation is motivated primarily by a desire to maintain the balance. England, like other nations, has been motivated by her own self-interest and has acted in world politics in such a way as to maintain her own preponderance of power.

6. Preponderant power in the hands of one nation or group of nations does not necessarily threaten world peace or the independence of small nations. Indeed, the great century of peace from 1815 to 1914 was a century of English and French preponderance. The greatest threats to world peace have come not from established nations (who have already used their preponderant power to establish a status quo satisfactory to them), but rather from less powerful challengers.

7. A balance of power does not bring peace. On the contrary, the greatest wars of modern history have occurred at times when one of these challengers most nearly balanced the power of the preponderant nations or when through miscalculation a challenger *thought* that its power was as great as that of its rivals.

We must reject the theory of the balance of power. Its concepts are fuzzy, it is logically unsound and contradicts itself, it is not consistent with the events that have occurred, and it does not explain them. One is reminded of the words of Richard Cobden:

The balance of power is a chimera! It is not a fallacy, a mistake, an imposture—it is an undescribed, indescribable, incomprehensible nothing; mere words, conveying to the mind not ideas, but sounds.[22]

[22] Richard Cobden, *Political Writings* (New York: Appleton, 1867), vol. 1, p. 258.

13

The Balance of Terror

❖❖❖❖❖❖❖❖❖❖❖❖❖❖❖❖❖❖❖❖❖❖❖

We have seen that the balance of power theory does not provide a key to the understanding of modern world politics. What then of "the balance of terror," a related but more recent theory, equally plausible and with a far more widespread and respectable band of followers? Is this, too, a myth? Or have we finally stumbled into a world where peace indeed depends upon a balance, not a balance of power in this case but a balance of terror where each side fears its opponent's known ability to unleash nuclear destruction? In other words, is not the conception of the balance of power a kind of prophecy that depended for its realization upon events its proponents could not possibly imagine but which have now come to pass in the balance of terror? Do we not have today a precarious but real equilibrium—and with it, peace—between the United States and the Soviet Union because each possesses the power to destroy the other and much of the rest of the world as well?

It would be comforting to believe that the present system of international politics is self-regulating, that it contains automatic safeguards, and that in pursuing their own nuclear preponderance the individual great nations are unwittingly erecting a system that will protect them from ever using those weapons. It is comforting—and very old-fashioned —to believe that the unrelenting pursuit of private advantage somehow guarantees the common welfare and that ever more horrible and more numerous weapons will somehow guarantee world peace. It is simply not true.

The reader must draw his own conclusions, but first let us examine the theory of the balance of terror with great care, for it is a major element in the shaky edifice of the theory of international politics today. And let us recall once more the criteria by which such theories must be judged. First, the conception should be clearly stated. Second, the statements should be logically sound and internally consistent. Third, the theory should be consistent with current happenings and should offer the best available explanation of them.

The Theory of the Balance of Terror

The new distribution of destructive power was baptized "the balance of terror" by master phrase-makers. Winston Churchill, urging Britain's Labour government to negotiate with the Soviet Union, planted the seeds of the new conception when he stated:

> Moralists may find it a melancholy thought that peace can find no nobler foundation than mutual terror but for my part I shall be content if these foundations are solid, because they will give us the extra time and the new breathing space for the supreme effort which has to be made for a world settlement.[1]

"Mutual terror" became the "balance" in a classic article by Albert Wohlstetter in 1959 entitled "The Delicate Balance of Terror."[2] The phrase found rapid favor and wide acceptance for the conception of international politics that it suggested. It was a plausible idea, it had the advantage of reducing the complexities of international politics to an awesome simplicity, and it held some promise of peace.

Even before Wohlstetter's article, throughout the 1950s and particularly in the latter part of the decade, a body of literature was growing up on "mutual deterrence,"[3] a term that can be used almost inter-

---

[1] Winston Churchill, Speech in the House of Commons, March 28, 1950.

[2] Albert Wohlstetter, "The Delicate Balance of Terror," Foreign Affairs, 37, 2 (January 1959), 211–34. The article actually dealt with the need for increasing American preparedness.

[3] Mutual deterrence is only one of a number of conceptions of deterrence, many of which are overlapping and confusing. Thus the literature indicates that deterrence can be passive, negative, positive, extended, graduated, basic, minimum, finite, stabilized, mutual, primary, secondary, and so on, new names outrunning new ideas by far.

changeably with "the balance of terror." This material, largely in the form of articles, reports, and monographs, was produced primarily by men concerned with American military policy and in particular with alternative means of investing in American military security, that is, conventional versus nuclear strategies, missiles versus bombers, tactical versus strategic weapons, and so on. It is often forgotten, however, that the theoretical formulations on deterrence were designed primarily to support specific policy choices and to meet the requirements of inter-service warfare and governmental decision-making. For the most part the authors of the early literature on deterrence were not concerned primarily with the creation of academic theory to explain international politics, though theorists in recent years have drawn upon their work and accepted much of their vocabulary and many of their ideas. Perhaps unavoidably, this has led to some confusion between the rationalization of American policy and the formation of sound theory and to an identification of the pursuit of American nuclear preponderance with the guaranteeing of world peace. One is reminded again of the balance of power, which was set forth as an explanation of British policy only to be elevated later to a fundamental law of international theory.

It is not easy to extract from this vast and often technical body of writings a coherent and generally agreed upon theory of the balance of terror. Experts differ in their approaches and in their conclusions. The composite summary below does not reflect the views of any one writer but has the merit of giving the reader an understanding of the essence of the problem.

The balance of terror, or mutual deterrence, means simply that two (or more) opposing nations are sufficiently frightened of one another that neither is willing to risk any action that would provoke a military attack by the other.[4] Appropriately, the root of the word "deterrent" comes from the Latin *terrere,* which means to terrify. "To deter" means to frighten someone away from doing something he would otherwise do. Mutual deterrence is said to be caused by the fact that each side possesses nuclear weapons in sufficient quantity to inflict unacceptable damage upon the other even after having absorbed a surprise attack. Therefore no aggressor can hope to escape punishment. It is the fear of nuclear punishment that acts as a deterrent.

Discussions of the balance of terror underline the fact that the

---

[4] Recently the argument has been presented that nuclear weapons were never meant to deter nonnuclear attacks but only nuclear aggression, but there is too much evidence to the contrary. For example, if nuclear weapons were meant to deter only nuclear aggression, why is it argued and accepted that between 1945 and 1956 American nuclear capability deterred the Russians from attacking Western Europe?

balance is not one of total power or even a balance of nuclear weapons but rather a balance of fear, for an even distribution of nuclear weapons has never existed. From the very first, the United States and its allies have been far ahead of the Communist nations in the quantity and in the quality of their nuclear armament, and although the degree of Western advantage has fluctuated, it has always been great. Table 1 offers some estimates of strategic strength in recent years. Although terror may be equalized, it shows a substantial American weapons advantage, most importantly in intercontinental ballistic missiles (ICBMs), where the American advantage is 3 to 1.

TABLE 1

Estimates of Comparative Strengths

	Western Alliance	Communist Powers
Early 1963		
ICBMs*	450–500	75+
MRBMs†	250	700
Long-range bombers	630	200
Medium-range bombers	1,630	1,400
Battleships and carriers	40	—
Nuclear submarines	32	12
Early 1967		
ICBMs	934	300
Fleet ballistic missiles	624	150
IRBMs,‡ MRBMs	—	750
Long-range heavy bombers	595	200
Medium bombers	222	1,200
Carriers	37	—
Nuclear submarines	70	50

* Intercontinental ballistic missiles.

† Medium-range ballistic missiles.

‡ Intermediate-range ballistic missiles.

SOURCES: 1963 data, Institute for Strategic Studies, *The Communist Bloc and the Western Alliances, the Military Balance, 1962–1963* (London: Institute for Strategic Studies, 1963), p. 26; 1967 data, Institute for Strategic Studies, *The Military Balance, 1966–1967* (London: Institute for Strategic Studies, 1967), p. 43.

It is fear, then, that is balanced, but it is nuclear weapons that generate this fear. The fundamental question always in dispute is thus: How many and what kind of nuclear weapons are necessary to generate the kind of fear that will deter an adversary from attack? Three related problems have been widely debated: (1) How great an arsenal of nuclear missiles is necessary to penetrate the defenses of an adversary in sufficient numbers under any and all circumstances? (2) How can the adversary be made to understand in advance that his attack will be resisted and that nuclear weapons will be used in retaliation? The problem of credibility is one that has long tortured those involved in security matters. (3) Should the nuclear weapons a nation possesses be aimed against the nuclear arsenal of the adversary in an attempt to limit the damage he can do or should nuclear retaliation have as a target the adversary's population centers in an attempt to dissuade him from attacking? And at this point another problem presents itself. Will enough nuclear power to destroy the five major cities, or the ten major cities, or the twenty major cities be enough? Must a nation be able to destroy 10 percent of the enemy's population, or a third, or half the population to deter? Experts wrangle endlessly over such problems.

Obviously the kind of nuclear arsenal required for a deterrent is related to the kind of nuclear punishment that the adversary will consider unacceptable. It is also related to the capacity of the enemy to inflict damage in a first strike and to defend itself against damage in a second strike. Let us review briefly two key concepts of the balance of terror: deterrence and unacceptable damage.

DETERRENCE

Since totally effective defense against a surprise attack does not exist, a nation's deterrent power depends upon its retaliatory force or its "second-strike capacity." This situation is due to the two technological revolutions in weaponry since the beginning of the nuclear age. The first was the development of thermonuclear warheads. Their destructive power—roughly a million times greater than that of conventional chemical explosives—made it feasible for a nation in a single attack to destroy a major portion of an enemy's arsenal, of its industrial centers, and of its population. However, as long as manned bombers were the sole means of delivering bombs on target, sufficient time remained between the identification of an attacking force and its actual strike to launch a counterattack.

The development of intercontinental ballistic missiles changed the situation. Now the thousands of miles from the launching pads to their most likely targets could be covered in 20 to 30 minutes, leaving the victim very little time indeed—probably only a few minutes—to ascertain that the attack was coming, and certainly too little time to activate a retaliatory blow before the bombs fell. The first blow could be delivered so quickly that in order to threaten to punish the attacker, the potential victim would have to ensure the survival of his nuclear retaliatory force in order that he might devastate his attacker in turn. Thus deterrent power does not depend upon the entire military capability of a country or upon all of its existing military establishment; it stems from that portion of the nuclear force that survives the attacker's first blow.

Retaliatory force, then, is the keystone of the balance of terror. If the existence of such retaliatory force on either side of the balance were ever in jeopardy, or even if its presence were doubted, the balance of terror would vanish. The consequences might well be disastrous, for if either side thought it could destroy or disarm its opponent with relative impunity, the temptation might be too great to resist. And knowing its adversary to be so tempted, the weaker side might be prodded to attack in despair before the enemy acted to disarm it. Security is certain only as long as each side believes that the other side knows it is incurring unacceptable damage if it attacks.

UNACCEPTABLE DAMAGE

The concept of unacceptable damage is also crucial to the theory of the balance of terror. It refers to casualties and physical destruction so vast that a government will not knowingly risk suffering such damage. For example, virtual extinction of the nation, its government, and its population would obviously be unacceptable damage.

It should be clear, however, that damage may be unacceptable long before a nation becomes extinct, and there is no way of knowing exactly where that point is. One is reminded of a famous table and a famous question in Herman Kahn's *On Thermonuclear War*. The table and the question are reproduced below.

Tragic but Distinguishable Postwar States

Dead	Economic Recuperation
2,000,000	1 year
5,000,000	2 years
10,000,000	5 years
20,000,000	10 years
40,000,000	20 years
80,000,000	50 years
160,000,000	100 years

Will the survivors envy the dead?[5]

[5] Herman Kahn, *On Thermonuclear War* (Princeton, N.J.: Princeton University Press, 1961), p. 34.

Americans asked by Kahn gave the impression that they considered a loss of between 10 and 60 million American lives (presumably not their own) an acceptable price to pay for the fulfillment of our commitment to Europe.[6] One is also reminded of Mao Tse-tung's reported assertion that China could afford to lose half its population in nuclear war if need be, for there would still be more than 300 million Chinese left. This is true, of course, but as the Poles observed on hearing of Mao's boast, would the hundreds of millions of Chinese spared by nuclear war still form a Communist nation?

An air of unreality surrounds the concept of unacceptable damage. A Communist leader might be in a position to "accept" more losses than a democrat, a big nation more than a small. And surely the reason for which the loss is incurred makes a difference. Is that loss suffered to defend one's ally or to defend one's own soil? Is that loss risked by attacking another nation first or is it the price of refusing to surrender to an enemy who attacks first? Who can calculate such losses in advance? Who knows what kind of an attack one's enemies can mount or how one's own defenses would actually work?

FINITE DETERRENCE VERSUS COUNTERFORCE STRATEGY

Among American nuclear strategists, argument has raged about the quantity of nuclear weapons required and the conditions under which they would be used. The dispute is based on two different conceptions of the balance of terror. The first group, those who advocate "finite deterrence," has held that the nuclear balance is in effect a nuclear stalemate where neither side is expected to use nuclear weapons. The second group, those who advocate "counterforce strategy," is not so optimistic. These two views are based upon different fundamental assumptions regarding nuclear war.

Those who advocate finite deterrence assume that since nuclear war is bound to lead to unacceptable damage, all energies and ingenuity should be turned to preventing it. They propose to maintain a sufficiently high degree of fear by planning a massive retaliatory strike against the total wealth and population of any nuclear aggressor. The assumption is that if nuclear war ever does occur, it will take the form of each side hurling at the other in one mighty blow the bulk of its nuclear force and there is thus little point in planning or preparing for the period after nuclear war has started. It is also assumed that the United States would never have the incentive to strike first but would hold its nuclear weapons in reserve to be used only in retaliation. Consequently, the nuclear arms race should stop when a nation possesses the second-strike capacity to inflict unac-

[6] *Ibid.,* p. 30.

ceptable damage upon its nuclear opponents. In other words, the number of atomic weapons required is finite and limited.

Such a policy has two admitted assets: It puts a limit on the expenditures required for atomic defense, and it shifts the burden of starting a nuclear war onto the shoulders of the enemy. Those who oppose finite deterrence point out that while it may deter all-out nuclear attack, there remain other forms of aggression and that it does not prepare the nation for the possible failure of deterrence.

The counterforce strategists reject the view that nuclear war need take the form of a spasm of total destruction and see instead a continuum of terror before the point of unacceptable damage is reached. Obviously, the United States must retain the ability to retaliate against a full nuclear strike, but it should also be able to inflict smaller amounts of nuclear damage for smaller offenses. Nuclear deterrence, in short, should also be available to deter nonnuclear or limited aggression.

The example usually given and the one for which the strategy was originally framed concerned the possibility that the USSR in the 1950s might use her vast land forces to attack Western Europe. Nuclear retaliation by the United States was proposed—not a blow aimed at destroying the Soviet Union, but rather an attack limited to her nuclear installations (counterforce), destroying her capacity to inflict unacceptable damage upon the United States. The destruction of cities would be threatened only if Russia refused to withdraw from Western Europe, which she would presumably then do. After the Soviets rebuilt their atomic arsenal, the balance of terror would be reestablished.

This is counterforce. In essence it exhibits a willingness, even a preference, for striking first; it proposes a gradual escalation of nuclear attacks to deter the enemy from a variety of actions both before and after the beginning of nuclear war; and it requires an immense, varied, and extremely expensive atomic arsenal. One must stay far ahead in the nuclear race, for vast power is required to be always in position to destroy or to blackmail an opponent. The primary objections to this policy have been that it is too expensive and that it endangers peace in itself, for an unrestrained nuclear race has a destabilizing effect upon the balance of terror.

The fundamental difference between these two strategies appears to lie in this simple fact. Finite deterrence is concerned primarily with preventing nuclear war, counterforce strategy with demonstrating a capacity for fighting it. United States policy in the mid-1960s apparently leaned to neither extreme but combined elements of both in a strategy that has been called "controlled, selective response." It aimed at the destruction of the enemy's military forces and specifically forbade bombing cities as long as the enemy did not bomb American cities and it included preferred first use of strategic nuclear weapons if war occurred, but the strategic nuclear forces were not so large as those called for in pure counterforce strategy.[7]

Comparison with the Balance of Power

Some similarities can be observed between the theory of the balance of terror and that of the balance of power. Both assume that the nations involved are seeking to maximize their power, and both assert that peace is most assured when an equality of power or terror is reached and most in danger when the balance is upset. Finally, both are popularly accepted theories that have been used to explain or to justify national policies that are too dangerous, too crass, or just too complicated to explain or to justify otherwise.

If for no other reason, some suspicion regarding the soundness of the balance of terror theory ought to be aroused by the fact that it can be and has been used to justify absolutely contradictory alternatives. For example, the Truman Administration resisted the advice of zealots to attack China during the Korean conflict at least in part on the grounds that to do so would increase the risk of a nuclear war with the Soviet Union. But when President Kennedy threatened Russia in 1962 in order to force her to remove her missiles from Cuba, he cited the need to preserve the nuclear balance. Similarly, those who have wished to continue the nuclear arms race have pleaded that the balance of terror required it if America wished to frighten her adversaries into keeping the peace. On the other hand, those who have wished to stop testing and stockpiling new nuclear weapons have argued that the balance of terror requires only second-strike retaliatory power and adequate anti-missile missiles and that to continue arming beyond this point may frighten adversaries into thinking we plan to attack.

The point here is not to determine which of these policies is correct, but rather to point out that the theory of the balance of terror can apparently be used to justify just about anything in political debate. Its similarity in this respect to the balance of power is striking.

There are, however, also major differences between the two theories:

1. Proponents of the new balance stress the difference in the nature of nuclear and nonnuclear weapons. Conventional weapons were used to conquer territory or to contest the conquest of territory

[7] Timothy W. Stanley, *NATO in Transition* (New York: Praeger, 1965), pp. 92–94.

by an opponent, but nuclear weapons are designed to punish the adversary who has attacked or who has conquered territory and to make him give up his prey. One is reminded of the difference in exercising power through punishment and through the use of force. (Force is used to compel an enemy to do something against his wishes, whereas punishment is threatened to prevent an action by raising its price, or if actually used, to prevent its recurrence by indicating that the threat was not a bluff.) Under the balance of power theory, nations were expected to use their armed forces in wars to maintain the balance if necessary. Under the balance of terror theory, nations are expected to hold their weapons as threats—or if they use them at all, to strike only once or twice. The difficulty, of course, is that any use of them would probably precipitate the very all-out war they are designed to prevent.

2. Under the old balance of power system the arms race was unlimited, with each side striving for ever greater military strength. In the new balance, however, there is a limit (never yet defined) to the quantity of offensive weapons required even in counter-force strategy. Once a nation possesses enough nuclear missiles and bombs to destroy the enemy totally even in a retaliatory attack, the rest is overkill. There is, of course, no end to the search for ever more effective anti-missile defenses and then for more effective missiles to evade the enemy's anti-missile missiles.

3. The role of alliances also differs in the two balances. Under the balance of power, alliances were a primary method by which each side increased its power and through which the balance was maintained. For the balance of terror, alliances have much less significance. They are not a means through which a nuclear nation can increase its nuclear strength, for only the United States and the USSR possess effective nuclear deterrent power. Although three other nations—England, France, and China—aspire to full nuclear status, none is likely to possess effective second-strike retaliatory power to inflict unacceptable damage upon the nuclear giants for some time, probably several decades in the case of China and possibly never in the case of England and France. Thus alliances cannot bring any radical addition to the nuclear capability of either of the two major nuclear powers. They remain useful for many other reasons: for economic ties, for political coordination, for assistance in conventional wars, and as a means of staking out territory that no enemy may attack unscathed, but they do not affect the balance of terror.

4. A final difference between the two balances lies in the fact that the balance of power was alleged to operate best with as many participants as possible and to have failed with bipolarization, whereas the balance of terror is a simple balance of two camps. Some contend that a complex balance of terror composed of many nuclear powers cannot successfully be maintained, but it does not seem logical to suppose that failure is more likely with three or four participants than it is with two.

Relative Nuclear Strengths

In order to evaluate the theory of the balance of terror, it is necessary to measure its claims against reality and to see if, in fact, the presence of nuclear weapons has had the effect upon international politics that is claimed for it. Before doing this, however, we must review briefly the time-table of nuclear development and get firmly in mind which nations had what nuclear capacity at what date. Estimates of the relative strength of the United States and the Soviet Union during the first two decades of nuclear history are not exact, but they provide the only possible empirical check of the balance of terror.

Table 2 provides a rough sketch of the relative strategic strength of the two great nuclear powers in the twenty years after World War II. It shows four distinguishable periods in the distribution of nuclear power:[8]

TABLE 2

Some Estimates of Comparative Strategic Strength,
U.S. and USSR, 1945–1966

United States	USSR
1945–1949	*1945–1949*
U.S. nuclear monopoly	Red Army considered response to
Atomic weapons scarcity	American atomic threat on both
No miniaturization	political and strategic levels
B-29 principal means of delivery	1947: Some TU4 long-range
	bombers
	1949: Atomic device exploded
[*Evaluation:* U.S. monopoly of nuclear power]	

[8] This division into periods is based on that of Raymond Aron, *The Great Debate* (Garden City, N.Y.: Doubleday, 1965), chap. 1.

1950–1956
1952: Test of thermonuclear bomb
Delivery by B-36 long-range bombers (383 by 1954) and B-47
medium-range bombers given intercontinental range by tankers
(2,041 by 1957)
1955: B-52 long-range bombers
became operational

1950–1956
Stepped-up production of fighters
in answer to U.S. bombers
1953: Thermonuclear bomb exploded
1955–1956: Bison long-range
bombers, 50–75; other new
bombers developed: Bears
(long-range), Badgers (medium-
range)

[*Evaluation:* U.S. monopoly lost but crushing superiority remained]

1957–1962
1957: ICBM tested
1959: B-52s replace B-36s
1960: Polaris (submarine launch-
able ballistic missile) operational; B-58 medium-range
bomber operational
Early 1962:

ICBMs (Atlas, Titan)	63
SLBMs (Polaris)	96
Long-range bombers	600
Medium-range bombers	880–90

1957–1962
1957: ICBM tested (sent up Sput-
nik)
1958–1960: Emphasis on production of MRBMs

Late 1961:

ICBMs	50
MRBMs	200
SLBMs	(no estimate)
Long-range bombers	190
Medium-range bombers	1,000

[*Evaluation:* U.S. advantage but increasingly vulnerable]

1963–present
Early 1963:

ICBMs (Atlas, Titan, Minutemen)	294
SLBMs (Polaris)	144+
Long-range bombers (B-52)	630
Medium-range bombers (B-47, B-58)	690+

Late 1966:

ICBMs (Titan, Minutemen)	904
SLBMs (Polaris)	656
Long-range bombers (B-52)	600
Medium-range bombers (B-47, B-58)	80

1963–present
Late 1963:

ICBMs	100+
IRBMs	(no estimate)
MRBMs	750
SLBMs	100
Long-range bombers	190
Medium-range bombers	1,400

Late 1966:

ICBMs	300
IRBMs and MRBMs	700–750
SLBMs	280
Long-range bombers	210
Medium-range bombers	900+

[*Evaluation:* Retaliatory capacity achieved on both sides]

SOURCE: Approximate estimates by the Institute for Strategic Studies, London, in annual publications on *The Military Balance,* 1961–1962 to 1966–1967.

In the first period the United States had a monopoly of nuclear power. The obvious advantages of this monopoly were qualified, however, by two fundamental limitations: one, atomic weapons were few in number and remained so until the end of the Korean War, and two, atomic weapons were still too big and too awkward for easy delivery by air. In addition, the major means of delivering nuclear bombs during this period was the relatively slow B-29 bomber, the plane that had carried the bombs to Hiroshima and Nagasaki.

In September, 1949, the Soviet Union exploded its first atomic bomb, ending America's monopoly. Then in 1952 and 1953 thermonuclear bombs were tested in rapid succession by the United States and the Soviet Union. In spite of losing her monopoly, however, the United States retained a massive lead throughout the second period. She was far ahead in making nuclear weapons smaller and therefore more usable; the United States Air Force, the major instrument for delivering nuclear bombs to their targets, was much stronger in numbers, equipment, and training than that of Russia; and the United States had ringed the Soviet Union with bases from which her air force could deliver mortal blows to any part of the USSR.

Russia, on the other hand, possessed a smaller number of unwieldy bombs and depended for their delivery upon a small number (not more than 200) of long-range bombers vulnerable to destruction on the ground. Russian inferiority during this period was so marked as to have made it practically impossible for her to have inflicted more than token punishment upon the United States.

The beginning of the end of this disparity as well as the end of the second period is conveniently marked by the successful testing of ballistic missiles by both countries and by the launching of the first Soviet satellite in 1957. The third period, which stretches roughly through 1962, was one of transition, with both sides beginning the shift from aircraft to missiles as the core of their attacking forces. By the end of the period there was already available a small number of missiles capable of delivering nuclear warheads to enemy targets five or six thousand miles away. Strangely enough, considering the theory of the balance of terror, the data for these years suggest that Soviet emphasis was on the construction of medium-range rather than intercontinental missiles, and it was perhaps in part because of this emphasis that America retained her advantage until roughly 1958 or 1959. After that date it was rapidly reduced.

The fourth period, beginning in 1963 and stretching to the present, shows a continuation of trends already quite visible in the third period. Increasingly, giant ICBMs have become the backbone of the nuclear attack forces. Because the new weapons can destroy nations in a matter of minutes, the emphasis has been on constructing missiles that could survive an attack, that is, missiles than can be protected, hidden, dispersed, and fired on an instant's notice. This trend has, of course, meant a marked reduction in the advantage the United States had earlier possessed.

In summary, we see that according to all evidence there was no nuclear balance in the first and second periods. The imbalance of weapons was such as to give an absolute and crushing superiority to the United States and should therefore have created also an imbalance of terror. In the third period, that is, by 1957 and certainly by 1958 or 1959, the United States became increasingly vulnerable to nuclear attack, and this situation finally created a balance of terror in the sense that the term is generally used. In the fourth period the conditions for the balance of terror were made more secure when both sides attained second-strike capacity. Although both sides scrambled for swift and secure retaliatory forces during this period, it does seem that there was greater frenzy and overt anxiety in the United States than in the Soviet Union. If true, this may be in part because the Soviet Union had been living with the possibility of nuclear destruction as a fact of life for twenty years, whereas the exposed position of the United States was new.

Effects of Nuclear Weapons on World Politics

President Kennedy once stated that the possession of nuclear weapons by both the United States and the Soviet Union "changes the problem. . . . It changes all the answers and all the questions."[9] We must ask: in what major ways have nuclear weapons changed world politics?

Five claims about the effects of nuclear weapons are frequently made. It is argued that they have changed the nature and the dimensions of armed conflict. Second, it is said that they have created terror in the hearts of both common people and their leaders. Third—and this is the core of the balance of terror theory—it is insisted that this terror has made the major nations cautious in dealing with each other and that fear of nuclear weapons is essential in preventing world war. Fourth, it is contended that nuclear weapons have affected the formation of blocs and the utility of alliances. Fifth, it is claimed that nuclear weapons have minimized or promise to minimize differences in power among nations. Some of these claims are true and some are not. A review of

[9] Theodore C. Sorensen, *Kennedy* (New York: Harper & Row, 1965), p. 512.

them will show some of the reasons why the balance of terror conception is not convincing.

CHANGES IN THE NATURE OF WARFARE

The first claim is obviously true. The latest thermonuclear missiles are completely different from any previous weapons in their destructive power, in their range, and in the speed with which they strike. In consequence the third world war, if it occurs, will be completely different from any previous war.

The explosive power of bombs has risen a million times since World War II. The atomic bomb increased explosive power a thousand times over conventional bombs, and thermonuclear bombs multiplied the previous thousandfold increase again a thousand times. However, the two revolutions—from conventional to atomic, and from atomic to thermonuclear—represent drastically different changes. One can compare the single plane and single bomb sorties over Hiroshima and Nagasaki with the full-blown raids over Tokyo of close to 300 bombers loaded with conventional bombs. Again, the 600,000 tons of high explosives dropped on Germany in 1944 could be equated with 300 Hiroshima bombs.[10] Horrible as they were, the first generation of nuclear weapons—uranium bombs operating through nuclear fission—did not completely alter the nature of modern warfare.

Thermonuclear bombs are of a different world. The hydrogen bombs, operating through nuclear fusion, release so much more destructive power that comparison is truly impossible. What in past experience can compare with a single 20-megaton bomb that contains within itself more explosive power than has been detonated in all the wars since the invention of gunpowder? What with a 100-megaton bomb (equivalent to 100 million tons of TNT) which is possible if not already in existence? One hydrogen bomb can utterly destroy the largest city. One cobalt bomb could set fire to half a continent.

The rocket delivery systems of the new weapons also defy comparison. The range of the latest ICBMs (and even the range of the new manned bombers) makes it possible for each of the combatants to lob nuclear warheads into any portion of the territory of the other. And the speed of the missiles (up to 18,000 miles per hour) makes total defense against them impossible. As recently as World War II it took months or even years to prepare and launch an invasion across the Atlantic or Pacific Oceans and even a few years ago it took hours for an air attack to cross the seas. There is probably no way to prevent some of the nuclear warheads from finding their targets, no way to evacuate

[10] Aron, *op. cit.*, p. 3.

314   PART TWO: WORLD RELATIONS

major cities before they are destroyed, no way to save most of a nation's war industries and much of its attacking forces when total destruction can be delivered in a few minutes.

It is difficult if not impossible to visualize the kind of war that would result from the use of nuclear weapons. Would one side surrender immediately after the damage of the first punch and counterpunch was assessed, or would both sides continue to hurl all the nuclear warheads they possessed? And, if so, what would remain? Certainly nuclear weapons have changed the nature of warfare.

THE CREATION OF TERROR

There is equally small doubt that nuclear weapons have spread terror. There seems no question that the mere existence of such weapons has substantially raised the level of anxiety in an already anxious world. It has magnified the importance of small crises and greatly increased the responsibilities of the chiefs of state of the nuclear powers. Most people simply do not spend much time thinking about what a nuclear war would mean to them in personal terms. The horror is too great to think about day after day. In small crises, they become very anxious; in a large one, they would probably panic.

The destructiveness and the horror of nuclear war cannot be denied, nor the terror that such a possibility has inspired. We must still determine, however, in what way the destructiveness, horror, and terror of nuclear war have influenced the behavior of nations in world politics.

NUCLEAR WEAPONS AS DETERRENTS

It is widely believed that fear of nuclear holocaust has made the leaders of major nations more cautious in dealing with each other, but this is difficult to prove. A look at the prenuclear period before World War II reveals, to be sure, examples of recklessness by Nazi Germany and by Imperial Japan that may be without parallel in the nuclear age, but it also reveals examples of excessive caution. The Russians under Stalin were immensely cautious with Hitler, and who can forget Chamberlain and Daladier at Munich? One is tempted to be malicious and suggest that had Hitler possessed atomic bombs, an untold amount of scholarship would have been devoted to proving that they were the cause of Western caution.

Similarly in nuclear times, it is possible to find examples of both caution and the taking of tremendous risks. A number of nations have risked or threatened nuclear war. Events in Cuba, Berlin, Korea, and Vietnam remind us that nations are still ready to fight, with nuclear weapons if need be. Unfortunately no clearly identifiable climate of caution exists to prove the influence of nuclear weapons on keeping the peace of the world.

Nor is it possible to read clearly the effect of nuclear weapons by comparing the actions of nations that possess them with the actions of those that do not. Let us examine closely the first two periods of the nuclear age, from 1945 through 1956, when the United States had first a monopoly and then a crushing superiority in nuclear power. One would expect some heightened assurance and assertion of interests on the part of the United States coupled with timidity and caution on the part of the Soviet Union, but in fact the very opposite seems to be the case. These are the years of the Communist coup in Czechoslovakia, the Berlin blockade, the Korean War, and the crushing of the Hungarian revolt. Throughout this period the United States was passive and defensive while Russia and China behaved aggressively—an odd commentary on the value of nuclear weapons.

Some argue that the Soviet Union would have behaved even *more* aggressively had it not been for American atomic power, that only "the bomb" deterred her from attacking and occupying all of Western Europe right after World War II. Hindsight suggests, however, that fears of a Soviet attack on Western Europe were based upon miscalculations of Soviet intentions and potentialities. Exhausted by a war that had devastated her cities, wrecked her economy, and cost her 20 million dead, the Soviet Union seems unlikely to have been interested in further military adventures at that time.

Strangely enough, Soviet restraint in her dealings with the United States seems to have *increased* in the years since she, too, has achieved nuclear strength, while China and North Vietnam, who possessed no atomic striking forces, certainly did not appear sufficiently intimidated by American nuclear might to change their aggressive behavior. Surely the hypothesis that nuclear weapons are effective deterrents should be examined with care.

Any attempt to test this hypothesis more exactly raises a fundamental problem: What kind of evidence shall we accept? Nuclear weapons are only one of many factors that contribute to a nation's total power. In a conflict where they are not even used, how are we to judge the contribution they have made to the outcome? Inevitably much of the argument in criticism and in defense of the balance of terror is speculative and anecdotal. Because we cannot rerun history to test hypotheses, it is impossible to hold constant all the other variables to see what difference the possession of nuclear power makes. It is even difficult to find similar cases at different periods of time, for the number of conflicts involving nuclear powers is small.

Obviously, we can only make the best of the evidence that exists. With full awareness of its shortcomings, let us examine three types of conflicts that may aid our analysis. We shall begin with conflicts between nations where the nuclear position of the contestants changed radically over time. In such conflicts, it could be argued, many of the other pertinent variables were held very roughly constant. Unfortunately, only the Berlin conflict meets these specifications.

A second type of conflict that will tell us something about the influence of nuclear power upon international behavior is a contest between a nuclear power and a country that has few or no atomic weapons. Here, of course, the other variables are not being held constant so that it is not possible to say with any precision what the influence of nuclear weapons has been. All that is possible is to compare the behavior of both parties with what one could expect it to be if the hypothesis of nuclear deterrence were true. It seems sensible to expect the nonnuclear power to be more cautious and compromising if not submissive and the nuclear power to be firm and demanding. And if this is not the behavior observed, it seems reasonable to argue that other factors have played a more significant role. The Iranian case of 1946, the Korean War, the 1956 Suez crisis, and the war in Vietnam are examples of this type of conflict.

A third type of conflict to be examined is a confrontation where both parties have effective nuclear weapons. For the evidence we seek, this is the least informative kind of case, but it may at least bring forth some indication of the other variables that are important in the outcome of conflicts among the nuclear giants. The Hungarian revolt and the Cuban missile crisis are clashes of this type.

¶ *The Berlin Case.* The Berlin conflict began in 1948 when the Russians and the East Germans blockaded the city, preventing Allied access to Berlin by the customary ground routes through East Germany. The blockade lasted 321 days. During the entire period the United States supplied West Berlin by air. At the end of that time, the Russians reopened the roads.

The conflict was revived in 1957 and lasted off and on until the building of the Berlin Wall in 1961. The causes of the revival of the conflict were many. Throughout the postwar years the presence of a Western enclave in the middle of East Germany was an annoyance to the Russians, both because it represented a showcase of Western freedom and wealth and because it served as a depot for the stream of refugees escaping East Germany. In addition, the Soviets wished to use Berlin as a lever to force the West to recognize East Germany. They proposed that the West give up its rights in the city and that Berlin become a free and demilitarized city. Unless the West agreed, the Russians threatened to sign a peace treaty with the East Germans and put them in sole charge of communication with Berlin, thereby forcing the Allies to deal with them and grant them at least implicit recognition. The West refused to agree to any new status for Berlin, and the dispute eventually petered out when the Soviet Union gave up its attempts to change the status quo.

The Berlin case provides the kind of test we wish to make. Here the United States and the USSR stood toe to toe. Second, the dispute was a prolonged one and during its existence the distribution of nuclear power changed substantially. In 1948 the United States enjoyed an atomic monopoly. In 1957–1961 both nations possessed thermonuclear bombs and the means of delivering them, though the United States still held a marked advantage. What effect did this change have upon the behavior of the contestants?

Surprisingly, the behavior of the United States and the Soviet Union was not at all what one would expect from the conception of nuclear deterrence and the balance of terror. In 1948 it was the USSR who provided the provocation and behaved aggressively while the United States was restrained and even timid. Suggestions that the United States push its way into Berlin with military forces in spite of the blockade were rejected, and the expensive and difficult airlift was undertaken instead. In 1957–1961, on the other hand, after the Soviet Union possessed nuclear weapons, her behavior as far as Berlin was concerned was much more subdued. During the second period of conflict the Communist side limited itself to minor temporary annoyances and threats, and it was the Soviet Union that finally adopted the defensive course of building the Wall. It is very difficult to see what possible role nuclear weapons played in the pattern of conflict over Berlin or in its outcome.

¶ *Conflict Between Nuclear and Nonnuclear Powers.* In the category of conflicts between nuclear and nonnuclear nations, there are more cases to examine. Let us look at four: Iran, Suez, Korea, and Vietnam, and see if the behavior of the parties fits our expectations.

In two of them, the Russo-American conflict over Iran in 1946, and the 1956 conflict over Suez between the French and English on the one hand and the Russians on the other, the nonnuclear parties acted as expected. In both cases the side possessing little or no atomic power capitulated, but there is no clear indication that the capitulation was due to nuclear threat.

In the Iranian case the Soviet Union had left troops in Iran after the war and was slow in removing them. In 1946, the Iranian government took its complaint to the United Nations Security Council where the United States strongly supported its demand that the Soviet troops be evacuated immediately. The Russians, though apparently procrastinating, insisted that they were planning to remove the troops anyway and did in fact evacuate them four and a half months later.

In the Suez crisis of 1956, Egypt nationalized the Suez Canal, whereupon England, France, and Israel launched a military attack upon Egypt. The Soviet Union issued a vague threat to defend Egypt by using rockets against England and France, and the United States replied that if its allies were attacked it would defend them. The dispute went to the United Nations where the United States and the Soviet Union both joined the majority in demanding an immediate end to hostilities. England, France, and Israel withdrew leaving Egypt in possession of the Canal.

Even today there are people in Moscow who believe that England and France withdrew from Egypt in response to the Soviet Union's nuclear threats, but a thorough reading of the case and especially of the testimony of English leaders suggests that the Western powers were much more influenced by their failure to win American support. Far from supporting England and France, the United States opposed the invasion strongly both in public statements and in private, where she is reported to have threatened England and France with financial reprisals if they did not end hostilities.[11] In short, the United States possessed more effective ways of punishing the British and the French than did the Soviets, who could only threaten war with all its consequences.

In the other two cases of conflict between nuclear and nonnuclear powers, the major parties are China and her satellites on one side and the United States on the other. Here the behavior of the combatants is difficult to explain if one accepts the deterrence theory, for it is almost exactly the opposite of what one would expect.

¶ *Korea.* In the Korean conflict, the Chinese, who possessed no nuclear weapons, took on in open combat the world's leading nuclear power. They did this with the Manchurian industrial complex, China's most important industrial area, close by and completely vulnerable to American air attack. Chinese troops for Korea assembled in Manchuria and Chinese fighter planes engaged American planes in combat over North Korea and then returned to their Chinese bases. Chinese ground soldiers humiliated the United States by fighting her forces to a standstill in

11 Terence Robertson, *Crisis* (New York: Atheneum, 1965), pp. 254–64.

battles highly costly in American equipment and casualties, and throughout the conflict there were strong factions in the United States—including the commander of American forces in Korea—who advocated carrying the war into Chinese territory. One cannot imagine a setting in which the Chinese could be more exposed to the risk of atomic attack. The Chinese were reportedly worried, but their concern did not affect their behavior.

Some maintain that Chinese behavior must be viewed in the light of the Soviet atomic umbrella, for the Soviet Union was obligated by treaty to help defend China if Chinese territory was attacked. In the years from 1950 to 1953, however, the USSR possessed little in the way of atomic arms. She had exploded her first atomic device only in 1949, possessed few long-range bombers and no missiles. It would probably have been impossible for her to launch an atomic attack that would have damaged the United States. President Truman may well have been reluctant to attack China and thus risk involving the Soviet Union, but his fear was not of Soviet *nuclear* strength.

Indeed, not only China's rashness but also America's restraint are simply not understandable in terms of the deterrence theory. American restraint may be—and has been—explained by the fear of getting bogged down in a war with 650 million Chinese, by the fear of being maneuvered into leaving Europe defenseless, and so on. The point, of course, is that the advantages of possessing nuclear weapons did not override these fears.

President Eisenhower, who came to power in 1953, has suggested that it was fear of American nuclear attack that finally brought the Chinese to agree to end the war. If so, this would represent a significant example of nuclear deterrence, but it is difficult to accept the suggestion at face value. President Eisenhower stated in his memoirs that in the spring of 1953 he was unwilling to accept any longer the stalemate in the Korean War and in the armistice talks with the North Koreans and the Chinese and that he definitely considered an atomic attack upon Chinese targets. In his words:

> One possibility was to let the Communist authorities understand that, in the absence of satisfactory progress, we intended to move decisively without inhibition in our use of weapons, and we would no longer be responsible for confining hostilities to the Korean Peninsula.[12]

He says that this warning was delivered to the Chinese and that in consequence they signed the armistice agreement.

[12] Dwight D. Eisenhower, *Mandate for Change 1953–1956* (New York: Doubleday, 1963), p. 181.

Without dismissing lightly the only hard bit of evidence of nuclear influence in the atomic age, we should note that the armistice talks were already well along before the Eisenhower threat and that the main outstanding issue between the two sides dealt not with territorial or political settlements but simply with the repatriation of Chinese prisoners of war. It is quite possible that the Chinese would have agreed to the armistice in any case. Second, it is not clear why the fear of nuclear attack that failed to deter the Chinese from entering the Korean War in the first place or from driving the Americans back to the 38th parallel in the second place should suddenly have deterred them from insisting that their prisoners be repatriated simply because the American government made explicit a danger which had always existed. Finally, although there can be no doubt of President Eisenhower's accuracy in reporting his own feelings and the actions of the American government, in the nature of things he could only guess why the Chinese behaved as they did. If American intelligence did not even know that the Chinese were going to enter the war, it is difficult to see how they knew why the Chinese finally agreed to an armistice.

The importance of the American nuclear threat in bringing the Chinese to a settlement can be variously estimated. At the minimum it had no influence but simply provided an explanation for actions caused by other factors. At the maximum it showed that a nuclear threat can hasten the end of wars already close to conclusion, as it did in Hiroshima and Nagasaki.

¶ *Vietnam.* In the case of Vietnam, the role of nuclear deterrence is even more difficult to locate. In fact, it might be said to be invisible.

The first conflict in Vietnam (then French Indochina) was between the French and the Communist rebels of Ho Chi Minh, neither of whom possessed nuclear weapons. The United States was involved, however, to the extent of providing massive military aid to the French and of caring deeply who won, since she viewed the creation of a Communist state in Southeast Asia as a direct threat to American interests.

It was precisely as the French were in the process of losing the war in Indochina that American Secretary of State John Foster Dulles enunciated the doctrine of "massive (that is, nuclear) retaliation." In January, 1954, Dulles stated that in case of aggression the United States could be expected to "depend primarily upon a great capacity to retaliate instantly by means and at places of our own choosing."[13] The doc-

13 John Foster Dulles, Speech before the Council on Foreign Relations, Jan. 12, 1954. *The New York Times,* Jan. 13, 1954, p. 2.

trine of massive retaliation was born (1) of the frustrations and high casualties of the Korean conflict and the resolve never again to be cornered into a fight of this nature, and (2) of the anxiety of the Eisenhower Administration over the financial cost of maintaining nonnuclear forces capable of stopping aggression and smothering rebellion anywhere in the world. The idea of massive retaliation against a Communist attack on Western Europe was not new, but now Dulles proposed to extend the doctrine to the rest of the world. Coming at the time that it did, the doctrine was widely interpreted as a serious warning to Ho Chi Minh and his backers.

The threat went unheeded, however. In May the rebels won the battle of Dienbienphu and the French forces in Indochina collapsed. The United States did nothing and in July agreed along with France to the end of the Indochinese War and the de facto creation of a Communist state in North Vietnam. Indeed, the doctrine of massive retaliation was never applied anywhere and was later replaced, as we have noted, by the idea of "controlled, selective response."

This doctrine, too, appears to have had no effect in Vietnam. Ten years later the United States found itself much more directly involved in fighting Ho Chi Minh, first by giving aid to South Vietnam in its struggle against northern-supported rebels, later by sending in American forces to take over the bulk of the fighting. This time no specific nuclear threat was made by the United States, but the Americans engaged in a steady, calculated escalation of the conflict through progressively severe bombing of North Vietnam as measures at each level failed to bring victory or to deter continued assistance to the rebels by North Vietnam.

Once again the awesome power of the world's greatest nuclear nation failed to deter aggression by even a minor nation. A French professor teaching in Hanoi in 1966 stated that North Vietnamese officials considered it a certainty that American bombers would sooner or later totally destroy their cities and industries, but that this alone would not ensure their defeat. It would bring the country back to where it had been when it defeated the French in 1954, but they believed that if this happened North Vietnam would receive massive aid from other Communist countries and that reconstruction would be rapid once hostilities were over.[14] This is, in fact, exactly what happened in North Korea.

Faced with vastly superior nuclear power, the North Vietnamese

[14] Charles Formau quoted by Bernard Fall, "The Other Side of the 17th Parallel," *The New York Times Magazine,* March 16, 1966.

leaders were consciously and intentionally willing to risk the total destruction of all their cities and industries. In short, they were not deterred.

¶ *Conflicts Between Nuclear Powers.* In the third category—conflicts between nuclear powers—there are two cases to be examined: the Hungarian revolt of 1956 and the Cuban missile crisis in 1962.

The Hungarian revolt arose out of the massive discontent with Soviet control latent throughout Eastern Europe. Nationalistic resentment at Russian domination and widespread discontent with the economic sacrifices imposed by the forced pace of industrialization made up an explosive situation that could have blown the Russians out of Eastern Europe. All that was needed was some indication that a revolt against them could succeed. This was a test case of great importance to the Soviet Union and to the West.

Why didn't the United States intervene? She had every excuse. For years American political leaders, especially Republicans, had been deploring the Soviet Union's hold upon her Eastern European satellites and promising their eventual liberation. Finally, in 1956, the Hungarian people revolted, hoping for, and even expecting, help from the West. The entire country was in an uproar and as Soviet tanks moved in to crush the rebellion, the president of Hungary declared his country neutral, withdrew it from the Warsaw Pact, and asked for military help from the West. The United States was still in a strong, superior position as far as nuclear power was concerned; indeed, 1956 was probably the last year in which America's nuclear advantage was decisive.

It was a golden opportunity, but the United States declined to act, and the Russians crushed the revolt. When Secretary Dulles was asked why the United States had not intervened, he stated that the danger of nuclear war with the Soviet Union had kept her from it.

¶ *Cuba I.* In the Cuban case six years later, however, the United States willingly risked nuclear war with the Soviet Union, and at a time when its power to attack America with atomic missiles was much greater than it had been in 1956. The Cuban case is an important one, for it offers many insights into the behavior of nuclear powers in a direct confrontation.

Let us begin with an earlier Cuban crisis—the episode of the Bay of Pigs. In 1961 a small band of Cuban exiles, recruited, trained, armed, and organized by the American Central Intelligence Agency, invaded Castro's Communist Cuba. It had been planned that the role of the United States in the invasion was to remain a secret and it had been hoped that the invasion would kick off a mass revolt which would result in the overthrow of the Castro government. Instead, the role of the United States was quite apparent, no mass revolt occurred, and the invaders were immediately in serious military difficulties. Nevertheless, President Kennedy stuck to his original resolve that there be no sizable direct American military support for the exiles and allowed the invasion to collapse.

The American government's resolve was not due to fear of the Soviet Union, which supported Castro. Although Khrushchev angrily denounced the invasion and promised Cuba "all necessary assistance," Kennedy's determination not to involve American forces predated this warning, and stemmed primarily from the fear of anti-American reaction in Latin America and in the United Nations. The United States chose not to use her power lest it damage her reputation as a peaceful and law-abiding nation. The result was a "victory" by Cuba over the United States.

¶ *Cuba II.* A year and a half later, however, a second dispute over Cuba had quite a different outcome, in spite of the fact that the Soviet Union was this time directly involved and in spite of a clear danger of nuclear war. In the fall of 1962 it became known to the American government that the Soviet Union was placing in Cuba nuclear missiles with a range that covered a large part of the United States. The moves were being made in secrecy and had been specifically denied by the highest Soviet authorities. President Kennedy and his top officials decided that immediate action was necessary before the missiles became operational, and six possible courses of action were discussed:[15]

1. Do nothing.
2. Use diplomatic pressures and negotiations. It was suggested the United States might agree to remove its missile bases in Turkey in exchange for the removal of the Cuban bases. Interestingly enough, some Pentagon advisors favored limiting American response to diplomatic action on the ground that both the United States and the Soviet Union had long lived within range of each other's nuclear missiles and that the United States should not react in such a way as to inflate the importance of the Cuban missiles.

[15] For full description of the Cuban confrontation, see Sorensen, *op. cit.,* chap. XXIV; Arthur Schlesinger, Jr., *A Thousand Days, John F. Kennedy in the White House* (Boston: Houghton Mifflin; London: André Deutsch, 1965), chaps. XXX, XXXI; Roger Hilsman, *To Move a Nation* (Garden City, N.Y.: Doubleday, 1967), part V.

3. Make a secret approach to Castro in an attempt to split him off from the Russians.
4. Set up a blockade of Cuba.
5. Deliver an air strike to destroy the missiles and their installations.
6. Mount an invasion of Cuba that would rid the United States of Castro as well as the missiles.

President Kennedy rejected alternatives one and two immediately, because, as he had once caustically remarked about Khrushchev, "That _____ won't pay any attention to words. He has to see you move."[16] Alternative three was also set aside because Kennedy rightly believed that this was a confrontation between the United States and the Soviet Union and that only the latter could remove the missiles. Alternative six, invasion, had few supporters and was considered perhaps a last step. It was felt that invasion more than any of the other alternatives would risk a world war, would tempt Soviet retaliation in Berlin or elsewhere, and would also ruin United States relations with Latin America. The choice soon narrowed down to alternatives four and five. Should America blockade the island or should it bomb the missile sites and present Khrushchev and the world with a fait accompli?

One incident in the American deliberations deserves special mention. In the literature on nuclear power there has been vigorous discussion of the possibility of a limited, rigorously controlled exchange of nuclear blows making it crystal clear that any further nuclear action will mean further escalation. Such an exchange of blows was christened Tit for Tat. Unbelievable though it may seem, Tit for Tat was actually proposed in the discussions on Cuba. As Theodore Sorensen tells it:

> The air-strike advocates did not shrink from the fact that a Soviet military riposte was likely. "What will the Soviets do in response?" one consultant favoring this course was asked. "I know the Soviets pretty well," he replied. "I think they'll knock out our missile bases in Turkey." "What do we do then?" "Under our NATO treaty, we'd be obligated to knock out a base inside the Soviet Union." "What will they do then?" "Why, then we hope everyone will cool down and want to talk." It seemed rather cool in the conference room as he spoke.[17]

The air-strike option was abandoned when it was realized that a so-called clean surgical strike (removal of the offensive installations with

[16] Schlesinger, op. cit., p. 391.
[17] Sorensen, op. cit., p. 685.

no injury to civilians or Russian soldiers) was not possible. Furthermore, no guarantee could be given that all of the missiles could be destroyed or that some of them would not fire first. If an air strike were carried out, it would have to be followed by an invasion.

The decision-makers chose a blockade against offensive weapons (that is, missiles and bombers) as the less pugnacious alternative. It was a limited, low-key military action that left Khrushchev a way to save face but that at the same time permitted controlled escalation of American action if necessary. The decision was announced by the President, the allies were informed, their support obtained, and the confrontation began. The rest is well known. Soviet ships headed for Cuba turned around and the delivery of additional nuclear weapons to Cuba ceased, but construction of the missile sites continued furiously. The United States prepared for an air strike and/or an invasion of Cuba and warned Moscow that the missiles must be removed or the United States would take military action. The Soviets then capitulated and agreed to remove the missiles in return for a rather vague American promise not to invade Cuba.

Three crucial observations must be made. First, the United States was ready to go to war, and nuclear war if need be, over the Cuban missiles. President Kennedy was almost certain that the Soviet Union would retaliate against the blockade, probably in Berlin, perhaps in Turkey or Iran. Everything was in combat readiness on both sides, and the danger of nuclear war was fully faced. After deciding to impose the blockade, President Kennedy asked his wife if she would not prefer to leave Washington and stay nearer the underground shelter to which the First Family would be evacuated in case of a Soviet attack (she chose to remain in Washington).[18]

Robert Kennedy said afterward, "We all agreed in the end that if the Russians were ready to go to nuclear war over Cuba, they were ready to go to nuclear war, and that was that. So we might as well have the show-down then as six months later."[19] The President himself later said that it seemed to him at the time that the odds that the Soviets would go all the way to war were "somewhere between one out of three and even."[20] Whatever the effect of American determination upon the Russians, it seems clear that the Americans were not deterred by fear of a Soviet nuclear attack.

Second, the major threat of the Soviet missiles in Cuba was not military. It is true that the medium- and intermediate-range ballistic

18 *Ibid.*, p. 693.
19 Schlesinger, *op. cit.*, pp. 829–30.
20 Sorensen, *op. cit.*, p. 705.

missiles placed in Cuba would have greatly increased Soviet striking capacity against American targets and would have virtually eliminated any warning between launch and strike, but this would still have left the United States with at least a 2-to-1 superiority in nuclear power targeted on the Soviet Union. As Sorensen has written:

> ... these Cuban missiles alone, in view of all the other megatonnage the Soviets were capable of unleashing upon us, did not substantially alter the strategic balance *in fact*. . . . But that balance would have been substantially altered *in appearance*; and in matters of national will and world leadership, as the President said later, such appearances contribute to reality.[21]

Third, the real threat to America was political. "The President," wrote Sorensen, "was concerned less about the missiles' military implications than with their effect on the global political balance."[22] What the United States was ready to fight about was its position in the world, its dominance over the international system outside the Communist bloc. The political balance was threatened because the establishment of a Soviet base in America's backyard would in the eyes of the world put the USSR and the United States on the same basis. What America had done on the Soviet Union's frontiers, the Soviet Union would do on America's. This was the change in the status quo that the United States would not tolerate. It was bad enough to have Cuba desert the American system; it was intolerable to have her become a Russian base. President Kennedy was perfectly clear on the matter in his speech to the nation:

> But this secret, swift and extraordinary build-up of Communist missiles, *in an area well known to have a special and historical relationship to the United States* and the nations of the Western Hemisphere, in violation of Soviet assurances, and *in defiance of American and hemispheric policy*—this sudden, clandestine decision to station strategic weapons for the first time outside of Soviet soil, is a *deliberately provocative and unjustified change in the status quo which cannot be accepted by this country.* [Italics added][23]

In short, the United States was ready to fight a nuclear war when her political position in the world was endangered and her domination of her international order threatened. The Soviet Union, on the other hand, was obviously deterred by the threat of nuclear war. Why? All the evidence points in one direction. She realized that the world did not

21 *Ibid.*, p. 678.
22 *Ibid.*, p. 683.
23 *Ibid.*, p. 703.

regard American missiles on Soviet borders and Soviet missiles on American borders in the same light. Again President Kennedy summarized the problem:

> I think there is a law of equity in these disputes. When one party is clearly wrong, it will eventually give way. . . . They had no business in putting those missiles in and lying to me about it. They were in the wrong and knew it. So, when we stood firm, they had to back down. But this doesn't mean at all that they would back down when they felt they were in the right and had vital interests involved.[24]

As Arthur Schlesinger, Jr., has commented:

> The Cuban missile crisis, he [Kennedy] pointed out, had three distinctive features: it took place in an area where we enjoyed local conventional superiority, where Soviet national security was not directly engaged and where the Russians lacked a case which they could plausibly sustain before the world. Things would be different, he said, if the situation were one where they had the local superiority, where their national security was directly engaged, and where they could convince themselves and others they were in the right.[25]

It is a perfect summary of the factors that decide the outcome in conflicts between nuclear powers.

We are now in better position to understand why the United States did not intervene in the Hungarian revolt, for the factors that operated in favor of America in Cuba operated in favor of the Soviet Union in Hungary. Here Russia's vital interests were threatened, and though weaker than the United States, she would probably have been prepared to fight to retain her hold on Eastern Europe. The West, the neutrals, and certainly the Russian people did not expect the Soviet leaders to sit by and let the Soviet empire disintegrate. There was, to be sure, widespread revulsion at the brutal repression of the revolt, but such action had long been standard for dominant nations whose dependencies threatened to revolt. (The fact that Britain and France were at that very time attacking Egypt over Suez made this reality clearer than usual.) Certainly the Russians themselves considered that they were in the right. Finally, the Soviet Union had military superiority at the point of conflict.

Our examination of conflicts involving at least one nuclear power leads to the disquieting conclusion that the presence of nuclear weapons does not appear to have changed the behavior of nations in any clearly

[24] Schlesinger, *op. cit.,* p. 831.
[25] *Ibid.*

visible way. It is certain that the weapons are terrible. It is certain that after they were used the world would be a vastly different place, *but in advance of their use they seem to have little effect upon the normal course of world politics.* World leaders are still willing to fight if the vital interests of their countries are involved. There is probably no statesman who worried more about the consequences of nuclear war than did President Kennedy, yet he was ready to risk such a war to safeguard American interests in Cuba.

Nor is it only political leaders who are ready to risk nuclear war. The public, too, is unwilling to see its country suffer insults, surrender to threats, or "be pushed around." Public support for Kennedy reached a peak after his successful confrontation with the Russians, and his action was applauded throughout the Western world. The United States and her allies would have pilloried Kennedy had he left the Soviet missiles in Cuba rather than take a chance.

One can therefore reasonably argue *that fear of nuclear war ought to deter the rulers of nations from taking the chances they do, but in fact it does not.* For all the agonizing that may precede their decisions, they continue to act in crises as they have always acted. It is terribly important that the United States in particular understand this fact, for in the gradual escalation of any conflict it is crucial to estimate correctly what the reaction of an adversary to each step will be. It would be tragic if the United States ever acted on the assumption that her nuclear preponderance could be used to blackmail her enemies—nuclear or nonnuclear—into submission. It cannot, and in this course lies the quickest route to the war we all seek to avoid.

NUCLEAR WEAPONS, BLOCS, AND ALLIANCES

Nuclear weapons, then, do not operate as deterrents, but there are still two other ways in which it is claimed they have influenced world politics. Let us examine first their effect upon blocs and alliances.

¶ *Blocs.* Not so long ago it was common to argue that nuclear weapons were in large measure responsible for the polarization of the world into tight blocs of East and West. In a world where only two nations had atomic bombs, it seemed natural that other nations should seek protection and accept the leadership of one of the nuclear powers. Later, when the blocs began to crack and split apart, it was argued that quarrels over nuclear weapons were at the core of America's difficulties with France and Russia's difficulties with China.

Such arguments, though plausible, should be approached with caution, for even a superficial review of the history of the formation of the two blocs indicates clearly that there were other and more important variables at work. The Russians, for example, began to make Eastern Europe into a political and economic tributary of the Soviet Union early in 1947, well in advance of Soviet nuclear capability and quite apart from any wish on the part of the satellites themselves. The Soviet bloc began to deteriorate visibly in 1956, a year which should have marked a high point in Communist fear of American nuclear strength. The United States had a crushing superiority in nuclear weapons and the Republican Party then in power had officially adopted as one of its foreign policy goals the liberation of Eastern Europe. In fact, the loosening of Eastern Europe's bonds with Russia had nothing to do with nuclear fears but stemmed from long-standing political and economic grievances that were allowed to surface under the relatively milder policies of Khrushchev.

The Sino-Soviet split, beginning in 1958 after almost a decade of close cooperation, stems fundamentally from the fact that China's size and growing strength threaten Russian domination of the Soviet bloc. It is true that China has nuclear aspirations and wanted Soviet weapons and help in developing her own nuclear industry, but it is wrong to think of this as the cause of the dispute. Were this the case China would hardly have purged those of her leaders who wanted to compromise with the Soviet Union in order to obtain Russian nuclear weapons; nor would the Soviet Union have failed so miserably in her attempts to make China conform to Russian policy by holding out nuclear bait.

In the West the situation is not quite so clear, for the Western bloc did form around the United States at a time when she possessed a nuclear monopoly. However, the economic ties among the nations of the Western bloc have always been far stronger than the military ties: NATO, for example, has been plagued with difficulties from its beginning, whereas the economic dependency of the bloc upon the United States, particularly in the years immediately following the war, was an overwhelming fact of European life. Difficulties within the bloc have been caused not only by nuclear proliferation but also by the fact that Western Europe has become increasingly able to stand on her own feet economically; under De Gaulle France, in particular, seems to have mistaken affluence for power.

After World War II, the United States and the Soviet Union were far and away the most powerful nations on earth, quite apart from the possession of nuclear weapons, and it was only natural that each should dominate the other nations in its camp. Within each bloc the leading nation had an overwhelming power advantage over its nearest rival. If gross national product is used as an index of power, the United States in 1950 had six times the power potential of Britain, and the Soviet

Union three times that of China. The formation of the Eastern and Western blocs is perfectly explainable without any reference to nuclear strength.

¶ *Alliances.* It is also argued that the introduction of nuclear weapons has greatly reduced the reliability and the desirability of alliances. The argument here is that fear of nuclear war has made allies less trustworthy than they used to be, that smaller nations lacking nuclear power may be reluctant to fulfill their commitments to a nuclear patron for fear of becoming a target of nuclear retaliation in a war of the giants, and that a nuclear patron may desert its clients rather than risk annihilation in defending them. Hans Morgenthau, for one, has argued:

> The availability of nuclear weapons has radically transformed these traditional relations among allies and the risks attending them. Nuclear nation A, which enters into an alliance with Nation B, nuclear or non-nuclear, runs a double risk different in kind from the risks facing a member of a traditional alliance. In honoring the alliance, it might have to fight a nuclear war against nuclear power C, thereby forfeiting its own existence. Or ally B may provoke a war with nuclear power C on behalf of interests other than those contemplated by the alliance and thereby force A's hand, involving it in a nuclear war on behalf of interests other than its own. That latter risk is magnified if B is also a nuclear power, of however small dimensions. If B were to threaten or attack C with nuclear weapons, C might, rightly or wrongly, consider B's military power as a mere extension of A's and anticipate and partly prevent the commitment of A through a first strike against A. Or A, anticipating C's reaction against itself or seeking to save B through nuclear deterrence, will commit its own nuclear arsenal against C. In either case, B, however weak as a nuclear power, has the ability to act as a trigger for a general nuclear war.
>
> B, on the other hand, faces a double risk, too. It may forfeit its existence in a nuclear war fought by A on behalf of its interests. Or it may find itself abandoned by A, who refuses to run the risk of its own destruction on behalf of the interests of B.[26]

It is concluded that the reliability of allies is smaller and the risks of alliances commensurably greater in the nuclear age.

This hypothesis seems entirely plausible—yet the evidence points the other way. In the first twenty years of the nuclear era few countries

[26] Hans J. Morgenthau, "The Four Paradoxes of Nuclear Strategy," *American Political Science Review,* LVIII, 1 (March 1964), 33.

have been abandoned by their allies. The United States defended Iran in 1946 and Turkey in 1947, and the Western powers have defended Berlin from 1948 to the present day. The United States defended South Korea in 1950 and the Chinese defended North Korea.

Or take one dramatic instance: the behavior of France in the Cuban missile crisis. Here was a confrontation between two nuclear giants where the danger of nuclear war was clear; here too was a situation that endangered only American security. Yet when the United States decided to stand up to the Soviet Union, all her allies stood firmly by her. De Gaulle, by that time a bitter critic of American policy and intent on breaking up the Western bloc, had not even been consulted on American action. And yet when informed, he simply said: "If there is a war, I will be with you."[27]

How different the behavior of allies in the prenuclear years before World War II: Austria abandoned by Italy to the Nazis; Ethiopia abandoned by all but a handful of the members of the League of Nations; Czechoslovakia abandoned by England and France and Russia. It is hard to find an instance, except for Poland, in which allies did abide by their agreements. On this evidence, it is difficult to argue that nuclear weapons have adversely affected the operation of alliances.

Finally, if alliances are useless in a nuclear age, they should be decreasing in number—yet the opposite is true. The United States is tied by alliances to 46 nations, and the Soviet Union to 11 more. It would appear that nuclear weapons have not had the predicted effect upon the behavior of nations in their alliances with each other.

NUCLEAR WEAPONS AND POWER

Still another effect of nuclear weapons on the behavior of nations is said to be their role as an equalizer of power. The notion here is that a small nation possessing a given number of atomic bombs is as powerful as any other nation on earth, for it can destroy its enemies no matter what their size. As a French theorist has written:

> . . . thermonuclear weapons neutralize the armed masses, equal-
> ize the factors of demography, contract distance, level the heights,
> limit the advantages which until yesterday the Big Powers derived
> from the sheer dimensions of their territory. . . . It is easy to prove
> that countries as different as Switzerland and Communist China are
> in the same boat when it comes to the nuclear threat.[28]

[27] Schlesinger, *op. cit.*, p. 815.
[28] Pierre Gallois, quoted by Aron, *op. cit.*, p. 102.

If this were true, it would indeed represent a revolution in international politics, for it would wipe out existing differences in power and completely alter the determinants of national power. However, it is not true. *If* Switzerland (or any other small country) *could* develop a nuclear arsenal as strong as that of the great nuclear powers, she would indeed become considerably more powerful than she is today, though even then she would be far from the equal of the great powers in possessing means of persuasion, reward, and punishment short of nuclear war. But this is precisely the point. Small countries can afford at best only a few nuclear bombs, not an arsenal; and the few by themselves are more a danger than a defense. As we have seen, it is necessary to have a retaliatory force that can cripple an enemy even after a surprise attack. This means not only possessing thermonuclear warheads in large quantity but also possessing the silos and the submarines in which to hide and disperse them if they are to survive attack, the latest and swiftest rockets with which to deliver them through the enemy's defenses, and anti-missile missiles more effective than the swiftest and newest enemy rockets. The industries, the skilled manpower, and the sheer cost of maintaining such an arsenal and keeping it constantly up to date are tremendous. Nuclear weapons are the most expensive weapons ever invented. They are beyond the resources of all but a very few nations.

It is no accident that the nations that possess nuclear power today—the United States, the Soviet Union, Britain, France, and China—were the Big Five even before they had nuclear weapons. And the only other countries with the capability of becoming nuclear powers in the near future—Germany and Japan—have also been great powers and owe their present weakened position to their defeat in World War II. Nor is it a coincidence that the only two nations with true retaliatory nuclear capability are nations whose GNP is over $200 billion. Below are two rankings of the great powers, one by their nuclear strength and the other by their gross national product. With the exception of West Germany, deliberately disarmed, the rankings are the same.

Nuclear Strength	Gross National Product
United States	United States
USSR	USSR
United Kingdom	West Germany
France	United Kingdom
China	France
	China

It seems obvious that the same factors that produce national power in the absence of nuclear weapons also make possible the possession of nuclear weapons. The weapons reinforce power, but it is the potential for power that brings the weapons, not the other way around.

We must still consider the further question of whether the possession of some nuclear weapons can at least improve the power position of a nation in relation to other nations of similar power. Even here, the answer is not very encouraging. France with her new atomic weapons has perhaps increased her prestige, but she has not noticeably improved her power position vis-à-vis either Britain or Germany and certainly not vis-à-vis the United States. China, on the other hand, does not seem to have been hindered in her spectacular rise in power by the fact that she had no nuclear weapons until 1965.

One is drawn to conclude that the hypothesis that nuclear weapons minimize differences in power is not borne out and to advance another hypothesis instead. Nuclear power has not and will not reverse existing trends in international politics. It will not deter nations from defending their national interests; it does not make alliances useless; and it does not remove the power differences that provide the framework of world politics. Quite the contrary: If there is any clear effect that nuclear weapons have had upon world politics in the last twenty years, it has been that they have reinforced fundamental existing trends.

THE REINFORCEMENT OF TRENDS

Numerous examples can be given of the way in which the appearance of nuclear weapons has speeded up trends that were already in existence. For example, nuclear weapons have permitted the USSR to gain in power in relation to the United States faster than would otherwise have been possible. It is important to note, however, that the Soviet Union was already increasing her power through rapid industrialization in the years before World War II, through victory in the war, and through renewed economic growth, territorial expansion, and consolidation of her hold on Eastern Europe in the postwar years. Russian achievements in the development of nuclear warheads and in advanced rocketry gave a dramatic boost to her military power and to her *reputation* for power (and, as we have noted, reputations in themselves increase the ability to influence others), but there is little doubt that she would have continued to gain on America even if atomic weapons had never been invented. The power gap between China and the other great powers has also been narrowing since 1949, but her achievement of nuclear retaliatory force—likely within the next few decades—will give Chinese power a similar conspicuous boost.

Nuclear weapons confer prestige as well as power, for they also play a role as status symbols. Here too they have a curiously reinforcing effect upon existing trends. Nuclear weapons have elevated those who can afford the entire arsenal to new peaks of international power, but their formidable costliness also operates as a silent and peaceful selector which lesser nations wishing to compete for greatness cannot ignore. France and England have both sought atomic arms more for their prestige value than for their military use, for neither can afford retaliatory power. Both countries have sought to hold on to the illusion of power by expensive means, and its very cost will hasten their decline because of the strain it places on the economy.

The Balance of Terror: An Appraisal

Let us review briefly the conception of the balance of terror. It is alleged that the possession of full nuclear power (that is, second-strike capability to inflict unacceptable damage upon an enemy even after absorbing a surprise attack) will so terrify any adversary as to deter it from action that would provoke a major military attack. When two or more opposing nations possess such nuclear power, there is said to exist a balance of terror that will prevent nuclear war through mutual deterrence.

The evidence now available for study leaves serious doubts about the validity of this conception or its usefulness in understanding world politics in the nuclear age. The misgivings stem not from any doubt of the ability of the United States and the USSR to destroy each other in battle, nor from any doubt that the horror of nuclear war has inspired fear in the hearts of the world's leaders and its masses, but from the claim that this fear has in turn produced dramatic changes in the behavior of nations in world politics.

The exponents of the balance of terror assume a connection between fear and behavior, and while they are quite precise about the potency of the weapons and their delivery systems, they are unavoidably vague about the political consequences of the military potential. They simply assume deterrence. They argue that if the threat of nuclear retaliation is credible, if the opponent is rational, if there is communication, if what is to be gained is not worth what is to be lost, and so on, then the adversary will be deterred.

There have been few tests of the matter in actual behavior, but the evidence that exists suggests strongly that the expected changes in international behavior have not occurred. Nuclear weapons have not revolutionized the power structure of the world; they have not removed the differences between great and small powers. On the contrary, they have exaggerated these differences, for only the largest and strongest of nations can afford the tremendous outlay of resources required to achieve a full nuclear arsenal. If anything, nuclear weapons have reinforced the existing patterns of international relations by hastening the rise of nations already growing in power and the decline of those already falling. Nuclear weapons have not leveled differences in power, they have not frightened nations into blocs or out of alliances, and most important of all, they have not deterred nations from fighting for their national interests.

In case after case of conflict involving one or more nuclear powers, the nations involved have not acted in accordance with the dictates of the balance of terror. And even without detailed examination of cases it should be perfectly obvious that over the years, when the United States had first an atomic monopoly and then a tremendous nuclear superiority, her deterrent did not seem to change the behavior of either the Russians or the Chinese. Indeed it seems the only nation deterred was the United States itself.

Why is it that America's deterrent apparently began to operate only after the Russians too possessed retaliatory power? Perhaps the answer really lies in the fact that there *is* no deterrent and that as long as only one party to a dispute has nuclear power it is often obvious that it does not deter, but when both parties have nuclear strength, a retreat by either side can be credited with plausibility to the nuclear deterrent of the other, even if this is not the case. Certainly the disputes we have examined provide no clear proof of nuclear deterrence; on the contrary, they offer numerous instances of behavior directly counter to the theory.

What then is the use of nuclear weapons? Why all this talk of deterrence if it is so doubtful that deterrence is in fact a consequence of nuclear threat? The value of nuclear weapons, of course, is in their being used. Atomic powers build their nuclear stockpiles in case such weapons have to be used either in aggression or in revenge; their utility in forestalling such action is quite doubtful. Perhaps these weapons will never be used, but no nation that can afford them dares not to have them, for they *might* be used.

Now to the second question: Why all this talk of deterrence? Again the answer seems fairly simple: The thought of nuclear war is intolerable and it is intolerable to believe that one's country is preparing to contribute to it. There are two ways to peace of mind: one is to change our national behavior; the other is to affirm that the behavior means the reverse of what it actually does. The latter course is obviously easier, and so we adopt it. Thus the American Air Force puts a sign on the gates of the Strategic Air Command, which would be in charge of a nuclear strike if it came to war, saying "Peace is our profession." The

American secretary of war is called the secretary of defense, and nuclear stockpiles are called a deterrent.

Agreed that nuclear weapons can spread death, agreed that they have spread terror, it is still doubtful that they have created deterrence. These findings are, of course, deeply disquieting. Any sane person would wish for some guarantee of world peace, or at least for some assurance that these new and most terrible weapons will never be used, but in fact there is no clear sign that nuclear arms held by one side deter the other from fighting. Other factors determine whether nations fight or not, and in the next chapter we shall focus on the forces that shape such behavior.

Our discussion of deterrence brings to mind the bitter judgment Tacitus passed upon the Romans: "They create a desert and call it peace." Amending only slightly to fit modern times, we can say: "They create terror and call it security."

14

The Power Transition

━━

Since World War II, tremendous emphasis has been placed upon military preparations. Aware that the balance of power does not seem to be working and afraid to trust in full the new international organizations that we have created, nation after nation has turned to military might in hopes of thereby guaranteeing the kind of world it wants. Coupled with the current arms race, we have also seen a scramble for allies—the creation of blocs and counterblocs, the wooing of neutrals, and endless conferences and agreements.

Yet the significant facts of international politics are not determined by military strength and alliances. To explain the major trends of international politics, one must turn away from such exciting and colorful problems as how many missiles the Russians have or what one head of state said to another at a summit meeting. The distribution of power among nations does not balance itself, as we have seen. Nor can a nation assure the distribution of power it wishes by arming and by holding conferences. We have learned that the major determinants of national power are population size, political efficiency, and economic development. It is shifts in such areas as these that lead to changes in the distribution of power.

The present instability of the international order is based on the fact that we live in a period when the population, political organization, and industrial strength of nations are changing rapidly. Newcomers are constantly challenging the established leaders of world politics, and if ever one of these challenges is successful, it will mean a huge transference of power from one group of nations to another—and a new international order. Some of the challengers of the recent past have been beaten back. Whether the current challenge will be successful or not remains to be seen, but one thing can be predicted with safety: the present challenge is by no means the last. Whoever wins the current contest will in time be faced by new challengers. We can even predict who they will be.

Behind the apparent chaos of this ever-shifting distribution of power in the world, certain regularities can be observed. If world politics is not a self-regulating mechanism or a chess game, neither is it a wild chaos or a free-for-all. It is the purpose of this chapter to describe the regularities and the major trends of modern international politics. In doing so, we shall try to provide a framework that fits the data more accurately and that affords a better basis for the prediction of future events than either the balance of power or the balance of terror.

Stages of the Power Transition

One main quarrel with the balance of power theory was the assumption that the strength of each nation was relatively constant unless it won a war or made new alliances. In fact, however, internal changes of the most momentous sort are constantly occurring within modern nations, and many of these changes have great significance in terms of national power. Industrialization and political modernization are particularly crucial in this respect. The most powerful nations in the world today are all politically modern and industrial. The established leaders are those who industrialized first, and those who challenge them for leadership are nations that have industrialized more recently. This is not an accident.

One of the most significant statements that can be made about modern times is that we live in the midst of a worldwide industrial revolution. It is not one, however, that all the nations of the world are going through together; it is a revolution that started in England in the eighteenth century, spread to France and to the rest of Northwestern Europe as well as to the United States in the nineteenth century, reached Southern and Eastern Europe and Japan in the first half of the twentieth century, and is only now erupting in China. Indeed, much of the world has barely been touched at all.

Of interest to us here is the fact that industrialization and political modernization bring a great increase in power to a nation. Of course, the gains to be made are proportionate to the base a nation starts with.

Nations that are small in size may find their power and influence increased through industrialization and political modernization, but they cannot hope to compete with the giants of international politics. Nonindustrial nations with large populations, however, can expect industrialization to pay great dividends in terms of national power. Even a moderately sized nation may gain handsomely, for, as we have seen, industrialization brings a sharp population increase. Furthermore, nations that industrialize successfully must develop effective national governments either in advance of industrialization or during the process. Thus a modernizing nation typically gains simultaneously in wealth and industrial strength, in population, and in efficiency of governmental organization. Since these are the three major determinants of national power, an increase in them inevitably results in a great increase of power for the particular nation. In fact, if we compare the power and influence of any nation before it has industrialized with its power and influence after the process is well under way, we will see this growth clearly.

Thus we can say that a nation that industrializes goes through a power transition in the course of which it passes from a stage of little power to one of greatly increased power. For convenience, the power transition can be divided into three distinct stages:

1. The stage of potential power
2. The stage of transitional growth in power
3. The stage of power maturity

THE STAGE OF POTENTIAL POWER

The first stage can be called the stage of potential power. In this stage, a nation is not industrial. Its people are primarily agricultural, and the great majority of them are rural. Economic productivity is low, and so are standards of living for the vast majority of the people. Industrial output is small or nonexistent. Technical skills are few and formal education unimportant. The population may be dense or sparse, but it is increasing in size; often at a rapid rate. Politically, the nation is still in the stage of primitive unification. Government is not very efficient. Often such a country is ruled by foreign conquerors or by a small aristocracy. Local loyalties are strong, and nationalistic sentiments are not usually marked until near the end of this stage. The governmental bureaucracy is neither large nor efficient. The common people do not participate much in national government except to pay taxes, nor do they have much interest in national politics. There are no institutions that can even begin to organize the human and material resources of the nation.

As a result, the power of such a nation is fairly stable but at a very low point. There may be some fluctuations—through conquest of other preindustrial states or through the policies of some exceptional ruler—but these are liable to be of short duration and are relatively minor compared to the great increase in power that is possible if such a nation industrializes. Such a nation may be extremely powerful in a world where no nation is industrial, but compared to any industrial nation, even a small one, its power is slight. The major part of its power is potential. If it is to be realized at all, it will be in the future.

The potential that the nation has is determined, of course, at least partly by its size in this preindustrial stage. If the nation is very small (that is, has a small population), its potentialities for power are small. Even if they are fully realized, the nation will remain a minor power. If the nation is large at the start, however, it can expect a huge increase in power by realizing its full potential. Let us take as examples Guatemala and India. Both these countries are in the first stage of the power transition. Both can expect to multiply the power they have many times if they succeed in industrializing. But Guatemala even fifty times more powerful than she is now will not be a nation of consequence. She may improve her living standards and have a rich culture; she may lord it over minuscule neighbors; but she will not be an important nation in world politics. An India even ten times stronger than she is today would be another matter altogether. Starting with what she has now, India by industrializing fully would become one of the most powerful nations in the world. Indeed, with the exception of China, there is no nation that could rival her in power. That is why such nations as China and India, and to a lesser extent Indonesia and Brazil, have as much influence in international councils as they do. They can cash in today on some of the power they may possess tomorrow, for the world is well aware of the power potential they possess.

THE STAGE OF TRANSITIONAL GROWTH IN POWER

The second stage of the power transition is the stage of transitional growth. During this stage, the nation is undergoing the transition from a preindustrial to an industrial stage, and in the process of this transition, its power increases rapidly relative to that of the other preindustrial nations it leaves behind and to that of the already industrialized nations it is beginning to catch up with.

During this stage, fundamental changes take place within the nation. There is a great growth in industry and in the cities. In occupations, large numbers of people move out of farming and into industry and service occupations. Geographically, they move from the countryside to the growing cities. Productivity rises, the gross national product goes up sharply, living standards improve. The death rate has dropped, and although the birth rate also drops somewhat, the population increases, often at a fairly rapid rate. Political institutions also change. In fact, political changes sometimes precede industrialization. The central national government grows in power and extends its control over the nation's life; the governmental bureaucracy expands. The general population is more affected by what the government does and comes to participate more in the activities of government, whether that government be totalitarian or democratic. Nationalism runs high and sometimes finds expression in aggressive action toward the outside. The form of government changes as new social classes rise in economic and political importance. Indeed, there is scarcely a single social institution that does not change drastically. Family structure changes, community organization takes on new forms, relations of church and state are altered, and religious beliefs change. Science progresses, education changes almost completely, new ideologies arise. In short, the entire way of life of the people of the nation changes.

What is important from our point of view in this chapter is that so many of these changes have the effect of increasing the ability of the nation's representatives to influence the behavior of other nations, that is, of increasing the nation's power. Industrialization, of course, is not a process that ends automatically once it reaches a certain point. Economic, political, and social institutions are continuing to change today, even in the most advanced nations, and in terms of economic and social efficiency, great gains still remain to be made. But the changes that occur at the beginning of the industrialization process are qualitative, not just quantitative. It is these first fundamental changes that bring the great spurt in national power.

Of course, the speed at which a nation gains power depends largely upon the speed with which it industrializes, and both these factors have a great influence on the degree to which the rise of a new power upsets the international community. The first nations to industrialize did so relatively slowly, whereas the nations that have industrialized most recently have done so quite rapidly. Their increase in power has been correspondingly sudden.

The Soviet Union provides an excellent example of a nation that has recently gone through the stage of transitional growth. The speed of her industrialization is legendary, and the rapid growth in her power is something that we have all witnessed. In the space of thirty years, the USSR rose from a large nation of perhaps fifth or sixth rank in the world to the second greatest nation on earth, surpassed in power only by the United States. The rise of China, which is now in the stage of transitional growth, promises to be equally spectacular.

The third stage of the power transition is the stage of power maturity. It is reached when the nation is fully industrial, as the United States and Western Europe are today. Technological change is still rapid in such nations and will probably continue to be rapid. Economic efficiency is high and will continue to increase. The GNP continues to rise, but at a slower *rate* than previously. Governmental organs are stronger and more efficient than ever. Bureaucratization seems to be increasing both in political and economic institutions. The family, the church, the community are changing still and will continue to change. There is room for much improvement in producing greater wealth and in distributing it more equitably and raising the living standards of all. And there is much room for social improvement, for gains in physical and mental health, for better education, for better race relations and more wholesome community life.

But the great burst of energy characteristic of nations in the early stages of industrialization lies in the past for mature nations. They cannot again double and triple and quadruple their capital investment as they did in the early years. Great cities will not again spring up overnight. Improvements in living standards will no longer seem to be miracles. The death rate cannot again be slashed as it was when the great epidemic diseases were first brought under control, and the population, although it may continue to grow, will not expand at the dizzy rate of the early days. National sentiment will not flame as it did in the first enthusiasm of growing power.

The internal qualities that give a nation international power do not disappear in the stage of power maturity. They may even continue to increase, but not at the rate they did before, and to slow down even a little in a race where everyone else is running forward is to run the risk of falling behind eventually. This is why the *power* of a nation may decline in the stage of power maturity, even though the nation continues to grow richer, more industrial, and more efficient.

We must remember that power is relative, not absolute. It is not a characteristic of the nation itself, but a characteristic of its relationships with other nations. If the rest of the world were standing still and only a single nation were industrializing, that nation would continue to grow more and more powerful indefinitely. It would soon have the power to rule the world. Indeed, England, the first nation to industrialize, practically did rule the world. At her peak she governed one-quarter of the earth's surface and controlled many of the activities of other nations as well. But the rest of the world does not stand still. It did not stand still for

England, and it will not stand still for the United States. Today, England has dropped to third place in terms of world power, and she will drop further and faster in the years to come.

The major reason that power declines in the third stage has nothing to do with the mature nation itself. Its *relative* power declines because other nations are entering the second stage of transitional growth, and as they do so, they begin to close the gap between themselves and the nations that industrialized before them. Had all the nations of the world gone through the Industrial Revolution at the same time and at the same speed, the result would have been a great change in international relations but not necessarily any major shift in the distribution of power among nations. There would have been no *power* transition. However, industrialization has proceeded unevenly throughout the world. The result has been that first one nation and then another has experienced a sudden spurt in power. It is like a race in which one runner after another goes into a brief sprint. Some of the runners are too small and too slow ever to have a chance of winning, but among the major contenders, these sprints may mean the difference between leading the pack and running sixth or eighth. It is these sudden sprints that keep upsetting the distribution of power in the world, threatening the established order of the moment and disturbing world peace. It is the differential spread of industrialization throughout the world and the resulting power transition, *not* some automatic balancing process, that provides the framework of modern international politics.

The Present Period in Perspective

Because we are still in the midst of this worldwide industrial revolution, the present period is an unusual one, differing markedly from the period that preceded it and differing also from the period that will follow. It may be useful to divide the history of international relations into three periods, though in so doing we must be careful not to confuse these three periods with the three stages of the power transition through which each nation passes. The difference should become clear as we proceed.

In the first period, there were as yet no industrial nations. Although the nations of the world differed in their economic and social development, all were still preindustrial, that is, they were all in stage 1 of the power transition, the stage of potential power. There were differences in power between one nation and another, but these differences were not based upon industrial strength. The same means of power—territorial consolidation and conquest, skillful alliances, military proficiency, and able political leadership—were available to all nations. This period extended from the creation of nation-states until roughly the middle of the eighteenth century, when England started to industrialize.

The second period, in which we still live, is the period of the industrial revolution. In this period some nations have industrialized and others have not. In terms of the power transition, some nations are in stage 1, some in stage 2, and some in stage 3. Differences in power between nations are tremendous. At the beginning of this period, the nations that industrialized first had a great power advantage over all the others, but as the period progressed, they began to be hard-pressed by other nations entering stage 2 behind them.

The third period still lies in the future. It will begin when all the nations of the world have become fully industrial, that is, when all have entered stage 3 of the power transition. At this point, the nations will again resemble each other more closely, as they did in the first period. Differences in power and in wealth will continue to exist, if nations continue to be the units of political organization, but whatever differences there are will not be based so heavily upon differential industrial advancement as they are today; they will be based upon other, as yet unknown, factors.

If the theory of the balance of power has any applicability at all, it is to the politics of the first period, that preindustrial, dynastic period when nations were kings and politics a sport, when there were many nations of roughly equivalent power, and when nations could and did increase their power largely through clever diplomacy, alliances, and military adventures. In terms of our determinants of power, differences in political efficiency were highly significant.

The theories of this book, and the theory of the power transition in particular, apply to the second period, when the major determinants of national power are population size, political efficiency, and industrial strength, and when shifts in power through internal development are consequently of great importance. Differential industrialization is the key to understanding the shifts in power in the nineteenth and twentieth centuries, but it was not the key in the years before 1750 or so, and it will not always be the key in the future.

The third period will require new theories. We cannot predict yet what they will be, for we cannot predict what the world will be like after all nations are industrialized. Indeed, we may not have nations at all. By projecting current trends we can make guesses about the near future, but we cannot see very far ahead. What will the world be like when China and India are the two major powers, as it seems likely they will be? What would the world be like after a major nuclear war? We cannot say. Bound by their own culture and their own experience, social scientists frame theories to explain the past and all too often blithely project them into the future as "universal laws," assuming that the assumptions on which they are based will continue to be true. Social theories may be adequate for their day, but as time passes, they require revision. One of the most serious criticisms that can be made of the balance of power theory is that it has not been revised to take into account new conditions. Concepts and hypotheses applicable to the sixteenth century and to the politics of such units as the Italian city-states have been taken and applied, without major revision, to the international politics of twentieth-century nations such as the United States, England, and the Soviet Union. We shall try not to repeat the error. The theories set forth here represent only an attempt to explain the international politics of the present age. They are based upon the events of the relatively recent past, and they should continue to be useful in the relatively near future, but that is all.

Shifts in the Distribution of Power

Let us return to the second period and examine it in more detail, for that is the period in which we now live and the period to which the theories of this book apply. It also happens to be a particularly fascinating period to study because of the rapid and dramatic changes that are occurring in it.

When we focus our attention on this period, it becomes clear how different it is from the imaginary world in which the balance of power would operate. Far from being stable, unchanging units, nations are constantly changing in power, and much of that change is generated from within. In this second period, the major ways in which individual nations have increased their power have been through industrialization, imperialism, and immigration. We have already described the growth of power through industrialization and we shall not repeat that description here. We should, however, note some of the problems created by the possibility of increasing power in this fashion.

PROBLEMS POSED BY POWER GROWTH THROUGH INDUSTRIALIZATION

For the neighbors or potential enemies of a nation that embarks upon this path to power, the increase in strength brought by industrialization is extremely discomforting, the more so since it is likely to be rapid and since there is little that other nations can do to stop it. Even a major power may find that it must stand by helplessly while a former subject or an inferior rival catches and surpasses it in power. What, after all, can a nation do to prevent another nation from increasing its economic productivity? How can it prevent the death rate from going down and the population from increasing in another state? How can it stop a foreign government from increasing the efficiency of its institutions? Granted that the increasing power of the industrializing nation constitutes a great threat to the neighbors, what can the neighbors do about it? This problem is a major one in international politics today. It results directly from the fact that the major source of power for many a nation lies within the possibilities of its own internal development.

This difficulty of modern international politics will stand out more clearly if one compares the ways in which a nation would handle an opponent's power gain in the previous period with those of the present period. In the preindustrial era, nations could not increase their power very much unless they acted outside their own boundaries. True, a nation could gain some power if its rulers administered it wisely and encouraged the national economy, if they did not bleed their subjects white with taxes, and if the people were satisfied and loyal. However, the amount of power that could be gained in this fashion was not great. If a nation wanted to increase its power substantially, the best way was to ally itself with a powerful neighbor or to undertake the difficult task of conquering a territory with a large and wealthy population. If a nation did either of these things, its opponents were given a clear indication of what it was trying to do and could take steps to counteract its moves. They could seek to break up the new alliances or form counteralliances. They were even justified in going to war to stop aggression that would result in a power increase for the aggressor.

Today, the situation is quite different. Wars may still be waged to stop outright military aggression, and alliances are still formed to counteract the alliances of rivals, but there is little that a nation can do to stop another nation from industrializing. One must not forget that industrialization is not only the road to power but also the road to wealth. To prevent a nation from gaining power by this method means preventing it from achieving a higher standard of living as well. Keeping one's competitors poor and helpless so that they will never be a threat is not a policy that appeals to many. If pursued, it would have to be disguised, and even so, it would probably earn hatred for those who pursued it.

In fact, there are only three alternatives that a nation can follow to meet the threat posed by a rival's industrialization, and none of them is altogether satisfactory. If the threatened nation is already powerful itself, it may try to smother its rival's attempt to industrialize at the start. If it controls the other country as a colony, it can prevent it from developing rival industries (political colonizers have always done just that). If it exercises more subtle influence through foreign aid and the control of credit, it can encourage its potential rival to concentrate on exporting agricultural products and raw materials or on developing light industries to produce luxury goods (both the United States and the USSR have had such policies in regard to economic dependencies and satellites). If neither of these policies is feasible, it can try to foster the internal subversion of the rival government and bring about its replacement by a more pliable regime. In the last analysis, it can even wage a preventive war to destroy a rival before it gets too strong. Such a policy has sometimes been advocated by fire-eating Americans upset by the growing might of Russia and China on the theory that it would be easier to defeat them now than later when their industrial and military strength has increased even further, although it is difficult to see how such a policy would make much sense from either a moral or a practical point of view. The Soviet Union is already too strong, and China will soon be, to be dusted off without getting ourselves buried in dust in the process. As far as we know, responsible officials have never considered such a policy.

The second alternative is to take half-measures and try to delay the industrialization of a rival without actually intervening in its affairs. Trade barriers, embargoes, and refusals to give aid will hurt a new, developing nation, but they will not stop its industrialization. Japan and the Soviet Union have proved to the world that industrialization is possible with a minimum of help from the outside. The price in human terms is great, but the nation determined to industrialize can succeed if it is willing to pay that price.

The United States has adopted this delaying tactic against the Soviet Union. For some years after World War II, the United States refused to send strategic goods to Russia and persuaded many of its allies to do likewise. Theoretically, the embargo was against strategic goods that would be used for military purposes, but actually such goods included a significant proportion of the items necessary for a developing, industrial economy; for example, all kinds of machine tools and even plans and information on techniques of drilling oil wells. True, machine tools can make arms, and oil is necessary for war, but of course any major industrial nation can divert much of its economy to war production. The only foolproof way of making sure it does not do so is to destroy its industrial might. There is no doubt that the American embargo hurt the USSR. We can deduce that from the constant requests for more trade that the Russians directed at the West. We pretended to be placing an embargo only on war goods, and the Russians pretended to be interested only in peaceful trade, but there is little doubt that both sides were aware that it is industrial strength, not military might alone, that will be decisive in the struggle for world power now going on.

In recent years, the embargo against the USSR has been considerably relaxed, but the United States has now adopted a similar policy toward Communist China. Americans may in all sincerity deplore the poverty and disease and backwardness of China, but our government has no intention of helping China to industrialize under a government that has taken up the role of being America's worst enemy.

The third alternative for a nation to take in dealing with the industrialization of another nation is to help that nation all it can in the hope that in gratitude it will remain friendly, even after it has become powerful enough to do as it pleases. But this alternative, so appealing from a moral point of view, also has its drawbacks. Certainly, if a now backward nation is going to surpass us in strength in the future, it would be better to guarantee its friendship than to have it as an enemy, but it would be best of all not to be surpassed. Even a friend will consider its own interests first and ours second, and if it is more powerful than we, it is not hard to predict who will win out whenever interests conflict.

England and the United States are a good case in point. English capital was extremely important in the early development of American industry, and the English navy protected the United States throughout the nineteenth century. England, in fact, remained friendly with the United States throughout the period while we industrialized, climbed in power, and eventually took England's place as the most powerful nation in the world. As a result, British and American interests are closely tied together, and we have stood by England in all her major conflicts. Our policies, however, have not always been to England's advantage. We have encouraged the dissolution of her empire, taken over much of her trade, and given her aid on condition that she follow our lead in dealing with other nations. When it came to a showdown over the Suez Canal, we humiliated the British and forced them to retreat militarily because we were not pleased with their seizure of the Canal. England's dependence upon the United States grows daily. There is no doubt that she is pleased to have the most powerful nation in the world for her friend rather than her enemy, but her lot is by no means as happy as it was when England was second to none.

IMPERIALISM AS A MEANS TO POWER

We noted earlier that there were possibilties of achieving power in this present period other than industrializing. One such means is through the conquest of colonies, a method that was particularly important in the early years of the present period. If we look at the actual history of the period, it appears that this means was not a substitute for industrialization but rather a supplement, for the first nations to industrialize also became the world's greatest colonial powers, supplanting the earlier colonial powers, sometimes even stealing their colonies from them.

As we said before, colonialism was possible only as long as there was a large discrepancy in power between the colonizer and the colonized. Such a discrepancy existed even in the years before the industrial revolution proper, for the economically more advanced European nations were considerably more powerful than the primitive world at large. With industrialization, however, the discrepancy grew tremendous. At the same time, the industrializing nations were undergoing a rapid growth in population, which provided a vast pool of colonists to migrate overseas to work and build themselves or to form an upper class to administer the government and supervise the work of the native population. With economic development, the need grew for cheap labor, cheap raw materials and markets, and for soldiers to defend the far-flung possessions of the colonizer. The colonies provided all of these.

The major colonial powers of the nineteenth and early twentieth centuries, although advanced economically, were not particularly large themselves, and there is no question that their great colonial empires added much to their wealth and power. Colonies, however, have proved to be a somewhat treacherous source of power, for the power they give does not spring from within the social organization of the colonizer but depends in large part upon the state of affairs in the colony, and as we have seen, colonialism itself causes changes in the colonies that eventually bring about the end of their political dependency. The conquest of colonies was a relatively easy way of gaining power in a hurry, but the loss of these same colonies substantially reduced the power of the colonizers in one stroke. England's loss of her major colonies has brought about a considerable decline in her fortunes, and the desperate fight that France put up to retain as much as she could of her empire was an indication of her realization that, stripped of her overseas possessions, she would lose a large part of her claim to great power status.

Imperialism, then, was an important additional source of power for the leading nations in the early part of the present period, but this possibility is coming to be ruled out as the economically backward areas of the world begin to modernize.

IMMIGRATION AS A SOURCE OF POWER

There is still one other important way in which nations have gained power during this present, second period of international history: through mass immigration. This way, too, is not directly related to industrialization, although some important connections can be traced. It is fairly certain, for example, that large numbers of European migrants would not have been available if Europe's population had not been growing so rapidly and if her home economy had not been undergoing such a drastic reorganization due to industrialization, and it is doubtful that the New World would have been able to absorb such a flood of immigration if it had not been industrializing itself. However, we can consider the effects of immigration separately from the effects of industrialization.

The major nation to gain power in this fashion was the United States, virtually all of whose people were originally migrants. Particularly toward the end of the nineteenth century and in the years just before World War I, her population grew at an astronomic rate, thanks in large part to immigration. In the peak years, the United States was admitting more than a million people a year. To a lesser degree, Canada, Australia, New Zealand, South Africa, and the nations of Latin America have gained in the same way. Israel is an even more recent example of a nation that has gained in power through immigration.

If population size is a major determinant of national power, immigration should be an important means of adding to a nation's strength, provided that the migrants arrive in large enough numbers and provided that they can be absorbed into the economy and the social system. This seems, however, to be a means to power that is fast vanishing. Free immigration ended with World War I, and although wars and political upheavals continue to stimulate a good deal of refugee movement from one country to another, both the countries of origin and the countries of destination pose formidable barriers to the free movement of individuals who would like to change their nationality. Countries such as Australia that still desire mass immigration are no longer able to obtain the kind of migrants they want, and they are not willing to admit those who are willing to come. Power based on mass immigration, like power based on imperialism, appears to be a phenomenon of the past.

The International Order

A second major characteristic of the present period is the growing strength and permanence of ties among nations. Relations among nations are no longer of the personal sort that were common among preindustrial monarchs, who could and did switch sides in much the way that ordinary people change their friends, not often to be sure, but occasionally if sufficiently provoked or disenchanted. Preindustrial rulers were relatively free to move from one side to another in a controversy, because they had only to take the royal court and the army along with them. The common people were not much interested in international affairs unless they were directly and immediately affected by them, and hence it was not necessary to change their sentiments for a nation to switch sides. Also, relations between nations in the preindustrial era were much more heavily political and less economic than they are today. If a nation's power interests would benefit from a switch, it could be made without any significant effect upon the national economy.

Not so today. Industrialization has greatly increased the economic relations among advanced nations and has created new kinds of mutual economic dependence between advanced nations and underdeveloped areas. Modern industries require raw materials that do not necessarily exist in sufficient quantity within the national boundaries; and once a company has made the necessary foreign contacts, ingratiated itself with the proper people, learned to conform to the necessary regulations (or, if necessary, paid off the proper political officials), established an agreeable price, and made all the arrangements for getting the material paid for and shipped from one country to the other, the company prefers that this arrangement be continued for some years. Certainly, its interests will be hurt by a political change that requires it to find new sources of supply in some other country.

Similar arrangements must be made by a company that depends upon exporting some of its products to other countries. Developing markets takes time. Again contacts must be made, rules learned, and money invested. A company may find that its foreign markets do not really begin to pay off until habits of long standing have been developed in foreign customers.

Underdeveloped nations may become particularly dependent upon advanced nations who help develop their resources by investing capital, providing managerial personnel, and handling all the marketing of the country's few significant exports. The national government itself may become dependent upon payments made by such a "friend," as in the case of Middle Eastern nations whose government revenues are provided almost entirely by payments for oil.

Over a long period of time, economic relations between nations do change. New resources are discovered and developed, new rivals win markets away from their competitors, new financing and shipping arrangements are made. But in the short run, any modern nation has a considerable interest in maintaining good relations with the nations with whom it deals economically and in seeing that its friends do not get too friendly with its rivals. A sudden switch, severing ties with its current friends and establishing new ties with its enemies instead, would be extremely dislocating. Indeed, it would ruin the economy of most nations to attempt such a thing.

Military ties between nations are also of a more permanent nature than they used to be. Modern warfare is so expensive that smaller nations become almost completely dependent upon larger nations for their defense. In 1957, such a major nation as England announced frankly that she could not hope to defend her territory in an atomic war and that she was relying largely upon the retaliatory power of the United States to protect her from the dangers of a Russian attack. Ten years later it was a serious question whether England could afford being a great power at all. Alliances are no longer simply a matter of exchanging plans and information and promises. It is now quite common for one ally to provide a major share of the military equipment for the other ally's forces. Expensive bases must be built and maintained on foreign territory, and troops must be stationed there. Equipment must be standardized. The task of military preparation is so complex today that often a division of labor is arrived at among allies, one providing the missiles, another the nuclear warheads, a third the bases to launch them from—or one providing the foot soldiers and the other the tanks and the air power, and so on.

Under such circumstances, a nation is not likely to make and break alliances lightly. Too much has been invested in the present system of alliances, and too long a time would have to elapse before new defenses could be built with new allies.

Finally, it should be noted that public opinion plays a new role in holding nations to their friends. Modern government and modern warfare both require mass support, and as a result, national governments find it necessary to mobilize popular sentiment behind any important move in international politics. Official and unofficial propaganda continuously drums home the message that the friends and allies of the nation are virtuous and the enemies evil. The average man in the street has a firm belief that the governments (and possibly the people as well) of certain nations are his friends in a very personal sense while others are his enemies. He is willing to pay high taxes, obey regulations that may be detrimental to his private interests, and even go to war and kill people in support of his nation's foreign policy. He would be shocked and horrified if his government suddenly asked him to alter all his opinions and fight on the side of the nations he dislikes against the nations he likes. Sudden changes are therefore made particularly difficult by the role of modern public opinion.

Because the ties between nations are much stronger and of longer duration than they used to be, we can say that the nations of the world are organized into systems or international orders which persist for a relatively long time. A powerful nation tends to set up a system of relations with lesser states that can be called an "order" because the relations are stabilized. In time, everyone comes to know what kind of behavior to expect from the others, habits and patterns are established, and certain rules as to how these relations *ought* to be carried on grow to be accepted by all the parties. Power is distributed in a recognized fashion. Certain nations are acknowledged as leaders, and the area of their leadership comes to be established through precedent. Trade is conducted along familiar channels according to generally agreed upon procedures. Diplomatic relations also fall into recognized patterns. Certain nations are expected to support other nations, and certain diplomats are expected to give deference to others. Even the minute courtesies come to be standardized: there are rules of diplomacy; there are even rules of war.

Nations that accept the given distribution of power and wealth and that abide by the same rules of trade, diplomacy, and war can be said to belong to the same international order. Sometimes there is only one such order in the world, but at other times, as at present, two or more competing international orders may exist simultaneously. Each system has its own patterns of behavior and its own rules, and each would distribute the power and wealth of the world in a different manner if it were dominant.

Nations are *not* free to shift from one international order to another without serious internal changes, involving usually a change in economic systems, a change in the predominant class, a change in the political system, and a change in ideology. Nations may jockey for position within the order to which they belong, and on minor matters they may have considerable freedom of movement. In such matters as an election in the United Nations, an invitation to a conference, the taking up of a question in the United Nations Security Council, or the wording of a communique, members of the same international order can and do intrigue against each other, giving and withdrawing support, and even abandoning their friends on occasion. Members of the same order may quarrel over who should pay what share of the military expenses or what strategy is preferable. They may even steal markets from each other. Certainly, they struggle for power over each other. But they cannot and do not switch sides lightly, deserting one international order for the other. Great or small, their whole way of life is geared to the order to which they belong. Its rules are their rules, and the most powerful people within each nation receive benefits that would be seriously threatened if a new set of rules were adopted for trade and politics and war.

These two fundamental facts, the great shifts in power through internal development of nations and the ties that bind nations into competing international orders, provide the framework for understanding recent international politics. Given these two major facts, we will find that, as a result, there are certain recurring patterns in the international history of the last two hundred years, patterns that are likely to be repeated in the future. Let us look at the history of international politics in the present, second period from this point of view.

BRITISH SUPREMACY

At the end of the first or preindustrial period, France was the most powerful nation in the world. England, who was the first to industrialize, caught up with France in the early years of the second period, fought her on a number of occasions, and defeated her conclusively in the Napoleonic Wars. England emerged from these wars the undisputed dominant power in Europe and in the world. Throughout the nineteenth century, she expanded and consolidated further a new, English-dominated international order. Her preponderance of power was immense. Her military strength was great, her economic might unchallenged. Her new, industrial economy seemed insatiable in its demand for commodities produced by the rest of the world, and much of the world in turn came to depend upon English industry for its manufactured goods. In addition, England's population was increasing rapidly, and large numbers of people unable to adjust to the socioeconomic changes at home migrated to new lands and helped spread English culture and English power. By 1900, England had conquered 12 million square miles of territory and 360 million people to make up the greatest empire in the world's history, and her economic and political influence were felt far beyond the one-quarter of the globe that she ruled formally. Most of the nations of the world were more or less in England's economic orbit. Brittania ruled the waves, and laissez faire ruled the markets. England and her order were supreme.

To defeated France, still a great power in her own right, England granted an important place in her international order. By 1900, France had an empire second only to that of Britain. French colonies covered over 4 million square miles and were inhabited by more than 60 million people. England and France were rivals in many spheres, but they played by the same set of rules, and both drew together to protect their common interests when threatened by outsiders. Their disputes were family quarrels, much like the quarrels of England and the United States today.

CHALLENGERS: THE UNITED STATES AND GERMANY

The power advantage that industrial England and France had over the rest of the world began to disappear around the middle of the nineteenth century, when other nations started to industrialize. Many of these nations were small, but two, the United States and Germany, were important, for they had the initially large population necessary to become great powers through industrialization. Both the United States and Germany entered the beginning of the transitional growth stage when England and France were approaching the end of that stage. This meant that the speed with which the United States and Germany gained power was more rapid than that of England and France. It was clear that if their rate of growth continued, they would eventually catch and even surpass England and France in power, and this is exactly what happened. The United States eventually passed all the European nations, while Germany passed France and caught up with England.

In the case of the United States, industrial growth and floods of immigration made for a rapid and spectacular growth in power. In population alone, the United States pulled ahead of five major European nations between the years 1840 and 1880: England, France, Germany, Italy, and Austria-Hungary. By 1880, Russia was the only nation in Europe with a larger population,[1] and her backward economy prevented her from being an effective rival in terms of power. England continued to be the recognized leader of the world until after World War I, but in actuality, the United States probably passed her in power some years before that war began. It is interesting to speculate why England allowed herself to be surpassed without giving battle to the United States, since this is not the usual behavior of dominant nations toward those who supplant them. We shall discuss this later in the chapter.

The case of Germany is somewhat different. Industrialization of some of the separate German states was followed by their unification into a single political unit in the years between 1866 and 1871. Although the most powerful German state, Prussia, was considerably less powerful than France, a united and industrial Germany was a serious rival. In fact, Germany challenged France and defeated her in the field in the Franco-Prussian War. The defeat of France came as a surprise, for no one had fully appreciated the disappearance of the power advantage that

[1] W. S. Woytinsky and E. S. Woytinsky, *World Population and Production* (New York: Twentieth Century Fund, 1953), p. 46.

France had had over the other continental powers. Germany and France were approximately equal in power at the time of the Franco-Prussian War, but Germany was still in the stage of transitional growth in power, while France was approaching the stage of power maturity. Not only was her industrialization further along, but in addition, for reasons peculiar to French culture, France never did experience as rapid a population growth as other nations going through the industrial revolution. By reducing her birth rate at a comparatively early date, France choked off the possibilities of population increase that came with a lowered death rate. Inevitably, Germany began to outdistance France. The power difference between the two was small in the nineteenth century, but after World War I, Germany pulled rapidly ahead, and on the eve of the second world conflict, Germany was considerably more powerful. Had France been the dominant power of the established international order, Germany, the challenger, would have achieved the dominance she sought. Unfortunately for Germany, it was not France with whom she had to contend, but England and the United States.

With England, Germany did not have such an easy time. It took more than seventy years to catch up with her. Imperial Germany never caught England; it was Nazi Germany that equaled and possibly even passed England in power for a few brief years. Just before World War I, Germany was still less powerful than England and only slightly more powerful than France. Thus the power advantage was still on the side of the Allies, but the gap had been narrowed substantially. Germany's more rapid growth and the confidence she felt because of it led to the first of her two armed bids for first place. Actually, by that time the German attempt was already hopeless, since even before the turn of the century, the Anglo-French international order was underwritten by the new American giant, but America's role was not clearly perceived. England's role was. Englishmen and Germans were both well aware that Germany's major enemy was not France but England.[2]

After her defeat in World War I, Germany suffered a temporary eclipse in power, losing what colonies she had managed to collect. How-

[2] Crowe, the British Under Secretary for Foreign Affairs, made this quite clear when he wrote in 1908: "The German (formerly Prussian) Government has always been most remarkable for the pains it takes to create a feeling of intense and holy hatred against a country with which it contemplates the possibility of war. It is undoubtedly in this way that the frantic hatred of England as a monster of personified selfishness and greed and absolute want of conscience, which now animates Germany, has been nursed and fed." G. P. Gooch and Harold Temperley (eds.), *British Documents on the Origin of the War 1898–1914* (London, H.M.S.O., 1928), vol. 6, p. 131, quoted in E. H. Carr, *The Twenty Years' Crisis 1919–1939* (London: Macmillan, 1954), p. 72.

ever, she retained her industrial strength and most of her base population, and with Nazi organization and conquest she rose again. Before World War II turned against her, Germany swollen with conquests was probably stronger than England and France combined, but as subsequent events proved conclusively, she was not stronger than the United States and Russia combined.

It would be most helpful if our impressions of the major power shifts in the eighteenth and nineteenth centuries could be checked by reference to GNP figures for England, France, Germany, and the United States during the periods in question. Unfortunately, such data simply do not exist. Interestingly enough, however, if we substitute data on the production of pig iron for the missing GNPs, our description of the power shifts seems on the whole to be confirmed (see Table 1). Pig-iron production is certainly not as good an indicator of national power as GNP, but it does at least suggest the progress of industrialization of a country, and this, as we have stated repeatedly, is one crucial determinant of the power of nations.

TABLE 1

Production of Pig Iron in Selected Countries

(thousands of tons) *

Year	U.K.	U.S.	France	Germany
1500	6		12	5
1700	12		22	10
1740	20	1	26	18
1790	68	30	40	30
1840	1,396	290	350	170
1870	5,964	1,665	1,178	1,391
1880	7,749	3,835	1,725	2,729
1890	7,904	9,203	1,970	4,685
1900	8,960	13,789	2,670	8,381
1910	10,217	27,384	4,038	14,793

* U.S., U.K., long tons; others in metric tons.

SOURCE: Norman S. Buchanan and Howard S. Ellis, *Approaches to Economic Development* (New York: The Twentieth Century Fund, 1955), p. 220.

The table indicates that France was preeminent until the middle of the eighteenth century when England caught up with and passed her decisively. Germany caught and had passed France by 1870, and she caught up with England in pig-iron production before World War I. The United States passed Germany as Germany was catching up with France and then caught and passed England in the 1880s. The data thus strongly support our interpretation.

Let us turn back again a few years. In the latter part of the nineteenth century, another major nation began to move through the power transition. The early growth of Japan passed almost unnoticed because, far from Europe and a nonparticipant in European quarrels, Japan did not engage anyone in an open test of power but simply and quietly grew from within by modernizing her political structure and by embarking upon industrialization with hitherto unknown speed. In 1905, Japan took on the decaying Russian Empire and administered a sharp defeat to her in the Russo-Japanese War. Japanese power was brought to the notice of all observers with a suddenness that was quite startling. Japanese power was perhaps magnified by the fact that Japan was surrounded by nations that were still in the preindustrial stage of potential power. When she attacked Russia and later China, her victims were peasant nations that could not resist the attack of a nation as modern as Japan, even though they were much larger. The early defeat of Russia should not have been a surprise.

Japan's choice of England, France, and the United States as allies in World War I avoided for Japan the necessity of a head-on clash with any first-class power. Between the two world wars, Japan increased its territory by annexing huge provinces of China. In World War II, however, Japan made the mistake of siding with the Axis nations in her bid for dominance in the Pacific. This involved Japan in direct conflict with England and France, but both were preoccupied in Europe and could not devote their full attention to Japan. In fact, Japan won a series of smashing victories in the early years of the war. Rapid growth and a series of victories over weak opponents made it appear to Japan that the power gap between herself and the United States was much smaller than it really was, and as a result, Japan attacked the United States. It was a mistake of the first magnitude. The Allied victory in World War II shattered German and Japanese aspirations to dominance.

Germany's years as a great power are not yet over, however. It is deeply ironic that German conflicts with England over first place and German defeats at English hands bled England white and destroyed her empire, so that two decades after World War II, Germany—though split—is at long last in position to pass England permanently in power. But German power will soon find its level. Even a reunited Germany lacks the population to contend for world rule in competition with such giants as the United States and Russia. Nor does Japan have any chance of dominating the Far East. She will continue to be a major Asian nation, but she cannot compete with American control of the Pacific, and on the Asian continent her place is already being taken by Communist China. Neither Germany nor Japan is likely to threaten the Anglo-American order again. Most likely they will accept a secondary place in that order, gaining what benefits they can from it and flirting with the Communist world occasionally for minor advantages.

NEW CHALLENGERS: THE SOVIET UNION AND CHINA

Today the Western order, now firmly led by the United States, is faced with new challengers—the Soviet Union and China. The Communist nations are still far behind the Western nations in power, although one might not think so if he took the newspaper reports and speeches of Western military and civilian leaders at face value. The sudden and startling revelation of Russia's supremacy in the development of long-range missiles and satellites threw the West into a temporary panic, but *sputniks* should not be allowed to obscure the fact that the United States is still much stronger than the USSR.

What worries the West is not so much the situation today, but rather that the Soviet Union is gaining on the United States and her allies. Some such gains are to be expected. The Western nations all completed their transitional growth in power some time ago, whereas Russia has just left that stage and is still growing more rapidly than the major Western nations in both wealth and population.[3]

The important question, of course, is how much longer Soviet growth rates will continue to exceed those of the West. There are indications that both economic growth and population increase are slackening off in the Soviet Union, and it is possible that the United States already has a sufficient power advantage so that the Soviets will not be able to close the gap separating them from the United States. Only future events will tell. One thing is sure, however: Arms alone will not keep the advantage that America now possesses.

It is doubtful that the Soviet Union will be successful in her attempts to establish her own international order as the dominant one, but it can be predicted that the pattern of growth and challenge will be repeated again and again. China has already taken up the role of challenger, vying with the Soviet Union for leadership of the Communist bloc while at the same time beginning to challenge the United States for world dominance. The Chinese challenge of Soviet leadership will take time but should be successful eventually if China is able to surmount her present political

[3] See Tables 2 and 3 in Chapter 9.

difficulties and to resume rapid industrialization. The USSR, after all, has already passed into the stage of power maturity while China has many years of transitional growth in power ahead. Given the huge Chinese population, the power of China ought eventually to become greater than that of the Soviet Union simply through internal development. If China is successful, control of the Communist order will pass to her, and the Western powers will find that the most serious threat to their supremacy comes from China.

Still other challenges lie in the distant future. India may well pose a serious threat to Chinese domination, and Africa, if she ever became a single, industrialized political unit, would be a power to reckon with. It is impossible to predict the exact course of events, but it seems fairly obvious that the Western powers will have an extremely difficult if not impossible time in maintaining the dominance of their own international order until the end of the second period, for as the rest of the world becomes industrial, Europe and America will lose the tremendous power advantage they now possess.

THE PATTERN

From this brief history and projection, it can be seen that a recurring pattern underlies international politics in the present period. At any given moment the single most powerful nation on earth heads an international order that includes some other major powers of secondary importance and some minor nations and dependencies as well. In the present period, the most powerful nation has always been an industrial nation. Thus England, the first large nation to industrialize, was the first leader. As new nations industrialized, the old leader was challenged. Sometimes the challenge came from within the same international order, as when the United States took over world leadership from England or when Germany challenged England and France in World War I. Sometimes the challenge came from outside, from a nation that wished to establish a competitive international order as the dominant order, as in the case of Nazi Germany and Japan, or the Soviet Union and China today.

Ordinarily, such challenges by newcomers result in war. Indeed, the major wars of recent history have all been wars involving the biggest power in the world and its allies against a challenger (or group of challengers) who had recently risen in power thanks to industrialization. One could almost say that the rise of such a challenger guarantees a major war.

THE PEACEFUL TRANSFER OF POWER

There is, however, one major exception that bears examination. This is the transfer of world leadership from England to the United States, a transfer that took place without armed conflict between the two. A number of explanations can be advanced as to why this unusual event occurred.

First of all, the United States did not seek world leadership. In fact, she was reluctant to accept it even after her power had grown to such a point that her dominant position was obvious to everyone. This made her rise to power much less offensive and much less obvious until after it was an accomplished fact.

Second, America's rapid growth in power was due almost entirely to internal developments that did not threaten England. Her territorial expansion was made at the expense of the American Indians and Mexico. Her imperialistic ventures were made at the expense of Spain, not England, and even they were few and hesitating. Her population growth was brought about by favorable conditions within the country and by free immigration which was as welcome in Europe as it was in the United States. Even American industrial development was profitable to England, for there was a great deal of English capital invested in American industry in the years before the two great wars. Thus America's growth in power before World War I was in no way detrimental to English interests. It did not challenge and defeat her; it merely passed her. Even today, when the supremacy of the United States is established and the power of Britain is visibly shrinking, the United States does not take markets or bases or territory or influence away from Britain. At most, we pick up what she lets go. There is a world of difference between the two. Britain has lost her possessions and her wealth because she is getting weaker, not because of the United States.

The major reason why England has allowed the United States to take her place without a struggle is because the United States has accepted the Anglo-French international order. It has not upset the working rules. It has not substituted new economic or political institutions or even a new ideology. It has not required internal revolutions in any of the old major powers, and those who benefited from the order when England ran it continue to benefit from it today, though to a lesser extent. Far from destroying the Anglo-French international order, the United States has given it a new lease on life by continuing to defend it after England and France alone no longer possessed the power to do so.

In practice, partnership with America has meant that America became the senior partner, a development which was not altogether welcome to England but which was accepted as unavoidable. There is bitterness today over the fact that America does not always exercise her leadership in the way that England would have her exercise it, but even this is viewed as distinctly preferable to accepting a rival international order dominated by any other nation. English acceptance of American domination has been made easier by the fact that the two nations have been staunch friends for many years, that they have fought two world wars together, and that they are tied to each other not only by economic and political ties, but also by language, culture, and a common history.

Finally, it should not be overlooked that even if England had objected to America's growing power, there was little she could have done about it. Until World War I, the United States was not a European power and took no part in European politics. Her growth was not fully appreciated until it was too late to stop it. When it became apparent that the United States was going to supplant England as the dominant power in the world, England was busy fighting Germany's first challenge, and the United States was her best ally. By the time World War I was over, America's top position in the world was assured, although another war was necessary before the United States accepted fully the responsibilities that went with her position.

To date, this has been the only instance of a challenger replacing a dominant nation without a fight. No one knows whether a similar shift in power within the Communist order (from the Soviet Union to China) is possible. In the 1950s, with Russia a heavy contributor to Chinese industrialization and with close ideological ties between the two countries, it seemed possible that the Anglo-American experience could be repeated. This seemed particularly likely because it appeared that the USSR would be preoccupied in competing with the West at the very time when China would be catching up with her in power. Since the end of the 1950s, however, relations between the two Communist countries have become very strained, largely as a result of China's open challenge to Soviet leadership. This premature declaration of Chinese aspirations so far in advance of the time when they can be realized has diminished the chances of a peaceful change within the Communist camp. On balance, it appears that China's overtaking of Russia will be full of difficulties. It would be rash, however, to predict that Russo-Chinese relations are heading inevitably toward armed conflict. One should wait and see whether Chinese defeats in foreign policy and a change in Chinese leadership will not convince the Communist newcomer that revolutionary fervor is no substitute for industrial strength.

The Conditions of Peace

We are now in position to understand more clearly why the usual distribution of power in the world has not been a balance but rather a preponderance of power in the hands of one nation and its allies. And we can understand why world peace has coincided with periods of unchallenged supremacy of power, whereas the periods of approximate balance have been the periods of war. Wars occur when a great power in a secondary position challenges the top nation and its allies for control. Thus the usual major conflict is between the top nation (and its allies) and the challenger about to catch up with it in power.

In some respects the international order has striking similarities with that of a national society; it is legitimized by an ideology and rooted in the power differential of the groups that compose it. Peace is possible only when those possessing preponderant power are in firm control and are satisfied with the status quo or with the way in which it promises to develop in a peaceful context. Peace is threatened whenever a powerful nation is dissatisfied with the status quo and is powerful enough to attempt to change things in the face of opposition from those who control the existing international order.

Degree of power and degree of satisfaction, then, become important national characteristics to be considered when trying to locate the nations that are most likely to disturb world peace. We can classify all the nations of the world in terms of these two characteristics, achieving four categories which turn out to be of major importance in international politics:

1. The powerful and satisfied
2. The powerful and dissatisfied
3. The weak and satisfied
4. The weak and dissatisfied

THE POWERFUL AND SATISFIED

The international order is best visualized if one thinks of a pyramid with one nation at the top and many nations at the bottom. Those at the top of the pyramid are most powerful and those at the bottom least powerful. As we move downward in terms of power, the number of nations in each layer is greater than the number in the layer above it. Figure 1 gives a first approximation of the pyramid.

At the very apex of the pyramid is the most powerful nation in the world, currently the United States, previously England, perhaps tomorrow Russia or China. This is the dominant nation, the nation that controls the existing dominant international order. Indeed, this is the nation that established that international order in the first place (or inherited it from its founders), and this is the nation that receives the greatest share of the benefits that flow from the existence of the international order.

The kind of relationship between the dominant nation and the lesser

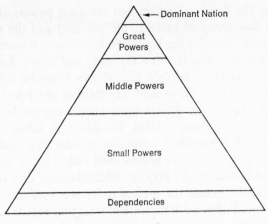

Dominant Nation

Great
Powers

Middle Powers

Small Powers

Dependencies

FIGURE 1

members of its international order varies from one order to another. It varies also according to the power of the lesser member. Thus the United States has a different kind of relationship with the nations of Western Europe than the Soviet Union has with the nations of Eastern Europe, and the United States benefits differently in its relations with Saudi Arabia than it does in its relations with England. All dominant nations attempt to appear disinterested in any benefits for themselves, but in fact the dominant nation always benefits disproportionately from any enterprises involving less powerful nations, be they friends or foes.

It is important to note that the power discrepancy between the dominant nation and the nations below it is usually great. The international order, like any other order, is based on power. A large power discrepancy between the dominant nation and the rest of the nations below it ensures the security of the leader and the stability of the order as a whole.

Just below the apex of the pyramid are the great powers. The difference between them and the dominant nation is to be found not only in their different abilities to influence the behavior of others, but also in the differential benefits they receive from the international order to which they belong. Great powers are, as their name indicates, very powerful nations, but they are less powerful than the dominant nation. They receive substantial benefits from the international order of which they are members, but they receive less benefits than the dominant nation. Because these nations are so important, the dominant nation requires the help of at least some of them to keep its international order running smoothly. Thus we find that some of the great powers are allied with the dominant nation, sharing in the leadership of the dominant international order and in the benefits that flow from it.

Together, the dominant nation and the great powers allied with it make up our first group of nations: the powerful and the satisfied. At present, this group includes the United States, Britain, France, and, since their defeat in World War II, West Germany and Japan. Satisfaction is, of course, a relative term, but in a general way it can be said that these nations are satisfied with the present international order and its working rules, for they feel that the present order offers them the best chance of obtaining the goals they have in mind. The dominant nation is necessarily more satisfied with the existing international order than with any other since it is to a large extent *its* international order. Other nations (such as England and France today) may be satisfied because they realized their full power potential before the present order was established, and thus their power assured them a full measure of what they regard as their rightful share of benefits. Still other great powers (such as the defeated Axis nations) may be considered satisfied because they can no longer hope to achieve the domination they once sought and are thus content to accept a place in the international order that seems likely to allow them substantial rewards.

THE POWERFUL AND DISSATISFIED

Some of the great powers, however, are not satisfied with the way things are run on the international scene, and they make up our second category, that of the powerful and dissatisfied. From this group come the challengers who seek to upset the existing international order and establish a new order in its place. When nations are dissatisfied and at the same time powerful enough to possess the means of doing something about their dissatisfaction, trouble can be expected.

As we have seen in our brief historical sketch, the powerful and dissatisfied nations are usually those that have grown to full power after the existing international order was fully established and the benefits already allocated. These parvenus had no share in the creation of the international order, and the dominant nation and its supporters are not usually willing to grant the newcomers more than a small part of the advantages they receive. Certainly they are unwilling to share the source of all their privileges: the rule of international society. To do so would be to abandon to a newcomer the preferred position they hold. As far as the dominant nation is concerned and, even more pointedly, as far as great nations that support the dominant nation are concerned, the challengers are to be kept in their place.

The challengers, for their part, are seeking to establish a new place for themselves in international society, a place to which they feel their increasing power entitles them. Often these nations have grown rapidly in power and expect to continue to grow. They have reason to believe that they can rival or surpass in power the dominant nation, and they are unwilling to accept a subordinate position in international affairs when dominance would give them much greater benefits and privileges.

A rapid rise in power thus produces dissatisfaction in itself. At the same time, it is likely to be accompanied by dissatisfaction of a different sort. In the present period such rapid rises have been brought about largely through industrialization. Rapid industrialization, however, produces many internal strains and grievances, and the temptation is great for the national government of a nation undergoing such changes to channel some of the dissatisfaction into aggressive attitudes and actions toward some outside nation in order to divert criticism from the government or other powerful groups within the nation. Industrialization is the source of much of the international trouble of the present period, for it expands the aspirations of men and helps to make them dissatisfied with their lot, while at the same time it increases their power to do something about their dissatisfactions, that is, to wrest a greater share of the good things of life from those who currently control them.

The role of challenger, of course, is not a permanent role, nor is it one that all great powers go through. Some of the great powers never fill it. These are the nations that accept a supporting role in the dominant international order, nations we have classified as "powerful and satisfied." Dissatisfied, powerful nations, however, are likely to become challengers, at least for a time. Those who succeed become dominant (and so satisfied) nations eventually. Those who fail conclusively may fall back and accept a secondary supporting role in the international order they have tried to overturn, as Germany appears to have done after two defeats, thus joining the ranks of the satisfied and the powerful by a different path. As long as they remain outside the dominant international order and have hopes of overturning it or taking over its leadership through combat, however, such nations are serious threats to world peace. It is the powerful and dissatisfied nations that start world wars.

THE WEAK AND SATISFIED

Below the great powers come the lesser nations, middle powers and small powers. Many of these nations have accepted the existing international order (or have had it imposed upon them and now accept it without question) and found a place in it that assures them certain benefits. We shall call them the weak and satisfied.

At the top of this group are the nations generally called second-rank powers, such as Canada, Australia, and Argentina today. Also in this classification are small but wealthy nations such as Belgium, Norway, and

Switzerland. Finally, the category includes those virtually powerless nations and dependencies that are tied to the existing international order and that accept it without question—for example, South Korea, Jamaica, and Liberia.

No trouble is to be expected from nations in this group, because they fill both the requirements of perfectly peaceful nations: (1) On the whole they are satisfied with the status quo; and (2) if they did desire to make changes upsetting others, they would lack the power to do so. The nations in this group do not benefit excessively from the existing international order, but they do have an established place in it that allows them certain benefits. Even if the benefits are not great, at least in the existing international order these nations know where they stand, whereas they have no guarantee that in a new scheme of things they might not be much worse off than they are. Because they are committed to the existing international order, these nations, too, will oppose a challenger.

THE WEAK AND DISSATISFIED

Our fourth and final category consists of those nations and dependencies that are profoundly dissatisfied with the current world order and their place in it but that lack the power to disturb world peace. Indonesia is an example of this type, as are many of the nations of Asia and Africa today.

Such nations may go along with the status quo, resenting the current international order, feeling that their share of its benefits is too small, but nevertheless accepting it. If they are dependencies, they may be forced to help defend the existing order from attack, but such help is usually given half-heartedly. Or these nations may attempt to establish an independent position, not identified with the dominant nation and its allies and not identified with the challengers. In fact, such a position usually has the effect of perpetuating the status quo, for a neutral stand in an uneven battle gives the victory to the stronger side. Nations in this category are not necessarily peaceful. Indeed, they may stir up quite a ruckus in their own corner of the world in the form of a revolt against colonial domination or an attack on a weaker neighbor, but they are not the major disturbers of world peace. They do not possess the power to overturn the international order by themselves: they are dangerous only collectively, if they join the side of a major challenger.

This category includes a disproportionate number of nations at the very bottom of the international pyramid, in particular nonindustrial nations and dependencies. Lacking power, these nations are most often exploited by stronger nations, and consequently they have the most obvious reasons for being dissatisfied with the existing international order. Indeed, many of the benefits that make this order so attractive to the dominant nation and its supporters exist *at the expense of* the nations on the bottom of the pyramid. They are indeed part of the existing international order: they provide the spoils.

POWER AND SATISFACTION

It should be clear from our classification that power and satisfaction do not go hand in hand, although they are related. The most powerful nation in the world, the dominant nation, is always "satisfied" in the sense of favoring the status quo, since it has already used its power to establish a world order to its satisfaction.

Other great powers may be either satisfied supporters of the dominant international order or dissatisfied challengers seeking to set up a rival order. It is usual at any given moment for most of the great powers to be on the side of the dominant nation, for if a great majority of them were to oppose that nation, its order could not survive for long.

Middle powers are also most likely to be found on the "satisfied" team of the dominant nation, for again their support is important, though some of the middle powers who have risen to that status recently may find that their interests are better served by siding with the challenger.

Small powers, backward nations, and dependencies, on the other hand, are most often "dissatisfied," for reasons we have discussed above. They may be compelled to act in support of the dominant nation and its allies, but their sympathies are often with the challenger.

If we superimpose the satisfaction-dissatisfaction distinction upon the power pyramid, we get the result shown in Figure 2. Figure 2, however, distorts the picture as far as the distribution of power is concerned, for

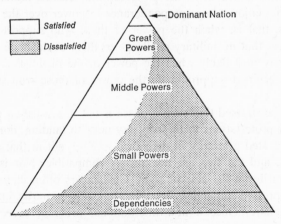

FIGURE 2

the dominant nation at the top is much stronger than all the bottom nations put together, although the area it represents in a pyramid is smaller. If power is represented by area as well as height, we get the result presented in Figure 3.

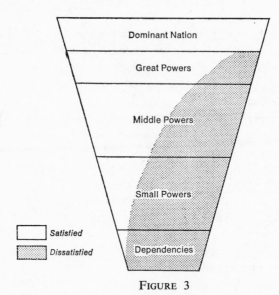

FIGURE 3

In a major international contest, the dominant nation is assured the support of the satisfied and of whatever dissatisfied nations it can compel to aid it. The challenger draws his support from the ranks of the dissatisfied, although he rarely can count upon them all. Peace, then, is most likely to be maintained when the powerful and satisfied nations together with their allies enjoy a huge preponderance in power over the challenger and its allies, that is, when the power of those who support the status quo is so great that no military challenge to them could hope to achieve success. War is most likely when the power of the dissatisfied challenger and its allies begins to approximate the power of those who support the status quo.

It must be stressed that such a peace is not necessarily a peace with justice. Their protestations to the contrary notwithstanding, dominant nations are interested primarily in their own welfare, not in that of the rest of the world, and the two are not always compatible. Nor is the challenger necessarily on the side of right. Challengers often claim to speak for all of oppressed humanity, but they, too, are primarily interested in their own welfare. Once a new international order is successfully established, the underdogs are likely to find that they are still underdogs who have merely exchanged one set of world leaders for another.

Peace is not synonymous with the maintenance of the status quo either. If there is one idea that we hope to put across, it is that change is constant. The international distribution of power is constantly shifting and with it many of the other arrangements that depend upon power. The possibilities of peaceful change should not be underestimated, but neither should the frequency with which major changes are brought about through war. As the challenger grows more powerful, it begins to demand new arrangements and changes in the international order that will give it a larger share of the benefits it desires. In theory, those who dominate the existing international order could make way for the newcomer and welcome it into the top ranks, giving up some of their privileges in the process. In practice, however, such action is rare. The challenger usually demands a place at the top and is rebuffed. Desiring change and unable to bring it about peacefully, the challenger all too often turns to war.

It might be expected that a wise challenger, growing in power through internal development, would wait to threaten the existing international order until it was as powerful as the dominant nation and its allies, for surely it would seem foolish to attack while weaker than the enemy. If this expectation were correct, the risk of war would be greatest when the two opposing camps were almost exactly equal in power, and if war broke out before this point, it would take the form of a preventive war launched by the dominant nation to destroy a competitor before it became strong enough to upset the existing international order.

In fact, however, this is not what has happened in recent history. Germany, Italy, and Japan attacked the dominant nation and its allies long before they equaled them in power, and the attack was launched by the challengers, not by the dominant camp. If history repeats itself, the next world war will be started by the Soviet Union and/or China, and it will be launched before the challenger is as powerful as the United States and its allies, thus diminishing the chances of a Communist victory. However, history may not repeat itself, for the Soviet Union and China are not Germany and Japan, and there are other factors involved besides the relative power of the two camps.

OTHER FACTORS FAVORING WAR OR PEACE

We have established that world peace is guaranteed when the nations satisfied with the existing international order enjoy an unchallenged supremacy of power and that major wars are most likely when a dissatisfied challenger achieves an approximate balance of power with the dominant nation. However, we have noted that in some cases (World Wars I and II) the challengers attacked before such a balance was reached, whereas in other cases (the transfer of power from Britain to the United States), the challenger passed the dominant nation without an armed conflict. Clearly, there are other factors at work. We have mentioned some of them in passing, but now the time has come to spell them out more carefully.

One factor influencing the likelihood of war is the power potential of the challenger when it begins its rise. All nations grow in power as they industrialize, and as they grow, seek a higher place in the international order. However, if a nation is too small to come anywhere near equaling the power of the dominant nation, even when it achieves full industrialization, friction between the two should not go beyond some minor problems of adjustment. The growing nation is too small to be an effective challenger. It will not become involved in a major war against the dominant nation unless it can team up with a real challenger of considerably greater strength. In short, there is no danger of war if the challenger is too small to be effective.

On the other hand, if the challenger is so large that its dominance, once it becomes industrial, is virtually guaranteed, the chances of conflict are also reduced. The future dominance of such a nation appears obvious and inevitable long before it is actually achieved, and this enables both the challenger and the dominant nation to adjust to the idea gradually. The challenger, for its part, need not attack the dominant nation openly but can surpass it in power through internal growth. The dominant nation, for its part, realizes that it will lose out whether it fights or not and so has a strong motive to avoid the costs of war and work out a peaceful adjustment instead. This factor undoubtedly played a role in the transfer of power from England to the United States, for by the time the growth of the United States was fully appreciated, England must have realized that she could not hope to compete successfully with the American giant. It may also play a role in the case of China. China's power today is very little, but her potential is obvious, and there is already considerable sentiment in Western Europe that we should adjust to allowing her a dominant role at least in the Far East. The risk of war, then, is also reduced if the challenger is so large that its future dominance is obvious to all.

It is between these two extremes that the factor of size may well be a source of trouble. If the size of the challenger is such that at its peak it will roughly equal the power of the dominant nation, the risk of war is great. Such a nation cannot hope to achieve obvious supremacy through internal development. It can secure a commanding position only by the voluntary surrender of the current dominant nation *or* by seizing it through victory in war. The chances of voluntary surrender, always tenuous, are even slimmer here, for there is nothing inevitable about the rise of such a challenger. By standing firm, the dominant nation may hold off such a challenger indefinitely. The challenger, however, blocked from any hope of achieving the position it seeks through peaceful adjustment, may turn to war. This seems to be what happened in the case of Germany in World War I and in the case of the Axis nations in World War II. It may well be the case for Russia if there is a third world war.

A second factor influencing the likelihood of war is the speed with which the challenger rises in power. It should be clear by now that it is the difference in relative rates of growth that is primarily responsible for upsetting international tranquillity. The more rapidly the challenger acquires power, the greater will be the international repercussions of this acquisition. If the rise of the challenger is extremely rapid, it will be more difficult for the dominant nation to make whatever peaceful adjustments may be in order. Within the lifetime of a single generation of statesmen, the relative power of the nations they represent may change quite drastically. It is difficult for men of power to accept such changes and deal with them effectively. A rapid rise in power may also create difficulties for the challenger, who has a new role to learn. Statements and behavior acceptable from a nation of middle rank are often not appropriate for a great power with major responsibilities. Thus the challenger may find that its actions are more offensive to others than it intends them to be.

In addition, as we have noted, the rapid industrialization that lies behind a rapid rise in power may create internal strains of such magnitude that goverment officials are led to provocative statements and actions toward other nations in an effort to distract attention from internal difficulties and fix the responsibility for internal troubles on "the outside." Sacrifices may be demanded in the name of national defense that would never be tolerated for the sake of internal development alone. Thus a certain amount of international tension may be positively useful to a nation that is industrializing rapidly. The Korean War, for example, was probably a benefit to Communist China, for it helped create national unity at a time when the government was carrying out wide changes, many of which were unpopular. The trick is not to let such controlled tensions get out of hand to the point of provoking prematurely a major conflict that would surely destroy the hopes of the challenger.

A final danger is that too rapid a rise in power may go to the challenger's head. A major spurt in power within a single lifetime may lead officials to compare their nation not with other nations, but with its own recent past. They can *see* the difference between what their nation was and what it is today; carried away with justifiable pride, they may be led to think that they have already reached what their nation will be tomorrow. Impatient at the reluctance of other nations to realize how powerful they have become, they may fool themselves into thinking they are more powerful than they are, and in the flush of overconfidence, deliberately start a major war that cooler analysis would clearly reveal they have no chance of winning. Both Italy and Japan seem to have suffered from such delusions in World War II. At present this seems to be a danger in the case of China.

A third factor influencing the likelihood of war is the flexibility of the dominant nation in adjusting to the changes required by the appearance of a new major nation. As we have noted, major concessions to a challenger are not always in order, particularly if the challenger is considerably weaker than the dominant nation. In the case of a challenger whose future dominance is assured, wise concessions made in advance may serve the double purpose of avoiding a world war and assuring the declining nation a higher place in the new international order than it would otherwise possess. England is the prime example of a nation that has retired from world leadership gracefully. She has applied this grace not only in her dealings with the United States, but also in her generous grant of independence to most of her colonies. France, on the other hand, represents a nation that has pursued an inflexible policy in dealing with shifts in the power of other nations. It is difficult to imagine which course the United States would adopt in such circumstances. A search for the determinants of flexibility of this sort would make an interesting study in itself. Suffice it to say here that the flexibility of the dominant nation does seem to be a factor in determining whether or not war occurs when a challenger rises in power.

Still another factor influencing the likelihood of war is the amount of friendship between the dominant nation and the challenger. We have already noted that in the case of England and the United States, this factor seemed to be an important one in allowing the transfer of power to take place peacefully. Such friendship leads the challenger to be less offensive and less obvious as it passes the dominant nation in strength. One of the reasons America's rise to power did not antagonize the British was that it was not accompanied by a stream of anti-British statements emanating from the United States. America, at least overtly, did not *want* world leadership, and she expressed no desire to take Britain's place. Germany, on the other hand, was quite hostile to Britain and was thoroughly aware of her rivalry. Her desire to unseat England was constantly emphasized by the German government and by the press. The same is true of Russia and, to an even greater extent, of China. Hostility toward the United States is manifest and is reciprocated. Hardly a day passes without American leaders reminding the American people of the danger that the Soviet

Union and China represent, while Soviet and Chinese leaders constantly measure their countries' achievements in terms of how far behind the United States they are. Such statements do not in themselves cause wars, but they are both symptom and cause of the kind of attitude that makes wars possible.

Underlying this attitude of friendship or animosity is an even more important factor, and again it is one that we have mentioned before: whether the challenger accepts the existing international order and merely wishes to take over its leadership, or whether the challenger aspires to create a new international order of its own. Peaceful adjustment is possible in the case of the challenger who is willing to continue the existing international order and abide by its rules, but it is much more difficult, if not impossible, in the case of a challenger who wishes to destroy the existing order. England and the United States might conceivably have come to terms with the Kaiser's Germany, but they could not have come to terms with Hitler. England had no choice but to fight Hitler, even though her victory was by no means assured when she went to war. Similarly, it is difficult to see how the West could ever adjust peacefully to Communist dominance, for such adjustment would require greater changes than nations are willing to make voluntarily even though faced with possibly superior force.

Summary

Let us review the regularities that underlie the current instability of international politics. We have divided the history of international relations into three periods: the first period, now past, when no nation was industrial; the second period, from about 1750 until some time in the future, when some nations are preindustrial, some industrializing, and some fully industrial; and the third period, not yet begun, in which all nations will be industrially advanced.

The present or second period is the period of the power transition. It differs markedly from the period that preceded it and from the period that will follow; it has been characterized by great and sudden shifts in national power caused primarily by the differential spread of industrialization throughout the world. As each nation industrializes, it experiences an increase in wealth, in population, and in the efficiency of its governmental organization. Since these are the major determinants of national power, it also experiences an increase in power.

The power transition through which each nation passes can be divided into three stages: (1) the stage of potential power, in which the nation is still preindustrial and possesses little power compared to any industrial nation; (2) the stage of transitional growth in power, during which the nation industrializes and experiences a great spurt in its power; and (3) the stage of power maturity, when the nation is fully industrial and when it continues to grow in wealth but declines in power in relation to that of other nations just entering stage 2.

The present period is also characterized by strong ties between nations binding them into competing international orders. Because of the importance of these ties, nations are *not* free without grave internal changes to shift from one international order to another.

These two characteristics—the shifts in power due to industrialization and the ties between nations—provide the basis for a recurring pattern that can be traced in recent international events. The most powerful nation in the world customarily heads an international order that includes other major nations (the powerful and satisfied) and also some minor nations and dependencies (the weak and satisfied and the weak and dissatisfied). As long as the satisfied nations enjoy a large preponderance of power over the rest of the world, peace is guaranteed. However, as new nations industrialize, the old leader is challenged. A recently industrialized nation may be dissatisfied with the existing international order because it rose too late to receive a proportionate share of the benefits, and it may succeed in drawing to its side lesser nations who are also dissatisfied because they are exploited by the nations that dominate the existing order.

Such a challenge usually results in war, although it is possible for world leadership to be transferred from one nation to another without a conflict. Certainly the major wars of recent history have all been wars involving the dominant nation and its allies against a challenger who has recently risen in power thanks to industrialization. In the recent past, such wars have occurred when the challenger had grown rapidly but *before* the challenger was as powerful as the dominant nation and its allies, and the wars were started by the challenger. Whether this pattern will continue remains to be seen.

Thus wars are most likely when there is an approaching balance of power between the dominant nation and a major challenger. Other factors also operate to make war more or less likely. Specifically, war is most apt to occur: if the challenger is of such a size that at its peak it will roughly equal the dominant nation in power; if the rise of the challenger is rapid; if the dominant nation is inflexible in its policies; if there is no tradition of friendship between the dominant nation and the challenger; and if the challenger sets out to replace the existing international order with a competitive order of its own.

15

Diplomacy

We have considered the underlying forces that shape relations among nations in the present period of world history. We turn now to consideration of the process through which the official portion of these relations is carried on, diplomacy, and to consideration of the men who represent their nations in these relations, the diplomats.

It is customary to consider these men and their activities as very important, but if the analysis of the previous chapters is correct, the scene is set and the script largely written before the diplomats appear upon the stage. Can one really believe that it was Metternich, as ambassador to Paris, who was responsible for keeping France and Austria at peace? Can one believe that by taking a different stand, American diplomats could have prevented China from falling to the Communists? Is it possible that a knowledgeable and clever diplomat in New Delhi today could alter the policy of India toward the United States or the policy of the United States toward India? If so, one can believe that the proper diplomat in the proper place at the proper time saying the proper things can play a major role in international politics, that a good diplomat sets the stage and writes the lines as well as performing before an admiring public.

François-Poncet, the French ambassador to Germany and Italy in the years before World War II, once wrote: "In fact, I was chiefly an informer and a mailman."[1] Such modesty, however, is unusual. Most diplomats, and those who are professional students of diplomacy as well, have a vested interest in believing that diplomacy is of more importance.

The historian A. J. P. Taylor has written: "A work of diplomatic history has to take diplomacy seriously; and perhaps it is enough to say that diplomacy helped men to remain at peace as long as they wished to do so."[2] Here, however, we need not take the importance of diplomacy for granted. On the contrary, in this chapter, we shall evaluate the contribution of diplomacy to maintaining peace and otherwise determining the course of world affairs, and stake out the limits beyond which the influence of diplomacy cannot reach. The very question Mr. Taylor bypasses is the one we seek to answer. *Does* diplomacy help?

Diplomacy Defined

The term "diplomacy" has been used to cover a surprisingly wide variety of ideas. Harold Nicolson has indicated the problem in his classic book on diplomacy:

> In current language this word "diplomacy" is carelessly taken to denote several quite different things. At one moment it is employed as a synonym for "foreign policy," as when we say "British diplomacy in the Near East has been lacking in vigour." At another moment it signifies "negotiation" as when we say "The problem is one which might be well solved by diplomacy." More specifically, the problem denotes the processes and machinery by which such negotiation is carried out. A fourth meaning is that of a branch of the Foreign Service, as when one says "my nephew is working for diplomacy." And a fifth interpretation which this unfortunate word is made to carry is that of an abstract quality or gift, which, in its best sense, implies the skill in the conduct of international negotiation; and, in its worse sense, implies the more guileful aspects of tact.[3]

We can reject several of these definitions immediately. The last meaning, that is, skill and guile in international negotiation, is too nar-

[1] André François-Poncet, *Souvenirs d'une ambassade à Berlin* (Paris: Flammerion, 1946), p. 12.

[2] A. J. P. Taylor, *The Struggle for Mastery of Europe 1848–1918* (Oxford: Clarendon Press, 1954), pp. 256–57.

[3] Harold Nicolson, *Diplomacy* (New York: Harcourt, Brace, 1939), pp. 13–14.

row,[4] for if it were accepted, it would exclude all diplomatic activity neither skillful nor guileful, creating the problem of what to call diplomatic activity that fell short of these standards. For example, the diplomacy of the Western democracies between the two world wars[5] and much of our own diplomacy toward England and France both in the past and today[6] was neither crafty nor intelligent, and yet it undeniably represented a major portion of the significant diplomatic activity of the period. Tact, skill, and guile can be considered *standards* or *criteria* of good diplomacy, but not characteristics that define diplomacy in general.

Neither is the definition of diplomacy as a diplomatic career of much use for our present purposes. It is true that the attractiveness and glamor of a diplomatic career help to explain why diplomacy is considered so important, but our interest in diplomacy is deeper than this. The definition of diplomacy as foreign policy, on the other hand, is too broad. Diplomacy is but one part of the process by which foreign policy is formulated and executed.

As we shall use it here, the word "diplomacy" is closer in meaning to Nicolson's second and third definitions, "negotiation . . . and the processes and machinery by which such negotiation is carried out." To pin the definition down completely, diplomacy refers to the process of negotiation carried on between the official governmental representatives of one nation and those of another (or others).

In modern times the diplomats who carry on these negotiations have been full-time occupational specialists in the paid employ of the national government they represent. In the past, however, such work was the occupation of aristocrats, often part-time and rarely paid. Even today, the top diplomatic posts of a nation like the United States entail expenses that are greater than the salaries they offer and are often given to men who have never worked for the government before and will never do so again.

A word should also be said about the process of negotiation before we leave the topic of definition. To negotiate is to have dealings with a view to coming to an agreement. Obviously, if complete agreement were

[4] This definition, however, has been adopted by no less an authority than Sir Ernest Satow, who defines diplomacy as "the application of intelligence and tact to the conduct of official relations between governments of independent states, extending sometimes also to their relations with vassal states." Sir Ernest Satow, *A Guide to Diplomatic Practice*, 3rd ed. (London: Longmans, Green, 1952), p. 1.

[5] See Paul Reynaud, *In the Thick of the Fight, 1930–1945* (New York: Simon and Schuster, 1955).

[6] For example, the events that led to the reoccupation of the Suez Canal in 1956. See *The New York Times,* Nov. 1, 1956, p. 1, cols. 5–7.

already present, there would be no need for negotiation, so diplomacy is used where there are areas of disagreement or misunderstanding, real or potential. On the other hand, the difference or disagreement must be of a type that can be resolved through a process of negotiation. This second fact points clearly to the major limitation of diplomacy: many of the disagreements among nations cannot be negotiated away.

The Limitations of Diplomacy

Diplomacy can be considered successful only if one party convinces the other or if each accepts part of the other's position, thus arriving at a compromise that is satisfactory to both. What are the conditions making for success in international negotiation? These conditions also define the outer limits beyond which diplomacy cannot have a major influence on international relations. Several factors appear to affect the success of diplomatic negotiation.

We have already discussed the ways in which one nation can influence the behavior of another in our discussion of national power. Negotiation, after all, is one special case in which two parties (or more) attempt to exercise power over each other. We have noted that the methods of influencing others include force, punishments, rewards, and persuasion. These methods are all available to diplomats in their negotiations with each other, but they are not of equal importance.

Only rarely is a diplomat an instrument of compulsion. He cannot, of course, use force himself, for international tiffs are not settled by diplomatic fisticuffs, appealing though such an idea may be. When the discrepancy in power between two nations is so great that the lesser nation is actually a dependency or a satellite, however, the representative of the greater power may give orders which are backed by force and which are obeyed without question.

When the power of the two nations is more equal and the lesser nation cannot be ordered about in this fashion, force must be used, not merely threatened, to be effective. Here, the role of the diplomat is limited to delivering the final ultimatum that leads to war or the formal declaration of war. Once hostilities begin, diplomatic relations with the enemy are severed, to be resumed only when it comes time to make peace and agreement is again required.

Persuasion is the major method employed in international diplomacy, and it is in the arts of persuasion that good diplomats are supposed to excel. In addition, whenever they can, diplomats support their arguments by promising rewards or threatening punishments.

The job of the diplomat, then, is to come to agreement with the representatives of other nations over specific differences that are considered suitable for negotiation. In attempting to win the others over to his nation's point of view, the diplomat exercises his persuasive powers, presenting arguments that from his knowledge of the other men and their nations he believes will be effective, appealing to sentiments that are shared, pointing out facts that the others may have overlooked. In addition, he must try to assess what rewards and punishments would be effective in influencing the others and suggest that his government use them. If his government is willing and able to back him up, he may then add to his argument the weight of offers of reward or threats of punishment. In addition, he responds to the arguments of other diplomats, altering his position in the light of new facts revealed in the process of negotiation, horse-trading a little if the rewards offered by other nations are attractive, retreating if a punitive action is feared. Finally, if negotiation breaks down completely, he may inform his government that further discussion would be useless, that the others cannot be brought into agreement with a position acceptable to his government, and that only force remains as a means of achieving his government's purpose. In the absence of willingness or ability to use force, a stalemate must be accepted.

Success in diplomacy will be influenced somewhat by the skill of the diplomat in understanding his opponents and bringing to bear the right arguments at the right time, by his skill in predicting how they will respond to rewards and punishments and thus offering neither too much nor too little, and by his skill in persuading his own home government to back him up, for the diplomat himself cannot reward or punish to any appreciable extent but must rely upon the actions of his government. Diplomatic skill is important, but the role it plays in bringing diplomatic negotiations to a successful conclusion has been greatly overrated. Other factors are more important.

Diplomats are always limited by the policies of the governments they represent. No matter how skilled, they cannot press for objectives their government does not share, they cannot offer rewards or punishments their government is unwilling to supply, they cannot compromise in areas where their government is unwilling to budge. Diplomats, it is true, have a voice in the formation of foreign policy, but it is by no means the determining voice. Foreign policy, like other governmental policies, is formed in accordance with the interests of the most powerful groups within the nation, and it is always limited by what the public will stand for. Particularly in a democracy, but even in a dictatorship, a large number of people participate in the formation of foreign policy, and none of their interests can be ignored. The diplomat represents a nation, and he must conform to the policies of its government. Diplomatic success, then, is influenced not only by the skill of the diplomat but also by the nature of the foreign policy he is called upon to implement.

Because the parties to the negotiation are nations and not individual diplomats, the area where persuasion alone can be effective is extremely small. It must be assumed that in any important international disagreement, each of the governments concerned has thought through its position fairly carefully and that the interests and responsibilities of each government and of the groups it represents have led the government to take the position it has chosen. Under these circumstances, it is highly doubtful that verbal arguments, no matter how cogent and well founded, will cause either party to alter its position substantially. In spite of the popular belief that international disagreement is caused by misunderstanding, this is seldom true. The parties involved usually understand each other all too well; they simply do not agree.

The ability of a diplomat to offer rewards and threaten punishments is also limited. A diplomat is essentially a bargainer, and he can bargain only with the means at his disposal. He cannot make use of rewards and punishments that his nation does not possess or is unwilling to use. He will be limited if his nation is weak, just as he will be limited if his government is stupid. Of the two, weakness is probably more crippling, for even the disadvantages of poor policy can be overcome if a nation possesses enough strength. In the last analysis, the effectiveness of American diplomacy today is due to American wealth and power, just as the effectiveness of English diplomacy in the nineteenth century was due to English wealth and power. France at her height also had a reputation for diplomatic skill. American diplomats today are quite capable of holding their own. Our fears that they will be outsmarted are an attitude that dates from the days when America was weak and England and France were powerful. We mistook power for skill and credited other nations with innate qualities we lacked. It is time we rectified the error.

From the point of view of the individual diplomat and his nation, success in diplomacy means victory in winning other nations over to one's point of view. From the point of view of the objective observer, success means the peaceful resolution of a dispute between the negotiating nations, regardless of which nation has made the major concessions. Success in this latter sense is influenced by still another factor: the amount of agreement that exists between the nations involved when they start negotiating.

If there is general agreement between two nations on ideology, on methods, and on the kind of world order they desire, it is not difficult to reconcile even a fairly major disagreement on a limited topic, but if two nations are in profound disagreement over most of the aims and methods of their foreign policies, even a minor difference may prove irreconcilable. Negotiation is conducted within a context, and one cannot predict the outcome simply from knowledge of the points being negotiated.

It also makes a difference how serious the disagreement is, quite apart from the general tenor of relations between the two nations. When a nation feels its vital interests are affected, it may refuse to compromise, no matter what arguments, rewards, and punishments are proposed. If two nations differ on a matter that is vital to them both, diplomacy will not be able to resolve the difference.

Diplomacy, then, is most useful in settling disagreements among friends and of only limited usefulness in dealing with conflicts among enemies. It is thus not fitted for the spectacular role that it is sometimes expected to play, for it is not the quarrels of friends that cause us most serious concern. Differences between the United States and Britain, the United States and France, or Indonesia and India can be and are solved through diplomatic channels. It is the major disagreements between powerful rivals such as Britain and Nazi Germany or the United States and the Soviet Union or China that concern us, for these are the differences that may lead to war, and although we sometimes look to diplomacy to solve them, we look in vain, for they lie beyond the boundaries of the area where diplomacy can operate effectively.

Our hypothesis that diplomacy can be successful only when a large area of agreement already exists is supported by a comparison between much of the nineteenth century, a period when diplomacy seemed able to head off international warfare, and the twentieth century, when negotiation has been unable to stem the tides of war. The success of nineteenth-century diplomats is attributable at least in part to the then existing fundamental international agreement and to the narrow limits within which disagreement was contained. It is essential to realize that this condition is the cause of diplomacy's success and not the result of diplomatic activity.

The nineteenth century, it will be recalled, was the high period of the bourgeois state, a period in which the new middle class dominated the political and economic life of all the most powerful nations. These men were united by a common ideology and a common view of the kind of international order they desired, although they might be rivals when it came to the place each nation desired for itself within the order. Their acceptance of the established framework made it relatively easy for differences of a minor nature to be settled through negotiation. Moreover, international agreement in the nineteenth century was securely founded on the overwhelming superiority in power of England and France. As long as these two nations together were so much more powerful than all others, other nations had to rely on negotiation as a means of solving differences, for the use of force against these giants would have been doomed to failure. The peculiar circumstances of the nineteenth century made men reasonable and negotiation fruitful.

On the other hand, diplomacy in the twentieth century has been a rather dismal failure and is likely to continue to be so because the prerequisites of diplomatic success no longer exist. The widespread agreement that bound together the dominant groups within the most powerful nations has disappeared. First Nazism and now communism have challenged the prevailing ideology of the Western democracies. First Germany and Japan and now Russian and China have challenged the power supremacy of the Western powers. These nations seek to establish a completely new world order, and their power is great enough that they cannot be compelled to come to agreement with the West. We noted earlier that the preponderant power of England and France in the nineteenth century was due to the fact that they were the first nations to industrialize, but that as industrialization spread to other nations, their preponderance disappeared. It is unfortunate, but one must realize that just as the socio-economic changes that destroyed acceptance of the old international order cannot be stopped, so the consequences of these changes cannot be avoided through diplomacy.

Let us review briefly the points that have been made. Success in diplomacy is furthered if skilled diplomats are guided by wise and flexible foreign policies, but success is not likely unless there is also a wide area of agreement between the negotiators at the start *or* unless there is a huge difference in power between them. Both of these latter requirements are missing today in most of the major diplomatic conferences. The international scene of the twentieth century is characterized by a lack of fundamental agreement among the major nations of the world and by drastic shifts in the distribution of power among nations which have the effect of reducing the power preponderance of the dominant nation.

Under these circumstances, even diplomatic skill and sound policy are not enough to guarantee diplomatic success in dealing with the major conflicts between the dominant nation and its challengers. To expect diplomacy to solve them is to engage in romantic illusions. Surely no one expects the United States to allow herself to be negotiated out of the position of dominance she now occupies, but as long as she enjoys this dominance, she will seek to perpetuate a world order that is unsatisfactory to the challengers. Similarly, no one expects Russia and China to be negotiated into giving up their challenge to the status quo, but as long as they insist on challenging it, their actions will be unsatisfactory to the United States and her allies.

This is not to say that attempts at diplomatic bargaining between such nations as the United States and Russia should be abandoned and the use of force given full play instead. If the disagreement is minor, diplomacy should certainly be utilized, and even in fairly major disagreements it may be worth a try, but it is foolish to expect all differences to be resolved. Whether we like it or not, the role that diplomacy can play in international affairs is necessarily modest. Not "bad diplomacy" but the formidable limitations imposed upon diplomacy are responsible for so many of the diplomatic failures of the present day. The choice is not between resolving all differences through diplomacy and going to war. There is a third alternative. We must learn to recognize both the horror of war and the limitations of diplomacy and to accept a world in which all differences are *not* resolved and all actions by other nations *not* satisfactory and still remain at peace.

Shopkeeper versus Warrior Diplomacy

Writers investigating the approach to diplomacy of various nations have noticed that these approaches differ significantly between one nation and another. Some nations have been reasonable in negotiation while others were not; some conciliatory, others truculent; some regarding diplomacy as a means of maintaining peace through compromise, others regarding it as an extension of warfare. The same nations have exhibited different approaches at different times, but by and large, two broad types of diplomacy have been distinguished, varieties that have been called "shopkeeper diplomacy" and "warrior diplomacy."

Even more interesting, it was noticed that in the long run, the nations with the peaceful approach got what they wanted, whereas the unreasonable and warlike nations ended in ruin. It was almost inevitable that writers, particularly those sharing the nationality of one of the successful nations, should give in to the temptation to explain success in diplomacy as due to the virtuous characteristics of the successful nations and the lack of virtue of those who failed. The whole analysis offered a tailor-made opportunity for a conclusion that virtue is rewarded, for outbursts of ill-disguised prejudice against other nations, and for a bath of moral self-approbation.

An example can be found in the writings of Harold Nicolson, the British scholar and diplomat. He writes:

[In] moments of enlightenment, [foreign critics] recognize that . . . the success of British diplomacy is to be explained by the fact that it is founded on the sound business principles of moderation, fair-dealing, reasonableness, credit, compromise, and a distrust of all surprises or sensational extremes.[7]

He concludes at a later stage: "I believe, in all sincerity, that it is on the whole the type which is most conducive to the maintenance of peaceful relations."[8] Shopkeeper diplomacy, then, is "best" both because it is most moral and because it is most successful. Success in international relations is credited to the type of diplomacy carried on by a nation and ultimately to the national background and the personality of the negotiators.

Phrased in these terms, the argument has a certain surface plausibility, but what are we to make of the parallel argument that qualities that ought by all logic to bring about disaster have also been an important cause of success? We refer to the British habit of "muddling through." The British have long been renowned as excellent diplomats, and their diplomacy has been regarded until comparatively recently as highly successful. On the other hand, it has been generally accepted that they muddled through difficult international problems. The British themselves seemed quite proud of the fact. "To muddle," of course, means "to confuse," "to cloud," "to make a mess." Thus by general agreement, the diplomacy of Britain was confused, vague, and disordered, and yet it is contended with a perfectly straight face that precisely this muddling made the British successful. Apparently it is permissible in certain cases to throw logic and common sense to the winds.

The error in this reasoning, though grave, is fairly common in the social sciences. It consists of taking two qualities that appear at the same time and treating them as cause and effect, when it fact both are due to other factors and may not even be related. In this case, the error lies in taking a national approach to diplomacy and considering it a cause of diplomatic success, whereas in actuality the explanation for both the success and the approach are to be found elsewhere, in the power of the nation and in its place in the international hierarchy.

The British have been successful in their past negotiations with other nations because they have been powerful. They have been successful in spite of the fact that they have muddled and not because of it. The role of power can be seen clearly in the Suez crisis that came to a head in 1956, in which Britain exhibited some truly first-class muddling, with-

[7] Nicolson, *op. cit.,* p. 132.
[8] *Ibid.,* p. 144.

drawing her troops from Suez; then standing by and fuming when Egypt nationalized the Canal; then belatedly attacking the Canal without consulting her major ally, the United States, and conquering half the Canal; then withdrawing again because of American objections, leaving the Canal blocked and in Egyptian hands, British-American relations severely strained, and Britain faced with the task of paying the bill for the expeditionary force and coping with a serious oil shortage as long as the Canal remained blocked. It is difficult to imagine a more complete fiasco. Here, British muddling led to disaster, not to success, and the reason was that Britain was no longer the most powerful nation involved in the dispute. The United States did its own share of muddling in the affair but emerged unharmed. The moral is clear. The strongest nation in the world can afford to muddle, but powers of second rank cannot. It is the power not the muddling that brings success.

Power, together with the position of a nation in the international hierarchy, is also responsible in large part for the approach to diplomacy adopted by a nation. The dominant nation and its allies will necessarily approach diplomacy in a different manner from a challenger. It should not be surprising that the former are reasonable and peacefully inclined whereas the latter are demanding and bellicose, or that the former view diplomacy as a means of reaching agreement whereas the latter use negotiation for propaganda purposes and consider each diplomatic victory merely as a stepping stone to new demands. The difference is explained not by national virtues and vices but by the fact that challengers are seeking to upset the status quo while the dominant nation and its allies are content to leave things as they are.

Challengers are unreasonable when they sit down to negotiate because reasonable demands would allow the international order to remain undisturbed, while what they are trying to do is change it. They are unreasonable and pugnacious because they are trying to break the rules that relegate them to second place when they seek to be first.

Dominant nations, on the other hand, are noted for the moderate and reasonable character of their demands, but one must realize that they have set up the rules by which reasonable conduct in international relations is defined. Since they are already relatively satisfied, their demands are few. Since the established order cannot be upset without the use of force against them, they are opposed to the use of force and insist upon the necessity for agreement, knowing full well that they will never agree to relinquish their position of power and privilege.

The diplomacy of nations seeking to maintain the existing order also appears more haphazard and more fumbling than the diplomacy of challengers. The British in the past and the Americans today have often been accused of not having clear aims in diplomatic negotiation. One can be amused at the exasperated complaint of an aide to Soviet Foreign Secretary Molotov who was dealing with United States Secretary of State James Byrnes. Said the Russian: "Why doesn't he [Byrnes] stop this talk about principles, and get down to business and start trading."[9]

The problem was that America really did not want anything she did not already have. She wished only that other nations would stop wanting things that didn't belong to them. Dominant nations, since the international order is already in accordance with their interests, do not find it necessary to know explicitly what they want. The world is generally satisfactory. They simply have not given much thought to what it is that makes it that way. It is enough to leave things as they are and to oppose any drastic changes suggested by the challengers.

Challengers, on the other hand, have much more specific objectives. To challenge the status quo means to formulate acceptable alternatives to things as they are. A challenger must present a convincing list of grievances against the existing order and a program of how things could be improved. A nation seeking to improve its position with the acquiescence of its rivals must know exactly what it is about.

To sum up, then, we have singled out two different approaches to diplomacy—one the cautious, peaceable, and reasonable approach of the shopkeeper, the other the brilliant, quarrelsome, and dynamic approach of the warrior—and we have noted that in diplomatic contests, the shopkeepers have the better of the match. However, we must part company with those who claim that their victory is caused by sweet reasonableness and sound character. Instead, both victory and approach follow from the fact that such nations are rich, powerful, and contented. It is their power that guarantees their diplomatic success in spite of conduct that is often far from skilled, and it is their power that guarantees them a place in the international order so fortunately situated that they can afford to sit back and brand as "unreasonable" anyone who seeks a change. The shopkeepers have fought their battles in the past. The warriors, in their turn, would be all too happy to be shopkeepers if only they could oust the present owners from the premises.

Secret versus Open Diplomacy

Another controversy that has marked the writings on diplomacy has been the question of whether secret or open diplomacy is preferable. Prior to World War I, diplomacy was largely secret—that is to say, the

[9] James F. Byrnes, *Speaking Frankly* (New York: Harper & Row, 1947), p. 281.

general public was not informed as to the nature of negotiations going on or told in full about the agreements reached. After the war the belief began to circulate that diplomacy should be open, that is, public.

It was only natural that in the postwar attempt to reconstruct the orderly world of the previous age, special attention should be given to diplomacy. Not only was diplomacy the symbol of international intercourse, it was also the means by which people believed the international order could be built again. Because diplomacy was believed to be responsible for war and peace, the search for causes of World War I found scholars of the day blaming the war upon the machinations and mistakes of diplomats. Diplomacy made an irresistible scapegoat, for if international conflicts could be avoided by simple changes in diplomatic technique, there existed an easy way out of postwar difficulties back into the peace and order of the prewar era. Obviously, if the misbehavior of diplomats in the decades preceding the war was responsible for bringing on that conflict, then what was needed was to keep an eye on diplomats in the future. The cloak of secrecy protecting their activities was to be torn away and international negotiation and its results subjected to continuous public scrutiny.

The attack on orthodox diplomacy was led by Woodrow Wilson, who publicly challenged the diplomatic procedure of the past in his famous Fourteen Points. The goal was stated clearly: "Open covenants of peace, openly arrived at, after which there will be no private understanding of any kind, but diplomacy shall proceed frankly and in the public view." The words, "open covenants openly arrived at" became the battle cry of those who sought to reform diplomacy.

In its simplest form, the argument in favor of open diplomacy is this: The people of a nation have a right to know what international commitments their government makes, because it is they who will be called upon to sacrifice their wealth and their lives to keep the pledges that their diplomats have made. In international as well as in internal affairs, democracy requires that governments be responsible to their people, but the people cannot exercise their rights unless they have full knowledge of what the government is doing. To the people of the world, battered and burned by a war of unprecedented horror which they felt had been foisted upon them by diplomats, such an argument had tremendous appeal. In the democratic nations it was irresistible.

The defenders of secret diplomacy soon conceded that the agreements made by diplomats should become public. To argue otherwise in democratic societies (and it was largely there that the debate was carried on) would have been indefensible. But they refused to concede that the negotiations themselves should be open to the public view. In other words, they accepted the idea of open covenants, but preferred to have them secretly arrived at. They argued with vigor that privacy was one of the prerequisites of success in international diplomacy, that secrecy allowed the negotiators to be frank and facilitated the making of concessions which might be embarrassing if they required a diplomat to reverse his position in public, that the glare of publicity would make diplomats into propagandists and force them to kowtow to momentary public prejudices.

Neither the arguments of the backers of open diplomacy nor those of the supporters of secret diplomacy are totally convincing if they are examined closely. The advocates of open diplomacy stake their entire case upon a single argument. It is one thing to argue that open diplomacy is more democratic and that democracy is to be valued as a goal in itself. What democrat can quarrel with this? But behind the idea that democratic control over international diplomacy is essential lies the assumption that popular control will increase the chances of peace. This may be true, but it is by no means proven. Indeed, it is open to serious question, considering the widespread popular support that warlike leaders frequently enjoy and the humiliating defeats all too often administered to men of peace, even in democratic countries. And even assuming the public is firm in its desire for peace, are we also to assume that it necessarily knows the technique of achieving its goal better than the professional diplomats? We may, indeed, prefer that the diplomatic process be subject to democratic control, but let us not therefore assume that the problem of war is solved.

The arguments in favor of secret diplomacy also cover some hidden assumptions. It is argued that a negotiator loses flexibility if he must negotiate in public, that having made a stand, he will not be able to retreat easily even though it might be to his nation's advantage as far as the total outcome of the bargaining is concerned. It is true that many a diplomatic conference has collapsed for want of enough concessions and for lack of a sufficiently flexible attitude on the part of the negotiators. But it is assumed that the major cause of the inflexibility of modern diplomats is the publicity to which their negotiations are exposed. And where is the evidence for this belief? It does not exist.

Would the deadlocks that have blocked agreement in the United Nations Security Council have disappeared if the doors had been locked and the press and radio sent home? We have no way of knowing, but it does not seem likely. Would the United States and the USSR have agreed on Greece or Iran or Korea if they could have talked about it privately? Hardly. Could the United States and Communist China make significant concessions to each other if only they could talk it over in seclusion?

Actual private contacts between the two nations through their representatives in Poland have given no indication that this would be the case. Private meetings between the representatives of the West and those of the Communist bloc have found the two sides every bit as inflexible and unwilling to compromise as in the public negotiations between them.

The assumption that private meetings would be more fruitful than public meetings rests on the fact that diplomacy in the nineteenth century, when meetings were strictly private, was considerably more successful than diplomacy in recent years, which has been partially public, but as we have seen, there are many reasons why the accomplishments of diplomacy appear more limited today than in the past. If evidence of the effectiveness of secret diplomacy is wanted, the other factors affecting diplomatic success must be held constant. It is no use comparing one century with another. Our examination must be limited to the period since open diplomacy has been in existence, and within that period we must compare public and private negotiations over roughly comparable disputes. In truth, the diplomacy of recent years, *both* secret and open, has been a failure. It is not a lack of privacy that prevents the West from coming to agreement with those who challenge the existing international order.

There is one circumstance in which a diplomat *is* freer in private than he is in public, one instance in which he can in fact make more concessions if the public gaze is not fixed upon him, and that is when he wishes to do something of which the public disapproves. Contend as they may that secret diplomacy is more effective and consequently in the public interest, the advocates of secret diplomacy cannot hide the fact that their argument is fundamentally undemocratic. The issue is popular control. The major advantage of secret diplomacy is that it is free of such control, completely free if diplomatic agreements can be kept secret even after they are concluded, but partially free if they can at least be made in private and presented to the public as *faits accomplis*. The hidden assumption here is that professional diplomats are better judges of the public interest than the public itself, that they know what is best for the nation and that they can most effectively pursue the national interest if the public stays out of their way. This may be true, but it is an undemocratic belief. Democratic theory demands that the government serve the wishes of the public, *even when the public is wrong*. It is considered that this is a lesser risk than placing the final decision as to what is good for the public into the hands of any elite group, no matter how well intentioned.

It can be argued, of course, that sometimes the interests of the majority can be served only if those of some particular minority suffer and that a diplomat can strike the best bargain for his country as a whole only if he is free to make concessions in one area in order to advantage his nation in another, a course which may prove impossible if that part of the nation that is affected adversely by the concession learns of it immediately and sets up a howl. The argument is probably correct, but here again, the procedure suggested is undemocratic. It is part of the democratic process that the conflicting interests of various parts of the public be worked out through open debate, not settled in secret by the autocratic decision of some public official. If democracy sometimes inconveniences the diplomat, that is too bad, but there is no way to avoid the inconvenience without lessening democratic control.

Advocates of secret diplomacy maintain, of course, that the requirements of democracy are fully met by making the agreements public after they are concluded. Full debate can be held at that time, and if necessary, representatives of the public can refuse to ratify the agreement if they do not like it. In the last analysis, the public in a democratic nation can refuse to reelect a government that makes unpopular agreements.

In a sense, however, the modern supporters of secret diplomacy defeat themselves, for by accepting the idea that there should be no secret agreements but only secret negotiations leading to agreements that are eventually made public, they give up the major advantage of secrecy. In these circumstances, public control is merely diminished and postponed, not eliminated, and the public is still present in the mind of each diplomat who knows he must submit the agreement he makes to public approval sooner or later. Under these circumstances, diplomats may indeed gain a certain shelter from the public eye, may refrain from the more long-winded varieties of propaganda when talking to each other, may indicate an awareness of certain facts of life that the public prefers to ignore, may even make exaggerated demands for bargaining purposes and then give them up without losing face, but these advantages are all of a limited nature. Privacy that lasts only as long as the negotiations are in progress does not free the diplomat from the pressure of public opinion nor greatly increase his power to make concessions.

Let us take a hypothetical example. Suppose the United States could regain Arab friendship in the Middle East and eliminate Soviet infiltration in that oil-rich area by promising to give no further support of any kind to Israel, and suppose further that the State Department decided that this would be the wisest thing to do. Such an agreement could certainly be made if it were done in absolute secrecy, but once the agreement were made, it could not be put into effect without the American supporters of Israel knowing about it and protesting.

Diplomats who must win public support for their actions cannot afford to make concessions that run against the interests of important and powerful groups within the nation, even though such concessions might contribute to the reaching of agreement. Secrecy in negotiation does not overcome this handicap; indeed, it may make matters worse. The government with an unpopular policy to sell would be better advised to take the public gently into its confidence, sound out the opposition in advance and disarm it if possible, line up support and give its most powerful supporters a feeling of participation in the formation of the policy, even invite them to observe the negotiations, certainly keep them informed. Such procedures are in fact increasingly popular with the diplomats of democratic nations, so that even the "secret" negotiations of today are only semi-secret. Diplomats may lament the lack of secrecy, but given the political realities of the day, there is no question that such measures help to ensure support for agreements reached. Ironically enough, the foremost advocate of open diplomacy, Woodrow Wilson, failed because he did not take important Americans into his confidence during the secret negotiations that resulted in the Treaty of Versailles ending World War I and in the League of Nations Covenant, with the result that the United States Senate refused to ratify them. The lesson learned so painfully was not forgotten when it came time to set up the United Nations.

The nature of national politics and the nature of diplomacy as well have changed in the past few centuries, with the result that the secrecy appropriate in the past is no longer appropriate today. The conditions necessary for secret diplomacy (that is, secret from the public) existed at a time when the general public did not participate in national government, when the majority of the population of a nation did not care, did not know, and did not *want* to know about either the course of international negotiations or the agreements that were made.

Diplomacy, however, has never been kept secret from those whose support was necessary to the diplomats. During the dynastic period, the ins and outs of diplomatic negotiation were always known to those affected by international relations, namely, the king and his court. And even in the mid-nineteenth century, as A. J. P. Taylor points out, "Though they [the diplomats] carried on the mysteries of secret diplomacy, there were few real secrets in the diplomatic world."[10]

Secret diplomacy in the old style has come to an end because the public now has a much greater role in national government and public support is required for major international decisions. This is particularly true in democratic nations. Dictatorships are better equipped to carry on secret diplomacy, for in them a smaller group participates in the

[10] Taylor, *op. cit.,* p. xxxii.

decision-making processes of government. Thus a dictatorship can keep the results of its negotiations secret and can compel its people to accept agreements that may be unpopular. However, even here, the secrecy allowable is limited. Even dictators spend considerable time and energy in preparing their people to accept decisions made in international politics. We know that the picture of international affairs drawn by such regimes for their people is often badly distorted, but they do find it necessary to give out *some* information. Like the democratic nations, they find it necessary to blame the other side for a lack of results and to claim spurious diplomatic victories. Not infrequently in recent years, it has been a totalitarian government that has broken the diplomatic rules and made public the nature of diplomatic conversations that the other parties considered to be secret. Such moves are indication enough that dictators too must worry about the public reaction to diplomatic negotiations.

It should not be thought, however, that increased public participation and interest in diplomacy have brought an end to secret conversations. Even today, the great majority of diplomatic negotiations are conducted in privacy from the press and public, although information about their progress is frequently "leaked." Even in such public bodies as the United Nations, all preparatory work is done in private, and there is considerable behind-the-scenes lobbying and consulting during the course of public discussions leading to important decisions. As in other democratic institutions—parliaments, congresses, conventions—the representatives are allowed to consult in private before making their positions public. Open diplomacy does not put an end to that modicum of secrecy necessary for the smooth functioning of an organization.

In conclusion, both sides of the debate over secret versus open diplomacy have made significant errors, the pro-secrecy group in assuming (1) that an elite group of diplomats is to be trusted more than the public to do what is in the national interest; (2) that the cause of recent diplomatic failures lies in their lack of secrecy; and (3) that secrecy of any duration or importance is possible in a world where diplomats represent governments that are responsible to popular control. Those favoring open diplomacy have erred for their part in assuming that popular control over diplomacy will bring about world peace.

Both groups have granted to diplomacy a far more important role in determining the course of events than it actually plays. We have seen that modern wars are due not to diplomatic errors, but to far-reaching changes that have upset the distribution of power among nations, leading the challengers to insist upon changes to which the dominant nation and its allies will not voluntarily agree. To expect diplomacy to resolve all such differences is to expect too much. To believe that the technique of opening diplomatic discussions to public scrutiny or the technique of holding them in strictest secrecy will bring about this happy consequence is to pin one's hopes on daydreams.

Changes in the Role of Diplomacy

We have already suggested that changes in the role of diplomacy are related to the shift from the dynastic to the bourgeois to the modern state. Let us spell this thought out in more detail. In broad outline, it can be said that in the dynastic state, diplomacy was at its height, and in that period diplomats could and did influence international events significantly. In the bourgeois period, diplomacy was in a transitional state: international negotiation was little changed in form but diplomats were less in control of what happened than they thought they were. In the present period, diplomacy has receded still further in importance, and the limitations on what it can accomplish are severe.

In short, as the number of people involved in and affected by international events has increased (that is, as the state has become truly national in character), the influence of diplomacy has waned.

THE DYNASTIC PERIOD

Throughout the dynastic period, the state could not do much on an international level, but the little it could do was done at the pleasure of the king. The monarch had virtually full freedom of action, for relatively few others were deeply affected by his international acts. The fortunes of individual rulers and their families and followers might rise and fall depending upon the international marriages contracted, the alliances formed, the battles waged, but the life of the peasant and even of the early businessman continued much the same. The international aims of the monarch could be translated into action without their cooperation.

Because monarchs could do as they wished, diplomacy was a highly personal business, and within well-defined limits, a skilled ambassador could have a great effect on international affairs. As the personal representative of one monarch to another, a diplomat's main task was to win the favor of the king at whose court he was stationed and to convince the king of the advantages of the policies favored by his own master. Diplomats spent much of their time in wooing the confidence and affection of the sovereign and in cultivating whatever favorites he had. Balls, receptions, parties, and tête-à-têtes were the major setting for diplomatic activity. Intrigue and manipulation, flirtations and the bribing of courtiers were means to diplomatic ends. Diplomacy was both colorful and important.

THE BOURGEOIS PERIOD

The conditions that made diplomacy so personal, so flexible, and so significant began to disappear at the end of the dynastic period. With the emergence of a new social and economic structure that was eventually to tie the whole nation into a single unit, the freedom of action of the crown became more limited. The will of the monarch began to be replaced as a motive for international action by the national interest, or at least by the interests of the bourgeoisie. Compromises and solutions of international conflicts that were injurious to the new dominant class became increasingly difficult to execute, for the new power groups found ways of being heard. In England, for example, as early as the beginning of the nineteenth century, foreign ministers found it necessary to contend with public opinion.

To be sure, the change took more than a hundred years to be completed. Two factors helped postpone the full impact of diplomacy's decline in importance. First of all, the separation of politics and economics on the international as well as on the domestic level allowed the solution of international social and economic conflicts to be achieved through channels other than diplomatic negotiation, but diplomacy still claimed the credit for the fact that things were running smoothly. Second, the population at large, although increasingly affected by international events, did not capture control of the political machinery of the state until the very end of this period.

The first reason was particularly important. The separation between economics and politics allowed the most important problems of the period to be solved informally without the national governments' being involved at all. On the other hand, the very fact that the problems that arose were dealt with elsewhere furthered the preservation of international peace and encouraged the feeling that diplomacy was accomplishing things. Ambassadors made statements, foreign ministers sent instructions to diplomats on the position to take on this or that European quarrel, diplomats whispered warnings to each other, conferences were called and foreign ministers traveled to distant capitals to sign the resulting agreements. Most of this activity, however, was on the periphery of international events, but the fact that grave international political problems did not arise prevented the usefulness of diplomacy from being put to the test.

The illusion that diplomacy could solve all international problems was shattered when the trends of the preceding period were carried to their conclusion. Increasing political mobilization meant that an ever larger number of people were involved and interested in international relations, that the national government had to consider the interests of many divergent groups in drawing up its foreign policy and in executing it through diplomatic activities. Much of the old flexibility vanished. No longer was it enough for a diplomat to convince a king. Now he must convince a minister who was dependent on a government that was dependent on mass support.

At the same time, the increasing role of national government, in particular the extension of its activities into social welfare and economic regulation or even outright ownership and operation of major economic enterprises, meant that the machinery of government was being used to deal with the major problems of national life. Diplomacy returned to the center of the stage, but its successful performance was made more difficult, for what was at stake in international negotiation was no longer the pride and the property of a king nor even the political interests of a dominant class. At stake now were the living standards and the way of life of the millions who made up the national population. Small wonder that the area of compromise grew narrower and that the solution of these problems often lay beyond the range of a few brief conversations between governmental representatives. In the present era, international relations are more important than ever before, but the role of diplomacy in these relations has diminished sharply.

The Decreasing Importance of the Diplomat

As diplomacy has decreased in importance, so too has the importance of the diplomat. Individual diplomats are no longer indispensable. In the days when diplomacy was highly personal, the gifts of a particular ambassador might well prove necessary to the success of the mission, for if he succeeded in ingratiating himself with a foreign sovereign, he could obtain concessions for his country that no other man could match. Personal charm counted for a great deal, and a man skilled in the art of handling people could be a real asset to his country.

Negotiation between modern governments, however, is conducted on a much less personal basis. Although it is undoubtedly more pleasant if an envoy is likable and popular, it is not essential. Charm, hospitality, generosity, and so on will not help two nations to get along nor prevent two nations from falling out. The boorishness of a diplomat may be a source of unpleasantness, but it will not ruin his country's relations with other nations. Indeed, today we would consider an ambassador a very poor diplomat if he allowed the boorishness of others to interfere with his work.

It is sometimes claimed, even in modern times, that the personal qualities of a diplomat have contributed greatly to his success. For example, William Bullitt, the American ambassador to France before World War II, was very much liked and respected in official circles in Paris, and it is said that his personal popularity gave him tremendous influence over the French government. But it is difficult to distinguish between the influence Bullitt had because he was well liked and that which he had because he was the official representative of the United States. On the whole, we must insist that the personal influence of the modern diplomat is considerably less than that of his predecessors in the sixteenth, seventeenth, and eighteenth centuries.

The importance of modern diplomats has been further reduced by the development of rapid means of communication and transportation. In the past, because of the long periods of time it took to communicate with the home government, the diplomatic agent stationed abroad was allowed considerable discretion in dealing with matters that arose on short notice. Where his government had no previous position, it was he who formed policy, and even in the implementation of policies formed at home, he had a good amount of leeway. Of course, we must not exaggerate. Even then, the opportunity to make policy and to take responsibility was seized only by men of vision and courage, and such men were as rare then as they are now. The vast majority of obscure men in diplomatic posts took advantage of the opportunity given to them by their isolation and the slowness of events not by making decisions but by doing nothing. Nevertheless, the opportunity was present for those who knew how to avail themselves of it, and this opportunity, too, has disappeared under modern conditions.

Today, by telegraph and telephone, an ambassador can be instructed in a matter of hours or even minutes in the most minute detail on what he is to say, which points to stress and what to omit. Almost every detail of negotiation can be directed and followed by the foreign office. The diplomat becomes somewhat of a glorified messenger boy. Indeed, he is lucky if he is not by-passed altogether, for the same rapid means of communication that have made it possible for his superiors to instruct him in detail have also made it possible for foreign ministers and national leaders to communicate with each directly. During World War II, Roosevelt, Churchill, and Stalin did not have to bother with the ambassadors at their respective capitals when things were important. They could and did get on the telephone or send telegrams directly to one another. In the Cuban missile crisis of 1962 and again in the Arab-Israeli War of 1967, the Soviet premier and the President of the United States conferred with each other directly over the so-called Hot Line.

Improved air travel has made things even more difficult for the diplomatic corps. Since they can get together so easily, foreign ministers, prime ministers, and presidents have made a practice of hopping around the world to confer in person about affairs of state. Hardly a month passes that some new foreign dignitary does not make the pilgrimage to Washington. John Foster Dulles logged more than 400,000 miles in the air during his term of office as American Secretary of State, and Secretary of State Dean Rusk probably did as well. The Russian team of Khrushchev and Bulganin set a new record for globe-trotting by visiting just about every foreign country that would invite them, and Chinese Premier Chou En-lai also traveled extensively. This kind of activity is bitterly resented by some of the permanent diplomats who see themselves shunted aside and who claim that their bosses do more harm than good by such sorties. Whether they are right or wrong, the trend is unmistakable.

In still another respect, diplomats have been pushed aside by modern developments. No longer is an ambassador the major source of news and information about the nation in which he holds his post. Today, there are many additional sources of information, and some of them are more reliable than the dispatches that come out of the diplomatic pouch. Newspaper and radio and television reporters ferret out information that diplomats overlook. Magazine writers spend months writing background articles. Scholars and analysts and research teams make careful studies of foreign governments and economies. The government itself employs intelligence agents who may at times operate out of the embassies and consulates but who are not part of the diplomatic service. Even the official communications handed directly to an ambassador for transmission to his home government are likely to be broadcast over the radio before he has time to send the message through official channels. It is a rare and skillful diplomat who can tell his government much that it does not already know.

In truth, the failure of the diplomats in their fact-gathering function is sometimes shocking. In the Suez crisis of 1956, the American ambassadors in England and in France are reported not to have known that these two nations were preparing to launch an offensive against Egypt.[11] In World War II, when the American and British military attachés in Moscow sent out their evaluation of the ability of the USSR to resist the Nazi invasion, it was their opinion that the entire resistance would crumble in a few weeks.[12] The Italian ambassador at the time did not even know that his allies, the Germans, were about to attack Russia, and he is said to have been indignant that the Germans did not tell him.[13] It is hardly surprising that governments find it is a good idea to supplement the fact-finding of their diplomats with other sources.

Finally, the diplomatic corps has also suffered in the eclipse of its symbolic function. Louis XIV was ready to declare war on Spain because the men accompanying the carriage of the Spanish ambassador and the men accompanying the carriage of the French ambassador had gotten into a fight over which carriage should go first at an official function in London.[14] This sort of thing no longer happens. Indeed, it strikes us as childish today. Questions of precedence and prestige were all systematized more than a century and a half ago. Today, the rules are followed, but nobody else really cares which diplomat sits where or who goes through a door first. Ambassadors still make the rounds, making speeches, opening exhibitions, appearing at dinners, giving balls and receptions, and being entertained in turn. All this may be important to them and to their wives, but it cannot be argued that such activities are crucial to the dealings of nations. Diplomats still represent one nation to another, but they are not the living symbols they once were.

Why Diplomacy Is Considered Important

If all we say its true, why then is diplomacy so widely considered to be important and why are diplomats so highly regarded? Surely, there must be good reasons for these beliefs. In fact, there are several.

Diplomacy has been considered important in part because the greatest amount of information we have about the international relations of the past has come from diplomatic documents. It must not be forgotten that one of the first areas of international relations to be investigated was the history of diplomacy. It was only natural that scholars trying to under-

[11] *The New York Times,* Nov. 1, 1956, p. 10, cols. 3, 4; Nov. 4, 1956, section IV, p. 1, cols. 4, 5, 6.
[12] Robert E. Sherwood, *Roosevelt and Hopkins* (New York: Harper & Row, 1948), pp. 304, 327, 330, 395–96.
[13] Dino Alfieri, *Dictators Face to Face* (New York: New York University Press, 1955), p. 138.
[14] Nicolson, *op. cit.,* p. 180.

stand international relations should pounce upon diplomatic dispatches, the letters of ambassadors, the memoirs of diplomats and foreign ministers and premiers. This was original source material. What is more, it was intimate, interesting, and highly colorful. For a long time, we have been accustomed to seeing international politics through the eyes of people who have at one time or another been engaged in diplomacy. Their view of events has been taken as authoritative, and their interpretation of history has permeated the outlook of those who study and describe international relations.

Government officials have other reasons for rating the importance of diplomacy so highly. It is, after all, the cheapest way of exercising power in international affairs. What is the cost of an international conference, no matter how elaborate, compared with the cost of even a small battle or the sortie of a score of planes? Even the poorest country can afford a modest diplomatic corps and keep it in reasonable style. It is the sort of thing on which one cannot lose.

Diplomacy is also valued precisely because there is no easy, objective check on whether it is important or not. Theoretically, one should be able to assess the value of agreements reached at a diplomatic conference, but practically, the people who go to conferences have ways of avoiding being pinned down. Statements are issued claiming that much has been accomplished, that there has been a "useful exchange of views," that the parties agreed on "general objectives." Friendship has always been strengthened, future misunderstandings avoided, a foundation for future cooperation laid. Read the next set of official statements after a major diplomatic meeting, not the news story about it, but the official statement that will probably be quoted in the story or perhaps printed in full. You will find that 90 percent of its contents could have been written before the conference took place and that most of the accomplishments listed are so vague that there is no possible way of checking on whether or not they were achieved.

This state of affairs has obvious advantages for a practicing politician. When the tide of political events is unfavorable to a government, there is no cheaper boost to morale and popularity than a diplomatic victory. If you represent a large nation and you have even a moderately skilled public relations organization at home, you can always claim that you have achieved a victory. If the meeting ends in total failure to agree on anything, you can always claim that your opponent tried to hoodwink you and that you saw through his ruse. If the meeting was with a friendly nation, you have "cemented the bonds of friendship between the two nations."

Finally, diplomacy is considered important because diplomats are so often important people. A writer has described a major modern meeting, the Summit Conference in Geneva in 1955, as follows:

> To the Geneva conference of the Four Powers in 1955 each national leader brought an ambassador or two and what Sir Winston Churchill described as "hordes of experts and officials drawn up in vast, cumbrous array." They filled the hotels. They rushed about in limousines. They tied up telephone and telegraph lines. Carrying thick briefcases, they conferred endlessly from early morning to midnight. They wrote memoranda that did not greatly deflect the course of history but gave their authors the intellectual satisfaction that often is the only reward of the professional diplomat.[15]

Not every man can travel to Geneva and tie up the transatlantic telephone. Diplomats fly on secret missions. They have their pictures taken before and after secret meetings. They are written about and discussed. They gather together in such places as Geneva, Paris, London, and New York. Their words, vague and meaningless though they may be, are reprinted widely and are always good for an editorial or two. Theirs is a life of travel and glamour and publicity. No wonder they feel important.

Finally, it should not be overlooked that diplomats are often aristocrats or people of social prominence. This in itself lends an aura of glamour and importance to diplomacy. Until very recently, and even to a large extent today, diplomacy has been the private preserve of the rich and the well-born. No one disputes that diplomatic positions in the past were an aristocratic monopoly or that the foreign service has been in more than one nation the last governmental stronghold of the nobility. John Bright described the British foreign office in the mid-nineteenth century as "neither more nor less than a gigantic system of outdoor relief for the aristocracy."[16] The foreign office of Imperial Germany was heavily staffed with aristocrats. The same was true of the diplomatic services of Italy, France, Austria-Hungary, Poland, and Tsarist Russia. Nor was blue blood the only requirement for a diplomatic career. Money, too, was necessary. The obvious exclusiveness of the profession is to be seen in the fact that the expenses of holding a diplomatic appointment were far in excess of any nominal salary received.

Defenders of diplomacy sometimes argue that this may be true of the past, but that it is no longer true today. Ability, not family background, is supposed to be the prime consideration today in recruiting members of the diplomatic corps. Democratization is said to have

[15] Harold Callender, *The New York Times Magazine*, Dec. 9, 1956, p. 15.
[16] Paul Seabury, *The Wilhelmstrasse* (Berkeley, Calif.: University of California Press, 1954), p. 4.

reached even here. It is true, of course, that two world wars have had a profound leveling influence on many nations. It would be strange if they had not shaken at all this great governmental citadel of privilege, but the cracks in the walls have been mended by those inside, and the change has not been as great as one would think. The nobility of various nations, for example, has kept its hold on the diplomatic corps. In the democratic Weimar Republic in Germany just before its death at Hitler's hands, exactly half the mission chiefs abroad were aristocrats. The aristocracy continued to hold many positions in Hitler's foreign office, and after the Nazi defeat, the same people were still running things. Italian diplomatic lists between the two world wars were well peppered with noble titles, and again much the same people are still in control. Even today, British diplomatic rolls contain a disproportionate number of men of noble rank.

Russia, of course, has abolished her traditional aristocracy, and the United States never had one, but in both these countries diplomacy is still the work of the local brand of elite. The USSR saves her major diplomatic posts for trusted Communist bureaucrats. The United States confers her choicest posts upon rich businessmen who have contributed to political campaigns and staffs the lower ranks with young men from good families and good schools. It is only fair to state that Soviet diplomats are highly skilled professionals as well as Communists and that a trend toward more career appointments for top posts is clearly visible in the United States, but neither of these two countries offers serious evidence to refute the statement that diplomacy is generally aristocratic work.

Not only do the elite make up the various diplomatic corps of the world, but these fortunate humans also rub shoulders with the equally fortunate of other countries, and this rubbing of shoulders seems to be important. If this were not the case, why should the most sought after posts in the American corps be the Court of St. James's, followed closely by Paris and Rome? If the importance of the nation were the prime criterion, the place to go would be to Moscow, but who wants to go to Moscow, where life is drab and dreary and where no one even dresses for dinner? In England, the exciting life of the English court is open to the diplomat of high rank. Wanting to go to Paris or Rome requires no lengthy explanation. The point is that the conduct of international relations has little to do with it. Diplomacy is considered important, at least in part, because its personnel traditionally has been drawn heavily from those who occupy the pinnacle of the social pyramid, and because the work involved, particularly in the upper reaches, resembles closely the life of the rich and idle.

Summary

Our treatment has accorded international diplomacy less importance than it is customarily given. Defining diplomacy as the process of negotiation carried on between the official governmental representatives of nations, we have noted that such negotiations are not of great importance in modern times in altering relations between nations. The large number of people interested in international affairs and exercising democratic controls over national governments has limited the flexibility of the diplomat, and the increased role of government in modern society has forced the diplomat to deal with the gravest of economic and social problems, many of which cannot be solved by conversation.

During most of the nineteenth century, diplomacy claimed the credit for a peaceful world, but in reality this peace was made possible by Britain's huge preponderance of power and by the fact that the dominant class in all the most powerful nations had a common outlook on life. During the twentieth century, these conditions have disappeared, and the limitations of diplomacy have become clear.

Since successful diplomacy depends upon the reaching of agreement, it is a technique best suited for settling relatively minor differences among friends. It should *not* be expected to solve major disputes between challengers and dominant nations. Neither shopkeeper nor warrior diplomacy, neither open nor secret diplomacy, can be expected to carry off this task.

Although both diplomacy and diplomats have declined in importance over the last few centuries, they are still considered important by most writers. The error occurs because so much of our knowledge of international relations comes from diplomatic documents, because diplomacy is a glamorous profession staffed by an elite group of people, because politicians find it convenient to inflate the significance of diplomacy in order to claim diplomatic victories, and because the general public wishes so desperately that there were some simple technique of solving the troubles of our age.

By all means, let us talk not fight, but let us not expect thereby that we can avoid the consequences of the unsettling shifts of power that characterize the twentieth-century world.

Part Three

INTERNATIONAL ORGANIZATIONS

16

Collective Security

Our study of international relations would not be complete if, in addition to examining the nature of nations and the forces underlying their actual relations with each other, we did not also consider the ways in which men have tried to alter these relations through the creation of international organizations. Two problems in particular have seemed to require solution. One, admittedly a problem limited to the dominant nation and its allies, is the question of how those who benefit from the existing international order are to protect that order against new challengers who threaten to upset it. The other problem, common to all, is how to avoid the devastating world wars that characterize our century.

One idea that has been proposed as a solution to these problems is the idea of collective security. As a theory, it formed the basis for the creation of the League of Nations, and many of its assumptions have been woven into the United Nations as well.

The Concept of Collective Security

The idea of collective security is simple enough: Its aim is to provide security for all nations. It seeks to do this by assuring the failure of any aggressive use of force in international relations. Nations would continue to have differences, of course, but they would have to find some other way of resolving them, for aggression would be severely punished. Under collective security, no one would care a whit why a war started or what the consequences of a victory for one side or the other might be. It would be a duty to oppose aggression, whoever committed it for whatever reason. The plan correctly calculates that an aggressor will not be stopped by reason or by humane feelings but that he will be stopped by superior force. Consequently, the nations of the world must pledge themselves to stand together against any aggressor nation, isolating it and overwhelming it with their superior power.

With collective security, peace is indivisible, and any attack on any nation, no matter how remote, is the beginning of a tear in the fabric of international law and order that automatically endangers the safety of nations everywhere. As the representative of Haiti told the League of Nations when Italy attacked Ethiopia in 1936: "Great or small, strong or weak, near or far, white or colored, let us never forget that one day we may be somebody's Ethiopia."[1] For just as any nation is capable of becoming a victim, so any nation is capable of becoming an aggressor. Collective security is not a scheme to keep some nations in check and not others. Rather, it is a plan by which *any* nation that uses force illegally will be defeated.

Perhaps the most attractive feature of collective security is the fact that if everything goes according to plan, force will not have to be used at all. The mere threat of action by the collectivity will be enough. It seems reasonable to assume that a potential aggressor faced with the certainty of universal opposition if he attacks would give up his aggressive plans, knowing that he was bound to fail. Even if he attacked anyway, it would be possible to make him withdraw without the use of force, for the nations of the world are so economically interdependent that no one nation could long survive if it were cut off from all its markets and sources of supply by a worldwide economic boycott. In short, by committing themselves in advance to stand by one another in case of aggression against any nation, the nations of the world would not only be able to stop aggression in its tracks; they would prevent it from occurring in the first place.

Upon first examination, the idea of collective security seems reasonable and logical enough, but more critical examination shows some severe weaknesses in the plan. In the pages that follow, we shall examine the explicit and implicit assumptions on which the plan rests. We shall consider what changes the end of armed combat would force upon

[1] Inis L. Claude, Jr., *Swords into Plowshares* (New York: Random House, 1955), p. 258.

international relations. Finally, we shall consider the machinery through which collective security was to be put into effect.

Underlying Assumptions

The idea of collective security rests upon five assumptions that must prove to be correct if the idea is to work out in practice. They are:

1. In any armed combat, all nations will agree on which combatant is the aggressor. What's more, they will reach this agreement immediately, since rapid and united action is necessary if aggression is to be brought to a halt before extensive damage is done.
2. All nations are equally interested in stopping aggression from whatever source it comes. Preventing aggression is a value that overrides all others in international relations. Neither friendship nor economic advantage will stand in the way of action against an aggressor.
3. All nations are free and able to join in action against an aggressor.
4. The combined power of the collectivity, that is, of all nations in the world except the aggressor, will be great enough to overwhelm the aggressor.
5. Knowing that overwhelming power stands ready to be used against it, an aggressor nation will either sheathe its sword or go down in defeat.

As we shall see, the fourth and fifth assumptions are essentially correct, but the first three are in error, and for this reason the system has never worked in practice.

AGREEMENT ON THE IDENTITY OF THE AGGRESSOR

Unfortunately for the operation of collective security, there is rarely unanimous agreement on which nation is the aggressor in an international squabble. The accused nation itself almost invariably denies the charge, often by claiming that it was provoked by the aggressive action of others. Friends of the aggressor agree. Friends of the victim protest. The final verdict of history is liable to depend upon who writes the account of the event. Historians have argued and will continue to argue over who was the aggressor in World War I. Most of the nations in the world have no doubt whatever that the Communist North Koreans started the Korean War by invading South Korea, but the Communist nations insist that the initial attack came from South Korea.

It seems quite likely that if a major war occurs between East and West, the ultimately accepted version of who was the aggressor will depend upon who wins the war.

Apart from the possibilities of falsifying history, there is an even more basic problem in the fact that there is no clear definition of aggression. It is frequently assumed that aggression is synonymous with the first use of military force by one nation against another. This diminishes but does not eliminate the difficulty of identifying the aggressor in many cases. In the past few decades we have witnessed a number of instances in which nations obviously spoiling for a fight have launched armed attacks so unprovoked, so open and so brutal, so lacking in regard for both the rules of warfare and the principles of human decency, that identification of the aggressor proved no problem. It was the Japanese who attacked the Americans in World War II and not the other way around. American forces were at breakfast and in church that morning in 1941 when Japanese planes without warning bombed and strafed the American fleet at Pearl Harbor. It was Germany that started the war in the first place by attacking Poland on the flimsiest of pretexts. It was Fascist Italy that attacked Ethiopia, Albania, and Greece and stabbed a dying France. It was the Russians who attacked the Finns. In all these cases, the practice of labeling as aggressor the first to use armed force seems to lay the blame at the proper door, but other cases are not always so simple.

What, for example, are we to make of Israel's attacks on Egypt in 1956 and again in 1967? In both instances, Israel was certainly the first to launch a major attack, but before that attack there had been almost nightly raids across the Israeli border by Arab commandos and a series of retaliatory raids by the Israelis. Who was the first to use force, then? Apparently, Egypt. But the amount of force was small, for the raiders did not do much damage, and they returned home after each foray. How *much* force must be used before it is to be considered aggression? A single border incident involving half a dozen raiders is clearly too small. An organized attack by a division is probably enough. But where is the dividing line? How many raids equal the attack of a division? There are no easy answers. In addition, Egypt in both years had precipitated Israel's attack by seizing and closing major waterways to Israeli ships (the Suez Canal in 1956, the Gulf of Aqaba in 1967).

In this particular case, identification of the aggressor is complicated by the fact that Israel steadily insisted she wished to live in peace with her neighbors, whereas Arab leaders stated officially and categorically that their aim was to erase Israel from the map. Do stated intentions count?

To complicate matters even further, Egypt was in the process of building up a force, armed with Russian planes and weapons, that would have been capable of putting the threats of her leader, Gamal Abdel Nasser, into effect. Is it aggression to attack a neighbor who is arming to annihilate you? The common sense answer would be: "No, not if it is certain he plans to attack as soon as he is strong enough. Yes, if there is a possiblity that he may not attack." But how are we to read the future? In a world where collective security was in full operation, we would wait until the aggressor actually attacked, knowing that the collectivity could turn him back with ease. Any previous action against him would itself be aggression. But in a world where collective security is by no means certain and every nation must defend itself, who can say with certainty that Israel was the aggressor?

Other problems are posed by the possibility of threatening force without using it. Suppose one nation threatens another and the weaker nation gives in without a fight. Hitler did not use force in taking over Czechoslovakia. His threats were enough to frighten the Western allies, and resistance on the part of Czechoslovakia alone would have been suicidal. The Germans marched in unopposed, but was that not aggression?

There are other equally vexing problems. How is one to judge the use of Russian troops to put down the Hungarian revolt of 1956? In view of the virtually unanimous resistance of the Hungarian people to Soviet domination, it is difficult to call the action anything but aggression. However, the Russian troops were *invited in* by the constitutional government of Hungary to help it put down an internal rebellion. If we are to classify this as aggression, it is difficult to classify in any other way the use of British troops to help Greece in putting down a Communist revolt sponsored by Moscow after the end of World War II or the use of American troops to help the government of South Vietnam. The difference may be crystal clear to us, but comparison shows that a legalistic definition of aggression may not be altogether satisfactory.

The Communist nations have devised other techniques that escape legal definition as aggression in their aid to "wars of national liberation." It is extremely difficult to detect aid that is given to revolutionaries in other countries to enable them to overthrow their own governments, particularly if such aid is largely in the form of military training and ideological indoctrination for a small number of leaders. Weapons and supplies can be identified, but can we classify the sale of arms to revolutionaries as aggression? Was the USSR an aggressor in Korea because she supplied the North Koreans with arms to attack their neighbors to the south? Are China and the USSR aggressors for helping North

Vietnam and the Vietcong fight in South Vietnam? Is the United States an aggressor for bombing North Vietnam?

The use of so-called volunteers is another technique plaguing those who seek a simple definition of aggression. Whole divisions or even armies that are called "volunteers" fool no one, but what about a relatively small number of high officers or specialists such as bomber pilots or submarine commanders? Does the nation that supplies these to another nation share in any aggression it commits? It becomes clear that even the identification of military aggression is by no means simple.

How much more difficult is our task if we consider economic and ideological aggression as well as the use of military force. After all, economic power can also be used for aggressive purposes. A nation can be strangled by an economically more powerful nation just as surely as she can be conquered by a nation that is more powerful militarily. Iran was brought to her knees by the Western refusal to buy her oil after she nationalized the industry and threw out the British. Hitler attacked the Balkans economically long before his armies began to cross their frontiers, and Soviet penetration of the Middle East and Africa to date has involved virtually no soldiers other than a few advisers.

Even ideological attack may be highly effective. Joseph Goebbels, Hitler's minister of propaganda, demonstrated how deadly such attacks can be in developing home-grown traitors and in weakening a victim's will to fight once military aggression occurs. Russia daily beams propaganda broadcasts to large areas of the world urging the undermining of pro-Western governments, and we, for our part, broadcast to the Russians and the satellite peoples, undermining Communist rule. Such actions are not customarily considered aggression, but their military value in case of an armed conflict may turn out to be substantial.

One final problem: Under collective security no nation is prejudged to be guilty. Only after the aggressor has actually struck can the collectivity act in its turn. Such procedure seems necessary if the system is to be absolutely fair and impartial, but it greatly impairs the efficiency of the scheme. Of course, if the aggressor is weak, no harm is done. No great preparation is required to deal with such an aggressor; one stern warning by the combined great powers will be sufficient to stop it dead in its tracks and make it reconsider. However, if the aggressor can be stopped only by great armed strength, it is necessary to know which nation is the aggressor some time in advance of any aggression it actually commits. Nations need time, perhaps even years, to weld their separate armies into one mighty fighting force. Germany defeated one nation after another and wrecked most of Europe before she was brought down in defeat because all the nations that eventually combined against her were not prepared to enter the fight at the start.

We are caught in a dilemma. For effective action, we must know in advance who the aggressor is, but to be perfectly fair, we can never be sure the aggressor is really going to attack until *after* he has done so. If the collectivity begins to prepare in advance of actual aggression, the potential aggressor will seize the opportunity and complain that it is they, not he, who plan aggression. Hitler complained that Germany was being surrounded and that his neighbors were planning to attack him. At the time, he was believed by some. The Soviet Union and China complain today that the United States and her allies are preparing war against them and point to the fact that they are surrounded by our air bases and a ring of unfriendly alliances directed against them. *We* may know that our intentions are peaceful and our bases and alliances defensive, but other nations do not always share our self-appraisal.

To spot an aggressor in advance requires great foresight. France, at the end of World War I, pointed to Germany as the next aggressor and begged the nations of the world to help keep Germany down in the name of collective security. Instead, France was amazed to learn that under the principles of collective security she and Germany were to be treated as equally capable of aggression. France proved to be right, but the evidence was her defeat and virtual ruin in World War II. Today, the United States points to Russia and China as the next aggressors. Perhaps she, too, is right, but the "uncommitted" nations refuse to jump to this conclusion. The operation of collective security would require that the world wait and see.

The assumption that all nations will agree on the identity of the aggressor is false. In the absence of a clear definition of aggression, aggressive acts can be disguised, and even when they are committed openly, claims and counterclaims can be launched as to which side started it all. It is unfair to identify an aggressor as such before he strikes, but once a major aggressor does move, it may be years before he can be put down again, even with the combined fighting strength of a united collectivity of nations.

UNIVERSAL INTEREST IN STOPPING AGGRESSION

The second assumption underlying the concept of collective security is that all nations are equally interested in preventing or stopping aggression. This, too, is belied by the facts, for in the course of recent history, aggressors have never found themselves friendless. It is curiously contradictory to assume on the one hand that all nations are equally capable of becoming aggressors and on the other that they are all equally interested in stopping aggression when it occurs. Nations that are contemplating aggression—or acts that other nations may consider aggression—obviously will not support schemes that will ensure their own future defeat. Nor will the friends who would benefit from their aggression turn against them.

Nevertheless, the belief that aggression is equally deplored by all is a popular belief, particularly in the periods immediately following wars, when the world hungers for perpetual peace, when the defeated lie punished and even the victorious are tired of combat. After World War I, a conflict that had shocked with its horror a generation less hard than ours, the truth of this assumption seemed particularly self-evident. Indeed, the whole concept of collective security carries the mark of the thinking common in the time when it was first proposed.

In the light of our previous analysis of the international order, it seems evident that some nations will be more interested in stopping aggression than others. We must not forget that to nations that are fundamentally satisfied with the existing order, that is, to the dominant nation and its major allies, peace and security mean the preservation of the privileges they have. As long as peace is preserved, the losses they suffer will be minimized and the tempo of their decline slowed down. To the dissatisfied, on the other hand, international peace means peace without justice. If such a nation becomes strong enough, it may become a challenger with much to gain from upsetting the existing order, by force of arms if no other way is possible. For the dissatisfied of little power, initiating aggression against larger nations is out of the question. Such nations must wait for the opportunity provided by the aggression of a larger challenger. Thus when a powerful and dissatisfied challenger strikes, it runs interference for many nations that are dissatisfied with their place in the existing order. For this reason, a major aggressor seldom fights alone.

Not even the dominant nation can be counted upon to oppose all acts of aggression with equal vigor. Unfortunately for collective security, the old refrain that peace is indivisible and that aggression anywhere threatens all nations everywhere is not really true. All nations are not equally afraid of being attacked. Appeals to the self-interest of nations, a major argument of those who favor collective security, miss the point. A major nation need not fear attack from any but a small handful of nations. Such a nation is understandably unwilling to make a priori commitments that it will fight on the side of anyone attacked anywhere in the world even if its own interests are not at stake.

Many acts of aggression threaten no one but the immediate victim. India's invasion and seizure of Hyderabad threatened no one outside Hyderabad. An attack by Russia upon Turkey or Greece would be quite a different matter, however. In short, the dominant nation and its friends can perhaps be counted upon to oppose aggression by a major challenger against a friendly nation, but they cannot be counted upon to intervene in every isolated case of aggression by one nation against another. Even an attack by a challenger will affect the interests of the dominant nations differently. England expressed much more concern over Egypt's nationalization of the Suez Canal than over the attack of North Korea on South Korea, while the United States, with interests in the Pacific and no direct interest in the Canal, considered the Korean attack far more serious. France, in the 1930s, was far more concerned with potential German aggression in Europe than with actual Italian aggression in Ethiopia.

It is obviously mistaken to believe that peace and security are universal goals of all nations, overriding all others. When nations are immediately and severely threatened, security may in fact take precedence over all other concerns, but in the normal run of events, security can be taken for granted, and peace is only one of many national goals. It is a sad fact but true that when the interests of the great powers are not directly threatened, aggressors may be left to devour their victims undisturbed.

UNIVERSAL ABILITY TO OPPOSE AGGRESSION

The successful operation of collective security assumes not only that all nations are *interested* in stopping aggression but also that they are *able* to do so, that is, that they are free to join with other members of the collectivity in taking action against the aggressor. This, too, is incorrect.

A small nation bordering on a potential aggressor will think twice before joining any move against its more powerful neighbor, for battles "to stop the aggressor" are quite likely to be fought upon its territory, destroying its industries and its homes as well as those of the aggressor. Such fears quite naturally may cool its ardor for seeing collective security work. It is true that certain nations, because of their location, are most exposed to aggression themselves, and one might think that they would have the most to gain from the successful operation of collective security. But they are often too weak to defend themselves successfully, and other nations are too distant to prevent their fall if the aggressor attacks. The most that other nations can promise is liberation after the conquest is completed, and liberation is likely to prove even more destructive than the initial conquest.

Because of this, such nations may attempt to take refuge in neutrality. Even great powers may resist lending a hand to stop aggression because of such fears. Many Germans, for example, opposed membership in the Western coalition against Russia even though their sympathies were firmly on the side of the West, for they feared that such behavior guaranteed that many of the major battles of a third world war, should one occur, would be fought upon their soil. They hoped by remaining neutral in the struggle between East and West to avoid such a fate.

There are other reasons why nations sometimes cannot join in action against an aggressor. Their troops may be committed elsewhere, far from the scene of aggression. At the time of the Korean War, France was heavily engaged in trying to defend her colony in Indochina from Communist rebels and could not spare many troops for Korea. When France tried to hold another rebellious colony, Algeria, she withdrew from Europe troops that were committed to the North Atlantic Treaty Organization.

Sometimes a nation requires the help of an aggressor to defend itself against possible aggression from other quarters. Again, France provides an example. At the time when Fascist Italy attacked Ethiopia, France was reluctant to move against her, for she still hoped that Italy might be won to her side in the coming battle against Germany. The facts turned out to be otherwise, but the hope is understandable.

When aggression is committed by one of a nation's most valued allies, the choice is even more difficult. Could the United States afford to oppose aggression committed by either England or France, whose help she requires in the strugggle against Russia? Events appear to prove she can, for when England and France attacked Egypt in an effort to seize back the nationalized Suez Canal, the United States opposed them and forced their withdrawal, much to the detriment of Allied relations. Perhaps the dominant nation in the world can afford to antagonize anyone. But could England or France afford to oppose aggression committed by the United States?

Finally, we must not overlook the strength of economic ties in binding nations together, even when one commits unwelcome aggression. Nations that are economically tied to an aggressor may not be able to sever their ties without great hardship. In addition to the initial hardship of having to rearrange an entire economy on short notice and convince the population to tighten its belts for the duration of the crisis, there is the danger that once the crisis is ended, it may prove impossible to reestablish the broken economic ties, for the aggressor may have shopped around and found more secure sources of supply or better markets elsewhere. The plan for collective security stresses the fact that an aggressor is economically dependent upon other nations and thus can be punished by economic sanctions. Once economically isolated, he will find it difficult to go on fighting. This is probably true, but we must not forget that interdependence is a two-way street; nations are also dependent upon the aggressor and thus unable to break away completely.

The first three assumptions, then, are incorrect. It cannot be assumed that nations will agree on what constitutes aggression or on which nation is the aggressor. Nor can it be assumed that all nations are either interested in stopping aggression or able to join in action against the aggressor. Under these circumstances, collective security cannot be expected to work, even though the remaining two assumptions are correct.

PREPONDERANT POWER OF THE COLLECTIVITY

All against one, the basic formula of collective security, is neither sporting nor heroic but it guarantees success in any trial of strength. The assumption that the collectivity, once united and once intent on preventing aggression, is strong enough to keep the peace, is essentially correct. It seems fairly obvious that no single nation is strong enough to win a victory against the combined strength of all the other nations in the world.

Still, some nations can come closer to achieving such a victory than others. Should the aggressor be a small nation, no great problem is posed. The intervention of a single great power will be enough to send its troops scurrying for home. But stopping aggression by one of the great powers is more difficult. Germany, for example, came close to victory in World War II. The case of Germany, however, proves our point. Germany did not fight alone, nor did she fight all her enemies at once. Particularly at the beginning, she picked off her victims one at a time, and her early successes rested on the fact that before the kill, she isolated each victim. For Austria and Czechoslovakia, Germany did not fight at all. The conquest of Poland did require the use of force, but Hitler was careful to neutralize Russia before he attacked. Then, with the Eastern front secure, he turned to the West and conquered all of Europe to the Channel. Only then did he turn and attack Russia. The combined strength of England, the United States, and the Soviet Union eventually defeated Germany, but not without a mighty and costly struggle.

Today, with the possible exception of the United States and the Soviet Union, there is no nation that could successfully resist a coalition of other great powers, surely not France or England, who withdrew from Suez rather than stand up to American opposition, surely not China, who dares not attack Formosa. Even the two superpowers probably could not stand up against the rest of the world combined. Russia today is not even as strong as the United States. Compared to the whole Western alliance, she is by far the weaker party. Deserted by China and the satellites, she would not stand a chance. Collective security, then, could take care of Soviet aggression, for with the whole world against her, Russia would not be half as dangerous as she appears today. The Soviet Union is dangerous precisely because the whole world is *not* combined against her and because the *potential* power of Russia *and* her allies is so great.

That leaves the United States. Could she defy the world? We think not. The matter will never be put to the test, so we cannot be sure, but the concern with which the United States tends her alliances with Western Europe, the energy she spends trying to win new allies from among the neutral nations, and the consternation with which she views the fall of any new nation to communism are clear enough indication that she fears to stand alone in any battle against world communism. The collectivity is also stronger than the United States.

Collective security is not really necessary unless the aggressor is one of the two great superpowers. The combined might of all the nations in the world is not required to put down aggression by lesser nations. Indeed, there is no nation on earth that dares to risk the severe displeasure of these two giants. Continued acts of aggression by small and medium-sized nations cannot be blamed upon a lack of collective security. Even without collective security, they would not be possible unless the two great powers both looked the other way *or* unless one of the great powers protected the aggressor against the other.

The assumption that no nation could successfully resist the combined might of all the others is correct. The difficulty is that in cases of small aggressors, this combined might is not necessary, and in the only cases where it *would* be necessary, that is, aggression by either the United States or Russia, such a force could not be gathered. One of these nations is the dominant nation in the existing international order, the other the major challenger. Each has its own group of followers, who would never admit that their leader was an aggressor and who would be neither interested not able to oppose it if it were.

PEACE BASED ON PREPONDERANT POWER

The fifth and final assumption underlying the concept of collective security is that a would-be aggressor faced with the certainty of united opposition from the rest of the world would give up its plans for aggression as hopeless. This assumption, too, is probably correct. We have seen in our previous study that peace is guaranteed when overwhelming power lies in the hands of those who favor the maintenance of the existing order. The period from 1815 to 1914 was a century of peace because of the tremendous power advantage enjoyed by Britain through most of those years. The years since 1914 have been marked by war because the preponderance of Britain and her new American partner has been challenged by new nations that have industrialized more recently.

In a sense, the whole idea of collective security is an attempt to re-create artificially the kind of imbalance of power that guaranteed world peace in the years before World War I. The crucial difference, of course, is that the earlier imbalance was caused by the power advantage of a specific group of three nations (Britain, France, and the United States) who controlled the dominant positions in an international order based on their supremacy. The imbalance hoped for by the advocates of collective security, on the other hand, is to be a completely artificial creation built upon the combined strength of whatever group of nations is left when the aggressor is subtracted. Its unity is to be provided by principle alone, not by any common interest in any particular kind of world.

The preponderant power of the collectivity would indeed be sufficient to prevent aggression *if* it could be mobilized on the side of peace, but it is here that the error of the first three assumptions is most telling, for as long as nations are governed by national interest rather than by principle, as long as they refuse to recognize that their friends may be aggressors and are not interested or not able to oppose them, so long will it be impossible to mobilize the kind of united force that would be necessary to make collective security work. We must conclude that the plan is fundamentally unworkable, noble though it may be in inspiration.

Collective Security and the International Order

Collective security has never been an operating reality, and yet it is interesting to speculate what the consequences would be if it were. What would be the effect upon the existing international order? Would collective security benefit the dominant nation or the challenger?

It is generally assumed that collective security would help to perpetuate the status quo, and to a certain extent, this is true. Collective security would certainly make impossible any armed challenge to the existing order; since challengers often rely upon the use of force to achieve their goals, it seems logical that serious challengers would oppose the full operation of collective security.

But it is easy to overestimate the extent to which ending armed aggression would prevent shifts in the distribution of power among nations and consequent changes in the international order. Although nations would be prevented from invading the territory or taking away the political independence of other nations, there would be nothing to prevent their gaining wealth and power through industrialization, population growth, and peaceful trade with others. Even without aggression, challengers can grow in power until they are stronger than the dominant nation. Indeed, if one excepts a few acts of aggression against Latin American nations, this is precisely what the United States did. It became the dominant nation in the world simply by growing and modernizing within its own boundaries and by utilizing its tremendous wealth in trade with other nations. World War I marked the emergence of the United States as the strongest nation in the world, but the war was not the cause of her power.

The Soviet Union's recent rise has been marked by aggressive expansion in Eastern Europe, but the amount of power gained in such moves is small compared to the vast increase in power gained through rapid industrialization. Had collective security been working properly, Russia could never have invaded Finland nor absorbed Lithuania, Latvia, and Estonia; nor would World War II have given her an opportunity to replace the governments of the European satellites and take over their control. Even without these actions, however, the Soviet Union would have risen in power to the point where she was the major challenger to the Western order, for her population is large and her modernization has been rapid. Nor would the operation of collective security prevent her from continuing to rise in power in the years to come. Without further aggression, it is doubtful whether she can pull abreast of the United States in power, but surely she can narrow the gap, for her economy is still backward in many respects and her population is continuing to grow. Collective security, then, would prevent aggressive attacks upon the dominant nation and its friends, but it could not prevent them from being eclipsed by new and powerful rivals, nor could it assure that the nations they dominate would not be bought or wooed away from them, destroying the international order they head.

In spite of the lack of guarantees, however, the picture of collective security that we have presented so far is one that is favorable to the dominant nation and unfavorable to the challenger, for the successful operation of collective security would eliminate at least *one* of the ways in which challengers could upset the existing international order.

Unfortunately for the dominant nation and its friends, this is not the whole story, for collective security would inhibit them as well. Indeed, if it were put into effect, the present international order could not exist for long. Any international order is based in part on differences in power among those nations that compose it, and the ability to use force is one of the most important ingredients of national power. It is true that power is only one of the main supports of an international order. No order can be maintained for long by force alone, and any stable order must assure that at least its major participants are satisfied with their place in it and with the rules by which it operates. At the very least, they must find their present circumstances favorable enough to be preferable to the risks involved in any attempt to change the status quo.

Nevertheless, the preponderant power of the dominant nation and its major partners is an important factor in maintaining the stability of the international order.

If collective security were to be effectively implemented, it would destroy at one stroke many of the advantages that come from superior strength. Deprived of the ability to use their superior military forces, the great powers would lose much of their ability to dominate weaker nations. America's domination of West Germany and Japan and her hold on Latin America would be seriously weakened. The advantage of Russia's being more powerful than her satellites would be considerably diminished.

Under present circumstances, dissatisfied nations of little power are totally unable to better their lot or to upset the international order. But if collective security were put into effect, they would be able with impunity to undermine the order to which they belong. It is difficult to estimate the extent of the possible damage, for we do not even know exactly how many such nations there are. The dominant nation and her coterie of powerful and satisfied followers portray the nations under their domination as blissfully contented, but this is not necessarily so. The Soviet Union proclaims that her satellites follow her lead by choice, but we know that this is not true. We do not even know many of the grievances of the small nations, for there is little point in their complaining about troubles that cannot be remedied.

It seems clear, however, that many of the weaker nations are far from satisfied with their position in the world or with their relations with the greater powers. Such nations now lack the power to threaten the existing order, but if collective security made them immune from military reprisal, they might well try to take away some of the privileges foreign nations enjoy within their territories. Nations rich in resources could seize the facilities owned by foreigners or make the foreigners pay more dearly for the resources they now get cut-rate. Nations whose foreign trade is monopolized by foreigners could look around for better customers. Nations in strategic locations could refuse to serve as bases for foreign troops. It would be quite a different world in which the mice no longer feared the cats.

Powerful nations would still be able to exercise economic and ideological power over weaker nations. They would still control the ability to reward and punish and persuade, but without the ability to exercise force for purely national purposes, their control over others would be considerably weakened. Economic superiority alone might be enough to maintain an international order for a time, but eventually, if weaker nations knew that force could not be used against them, they would do away with some of the economic privileges of the great powers.

Thus collective security would prevent the most powerful nations from reinforcing their hold on weaker nations or from extending their hold to new nations. Both the dominant nation and the major challenger would lose many of their followers, and for this reason, both would be opposed to the effective operation of collective security, whatever they might say to the contrary as long as it is not a serious possibility.

Collective Security and International Organization

The instrument designed to translate collective security from blueprint into reality was the international organization, first the League of Nations, created at the end of World War I, then the United Nations, created at the end of World War II. Both organizations when they were new created the illusion that from then on the world would be secure, but as instruments of collective security, both have failed. The aggressors of the past were members of the League, and the aggressors of the future will in all probability be members of the United Nations.

The failure of these organizations to implement collective security should not be surprising in view of the fallacious assumption upon which the whole idea is based. International organizations, after all, are no more than machinery to be used by the member nations as they see fit, and as long as the member nations do not wish to unite against aggression, no amount of structures and procedures can make them do so. Indeed, the defects of structure and procedure are important less as causes of failure than as indications of how far (or rather, how short a way) the member states are willing to go in their support of collective security. These defects are not entirely mistakes. Rather, they are ways in which nations have protected themselves against a kind of international security that might be detrimental to their interests.

It should be noted that both major international organizations to date were created at the end of wars, at a time when it was not yet clear who the next aggressor would be. If the new aggressor was among the victors, he had not yet shown his hand. Thus neither of the two great world organizations were formed as coalitions against any one state in particular. They were supposed to oppose aggression from any quarter. No nation capable of committing aggression or of being accused of aggression could feel comfortable if the organization worked too well.

The fear that the collectivity might be turned against one of them (and they did not know which one) was particularly strong among the great powers. It would be fine if the future aggressor were known in advance and if it were clear that the organization was designed to keep *him* down and no one else. France was willing and eager to give force to the League if it were clearly understood that the purpose was to keep Germany in check. The United States today might be only too willing to give more power to the United Nations to keep Russia and China in their places. Indeed, she has made moves in this direction by shifting the main task of supervising security away from the Security Council, where Russia has a veto, to the General Assembly, where she is frequently outvoted.

It is quite another matter for a great power to agree to grant to an organization real power that may be used against its *own* interests. Quite correctly, each great power fears that if it found it necessary to fight for its rights and privileges, a hostile collectivity might call this aggression and turn against it. When the United Nations was formed, Great Britain had an empire to defend against the depredations of the Russians and against the ideals of her American ally. The Soviet Union had reason to worry that England and the United States would stick together and that she would be the one to be accused of upsetting the peace.

The United States also feared the possibility that the collectivity might be turned against her (and, in fact, did later oppose UN involvement in Latin America, where her actions were unpopular), but this was not her major worry. What gave her more concern was the possibility that her armed forces might be voted into action for the purpose of putting down every minor disorder on the face of the globe, including those in which the United States had no particular interest. It is highly unlikely that the American Senate would ever have ratified a United Nations Charter that could commit the forces of the United States without express American consent.

The fears of the great powers that the new international organizations might be used against them were quieted by denying the organizations the ability to act without their permission. Important decisions in the League required a unanimous vote. Important decisions in the United Nations require the approval of each of the Big Five (the United States, the USSR, Britain, France, and China). This solved the problems as far as the great powers were concerned, but of course it torpedoed any possibility of putting collective security into effect. No act of aggression committed by any of the big powers or by any smaller nation that a great power chose to protect could be touched.

We have noted before that only the greatest of nations are capable of launching aggression serious enough to require collective action, and it was precisely in such cases that both organizations were prevented from acting. Whatever else they may have accomplished, the League of Nations and the United Nations have not succeeded in making collective security a reality.

Summary

We have opened our discussion of the ways in which men have tried to improve modern international relations with a study of collective security, a scheme whereby the combined might of all the nations in the world would be turned against any nation that committed aggression.

The whole idea is based upon the correct assumptions that peace can best be preserved by a preponderance of power, that the combined strength of all the nations except a single aggressor would always equal such a preponderance, and that an aggressor faced with such overwhelming force would give up, probably in advance.

Unfortunately, however, the scheme is also based upon three incorrect assumptions: (1) the assumption that nations would all agree upon who was the aggressor, when in fact they have not done so; (2) the assumption that all nations are equally interested in stopping aggression, when in fact there are always some nations that side with the aggressor; and (3) the assumption that all nations are able to join in action against the aggressor, when in fact there are always nations that cannot do so because they are afraid of the aggressor, because they need his help, or because they are tied to him economically.

We have explored the consequences that would follow if collective security were ever put into effect, and we have found that they would be in many ways detrimental both to the dominant nation and to the major challenger, for collective security would prevent the challenger from using force in his bid for power, and the dominant power from using force or the threat of force to uphold the international order it heads or to protect its privileges.

Finally, we have seen that international organizations, supposedly created to put collective security into practice, have in fact been made incapable of action in the only cases where collective security would be required. This is but one instance of the curious discrepancy between the promise and the fulfillment of the great world organizations of the twentieth century, the topic of the next two chapters.

17

Background for a Puzzle

❖❖❖❖❖❖❖❖❖❖❖❖❖❖❖❖❖❖❖❖❖❖❖❖❖❖❖❖❖❖❖❖❖

There is a fundamental contradiction in international organization, a contradiction that runs right through its history, sets limits to its present operations, and, unless unforeseeable changes occur, will shape its future development. The contradiction can be seen by looking at such bodies as the United Nations or the League of Nations before it. These organizations, housed in impressive chambers, staffed by important diplomats, and encouraged by worldwide publicity, lack the crucial powers to put their goals into effect; and the member nations, while meeting in council to keep peace, continue to pursue the policies that lead to war. The effect is somewhat puzzling.

It would be easy to lay the blame on "evil nations" or on "hypo-critical diplomats," but the problem is deeper than that. The inconsistency that plagues international organizations grows out of the attempt to reconcile two contradictory forces: national sovereignty and international interdependence, for these forces represent the desire of nations to pursue, at one and the same time, two mutually exclusive ways of life.

The conflict between sovereignty and interdependence has left its mark on international institutions. Its brand is clearly to be seen in the structure, in the powers, and in the procedures of international bodies. The desire to escape the uncomfortable contradiction between sovereignty and interdependence has led people to forsake reality by demanding that one of these forces give way to the other. The solution is appealing in its simplicity, but unfortunately, it is impossible to do away with either. National sovereignty and international interdependence are the products of a lengthy evolution, and they have their roots in political, economic, psychological, and social realities. Misjudgment of the potency of either force leads to absurd expectations and thence to disillusionment. We therefore begin our study of international organization with a short analysis of sovereignty and interdependence.

Sovereignty

"Sovereignty" is a word on many tongues. It is preached by antediluvian nationalists who would board up the United Nations and send its members packing. It is promised by politicians most publicly committed to closer international cooperation. It has been the center of many a long and heated controversy. At one time, philosophers and lawyers who believed in the supremacy of the national state maintained that no limitation of sovereignty was possible. For them, not even the smallest portion of sovereignty could be given away, since sovereignty, like virtue, could only be kept intact or lost forever.[1] Others more partial to international organization have argued that sovereignty is divisible and that the very act of giving it away is a legitimate exercise of a nation's sovereign power.[2] Still others have argued that sovereignty no longer exists today, whereas the United Nations Charter stoutly declares that its members are sovereign states.

Under the circumstances, it is wisest to admit that a number of different concepts have been stuck with the same label. There is not much point in arguing over which label has been properly placed. In this book we choose to define sovereignty as the possession of supreme power, but this is not to say that this definition is "correct." The reader may define the term as he wishes, as long as he remembers what is meant when the term is used here.

We have already defined power as the ability to influence the behavior of others in accordance with one's own ends. Sovereign power

---

[1] For a discussion of this school of thought, see Clyde Eagleton, *International Government* (New York: Ronald Press, 1948), p. 24.
[2] See Philip C. Jessup, *A Modern Law of Nations* (New York: Macmillan, 1949), p. 41. See also Frederick S. Dunn, *The Practice and Procedure of International Conferences* (Baltimore, Md.: Johns Hopkins Press, 1929), p. 126.

is supreme power, and within its territorial jurisdiction, the national government is sovereign, since it controls more power than any other group or individual. The nation is also sovereign in its dealings with other nations, since it recognizes no authority above itself.

It may be useful to distinguish between legal sovereignty and the actual control of supreme power. In a legal sense, all independent nations are sovereign, but if we look at the practice of politics, we may seriously question the actual sovereignty of some of the satellites and economic dependencies. We must question the sovereignty of Iran during the period when a British oil company interfered freely in parliamentary elections and helped to choose cabinet members.[3] We may deny altogether the sovereignty of Rumania in 1945, when King Michael appointed a Communist-backed prime minister after Russia's Andrei Vishinski had told him he had just two hours and five minutes to fire the old one.[4] In both cases, the greatest power within the nation was controlled by foreigners, in one case by a British oil company, in the other by the Russian Army. The actual distribution of power within a nation can be determined only after careful study. Particularly in the case of the economic dependencies, it is often difficult to tell whether the national government or foreign interests are in control. All the major nations of the world, however, are sovereign in fact as well as law.

National sovereignty has two characteristics that will prove to be important when we come to an examination of international organizations. First, power—and sovereign power is no exception—is always exercised in the interests of the powerful as they see that interest. Second, national power is rarely relinquished consciously and voluntarily.

The first statement is not really open to argument. If power is defined as the ability to influence the behavior of others in accordance with one's own ends, then to exercise power means simply that one *does* influence the behavior of others in accordance with one's own ends. Of course, it is conceivable that a nation could be genuinely unselfish, that the goals of its foreign policy might be the welfare of humanity whether or not this benefited the nation concerned. In actuality, no national government has ever *claimed* to be pursuing such a policy, and if it did, it could be sure that a sizable delegation of its citizens would descend upon the capital in rage, demanding that the government stop "selling out"

[3] See the statement of Iranian Premier Mohammed Mossadegh to the United Nations Security Council. *Official Records of the Security Council,* 6th year, 560th meeting (Oct. 15, 1951), pp. 14ff.
[4] James F. Byrnes, *Speaking Frankly* (New York: Harper & Row, 1947), pp. 50–53.

the nation. What passes for national unselfishness is the kind of policy that benefits others without causing any damage at home, what Americans are fond of calling "enlightened self-interest" since it is supposed to result in long-range benefits for the nation in the form of good will, trade, and possibly alliances. In short, whether they are selfish or unselfish, far-sighted or shortsighted, the ends for which national power is exercised are the goals of those who wield the power.

National policies do not necessarily benefit everyone within the nation. Englishmen of wealth are hard hit by government restrictions on spending their money abroad, and American consumers are hurt by tariffs that keep out cheap foreign goods. Some governments do not even begin to represent the interests of the entire nation but operate instead for the benefit of the few—a racial or religious minority, a military clique perhaps, or powerful business interests. Satellites and economic dependencies may even be administered primarily in the interests of other nations. But whether the power-wielding group is or is not representative of the entire nation does not concern us here. Whether power is wielded for the sake of the few or the welfare of the many, for a dictator's dream or a common goal, the fact remains unchanged that power is exercised in the interests of the powerful and those they represent.

It follows that national power is rarely given up consciously and voluntarily, for if power is used to reach the goals of those who hold it, what reason can there be for giving it to others who may use it otherwise? Power changes hands, but it usually does so without the consent of those who lose it.

It must be understood that national sovereignty is not simply a matter of interest to diplomats and other government officials. The sovereign power of the national state deeply affects the everyday lives of the citizens who make up the nation. The state uses its power to organize the national society, to enforce the accepted ways of behavior, and to uphold a particular division of goods and services, offices and honors. On the international level, the national government uses its power to improve the well-being of its citizens, perhaps at the expense of others, and to protect their way of life as much as possible from outside interference. There is not a citizen whose life would not be influenced if his national government were to give up its sovereignty, for international and domestic power are but two sides of the same coin. One cannot give up power in international affairs and keep it at home.

Those who benefit from the existing distribution of power will oppose any shift that might injure them, but it is not primarily because of their interests that citizens support the nation-state. The tie between the individual and the nation is far stronger than is realized by those who would explain it away by proving that the true interests of all individuals would best be served by a world state based upon a world community. The greatest obstacle to the abolition of national sovereignty lies not in the national self-interest of individuals, but in the sentiments of nationalism, for citizens would not submit so willingly to the power of the state at home nor cheer so heartily its acts abroad if they did not feel a tremendous psychological commitment to the nation. If nationalism is to be done away with, some other way of satisfying these deep psychological needs must be found. Perhaps in the course of time the present attachment to the nation will be transferred to some other entity, but for the moment, nationalism carries the field, nor does it show any signs of withering away. The forces favoring nationalism have powerful means at their disposal. The road to larger unities appears long indeed.

This, then, is the reality of sovereignty. Supreme power within the nation is possessed by the national government, which exercises that power both internally and internationally in the interests of those it represents. Therefore the most important groups within each nation are reluctant to see their government relinquish any of its power to other states or to international agencies unless the compensating advantage to be gained is clear and immediate. In addition, the citizens of modern nations have a strong emotional commitment to the nation as it exists today.

Interdependence

Interdependence is the second reality that lies behind the charters of international organizations. As the strength of national sovereignty is sometimes underestimated by those who would rush into a world state, so the extent of international interdependence is underestimated by those who would linger too long with the forms of the past. Interdependence, like sovereignty, deserves our full consideration.

It is in the world of commerce, of trade and payments and markets and machines, that the interdependence between nations is most obvious. Modern industrialism from its earliest beginnings has reached out beyond the boundaries of the nation, and as industrialism has grown—demanding more materials, more markets, new goods and skills—it has pulled nation after nation within its grasp, tying nations to each other with thousands of invisible threads. Today even the most underdeveloped areas find that their fortunes rise and fall with those of the industrial world.

Modern production requires huge quantities of raw materials which Nature has not provided every nation: Coal and iron, oil and copper, tin, chromium, sulfur, graphite, and now uranium. The list is long, and modern industry requires them all. The most common object in daily use may be made of raw materials from many countries. A telephone, for example, requires raw materials from seventeen different countries in five continents.[5] The lack of a few crucial materials can cripple a national economy.

As machines require a varied diet, so do the men who run them. In a peasant economy, each family and each village grows most of the food it eats, but modern cities draw their foodstuffs from afar, and a small, industrial nation may be dependent upon foreign sources for the very sustenance of its population. England is the classic case in point, but Japan might be mentioned as well.

Machine production requires world markets as well as world sources of supply, for the economies of mass production are not possible unless large quantities of goods are turned out at once. Few nations possess within their borders customers enough to keep their factories running at full tilt. The mills of Manchester are busy turning out material for the dresses of housewives from Kansas to Nigeria. Even a nation as car-conscious as the United States does not drive all the automobiles it produces but exports its Cadillacs to foreign potentates and its trucks to businessmen the world over.

The greatest portion of international trade is between industrialized nations who trade their specialties with one another, but even in advance of industrialization, a nation may have many needs that can only be met from outside. In their attempt to develop their potentialities, under-developed countries also require help from outside in the form of machinery, capital, and technological and managerial skills. The foreign expert is as valuable an export as any other item on the market.

The economic interdependence of nations may best be analyzed in terms of balances of trade and international payments, but it can also be seen in human terms. The beef ration of an Englishman depends upon politics in the Argentine, a peasant in Ceylon sprays his crops with American insecticide, and a copper miner in the Congo finds that the money for his bride-price depends upon the purchasing policies of a German firm. Trade is no respecter of political boundaries, and this fact more than any other has led people to believe that the division of the world into nations is antiquated and that political barriers blocking trade and prosperity should be abolished.

The technology of war has also had startling effects upon the interdependence of nations. In an age when missiles can cross the ocean in minutes, when bombers can strike and return in the time it takes a general

[5] Eugene Staley, *World Economy in Transition* (New York: Council on Foreign Relations, 1939), pp. 23, 27, 29, charts V, VI.

to drive to his headquarters, a nation can no longer consider its own borders as its first line of defense. Bases and warning stations must be built far from home, and they must be protected by friendly troops. In the days since Pearl Harbor, American naval and air bases have sprung up like mushrooms around the world.

Alliances have always been cemented long before the fighting starts, but today much more than a promise of assistance is required. The necessities of modern warfare make long-range planning imperative. Military budgets must be coordinated, numbers, types, and distributions of troops decided upon, weapons and supplies collected at strategic places, equipment and training standardized. Because these preparations are required and because so many of them must be carried out by foreigners on foreign soil, what happens in other nations becomes a matter of prime concern, even from a strictly military point of view. Friendly governments, economic development, social stability—in short, other peoples' affairs—become the aims of national military policy, aims to be furthered by advice, assistance, and if necessary by direct interference.

The projects set in motion by military planners have still other effects upon the relations between nations. Military purchases may be used to bolster the economies of one's allies, and considerable economic benefits may flow to countries on whose soil armies assemble and train. In England, the amount paid by the American government for the maintenance of its bases is but a small part of Britain's national income, but in Morocco, when American military air bases were there, the American government was the largest single employer in the country.

The stationing of large bodies of troops on foreign soil leads to personal as well as economic ties. It is a platitude that soldiers do not always behave in ways designed to endear them to the local population, but occasional flare-ups of ill will should not be allowed to obscure the very real influence which results from protracted contact between the people of two different nations. Arabs exposed to an American Army mess for the first time in their lives may find their ideas of dietary sufficiency altered considerably, and G.I.s exposed to the countryside of France may wonder why Americans can't take time "to fix things up a little." More Americans have been to Paris at Uncle Sam's expense than have gone on Cook's tours, and for many Russians the march to Berlin was their first and last experience in foreign travel. The influence of the military does not end on the battlefield.

Revolutionary changes in the technology and techniques of communication have made possible what might be called an interdependence of ideas even among those who never meet their international neighbors. A century ago news traveled no faster than man himself could travel;

today men at opposite ends of the earth may communicate in a matter of seconds. The influence of American movies, for better or for worse, is felt round the world. Russian books and pamphlets may be found in the remotest corners of the earth. Books, magazines, newspapers, films, telegraph, radio, and television put the people of one nation in direct touch with the ideas of another.

Radio, in fact, provides a way for governments to reach directly the people of other nations whether their own governments like it or not. How important this may be is illustrated by the persistence of Anglo-American efforts to broadcast to the Soviet Union and by the equal perseverance of the Soviet government in attempting to block reception of these broadcasts. No longer can a culture remain in isolation from its neighbors. We are all exposed to the opinions of others, to their differing ways of life, and to the various values by which they live, and bit by bit we are all changing in adjustment to one another. International interdependence is a growing reality in the realms of trade and defense and in the world of ideas as well. Surely this fact must be reflected in international politics.

It is commonly stated that the ever-growing interdependence of nations is the main force that drives them to form international organizations.[6] This, of course, is true, but it is equally true that all nations are not dependent upon each other to the same degree or in the same way. Bulgaria is much more dependent upon the Soviet Union than the Soviet Union is dependent upon Bulgaria, and the United States depends upon its enemies in a different way than it depends upon its allies. These differences all fall within the realm of international interdependence, but the differences are significant when it comes to accounting for the kinds of organizations nations form and for the ways in which they use them.

There are some forms of interdependence that are not expressed in international organization at all. Certainly, the United States and Chile are interdependent, since the copper mined in Chile provides the sinews for many an American industry while the dollars earned from America provide Chile's major means of becoming a modern nation. Both nations need each other, but the need is by no means equal. Although the United States would be seriously inconvenienced if Chile were to hold out for a higher price or refuse to sell her copper, the Chilean economy would collapse if the United States refused to buy. Uncle Sam does not have to work through an international organization in order to influence Chile. The Yankee dollar speaks for itself.

The United States is not the only nation to meddle in its smaller

[6] See Werner Levi, *Fundamentals of World Organization* (Minneapolis: University of Minnesota Press, 1950), pp. 8, 46.

neighbors' business upon occasion, nor is money the only way to a nation's heart. As we have seen, the ways in which a major power can
dominate a small nation dependent upon it are many and subtle. The
point to be made here is that this kind of interdependence does not necessarily lead to the creation of international organizations. In the first
place, the dependence is bilateral; that is, it concerns only two nations,
and thus does not require any elaborate structures or formal organizations.
In the second place, it is so one-sided that the larger state can exercise
its influence directly without the necessity of invoking any international
principles or of bringing any other nations into the affair.

International organizations are formed where a number of nations
are involved and where each one feels it has something to gain by working
through a formal organization. A nation joins an international organization because it is aware that it depends upon other nations for the
achievement of some of its goals and because it sees in the organization
an essential means of cooperating with those with whom it agrees and
a useful channel for exerting pressure upon those with whom it disagrees.

More often than not, the nations that join together to form international organizations are already on friendly terms—they have come to
depend upon each other in many areas, and they are also likely to have
common goals. Yet unfriendly nations may also find reasons for forming
organizations with each other. A wise nation, like a wise man, keeps an
eye on what its enemies are doing, for enemies as well as friends are tied
together in this interdependent world. Unfriendly states may carefully
avoid entangling ties of trade and ideology, but within the military sphere,
they are securely bound to each other. London, Paris, and Bonn may
pressure Washington and may influence American military policy, but
in the last analysis it is our probable enemies who call the tune. Decisions
in Moscow and Peking determine the size of our armies, the location of
our bases, and the number of our allies. They set the odds that an American boy will be a G.I. before he's a B.A., that an American worker
will have a job making warplanes instead of washing machines, and they
ensure that Americans will groan when it comes time to pay their income
tax.[7]

Unfriendly states may be deeply affected by each other's actions, but
they lack the opportunities to influence each other through informal
channels that friends possess. They cannot send their leaders flying to
each other's capitals to talk things over without grave loss of face. Their
diplomats and businessmen do not maintain the myriad personal contacts

[7] In the United States budget proposed for fiscal 1969, 54 cents out of every budget
dollar went for national defense. United States Bureau of the Budget, *Budget of the
United States Government: Fiscal Year, 1969* (Washington, D.C., 1968), p. 542.

through which information and advice can be exchanged. Unfriendly states do not often belong to the same international organizations, but when they do, their common membership becomes all the more important since it provides one of the few and crucial links between them.

Both the League of Nations and the United Nations have included states that suspected, disliked, and even fought each other. This has not made things any easier for the organizations. The League, in fact, fell apart under the strain. As long as they can stand the tension, however, such organizations are of great importance. They are the sole expression of the interdependence that ties the fates of enemies together, and they provide one of the few avenues through which one rival power can influence another with any means but force or threat of force.

International interdependence is as much a reality as national sovereignty. National prosperity depends upon foreign raw materials, foreign markets, foreign financing, and foreign skills. National defense depends upon foreign bases, foreign friends and enemies. And national opinion depends at least in part upon foreign attitudes and values. Because of the many ties with other nations, national governments find that the achievement of their goals depends upon the behavior of others. This leads them to join international organizations, but they come to these organizations with all their sovereign powers, anxious to cooperate where they agree and to influence where they do not, but unwilling to yield what powers they have to any other group. To this unresolved conflict between national sovereignty and international interdependence we now turn our attention.

International Organization—The Great Inconsistency

Because nations are interdependent, they join international organizations, each one seeking an opportunity to influence or to control the decisions made by others in areas affecting it. Because nations are sovereign, each refuses to give to others the ability to control its actions and refuses to submit to the influence of others unless it will benefit from doing so, even in areas of vital interest to other nations. From the point of view of any one nation, this is perfectly consistent. To influence and not be influenced, to control and not be controlled, these are the aims of foreign policy.

From the point of view of the whole international community, however, such a situation is impossible. No one nation can control its destiny to the extent it wishes in an interdependent world as long as every other nation reserves the right to act as it chooses and retains the power to back up its choice. When nations are in agreement with each other, the inconsistency is not apparent. If your goals are my goals it does not matter that we each have the power to do as we please. But when nations disagree, the inconsistency is crucial, and because nations are so often in disagreement, the contradiction between sovereignty and interdependence has led to a series of curious compromises in the goals, in the powers, and in the procedures of international organizations.

The goals of international organizations both past and present may best be described as vague. The goal of the League of Nations as expressed in its Covenant was "to promote international cooperation and to achieve international peace and security." The United Nations' stated purpose is "to maintain international peace and security . . . to develop friendly relations among nations . . . to achieve international cooperation." The Charter of the World Health Organization, after having described health as "a state of complete physical, mental and social well-being and not merely the absence of disease or infirmity," declares the organization's objective to be "the attainment by all peoples of the highest possible level of health"; while collaboration among nations and universal respect for justice, for the rule of law, for human rights and fundamental freedoms are the goals of UNESCO.[8]

Some of the more specialized organizations, such as the International Labour Organisation, the International Bank, and the International Telecommunications Union have more specific goals, for the effects of the contradiction between sovereignty and interdependence are not so marked where the members of an organization can agree at least for certain special purposes. But where there is fundamental disagreement among the members, the effect upon the goals of international organizations has been to generate a fog of vagueness difficult to surpass.

Goals are left vague partly to make it easier to arouse worldwide public support for the new organizations. Justice, freedom, and security are time-worn words familiar to individuals the world over and possessed of many pleasant connotations. The appeal to a love of peace is not surprising when one considers that the major international organizations were formed during and immediately after man's most dreadful wars. The use of such universally accepted language does not in itself betoken any state of indecision. The failure to spell out these goals in any more definite fashion, however, must be viewed more seriously.

The major reason for the vagueness of international goals lies in the need to gloss over the divergent interests of the member nations. In an area where nations disagree, the more specific the goal, the smaller

[8] See United Nations, Department of Public Information, *Handbook of the United Nations and the Specialized Agencies* (New York: United Nations, 1949) for the goals of these and other organizations.

the group that will pledge itself to its pursuit. Colonial powers will not join an organization dedicated to the eradication of colonialism, and former colonies will shy away from a body designed to perpetuate the empires from which they have escaped, but everyone—colonizer, ex-colony, and colonized—will join an organization dedicated to freedom, for each may interpret the term in his own fashion.

Interdependent nations wishing to work together form international organizations, but in the cordial atmosphere of charter-signing, they often find it expedient to avoid immediate quarrels by not specifying too exactly just what the organization is for. "Who knows?" each nation thinks. Perhaps its view will triumph in the end, and for the moment there is nothing to lose and much to gain by agreeing to discuss the matter further at a later date. Vague goals make it possible for sovereign nations to talk and work together, even in areas where they are not in complete agreement.

Here we encounter a vicious circle, for if the goals of an organization are vague, nations will not give it the power to act. They have no assurance how these powers will be used, and blank checks are no more favored in international politics than elsewhere. If an organization deals with controversial matters and if it wants to include nations with varying points of view, its goals must be vague and its powers will consequently be slim. On the other hand, if an organization is to possess the power to act, its goals must be specific, and this will limit its membership to those nations that are already in agreement within a fairly narrow area. Hope for a worldwide organization with power to act in controversial areas would appear to be nil as long as nations persist in relinquishing power only for specific actions of which they already approve.

The conflict between sovereignty and interdependence is clear when nations are faced with the problem of giving power to the international organizations they create. With very few exceptions, the only power they see fit to grant is the power to recommend. Thus international bodies collect statistics, receive reports, record agreements, undertake research, consider principles, study programs, discuss disputes, draw up plans, develop programs, give advice, and prepare draft treaties for nations to sign, but on the whole, they do not act. They cannot put their recommendations into effect without the aid of each affected nation, and each member has retained its right to reject international recommendations if it wishes—or not to pay any attention to them at all.

It can, of course, be argued that members of an organization have a moral commitment to carry out its recommendations, particularly if the recommendations represent the opinion of the majority of the international community. This may be true. Certainly, the fact that an action is likely to arouse widespread disapproval among other nations is a fact that must be taken into account when a nation plans its policies. Unfortunately, experience has shown that moral commitments are not enough to deter nations from courses they find to their advantage. They avail themselves quite freely of their right to disregard the recommendations of the international bodies to which they belong.

Some of the specialized organizations have power to take action on their own, for their goals are more specific and their membership more limited, but even here the power to act is carefully limited to areas of agreement.

The major exception to the rule that international bodies can do no more than recommend is the United Nations Security Council, which can order certain actions taken to deal with a threat to the peace or an act of aggression, but here, too, the sovereignty of nations is protected. Council "orders" must be enforced by national governments, and even more important, the Council can issue no orders at all if just one of the five permanent members—the United States, Russia, Britain, France, or China—disagrees.

What nations have granted with one hand they have taken away with the other. Where international bodies have been given the power to act, the decision to exercise that power has been made subject to the individual approval of the body's most important members through a special voting procedure. A simple majority vote may be allowed for decisions of no particular importance, but major decisions require unanimous approval or the consent of all the great nations or the approval of the nation affected. These voting procedures are quite various, but they all boil down to a veto power for at least the major members and possibly for all. By one means or another, by a limitation of powers or by a crippling voting procedure, international organizations have been prevented from taking action contrary to the interests of their sovereign members.

As an American representative to the United Nations once stated candidly:

> The United Nations is *not* able to involve the United States in actions against our interests. There is only one organ of the United Nations that can take action which is legally binding. It is the Security Council, and there the United States is protected by the veto power. No other United Nations decision can be anything but recommendatory.[9]

[9] Henry Cabot Lodge, Jr., "An Answer to Critics of the U.N.," *The New York Times Magazine,* Nov. 22, 1953, p. 12.

The same could be said for the rest of the family of international or-ganizations.

The contradiction between national sovereignty and international interdependence has led nations to agree upon joint goals but to keep these goals as vague as possible. It has led nations to form organizations to carry out their goals but to withhold from these organizations the power to compel. This is no criticism of the organizations, for they merely mirror the world of international politics as it is. Those who find the organizations lacking cannot change the world by drawing up new charters, for behind the institutions lie the forces that have shaped them. It is these which must be altered. In the meantime, the international organizations that exist today may be extremely useful, even in this presently imperfect world, provided one does not expect them to behave as if the millennium had already arrived.

18

International Organizations

Given an understanding of the forces that have shaped modern international organizations and an awareness of the limitations on what we can expect of them, the task of the present chapter is relatively simple. We turn now to what is primarily a factual treatment of international organizations, beginning with a brief history, moving on to a description of the structure and procedures of the two great modern organizations, the League of Nations and the United Nations, pausing to look at the way in which they actually work, and concluding with an evaluation of the role such organizations play in international relations.

It is possible to trace the roots of international organization as far back as the ancient world, but for present purposes we will restrict ourselves almost entirely to the world that has existed since nation-states became the dominant form of political unit and since industrialization began to give international relations a new flavor.

The first modern steps toward international organization were taken, haltingly, at the end of the Napoleonic Wars. The timing was not a mere coincidence, for fear of war and of the collapse of the international order that so often accompanies war has been a major motive in driving nations to seek closer cooperation with each other.

Ad Hoc Conferences

Before Napoleon, in what was primarily a preindustrial era, nations were much less interdependent than they are today, and international co-operation was limited largely to the waging of wars and the division of the spoils after a war had been won. When the necessity arose, repre-sentatives of various nations met in a conference called especially for the occasion. After the business at hand was completed, the conference broke up, and a new conference was not called until a new group of nations felt it necessary to meet for some other specific purpose. Thus, the ad hoc conferences were occasional and haphazard. Certain pro-cedural etiquette was followed, but those who attended did not make any commitments in advance. They did not join any permanent organiza-tion. They were not pledged to reach any agreement. They were not even under any obligation to meet. They met as representatives of sovereign nations, and if they made any agreements, it was because it seemed in their interest to do so.

Periodic Conferences

The Napoleonic Wars, however, profoundly changed European politics. In several ways, these wars differed from previous conflicts. First of all, they involved a much larger number of fighting men than previous wars had. The effort to defeat Napoleon forced the other European nations to strain their human and material resources. In addition, the French armies had sown everywhere the seeds of revolution. Peace was neces-sary if the autocracies of Europe were to survive. The victorious powers who met at the Congress of Vienna decided that something more than occasional ad hoc conferences was required if they were to coordinate their efforts in enforcing peace, and so they agreed to meet periodically. Four meetings were held from 1818 to 1822. The meetings accomplished little, for the great powers could not agree, and they were abandoned after 1822, but they proved an interesting forerunner of the more formal organization created a hundred years later after another great war had shaken Europe and the world.

These early periodic conferences were limited to the great powers. After a series of unfortunate experiences with rebellious small powers at the Congress of Vienna, the great powers decided that their purposes could be better achieved if they restricted the membership to themselves.

The periodic conferences failed, for the great powers could not agree even among themselves, but the myth persists to this day that the great powers can accomplish most and reach the highest level of agreement if they are allowed to discuss world problems in secret, unencumbered by the presence of other nations.

After the periodic conferences were abandoned, nations returned to the old technique of meeting ad hoc on rare occasions when they felt a meeting was necessary. This system continued throughout the nineteenth century and was the only form of international political coordination until the League of Nations was created. Even today, ad hoc meetings of the great powers continue side by side with the more regular meetings of the United Nations.

Functional Organizations

Meanwhile a new form of organization made its appearance—the functional organization. Unlike the political conferences that preceded them and the worldwide political organizations that were to follow, the functional organizations were not concerned primarily with power relations among nations or with the maintenance of peace and security. These organizations had far more limited purposes. They were technical organizations designed to provide machinery by which a number of nations could cooperate on specific common problems. Specific organizations included the International Statistical Institute, founded in 1853; the European Danube Commission, set up by treaty in 1856; the Geodetic Union, formed in 1864; the Universal Postal Union (1874); the International Bureau of Weights and Measures (1875); the International Union of Railway Freight Transportation (1890); the International Institute of Agriculture (1905); and the International Office of Public Health (1907), to name only a few of the earliest and most important of a long list of organizations.

The appearance of these new organizations was an indication of the increasing interdependence of modern nations. No matter how bitterly they might oppose each other, nations were finding that their increased communication and trade with each other made it necessary for them to cooperate, at least within very limited spheres.

Individual functional organizations have come and gone, but on the whole, this form of international organization has flourished. When the League of Nations was created, several functional organizations were put under its direction and others continued to exist alongside it. Many of the earlier organizations continue to operate to this day, and in addition a group of the most important functional organizations, some of them new, have been integrated into the United Nations system, where they are known as specialized agencies. Although it may be chronologically a bit out of place, it will perhaps be best to discuss the specialized agencies here, for the things that we have to say about the other functional organizations apply to them as well. There are at present fourteen specialized agencies. They are:

The International Labour Organisation (ILO), which circulates information, sends out technical experts, and draws up conventions (treaties) and regulations concerning labor problems such as wages, working conditions, employment, and the right to organize. The conventions and regulations, however, must be ratified by the member nations before they go into effect.

The World Health Organization (WHO), which also draws up conventions for ratification by members, makes regulations regarding sanitary and quarantine requirements and other procedures to prevent the spread of disease, and adopts standards for the safety, purity, potency, labeling, and advertising of medicines moving in international trade. WHO also offers technical assistance to nations requesting it and gives some emergency aid to nations stricken with epidemics or the like.

The International Monetary Fund (IMF), which buys and sells currencies in an attempt to stabilize exchange and also tries to discourage competitive import restrictions and currency devaluation (without much success so far).

The International Bank for Reconstruction and Development (or World Bank), which makes loans to governments or private parties and also offers some technical assistance in financial matters. The Bank has been accused of being overly cautious. Both the Monetary Fund and the Bank have weighted voting systems which allow them, practically speaking, to be dominated by the United States. Two other specialized agencies affiliated with the Bank are The International Development Association (IDA) and The International Finance Corporation (IFC).

The Food and Agriculture Organization of the United Nations (FAO), which has proposed some ambitious schemes for the international distribution of food, none of which has been accepted, and which consequently has had to content itself largely with circulating information and instruction on techniques for improving agricultural production. FAO also participates in technical assistance projects.

The United Nations Educational, Scientific and Cultural Organization (UNESCO), an organization which encourages educational and cultural cooperation through a rather diffuse set of activities. It is best noted for making studies and for some pilot projects in promoting literacy.

The International Civil Aviation Organization (ICAO), which draws up conventions, recommends standards, and circulates information about a kind of international cooperation that, in practice, is carried on mainly outside the ICAO by means of bilateral agreements and national laws.

The Universal Postal Union (UPU), one of the most successful of international organizations. It regulates international mail exchange and includes among its members nearly every nation in the world.

Other specialized agencies whose work does not require description are: The International Telecommunications Union (ITU), The World Meteorological Organization (WMO), The Inter-governmental Maritime Consultative Organization (IMCO), and the International Atomic Energy Agency.

In addition, there are two former specialized agencies, now defunct: The United Nations Relief and Reconstruction Administration (UNRRA), which spent nearly $4 billion on postwar relief before it was terminated in 1947; and The International Refugee Organization (IRO), which ran camps for war refugees and helped to get them repatriated or resettled in other countries. It was ended in 1951.

An International Trade Organization (ITO), planned when the UN was set up, did not come into existence because of the United States' refusal to join it. Some of its aims, however, were embodied in the General Agreement on Tariffs and Trade (GATT), a multilateral agreement establishing ground rules for international trade. Members of GATT meet periodically and the organization serves as a center for negotiations to reduce trade barriers and to settle trade disputes. It is not, however, a specialized agency of the United Nations. Neither are the United Nations Industrial Development Organization (UNIDO), concerned with the stimulation of industrial activities, nor the United Nations Conference on Trade and Development (UNCTAD). Both were created by the UN General Assembly, the latter on the initiative of the less developed countries in reaction to what they considered a lack of action from GATT in dealing with their special trade problems.

The functional organizations differ from ordinary international conferences in several important respects. Most important and most obvious, they are permanent organizations whose members meet regularly whether or not there is any particular problem requiring attention. In this respect, they are natural successors to the earlier periodic conferences.

A second difference is that the functional organizations have permanent offices and staffs that continue to conduct the affairs of the organization between meetings. Sometimes these staffs do little more than keep records and write letters to the member governments, but in other cases they carry on extensive activities that represent the heart of the work of the organization.

A third difference is that the decisions of functional organizations are often reached by majority vote. In theory, this is an important distinction. At an ordinary international conference, the representatives of nations meet and talk, but no decisions are binding upon nations that do not wish to be bound. A recalcitrant nation may be put in the embarrassing position of being a minority of one. It may even break up the conference and be blamed publicly for its failure, but it cannot be compelled to participate in any decision it does not like. Each nation, in effect, has a veto. Decisions can be reached only by unanimous vote. In the functional organizations, on the other hand, decisions can be made *even over the objections of some of the members.*

In practice, however, the difference is not as great as it seems, for the powers of the functional organizations are limited primarily to making recommendations. The conventions drawn up are only draft conventions. They must still be ratified by the member states before they go into effect. The regulations made are subject to the approval of the nations whose activities are to be regulated. The standards set are only recommendations. The technical assistance goes only to nations that request it for purposes they approve. With the single exception of the Postal Union,[1] membership in a functional organization does not commit the members to anything in advance. They may be voted down when it comes to making recommendations, but no one can force them to do what is recommended against their wishes.

The important thing, of course, is that the members of functional organizations often wish to cooperate. Because functional organizations deal with technical matters and because their aims are specific and their membership limited to interested nations, a fairly high level of agreement can often be maintained among the members. This is particularly true in the more technical and less controversial of the organizations, such

[1] Conventions can be adopted by the Postal Union by majority vote and if they are ratified by a majority of the members, they go into effect automatically, even for those nations that oppose them. A nation that objects can, of course, withdraw from the Union, but to do so would deprive the nation of mail communication with the rest of the world.

as those dealing with communication. The more ambitious organizations that deal with matters closer to the core of power, such as trade, tariffs, the distribution of food and commodities, and currency regulation, have met with less success. The refusal of nations to agree on these matters or to give up their national prerogatives has led them to withhold all real power from the organizations concerned.

THE FUNCTIONAL APPROACH

It is sometimes suggested that because the functional organizations seem to operate more effectively than the political organizations such as the major bodies of the League and the United Nations, it would be wise to concentrate more on them and less on the political organs. The argument runs: Nations at present may fail to agree and cooperate on the solution of political problems, but to attempt to solve these problems first is to put the cart before the horse. One must begin in areas where nations already agree. If nations cooperate in these areas, ties among them will multiply, and eventually perhaps they can even solve their political problems. Making progress where progress can be made will help to create the foundations for an international community. Only after this foundation is sufficiently stable can we create the kind of framework within which political problems can be solved successfully. The "functionalists" see the nonpolitical approach of the functional organizations as offering the greatest hope for the eventual solution of political problems.

The argument has a certain appeal. Full-scale cooperation on matters of trade and production and health and transportation and a thousand other "technical" matters *would* have a salutary effect upon political cooperation. The two areas are certainly related, and progress in one area should affect the other, but—and here is the catch—by the same token, failure in one area should also affect the other. The fact is that the nations of the world do *not* agree on matters of politics, and whether their disagreements are fought out in international political organizations like the United Nations Security Council or at old-time international conferences or on the battlefields, their political disagreement impedes cooperation in other spheres.

Food distribution and trade, for example, are not as "technical" and "nonpolitical" as one might think. True, there is general agreement that people should not starve, but the availability of food depends upon methods of production and distribution, and on both of these there is serious disagreement. High production of foodstuffs is not simply a matter of introducing better tools and a few simple techniques: it is influenced by the size of the landholdings, by the form of land tenure, by whether landlords are absentee or owner-operators, by the kind of incentives given to agricultural labor, by the kind of education given to those who manage agricultural enterprises, in short, by the entire social structure. Distribution of food is an even touchier matter, for it is but one facet of the larger problem of the distribution of wealth, both within each nation and among the nations of the world. It is hard to think of a problem more "political" than this.

World trade is also highly political, for nations use their power to improve their terms of trade, to exploit their dependencies economically, and to protect themselves from the competition of others. Such matters as tariffs, import restrictions, commodity control, and dumping are heavily influenced by internal politics and by the power of various economic interests within each nation. It is impossible to separate these matters from politics.

Even health may have its political aspects, as the withdrawal of the Soviet bloc from WHO and its subsequent return indicate quite clearly. Communists and non-Communists may agree on mail deliveries, but they find it difficult to agree on matters touching the economic system or social welfare. Indeed, Communist participation in the specialized agencies has been extremely spotty. They are, on the whole, organizations of the Western and uncommitted nations, and even these nations have not been able to agree enough to grant the organizations wide powers.

The simple truth is that politics is not an area removed from economic and social arrangements. Nations use their power to achieve economic and social goals, and their economic wealth and social well-being are, in turn, sources of power. Like it or not, the functional organizations are involved in politics, and as long as political disagreement divides nations, their work will suffer. Political disagreement impedes the work of the functional organizations, just as economic and social disagreement impedes the work of the security organizations. There appears to be no escape from the conclusion that so-called political and nonpolitical problems must be solved together. We could not, if we wished, confine our efforts to one area and expect progress in the other to follow automatically.

Limited International Organizations

In addition to the functional organizations, which are limited in purpose, there exist a number of international organizations that are limited in membership as well. Often, but not always, they are regional organizations, and often too, their membership is limited to a small number of states. The several dozen such organizations are a heterogeneous lot, but it is possible to classify the most important into three broad groups: those concerned primarily with security; those concerned with economic cooperation; and those with broad purposes such as unity and general coordination of activities among the members.

The security organizations are probably the most studied and the most often discussed. Among the most important are the North Atlantic Treaty Organization (NATO), the Southeast Asia Treaty Organization (SEATO), the Organization of American States (OAS), and the Warsaw Pact.

NATO, formed in 1949, allies thirteen Western European nations (Belgium, Denmark, France, Greece, Iceland, Italy, Luxembourg, the Netherlands, Norway, Portugal, Turkey, the United Kingdom, and West Germany) with the United States and Canada in a mutual promise to consider an armed attack against any one of them as an attack against all. The defense policies, strategies and operational activities of all except France are closely coordinated through a permanent council, a secretariat, a military committee composed of the fourteen chiefs of staff, and several combined commands.

SEATO, formed in 1954, was designed as a parallel alliance against possible Communist aggression in Southeast Asia and the Southwest Pacific. It joins Australia, New Zealand, Pakistan, Thailand, and the Philippines with the United States, the United Kingdom, and France in a treaty of mutual defense. It has proved an ineffective alliance because of the refusal of such major Southeast Asian nations as India, Indonesia, and Burma to join it and because the members have not agreed on military policy in the area, for example, in the Vietnamese war.

The OAS is an organization of wide aims formed by the United States and nineteen Latin-American states in 1948. As a security organization, it pledges its members to peaceful settlement of their own differences and to mutual assistance against aggression, armed or otherwise, against any member. Cooperation in matters of security is coordinated through the Inter-American Defense Board in Washington. The OAS supported the United States in the Cuban missile crisis of 1962 and in its intervention in the Dominican Republic in 1965.

The Warsaw Pact is the Communist equivalent to NATO. Formed in 1955 to counter West Germany's admission to NATO, it links the Soviet Union and the East European nations in a mutual defense pact and coordinates their military activities through a Joint Armed Forces Command with a Soviet commander-in-chief. Common policies are formed by a Political Consultative Committee.

I LOVE BILL

All these security organizations have in common the fact that they ally the dominant nation of an international order (either the United States or the Soviet Union) with other members of the order who may wish its military assistance. Some of the arrangements seem designed to maximize the military power of the collectivity; others have the effect of giving the dominant nation a legal basis for military intervention in a crisis. In all these organizations, the dominant nation has a privileged status in spite of the fact that formal equality prevails among the members, and this privileged position has led to dissension within both the Western alliances and the Warsaw Pact. Perhaps the most dramatic evidence of this dissension has been the withdrawal of France from the military (though not the political) organization of NATO.

Some of the limited organizations have concerned themselves with economic as well as military and political problems. This is particularly true of the Organization of American States, which maintains a close relationship with the Inter-American Development Bank, the United Nations Economic Commission for Latin America, and the Alliance for Progress. In Western Europe, economic organizations have for the most part excluded the United States and have formed around two groups: the Community of the Six (France, West Germany, Italy, Belgium, the Netherlands, and Luxembourg); and the Outer Seven or European Free Trade Association (the United Kingdom, Denmark, Norway, Sweden, Austria, Portugal, and Switzerland). Both groups are joined in the Organization for Economic Cooperation and Development (OECD) along with some other nations, but they have not formed a single economic community. The most effective group is the Community of the Six, which has formed three constituent groups: the Common Market or European Economic Community (EEC); the Coal and Steeel Community (ECSC); and the European Atomic Energy Community (Euratom). The Soviet Union has formed a roughly parallel organization in Eastern Europe, the Council for Mutual Economic Assistance (COMECON), but it has been troubled by dissension and by the withdrawal of Albania and Rumania.

Still other limited international organizations are composed of members brought together by cultural, historic, economic, and political affinities, but for less clearly defined purposes. The League of Arab States provides a good example. Its members include Arab states from

Iraq to Morocco, but they have been able to agree on little save enmity toward Israel. The Organization of African Unity, a similar grouping, has also been relatively unsuccessful in creating greater unity among its members. Also included in this category would be the British Commonwealth, a remnant of empire without any central control in which former British colonies cooperate and consult with each other and with Britain on almost any matter that concerns them. The French Community, which was formed in 1959 to retain a tie between France and her former African colonies, is no longer very effective.

A survey of the organizations of limited membership suggests several tentative conclusions: First, international organizations with limited membership and narrow purposes are no more successful than more universal and broader organizations. Second, although the usefulness of such organizations is often of fairly brief duration, the members usually refuse to let them die. Third, the benefits derived from international organizations are in direct proportion to the degree of political and economic development of their members.

The League of Nations

Of greater significance than any of the organizations thus far discussed is the kind of permanent worldwide organization that first appeared after World War I in the form of the League of Nations. Before that time, the great powers had joined functional organizations, made alliances, and met and made joint decisions whenever particular diplomatic crises arose, but they had felt no need for a permanent general organization.

The eruption of World War I brought a sudden end to a century of relative peace and nearly brought down the Anglo-French international order as well. The war threw Russia into the arms of bolshevism, left Italy and Germany so weakened that they soon fell prey to totalitarianism, exhausted France, and revealed, for the first time, England's dependence upon the United States. The old order emerged victorious, but it was clear to the winners that the order itself might not survive another such war. There were imperative reasons for preventing such a conflict.

Ideas of worldwide international organization had long been discussed. Now was the time to put them into effect. Hungry for permanent peace, the victorious Allies created the League of Nations and looked to it to preserve their security through the operation of open diplomacy and collective security.

At first the League was an organization of the war victors, but the expectation was that it should eventually include all the nations of the world. It never did. Most of the major nations joined the League (Germany was finally admitted in 1926), but the United States refused. President Wilson had been one of the major architects of the League, and many of its provisions had been designed to offset possible American objections. The decision of the Senate not to ratify the Treaty of Versailles, which contained the Covenant of the League of Nations, can best be explained as due to internal American politics, but it was a devastating blow to the new international organization. The membership of the League was further depleted when Germany, Italy, and Japan withdrew in order to be free to challenge the existing order, and when Russia was expelled in 1939 for attacking Finland.

Throughout its history, then, the League was dominated by the Western powers. It owed its creation primarily to the United States, Britain, and France, and in its operation it was dominated by the British and the French. It was from the beginning an organization designed not only to ensure world peace but also to perpetuate the international order headed by the three great Western powers.

It must be clearly understood that the League was not an international government. Like the functional organizations before it, it was a voluntary association of sovereign states whose members accepted certain moral and financial responsibilities set forth in the Covenant but nothing more. The League possessed no power to compel its members to do anything. Indeed, it could not even reach important decisions without a unanimous vote of all its members, a distinct step backward compared to some of the functional organizations. Once a decision had been reached by the League, it could be put into effect only through the efforts of the individual members. One cannot help wondering what the United States feared in refusing to join such a weak organization.

Three separate bodies were included in the League of Nations system: the League itself; the International Labour Organisation, now one of the specialized agencies of the United Nations; and the Permanent Court of International Justice, which could give advisory opinions on international law when it was asked and could rule on legal disputes between nations provided the nations agreed to accept its jurisdiction. We shall concentrate here on the League itself, which consisted of an assembly, a council, and a secretariat.

THE SECRETARIAT

The secretariat was a permanent staff of international civil servants who did not themselves make policy but who serviced the other organs of the League. It was headed by a Secretary-General and at its height included more than 700 individuals of many different nationalities. Ideally, these people in their official work for the League were supposed to have primary allegiance to the international organization, not to the state of which they were nationals. This is an important point, for the ability of international organizations to grow in effectiveness depends in part upon the ability of all men everywhere to transfer their allegiance to international institutions. It was hoped that a truly international secretariat would represent a modest step in that direction.

National governments, however, particularly those of the great powers, were not willing to relinquish control, even over the secretariat. In spite of repeated declarations that the first loyalty of the secretariat was to the League, many of the most important officials continued to act, in effect, as representatives of their nations. A system was worked out whereby each of the great powers in the League could select a national who was then officially appointed an Under-Secretary of the League. Lesser officials were supposed to be appointed for their ability and character alone, but in practice, care was taken to see that various nationalities were represented by an appropriate number of appointments, and loyalty to the nation of origin was considered an essential qualification for appointment to the secretariat. The Italian and German governments, in particular, sought to maintain strict control over all their citizens who worked for the League.

THE ASSEMBLY

The two main organs of the League were the assembly and the council. The assembly was the larger of the two, for it included representatives of every member nation. In many ways, the assembly resembled a periodic international conference. It met regularly once a year (and also held occasional special sessions), each nation had one vote, and all decisions except procedural questions required a unanimous vote. In other words, it was a place where the diplomatic representatives of nations could exchange views and arrive at agreements if they wished to. Like an international conference, the assembly sometimes drew up treaties for ratification by the member nations. It also passed resolutions that were, in effect, recommendations as far as the members were concerned.

The assembly had fairly broad authority. Indeed, in most matters, no clear line separated its work from that of the council. A dispute between the members of the League, for example, could be brought before either the assembly or the council. However, the assembly alone had the power to admit new members of the League, to elect the nonpermanent members of the council, to advise reconsideration of existing treaties, and to control the finances of the League.

In spite of the broad responsibilities of the assembly, the council was the more important body. Designed originally as a nine-nation body, it eventually was enlarged to include representatives of fourteen nations. The great powers (Great Britain, France, Italy, Japan, and later, Germany and the Soviet Union) were given permanent seats on the council,[2] and the other members were elected by the assembly for short terms.

As in the assembly, each member of the council had one vote, and unanimous approval was required for nonprocedural decisions. Thus the council meetings resembled periodic conferences of the world's great powers (except for the United States) with a few smaller nations allowed to attend and take part in the deliberations. The importance of the council stemmed not from its powers, which were much like those of the assembly, but from the fact that it was dominated by the great nations who, in fact, dominated world politics. Nations usually sent their foreign ministers or their prime ministers to council meetings, which were therefore brilliant diplomatic gatherings including many of the most prominent statesmen of the day. The council was required to meet at least once a year, but actually it met more often. Undoubtedly these frequent meetings of top diplomats afforded the major nations of the world an unparalleled opportunity to cooperate with each other, had they wished to do so. In the absence of such a wish, however, there was little that the council could do.

The council had a number of powers that were not granted to the assembly. It approved staff appointments to the secretariat, it supervised the holding of mandates, and according to the Covenant, it was given primary responsibility for the series of steps by which disputes between nations were to be settled, although the assembly too could consider disputes and suggest settlements. The handling of wars or threats of war and the punishment of aggressors was the business of the council, although it must be stressed that the only action the council could take in such cases was "to advise upon the means" by which aggression could be prevented and "to recommend to the several Governments concerned what effective military, naval or air force the Members of the League shall severally contribute" to protect the victim of aggression. The action itself would be taken by the national governments *if* they chose to heed the advice and follow the recommendations.

[2] A permanent seat on the council had also been planned for the United States.

The League of Nations accomplished a good deal in its relatively brief existence. It published many useful reports and studies, it administered the Saar Territory until that region voted to return to Germany, it administered the Free City of Danzig until Hitler seized it, and it maintained at least some supervision over the governing of the mandates. The League also helped a great many Russian, Greek, Armenian, and Turkish refugees to find new homes.

But the League failed dismally in its major task, the maintenance of international peace. When the final tally was made, the League had a few minor successes to its credit. It had settled a dispute between Sweden and Finland over some islands; it had drawn a new boundary for Upper Silesia; it had averted a war between Greece and Bulgaria over a border shooting; it had stopped a war between Peru and Colombia over a disputed border area.

Its failures, unfortunately, were more impressive. A dispute between Poland and Lithuania continued for ten years or more despite efforts of the League to settle it, as did a later war between Bolivia and Paraguay. A dispute between Hungary and Rumania remained on the council agenda for seven years before it was finally settled. When Italy seized Corfu from Greece in 1923, Greece was left to surrender to Italian pressure.

The most serious failures, however, involved the growing challenge of the Axis nations. When Japan seized Manchuria from China in 1931, the League council asked Japan to withdraw her troops. Japan refused. The council then sent a commission of inquiry which made recommendations. Japan ignored them. The assembly then condemned Japan, and she withdrew from the League of Nations, keeping Manchuria.

When Italy invaded Ethiopia in 1935, the story was repeated. The council ruled that Italy had resorted to war contrary to the Covenant and called for economic sanctions, but England and France were opposed to strong action against Italy, and the United States was aloof. Meanwhile, Italy conquered Ethiopia. In 1936 the sanctions were lifted, leaving Italy in possession of her prey.

When the Spanish Civil War broke out in 1936 and Germany and Italy recognized and began to aid General Franco's rebels, the Spanish government appealed to the League council. The council, however, considered the dispute a domestic affair and took no action.

The League *did* act against the Japanese invasion of China in 1937, but to no avail. When China appealed to the council, the council condemned the Japanese bombing of open towns and the assembly passed a resolution calling a conference which the Japanese refused to attend. The conference met and reaffirmed some moral principles; the council later passed a resolution deploring the situation, but the Japanese advance continued.

When Germany seized Danzig in 1939, the League did not move; and when Germany invaded Poland in the same year, no one even thought of appealing to the League. The League was dead, although it lingered on, a legal ghost, until the United Nations took its place.

In retrospect, it is perfectly clear that the League should not have been expected to succeed. Armed only with the weapons of diplomacy, it was sent into battle against the toughest challengers the international order had yet met. Persuasion was fine for nations that wanted to reach agreement, but it was of no avail against those that did not. Presumably, the League might have succeeded in its task had its members been willing to put collective security into practice, but of course they were not. Germany did not act alone. She had the support of Italy and Japan, and together these three constituted a force so powerful that mere warnings of collective action would not have turned them back. Censure by the League was meaningless when the United States looked the other way and Britain and France were afraid to act and Russia made deals with the aggressors. By the time the Western powers finally rose to meet with force the challenge to their order, the League was dead and the challenge could be put down only through the very war the League had been designed to prevent.

The United Nations

While the war was still in progress, the Allies determined that a new international organization should be created to take the place of the League, and even before Germany surrendered, the essentials of the new organization were hammered out by the United States, Britain, Russia, and China at the Dumbarton Oaks meeting in 1944. Again the international organization was the creation of the victors of a world war, but this time it included among its members from the very start both the dominant nation of the world (the United States) and the major challenger of the future (the Soviet Union).

The United Nations was officially born at San Francisco in 1945. Although its original members were all nations that had either fought against the Axis or that had at least declared their sympathies by becoming theoretical combatants at the last moment, it was intended that the organization have universal membership, and in fact, most of the other nations in the world were admitted in the years that followed. Two major nations still remain outside the United Nations: Germany, her admission delayed by her division into East and West Germany; and Communist China, her admission delayed by American insistence that the Chinese Nationalists on Formosa are still the legal government of China. However, it is likely that both nations will be admitted to the United Nations in the not too distant future.

The United Nations differs from the League in several respects, but the most important difference is that the United Nations has as a member the most powerful nation on earth. Since both the principles and the interests of the United States at present are firmly opposed to allowing the United Nations to be destroyed, the new organization has a considerably better chance for survival than its unfortunate predecessor. The United Nations also places greater emphasis upon economic and social problems. The League, of course, did provide for work on such problems, but it was primarily a security organization. When the United Nations was being planned, Britain and Russia were concerned mainly with its security functions, but thanks largely to American influence, the scope of United Nations' activities was extended to include economic and social problems.

The major organs of the United Nations are the General Assembly, similar in many respects to the assembly of the League; three councils: the Security Council, the Trusteeship Council, and the Economic and Social Council; and the International Court of Justice, in reality a continuation of the older court under a slightly different name. The United Nations also has a large secretariat staff compared to the relatively small number who served the League of Nations.

THE GENERAL ASSEMBLY

The General Assembly, like the assembly of the League, consists of representatives of every nation that belongs to the international organization, and each nation has one vote, no matter how small and powerless it may be. Unlike the League, however, unanimity is not required to reach decisions. The General Assembly operates by majority rule, some matters requiring a simple majority, others a two-thirds majority, but none unanimous consent. Thus it is possible for even the United States to be outvoted in the General Assembly, although such an event has not often occurred.

Given the voting system, one would not expect the General Assembly to have extensive powers, for the United States, Britain, and Russia would never grant much power to a body in which their combined voting strength was no greater than that of Lebanon, Liberia, and Luxembourg, for example. And in fact, the assembly, like its predecessor, can only recommend; the members are left completely free to accept or disregard the recommendations as they please.

The General Assembly has a regular session each year and has also held a number of special sessions, for the regular meetings have not proved sufficient to deal with the avalanche of matters brought before it. The jurisdiction of the assembly is extremely broad, for it can discuss and make recommendations on any international matter that falls within the purview of the United Nations. It is the assembly's job to coordinate and supervise the work of all the councils. It receives reports from each of them and exercises control over their budgets and finances. It shares with the Security Council the job of admitting and expelling members and the choosing of the Secretary-General, who heads the secretariat. Alone, it elects the nonpermanent members of all three councils.

In addition, the assembly has usurped some of the powers originally intended for the Security Council. The United Nations Charter clearly gave the Security Council primary responsibility for the maintenance of peace and security, although it granted the assembly secondary responsibility in this area. Because the Security Council itself was so often deadlocked by disagreement among the great powers, a tendency arose to shift to the General Assembly matters that became stalemated in the Security Council, or even to take disputes directly to the assembly in order to avoid a deadlock that could be foreseen. In 1950, the assembly, prodded by the United States, passed what is known as the "Uniting for Peace Resolution," in which it served notice that if the Security Council was prevented by the veto from acting against an aggressor, the assembly would step in and make recommendations to the members on what action they should take. For the next decade, the assembly seemed to have gained the upper hand over the Security Council. In recent years, however, the council has resumed some of its former importance. Before examining the reasons for these somewhat unexpected shifts, we had best examine the workings of the Security Council in more detail.

THE SECURITY COUNCIL

The Security Council was designed for speed and given what appeared to be extensive powers. Only 15 nations are members of the council, 5 permanent members (the United States, the Soviet Union, Britain, France, and China) and 10 other members elected by the General Assembly for two-year terms. Each member of the council is supposed to keep a representative at UN headquarters at all times so that the council can act quickly if the need arises.

The Security Council is empowered by the Charter to recommend the means by which nations in dispute should settle their differences peacefully or to recommend the terms of settlement if other methods fail. If a nation threatens the peace, breaks the peace, or commits an act of aggression, the council may call upon the members of the United Nations to apply whatever sanctions it feels are necessary, including the severance of diplomatic relations, economic sanctions, and military measures. The members of the United Nations agreed, when they signed the Charter, to make agreements with the Security Council so that armed forces of all the members would be made available to the council for use in maintaining peace.

Certainly, these appear to be real powers. Furthermore, because the Security Council is dominated by the great powers, a decision, once taken, should mean action. But these same great powers, as one would surely expect, have protected themselves with a number of safeguards, and these safeguards have all but completely destroyed the effectiveness of the council in maintaining international peace.

The Security Council can only "recommend" the peaceful settlement of international disputes, and although it can "call upon" the member nations to apply sanctions against an aggressor, there is nothing to guarantee that nations will heed the call. Significantly enough, the agreements by which armed forces were to be made available to the Security Council have never been negotiated.

The major protection of the great powers, however, lies in the famous veto. Decisions in the Security Council are made by a majority vote of nine members. If the decision concerns a matter of substance and not a mere question of procedure, however, the majority *must* include all five of the permanent members. In other words, by its single negative vote or "veto," any one of the five great powers can prevent a decision.

The arguments presented at San Francisco by the great powers in justification of the veto read today as an amazing example of hypocrisy. The great powers argued then that the veto was a privilege proportionate to their greater responsibility in keeping world peace. It is certainly true that the great powers do have a greater responsibility, but it is difficult to see how the veto helps them to discharge it. When a great power votes affirmatively to have the council take action to maintain world peace, its vote counts no more than that of any other nation; but when a great power votes "no" to prevent the council from acting, its single vote counts more than that of all the other members combined. The veto was designed to prevent action, not to further it, as everyone at San Francisco knew perfectly well. It was also argued by the great powers that the veto would force them to compromise and to agree, but it has not worked out this way in practice. On the contrary, knowing that no action can be taken against its wishes, a great power in the minority has no reason to budge an inch.

The representatives of the small powers at San Francisco bitterly fought the veto, but their logical arguments were to no avail. What gave the great powers their victory was their clear statement on more than one occasion that they would not join the United Nations unless they were assured a veto.

The Security Council was built upon the hopeful assumption that the great powers would agree and upon the fatalistic assumption that if they did not agree, there was nothing the rest of the world could do about it anyway. Agreement among the Big Five was considered essential to peace and progress in international relations. The Security Council was supposed to offer the best possible conditions for producing such agreement, for it provided frequent occasions for high-ranking diplomats of these nations to meet together without too many small nations to clutter up the meeting table.

In practice, the council has been used for quite different purposes. Disagreements between the dominant Western powers and the Russian challenger soon flared into the open, and the West found that it commanded a permanent majority in both the Security Council and the General Assembly. Council discussions were rarely used to reach compromises. They became instead a series of bitter debates at the end of which the Western nations pushed their proposals to a vote, forcing the Russians to use their veto and expose themselves to unfavorable public opinion, in the West at least. In time, however, the game became tiresome. Faced with a string of Soviet vetoes, the Security Council could not act. It could not even recommend that Communist nations be censured for misbehavior.

In these circumstances, the United States turned to the General Assembly to accomplish what the Security Council could not. In the assembly, the numerical majority that could be mustered by the West was even greater, and decisions detrimental to Russian interests could not be vetoed. True, the assembly could take no action on its own, but it could put the Russians legally and politically in the wrong. With this end in view, the Western powers encouraged the General Assembly to take on new powers, and the Security Council went into an eclipse from which it has only recently begun to emerge. The Western powers particularly have had cause to regret the increased power they have given to the assembly, for the one-nation–one-vote rule enables the small powers to outvote the great. When the assembly was given this added moral power at the instigation of the West, the members could be counted upon to vote with the West, and particularly with the United States, upon demand. But the admission of many new nations to the membership in recent years has made the American hold on the General Assembly somewhat uncertain. On issues that affect their lives, the new nations have had little hesitation in bolting the ranks. The United States is finding it more and more difficult to keep control, and this situation is likely to continue.

THE ECONOMIC AND SOCIAL COUNCIL

The Economic and Social Council is a departure from League experience and a step forward, for the aggressive entrance of the world's major international organization into the economic and social fields was long overdue. The Economic and Social Council has twenty-seven members elected by the General Assembly. In theory, there are no permanent members, but in practice, the Big Five have always been reelected. The Economic and Social Council operates by simple majority vote on all questions, but it can do no more than make recommendations and studies.

Specifically, the council is empowered to make studies and reports on "international economic, social, cultural, educational, health, and related matters" and to make recommendations about these matters and about "human rights and fundamental freedoms." It can also prepare draft conventions and call international conferences. Whatever judgment one may make of the activities of the Economic and Social Council or of the effectiveness of the United Nations as a whole, there is general agreement that many of the studies made under the auspices of this council have brought forth important and interesting information on major economic and social problems. Such studies in themselves will not solve the problems, but the knowledge gained through studies of this kind is necessary if the problems are ever to be solved.

The Economic and Social Council is also entrusted with the task of coordinating the activities of the specialized agencies, a task that has not been marked by great success, for the agencies, on the whole. have preferred to guard their independence.

One unique feature of the council is the fact that it is not limited to dealing with the representatives of national governments but allows the representatives of nongovernmental organizations to participate in its deliberations. These private individuals cannot speak or vote, but they can attend meetings and propose items for the council to consider along with written statements in support of their proposals. Whether or not this will set an important precedent for international organizations remains to be seen.

The Trusteeship Council has been the organ responsible for supervising the administration of trust territories by members of the United Nations. We have already noted in Chapter 10 that the trust territories, despite their new legal status, have been little different from ordinary colonies in actuality. Because the trust territories—with few exceptions—have become independent, the Trusteeship Council itself is now in a state of limbo.

The trust areas originally assigned to the council included all former mandates that had not yet achieved their independence (except for South-West Africa, which the Union of South Africa has refused to put under trusteeship) and two territories that were conquered from the Axis nations during World War II: Somaliland, a former Italian colony in Africa that was administered by Italy as a trust territory, and the Trust Territory of the Pacific Islands, former Japanese colonies now administered by the United States. These last islands, however, are not a regular trust territory supervised by the Trusteeship Council but are instead a "strategic trust area" supervised by the Security Council. This arrangement was insisted upon by the United States in order to give herself fuller control of these strategic islands. The United Nations Charter also provides that any nation can voluntarily place territories it administers under trusteeship, but there have been no such offers to date, nor is it likely that there will be.

Trust territories, like colonies, have been administered by the nation that controlled them. The "supervision" exercised by the Trusteeship Council consisted of sending a questionnaire to the administering nations each year, discussing the answers, and making recommendations that were then submitted to the General Assembly. In addition, the Trusteeship Council sent visiting missions to each trust territory every three years or so and considered petitions from people who live in the trust territories. The council could submit an administering nation to unpleasant publicity and uncomfortable questioning, but it could not compel it to change its behavior in any way.

In practice, the Trusteeship Council has been fairly soft upon the administering nations. This is partly because of the composition of the council. It has included as permanent members all the nations that administer a trust territory, as well as all the Big Five, even those who do not administer any territories (Russia and China). It has also included a number of nonpermanent members elected by the General Assembly. It was specified originally that there had to be always an equal number of administering and nonadministering nations on the Trusteeship Council.

Since the council operated by majority rule and the administering nations customarily voted together as a bloc, this had the effect of deadlocking the council if it ever attempted to become overly critical of the way trust territories were administered. Indeed, the anticolonial countries, in their drive to help all peoples under colonial rule become free, had to bypass the Trusteeship Council and use their voting power in the General Assembly to obtain from the United Nations the moral support they sought.

The Operation of the United Nations

We see, then, that the United Nations, like the League before it, possesses no power to influence the behavior of nations by any means except persuasion. The powers of material reward and punishment and force it nominally possesses are in actuality controlled by the separate national members, particularly by the great powers. Indeed the domination of the great powers is even more marked in the United Nations than it was in the League. Officially, the great powers had only one advantage in the League, permanent membership in the council. They had one vote each, like other nations, and the veto they possessed was shared by every nation in the organization.

In the United Nations, however, great power domination is quite obvious. In the General Assembly, the great powers are nominally equal with other nations, but in the Security Council, they and they alone possess the veto. Only the great powers are permanent members of all three councils, a status guaranteed by the Charter for the Security Council and the Trusteeship Council and granted by a sensible General Assembly for the Economic and Social Council. These formal privileges, however, are but a pale reflection of the real power they exercise.

No impartial observer can escape the conclusion that one or more of the great powers is behind almost every decision taken by the United Nations. Even in the General Assembly, it is not difficult to distinguish between the formal power structure, in which each nation has a right to speak and vote and decisions are reached by majority rule, and the informal power structure, in which the great powers pull the strings. After all, small nations dependent upon great powers outside the organization are not suddenly going to become independent within it simply because the Charter gives them equal voting rights. They know too well that the great powers possess the ability to reward or punish them for their behavior in the assembly, and on the whole, they mind their Ps and Qs. In almost any major case that has come before the United Nations, it is possible to see the informal leaders operating in the background (and occasionally in the open), pulling the levers and throwing the switches that move the formal machinery of the United Nations or prevent it from moving at all. A few examples will suffice.

In the Indonesian case, attempts by the Dutch to regain control over a rich colonial area that had been conquered by the Japanese and now insisted upon its independence resulted in armed hostilities. Since the Netherlands had at one point recognized the new Republic of Indonesia as a de facto government, the quarrel was brought before the Security Council as a dispute between two nations that threatened international peace. The council took action and eventually called upon the Netherlands to set up an independent United States of Indonesia, a proposal to which the Dutch later agreed. The United Nations is sometimes given credit for stopping the hostilities and for bringing about the independence of Indonesia, but such a view does not give proper weight to the activities of the United States, which desired the independence of Indonesia and subjected the Dutch to economic pressures in order to achieve its aim.

The Korean War presents an even clearer example of a great power operating through the United Nations to give international sanction to what was, in effect, a national action. When Communist North Korea invaded South Korea in 1950, the United States decided to resist this instance of Communist aggression with military force. The action, however, was taken in the name of the United Nations, and the troops that fought against the Communists, although in reality almost exclusively American and South Korean, were nominally a United Nations force.

The United Nations operated in this way: Because the Soviet Union was temporarily absent, the Security Council was able to vote immediately that a breach of the peace existed and call for an end to hostilities. Two days later, the council recommended that member nations help South Korea repel the Communist attack. The council later set up a unified United Nations command under the United States, and sixteen nations contributed military forces. When Communist China entered the war some months later on the side of North Korea, the Soviet representative was back in the Security Council, where his veto power prevented the council from acting. The United States then turned to the General Assembly, which declared that China was an aggressor and eventually adopted an embargo against her.

Legally, the United Nations was repelling aggression and restoring international peace and security. In reality, however, the United States and Communist China were engaged in a limited war. The American decision to resist force by force was made before the Security Council voted, and American troops were ordered into action before the council called upon members of the United Nations to aid South Korea. It seems quite certain that American troops would have gone into action no matter what the council had voted, although the American government certainly desired UN approval. The forces that fought in Korea were predominantly American; other nations sent only token forces. America's military contribution, in fact, was even greater than that of South Korea. The general of the United Nations unified command was the American General Douglas MacArthur, who received his orders from the American government, *not* from the United Nations. Communications from the Secretary-General were funneled through the American government, and the sixteen nations that contributed troops did not participate at all in making policy. The dominant role of the United States could not have been clearer.

We have seen how it is possible for great powers to use the United Nations in pursuit of national aims, but more often the great powers have used their domination of the United Nations to *prevent* the organization from acting against their national interests. When the Security Council proposed to send a committee to investigate the coup d'état by which the Communists took over Czechoslovakia in 1948, Russia vetoed the proposal. When the General Assembly proposed to discuss the situation in Algeria in 1955, the French withdrew from the assembly and hinted that they would also quit the United Nations. The assembly dropped the matter. Even the United States, firm opponent of Russian vetoes, made it clear on at least one occasion that she would not hesitate to use the veto if the Security Council tried to seat Communist China against her wishes.

In still other cases, the United Nations has taken action and made definite recommendations but has been unable to enforce them because of a lack of support from the great powers. The Palestine case was long and complicated and we cannot begin to trace its complexities here, but it must be noted that the detailed plans of the General Assembly for partitioning Palestine between the Arabs and the Jews were completely ignored when war broke out and the war resulted in other boundaries. For many years American policy in this area of the world consisted of a precarious effort to offend neither Israel nor the Arab nations. American indecision made it impossible for the United Nations to impose any clearcut settlement of the dispute. Similarly in the cases of Hyderabad and Kashmir, the unwillingness of the great powers to offend either India or Pakistan left disputes over these areas unsettled until India finally imposed a settlement by force. The border dispute between China and India in 1962 was never even taken to the United Nations for discussion.

If the great powers disagree or are indecisive about the course they wish to follow, that is to say, if the informal power structure does not act, the formal power structure of the United Nations is helpless. Decisions may be taken, but in these circumstances they represent little more than pious wishes. Differences between the formal and informal power structures are most obvious when a great power must act alone to block the organization from acting, but the two situations are not so different as they appear. In both instances, it is the policies and interests of the great powers that explain the action or inaction of the United Nations.

The Functions of International Organizations

In making a final evaluation of the work of such international organizations as the League of Nations and the United Nations, we should keep in mind the kind of accomplishments that can reasonably be expected of them. To some extent, the founders of these organizations, in trying to arouse the support required to bring them into being, oversold them. The result has been disillusionment when the organizations failed to live up to expectations. The fault lies with the salesmen, not the product.

Perhaps the most unfortunate illusion has been the belief that such organizations can guarantee world peace. The proof that they cannot lies in World War II, which buried the League along with its other war dead, and in the lesser conflicts that have wounded but not felled the United Nations. Surely it was unrealistic to have expected the League to prevent World War II or to have expected the United Nations to prevent such wars as those in Korea and Vietnam. As long as national governments have the power to make war, no international body can have the power to keep peace. That power still resides with the governments of nations and with the groups to which they are responsible.

But it is nonsense to argue that international organizations perform *no* function in world politics. On the contrary, they have important consequences, even in the realm of peacekeeping. At least three major functions can be identified, and all are clearly visible in the workings of the United Nations. The first major function is the legitimization of the dominant international order. The second is the reduction of conflict, particularly armed conflict, within the dominant international order. The third is the facilitation of increased communication and participation in world politics by the less powerful nations. Let us consider each of these functions briefly.

LEGITIMIZATION

It has often been noted that international organizations seem primarily to produce talk and not action, but talk can be important. In the earlier discussion of the power transition it was suggested that no international order can operate effectively unless it is accepted and supported (either actively or passively) by a substantial proportion of the members of the order, particularly the more powerful members. The talk that constitutes the main activity of international organizations is an important element in the process through which such acceptance and support are generated.

The contention that the major international organizations serve primarily as instruments of legitimization is reinforced by the timing of their appearance at the end of the Napoleonic Wars and after World Wars I and II. Each of these periods saw the rise of a new dominant nation and significant changes in the dominant international order. Each was a time when new attitudes and new patterns of behavior were being established in international relations and when the need for legitimization was therefore most acute, a time when the new dominant nation was seeking ways to gain legitimacy for its own privileges and power and for the power structure it had come to head.

That the new international organizations helped to meet this need should not surprise us. They do, after all, spend a great part of their time generating official statements of attitudes and policies by members; these range from close support for the dominant nation to bitter criticism and hostility, but if the continuous discussions and resolutions are followed closely, it becomes apparent that on important questions—particularly those touching on the role of the dominant nation—the views that are adopted by the organization as its own generally express support, either mild or strong. Criticism of the dominant international power structure tends to be filtered out. This support is not automatic; it is the result of endless patience and hard work. The dominant nation and its important friends are prime movers in the formulation of the favorable views adopted by the collectivity, and they are indefatigable in their efforts to prevent the official adoption of any views challenging their position. Thus one major function of international organization is to help transform the existing international power structure into a system of legitimate authority.

The relationship of the United States to the United Nations illustrates this point quite well. The United Nations was created at a time when the United States had clearly ascended to the position of dominant nation in the dominant international order. As such she faced two problems: the legitimization of her own role as leader—a role challenged by the Soviet Union—and the formation and acceptance of a new pattern of international dealings that reflected more clearly her past, her ideology, her capabilities, and her needs. This meant, among other things, unraveling the more primitive, more vulnerable, and more rigid international system of political colonialism that had been led by Britain. It is striking how well the United Nations was adapted to fill both needs. In the first ten years after World War II, when American rule was most insecure, the United States continually used that organization to demand, and to obtain, the formal backing of the United Nations for her own leadership and the sharp condemnation of all Soviet challenges to that leadership. The attempt to legitimize the American position and to isolate and condemn the challenger is now quite obvious.

The United Nations was also extremely useful in facilitating the dismantling of the old colonial system and its replacement by more flexible, less visible, and therefore less vulnerable ties between the weak nations and the strong, between the underdeveloped and the highly developed, between the producers and the processors of raw materials. International organizations, of course, did not cause the end of political colonialism: Colonialism crumbled because conditions changed—because the colonies were experiencing primitive unification, and because the extreme economic underdevelopment that had invited the crude exploitation of their wealth was giving way to at least a moderate degree of economic modernization. In short, political colonialism was killed by many of the same forces that created international organizations, not by the United Nations.

What the United Nations did was to ease the process. This international organization provided the publicity necessary to make it difficult for the colonial powers to quell their rebellions by force. It gave rebel leaders in exile an international forum. It permitted nations sympathetic with the rebels to pool their voices in calling for political independence for the colony. Most important, it gave the United States, which could remain neutral in the UN, the opportunity to encourage colonial liberation without a great deal of overt action that would alienate the colonial powers, who are after all her closest lieutenants in the new international order.

PEACEKEEPING

A second function of the major international organizations is peacekeeping or, more exactly, the reduction of armed conflict, for no organization has succeeded in preventing armed conflict entirely. It must be stressed, however, that this function is discharged only within the international order legitimized by the organization. Conflicts lying entirely outside the dominant international order and conflicts involving members of the dominant system and outsiders are handled differently.

In dealing with armed conflicts entirely outside the dominant international order, the international organization is generally quite helpless. The Hungarian revolt of 1956 provides a good example. After Soviet troops intervened to put down the Hungarian revolt, the General Assembly passed a number of resolutions demanding that the USSR withdraw; the Russians ignored the demands. A UN commission investigating the situation was refused admission to Hungary. After its report that the rights of the Hungarian people had been brutally violated, the UN took no further action.

In military disputes between members of the dominant order and outsiders, the international organization is also incapable of restoring peace, but it can and often does act to legitimize the position or actions of the members of the dominant order. In the Korean War, for example, the United Nations identified itself with South Korea and the United States in their dispute with North Korea and China, and the troops of the former and their allies became United Nations troops in name though not in reality, for their chain of command ended in Washington.

Such legitimizing action can be taken only if the member involved can win the support of the other important members of the dominant order. In the Vietnamese conflict, for example, the United States also used the United Nations as a forum to present its views and called upon the UN to take various actions in its support. North Vietnam and the USSR, however, firmly refused to accept any UN role in the dispute, apparently fearing the very legitimization that the United States sought. The United States, for its part, was unable to muster sufficient support from its customary allies to achieve UN legitimization in the face of Communist opposition.

The peacekeeping function of the United Nations is exercised effectively only in instances in which all parties to the armed conflict are members of the dominant international order, because it is in such cases that the dominant nation is most interested in keeping peace (as opposed to winning the conflict) and possesses the power to control the combatants. In these circumstances the international organization can be of immense help to the dominant nation in running its order. It is clear that armed strife among members of the same order is a threat to the fabric of the whole system. But although the dominant nation considers it essential that fighting be terminated as soon as possible, it may nevertheless be reluctant to intervene directly. At best, intervention would win the enmity of at least one party. A worse possibility is that the dominant nation could become mired in such a conflict and have to maintain troops in the region to keep the combatants apart. Still worse is the possibility that intervention by the dominant nation may bring the challenger into the conflict, thus escalating the significance of the quarrel.

It is therefore extremely helpful to the dominant nation if its own views of the conflict can be generally accepted and presented to the disputants as the views of the collectivity. It is also helpful if enforcement of the peace settlement can be handled by soldiers of other nations through the medium of the international organization. The organization thus permits the power structure of the dominant international order to suggest solutions and have them executed without exposing the dominant nation to as much hostility as it would meet if it solved the dispute directly.

This is exactly what happened in the Israeli-Arab wars in 1948 and 1956, and to a lesser extent in 1967. In all three outbreaks, military action was quickly snuffed out in large part because of American pressure, for most of the combatants were heavily dependent upon the United States, but the formal cease-fires were arranged by the United Nations, and UN armed personnel furnished by the smaller powers enforced the peace. Similar action was taken in the dispute between Turkey and Greece over Cyprus in 1964.

INCREASED INTERNATIONAL PARTICIPATION

The third major function of international organizations is to increase the participation of the less powerful nations in world politics. This was not true of the early international conferences. The demand by the smaller powers of Europe at the Congress of Vienna that they be allowed to participate in important decisions after the Napoleonic Wars so confused England and so angered the other great powers that they excluded the small powers from any further decision-making. England, with the help of France, ran the dominant international order of that day from her own foreign office. This was possible because the nineteenth-century world was relatively underdeveloped and relations, even among the more advanced nations were relatively few, slow, and casual. The most frequent and significant international relations were economic in nature and these were largely independent of political authorities or political decisions. Thus political direction of the dominant international order did not put undue strain upon the British diplomatic apparatus.

The situation had changed radically by the time the United States took over leadership of the dominant international order. Increased economic development, military interdependence, and the disintegration of political colonialism had vastly increased the number and complexity of international relations. Many new nations had been created, and two world wars had given the less powerful nations both the desire and the opportunity for greater participation in international decisions.

Both the League of Nations and the United Nations provided ideal channels for participation by the smaller powers without doing any real violence to the operating power structure. The participation of the small powers was and is largely symbolic, but within the formal structure of many League and UN bodies they are recognized as equal. Their representatives are given an opportunity to express their nations' views on important topics, to vote on decisions, and to exert whatever diplomatic pressure they are capable of exerting. Collectively, they are capable of influencing even the major powers somewhat by their refusal to legitimize activities and decisions of which they do not approve. Major decisions, however, continue to be made by the great powers, and where international legitimization is withheld, the great powers act without it if they feel their vital interests are at stake.

The increased participation of the lesser nations is an advantage not only to them but to the great powers as well, for the international organizations act to some extent as giant screens upon which the attitudes of the members are projected. They are, in short, communication centers where any nation can easily and efficiently learn the opinion of other nations on any important international issue without going to the expense, and perhaps the humiliation, of making a direct inquiry of every other government concerned. This is especially helpful to the dominant nation in its task of supervising relations within the dominant international order.

One word of comment upon the relations between the United States and the United Nations seems imperative. One really wonders what the American critics of the United Nations have in mind when they say that the United States has lost her freedom of maneuver and gained nothing but bills from being involved with the UN. Upon analysis the United Nations is revealed as an aid to keeping peace within the dominant international order, as a means of obtaining information needed to govern relations among the lesser members of the order, and, most important of all, as an agency for legitimizing American domination of her international order. All members of the United Nations stand to gain something, but the gains are weighted heavily in favor of the dominant international order and are roughly proportionate to the power of the nation concerned. It is the United States that gains most of all.

In summary, international organizations are an important part of the system of international politics. Although in form they may be precursors of some future form of world government, in practice they are functioning parts of the international system as it is, operating primarily as adjuncts of the dominant international order. It would be foolish to overestimate what international organizations can accomplish today in a world of sovereign states, but it would be equally foolish to discount the very real role in world politics now played by international organizations.

CONCLUSION

19

What of the Future?

❖❘❮❖

We have traced out the major patterns of international relations. We have come to know the major actors, and we have watched them play their parts upon the stage. And yet the drama goes on, forever unfolding new acts as the earlier scenes are lost to memory. Can we guess what the future will bring?

Prediction is a risky business. Prudence would dictate that we rise here, sigh and close the book. The future will be upon us soon enough, and we shall see then what it brings. Yet one cannot probe the past and present deeply without arriving at conclusions about the future as well. If the generalizations we have made were worth the making, they will continue to hold true beyond the present hour, and if they do hold true, there is much that we already know about the future.

There is, of course, the fear of being wrong. It is one thing to provide plausible interpretations of the past and quite another to throw one's theories into the crucible of the living future, where one quick turn of events can make a mockery of the tidiest of theories. The danger is real, but silence will not destroy it. We have, in the very act of exploring the past, made conclusions about the future. They may, of course, be wrong, but if so, withholding them from the reader will not make them correct.

We propose, then, to review briefly some of the most significant patterns of international relations that have been identified throughout the book. On the basis of these patterns, we shall make our predictions.

Significant Patterns

THE IMPORTANCE OF NATIONS

The major unit in world affairs today is the nation-state: no other group can fill its functions and take its place. The ties that bind each national group together are many and strong—a common government, a common political ideology, economic unity, the bonds of culture, language, and heritage, and sometimes a common religion as well. These make the nation unified, resistant to attack, resilient, and highly durable. The few, slim cracks are plastered over with a common sentiment of group identity. As we have seen, such feelings fill deep psychological needs for modern man. Personal relationships that make strong emotional demands upon the individual's allegiance do not usually cut across national lines. In fact, the sentiments born within the family are later transferred through the use of symbols to the national group.

Those qualities that unite the nation also separate it from other nations. The chasm between modern nations is still wide and deep. Variations in culture between nations, even neighbors, leap to the eye, and the people of one nation find real or imaginary characteristics to differentiate themselves from others.

The most corrosive force at work on nationalism is the increasing interdependence of nations, particularly in the realms of world trade and world security. Economic interdependence enmeshes men from many nations, but economic interdependence *within* the nation is still much greater. The average person still depends more heavily upon his fellow nationals than upon the people of other nations. What is true of economic relations is doubly true when it comes to security. We have stressed the dependence of modern nations upon their allies and even upon their enemies, but fundamentally, each nation must defend itself. It is to his own government that modern man looks for protection against war, conquest, and impoverishment.

The nation, in short, is the most important unit of action in world politics today as in the past.

GOALS AND POWER AS DETERMINANTS OF NATIONAL BEHAVIOR

The behavior of nations in their relations with each other is determined by their goals and by their power to achieve their goals.

Major goals are peace, power, wealth, and cultural welfare, and to a certain extent, every nation pursues them all. Every nation desires at least occasional peace, enough power to maintain its national existence and control its own affairs, enough wealth to provide a comfortable living for those the national government represents, and at least the preservation of its national culture. Above this bare minimum, however, the emphasis on one goal or another varies. National goals may be pursued in competition with other nations or as absolute goals. They may be unified or divergent, humanitarian or strictly national, long-range or immediate, general or specific, stated or actual, and they may involve perpetuation or destruction of the international status quo.

National goals are determined by the interests of the most powerful groups and individuals within the nation, by the power position of the nation, and by the general climate of the times. Our knowledge of the determinants of national goals is not as extensive as we might wish, but some generalizations can be made:

Peace is less important to nations that are growing in power than to declining nations or nations at their peak. Power is most often sought by strong nations, wealth by the rich. However, the Industrial Revolution has increased the general emphasis on wealth for all nations, just as the heightened destructiveness of war has increased the importance of peace.

Powerful, expanding nations have more competitive goals than weak or declining nations. Nations growing in power are most likely to have goals that demand a change in the status quo. Powerful nations can most easily afford to have goals that are narrowly nationalistic, but all nations fall back on nationalistic goals when a high degree of sacrifice is required of the national population to achieve them. Totalitarian nations are more apt to have unified and long-range goals than democratic nations, and goals are most likely to be specific when the nation is unified.

Successful achievement of a nation's goals depends primarily upon the power possessed, that is, upon the ability of the nation to influence the behavior of other nations by utilizing persuasion, offering rewards, threatening punishments, and using force. The main determinants of national power are the size of a nation's population, the efficiency of its political organization, and the level of its economic development. To a lesser extent, power is influenced by national morale, resources, and geography.

Population is the most important of the determinants of power, for the number of people in a nation—particularly the number of those of working and fighting age—sets a limit to the size of the nation's military establishment, the major means by which it exercises force on other nations and resists the use of force by others. Population size also sets limits on the labor force and on the national market, thus influencing the economic rewards and punishments a nation can command. Finally, a large and growing population gives a nation confidence in its future and in its relations with others. The importance of population is clearly indicated by the fact that there is no major world power with a population of less than 50 million.

We have rated political development second in importance as a determinant of nation power, for it is through the national government that the human and material resources of a nation are mobilized to influence the behavior of other nations. Governmental decisions have a crucial effect upon the national economy and upon the size, nature, and effectiveness of the nation's military forces. Governmental agencies form foreign policy and put it into effect through diplomatic and military action.

Almost as important as political development—perhaps even equally important—is economic development, or more specifically, the degree to which a nation is industrial. Economic efficiency contributes greatly to a nation's power, for it is the economy that produces the weapons and supplies for the military, the consumer goods and capital equipment for trade and aid, the technical experts who can provide assistance to others, the markets for the goods of other nations, the means of mass communication for propaganda, and the high standard of living that helps create a loyal population. Recent history has provided obvious evidence of the tremendous boost to national power provided by industrialization.

An index of national power that clearly reflects the influence of two of these three major determinants is the gross national product. The size of a nation's GNP, like its power, depends upon both the number of people in the nation and the level of their economic efficiency. Other determinants of power are reflected to some extent, but the index is deficient in that it does not give sufficient weight to the efficiency of political organization. Nevertheless, it is the best index of power available.

The determinants of national power are interrelated and tend to change together. Industrialization is accompanied by population growth and is closely related to improvements in political efficiency. "Industrialization" in the broadest sense of the term implies a change in an entire way of life, a change that is accompanied by a great increase in national power.

THE POWER TRANSITION

Because of the differential spread of industrialization throughout the world, the period in which we live has been characterized by great and sudden shifts in the distribution of power among nations. In this respect it differs from the period that preceded it, when no nation was industrial, and from the period that will follow when all nations are economically developed.

As each nation industrializes, it goes through a power transition that can be divided into three stages: (1) the stage of potential power, in which the nation is still preindustrial and possesses little power compared to industrial nations; (2) the stage of transitional growth in power, during which the nation industrializes and grows rapidly in power; and (3) the stage of power maturity, when the nation is fully industrial and continues to grow in wealth but declines in power relative to nations that are in stage 2. In other words, as each nation goes through the process of industrialization with its accompanying population growth and governmental modernization, it goes into a sudden sprint in the race for power, leaving far behind the nations that have not yet industrialized and narrowing the distance between it and the nations that have industrialized ahead of it. If the nation is large to begin with, its sprint may upset the existing international order.

We have already seen a number of major nations go through the power transition. England was the first, and her new industrial strength gave her the leadership of the world. France, Germany, and the United States came next along with the rest of Northwestern Europe and the European-peopled members of the British Commonwealth. Japan, Italy, and the Soviet Union followed later and are now in the stage of power maturity. Spain and most of Southeastern Europe started still later and are now in the stage of transitional growth in power. China has just in the last few years begun her transitional growth.

The first group of nations to industrialize did so fairly slowly under democratic forms of government. The most recent nations to industrialize have done so rapidly under totalitarian governments. Unfortunately, the association is not an accident. In a world where sufficient capital to industrialize rapidly cannot be borrowed but must be provided by raising production through inhuman work conditions and by cutting consumption through reducing the standard of living, a totalitarian government has marked advantages. The price in terms of human happiness and freedom is one that no true democrat will pay, but the leaders of nations in a hurry to industrialize are all too often willing to forsake democracy to reach their goal.

THE COLONIAL TRANSITION

The present era has also seen the rise and fall of classic colonialism. Fundamentally a relationship between the strong and the weak, colonial domination on a world scale was made possible by the preponderance of power over the rest of the world that Western Europe gained through early industrialization. Political colonialism is a self-liquidating process, and we have seen most of the former colonial world become politically independent, even in advance of its own industrialization.

The steps through which most colonies achieve their independence are these: In the process of conquering, controlling, and developing a colony, the colonizer unifies the native population politically and gives it a feeling of national identity if it did not have one before—in short, aids its primitive unification. The colonizer also provides the colony with nationalistic leaders opposed to colonial rule. This is the first step to freedom. The second step is taken when native leaders begin to appeal to the colonial rulers in terms of their own values, demanding basic human rights and an end to the more openly exploitative and repressive features of colonial rule. The demands are usually granted, at least to some extent. The third step consists of demands for political rights culminating in demands for political independence. Full independence is not always granted voluntarily by the colonial rulers, but political "reforms" are often made at this time in an effort to head off demands for independence. In effect, however, they merely speed the process.

With the completion of the third step, the colony achieves its political independence, sometimes after a long and bloody struggle. At this point, however, the colony usually becomes an economic dependency, for its economy continues to be controlled either by its former rulers or by the people of some other more advanced and more industrial nation.

A new form of colonialism that has appeared but recently is that exemplified by the Soviet satellites. Here again, the relationship is based upon a power difference, but both colony and master are of similar culture and race. Both economic dependencies and satellites may also be militarily dependent upon stronger nations.

The decline of the old colonial empires and the rise of the new economic dependencies (an American specialty) and of the satellites (a Soviet specialty) have had a marked effect upon the distribution of power among nations.

THE INTERNATIONAL ORDER

Relations among nations are not chaotic but are ordered in accordance with established patterns. There is at any given time an international order based upon the existing distribution of power and wealth and consisting of recognized habits and rules of international behavior. Those nations that accept the distribution of power and wealth and abide by the rules of trade, diplomacy, and war can be said to belong to the same international order. Sometimes, as during most of the nineteenth century, there is but one international order in the world. At other times, as at present, there may be two or more competing international orders, although one is always dominant.

The main international order is headed by the most powerful nation in the world, the dominant nation, as we have called it. Since this nation has usually created the order in the first place, used its power to obtain the lion's share of whatever benefits there may be, and designed the rules to perpetuate its privileges, the dominant nation is highly satisfied with the status quo. Allied with the dominant nation are other powerful and satisfied nations that occupy top positions in the international order. Beneath them are the lesser powers who accept the international order willingly because of the benefits it allows them or unwillingly because they are weak and have no choice. At the bottom of the order are the weakest nations and the dependencies. They, too, are part of the international order, for they provide the spoils.

THE ROLE OF THE CHALLENGER

There may, however, be other powerful nations that are not satisfied with the existing international order and seek to overturn it. These nations are the challengers. They have become powerful too late to receive a proportionate share of the benefits but are unwilling to get in line behind the nations that reached great-power status before them. They are unwilling to accept an international order that relegates them to fourth or fifth or sixth place when they feel they should be first.

Challengers are usually populous nations that are in the midst of or have recently gone through rapid industrialization and consequently have experienced a rapid and recent rise in power. Their privileges and position have not kept pace with their increase in power, and they feel, quite rightfully, that they are entitled to more. However, the swift rise from weakness to great power is often intoxicating, and challengers frequently demand much more than their power warrants. Such demands meet a wall of resistance from the established powers, who are reluctant to grant the challenger its just deserts, let alone its most extravagant demands. Denied the place to which it feels entitled, the challenger may turn to war in an attempt to replace the existing international order with one more to its liking. The challenger may succeed in gathering to its side some of the lesser nations that are dissatisfied with the existing order, and together these nations may form the basis for a competing international order.

Nations do not remain challengers forever, nor do all newly powerful nations challenge the existing order. Some accept a secondary role and do not even try to fight for more. Germany, a challenger of yesterday, seems finally to have given up her dreams of world domination and to have accepted, after two defeats, a position a level below her earlier aspirations. Such is the fate of challengers who lose. Even world leadership can be transferred from one nation to another without a conflict as has happened with England and the United States.

Typically, however, newly powerful nations are international trouble-makers. It is they who have been the aggressors of the past. All the major wars of recent history have seen the dominant nation and its allies arrayed on one side against the group led by a challenger who has recently risen in power thanks to industrialization. To date, the challengers, after whetting their appetite on a few minor victims, have challenged the dominant group *before* they equaled it in strength, and so have lost.

CONDITIONS LEADING TO WAR

War between challenger and dominant nation, then, appears most likely when the challenger approaches but has not quite overtaken the dominant nation in power. In other words, an approximate balance of power increases the danger of war, whereas a clear preponderance of power in the hands of the satisfied nations assures world peace. Other factors, however, also play a role.

War is especially likely if the challenger at its peak will roughly equal the dominant nation in power. Such a nation cannot hope to obtain a clear supremacy through internal development. Its only hope of taking the dominant nation's place is to unseat it in battle.

The threat of war is greater if the rise of the challenger is rapid, for not only does such a rapid change make peaceful adjustment by the dominant nation more difficult, but it also creates internal strains within the challenger nation that may be turned against the outside world in aggressive action. If great change occurs within a single lifetime, both challenger and dominant nation may find it difficult to estimate their relative power correctly and may stumble into a war that would never have been fought if both sides had foreseen where the victory would lie.

Inflexibility on the part of the dominant nation may also increase the danger of war. Concessions to a challenger are not always in order, but if the challenger is of such a size that through internal development alone it is certain to surpass the dominant nation, wise concessions may avert a senseless war. It is a flexible nation indeed, however, that can give up world leadership gracefully; the only modern example we have is England.

A long-standing friendship between dominant nation and challenger may make it easier for world leadership to change hands peacefully. If the two rivals are real friends, their mutual affection will absorb some of the strain that is certain to arise as the challenger passes the older ruler. But if there is no tradition of friendship between them, the rivalry will be open and bitter, and both nations will be more inclined to fight.

Finally, and perhaps most important of all, war will be much more likely if the challenger aspires to create a new international order than if it simply wishes to take over the leadership of the existing order. Peaceful adjustment is difficult in either case, but it is at least possible if the challenger is willing to continue to abide by the set of rules that favors the interests of powerful groups within the dominant nation and its allies. Such adjustment is virtually impossible if the challenger insists on changes that would upset not only the international distribution of power but also the distribution of power and wealth within each nation.

THE LIMITATIONS OF NUCLEAR POWER

The fundamental patterns of international relations will not be altered by nuclear arms. Military strength is, of course, an important form of national power, but it cannot exist in isolation from other sources of power. Today, as in the past, the greatest military might belongs to nations that are large, wealthy, and well-organized. The great atomic superpowers are precisely those nations that would be the most powerful if the new weapons did not exist.

Nuclear weapons have not had much effect upon the relative power of nations. They cannot prevent new challengers from growing in strength through internal development. They do not deter either challengers or defenders of the existing order from fighting for their vital national interests. In short, nuclear arms do not guarantee either peace or the status quo.

THE LIMITATIONS OF DIPLOMACY

The fundamental patterns of international relations will not be altered by skillful, reasonable, or sincere talk. Diplomacy is a negotiation process through which the representatives of nations settle differences through persuasion. It is suitable for the settlement of relatively minor disputes between friends, but it should not be expected to solve major disputes between challengers and dominant nations. Once such differences have been settled by other means, diplomacy may seal the bargain, but the victory has usually been won on the battlefield or in the counting houses before diplomacy claims it as its own.

Diplomacy enjoyed its greatest importance in the dynastic period before industrialization altered the nature of relations among nations. Today, however, the diplomat has seen his personal gifts depreciated by the impersonality of government, his unique information duplicated by other agencies, and his flexibility limited by democratic controls. At the same time, the increased role of modern government has forced the diplomat to deal with basic economic and social problems, many of which cannot be solved by conversations between governmental representatives.

Nineteenth-century diplomats claimed the credit for a century of peace, but we have seen that the underlying cause of peace was Britain's huge preponderance of power and the unified international order that was based upon it. Today, these conditions have vanished. It is too much to ask diplomacy to bring them back.

THE MYTH OF COLLECTIVE SECURITY

The dominant nation and its friends, in a search for a way to perpetuate their dominance and protect their international order from the devastating wars that threaten to upset it, have devised the idea of collective security —a system whereby the combined might of all the nations in the world would be turned against any challenger who sought to use force to upset the existing order. The idea, of course, is not appealing to a potential challenger, but twice in recent history, after wars that had temporarily removed the previous challenger from a policy-making position, the victors have written the idea of collective security into an international organization.

The difficulty, of course, is that collective security, properly applied, would deny the use of international force not only to the challenger but to the dominant nation as well. Freed from the fear of aggressive and punitive action against them, followers of both the dominant nation and the major challenger would desert in droves. For this and other reasons, no major nation has been willing to give up its ability to use force when and where it pleases.

In practice, collective security has not worked. It is quite true that peace is guaranteed by a preponderance of power, but preponderant power must lie in the hands of those nations that make up the dominant international order, and within that order, preponderant power must lie in the hands of the nations that head the order. An artificial preponderance created by lumping together all the nations of the world except for a single aggressor will never keep the peace, for such a group of nations will never act in concert. The nations of the world have never agreed upon who was the aggressor, nor are they all equally interested in stopping aggression. There will always be some nations that side with the disturber of the peace and others that dare not oppose him.

THE NATURE OF INTERNATIONAL ORGANIZATION

Despite all allegations to the contrary, international organizations are *not* machinery for putting collective security into operation. If we regard their acts and not their charters, it becomes perfectly clear that international organizations are instruments of diplomacy, subject to most of the limitations of conventional diplomacy.

Because they are increasingly interdependent, nations have created international organizations through which their representatives may keep in constant touch with one another. But because they are sovereign and wish to remain so, nations have withheld from these organizations the power to compel any nation to act against its wishes. The power to coerce, reward, and punish, even the power to persuade, remains in the hands of individual nations, where it is exercised by each national government in the interests of the dominant groups within the nation.

International organizations are primarily an aid to diplomatic negotiation and operate most effectively when concerned with relations among members of the dominant international order. They centralize diplomacy, providing their members information about each others' views. They often supplement the dominant nation's efforts to control the actions of the lesser members of the dominant international order and to keep peace among them. Most important of all, they serve to legitimize the dominant international order, that is, to transform the international power structure into a system of legitimate authority.

But international organization, like diplomacy and nuclear strength, can neither guarantee the peace nor perpetuate the existing international order, for it cannot prevent the shifts of power that undermine them both.

Predictions

The predictions that follow require one preliminary qualification: They extend only to the second period of international relations in which we now live, a period that will come to an end when the last nation in the world becomes industrialized. Some years of this period still remain. It is difficult to say exactly how many—surely at least seventy or eighty years, probably more, perhaps many more. Once the entire world has industrialized, the nature of international relations will change, and with it the theories required to understand it. The theories of this book apply to the second period.

CONTINUED IMPORTANCE OF NATIONS

The first prediction is that nations will continue to be the significant units of action in world affairs throughout the second period.

Increasing economic and military interdependence will multiply the ties among nations within each of the two world orders and within smaller regional groups. The nations of Western Europe will draw closer together economically, but it is extremely unlikely that the age-old dream of European union will be soon realized. The nations of Western Europe will keep their separate national identities and their independence of political action. Nor will there be any political unification within the Communist bloc. National independence will continue to characterize the nations of Latin America and the new nations of Asia and Africa, where nationalism is at its height. There may be some shifts in the identity of nations in the Near East, where many of the political units today resemble the old dynastic states of Europe more than modern nations.

The forces of nationalism will continue to be strong throughout the second period, perhaps declining somewhat in the older nations but growing even more powerful than at present in the new nations carved out of the colonial world as they complete their primitive unification.

World government is still a long way off. The United Nations will continue to exist as long as the United States is the dominant nation in the world, perhaps even longer, and the *forms* of international government —a world legislature, international law, a world court—will continue to grow within the United Nations system, but the *substance* of international government will not be much increased in the remaining decades of the second period. The creation of a world government through the voluntary agreement of existing nations is so unlikely that we can say flatly that it will never happen. World government through military conquest of the world by a single nation is also impossible at present, for no one nation controls a great enough preponderance of power to pull off such a feat.

For the remainder of the second period, then, there will be no world government. Regional groupings and blocs may become more closely unified, but nations will remain the major units of action. World affairs will continue to be inter*national* relations.

CONTINUING SHIFTS IN POWER

The second prediction is that the distribution of power among nations will continue to shift throughout the second period and that the shift will be away from the nations of the Western world.

Recent changes in national power have been largely the result of political mobilization and industrialization. Since the industrial way of life will continue to spread throughout the world, the distribution of power will also continue to change. It will not stabilize until the entire world is economically developed.

The West has already suffered a decrease in power through the loss of its colonial empires. In a very few years, political colonialism will be ended altogether. True, many of the colonies will remain economic dependencies of the West for some years to come, but the control exercised over an economic dependency is considerably less than that exercised over a political colony. Some of the larger economic dependencies will eventually achieve full economic independence by industrializing, but this will take a long time and will probably not occur until near the end of the second period. The nations that turn to communism will industrialize rapidly but will lose a good deal of their freedom of action.

In the case of the largest dependencies, the potential power realized through their industrialization will be great enough to cause profound disturbances in international relations. The disturbance will be particularly great if any of these large dependencies of the West switch to the Communist international order. The danger that they may do so is great, for the promise of quick industrialization and power is a potent one. And the danger of their defection will remain great until their own industrialization is well under way.

Even more important will be the shifts in power among the great nations of the world. The power of Britain and France, already declining, will continue to fall, for the advantages bestowed upon them by early industrialization will continue to vanish as the process spreads to other nations. Germany will probably increase her strength further as memories of World War II fade and the other great powers relax somewhat the artificial restrictions they have placed upon her free exercise of power.

The Soviet Union, China, and India will rise in strength in the years ahead. Russia has already experienced most of the spurt of power that comes with rapid industrialization, but she will increase her power still further before her growth is spent. China has only recently entered the stage of transitional growth in power. If she recovers successfully from the political chaos of the Cultural Revolution, her rise should be the most significant event of the next few decades. India has not yet started to industrialize in earnest, but her size alone guarantees that the power potential to be realized is immense.

The United States will continue to hold her predominant position within the Western international order, unchallenged by any competitor from within that order. She may even increase her power over other Western nations through economic penetration and military aid, and she will probably gain at least some new economic dependencies as former colonies of Britain and France continue to drift further away from their old masters. The commanding lead that the United States now enjoys over her Communist competitors, on the other hand, will be cut by the growing strength of Russia and China.

The question that interests us most is whether or not the United States will be able to retain her position of world leadership until the third period, when the distribution of power among nations will become more stable. Only three nations—the Soviet Union, China, and India—have a population base large enough to enable them to threaten the supremacy America now enjoys. Let us examine the prospects of each.

The Soviet Union may catch up with the United States, but it is doubtful that she will surpass her. True, her population is somewhat larger than that of the United States, and if she could equal American productivity, it would appear that her power should be greater. The United States, however, will not be standing still while the USSR completes the modernization of her economy, but will be improving her economic efficiency and increasing her wealth. Moreover, America's head start is so great that it will be many years—if ever—before Russian strength equals that of the United States. It must be remembered that Russia, too, has reached the stage of power maturity, when her rate of growth will slacken. It can be predicted that the Soviet Union will eventually offset much of the power advantage of the United States, but not all, and that she will level off at a point slightly below the United States in gross national product and in power.

China is another story. Her power potential is almost incalculable. With a population of some 700 million people, which will continue to increase rapidly as she industrializes, she is so large that with even a modest improvement in economic efficiency she will pass Russia (population, 230 million) with ease. And she will eventually pass the United States as well. The question is not whether China will become the most powerful nation on earth, but rather how long it will take her to achieve this status.

Prediction is difficult, however, for the second decade of Communist rule has been as disastrous for China as the first was promising. After an exceptionally rapid spurt of development, her economy was over-extended in the Great Leap Forward (1957–1960), faltered badly, and had barely regained its balance when it was disrupted by the political turmoil of the Cultural Revolution. The political institutions that had permitted Peking to mobilize the Chinese masses were in complete disarray. China's challenging posture had alienated the Soviet Union, the only nation in the world that could provide massive aid to Chinese modernization. And Chinese adventures abroad—an abortive coup in

Indonesia and an attack on India—plus her disorder at home had lost her the admiration and friendship of her neighbors. In the short run, these events have certainly slowed Chinese modernization, possibly for decades.

It is as dangerous, however, to project ahead the present unfavorable trends as it was to project the successes of the 1950s. It seems more prudent to suggest that the trends of the 1950s and the 1960s together indicate that the Chinese will eventually produce a modern nation and that this event will occur sooner than most Westerners expect and considerably later than the founders of Communist China foresee or find acceptable, probably sometime in the twenty-first century.

India, too, has an extraordinarily large population base, sufficient to enable her to surpass both the United States and Russia in power if she industralizes successfully. However, she will not be able to equal the power of China, for China is much larger in population, has completed her primitive unification, and has thrown her full effort into rapid industrialization some years ahead of India. If India industrializes in the Western manner and remains oriented primarily toward the West, she will eventually become the most powerful non-Communist nation in the world, making it difficult for the United States to maintain her present leadership of the democratic camp. If India takes the Communist road of industrialization, that international order will have won a vast preponderance of power. India, however, will not achieve industrial status until near the end of the period we are discussing, certainly not until well into the twenty-first century.

It is predicted, then, that the United States will retain world leadership for at least the remainder of the twentieth century, perhaps for even a longer time, but that the position will eventually pass to China. This prediction does not envisage world conquest by the Chinese any more than the present position of the United States is based upon world conquest, nor is it likely that the advanced Western democracies will ever have Communist governments, either by choice or by imposition. More likely, the relative power of the United States and China will slowly shift —as it has already begun to shift. The area within the American international order will slowly shrink, and the degree of American control over nations within its order will slowly lessen. Even with preponderant power passing to a Communist international order dominated by China, it is possible to imagine the American international order continuing as a rival order with considerable influence upon the Communist world and with even greater negative power to prevent unwanted interference within its own domain.

One crucial question remains: Will there be a third world war? If we apply the model constructed in this book, the probability of world war will be governed in large part by the differential rates of growth in power of the major nations, and the danger of war should be greatest when one of America's challengers—either the Soviet Union or China—arrives at a point where its power begins to approximate that of the United States. The recent slackening of Russian rates of economic growth would appear to postpone this period of danger from earlier estimates of the late 1970s or early 1980s until considerably later. In the meantime, the USSR has run into an unexpectedly early challenge from China for leadership of the Communist world.

Were it not for China, one would be forced to conclude that war between the Soviet Union and the United States was likely—although not for at least several decades—for the USSR is a challenger whose power at its peak will roughly equal that of the United States, her rise has been rapid, there is no long tradition of friendship to mitigate friction, and the USSR seeks not only to dethrone the United States but also to replace the existing international order with a Communist world order. In short, nearly all the relevant factors identified earlier would appear to maximize the chances of war.

China's recent provocative behavior, however, has altered the international picture, increasing the chances that the challenger America will face will be China and not the USSR. Let us be clear. Chinese power as yet is nowhere near equal that of the Soviet Union. Her present bid for domination of the Communist order is highly premature and virtually certain to be turned back, but it has split the Communist camp and diminished Russia's challenge to the West. It has also served notice that the ambitions of China's present leaders are not appropriate to the level of her power. If the next generation of Chinese leaders perpetuates this tendency, the likelihood of an early Chinese challenge to the United States is great. Thus the chances of war between China and the United States are high. At least six facts support this conclusion.

1. China is a country that will sooner or later equal the United States in power.
2. China's rise in power has been spectacular, and both she and the United States have found it difficult to approach realistically the new facts of international life. Indeed, at this writing the United States does not even legally recognize that the Communists govern mainland China.

3. Both the Chinese and the Americans have exhibited considerable inflexibility in their dealings with other nations. It is difficult to imagine either making concessions gracefully.
4. Present Chinese leadership may well believe that appeals to force have benefited China's international position. Certainly her claims to great-power status have been helped by her performance in armed conflicts with India and with the United States in Korea.
5. There is no tradition of friendship between the two nations that can be counted on to minimize bad feeling. Whatever good will America had generated in China through her missionaries and her past assistance has been rigorously stamped out by Chinese officials in an orgy of hatred with racial as well as ideological overtones.
6. China, like the Soviet Union, does not seek simply to replace the United States as the leading nation in the world but also seeks to destroy the international order she heads. China's leaders are unwilling and unable to accept the rules of the Western international order while the West finds equally unacceptable the adjustments that would be required if communism were imposed upon the world.

For the West, chances of averting war with China rest on two slim hopes. First is the cruel hope that China will not be able to modernize, that political disorganization and excessively rapid population growth will prevent her from industrializing and realizing her power potential. This seems unlikely if one considers the distant as well as the immediate future.

The second possibility is hardly hope at all for the West. If China can complete her industrialization rapidly and hold off her challenge to the USSR and to the West until her superiority in power is clear to all, no war will be required for her to achieve dominant status. If China can burst her peasant bonds and rise to her full industrial strength, no power on earth will be able to stop her. Simply by industrializing, she can leave America far behind in any race for power. It is the certainty of her dominance that may prevent a war, for if the United States understands that she cannot stop the rise of China, she may resign herself to the inevitable and let her pass in peace.

The moment of passage will still have its dangers, and if China's eventual victory is not to be marked by violence, she must thread her way with care. If she demands too much too soon, if she arouses fears by absorbing her Asian neighbors, if she wounds America's pride by seizing her outposts of power, or if, worst of all, she attacks America's friends, the United States will fight. Such a war would be in vain, for although it might postpone it could not prevent the day when China will dominate the world, but it would not be the first war to lay waste the world without altering its destiny.

In the past, challengers who have found it necessary to fight for world supremacy have lost. Germany, Italy, and Japan failed in their effort to seize by force the power they could not achieve through growth. In the one successful transfer of world leadership, from Britain to America, no battle was necessary. Perhaps the pattern will be repeated, for Russia cannot win world dominance with or without a war; China, on the other hand, need not fight to become the most powerful nation on earth. World wars, though likely, will not alter the underlying shifts of power ahead.

Strangely enough, small wars may make a difference. In nation after nation, internal struggles will develop between those who wish to take the Communist road to national welfare and abundance and those who prefer the way of the West. In some of these nations, shooting wars will follow, as they have in Korea and in Vietnam. Such struggles may decide the fate of a considerable number of nations now tied to the West.

More important than wars, however, will be the daily course of political, economic, and social modernization—in the advanced Western nations, who may prolong their moment of power; in the challengers, who may hasten their succession; and in the uncommitted nations, whose vulnerability to Communist lures will lessen once they become economically developed.

We are all too crisis-oriented and far too impressed with the value of war. The tides of world politics rise and fall with all the myriad decisions that affect each nation's power, and we must understand all these component factors before we can hope to influence them effectively. Even then, one nation's influence is small.

Certainly it is of no more avail for the United States than it was for Canute to stand upon the beach and command the tides to stop. Athenians, Romans, Arabs and Turks, Zulus and Sioux, Spaniards and Swedes, even Frenchmen and Englishmen have found it possible to continue living with their days of greatest power past. Perhaps Americans will find it possible as well.

BIBLIOGRAPHY

Bibliography

This bibliography is not an exhaustive list of the writings in the field, or of all the sources I have consulted. It represents, rather, a listing of those writings that have influenced my thinking most and are also readily available in the English language.

On the Study of International Relations

Brams, Steven J. "Transaction Flows in the International System," *The American Political Science Review*, LX, 4 (December 1966), 880–98.

Coplin, William D. "Inter-Nation Simulation and Contemporary Theory of International Relations," *The American Political Science Review*, LX, 3 (September 1966), 562–78.

Dahl, Robert. *Modern Political Analysis*. Englewood Cliffs, N.J.: Prentice-Hall, 1963.

Deutsch, Karl W. "Toward an Inventory of Basic Trends and Patterns in Comparative and International Politics," *The American Political Science Review*, LIV, 1 (March 1960), 34–57.

———. *Political Community at the International Level: Problems of Definition and Measurement*. Foreign Policy Analysis Series No. 2. Princeton: Princeton University Press, 1953.

Fox, W. T. R. "Fredrick Sherwood Dunn and the American Study of International Relations," *World Politics*, XV, 1 (October 1962), 1–19.

———. *Theoretical Aspects of International Relations*. South Bend, Ind.: University of Notre Dame Press, 1959.

———. "Interwar International Relations Research: The American Experience," *World Politics,* II, 1 (October 1949), 67–79.

———, and Annette Baker Fox. "The Teaching of International Relations in the United States," *World Politics,* XIII, 3 (April 1961), 339–59.

Hoffman, Stanley, ed. *Contemporary Theory in International Relations.* Englewood Cliffs, N.J.: Prentice-Hall, 1960.

Holsti, Ole R. "The 1914 Case," *The American Political Science Review,* LIX, 2 (June 1965), 365–78.

Kaplan, Morton A. "The New Great Debate: Traditionalism *vs.* Science in International Relations," *World Politics,* XIX, 1 (October 1966), 1–20.

Kelman, Herbert C., ed. *International Behavior.* New York: Holt, Rinehart and Winston, 1965.

Knorr, Klaus. "Economics and International Relations: A Problem in Teaching," *Political Science Quarterly,* LXII, 4 (December, 1947), 552–68.

Manning, C. A. *General Report on the Teaching of International Relations.* Paris: UNESCO, SS/Conf. 6/1, 1952.

Robinson, James A., Lee F. Anderson, Margaret G. Hermann, and Richard C. Snyder. "Teaching with Inter-Nation Simulation and Case Studies," *The American Political Science Review,* XL, 1 (March 1966), 53–65.

Rosenau, James N., ed. *International Politics and Foreign Policy.* New York: Free Press, 1961.

Singer, J. David, ed. *Human Behavior and International Politics.* Chicago: Rand McNally, 1965.

Snyder, Richard C., H. W. Bruck, and Burton Sapin. *Decision-making as an Approach to the Study of International Politics.* Foreign Policy Analysis Series No. 3. Princeton: Princeton University Press, 1954.

Thompson, Kenneth W. "The Study of International Politics: A Survey of Trends and Developments," *The Review of Politics,* XIV, 4 (October 1952), 433–67.

Van Wagenen, Richard W. *Research in the International Organization Field.* Princeton: Princeton University Press, 1952.

Verba, Sidney. "Simulation, Reality and Theory in International Relations," *World Politics,* XVI, 3 (April 1964), 490–520.

World Politics, XIV, 1 (October 1961).

On the Nation-State

Armstrong, John A. "Sources of Administrative Behavior: Some Soviet and Western European Comparisons," *The American Political Science Review,* LIX, 3 (September 1965), 643–55.

Barker, Sir Ernest. *National Character and the Factors in Its Formation.* London: Methuen, 1948.

Benedict, Ruth. *The Chrysanthemum and the Sword.* Boston: Houghton Mifflin, 1946.

Binder, Leonard. "National Integration and Political Development," *The*

American Political Science Review, LVIII, 3 (September 1964), 622–31.

Brogan, D. W. *The American Character*. New York: Knopf, 1944.

Brzezinski, Zbigniew. "Totalitarianism and Rationality," *The American Political Science Review*, L, 3 (September 1956), 751–63.

Carr, Edward H. *Nationalism and After*. New York: Macmillan, 1945.

Coleman, James S. "Nationalism in Tropical Africa," *The American Political Science Review*, XLVIII, 2 (June 1954), 404–26.

Commager, Henry Steele. *The American Mind*. New Haven: Yale University Press, 1950.

Dahl, Robert A. "A Critique of the Ruling Elite Model," *The American Political Science Review*, LII, 2 (June 1958), 463–69.

Deutsch, Karl. *The Nerves of Government*. New York: Free Press, 1963.

———. *Nationalism and Social Communication*. New York: Wiley, 1953.

Easton, David, and Jack Dennis. "The Child's Acquisition of Regime Norms: Political Efficacy," *The American Political Science Review*, LXI, 1 (March 1967), 25–38.

Eisenstadt, S. N. *Modernization: Protest and Change*. Englewood Cliffs, N.J.: Prentice-Hall, 1966.

———. "Modernization and Conditions of Sustained Growth," *World Politics*, XVI, 4 (July 1964), 576–94.

———. *The Political Systems of Empires*. New York: Free Press, 1963.

Field, Lowell. *Comparative Political Development*. Ithaca, N.Y.: Cornell University Press, 1967.

Friedrich, Carl J., and Zbigniew K. Brzezinski. *Totalitarian Dictatorship and Autocracy*. Cambridge: Harvard University Press, 1956.

Gregg, Phillip M., and Arthur S. Banks. "Dimensions of Political Systems: Factor Analysis of a Cross-Polity Survey," *The American Political Science Review*, LIX, 3 (September 1965), 602–14.

Haas, Ernst B. *Beyond the Nation State: Functionalism and International Organization*. Stanford: Stanford University Press, 1964.

Hayes, Carleton J. *The Historical Evolution of Modern Nationalism*. New York: R. R. Smith, 1931.

Herman, Leon M. "The Limits of Forced Economic Growth in the USSR," *World Politics*, XVI, 3 (April 1964) 407–17.

Hertz, Fredrick. *Nationality in History and Politics*. New York: Oxford University Press, 1944.

Holt, Robert T., and John E. Turner. *The Political Basis of Economic Development*. Princeton: Van Nostrand, 1966.

Huntington, Samuel P. "The Political Modernization of Traditional Monarchies," *Daedalus*, 95, 3 (Summer 1966), 763–88.

———. "Political Modernization: America vs. Europe," *World Politics*, XVIII, 3 (April 1966), 378–414.

———. "Political Development and Political Decay," *World Politics*, XVIII, 3 (April 1965) 386–430.

Janowitz, Morris. *The Military in the Political Development of New Nations*. Chicago: The University of Chicago Press, 1964.

Johnson, Chalmers. *Revolutionary Change*. Boston: Little, Brown, 1966.

Kohn, Hans. *American Nationalism: An Interpretative Essay*. New York: Macmillan, 1957.

————. *The Idea of Nationalism*. New York: Macmillan, 1944.

Lipset, Seymour M. *Political Man*. Garden City, N.Y.: Doubleday, 1960.

————. "Some Social Requisites of Democracy," *The American Political Science Review*, LIII, 1 (March 1959), 69–105.

Madariaga, Salvador de. *Englishmen, Frenchmen, Spaniards*. London: Oxford University Press, 1937.

May, John D. "Democracy, Organization, Michels," *The American Political Science Review*, LIX, 2 (June 1965), 417–29.

Mead, Margaret. "National Character," in A. L. Kroeber, ed., *Anthropology Today*. Chicago: The University of Chicago Press, 1953.

Moore, Barrington, Jr. *Social Origins of Dictatorship and Democracy: Lord and Peasant in the Making of the Modern World*. Boston: Beacon Press, 1966.

Needler, Martin. "Political Development and Military Intervention in Latin America," *The American Political Science Review*, LX, 3 (September 1966), 616.

Niebuhr, Reinhold. *Moral Man and Immoral Society*. New York: Scribner's, 1948.

Nieburg, H. L. "The Threat of Violence and Social Change," *The American Political Science Review*, LVI, 4 (December 1962), 865–73.

Organski, A. F. K. *The Stages of Political Development*. New York: Knopf, 1965.

Pye, Lucian W. *Politics, Personality and Nation Building: Burma's Search for Identity*. New Haven: Yale University Press, 1962.

Rosenblatt, Paul C. "Origins and Effects of Group Ethnocentrism and Nationalism," *The Journal of Conflict Resolution*, VIII, 2 (June 1964), 131–46.

Rostow, W. W. *The Stages of Economic Growth*. Cambridge: At the University Press, 1961.

Rudolph, Lloyd I. "The Modernity of Tradition: The Democratic Incarnation of Caste in India," *The American Political Science Review*, LIX, 4 (December 1965), 975–89.

Shils, Edward. "The Intellectuals in the Political Development of New States," *World Politics*, XIII, 3 (April 1960), 329–68.

Silvert, Kalman, ed. *The Expectant Peoples*. New York: Random House, 1963.

Stoetzel, Jean. *Without the Chrysanthemum and the Sword: A Study of the Attitudes of Youth in Post-war Japan*. New York: Columbia University Press, 1955.

Ward, Robert E. "Political Modernization and Political Culture in Japan," *World Politics*, XV, 4 (July 1963), 569–96.

Weinert, Richard S. "Violence in Pre-modern Societies: Rural Colombia," *The American Political Science Review*, LX, 2 (June 1966), 340–47.

Wurfel, David. "Foreign Aid and Social Reform in Political Development: A Philippine Case Study," *The American Political Science Review*, LIII, 2 (June 1959), 456–82.

and Peking's International Behavior," *The American Political Science Review*, LIX, 1 (March 1965), 80–99.

Wolfers, Arnold. " 'National Security' as an Ambiguous Symbol," *The Political Science Quarterly*, LXVII, 4 (December 1952), 481–502.

———. "Statesmanship and Moral Choice," *World Politics*, I, 2 (January 1949), 175–95.

On National Power and Its Determinants

Bachrach, Peter, and Morton S. Baratz. "Two Faces of Power," *The American Political Science Review*, LVI, 4 (December 1962), 947–52.

Bentley, Arthur. *The Process of Government*. Chicago: University of Chicago Press, 1908.

Bergson, Abram. *The Economics of Soviet Planning*. New Haven: Yale University Press, 1964.

———, and Simon Kusnetz, eds. *Economic Trends in the Soviet Union*. Cambridge: Harvard University Press, 1963.

Brzezinski, Zbigniew, and Samuel P. Huntington. *Political Power USA/USSR*. New York: Viking Press, 1964.

Buchanan, Norman S., and Howard S. Ellis. *Approaches to Economic Development*. New York: The Twentieth Century Fund, 1955.

Carr-Saunders, Alexander M. *The Population Problem: A Study in Human Evolution*. Oxford: The Clarendon Press, 1922.

Dahl, Robert A. *Modern Political Analysis*. Englewood Cliffs, N.J.: Prentice-Hall, 1963.

———. "The Concept of Power," *Behaviorial Science*, II, 3 (July 1957), 201–15.

Davis, Kingsley. *The Population of India and Pakistan*. Princeton: Princeton University Press, 1951.

———. "A Conceptual Analysis of Stratification," *American Sociological Review*, VII, 3 (June 1942), 309–21.

Frankel, Herbert S. *The Economic Impact on Underdeveloped Societies*. Cambridge: Harvard University Press, 1953.

Friedrich, Carl J. *Constitutional Government and Democracy*. Boston: Ginn, 1950.

———. "Some Observations on Weber's Analysis of Bureaucracy," in Robert K. Merton *et al.*, eds., *Reader in Bureaucracy*. New York: The Free Press, 1952.

Gagdil, D. R. "Pre-conditions of Economic Development," *Indian Economic Review*, I, 1 (February 1952), 14–20.

German, Clifford F. "A Tentative Evaluation of World Power," *The Journal of Conflict Resolution*, IV, 1, (March 1960), 138–44.

Goldhamer, Herbert, and Edward A. Shils. "Types of Power and Status," *The American Journal of Sociology*, 45, 2 (September 1939), 171–82.

Gottman, Jean. "Geography and International Relations," *World Politics*, III, 2 (January 1951), 153–73.

On National Goals and Their Determinants

Bauer, Raymond A. "Problems of Perception and the Relations Between the United States and the Soviet Union," *The Journal of Conflict Resolution,* V, 3 (September 1961), 223–29.

Beard, Charles A. *The Idea of National Interest.* New York: Macmillan, 1934.

Boulding, K. E. "National Image and International Systems," *The Journal of Conflict Resolution,* III, 2 (September 1959), 120–31.

Converse, Philip R., Aage R. Clausen, and Warren E. Miller. "Electoral Myth and Reality: The 1964 Election," *The American Political Science Review,* LIX, 2 (June 1965), 321–36.

Cook, Thomas I., and Malcolm Moos. "The American Idea of International Interest," *The American Political Science Review,* XLVII, 1 (March 1953), 28–44.

Deutsch, Karl W. "Integration and Arms Control in the European Political Environment: A Summary Report," *The American Political Science Review,* LX, 2 (June 1966), 354–65.

Good, Robert C. "Changing Patterns of African International Relations," *The American Political Science Review,* LVIII, 3 (September 1964), 632–41.

Klineberg, Otto. *Tensions Affecting International Understanding.* New York: Social Science Research Council, 1950.

Knight, Maxwell. *The German Executive 1890–1933.* Hoover Institute Elite Studies. Stanford: Stanford University Press, 1952.

Lasswell, Harold D. *et al. The Comparative Study of Elites.* Hoover Institute Elite Studies. Stanford: Stanford University Press, 1952.

———. *A Study of Power.* New York: Free Press, 1950, Part I.

Lerner, Daniel. *The Nazi Elite.* Hoover Institute Elite Studies. Stanford: Stanford University Press, 1951.

McNeil, Elton B. "Psychology and Aggression," *The Journal of Conflict Resolution,* III, 3 (September 1959), 195–293.

Morgenthau, Hans J. "A Political Theory of Foreign Aid," *The American Political Science Review,* LVI, 2 (June 1962), 301–9.

———. "Another 'Great Debate': The National Interest of the United States," *The American Political Science Review,* LVI, 4 (December 1952), 961–88.

———. *In Defense of the National Interest.* New York: Knopf, 1951.

North, Robert C. *Kuomintang and Chinese Communist Elites.* Hoover Institute Elite Studies. Stanford: Stanford University Press, 1952.

Osgood, Robert E. *Ideals and Self-interest in America's Foreign Relations: The Great Transformation of the Twentieth Century.* Chicago: The University of Chicago Press, 1953.

Schumpeter, Joseph. *The Sociology of Imperialism.* New York: Meridian Books, 1955.

Tsour, Tang, and Morton H. Halperin. "Mao Tse-tung's Revolutionary Strategy

Hoselitz, Bert F., ed. *The Progress of Underdeveloped Areas*. Chicago: The University of Chicago Press, 1952.

Huntington, Samuel P. "Interservice Competition and the Political Roles of the Armed Services," *The American Political Science Review*, LV, 1 (March 1961), 40–52.

———. *The Soldier and the State*. Cambridge: Belknap Press, 1957.

Khadduri, Majid. "The Role of the Military in Middle East Politics," *The American Political Science Review*, XLVII, 2 (June 1953), 511–24.

Kindleberger, Charles P. *Economic Development*. New York: McGraw-Hill, 1958.

Kish, George, and J. David Singer, eds. "The Geography of Conflict," *The Journal of Conflict Resolution*, IV, 1 (March 1960), 1–161.

Ladejinsky, Wolf. "Carrot and Stick in Rural China," *Foreign Affairs*, 36, 1 (October 1957), 91–104.

Landis, Paul H. *Population Problems*. New York: American Book, 1943.

Lasswell, Harold D. *Power and Personality*. New York: Norton, 1948.

———, and Abraham Kaplan. *Power and Society*. New Haven: Yale University Press, 1950.

Lerner, Daniel. *The Passing of Traditional Society: Modernizing the Middle East*. New York: Free Press, 1958.

Levy, Marion J., Jr. "Contrasting Factors in the Modernization of China and Japan," *Economic Development and Cultural Change*, II (October 1953), 161–97.

Lipset, Seymour M., and Reinhard Bendix. "Social Status and Social Structure, a Reexamination of the Data and Interpretations: II," *The British Journal of Sociology*, II, 3 (September 1951), 230–54.

Liu, F. F. *A Military History of Modern China, 1924–1949*. Princeton: Princeton University Press, 1956.

Lockwood, William W. *The Economic Development of Japan: Growth and Structural Change 1868–1938*. Princeton: Princeton University Press, 1954.

Mackinder, Sir Halford J. *Democratic Ideals and Reality*. New York: Holt, Rinehart and Winston, 1942.

———. "The Geographical Pivot of History," *Geographical Journal*, XXIII, 4 (April 1904), 421–37.

Maddison, Angus. *Economic Growth in the West: Comparative Experience in Europe and North America*. New York: The Twentieth Century Fund, 1964.

Malthus, Thomas R. *An Essay on Population*. Two vols. London: J. M. Dent; New York: Dutton, n.d. (Everyman's Library, No. 692, reprinted from the 7th edition).

March, James G. "An Introduction to the Theory and Measurement of Influence," *The American Political Science Review*, 49, 2 (June 1955), 431–51.

McIntosh, Donald S. "Power and Social Control," *The American Political Science Review*, LVII, 3 (September 1963), 619–31.

Mead, Margaret, ed. *Cultural Patterns and Technical Change*. Paris: UNESCO, 1953.

Moore, Barrington, Jr. *Political Power and Social Theory*. Cambridge: Harvard University Press, 1958.

Nurkse, Ragnar. *Problems of Capital Formation in Underdeveloped Countries*. New York: Oxford University Press, 1960.

Organski, Katherine, and A. F. K. Organski. *Population and World Power*. New York: Knopf, 1961.

Price, A. Grenfell. *White Settlers in the Tropics*. New York: American Geographical Society, 1939.

Puerto Rico, Office of Economic Research, Economic Development Administration. *The Net Income of the Commonwealth of Puerto Rico*. San Juan, 1953.

Robinson, E. A. G. *Economic Consequences of the Size of Nations*. New York: St. Martin's Press, 1960.

Rostow, W. W. *The Stages of Economic Growth*. Cambridge: At the University Press, 1960.

Samuelson, Paul A. *Economics*. New York: McGraw-Hill, 1964.

Schwartz, Solomon. *Labor in the Soviet Union*. New York: Praeger, 1952.

Shimkin, Demitri B. *Minerals: A Key to Soviet Power*. Cambridge: Harvard University Press, 1953.

Simon, Herbert. "Notes on the Observation and Measurement of Political Power," *Journal of Politics,* 15, 4 (November 1953), 500–16.

Sprout, Harold, and Margaret Sprout, eds. *The Foundations of National Power*. Princeton: Van Nostrand, 1951.

Spulber, Nicholas. *Foundations of Soviet Strategy for Economic Growth*. Bloomington: Indiana University Press, 1964.

Staley, Eugene. *The Future of Underdeveloped Countries*. New York: Harper & Row, 1954.

Tawney, R. H. *Religion and the Rise of Capitalism*. New York: Mentor Books, New American Library, 1953.

United Kingdom, Royal Commission on Population. *Report*. Cmd. 7695. London, H.M.S.O., 1949.

United Nations, Statistical Office, Department of Economic and Social Affairs. *Demographic Yearbook*. New York: United Nations, 1956, 1964, 1965, 1966.

———, Department of Social Affairs. *Population and Vital Statistics*. Reports, Statistical Papers, Series A, Vol. III, Nos. 3–4. New York: United Nations, 1951. 1950 mid-year estimates.

———. *World Iron Resources and Their Utilization*. New York: United Nations, 1950.

Vagts, Alfred. *Defense and Diplomacy: The Soldier and the Conduct of Foreign Relations*. New York: Columbia University Press, 1956.

Waltz, Kenneth W. "Kant Liberalism and War," *The American Political Science Review,* LVI, 2 (June 1962), 331–40.

Weber, Max. *The Protestant Ethic and the Spirit of Capitalism*. London: Allen and Unwin, 1930.

———. "The Essentials of Bureaucratic Organization: An Ideal-type Construction," in Robert K. Merton *et al.,* eds., *Reader in Bureaucracy*. New York: Free Press, 1952.

Wheeler-Bennett, John. *The Nemesis of Power: The German Army in Politics, 1918–1945.* London: Macmillan, 1953.

Winslow, C. E. A. *The Cost of Sickness and the Price of Health.* Geneva: World Health Organization, Monograph Series No. 7, 1951.

Woytinsky, W. S., and E. S. Woytinsky. *World Population and Production.* New York: The Twentieth Century Fund, 1953.

On Colonialism

Aniden, Rita. *Empire and After: A Study of British Imperial Attitudes.* London: Essential Books, 1949.

Apter, David. *The Gold Coast in Transition.* Princeton: Princeton University Press, 1955.

Bidwell, Percy W. *Raw Materials: A Study of American Policy.* New York: Harper & Row, 1958.

Brzezinski, Zbigniew. "Russia and Europe," *Foreign Affairs,* 42, 3 (April 1964), 428–44.

———. "The Challenge of Change in the Soviet Bloc," *Foreign Affairs,* 39, 3 (April 1961), 430–43.

———. *The Soviet Bloc: Unity and Conflict.* Cambridge: Harvard University Press, 1960.

Caroe, Sir Olaf. "Soviet Colonialism in Central Asia," *Foreign Affairs,* 32, 1 (October 1953), 135–44.

Coleman, James S. "Nationalism in Tropical Africa," *The American Political Science Review,* XLVIII, 2 (June 1954), 404–26.

Dedijer, Vladimir. "Albania, Soviet Pawn," *Foreign Affairs,* 30, 1 (October 1951), 103–11.

Duchacek, Ivo. "The Strategy of Communist Infiltration: Czechoslovakia, 1944–48," *World Politics,* II, 3 (April 1950), 345–72.

Eagleton, Clyde. "Excesses of Self-determination," *Foreign Affairs,* 31, 4 (July 1953), 592–604.

Emerson, Rupert. *From Empire to Nation.* Cambridge: Harvard University Press, 1960.

———. *Representative Government in Southeast Asia.* Cambridge: Harvard University Press, 1955.

Furnivall, J. S. *Colonial Policy and Practice.* Cambridge, Eng.: University Press, 1948.

Hailey, Malcom, 1st Baron. *An African Survey.* London: Oxford University Press, 1938.

Hammer, Ellen J. *The Struggle for Indochina, 1940–1955.* Stanford: Stanford University Press, 1954.

Haring, C. H. *The Spanish Empire in America.* New York: Oxford University Press, 1947.

Hurewitz, J. C. *Middle East Dilemmas.* New York: Harper & Row, 1953.

Kertesz, Stephen D. "The Methods of Communist Conquest: Hungary 1944–1947," *World Politics,* III, 1 (October 1950), 20–54.

Kuczynski, Robert R. *Colonial Population*. London: Oxford University Press, 1937.

Laqueur, Walter Z. *Communism and Nationalism in the Middle East*. New York: Praeger, 1956.

Montias, John Michael. "Communist Rule in Eastern Europe," *Foreign Affairs*, 43, 2 (January 1965), 331–48.

Renouvin, Pierre. *Les Politiques d'expansion imperialiste, colonies et empires*. Paris: Presses Universitaires, 1949.

Rosa, R. A. "The Soviet Theory of 'People's Democracy,'" *World Politics*, I, 4 (July 1949), 489–510.

Royal Institute of International Affairs. *The Colonial Problem*. London: Oxford University Press, 1937.

Schmokel, Wolfe W. *Dream of Empire: German Colonialism, 1919–1945*. New Haven: Yale University Press, 1964.

Schwartz, Harry. *Russia's Soviet Economy*. Second edition. Englewood Cliffs, N.J.: Prentice-Hall, 1954.

Ulam, Adam B. "The Cominform and the People's Democracies," *World Politics*, III, 2 (January 1951), 200–17.

Wainhouse, David W. *Remnants of Empire: The United Nations and the End of Colonialism*. New York: Harper & Row, 1964.

Watnick, Morris. "The Appeal of Communism to the Underdeveloped Peoples," in Bert F. Hoselitz, ed., *The Progress of Underdeveloped Countries*. Chicago: The University of Chicago Press, 1952.

Wellisz, Stanislaw. *The Economics of the Soviet Bloc*. New York: McGraw-Hill, 1964.

Woytinsky, W. S., and E. S. Woytinski. *World Commerce and Governments*. New York: The Twentieth Century Fund, 1955.

Zsoldos, Laszlo. *The Economic Integration of Hungary into the Soviet Bloc: Foreign Trade Experience*. Columbus: Bureau of Business Research, Ohio State University, 1963.

On the Balance of Power

Buehrig, Edward H. *Woodrow Wilson and the Balance of Power*. Bloomington: Indiana University Press, 1955.

Burns, Arthur L. "From Balance to Deterrence," *World Politics*, IX, 4 (July 1957), 494–529.

Carleton, William G. "Ideology or Balance of Power?" *The Yale Review*, XXXVI, 4 (June 1947), 590–602.

Claude, Inis L., Jr. *Power and International Relations*. New York: Random House, 1962.

Cobden, Richard. *Political Writings*. New York: Appleton, 1867. Vol. I.

Deutsch, Karl W., and J. David Singer. "Multipolar Systems and International Stability," *World Politics*, XVI, 3 (April 1964), 390–406.

Dinerstein, Herbert S. "The Transformation of Alliance Systems," *The American Political Science Review*, LIX, 3 (September 1965), 589–601.

Friedrich, Carl J. *Foreign Policy in the Making*. New York: Norton, 1938.

Garthoff, R. L. "The Concept of the Balance of Power in Soviet Policy-Making," *World Politics*, IV, 1 (October 1951), 85–111.

Gooch, G. P., and Harold Temperley, eds. *British Documents on the Origin of the War 1898–1914*. London: H.M.S.O., 1928. Vol. XI.

Grant, A. J., and Harold Temperley. *Europe in the Nineteenth and Twentieth Centuries, 1789–1950*. New York: Longmans, Green, 1952.

Haas, Ernst B. "Types of Collective Security: An Examination of Operational Concepts," *The American Political Science Review*, XLIX, 1 (March 1955), 40–62.

———. "The Balance of Power: Prescription, Concept, or Propaganda?" *World Politics*, V, 4 (July 1953), 442–77.

Kaplan, Morton A. "Balance of Power, Bipolarity and Other Models of International Systems," *The American Political Science Review*, LI, 3 (September 1957), 684–95.

———. *System and Process in International Politics*. New York: Wiley, 1957.

———, and Nicholas D. Katzenbach. "The Patterns of International Politics and International Law," *The American Political Science Review*, LIII, 3 (September 1959), 693–712.

Langer, William L. *European Alliances and Alignments, 1871–1890*. New York: Knopf, 1956.

Palmer, Norman D., and Howard C. Perkins. *International Relations*. Boston: Houghton Mifflin, 1953.

Speeches of the Right Honourable George Canning. Six vols. London: J. Ridgway, 1828.

Strausz-Hupé, Robert, and Stefan T. Possony. *International Relations in the Age of Conflict between Democracy and Dictatorship*. New York: McGraw-Hill, 1954.

Vagts, Alfred. "The Balance of Power: Growth of an Idea," *World Politics*, I, 1 (October 1948), 82–101.

———. "The United States and the Balance of Power," *The Journal of Politics*, 3, 4 (November 1941), 401–49.

Webster, Charles K. *The Foreign Policy of Castlereagh, 1815–1822*. London: Bell, 1947.

Wight, Martin. *Power Politics*. London: Royal Institute of International Affairs, 1946. "Looking Forward" Pamphlets No. 8.

On Nuclear Conflict

Aron, Raymond. *The Great Debate: Theories of Nuclear Strategy*. Garden City, N.Y.: Doubleday, 1965.

Barnet, Richard J. *Who Wants Disarmament?* Boston: Beacon Press, 1960.

Beaufre, André. *Deterrence and Strategy*. New York: Praeger, 1966.

Boulding, Kenneth A. *Conflict and Defense*. New York: Harper & Row, 1962.

Brodie, Bernard. *Strategy in the Missile Age*. Princeton: Princeton University Press, 1959.

Burns, Arthur Lee. "From Balance to Deterrence: A Theoretical Analysis," *World Politics,* IX, 4 (July 1957), 494–529.

Gallois, Pierre. *The Balance of Terror.* Boston: Houghton Mifflin, 1961.

Garthoff, Raymond L. *Soviet Strategy in the Nuclear Age.* New York: Praeger, 1962.

———. *The Soviet Image of Future War.* Washington: Public Affairs Press, 1959.

Halperin, Morton H. *China and the Bomb.* New York: Praeger, 1965.

———. *Limited War in the Nuclear Age.* New York: Wiley, 1963.

———. "Nuclear Weapons and Limited War," *The Journal of Conflict Resolution,* V, 2 (June 1961), 146–66.

Heer, David M. *After a Nuclear Attack: A Demographic Inquiry.* New York: Praeger, 1965.

Herz, John H. *International Politics in the Atomic Age.* New York: Columbia University Press, 1959.

Hoopes, Townsend, "Overseas Bases in American Strategy," *Foreign Affairs,* 37, 1 (October 1958), 69–82.

Horelick, Arnold L. "The Cuban Missile Crisis: An Analysis of Soviet Calculation and Behavior," *World Politics,* XVI, 3 (April 1964), 363–89.

Hsieh, Alice L. *Communist China's Strategy in the Nuclear Era.* Englewood Cliffs, N.J.: Prentice-Hall, 1962.

Huntington, Samuel P. *The Common Defense: Strategic Programs in National Politics.* New York: Columbia University Press, 1961.

Kahn, Herman. *On Thermonuclear War.* Princeton: Princeton University Press, 1961.

Kaplan, Morton A. "The Calculus of Deterrence," *World Politics,* XI, 1 (October 1958), 20–43.

Kaufmann, William W. *The McNamara Strategy.* New York: Harper & Row, 1964.

Kissinger, Henry A. *The Necessity for Choice.* New York: Harper & Row, 1961.

———. "Nuclear Testing and the Problem of Peace," *Foreign Affairs,* 37, 1 (October, 1958), 1–18.

Kolodziej, Edward A. "French Strategy Emergent: General André Beaufre— A Critique," *World Politics,* XIX, 3 (April 1967), 417–42.

Lieuwen, Edwin. *Arms and Politics in Latin America.* New York: Praeger, 1961.

Martin, Laurence W. "The Market for Strategic Ideas in Britain," *The American Political Science Review,* LVI, 1 (March 1962), 23–41.

Morgenstern, Oskar. *The Question of National Defense.* New York: Random House, 1959.

Morgenthau, Hans J. "The Four Paradoxes of Nuclear Strategy," *The American Political Science Review,* LVIII, 1 (March 1964), 23–35.

Osgood, Robert S. "Stabilizing the Military Environment," *The American Political Science Review,* LV, 1 (March 1961), 24–39.

———. "NATO: Problems of Security and Collaboration," *The American Political Science Review,* LIV, 1 (March 1960), 106–29.

Powell, Ralph. "China's Bomb: Exploitation and Reactions," *Foreign Affairs,* 43, 4 (July 1965), 616–25.

Schelling, T. C. "Nuclear Strategy in Europe," *World Politics,* XIV, 3 (April 1962), 421–32.

———. *The Strategy of Conflict.* Cambridge: Harvard University Press, 1960.

Schilling, Warner R. "Scientists, Foreign Policy, and Politics," *The American Political Science Review,* LVI, 2 (June 1962), 287–300.

Snyder, Glenn H. *Deterrence and Defense.* Princeton: Princeton University Press, 1961.

Taylor, Maxwell D. *The Uncertain Trumpet.* New York: Harper & Row, 1959.

Wohlstetter, Albert. "Nuclear Sharing: NATO and the N + 1 Country," *Foreign Affairs* 39, 3 (April 1961), pp. 355–87.

———. "The Delicate Balance of Terror," *Foreign Affairs,* 37, 2 (January 1959), pp. 211–34.

Wohlstetter, Roberta. "Cuba and Pearl Harbor: Hindsight and Foresight," *Foreign Affairs,* 43, 4 (July 1965), 691–707.

Wolfe, Thomas W. "Shifts in Soviet Strategic Thought," *Foreign Affairs,* 42, 3 (April 1964), pp. 475–86.

———. *Soviet Strategy at the Crossroads.* Cambridge: Harvard University Press, 1964.

On the International Power Transition

Bowles, W. Donald. "Soviet Russia as a Model for Underdeveloped Areas," *World Politics,* XIV, 3 (April 1962), 483–504.

Carr, Edward H. *The Twenty Years' Crisis 1919–1939.* London: Macmillan, 1954.

———. *The Soviet Impact on the Western* World. New York: Macmillan, 1947.

Cheng, Chu-yüan. *Economic Relations Between Peking and Moscow 1949–1963.* New York: Praeger, 1964.

Cook, Thomas I. "Democratic Psychology and a Democratic World Order," *World Politics,* I, 4 (July 1949), 553–64.

———, and Malcolm Moos. *Power Through Purpose.* Baltimore: Johns Hopkins, 1954.

Crozier, Brian. *The Rebels.* London: Chatto and Windus, 1960.

Deutsch, Karl W., and Alexander Eckstein. "National Industrialization and the Declining Share of the Economic Sector, 1890–1959," *World Politics,* XVII, 2 (January 1961), 267–99.

———, and Lewis J. Edinger. *Germany Rejoins the Powers.* Stanford: Stanford University Press, 1959.

Eckstein, Alexander. "On the Economic Crisis in Communist China," *Foreign Affairs,* 42, 4 (July 1964), 655–68.

Eden, Anthony. *Full Circle: The Memoirs of Anthony Eden.* Boston: Houghton Mifflin, 1960.

Fox, Annette B. *The Power of Small States.* Chicago: The University of Chicago Press, 1959.

Fox, William T. R. *The Super-powers*. New York: Harcourt, Brace & World, 1944.

Galuson, Walter. *Labor Productivity in Soviet and American Industry*. New York: Columbia University Press, 1955.

Hollister, William W. *China's Gross National Product and Social Accounts 1950–1957*. New York: Free Press, 1958.

Holsti, Ole R. "The Belief System and National Images: A Case Study," *The Journal of Conflict Resolution*, VI, 3 (September 1962), 244–52.

Hudson, G. F. "Russia and China, The Dilemmas of Power," *Foreign Affairs*, 39, 1 (October 1960), 1–10.

Jones, F. C. *Japan's New Order in East Asia*. New York: Oxford University Press, 1954.

Kautsky, John. "The New Strategy of International Communism," *The American Political Science Review*, XLIX, 2 (June 1955), 478–86.

Kennan, George F. "Peaceful Coexistence: A Western View," *Foreign Affairs*, 38, 2 (January 1960), 171–90.

————. *Russia Leaves the War*. Princeton: Princeton University Press, 1956.

————. *Realities of American Foreign Policy*. Princeton: Princeton University Press, 1954.

————. *American Diplomacy, 1900–1950*. Chicago: The University of Chicago Press, 1951.

Khrushchev, Nikita S. "On Peaceful Coexistence," *Foreign Affairs*, 38, 1 (October 1959), 1–18.

Kissinger, Henry A. "Military Policy and Defense of the 'Gray Areas,'" *Foreign Affairs*, 33, 3 (April 1955), 416–28.

Legislative Reference Service of the Library of Congress. *Soviet Economic Growth: A Comparison with the United States*. A Study prepared for the Subcommittee on Foreign Economic Policy of the Joint Economic Committee. 85th Congress, 1st Session. Washington, D.C., 1957.

————. *Trends in Economic Growth: A Comparison of the Western Powers and the Soviet Bloc*. A Study prepared for the Joint Committee on the Economic Report. 83rd Congress, 2nd Session. Washington, D.C., 1955.

Liu, Ta-chung, and Kung-chia Yeh. *The Economy of the Chinese Mainland: National Income and Economic Development 1933–1959*. Princeton: Princeton University Press, 1965.

Miller, Lynn W. "The Contemporary Significance of the Doctrine of Just War," *World Politics*, XVI, 2 (January 1964), 258–86.

Mosely, Philip E. "The Chinese-Soviet Rift: Origins and Portents," *Foreign Affairs*, 42, 1 (October 1963), 11–24.

————. "How 'New' Is the Kremlin's New Line?" *Foreign Affairs*, 33, 3 (April 1955), 376–86.

Niebuhr, Reinhold. "A Protest Against a Dilemma's Two Horns," *World Politics*, II, 3 (April 1950), 338–44.

Shiskin, Julius. U.S. Bureau of the Census. *Long Term Economic Growth*. Washington, D.C., 1966.

Spector, Ivar. *The Soviet Union and the Muslim World, 1917–1958*. Seattle: The University of Washington Press, 1959.

Walker, Richard. *China Under Communism: The First Five Years.* New Haven: Yale University Press, 1955.

Whiting, Allen S. *China Crosses the Yalu.* New York: Macmillan, 1960.

Zagoria, Donald S. *The Sino-Soviet Conflict, 1956–1961.* Princeton: Princeton University Press, 1962.

————. "Strains in the Sino-Soviet Alliance," *Problems of Communism,* IX, 3 (May-June, 1960), 1–11.

Zaninovich, M. George. "Pattern Analysis of Variables Within the International System: The Sino-Soviet Example," *The Journal of Conflict Resolution,* VI, 3 (September 1962), 253–68.

On Diplomacy

Alfieri, Dino. *Dictators Face to Face.* New York: New York University Press, 1955.

Byrnes, James F. *Speaking Frankly.* New York: Harper & Row, 1947.

Cambon, Jules. *Le Diplomate.* Paris: Hachette, 1926.

Ciano, Galeazzo. *The Ciano Diaries, 1939–1943.* Garden City, N.Y.: Garden City Publishing Company, 1947.

Corbett, Percy E. *Law in Diplomacy.* Princeton: Princeton University Press, 1959.

Craig, Gordon A., and Felix Gilbert, ed. *The Diplomats, 1919–1939.* Princeton: Princeton University Press, 1953.

Davies, Joseph. *Mission to Moscow.* New York: Simon and Schuster, 1941.

François-Poncet, André. *Souvenirs d'une ambassade à Berlin.* Paris: Flammerion, 1946.

Kissinger, Henry A. "Coalition Diplomacy in a Nuclear Age," *Foreign Affairs,* 42, 4 (July 1964), 525–45.

Kuhn, Harold, ed. "Game Theory, Bargaining, and International Relations," *The Journal of Conflict Resolution,* VI, 1 (March 1962), 1–76.

Lall, Arthur. *Modern International Negotiation.* New York: Columbia University Press, 1966.

Mowat, R. B. A. *A History of European Diplomacy, 1451–1789.* London: E. Arnold, 1928.

Nicolson, Harold G. *Diplomacy.* New York: Oxford University Press, 1963.

Reynaud, Paul. *In the Thick of the Fight, 1930–1945.* New York: Simon and Schuster, 1955.

Satow, Ernest. *A Guide to Diplomatic Practice.* London: Longmans, Green, 1957.

Seabury, Paul. *The Wilhelmstrasse.* Berkeley: University of California Press, 1954.

Sherwood, Robert. *Roosevelt and Hopkins.* New York: Harper & Row, 1948.

Sterling, Richard W. *Ethics in the World of Power.* Princeton: Princeton University Press, 1958.

Stilwell, Joseph W. *The Stilwell Papers.* New York: William Sloan Associates, 1948.

Taylor, A. J. P. *The Struggle for Mastery in Europe 1848–1918*. Oxford: The Clarendon Press, 1954.

Thayer, Charles W. *Diplomat*. New York: Harper & Row, 1959.

Webster, Charles K. *The Congress of Vienna*. London: Bell, 1945.

Williams, William A. *The Tragedy of American Diplomacy*. Cleveland: World, 1959.

Winant, John G. *Letter from Grosvenor Square*. Boston: Houghton Mifflin, 1947.

On Collective Security

Jessup, Philip C. *International Security*. New York: Council on Foreign Relations, 1935.

Martin, Andrew. *Collective Security*. Paris: UNESCO, 1952.

Mitrany, David. *The Problem of International Sanctions*. New York: Oxford University Press, 1925.

Royal Institute of International Affairs. *International Sanctions*. London: Oxford University Press, 1938.

Thompson, Kenneth W. "Collective Security Reexamined," *The American Political Science Review*, XLVII, 3 (September 1953) 753–72.

Wolfers, Arnold. *Britain and France Between Two Wars*. New York: W. W. Norton, 1966.

On International Organization

Alker, Hayward, Jr. "Dimensions of Conflict in the General Assembly," *The American Political Science Review*, LVIII, 3 (September 1964), 642–57.

Alker, Hayward, Jr. and Bruce Russet. *World Politics in the General Assembly*. New Haven: Yale University Press, 1965.

Claude, Inis L., Jr. "United Nations Use of Military Force," *The Journal of Conflict Resolution*, VII, 2 (June 1963), 117–29.

———. *Swords Into Plowshares*. New York: Random House, 1964.

Eagleton, Clyde. *International Government*. Third edition. New York: Ronald Press, 1957.

Goodrich, Leland M., and Edvard Hambro. *Charter of the United Nations*. Second edition. Boston: World Peace Foundation, 1949.

Gordenker, Leon. "Policy Making and Secretariat Influence in the UN General Assembly: The Case of Public Information," *The American Political Science Review*, LIV, 2 (June 1960), 359–73.

Koo, Wellington, Jr. *Voting Procedures in International Political Organizations*. New York: Columbia University Press, 1947.

Levi, Werner. *Fundamentals of World Organization*. Minneapolis: University of Minnesota Press, 1950.

Lijphart, Arend. "The Analysis of Bloc Voting in the General Assembly," *The American Political Science Review*, LVII, 4 (December 1963), 902–917.

Marshall, Charles B. "Character and Mission of a United Nations Peace Force, Under Conditions of General and Complete Disarmament," *The American Political Science Review*, LIX, 2 (June 1965), 350–64.

Miller, D. H. *The Drafting of the Covenant*. Two vols. New York: Putnam's, 1928.

Mitrany, David. *A Working Peace System*. Fourth edition. London: National Peace Council, 1946.

Riches, Cromwell A. *Majority Rule in International Organization*. Baltimore: Johns Hopkins, 1940.

————. *The Unanimity Rule and the League of Nations*. Baltimore: Johns Hopkins, 1933.

Russet, Bruce M. "Discovering Voting Groups in the United Nations," *The American Political Science Review*, XL, 2 (June 1966), 327–39.

Sayre, Wallace S. *The United Nations Secretariat*. New York: Carnegie Endowment for International Peace, 1950.

INDEX

Index

A Note on the Type

The text of this book was set on the Linotype in a face called TIMES ROMAN, designed by Stanley Morison for The Times (London), and first introduced by that newspaper in 1932.

Among typographers and designers of the twentieth century, Stanley Morison has been a strong forming influence, as typographical advisor to the English Monotype Corporation, as a director of two distinguished English publishing houses, and as a writer of sensibility, erudition, and keen practical sense.

Composed, Printed and Bound by the Haddon Craftsmen, Inc. Scranton, Pa. Typography and Binding design by Winston Potter.